TEACHER'S EDITION

MOSAIK 2

German Language and Culture

Boston, Massachusetts

On the cover: Houses by Friedensreich Hundertwasser, Vienna, Austria

Publisher: José A. Blanco
Professional Development Director: Norah Lulich Jones
Editorial Development: Brian Contreras, Sharla Zwirek
Project Management: Sally Giangrande
Rights Management: Ashley Dos Santos, Annie Pickert Fuller
Technology Production: Fabián Montoya, Paola Ríos Schaaf, Erica Solari
Design: Radoslav Mateev, Gabriel Noreña, Andrés Vanegas
Production: Manuela Arango, Oscar Díez, Adriana Jaramillo Ch.

Student Text ISBN: 978-1-68005-094-3
Teacher's Edition ISBN: 978-1-68005-114-8
Library of Congress Control Number: 2016947899

1 2 3 4 5 6 7 8 9 WC 21 20 19 18 17 16

Contents

Teacher's Edition Front Matter

Student Edition Front Matter

Scope and Sequence: MOSAIK 1

	KONTEXT	FOTOROMAN	KULTUR	STRUKTUREN	WEITER GEHT'S
KAPITEL 1 — LEKTION 1A Hallo! Wie geht's?	**Kontext:** Wie geht's? **Aussprache und Rechtschreibung:** The German alphabet	**Folge 1:** Willkommen in Berlin!	**Im Fokus:** Hallo, Deutschland! **Porträt:** Das Brandenburger Tor	**1A.1** Gender, articles, and nouns **1A.2** Plurals **1A.3** Subject pronouns, **sein**, and the nominative case **Wiederholung** **Zapping:** *Deutsche Bahn*	**Panorama:** Die deutschsprachige Welt **Lesen:** Adressbuch **Hören** **Schreiben** **Wortschatz**
KAPITEL 1 — LEKTION 1B	**Kontext:** In der Schule **Aussprache und Rechtschreibung:** The vowels **a**, **e**, **i**, **o**, and **u**	**Folge 2:** Oh, George!	**Im Fokus:** Die Schulzeit **Porträt:** Der Schultag	**1B.1 Haben** and the accusative case **1B.2** Word order **1B.3** Numbers **Wiederholung**	
KAPITEL 2 — LEKTION 2A Schule und Studium	**Kontext:** An der Universität **Aussprache und Rechtschreibung:** Consonant sounds	**Folge 3:** Checkpoint Charlie	**Im Fokus:** Uni-Zeit, Büffel-Zeit **Porträt:** Uni Basel	**2A.1** Regular verbs **2A.2** Interrogative words **2A.3** Talking about time and dates **Wiederholung** **Zapping:** *TU Berlin*	**Panorama:** Berlin **Lesen:** Karlswald-Universität **Hören** **Schreiben** **Wortschatz**
KAPITEL 2 — LEKTION 2B	**Kontext:** Sport und Freizeit **Aussprache und Rechtschreibung:** Diphthongs: **au**, **ei/ai**, and **eu/äu**	**Folge 4:** Ein Picknick im Park	**Im Fokus:** Skifahren im Blut **Porträt:** Mesut Özil	**2B.1** Stem-changing verbs **2B.2** Present tense used as future **2B.3** Negation **Wiederholung**	
KAPITEL 3 — LEKTION 3A Familie und Freunde	**Kontext:** Johanna Schmidts Familie **Aussprache und Rechtschreibung:** Final consonants	**Folge 5:** Ein Abend mit der Familie	**Im Fokus:** Eine deutsche Familie **Porträt:** Angela Merkel	**3A.1** Possessive adjectives **3A.2** Descriptive adjectives and adjective agreement **Wiederholung** **Zapping:** *Bauer Joghurt*	**Panorama:** Die Vereinigten Staaten und Kanada **Lesen:** Hunde und Katzen **Hören** **Schreiben** **Wortschatz**
KAPITEL 3 — LEKTION 3B	**Kontext:** Wie sind sie? **Aussprache und Rechtschreibung:** Consonant clusters	**Folge 6:** Unsere Mitbewohner	**Im Fokus:** Auf unsere Freunde! **Porträt:** Tokio Hotel	**3B.1** Modals **3B.2** Prepositions with the accusative **3B.3** The imperative **Wiederholung**	
KAPITEL 4 — LEKTION 4A Essen	**Kontext:** Lebensmittel **Aussprache und Rechtschreibung:** The German **s**, **z**, and **c**	**Folge 7:** Börek für alle	**Im Fokus:** Der Wiener Naschmarkt **Porträt:** Wolfgang Puck	**4A.1** Adverbs **4A.2** The modal **mögen** **4A.3** Separable and inseparable prefix verbs **Wiederholung** **Zapping:** *Yello Strom*	**Panorama:** Österreich **Lesen:** Die ersten Monate in Graz **Hören** **Schreiben** **Wortschatz**
KAPITEL 4 — LEKTION 4B	**Kontext:** Im Restaurant **Aussprache und Rechtschreibung:** The German **s** in combination with other letters	**Folge 8:** Die Rechnung, bitte!	**Im Fokus:** Wiener Kaffeehäuser **Porträt:** Figlmüller	**4B.1** The dative **4B.2** Prepositions with the dative **Wiederholung**	

	KONTEXT	FOTOROMAN	KULTUR	STRUKTUREN	WEITER GEHT'S
	ÜBERBLICK Reviews material from MOSAIK 1				
KAPITEL 1	**LEKTION 1A Feiern**				
KAPITEL 1	**Kontext:** Feste feiern **Aussprache und Rechtschreibung:** The consonantal **r**	**Folge 1:** Frohes neues Jahr!	**Im Fokus:** Das Oktoberfest **Porträt:** Die Sternsinger	**1A.1** The **Perfekt** (Part 1) **1A.2** Accusative pronouns **1A.3** Dative pronouns **Wiederholung** **Zapping:** *Penny*	**Panorama:** Bayern **Lesen:** Deutschland heute **Hören** **Schreiben** **Wortschatz**
KAPITEL 1	**LEKTION 1B**				
KAPITEL 1	**Kontext:** Kleidung **Aussprache und Rechtschreibung:** The letter combination **ch** (Part 1)	**Folge 2:** Sehr attraktiv, George!	**Im Fokus:** Deutsche Modewelt **Porträt:** Rudolf Moshammer	**1B.1** The **Perfekt** (Part 2) **1B.2 Wissen** and **kennen** **1B.3** Two-way prepositions **Wiederholung**	
KAPITEL 2	**LEKTION 2A Trautes Heim**				
KAPITEL 2	**Kontext:** Zu Hause **Aussprache und Rechtschreibung:** The letter combination **ch** (Part 2)	**Folge 3:** Besuch von Max	**Im Fokus:** Fribourg **Porträt:** César Ritz	**2A.1** The **Präteritum** **2A.2 Da-**, **wo-**, **hin-**, and **her-** compounds **2A.3** Coordinating conjunctions **Wiederholung** **Zapping:** *Hausarbeit*	**Panorama:** Die Schweiz und Liechtenstein **Lesen:** Schweizer Immobilien **Hören** **Schreiben** **Wortschatz**
KAPITEL 2	**LEKTION 2B**				
KAPITEL 2	**Kontext:** Hausarbeit **Aussprache und Rechtschreibung:** The German **k** sound	**Folge 4:** Ich putze gern!	**Im Fokus:** Haushaltsgeräte **Porträt:** Johanna Spyri	**2B.1 Perfekt** versus **Präteritum** **2B.2** Separable and inseparable prefix verbs in the **Perfekt** **Wiederholung**	
KAPITEL 3	**LEKTION 3A Urlaub und Ferien**				
KAPITEL 3	**Kontext:** Jahreszeiten **Aussprache und Rechtschreibung:** Long and short vowels	**Folge 5:** Berlin von oben	**Im Fokus:** Windenergie **Porträt:** Klima in Deutschland	**3A.1** Separable and inseparable prefix verbs (**Präteritum**) **3A.2** Prepositions of location; Prepositions in set phrases **Wiederholung** **Zapping:** *Urlaub im grünen Binnenland*	**Panorama:** Schleswig-Holstein, Hamburg und Bremen **Lesen:** Die Nordseeküste Schleswig Holsteins in 6 Tagen **Hören** **Schreiben** **Wortschatz**
KAPITEL 3	**LEKTION 3B**				
KAPITEL 3	**Kontext:** Reisen **Aussprache und Rechtschreibung:** Pure vowels versus diphthongs	**Folge 6:** Ein Sommer in der Türkei?	**Im Fokus:** Flughafen Frankfurt **Porträt:** Der ICE	**3B.1** Infinitive expressions and clauses **3B.2** Time expressions **3B.3** Indefinite pronouns **Wiederholung**	
KAPITEL 4	**LEKTION 4A Verkehrsmittel und Technologie**				
KAPITEL 4	**Kontext:** Auto und Rad fahren **Aussprache und Rechtschreibung:** Long and short vowels with an **Umlaut**	**Folge 7:** Ein Ende mit Schrecken	**Im Fokus:** Die deutsche Autobahn **Porträt:** Clärenore Stinnes	**4A.1 Das Plusquamperfekt** **4A.2** Comparatives and superlatives **Wiederholung** **Zapping:** *Mercedes Benz*	**Panorama:** Hessen und Thüringen **Lesen:** Vierfarbdrucker Installationsanleitung **Hören** **Schreiben** **Wortschatz**
KAPITEL 4	**LEKTION 4B**				
KAPITEL 4	**Kontext:** Technik und Medien **Aussprache und Rechtschreibung:** The German **l**	**Folge 8:** Ein Spaziergang durch Spandau	**Im Fokus:** Max-Planck-Gesellschaft **Porträt:** Darmstadt	**4B.1** The genitive case **4B.2** Demonstratives **Wiederholung**	

	KONTEXT	FOTOROMAN	KULTUR	STRUKTUREN	WEITER GEHT'S
	ÜBERBLICK Reviews material from MOSAIK 2				
KAPITEL 1	**LEKTION 1A Gesundheit**				
	Kontext: Die Alltagsroutine **Aussprache und Rechtschreibung:** Vocalic **r**	**Folge 1:** Guten Morgen, Herr Professor!	**Im Fokus:** Die Kur **Porträt:** Nivea	**1A.1** Reflexive verbs with accusative reflexive pronouns **1A.2** Reflexive verbs with dative reflexive pronouns **1A.3** Reciprocal verbs and reflexives used with prepositions **Wiederholung** **Zapping:** *Central Krankenversicherung*	**Panorama:** Mecklenburg-Vorpommern und Brandenburg **Lesen:** Andis Blog / Fit in 10 Minuten! **Hören** **Schreiben** **Wortschatz**
	LEKTION 1B				
	Kontext: Beim Arzt **Aussprache und Rechtschreibung:** Syllabic stress	**Folge 2:** Im Krankenhaus	**Im Fokus:** Apotheken **Porträt:** Röntgen	**1B.1 Der Konjunktiv II** **1B.2 Würden** with the infinitive **Wiederholung**	
KAPITEL 2	**LEKTION 2A Stadtleben**				
	Kontext: Besorgungen **Aussprache und Rechtschreibung:** The glottal stop	**Folge 3:** Gute Neuigkeiten	**Im Fokus:** Fußgängerzonen **Porträt:** Die Deutsche Post	**2A.1** Subordinating conjunctions **2A.2** Adjectives used as nouns **2A.3 Das Futur I** **Kurzfilm:** *Fanny*	**Panorama:** Niedersachsen und Nordrhein-Westfalen **Lesen:** Hermann Hesse, *Allein*; Paul Celan, *Todesfuge* **Hören** **Schreiben** **Wortschatz**
	LEKTION 2B				
	Kontext: In der Stadt **Aussprache und Rechtschreibung:** Loan words (Part 1)	**Folge 4:** Sabites Nacht	**Im Fokus:** Kabarett **Porträt:** Pina Bausch	**2B.1** Prepositions of direction **2B.2** Talking about nationality **Wiederholung**	
KAPITEL 3	**LEKTION 3A Beruf und Karriere**				
	Kontext: Im Büro **Aussprache und Rechtschreibung:** Loan words (Part 2)	**Folge 5:** Sag niemals nie	**Im Fokus:** Familienunternehmen **Porträt:** Robert Bosch	**3A.1** Relative pronouns **3A.2** The past tenses (review) **Wiederholung** **Kurzfilm:** *Die Berliner Mauer*	**Panorama:** Baden-Württemberg, das Saarland und Rheinland-Pfalz **Lesen:** Peter Bichsel, *Der Erfinder* **Hören** **Schreiben** **Wortschatz**
	LEKTION 3B				
	Kontext: Berufe **Aussprache und Rechtschreibung:** Recognizing near-cognates	**Folge 6:** Schlechte Nachrichten	**Im Fokus:** Sozialversicherungen **Porträt:** Der Marshallplan	**3B.1 Das Futur II** **3B.2** Adjective endings (review) **Wiederholung**	
KAPITEL 4	**LEKTION 4A Natur**				
	Kontext: In der Natur **Aussprache und Rechtschreibung:** Intonation	**Folge 7:** In der Kunstgalerie	**Im Fokus:** Landschaften Deutschlands **Porträt:** Alexander von Humboldt	**4A.1 Der Konjunktiv der Vergangenheit** **4A.2 Das Partizip Präsens** **Wiederholung** **Kurzfilm:** *Bienenstich ist aus*	**Panorama:** Sachsen-Anhalt und Sachsen **Lesen:** Rose Ausländer, *Meine Nachtigall*; Rainer Maria Rilke, *Der Panther* **Hören** **Schreiben** **Wortschatz**
	LEKTION 4B				
	Kontext: Die Umwelt **Aussprache und Rechtschreibung:** Tongue twisters	**Folge 8:** Auf Wiedersehen, Berlin!	**Im Fokus:** Grüne Berufe in Sachsen **Porträt:** Michael Braungart	**4B.1 Der Konjunktiv I** and indirect speech **4B.2** The passive voice **Wiederholung**	

There's more to **Mosaik** than meets the page

The **Mosaik** Supersite provides a learning environment designed especially for world language instruction. Password-protected and program-specific, this website provides seamless textbook-technology integration that helps build students' love for language learning.

For students:

- engaging media
- motivating user experience
- superior performance
- helpful resources
- plenty of practice

For educators:

- proven instructional design
- powerful course management
- time-saving tools
- enhanced support

Integrated content means a more powerful student experience

- Streaming videos—episodic dramatic series, authentic TV clips, and authentic short films
- All program audio in downloadable MP3 format
- Textbook activities and additional online-only practice—most with automatic feedback
- Video Chat and Partner Chat activities for conversational skills practice
- My Vocabulary for personalized language study
- Audio-sync readings for all **Lesen** selections
- Cultural readings in all levels and literary selections in **Mosaik 3**
- Online Student Activities Manual fully integrated with the Supersite gradebook

Specialized resources ensure a successful implementation

- Online assessments and Testing Program files in an editable format
- Audioscripts and videoscripts with English translations
- Grammar presentation slides
- Editable block and standard lesson plans
- IPAs with grading rubrics
- Digital Image Bank
- Answer keys
- "I Can" worksheets

Educator tools facilitate instruction and save time

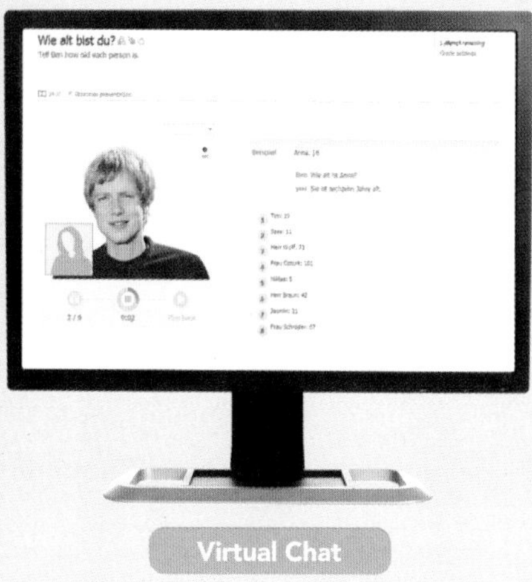

Virtual Chat

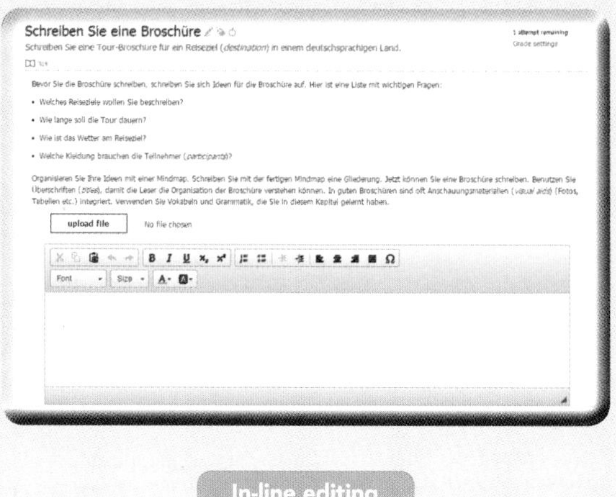

In-line editing

Easy course management

A powerful setup wizard lets you customize your class settings, copy previous courses to save time, and create your all-in-one gradebook. Grades for teacher-created assignments (e.g., pop quizzes, class participation) can be incorporated for a true, up-to-date cumulative grade.

Customized content

Tailor the Supersite to fit your needs. Create your own open-ended or video Partner Chat activities, add video or outside resources, and modify existing content with your own personalized notes.

Grading tools

Grade efficiently via spot-checking, student-by-student, and question-by-question options. Use in-line editing tools to give targeted feedback and voice comments—it's the perfect tool for busy language educators!

Assessment solutions

Administer online quizzes and tests. Use any pre-built assessment "as is" or customize them to meet your specific needs, including: adding or removing questions from a section, reordering sections or questions, and changing point values for questions.

Plus!

- A communication center for announcements, notifications, and student help requests
- Voiceboards for oral assignments, group discussions, homework, and more
- Reporting tools for summarizing student data
- Single sign-on for easy integration with your school's Learning Management System*
- Live Chat for video chat, audio chat, and instant messaging with students

* available for select LMSs

Content and tools delivered your way

Learning doesn't just happen in the classroom. With **Mosaik**, we provide you with a number of digital format options.

vText (Online)

- Browser-based electronic text for online viewing
- Links to all mouse-icon textbook activities*, audio, and video
- Access to all Supersite resources
- Highlighting and note taking
- Easy navigation with searchable table of contents
- iPad®-friendly*
- Single- and double-page view and zooming
- Automatically adds auto-graded activities to the gradebook

Available on any PC or device that has Internet connectivity.

eBook (Downloadable)

- Downloadable electronic text for offline viewing
- Embedded audio for anytime listening
- Easy navigation with searchable table of contents
- Highlighting and note taking
- Single-page view and zooming

When student is connected online:

- Links to all mouse-icon textbook activities*, audio, and video
- Access to all Supersite resources
- Automatically adds auto-graded activities in teacher gradebook

Available for a maximum of 2 computers and 2 mobile devices.

Visit **vistahigherlearning.com/interactive-texts** to learn more.

*Students must use a computer for audio-recording.

For the **Teacher**: Plan

COMPONENT TITLE	WHAT IS IT?			DVD
Teacher's Edition	Teacher support for core instruction	•	•	
Audioscripts	Scripts for all audio selections: • Textbook audioscripts • Lab audioscripts • Testing audioscripts • Virtual Chat audioscripts		•	•
Essential Questions	Chapter-level Essential Questions to guide instruction		•	•
Index of AP® Themes & Contexts	Listing of where the German AP® Themes and Contexts are addressed in each chapter	•	•	•
Lesson Plans	Editable block and standard schedules for every lesson		•	•
Pacing Guides	Guidelines for how to cover the instructional material for a variety of scenarios (standard and block schedules)	•	•	•
Scope & Sequence	Suggested sequence of study broken out by chapters and sections	•	•	•
Videoscripts and Translations	Scripts and translations for all videos: • *Fotoroman* • *Zapping*		•	•

For the **Teacher**: Teach

COMPONENT TITLE	WHAT IS IT?			DVD
Digital Image Bank	Images and maps from the text to use for presentation in class, plus a bank of illustrations to use with teacher-generated content		•	•
Grammar Presentation Slides	Textbook grammar presentation in an editable PowerPoint format		•	•
Info Gap Activities with Answer Key	Info Gap activity worksheets and answer key		•	•
Program Audio	• Textbook Audio • Lab Program Audio		•	•
Student Activities Manual Answer Key	Answers to all activities in the Student Activities Manual (Workbook/Lab Manual/Video Manual)		•	•
Textbook Activity Worksheets	Supplemental spoken and written activities in an editable format		•	•
Video Collection	Program video, including: • *Fotoroman* • *Zapping*		• •	•

For the **Teacher**: Assess

COMPONENT TITLE	WHAT IS IT?			DVD
"I Can" Worksheets	Lesson objectives broken down by chapter section and written in a student-friendly "I Can" statement format		•	•
Integrated Performance Assessments	IPA tasks with grading rubrics		•	•
Testing Program with Answer Key	Lesson quizzes, chapter tests, and cumulative exam		•	•
Testing Program Audio	Audio to accompany all assessments		•	•

For the **Student**

COMPONENT TITLE	WHAT IS IT?	Print	Supersite	DVD
Student Edition	Core instruction for students	•	•	
Audio-synced Readings	Audio to accompany all *Lesen* sections		•	
Dictionary	Easy digital access to a dictionary		•	
eBook	Downloadable Student Edition		•	
End-of-lesson Vocabulary Lists	Core vocabulary for each lesson, with linked audio online		•	
Flashcards	Provide an easy way to study vocabulary (available as part of My Vocabulary)		•	
Fotoroman Video	Engaging storyline video		•	•
Lab Manual Activities Audio	Audio to accompany the Lab Manual portion of the Student Activities Manual		•	•
My Vocabulary	A variety of tools to practice vocabulary		•	
Partner Chats	Work with a partner online to record a conversation via video or audio and submit for grading		•	
Student Activities Manual	Combined Workbook/Lab Manual/Video Manual aligned to each lesson	•	•	
Textbook Audio	Audio to accompany all textbook listening activities		•	
Textbook Mouse Activities	Textbook activities that can also be completed digitally; many provide immediate feedback		•	
Virtual Chats	Record and submit a simulated video or audio conversation with a native speaker for online grading		•	
Vocabulary Hot Spots	Vocabulary presentations with embedded audio		•	
Voiceboards	Collaborative spaces for oral assignments, group discussions, homework, and projects		•	
vText	Virtual interactive textbook for browser-based exploration • Links to all mouse-icon activities, audio, and video • Note-taking capabilities		•	
WebSAM	Online version of the Student Activities Manual, embedded in the online gradebook, with many auto-graded options		•	
Web-only Activities	Additional online practice for students		•	
Zapping Video	Authentic TV clips from across the German-speaking world		•	

Print Supersite Teacher's DVD Set

Beginning with the **student in mind**

Verkehrsmittel und Technologie

KAPITEL 4

LEKTION 4A

Kontext Seite 156–159
- **Auto und Rad fahren**
- Long and short vowels with an **Umlaut**

Fotoroman Seite 160–161
- **Ein Ende mit Schrecken**

Kultur Seite 162–163
- **Die deutsche Autobahn**

Strukturen Seite 164–173
- **4A.1 Das Plusquamperfekt**
- **4A.2** Comparatives and superlatives
- **Wiederholung**
- **Zapping**

LEKTION 4B

Kontext Seite 174–177
- **Technik und Medien**
- The German **l**

Fotoroman Seite 178–179
- **Ein Spaziergang durch Spandau**

Kultur Seite 180–181
- **Max-Planck-Gesellschaft**

Strukturen Seite 182–191
- **4B.1** The genitive case
- **4B.2** Demonstratives
- **Wiederholung**

WEITER GEHT'S

Seite 192–198
Panorama: Hessen und Thüringen
Lesen: Read instructions for a new printer.
Hören: Listen to a conversation about cell phones.
Schreiben: Write a review of a car.
Kapitel 4 Wortschatz

Chapter opener photos highlight scenes from the **Fotoroman** that illustrate the chapter theme. They are snapshots of the characters that students will come to know throughout the program.

Content lists break down each chapter into its two lessons and one **Weiter Geht's** section, giving an at-a-glance summary of the vocabulary, grammar, cultural topics, and language skills covered.

Supersite

Supersite resources are available for every section of each chapter at **vhlcentral.com**. Icons show you which textbook activities are also available online, and where additional practice activities are available. The description next to the Ⓢ icon indicates what additional resources are available for each section: videos, audio recordings, readings, presentations, and more!

Setting the stage
for communication

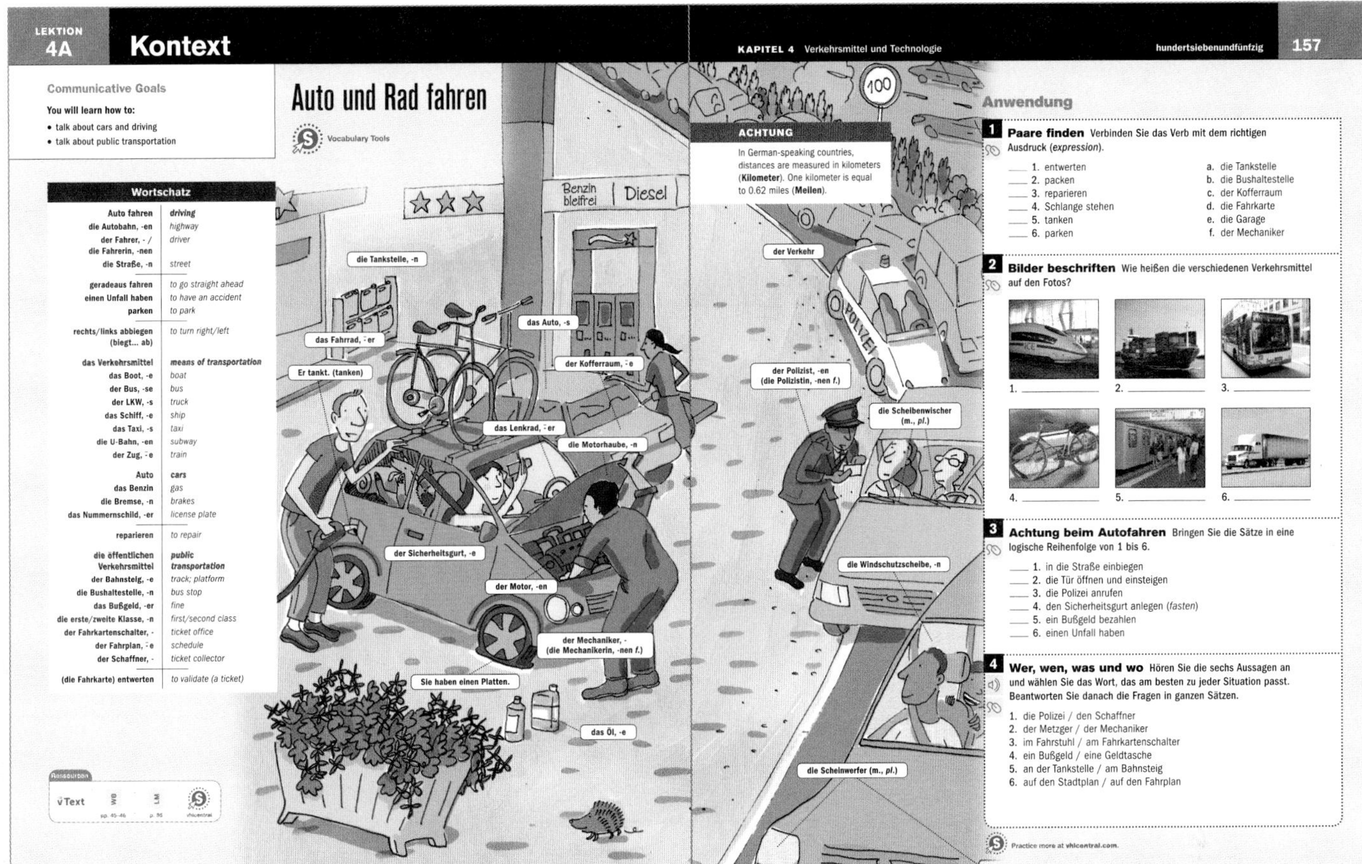

LEKTION 4A **Kontext**

KAPITEL 4 Verkehrsmittel und Technologie · hundertsiebenundfünfzig 157

Communicative Goals

You will learn how to:

- talk about cars and driving
- talk about public transportation

Wortschatz

Auto fahren	***driving***
die Autobahn, -en	*highway*
der Fahrer, - / die Fahrerin, -nen	*driver*
die Straße, -n	*street*
geradeaus fahren	*to go straight ahead*
einen Unfall haben	*to have an accident*
parken	*to park*
rechts/links abbiegen (biegt... ab)	*to turn right/left*
das Verkehrsmittel	***means of transportation***
das Boot, -e	*boat*
der Bus, -se	*bus*
der LKW, -s	*truck*
das Schiff, -e	*ship*
das Taxi, -s	*taxi*
die U-Bahn, -en	*subway*
der Zug, ¨-e	*train*
Auto	***cars***
das Benzin	*gas*
die Bremse, -n	*brakes*
das Nummernschild, -er	*license plate*
reparieren	*to repair*
die öffentlichen Verkehrsmittel	***public transportation***
der Bahnsteig, -e	*track; platform*
die Bushaltestelle, -n	*bus stop*
das Bußgeld, -er	*fine*
die erste/zweite Klasse, -n	*first/second class*
der Fahrkartenschalter, -	*ticket office*
der Fahrplan, ¨-e	*schedule*
der Schaffner, -	*ticket collector*
(die Fahrkarte) entwerten	*to validate (a ticket)*

Ressourcen: vText · WB pp. 45–46 · LM p. 95 · vhlcentral

Auto und Rad fahren

Vocabulary Tools

ACHTUNG

In German-speaking countries, distances are measured in kilometers (**Kilometer**). One kilometer is equal to 0.62 miles (**Meilen**).

Anwendung

1 Paare finden Verbinden Sie das Verb mit dem richtigen Ausdruck (*expression*).

____ 1. entwerten	a. die Tankstelle
____ 2. packen	b. die Bushaltestelle
____ 3. reparieren	c. der Kofferraum
____ 4. Schlange stehen	d. die Fahrkarte
____ 5. tanken	e. die Garage
____ 6. parken	f. der Mechaniker

2 Bilder beschriften Wie heißen die verschiedenen Verkehrsmittel auf den Fotos?

1. ________ 2. ________ 3. ________
4. ________ 5. ________ 6. ________

3 Achtung beim Autofahren Bringen Sie die Sätze in eine logische Reihenfolge von 1 bis 6.

____ 1. in die Straße einbiegen
____ 2. die Tür öffnen und einsteigen
____ 3. die Polizei anrufen
____ 4. den Sicherheitsgurt anlegen (*fasten*)
____ 5. ein Bußgeld bezahlen
____ 6. einen Unfall haben

4 Wer, wen, was und wo Hören Sie die sechs Aussagen an und wählen Sie das Wort, das am besten zu jeder Situation passt. Beantworten Sie danach die Fragen in ganzen Sätzen.

1. die Polizei / den Schaffner
2. der Metzger / der Mechaniker
3. im Fahrstuhl / am Fahrkartenschalter
4. ein Bußgeld / eine Geldtasche
5. an der Tankstelle / am Bahnsteig
6. auf den Stadtplan / auf den Fahrplan

Practice more at vhlcentral.com.

Communicative goals highlight the real-life tasks students will be able to carry out in German by the end of each lesson.

Illustrations introduce high-frequency vocabulary through expansive, full-color images.

Wortschatz sidebars call out important theme-related vocabulary in easy-to-reference German-English lists.

Ressourcen boxes indicate what print and technology ancillaries reinforce and expand on every section of every lesson.

Achtung boxes provide additional information about how and when to use certain vocabulary words or grammar structures.

Kontext always contains an audio activity that accompanies either the **Anwendung** or the **Kommunikation** practice activities. **Anwendung** follows a pedagogical sequence that starts with simpler, shorter, discrete recognition activities and builds toward longer, more complex production activities.

Supersite

- Audio recordings of all vocabulary items
- Audio for **Kontext** listening activity
- Image-based vocabulary activity with audio
- Textbook activities
- Additional online-only practice activities

Engaging students in **active communication**

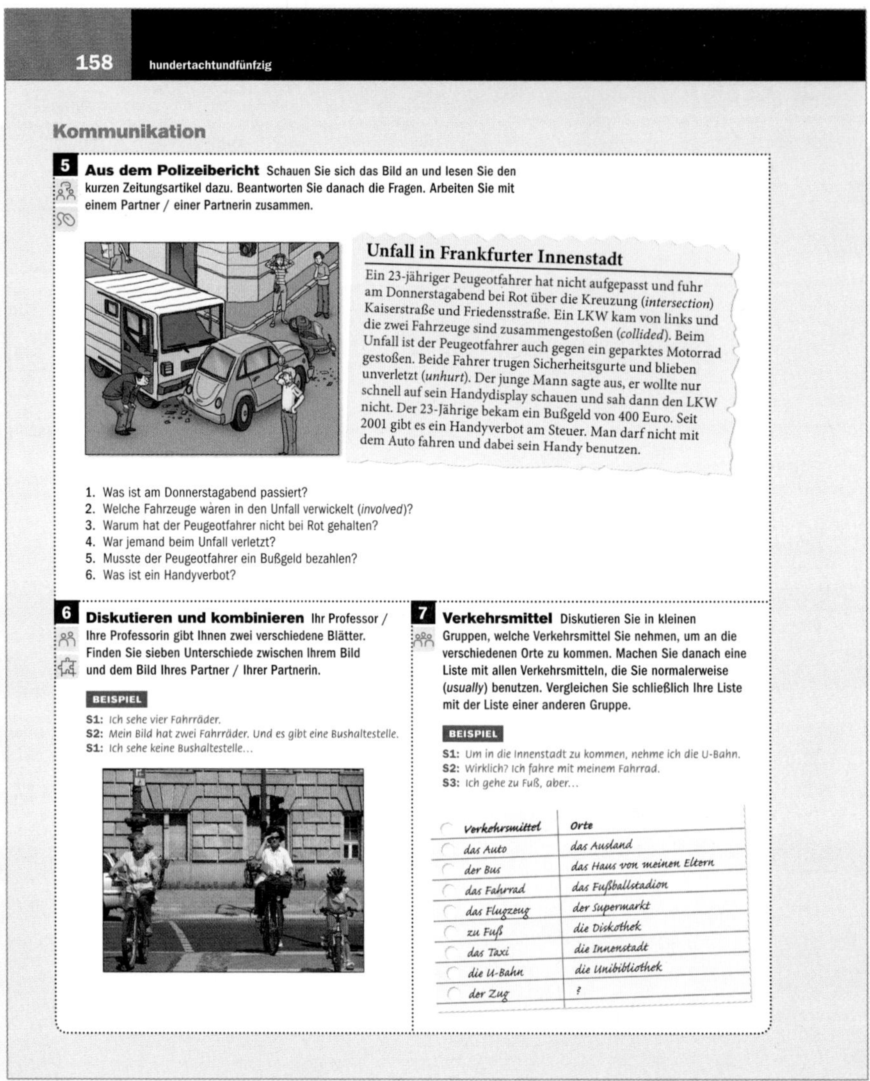

Kommunikation

5 Aus dem Polizeibericht Schauen Sie sich das Bild an und lesen Sie den kurzen Zeitungsartikel dazu. Beantworten Sie danach die Fragen. Arbeiten Sie mit einem Partner / einer Partnerin zusammen.

Unfall in Frankfurter Innenstadt

Ein 23-jähriger Peugeotfahrer hat nicht aufgepasst und fuhr am Donnerstagabend bei Rot über die Kreuzung (*intersection*) Kaiserstraße und Friedensstraße. Ein LKW kam von links und die zwei Fahrzeuge sind zusammengestoßen (*collided*). Beim Unfall ist der Peugeotfahrer auch gegen ein geparktes Motorrad gestoßen. Beide Fahrer trugen Sicherheitsgurte und blieben unverletzt (*unhurt*). Der junge Mann sagte aus, er wollte nur schnell auf sein Handydisplay schauen und sah dann den LKW nicht. Der 23-Jährige bekam ein Bußgeld von 400 Euro. Seit 2001 gibt es ein Handyverbot am Steuer. Man darf nicht mit dem Auto fahren und dabei sein Handy benutzen.

1. Was ist am Donnerstagabend passiert?
2. Welche Fahrzeuge wären in den Unfall verwickelt (*involved*)?
3. Warum hat der Peugeotfahrer nicht bei Rot gehalten?
4. War jemand beim Unfall verletzt?
5. Musste der Peugeotfahrer ein Bußgeld bezahlen?
6. Was ist ein Handyverbot?

6 Diskutieren und kombinieren Ihr Professor / Ihre Professorin gibt Ihnen zwei verschiedene Blätter. Finden Sie sieben Unterschiede zwischen Ihrem Bild und dem Bild Ihres Partner / Ihrer Partnerin.

BEISPIEL

S1: *Ich sehe vier Fahrräder.*
S2: *Mein Bild hat zwei Fahrräder. Und es gibt eine Bushaltestelle.*
S1: *Ich sehe keine Bushaltestelle...*

7 Verkehrsmittel Diskutieren Sie in kleinen Gruppen, welche Verkehrsmittel Sie nehmen, um an die verschiedenen Orte zu kommen. Machen Sie danach eine Liste mit allen Verkehrsmitteln, die Sie normalerweise (*usually*) benutzen. Vergleichen Sie schließlich Ihre Liste mit der Liste einer anderen Gruppe.

BEISPIEL

S1: *Um in die Innenstadt zu kommen, nehme ich die U-Bahn.*
S2: *Wirklich? Ich fahre mit meinem Fahrrad.*
S3: *Ich gehe zu Fuß, aber...*

Verkehrsmittel	Orte
das Auto	das Ausland
der Bus	das Haus von meinen Eltern
das Fahrrad	das Fußballstadion
das Flugzeug	der Supermarkt
zu Fuß	die Diskothek
das Taxi	die Innenstadt
die U-Bahn	die Unibibliothek
der Zug	?

Kommunikation activities make use of discourse-level prompts, encouraging the creative use of vocabulary in interactions with a partner, a small group, or the entire class.

Pair and group icons indicate communicative activities—such as role play, games, personal questions, interviews, and surveys—for interpersonal and presentational practice.

- Chat activities for conversational skill-building and oral practice

Authenticity
in pronunciation and spelling

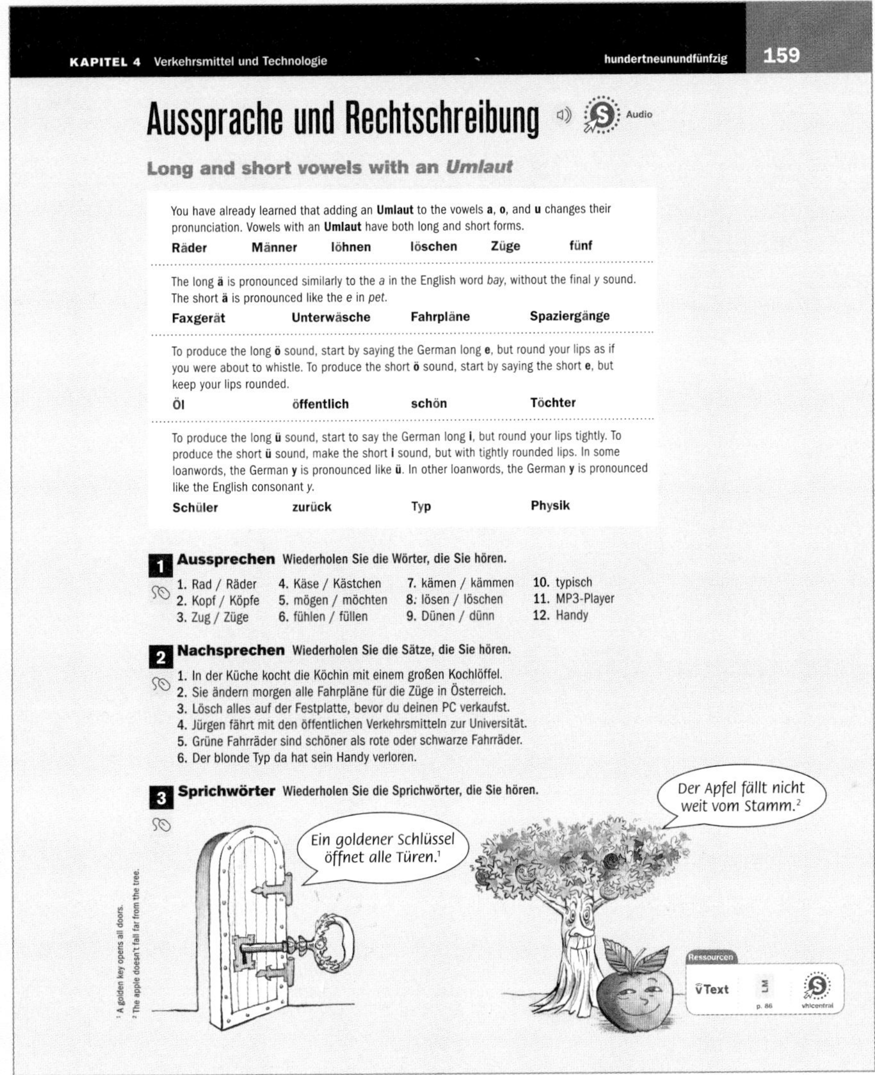

KAPITEL 4 Verkehrsmittel und Technologie — hundertneunundfünfzig 159

Aussprache und Rechtschreibung

Audio

Long and short vowels with an *Umlaut*

You have already learned that adding an **Umlaut** to the vowels **a**, **o**, and **u** changes their pronunciation. Vowels with an **Umlaut** have both long and short forms.

Räder **Männer** **löhnen** **löschen** **Züge** **fünf**

The long **ä** is pronounced similarly to the *a* in the English word *bay*, without the final *y* sound. The short **ä** is pronounced like the *e* in *pet*.

Faxgerät **Unterwäsche** **Fahrpläne** **Spaziergänge**

To produce the long **ö** sound, start by saying the German long **e**, but round your lips as if you were about to whistle. To produce the short **ö** sound, start by saying the short **e**, but keep your lips rounded.

Öl **öffentlich** **schön** **Töchter**

To produce the long **ü** sound, start to say the German long **i**, but round your lips tightly. To produce the short **ü** sound, make the short **i** sound, but with tightly rounded lips. In some loanwords, the German **y** is pronounced like **ü**. In other loanwords, the German **y** is pronounced like the English consonant *y*.

Schüler **zurück** **Typ** **Physik**

1 Aussprechen Wiederholen Sie die Wörter, die Sie hören.

1. Rad / Räder
2. Kopf / Köpfe
3. Zug / Züge
4. Käse / Kästchen
5. mögen / möchten
6. fühlen / füllen
7. kämen / kämmen
8. lösen / löschen
9. Dünen / dünn
10. typisch
11. MP3-Player
12. Handy

2 Nachsprechen Wiederholen Sie die Sätze, die Sie hören.

1. In der Küche kocht die Köchin mit einem großen Kochlöffel.
2. Sie ändern morgen alle Fahrpläne für die Züge in Österreich.
3. Lösch alles auf der Festplatte, bevor du deinen PC verkaufst.
4. Jürgen fährt mit den öffentlichen Verkehrsmitteln zur Universität.
5. Grüne Fahrräder sind schöner als rote oder schwarze Fahrräder.
6. Der blonde Typ da hat sein Handy verloren.

3 Sprichwörter Wiederholen Sie die Sprichwörter, die Sie hören.

[1] A golden key opens all doors.
[2] The apple doesn't fall far from the tree.

Explanations of German pronunciation and spelling are presented clearly, with abundant model words and phrases. The red highlighting feature focuses students' attention on the target structure.

Practice pronunciation and spelling at the word- and sentence-levels. The final activity features illustrated sayings and proverbs that present the target structures in an entertaining cultural context.

The audio icon at the top of the page indicates that the explanation and activities are recorded for convenient use in or outside of class.

Supersite

- Audio recording of the **Aussprache und Rechtschreibung** presentation
- Record-and-compare activities

Fotoroman
bridges language and culture

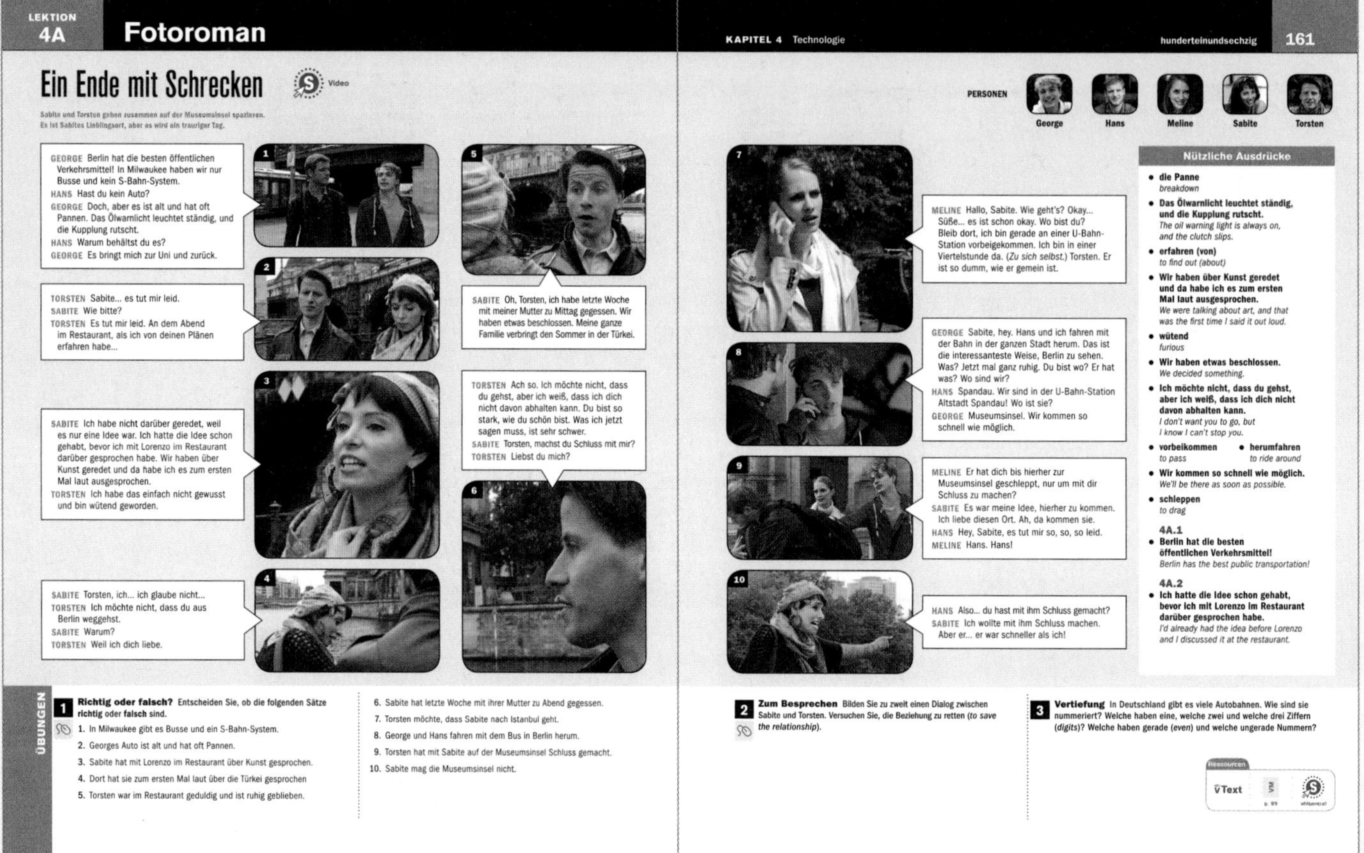

LEKTION 4A **Fotoroman**

KAPITEL 4 Technologie — hunderteinundsechzig 161

Ein Ende mit Schrecken

Video

Sabite und Torsten gehen zusammen auf der Museumsinsel spazieren. Es ist Sabites Lieblingsort, aber es wird ein trauriger Tag.

PERSONEN: George, Hans, Meline, Sabite, Torsten

Nützliche Ausdrücke

- **die Panne**
  breakdown
- **Das Ölwarnlicht leuchtet ständig, und die Kupplung rutscht.**
  The oil warning light is always on, and the clutch slips.
- **erfahren (von)**
  to find out (about)
- **Wir haben über Kunst geredet und da habe ich es zum ersten Mal laut ausgesprochen.**
  We were talking about art, and that was the first time I said it out loud.
- **wütend**
  furious
- **Wir haben etwas beschlossen.**
  We decided something.
- **Ich möchte nicht, dass du gehst, aber ich weiß, dass ich dich nicht davon abhalten kann.**
  I don't want you to go, but I know I can't stop you.
- **vorbeikommen**
  to pass
- **herumfahren**
  to ride around
- **Wir kommen so schnell wie möglich.**
  We'll be there as soon as possible.
- **schleppen**
  to drag

4A.1

- **Berlin hat die besten öffentlichen Verkehrsmittel!**
  Berlin has the best public transportation!

4A.2

- **Ich hatte die Idee schon gehabt, bevor ich mit Lorenzo im Restaurant darüber gesprochen habe.**
  I'd already had the idea before Lorenzo and I discussed it at the restaurant.

ÜBUNGEN

1 Richtig oder falsch? Entscheiden Sie, ob die folgenden Sätze **richtig** oder **falsch** sind.

1. In Milwaukee gibt es Busse und ein S-Bahn-System.
2. Georges Auto ist alt und hat oft Pannen.
3. Sabite hat mit Lorenzo im Restaurant über Kunst gesprochen.
4. Dort hat sie zum ersten Mal laut über die Türkei gesprochen
5. Torsten war im Restaurant geduldig und ist ruhig geblieben.
6. Sabite hat letzte Woche mit ihrer Mutter zu Abend gegessen.
7. Torsten möchte, dass Sabite nach Istanbul geht.
8. George und Hans fahren mit dem Bus in Berlin herum.
9. Torsten hat mit Sabite auf der Museumsinsel Schluss gemacht.
10. Sabite mag die Museumsinsel nicht.

2 Zum Besprechen Bilden Sie zu zweit einen Dialog zwischen Sabite und Torsten. Versuchen Sie, die Beziehung zu retten (*to save the relationship*).

3 Vertiefung In Deutschland gibt es viele Autobahnen. Wie sind sie nummeriert? Welche haben eine, welche zwei und welche drei Ziffern (*digits*)? Welche haben gerade (*even*) und welche ungerade Nummern?

Ressourcen: vText; VM p. 99; vhlcentral

Fotoroman is a versatile episodic video that can be assigned as homework, presented in class, or used as review.

Conversations reinforce vocabulary from **Kontext**. They also preview structures from the upcoming **Strukturen** section in context.

Personen features the cast of recurring **Fotoroman** characters, including four students living in Berlin: George, Sabite, Meline, and Hans.

Nützliche Ausdrücke calls out the most important words and expressions from the **Fotoroman** episode that have not been formally presented. This vocabulary is not tested. The blue numbers refer to the grammar structures presented in the lesson.

Übungen activities include comprehension questions, a communicative task, and a research-based task.

Supersite

- Streaming video for all episodes of the **Fotoroman**
- End-of-video **Zusammenfassung** section where key vocabulary and grammar from the episode are called out
- Textbook activities

Culture
presented in context

LEKTION 4A **Kultur**

KAPITEL 4 Verkehrsmittel und Technologie — hundertdreiundsechzig 163

IM FOKUS

Die deutsche Autobahn

Reading

TIPP

The German **Autobahn** is toll-free for cars, but Austria and Switzerland charge a toll (**eine Maut**) for use of all limited-access highways. Cars in each country must display a toll sticker (**eine Mautvignette**) in their windshields to show that they have paid an annual fee to use the country's **Autobahnnetz**.

DIE GESCHICHTE DER DEUTSCHEN Autobahn geht mehr als 80 Jahre zurück. Die AVUS (Automobil-Verkehrs- und Übungs-Straße), heute Teil der Autobahn A115, war die erste nur für Autos zugelassene° Straße Europas. Schon seit 1921 erstreckte sie sich° zwischen den Berliner Stadtteilen Charlottenburg und Nikolassee. Um einmal darüber zu fahren, musste man zehn Mark bezahlen. Damals war das ziemlich teuer!

Am 6. August 1932 eröffnete der Kölner Oberbürgermeister Konrad Adenauer die erste so genannte „Autobahn". Ihr Bau hatte drei Jahre gedauert. Sie war 20 Kilometer lang und erstreckte sich zwischen Köln und Bonn. In beide Fahrtrichtungen war sie zweispurig° und kreuzungsfrei° Damit entsprach° sie einer Autobahn, wie wir sie heute kennen, mit einem Unterschied: Es gab keinen Mittelstreifen°. Deshalb bekam der Abschnitt erst 1958, nach weiterem Ausbau°, den offiziellen Status der Autobahn.

Heute hat Deutschland eines der dichtesten Autobahnnetze° der Welt und der Bau geht immer weiter. Es gilt zwar in Deutschland eine Richtgeschwindigkeit° von 130 Kilometern pro Stunde, ein generelles Tempolimit° gibt es aber nicht. Trotzdem haben 45 Prozent aller deutschen Autobahnkilometer Tempolimits. An fast allen Autobahnen gibt es mittlerweile komfortable Raststätten°, wo es neben Tankstellen, Hotels, Restaurants und Läden sogar Kinderspielplätze gibt.

Längste Autobahnnetze der Welt

Land	Strecke°
USA	97.355 km
China	75.932 km
Spanien	16.204 km
Deutschland	12.917 km

zugelassene *permitted* **erstreckte... sich** *extended* **zweispurig** *two-lane* **kreuzungsfrei** *intersection-free* **entsprach** *conformed to* **Mittelstreifen** *median strip* **Ausbau** *extension* **Autobahnnetze** *interstate highway networks* **Richtgeschwindigkeit** *target speed* **Tempolimit** *speed limit* **Raststätten** *service areas* **Strecke** *distance*

DEUTSCH IM ALLTAG

Verkehrsschilder

die Kreuzung	*intersection*
das Stoppschild	*stop sign*
(die) Ausfahrt	*exit*
(die) Baustelle	*construction zone*
(die) Einbahnstraße	*one-way street*
(die) Umleitung	*detour*

DIE DEUTSCHSPRACHIGE WELT

Fahrrad fahren

In Deutschland besitzen mehr Haushalte° Fahrräder als ein Auto. Bei Familien haben sogar 96% der Haushalte Fahrräder. Deshalb gibt es in vielen Städten separate Fahrradwege°. Für das Fahrradfahren gibt es besondere Regeln°: Wenn es keinen Fahrradweg gibt, müssen Fahrradfahrer, die über 11 Jahre alt sind, auf der rechten Seite der Straße fahren. Besondere Schilder zeigen, wann Fahrradfahrer in Einbahnstraßen entgegen der Fahrtrichtung° fahren dürfen. In Fußgängerzonen° dürfen Radfahrer nur im Schritttempo° fahren. Außerdem muss jedes Fahrrad ein festes Fahrradlicht haben.

Haushalte *households* **Fahrradwege** *bike lanes* **Regeln** *rules* **entgegen der Fahrtrichtung** *against the flow of traffic* **Fußgängerzonen** *pedestrian zones* **Schritttempo** *walking speed*

PORTRÄT

Fräulein Stinnes' Weltreise°

Clärenore Stinnes kommt am 21. Januar 1901 als Tochter eines Großindustriellen zur Welt. Mit 24 Jahren nimmt sie zum ersten Mal an einem Autorennen° teil. Bis 1927 gewinnt sie 17 Rennen, darunter auch eine internationale Rallye in Russland. Sie ist die einzige Frau unter 53 Teilnehmern! Im Mai 1927 bricht Clärenore zu einer Weltreise auf. Sie finanziert die Reise mit Sponsoren wie Bosch und Aral. Auch das Außenministerium° und deutsche Auslandsvertretungen° unterstützen sie. Sie legt 47.000 Kilometer zurück und ist zwei Jahre und einen Monat unterwegs. Das Auto, ein Adler Standard 6, steht heute im Deutschen Museum in München.

Weltreise *world tour* **Autorennen** *car race* **Außenministerium** *Ministry of Foreign Affairs* **Auslandsvertretungen** *embassies*

IM INTERNET

Suchen Sie Informationen zu der Internationalen Automobil-Ausstellung (IAA). Wo und wann war die letzte Ausstellung?

Find out more at **vhlcentral.com**.

ÜBUNGEN

1 Richtig oder falsch? Sind die Aussagen richtig oder falsch? Korrigieren Sie die falschen Aussagen.

1. Die Geschichte der deutschen Autobahn geht 60 Jahre zurück.
2. Konrad Adenauer eröffnete 1921 die erste so genannte „Autobahn".
3. Die AVUS erstreckte sich zwischen Köln und Bonn.
4. Man baute die erste so genannte „Autobahn" in drei Jahren.
5. Eine Autobahn muss zweispurig und kreuzungsfrei sein.
6. Deuschland hat das dichteste Autobahnnetz der Welt.
7. In Deutschland gibt es eine Richtgeschwindigkeit von 130 Kilometern pro Stunde.
8. Es gibt auf deutschen Autobahnen keine Tempolimits.
9. Heute umfasst das Autobahnnetz in Deutschland mehr als 75.000 Kilometer.
10. Nach Spanien hat Deutschland das längste Autobahnnetz Europas.

Practice more at **vhlcentral.com**.

2 Was fehlt? Ergänzen Sie die Sätze.

1. In deutschen Haushalten gibt es öfter ________ als ein Auto.
2. In vielen Städten gibt es seperate ________ für Fahrräder.
3. Jedes Fahrrad in Deutschland muss ________ haben.
4. Ihre Weltumrundung hat ________ und einen Monat gedauert.
5. Das Auto, das Clärenore Stinnes bei ihrer Weltreise gefahren hat, kann man heute im ________ in München finden.

3 Lieblingstransportmittel Diskutieren Sie mit einem Partner / einer Partnerin Ihr Lieblingstransportmittel. Wie bewegen Sie sich am liebsten fort? Sind Sie ein Fan von Fahrrad, Auto oder Bus? Gehen Sie am liebsten zu Fuß? Warum bewegen Sie sich gerne so fort? Was sind die Vorteile und Nachteile?

Ressourcen — vText — vhlcentral

Im Fokus presents an in-depth reading about the lesson's cultural theme. Full-color photos bring to life important aspects of the topic, while charts support the main text with statistics and additional information.

Tipp boxes provide helpful tips for reading and understanding German.

Porträt spotlights notable people, places, events, and products from the German-speaking world. This article is thematically linked to the lesson.

Deutsch im Alltag presents additional vocabulary related to the lesson theme, showcasing words and phrases used in everyday spoken German. This vocabulary is not tested.

Die deutschsprachige Welt focuses on the people, places, dialects, and traditions in regions where German is spoken. This short article is thematically linked to the lesson.

Im Internet boxes, with provocative questions and photos, feature additional cultural explorations online.

Supersite

- **Kultur** reading
- **Im Internet** research activity expands on the chapter theme
- Textbook activities
- Chat activities for conversational skill-building and oral practice

Grammar
as a tool not a topic

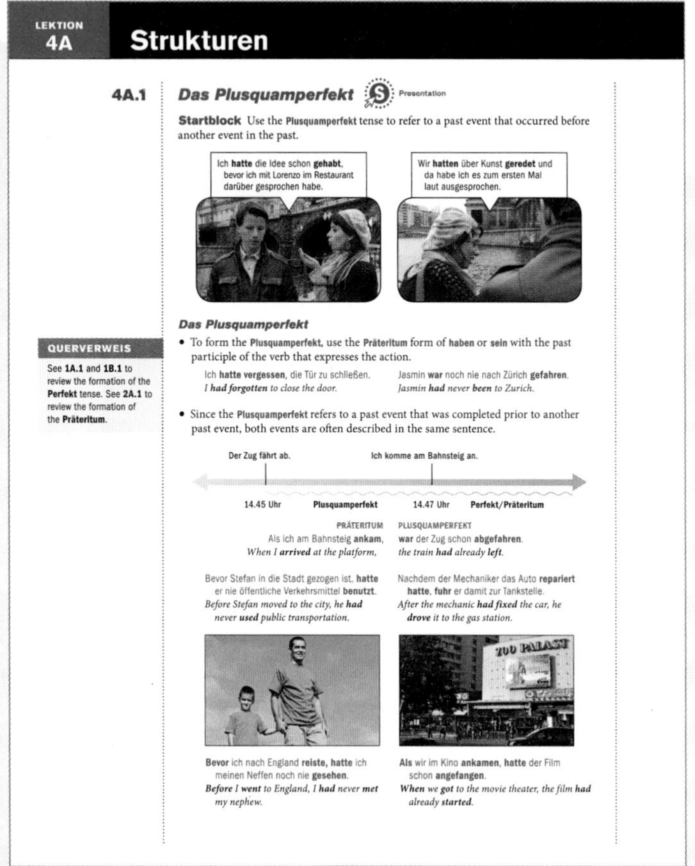
LEKTION 4A **Strukturen**

4A.1 ***Das Plusquamperfekt*** Presentation

Startblock Use the **Plusquamperfekt** tense to refer to a past event that occurred before another event in the past.

Das Plusquamperfekt

- To form the **Plusquamperfekt**, use the **Präteritum** form of **haben** or **sein** with the past participle of the verb that expresses the action.

Ich **hatte vergessen**, die Tür zu schließen.
*I **had forgotten** to close the door.*

Jasmin **war** noch nie nach Zürich **gefahren**.
*Jasmin **had** never **been** to Zurich.*

- Since the **Plusquamperfekt** refers to a past event that was completed prior to another past event, both events are often described in the same sentence.

PRÄTERITUM	PLUSQUAMPERFEKT
Als ich am Bahnsteig **ankam**,	**war** der Zug schon **abgefahren**.
*When I **arrived** at the platform,*	*the train **had** already **left**.*

Bevor Stefan in die Stadt gezogen ist, **hatte** er nie öffentliche Verkehrsmittel **benutzt**.
*Before Stefan moved to the city, he **had** never **used** public transportation.*

Nachdem der Mechaniker das Auto **repariert hatte**, **fuhr** er damit zur Tankstelle.
*After the mechanic **had fixed** the car, he **drove** it to the gas station.*

Bevor ich nach England **reiste, hatte** ich meinen Neffen noch nie **gesehen**.
***Before** I **went** to England, I **had** never **met** my nephew.*

Als wir im Kino **ankamen**, **hatte** der Film schon **angefangen**.
***When** we **got** to the movie theater, the film **had** already **started**.*

QUERVERWEIS

See **1A.1** and **1B.1** to review the formation of the **Perfekt** tense. See **2A.1** to review the formation of the **Präteritum**.

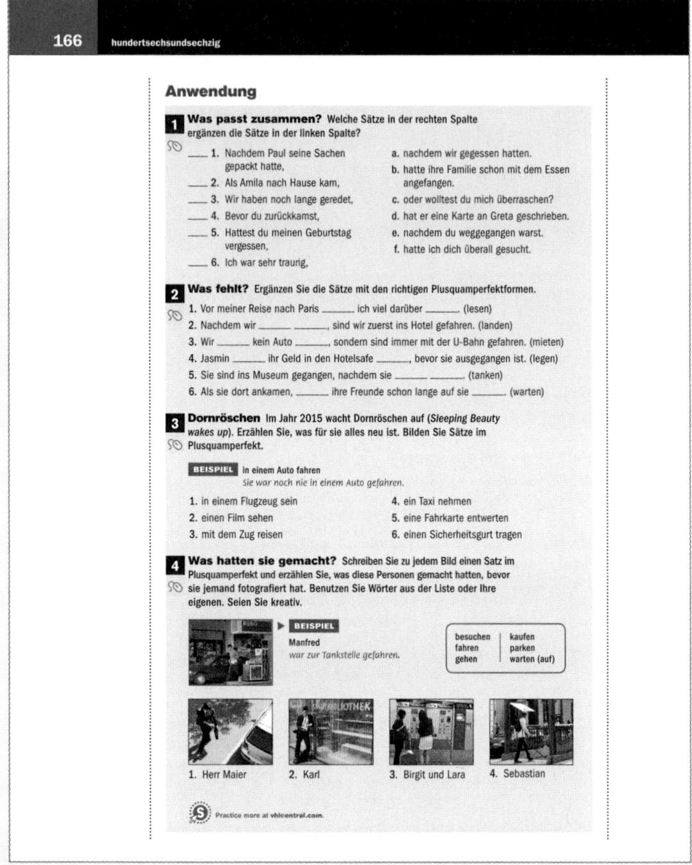
166 hundertsechsundsechzig

Anwendung

1 Was passt zusammen? Welche Sätze in der rechten Spalte ergänzen die Sätze in der linken Spalte?

___ 1. Nachdem Paul seine Sachen gepackt hatte,
___ 2. Als Amila nach Hause kam,
___ 3. Wir haben noch lange geredet,
___ 4. Bevor du zurückkamst,
___ 5. Hattest du meinen Geburtstag vergessen,
___ 6. Ich war sehr traurig,

a. nachdem wir gegessen hatten.
b. hatte ihre Familie schon mit dem Essen angefangen.
c. oder wolltest du mich überraschen?
d. hat er eine Karte an Greta geschrieben.
e. nachdem du weggegangen warst.
f. hatte ich dich überall gesucht.

2 Was fehlt? Ergänzen Sie die Sätze mit den richtigen Plusquamperfektformen.

1. Vor meiner Reise nach Paris ______ ich viel darüber ______. (lesen)
2. Nachdem wir ______ ______, sind wir zuerst ins Hotel gefahren. (landen)
3. Wir ______ kein Auto ______, sondern sind immer mit der U-Bahn gefahren. (mieten)
4. Jasmin ______ ihr Geld in den Hotelsafe ______, bevor sie ausgegangen ist. (legen)
5. Sie sind ins Museum gegangen, nachdem sie ______ ______. (tanken)
6. Als sie dort ankamen, ______ ihre Freunde schon lange auf sie ______. (warten)

3 Dornröschen Im Jahr 2015 wacht Dornröschen auf (*Sleeping Beauty wakes up*). Erzählen Sie, was für sie alles neu ist. Bilden Sie Sätze im Plusquamperfekt.

BEISPIEL in einem Auto fahren
Sie war noch nie in einem Auto gefahren.

1. in einem Flugzeug sein
2. einen Film sehen
3. mit dem Zug reisen
4. ein Taxi nehmen
5. eine Fahrkarte entwerten
6. einen Sicherheitsgurt tragen

4 Was hatten sie gemacht? Schreiben Sie zu jedem Bild einen Satz im Plusquamperfekt und erzählen Sie, was diese Personen gemacht hatten, bevor sie jemand fotografiert hat. Benutzen Sie Wörter aus der Liste oder Ihre eigenen. Seien Sie kreativ.

BEISPIEL
Manfred
war zur Tankstelle gefahren.

besuchen	kaufen
fahren	parken
gehen	warten (auf)

1. Herr Maier 2. Karl 3. Birgit und Lara 4. Sebastian

Practice more at vhlcentral.com.

Startblock eases into each grammar explanation, with definitions of grammatical terms and reminders about grammar concepts which are already familiar.

Querverweis boxes call out information covered in earlier lessons or provide cross-references to related topics that will be covered in future lessons.

Achtung boxes clarify potential sources of confusion and provide supplementary information.

Jetzt sind Sie dran! is the first opportunity to practice the new grammar point.

Anwendung offers a wide range of guided activities that combine lesson vocabulary and previously learned material with the new grammar point.

Kommunikation activities provide opportunities for self-expression using the lesson grammar and vocabulary. These activities feature interaction with a partner, in small groups, or with the whole class.

- Grammar presentations
- Textbook activities
- Additional online-only practice activities
- Chat activities for conversational skill-building and oral practice

Carefully scaffolded lesson review

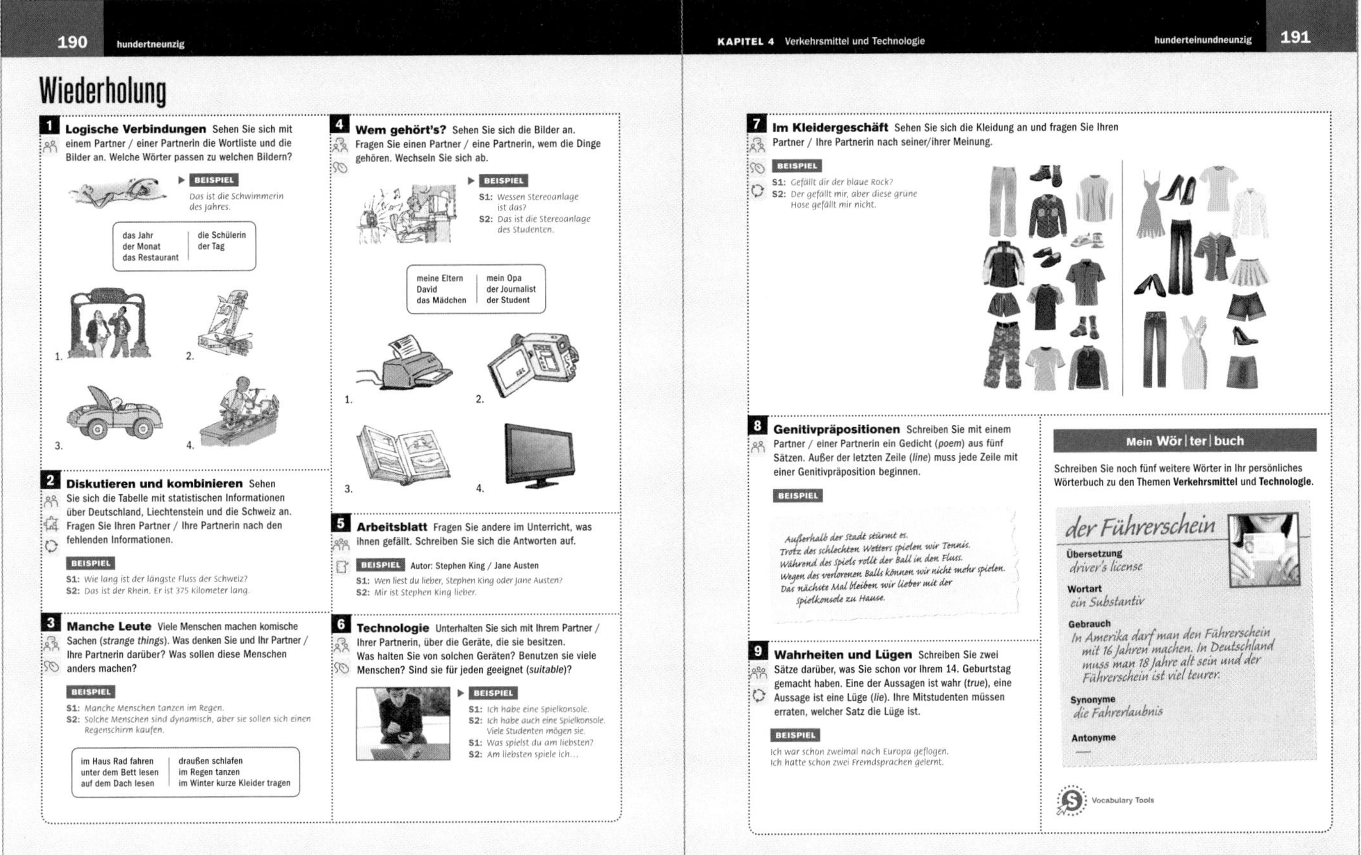

190 hundertneunzig

Wiederholung

1 Logische Verbindungen Sehen Sie sich mit einem Partner / einer Partnerin die Wortliste und die Bilder an. Welche Wörter passen zu welchen Bildern?

BEISPIEL
Das ist die Schwimmerin des Jahres.

das Jahr der Monat das Restaurant	die Schülerin der Tag

1. 2. 3. 4.

2 Diskutieren und kombinieren Sehen Sie sich die Tabelle mit statistischen Informationen über Deutschland, Liechtenstein und die Schweiz an. Fragen Sie Ihren Partner / Ihre Partnerin nach den fehlenden Informationen.

BEISPIEL
S1: *Wie lang ist der längste Fluss der Schweiz?*
S2: *Das ist der Rhein. Er ist 375 Kilometer lang.*

3 Manche Leute Viele Menschen machen komische Sachen (*strange things*). Was denken Sie und Ihr Partner / Ihre Partnerin darüber? Was sollen diese Menschen anders machen?

BEISPIEL
S1: *Manche Menschen tanzen im Regen.*
S2: *Solche Menschen sind dynamisch, aber sie sollen sich einen Regenschirm kaufen.*

im Haus Rad fahren unter dem Bett lesen auf dem Dach lesen	draußen schlafen im Regen tanzen im Winter kurze Kleider tragen

4 Wem gehört's? Sehen Sie sich die Bilder an. Fragen Sie einen Partner / eine Partnerin, wem die Dinge gehören. Wechseln Sie sich ab.

BEISPIEL
S1: *Wessen Stereoanlage ist das?*
S2: *Das ist die Stereoanlage des Studenten.*

meine Eltern David das Mädchen	mein Opa der Journalist der Student

1. 2. 3. 4.

5 Arbeitsblatt Fragen Sie andere im Unterricht, was ihnen gefällt. Schreiben Sie sich die Antworten auf.

BEISPIEL Autor: Stephen King / Jane Austen
S1: *Wen liest du lieber, Stephen King oder Jane Austen?*
S2: *Mir ist Stephen King lieber.*

6 Technologie Unterhalten Sie sich mit Ihrem Partner / Ihrer Partnerin, über die Geräte, die sie besitzen. Was halten Sie von solchen Geräten? Benutzen sie viele Menschen? Sind sie für jeden geeignet (*suitable*)?

BEISPIEL
S1: *Ich habe eine Spielkonsole.*
S2: *Ich habe auch eine Spielkonsole. Viele Studenten mögen sie.*
S1: *Was spielst du am liebsten?*
S2: *Am liebsten spiele ich…*

KAPITEL 4 Verkehrsmittel und Technologie hunderteinundneunzig 191

7 Im Kleidergeschäft Sehen Sie sich die Kleidung an und fragen Sie Ihren Partner / Ihre Partnerin nach seiner/ihrer Meinung.

BEISPIEL
S1: *Gefällt dir der blaue Rock?*
S2: *Der gefällt mir, aber diese grüne Hose gefällt mir nicht.*

8 Genitivpräpositionen Schreiben Sie mit einem Partner / einer Partnerin ein Gedicht (*poem*) aus fünf Sätzen. Außer der letzten Zeile (*line*) muss jede Zeile mit einer Genitivpräposition beginnen.

BEISPIEL
Außerhalb der Stadt stürmt es.
Trotz des schlechten Wetters spielen wir Tennis.
Während des Spiels rollt der Ball in den Fluss.
Wegen des verlorenen Balls können wir nicht mehr spielen.
Das nächste Mal bleiben wir lieber mit der Spielkonsole zu Hause.

9 Wahrheiten und Lügen Schreiben Sie zwei Sätze darüber, was Sie schon vor Ihrem 14. Geburtstag gemacht haben. Eine der Aussagen ist wahr (*true*), eine Aussage ist eine Lüge (*lie*). Ihre Mitstudenten müssen erraten, welcher Satz die Lüge ist.

BEISPIEL
Ich war schon zweimal nach Europa geflogen.
Ich hatte schon zwei Fremdsprachen gelernt.

Mein Wör|ter|buch

Schreiben Sie noch fünf weitere Wörter in Ihr persönliches Wörterbuch zu den Themen **Verkehrsmittel** und **Technologie**.

der Führerschein
Übersetzung *driver's license*
Wortart *ein Substantiv*
Gebrauch *In Amerika darf man den Führerschein mit 16 Jahren machen. In Deutschland muss man 18 Jahre alt sein und der Führerschein ist viel teurer.*
Synonyme *die Fahrerlaubnis*
Antonyme —

Vocabulary Tools

Wiederholung activities integrate the lesson's grammar points and vocabulary with previously learned vocabulary and structures, providing consistent, built-in review.

Pair and group icons indicate communicative activities—such as role play, games, personal questions, interviews, and surveys for interpersonal and presentational practice.

Information gap activities, identified by interlocking puzzle pieces, engage partners in problem-solving situations.

Recycling icons call out activities that practice the lesson's grammar and vocabulary along with previously learned material.

Mein Wörterbuch in the B lesson of each chapter offers the opportunity to increase vocabulary comprehension and the contextualization of new words.

- Chat activities for conversational skill-building and oral practice

Authentic cultural media
for interpretive communication

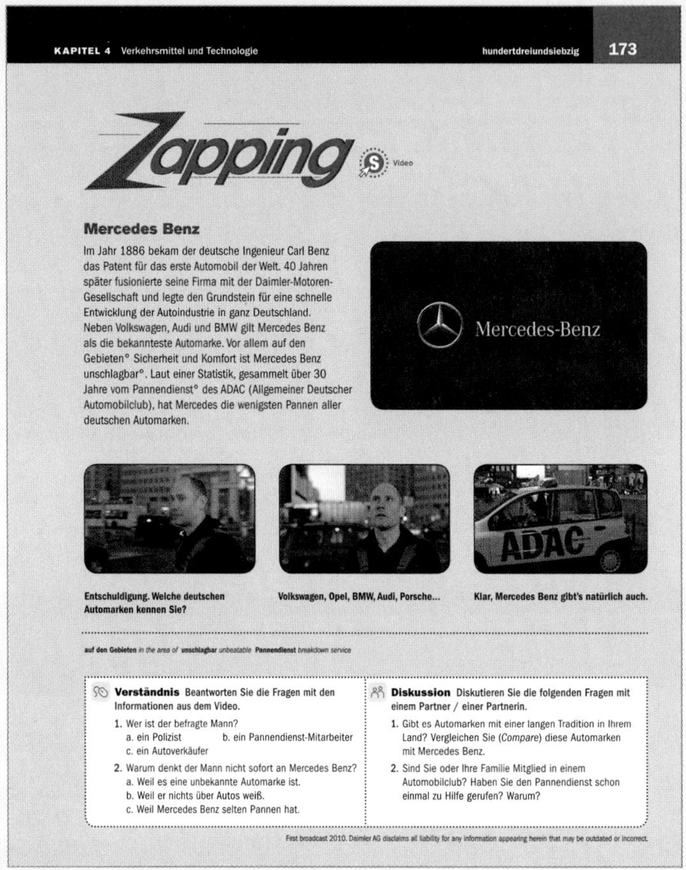

KAPITEL 4 Verkehrsmittel und Technologie — hundertdreiundsiebzig 173

Zapping — Video

Mercedes Benz

Im Jahr 1886 bekam der deutsche Ingenieur Carl Benz das Patent für das erste Automobil der Welt. 40 Jahren später fusionierte seine Firma mit der Daimler-Motoren-Gesellschaft und legte den Grundstein für eine schnelle Entwicklung der Autoindustrie in ganz Deutschland. Neben Volkswagen, Audi und BMW gilt Mercedes Benz als die bekannteste Automarke. Vor allem auf den Gebieten° Sicherheit und Komfort ist Mercedes Benz unschlagbar°. Laut einer Statistik, gesammelt über 30 Jahre vom Pannendienst° des ADAC (Allgemeiner Deutscher Automobilclub), hat Mercedes die wenigsten Pannen aller deutschen Automarken.

Entschuldigung. Welche deutschen Automarken kennen Sie?

Volkswagen, Opel, BMW, Audi, Porsche...

Klar, Mercedes Benz gibt's natürlich auch.

auf den Gebieten *in the area of* **unschlagbar** *unbeatable* **Pannendienst** *breakdown service*

Verständnis Beantworten Sie die Fragen mit den Informationen aus dem Video.

1. Wer ist der befragte Mann?
   a. ein Polizist b. ein Pannendienst-Mitarbeiter
   c. ein Autoverkäufer
2. Warum denkt der Mann nicht sofort an Mercedes Benz?
   a. Weil es eine unbekannte Automarke ist.
   b. Weil er nichts über Autos weiß.
   c. Weil Mercedes Benz selten Pannen hat.

Diskussion Diskutieren Sie die folgenden Fragen mit einem Partner / einer Partnerin.

1. Gibt es Automarken mit einer langen Tradition in Ihrem Land? Vergleichen Sie (*Compare*) diese Automarken mit Mercedes Benz.
2. Sind Sie oder Ihre Familie Mitglied in einem Automobilclub? Haben Sie den Pannendienst schon einmal zu Hilfe gerufen? Warum?

First broadcast 2010. Daimler AG disclaims all liability for any information appearing herein that may be outdated or incorrect.

Zapping presents TV commercials from the German-speaking world. Post-viewing activities check comprehension.

Summary provides context for each video clip.

Photos and captions provide key information to facilitate comprehension.

Analyse post-viewing activities encourage exploration of the broader idea presented in each video clip.

- Streaming video of the TV clip with teacher-controlled subtitle options
- Textbook activities

Perspective
through geography

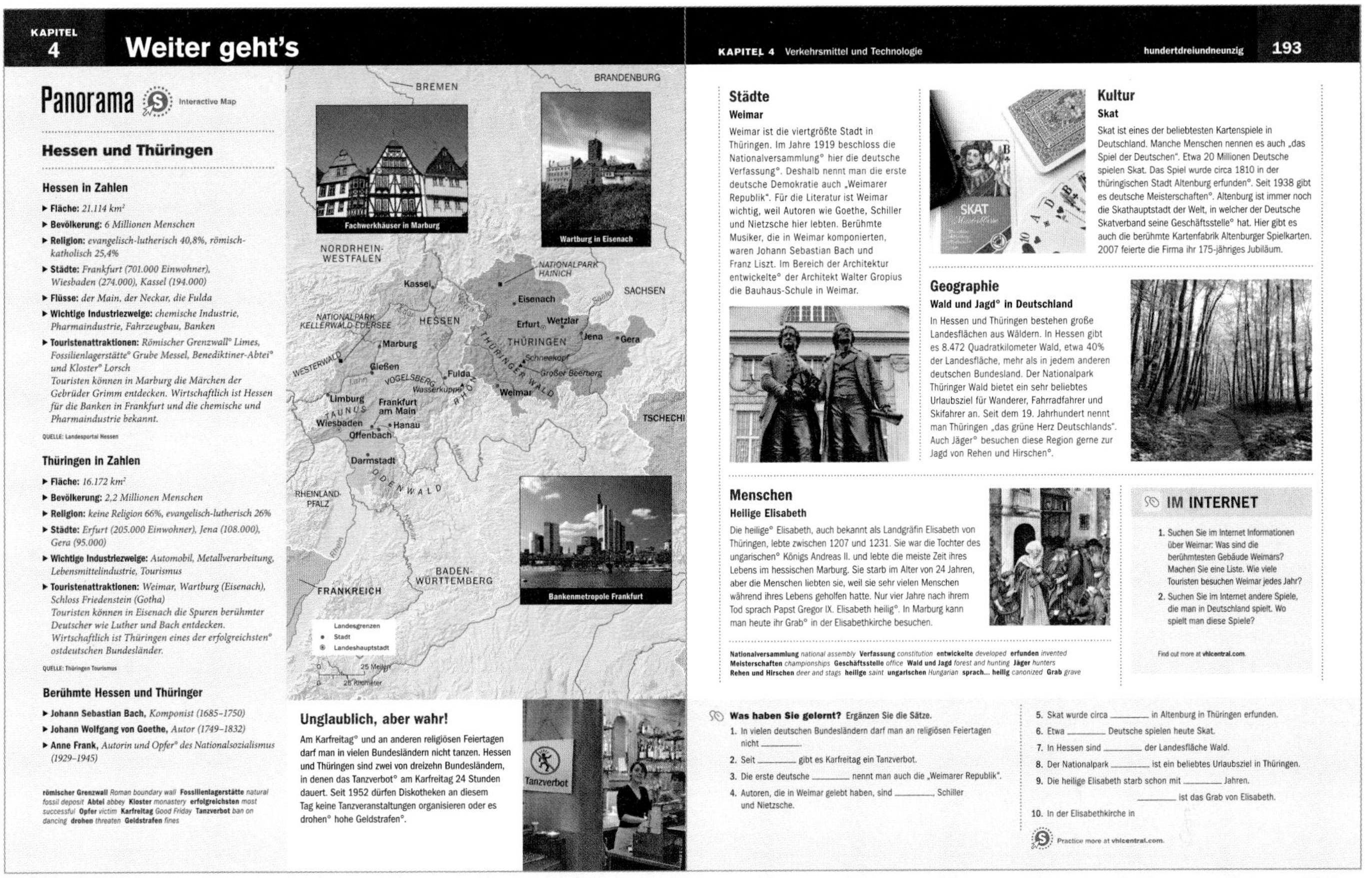

KAPITEL 4 **Weiter geht's**

Panorama
Interactive Map

Hessen und Thüringen

Hessen in Zahlen

- **Fläche:** *21.114 km²*
- **Bevölkerung:** *6 Millionen Menschen*
- **Religion:** *evangelisch-lutherisch 40,8%, römisch-katholisch 25,4%*
- **Städte:** *Frankfurt (701.000 Einwohner), Wiesbaden (274.000), Kassel (194.000)*
- **Flüsse:** *der Main, der Neckar, die Fulda*
- **Wichtige Industriezweige:** *chemische Industrie, Pharmaindustrie, Fahrzeugbau, Banken*
- **Touristenattraktionen:** *Römischer Grenzwall° Limes, Fossilienlagerstätte° Grube Messel, Benediktiner-Abtei° und Kloster° Lorsch*
  Touristen können in Marburg die Märchen der Gebrüder Grimm entdecken. Wirtschaftlich ist Hessen für die Banken in Frankfurt und die chemische und Pharmaindustrie bekannt.

QUELLE: Landesportal Hessen

Thüringen in Zahlen

- **Fläche:** *16.172 km²*
- **Bevölkerung:** *2,2 Millionen Menschen*
- **Religion:** *keine Religion 66%, evangelisch-lutherisch 26%*
- **Städte:** *Erfurt (205.000 Einwohner), Jena (108.000), Gera (95.000)*
- **Wichtige Industriezweige:** *Automobil, Metallverarbeitung, Lebensmittelindustrie, Tourismus*
- **Touristenattraktionen:** *Weimar, Wartburg (Eisenach), Schloss Friedenstein (Gotha)*
  Touristen können in Eisenach die Spuren berühmter Deutscher wie Luther und Bach entdecken. Wirtschaftlich ist Thüringen eines der erfolgreichsten° ostdeutschen Bundesländer.

QUELLE: Thüringen Tourismus

Berühmte Hessen und Thüringer

- **Johann Sebastian Bach,** *Komponist (1685–1750)*
- **Johann Wolfgang von Goethe,** *Autor (1749–1832)*
- **Anne Frank,** *Autorin und Opfer° des Nationalsozialismus (1929–1945)*

römischer Grenzwall *Roman boundary wall* **Fossilienlagerstätte** *natural fossil deposit* **Abtei** *abbey* **Kloster** *monastery* **erfolgreichsten** *most successful* **Opfer** *victim* **Karfreitag** *Good Friday* **Tanzverbot** *ban on dancing* **drohen** *threaten* **Geldstrafen** *fines*

Fachwerkhäuser in Marburg

Wartburg in Eisenach

Bankenmetropole Frankfurt

Landesgrenzen
Stadt
Landeshauptstadt

Unglaublich, aber wahr!

Am Karfreitag° und an anderen religiösen Feiertagen darf man in vielen Bundesländern nicht tanzen. Hessen und Thüringen sind zwei von dreizehn Bundesländern, in denen das Tanzverbot° am Karfreitag 24 Stunden dauert. Seit 1952 dürfen Diskotheken an diesem Tag keine Tanzveranstaltungen organisieren oder es drohen° hohe Geldstrafen°.

KAPITEL 4 Verkehrsmittel und Technologie — hundertdreiundneunzig 193

Städte
Weimar

Weimar ist die viertgrößte Stadt in Thüringen. Im Jahre 1919 beschloss die Nationalversammlung° hier die deutsche Verfassung°. Deshalb nennt man die erste deutsche Demokratie auch „Weimarer Republik". Für die Literatur ist Weimar wichtig, weil Autoren wie Goethe, Schiller und Nietzsche hier lebten. Berühmte Musiker, die in Weimar komponierten, waren Johann Sebastian Bach und Franz Liszt. Im Bereich der Architektur entwickelte° der Architekt Walter Gropius die Bauhaus-Schule in Weimar.

Kultur
Skat

Skat ist eines der beliebtesten Kartenspiele in Deutschland. Manche Menschen nennen es auch „das Spiel der Deutschen". Etwa 20 Millionen Deutsche spielen Skat. Das Spiel wurde circa 1810 in der thüringischen Stadt Altenburg erfunden°. Seit 1938 gibt es deutsche Meisterschaften°. Altenburg ist immer noch die Skathauptstadt der Welt, in welcher der Deutsche Skatverband seine Geschäftsstelle° hat. Hier gibt es auch die berühmte Kartenfabrik Altenburger Spielkarten. 2007 feierte die Firma ihr 175-jähriges Jubiläum.

Geographie
Wald und Jagd° in Deutschland

In Hessen und Thüringen bestehen große Landesflächen aus Wäldern. In Hessen gibt es 8.472 Quadratkilometer Wald, etwa 40% der Landesfläche, mehr als in jedem anderen deutschen Bundesland. Der Nationalpark Thüringer Wald bietet ein sehr beliebtes Urlaubsziel für Wanderer, Fahrradfahrer und Skifahrer an. Seit dem 19. Jahrhundert nennt man Thüringen „das grüne Herz Deutschlands". Auch Jäger° besuchen diese Region gerne zur Jagd von Rehen und Hirschen°.

Menschen
Heilige Elisabeth

Die heilige° Elisabeth, auch bekannt als Landgräfin Elisabeth von Thüringen, lebte zwischen 1207 und 1231. Sie war die Tochter des ungarischen° Königs Andreas II. und lebte die meiste Zeit ihres Lebens im hessischen Marburg. Sie starb im Alter von 24 Jahren, aber die Menschen liebten sie, weil sie sehr vielen Menschen während ihres Lebens geholfen hatte. Nur vier Jahre nach ihrem Tod sprach Papst Gregor IX. Elisabeth heilig°. In Marburg kann man heute ihr Grab° in der Elisabethkirche besuchen.

Nationalversammlung *national assembly* **Verfassung** *constitution* **entwickelte** *developed* **erfunden** *invented* **Meisterschaften** *championships* **Geschäftsstelle** *office* **Wald und Jagd** *forest and hunting* **Jäger** *hunters* **Rehen und Hirschen** *deer and stags* **heilige** *saint* **ungarischen** *Hungarian* **sprach... heilig** *canonized* **Grab** *grave*

IM INTERNET

1. Suchen Sie im Internet Informationen über Weimar: Was sind die berühmtesten Gebäude Weimars? Machen Sie eine Liste. Wie viele Touristen besuchen Weimar jedes Jahr?
2. Suchen Sie im Internet andere Spiele, die man in Deutschland spielt. Wo spielt man diese Spiele?

Find out more at **vhlcentral.com**.

Was haben Sie gelernt? Ergänzen Sie die Sätze.

1. In vielen deutschen Bundesländern darf man an religiösen Feiertagen nicht ________.
2. Seit ________ gibt es Karfreitag ein Tanzverbot.
3. Die erste deutsche ________ nennt man auch die „Weimarer Republik".
4. Autoren, die in Weimar gelebt haben, sind ________, Schiller und Nietzsche.
5. Skat wurde circa ________ in Altenburg in Thüringen erfunden.
6. Etwa ________ Deutsche spielen heute Skat.
7. In Hessen sind ________ der Landesfläche Wald.
8. Der Nationalpark ________ ist ein beliebtes Urlaubsziel in Thüringen.
9. Die heilige Elisabeth starb schon mit ________ Jahren.
10. In der Elisabethkirche in ________ ist das Grab von Elisabeth.

Practice more at **vhlcentral.com**.

Panorama offers interesting facts about the featured city, region, or country.

Maps point out major geographical features and situate the featured region in the context of its immediate surroundings.

Readings explore different aspects of the featured region's culture, such as history, landmarks, fine art, literature, and insight into everyday life.

Unglaublich, aber wahr! highlights an intriguing fact about the featured region.

Comprehension questions check understanding of key ideas.

- Map with statistics and cultural notes
- **Im Internet** research activity
- Textbook activities

Reading skills
developed in context

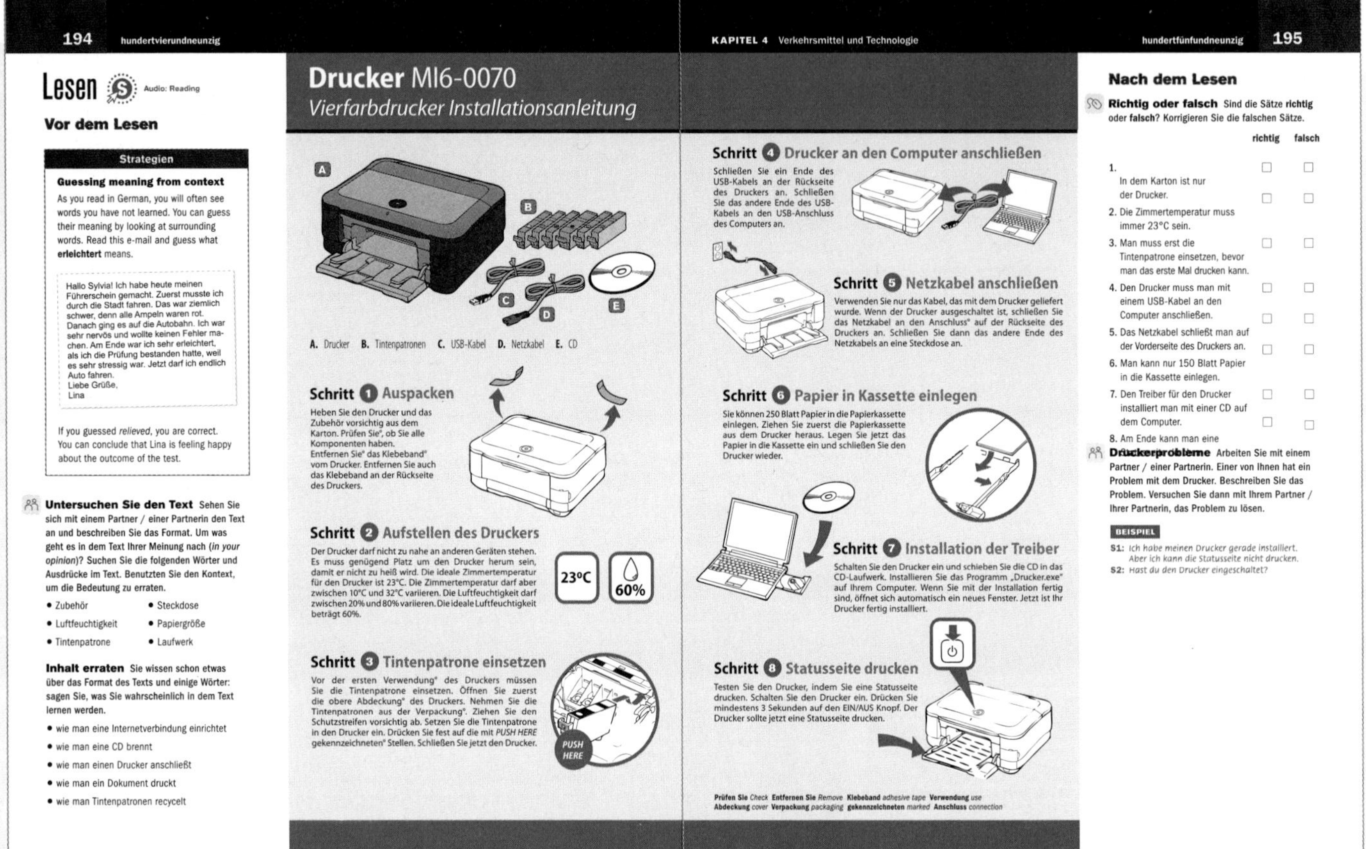
194 hundertvierundneunzig

Lesen Audio: Reading

Vor dem Lesen

Strategien

Guessing meaning from context

As you read in German, you will often see words you have not learned. You can guess their meaning by looking at surrounding words. Read this e-mail and guess what **erleichtert** means.

Hallo Sylvia! Ich habe heute meinen Führerschein gemacht. Zuerst musste ich durch die Stadt fahren. Das war ziemlich schwer, denn alle Ampeln waren rot. Danach ging es auf die Autobahn. Ich war sehr nervös und wollte keinen Fehler machen. Am Ende war ich sehr erleichtert, als ich die Prüfung bestanden hatte, weil es sehr stressig war. Jetzt darf ich endlich Auto fahren.
Liebe Grüße,
Lina

If you guessed *relieved*, you are correct. You can conclude that Lina is feeling happy about the outcome of the test.

Untersuchen Sie den Text Sehen Sie sich mit einem Partner / einer Partnerin den Text an und beschreiben Sie das Format. Um was geht es in dem Text Ihrer Meinung nach (*in your opinion*)? Suchen Sie die folgenden Wörter und Ausdrücke im Text. Benutzten Sie den Kontext, um die Bedeutung zu erraten.

- Zubehör
- Luftfeuchtigkeit
- Tintenpatrone
- Steckdose
- Papiergröße
- Laufwerk

Inhalt erraten Sie wissen schon etwas über das Format des Texts und einige Wörter: sagen Sie, was Sie wahrscheinlich in dem Text lernen werden.

- wie man eine Internetverbindung einrichtet
- wie man eine CD brennt
- wie man einen Drucker anschließt
- wie man ein Dokument druckt
- wie man Tintenpatronen recycelt

Drucker MI6-0070
Vierfarbdrucker Installationsanleitung

A. Drucker **B.** Tintenpatronen **C.** USB-Kabel **D.** Netzkabel **E.** CD

Schritt 1 Auspacken
Heben Sie den Drucker und das Zubehör vorsichtig aus dem Karton. Prüfen Sie°, ob Sie alle Komponenten haben. Entfernen Sie° das Klebeband° vom Drucker. Entfernen Sie auch das Klebeband an der Rückseite des Druckers.

Schritt 2 Aufstellen des Druckers
Der Drucker darf nicht zu nahe an anderen Geräten stehen. Es muss genügend Platz um den Drucker herum sein, damit er nicht zu heiß wird. Die ideale Zimmertemperatur für den Drucker ist 23°C. Die Zimmertemperatur darf aber zwischen 10°C und 32°C variieren. Die Luftfeuchtigkeit darf zwischen 20% und 80% variieren. Die ideale Luftfeuchtigkeit beträgt 60%.

23ºC 60%

Schritt 3 Tintenpatrone einsetzen
Vor der ersten Verwendung° des Druckers müssen Sie die Tintenpatrone einsetzen. Öffnen Sie zuerst die obere Abdeckung° des Druckers. Nehmen Sie die Tintenpatronen aus der Verpackung°. Ziehen Sie den Schutzstreifen vorsichtig ab. Setzen Sie die Tintenpatrone in den Drucker ein. Drücken Sie fest auf die mit *PUSH HERE* gekennzeichneten° Stellen. Schließen Sie jetzt den Drucker.

PUSH HERE

KAPITEL 4 Verkehrsmittel und Technologie

Schritt 4 Drucker an den Computer anschließen
Schließen Sie ein Ende des USB-Kabels an der Rückseite des Druckers an. Schließen Sie das andere Ende des USB-Kabels an den USB-Anschluss des Computers an.

Schritt 5 Netzkabel anschließen
Verwenden Sie nur das Kabel, das mit dem Drucker geliefert wurde. Wenn der Drucker ausgeschaltet ist, schließen Sie das Netzkabel an den Anschluss° auf der Rückseite des Druckers an. Schließen Sie dann das andere Ende des Netzkabels an eine Steckdose an.

Schritt 6 Papier in Kassette einlegen
Sie können 250 Blatt Papier in die Papierkassette einlegen. Ziehen Sie zuerst die Papierkassette aus dem Drucker heraus. Legen Sie jetzt das Papier in die Kassette ein und schließen Sie den Drucker wieder.

Schritt 7 Installation der Treiber
Schalten Sie den Drucker ein und schieben Sie die CD in das CD-Laufwerk. Installieren Sie das Programm „Drucker.exe" auf Ihrem Computer. Wenn Sie mit der Installation fertig sind, öffnet sich automatisch ein neues Fenster. Jetzt ist Ihr Drucker fertig installiert.

Schritt 8 Statusseite drucken
Testen Sie den Drucker, indem Sie eine Statusseite drucken. Schalten Sie den Drucker ein. Drücken Sie mindestens 3 Sekunden auf den EIN/AUS Knopf. Der Drucker sollte jetzt eine Statusseite drucken.

Prüfen Sie *Check* **Entfernen Sie** *Remove* **Klebeband** *adhesive tape* **Verwendung** *use* **Abdeckung** *cover* **Verpackung** *packaging* **gekennzeichneten** *marked* **Anschluss** *connection*

hundertfünfundneunzig 195

Nach dem Lesen

Richtig oder falsch Sind die Sätze **richtig** oder **falsch**? Korrigieren Sie die falschen Sätze.

	richtig	falsch
1. In dem Karton ist nur der Drucker.	☐	☐
2. Die Zimmertemperatur muss immer 23°C sein.	☐	☐
3. Man muss erst die Tintenpatrone einsetzen, bevor man das erste Mal drucken kann.	☐	☐
4. Den Drucker muss man mit einem USB-Kabel an den Computer anschließen.	☐	☐
5. Das Netzkabel schließt man auf der Vorderseite des Druckers an.	☐	☐
6. Man kann nur 150 Blatt Papier in die Kassette einlegen.	☐	☐
7. Den Treiber für den Drucker installiert man mit einer CD auf dem Computer.	☐	☐
8. Am Ende kann man eine	☐	☐

Druckerprobleme Arbeiten Sie mit einem Partner / einer Partnerin. Einer von Ihnen hat ein Problem mit dem Drucker. Beschreiben Sie das Problem. Versuchen Sie dann mit Ihrem Partner / Ihrer Partnerin, das Problem zu lösen.

BEISPIEL

S1: *Ich habe meinen Drucker gerade installiert. Aber ich kann die Statusseite nicht drucken.*
S2: *Hast du den Drucker eingeschaltet?*

Vor dem Lesen presents useful strategies and activities that help develop stronger reading abilities.

Readings are tied to the chapter theme. The selections recycle vocabulary and grammar learned.

Nach dem Lesen consists of post-reading activities that check comprehension.

Supersite

- Audio-sync reading that highlights text as it is being read
- Textbook activities
- Chat activities for conversational skill-building and oral practice

Listening and writing skills
developed in context

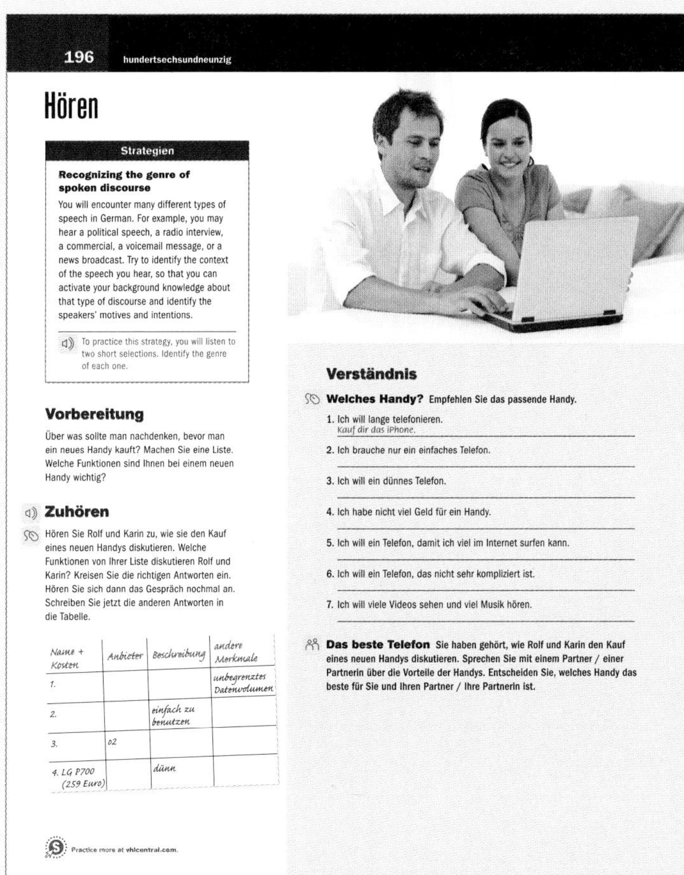

196 hundertsechsundneunzig

Hören

Strategien

Recognizing the genre of spoken discourse

You will encounter many different types of speech in German. For example, you may hear a political speech, a radio interview, a commercial, a voicemail message, or a news broadcast. Try to identify the context of the speech you hear, so that you can activate your background knowledge about that type of discourse and identify the speakers' motives and intentions.

To practice this strategy, you will listen to two short selections. Identify the genre of each one.

Vorbereitung

Über was sollte man nachdenken, bevor man ein neues Handy kauft? Machen Sie eine Liste. Welche Funktionen sind Ihnen bei einem neuen Handy wichtig?

Zuhören

Hören Sie Rolf und Karin zu, wie sie den Kauf eines neuen Handys diskutieren. Welche Funktionen von Ihrer Liste diskutieren Rolf und Karin? Kreisen Sie die richtigen Antworten ein. Hören Sie sich dann das Gespräch nochmal an. Schreiben Sie jetzt die anderen Antworten in die Tabelle.

Name + Kosten	Anbieter	Beschreibung	andere Merkmale
1.			unbegrenztes Datenvolumen
2.		einfach zu benutzen	
3.	O2		
4. LG P700 (259 Euro)		dünn	

Practice more at vhlcentral.com.

Verständnis

Welches Handy? Empfehlen Sie das passende Handy.

1. Ich will lange telefonieren. *Kauf dir das iPhone.*
2. Ich brauche nur ein einfaches Telefon.
3. Ich will ein dünnes Telefon.
4. Ich habe nicht viel Geld für ein Handy.
5. Ich will ein Telefon, damit ich viel im Internet surfen kann.
6. Ich will ein Telefon, das nicht sehr kompliziert ist.
7. Ich will viele Videos sehen und viel Musik hören.

Das beste Telefon Sie haben gehört, wie Rolf und Karin den Kauf eines neuen Handys diskutieren. Sprechen Sie mit einem Partner / einer Partnerin über die Vorteile der Handys. Entscheiden Sie, welches Handy das beste für Sie und Ihren Partner / Ihre Partnerin ist.

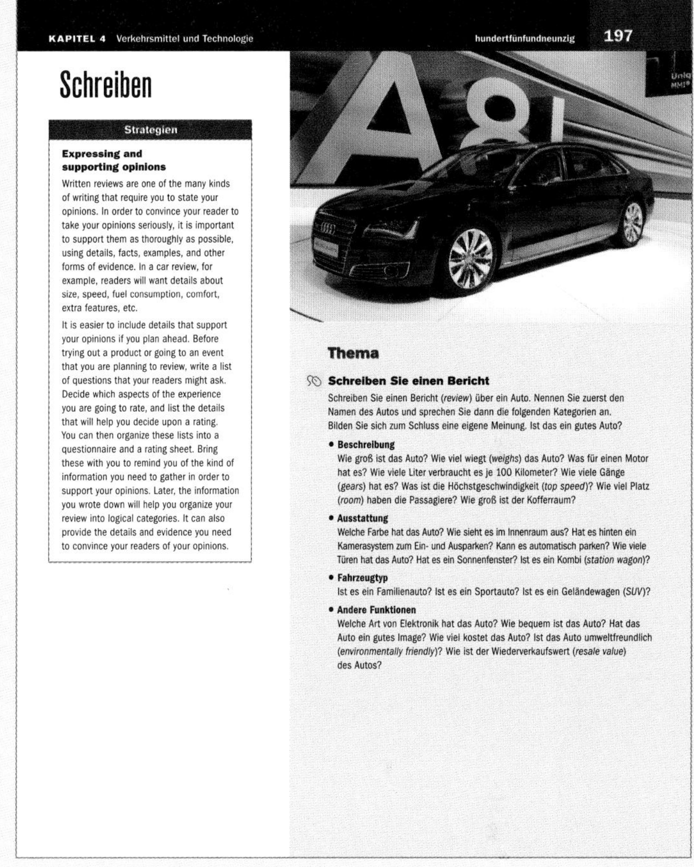

KAPITEL 4 Verkehrsmittel und Technologie hundertfünfundneunzig 197

Schreiben

Strategien

Expressing and supporting opinions

Written reviews are one of the many kinds of writing that require you to state your opinions. In order to convince your reader to take your opinions seriously, it is important to support them as thoroughly as possible, using details, facts, examples, and other forms of evidence. In a car review, for example, readers will want details about size, speed, fuel consumption, comfort, extra features, etc.

It is easier to include details that support your opinions if you plan ahead. Before trying out a product or going to an event that you are planning to review, write a list of questions that your readers might ask. Decide which aspects of the experience you are going to rate, and list the details that will help you decide upon a rating. You can then organize these lists into a questionnaire and a rating sheet. Bring these with you to remind you of the kind of information you need to gather in order to support your opinions. Later, the information you wrote down will help you organize your review into logical categories. It can also provide the details and evidence you need to convince your readers of your opinions.

Thema

Schreiben Sie einen Bericht

Schreiben Sie einen Bericht (*review*) über ein Auto. Nennen Sie zuerst den Namen des Autos und sprechen Sie dann die folgenden Kategorien an. Bilden Sie sich zum Schluss eine eigene Meinung. Ist das ein gutes Auto?

- **Beschreibung**
  Wie groß ist das Auto? Wie viel wiegt (*weighs*) das Auto? Was für einen Motor hat es? Wie viele Liter verbraucht es je 100 Kilometer? Wie viele Gänge (*gears*) hat es? Was ist die Höchstgeschwindigkeit (*top speed*)? Wie viel Platz (*room*) haben die Passagiere? Wie groß ist der Kofferraum?
- **Ausstattung**
  Welche Farbe hat das Auto? Wie sieht es im Innenraum aus? Hat es hinten ein Kamerasystem zum Ein- und Ausparken? Kann es automatisch parken? Wie viele Türen hat das Auto? Hat es ein Sonnenfenster? Ist es ein Kombi (*station wagon*)?
- **Fahrzeugtyp**
  Ist es ein Familienauto? Ist es ein Sportauto? Ist es ein Geländewagen (*SUV*)?
- **Andere Funktionen**
  Welche Art von Elektronik hat das Auto? Wie bequem ist das Auto? Hat das Auto ein gutes Image? Wie viel kostet das Auto? Ist das Auto umweltfreundlich (*environmentally friendly*)? Wie ist der Wiederverkaufswert (*resale value*) des Autos?

Hören uses a recorded conversation or narration to develop listening skills in German, while **Strategien** and **Vorbereitung** are preparation for an audio listening activity.

Zuhören serves as a guide to the recorded segment, and **Verständnis** checks comprehension.

In the **Schreiben** section, **Strategien** provides useful preparation for the writing task presented in **Thema.**

Thema presents a writing topic and includes suggestions for approaching it. It also provides words and phrases that may be useful in writing about the topic.

- Audio for **Hören** activities
- Textbook activities
- Additional online-only practice activity
- Composition writing activity for **Schreiben**
- Chat activities for conversational skill-building and oral practice

Vocabulary

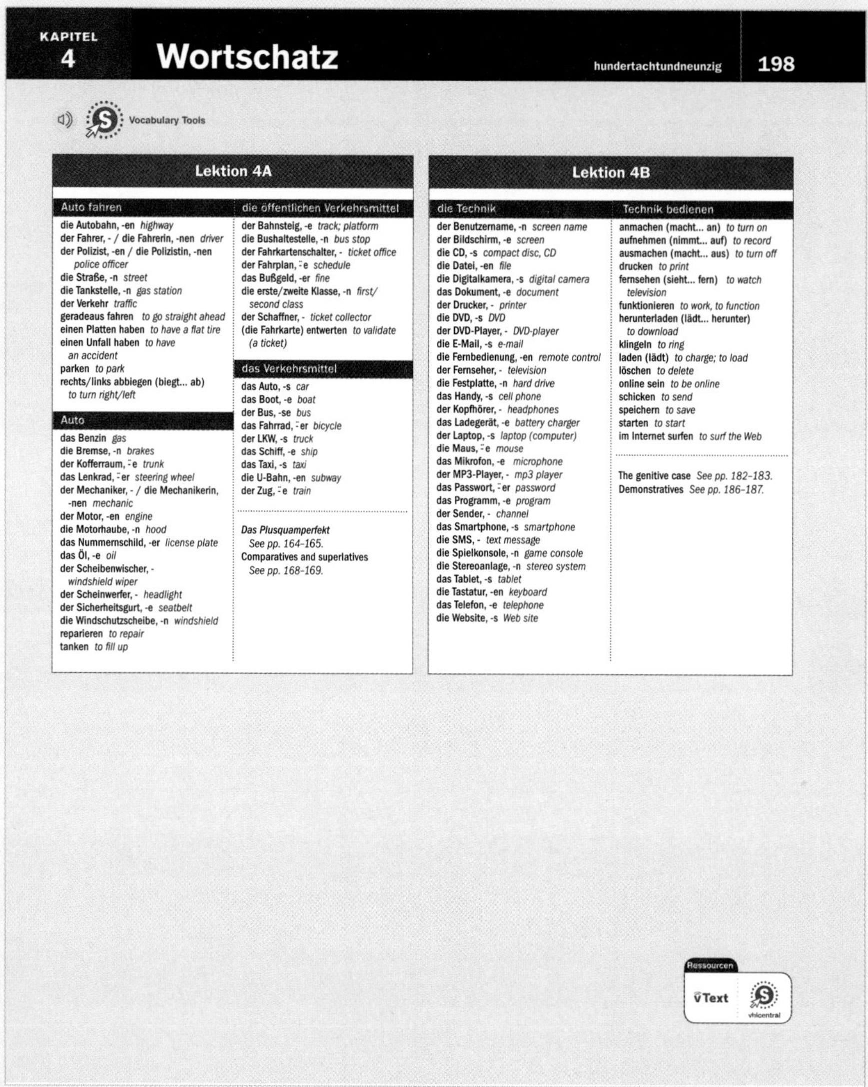

KAPITEL 4 **Wortschatz** hundertachtundneunzig 198

Vocabulary Tools

Lektion 4A

Auto fahren

die Autobahn, -en *highway*
der Fahrer, - / die Fahrerin, -nen *driver*
der Polizist, -en / die Polizistin, -nen *police officer*
die Straße, -n *street*
die Tankstelle, -n *gas station*
der Verkehr *traffic*
geradeaus fahren *to go straight ahead*
einen Platten haben *to have a flat tire*
einen Unfall haben *to have an accident*
parken *to park*
rechts/links abbiegen (biegt... ab) *to turn right/left*

Auto

das Benzin *gas*
die Bremse, -n *brakes*
der Kofferraum, ¨e *trunk*
das Lenkrad, ¨er *steering wheel*
der Mechaniker, - / die Mechanikerin, -nen *mechanic*
der Motor, -en *engine*
die Motorhaube, -n *hood*
das Nummernschild, -er *license plate*
das Öl, -e *oil*
der Scheibenwischer, - *windshield wiper*
der Scheinwerfer, - *headlight*
der Sicherheitsgurt, -e *seatbelt*
die Windschutzscheibe, -n *windshield*
reparieren *to repair*
tanken *to fill up*

die öffentlichen Verkehrsmittel

der Bahnsteig, -e *track; platform*
die Bushaltestelle, -n *bus stop*
der Fahrkartenschalter, - *ticket office*
der Fahrplan, ¨e *schedule*
das Bußgeld, -er *fine*
die erste/zweite Klasse, -n *first/second class*
der Schaffner, - *ticket collector*
(die Fahrkarte) entwerten *to validate (a ticket)*

das Verkehrsmittel

das Auto, -s *car*
das Boot, -e *boat*
der Bus, -se *bus*
das Fahrrad, ¨er *bicycle*
der LKW, -s *truck*
das Schiff, -e *ship*
das Taxi, -s *taxi*
die U-Bahn, -en *subway*
der Zug, ¨e *train*

Das Plusquamperfekt *See pp. 164–165.*
Comparatives and superlatives *See pp. 168–169.*

Lektion 4B

die Technik

der Benutzername, -n *screen name*
der Bildschirm, -e *screen*
die CD, -s *compact disc, CD*
die Datei, -en *file*
die Digitalkamera, -s *digital camera*
das Dokument, -e *document*
der Drucker, - *printer*
die DVD, -s *DVD*
der DVD-Player, - *DVD-player*
die E-Mail, -s *e-mail*
die Fernbedienung, -en *remote control*
der Fernseher, - *television*
die Festplatte, -n *hard drive*
das Handy, -s *cell phone*
der Kopfhörer, - *headphones*
das Ladegerät, -e *battery charger*
der Laptop, -s *laptop (computer)*
die Maus, ¨e *mouse*
das Mikrofon, -e *microphone*
der MP3-Player, - *mp3 player*
das Passwort, ¨er *password*
das Programm, -e *program*
der Sender, - *channel*
das Smartphone, -s *smartphone*
die SMS, - *text message*
die Spielkonsole, -n *game console*
die Stereoanlage, -n *stereo system*
das Tablet, -s *tablet*
die Tastatur, -en *keyboard*
das Telefon, -e *telephone*
die Website, -s *Web site*

Technik bedienen

anmachen (macht... an) *to turn on*
aufnehmen (nimmt... auf) *to record*
ausmachen (macht... aus) *to turn off*
drucken *to print*
fernsehen (sieht... fern) *to watch television*
funktionieren *to work, to function*
herunterladen (lädt... herunter) *to download*
klingeln *to ring*
laden (lädt) *to charge; to load*
löschen *to delete*
online sein *to be online*
schicken *to send*
speichern *to save*
starten *to start*
im Internet surfen *to surf the Web*

The genitive case *See pp. 182–183.*
Demonstratives *See pp. 186–187.*

Ressourcen
vText
vhlcentral

Wortschatz presents the chapter's active vocabulary in logical groupings, including notation of plural forms. Words are separated by corresponding A and B lessons.

- Audio recordings of all vocabulary items
- My Vocabulary

World-Readiness Standards for Learning Languages

Mosaik blends the underlying principles of ACTFL's World-Readiness Standards with features and strategies tailored specifically to build students' language and cultural competencies.

THE FIVE C'S OF FOREIGN LANGUAGE LEARNING	
Communication	**Students:** 1. Interact and negotiate meaning in spoken, signed, or written conversations to share information, reactions, feelings, and opinions. (Interpersonal mode) 2. Understand, interpret, and analyze what is heard, read, or viewed on a variety of topics. (Interpretive mode) 3. Present information, concepts, and ideas to inform, explain, persuade, and narrate on a variety of topics using appropriate media and adapting to various audiences of listeners, readers, or viewers. (Presentational mode)
Cultures	**Students use German to investigate, explain, and reflect on:** 1. The relationship of the practices and perspectives of the culture studied. 2. The relationship of the products and perspectives of the culture studied.
Connections	**Students:** 1. Build, reinforce, and expand their knowledge of other disciplines while using German to develop critical thinking and to solve problems creatively. 2. Access and evaluate information and diverse perspectives that are available through German and its cultures.
Comparisons	**Students use German to investigate, explain, and reflect on:** 1. The nature of language through comparisons of the German language and their own. 2. The concept of culture through comparisons of the cultures studied and their own.
Communities	**Students:** 1. Use German both within and beyond the school to interact and collaborate in their community and the globalized world. 2. Set goals and reflect on their progress in using languages for enjoyment, enrichment, and advancement.

Adapted from ACTFL's *Standards for Foreign Language Learning in the 21st Century*

Six-step instructional design

Take advantage of the unique, powerful six-step instructional design in **Mosaik**. With a focus on personalization, authenticity, cultural immersion, and the seamless integration of text and technology, language learning comes to life in ways that are meaningful to each and every student.

STEP 1

Context

Begin each lesson by asking students to provide from their own experience words, concepts, categories, and opinions related to the theme. Spend quality time evoking words, images, ideas, phrases, and sentences; group and classify concepts. You are giving students the "hook" for their learning, focusing them on their most interesting topic—themselves—and encouraging them to invest personally in their learning.

STEP 2

Vocabulary

Now turn to the vocabulary section, inviting students to experience it as a new linguistic code to express what they already know and experience in the context of the lesson theme. Vocabulary concepts are presented in context, carefully organized, and frequently reviewed to reinforce student understanding. Involve students in brainstorming, classifying and grouping words and thoughts, and personalizing phrases and sentences. In this way, you will help students see German as a new tool for self-expression.

STEP 3

Media

Once students see that German is a tool for expressing their own ideas, bridge their experiences to those of German speakers through the **Fotoroman** section. The **Fotoroman** storyline video presents and reviews vocabulary and structure in accurate cultural contexts for effective training in both comprehension and personal communication.

STEP 4

Culture

Now bring students into the experience of culture as seen from the perspective of those living in it. Here we share German-speaking cultures' unique geography, history, products, perspectives, and practices. Through **Zapping** (authentic video) students experience and reflect on cultural experiences beyond their own.

STEP 5

Structure

Through context, media and culture, students have incorporated both previously learned and new grammatical structures into their personalized communication. Now a formal presentation of relevant grammar demonstrates that grammar is a tool for clearer and more effective communication. Clear presentations and invitations to compare German to English build confidence, fluency, and accuracy.

STEP 6

Skill synthesis

Pulling all their learning together, students now integrate context, personal experience, communication tools, and cultural products, perspectives, and practices. Through extended reading, writing, listening, speaking, and cultural exploration in scaffolded progression, students apply all their skills for a rich, personalized experience of German.

Learning to Use Your **Teacher's Edition**

Mosaik offers you a comprehensive, thoroughly developed Teacher's Edition (TE). It features student text pages overprinted with answers to all activities with discrete responses. Each page also contains annotations for a few selected activities that were written to complement and support varied teaching styles, to extend the already rich contents of the student textbook, and to save you time in class preparation and course management.

Because the **Mosaik** TE is different from teacher's editions available with other German programs, this section is designed as a quick orientation to the principal types of teacher annotations it contains. As you familiarize yourself with them, it is important to know that the annotations are suggestions only. Any German question, sentence, model, or simulated teacher-student exchange is not meant to be prescriptive or limiting. You are encouraged to view these suggested "scripts" as flexible points of departure that will help you achieve your instructional goals.

For the Chapter Opening Page

- **Suggestion** A discussion topic idea, based on the Chapter Opener photo

For the Lessons

- **Suggestion** Teaching suggestions for working with on-page materials, carrying out specific activities, and presenting new vocabulary or grammar
- **Expansion** Expansions and variations on activities
- **Vorbereitung** Suggestions for talking about the **Fotoroman** pages before students have watched the video or studied the pages
- **Nützliche Ausdrücke** A list of expressions taken from the **Fotoroman** that students may need to study before watching the episode
- **Partner and Virtual Chats** Assignments that develop students' communication skills with the convenience of the Supersite
- **Communication Icons** are tagged to activities that engage students in one of the three different modes of communication:

Interpretive communication Exercises that target students' reading or listening skills and assess their comprehension

Presentational communication Ideas and contexts that require students to produce a written or verbal presentation in the target language

Interpersonal communication Activities that provide students with opportunities to carry out language functions in simulated real-life contexts or engage in personalized communication with others

Please check the **Mosaik** Supersite at **vhlcentral.com** for additional teaching support.

Differentiation

Knowing how to appeal to learners of different abilities and learning styles will allow you to foster a positive teaching environment and motivate all your students. Here are some strategies for creating inclusive learning environments. Extension and expansion activities are also suggested.

Learners with Special Needs

Learners with special needs include students with attention priority disorders or learning disabilities, slower-paced learners, at-risk learners, and English language learners. Some inclusion strategies that work well with such students are:

Clear Structure By teaching concepts in a predictable order, you can help students organize their learning. Encourage students to keep outlines of materials they read, classify words into categories such as colors, or follow prewriting steps.

Frequent Review and Repetition Preview material to be taught and review material covered at the end of each lesson. Pair proficient learners with less proficient ones to practice and reinforce concepts. Help students retain concepts through continuous practice and review.

Multi-sensory Input and Output Use visual, auditory, and kinesthetic tasks to add interest and motivation, and to achieve long-term retention. For example, vary input with the use of audio recordings, video, guided visualization, rhymes, and mnemonics.

Additional Time Consider how physical limitations may affect participation in special projects or daily routines. Provide additional time and recommended accommodations.

Different Learning Styles

Visual Learners learn best by seeing, so engage them in activities and projects that are visually creative. Encourage them to write down information and to think in pictures as a long-term retention strategy. Reinforce their learning through visual displays such as diagrams, videos, and handouts.

Auditory Learners best retain information by listening. Engage them in discussions, debates, and role-playing. Reinforce their learning by playing audio versions of texts or reading aloud passages and stories. Encourage them to pay attention to voice, tone, and pitch to infer meaning.

Kinesthetic Learners learn best through moving, touching, and doing hands-on activities. Involve such students in skits and dramatizations; to infer or convey meaning, have them observe or model gestures such as those used for greeting someone or getting someone's attention.

Advanced Learners

Advanced Learners have the potential to learn language concepts and complete assignments at an accelerated pace. They may benefit from assignments that are more challenging than the ones given to their peers. The key to differentiating for advanced learners is adding a degree of rigor to a given task. Examples include sharing perspectives on texts they have read with the class, retelling detailed stories, preparing analyses of texts, or adding to discussions. Here are some other strategies for engaging advanced learners:

Timed Answers Have students answer questions within a specified time limit.

Persuading Adapt activities so students have to write or present their points of view in order to persuade an audience. Pair or group advanced learners to form debating teams.

Best Practices

The creators of **Mosaik** understand that there are many different approaches to successful language teaching and that no one method works perfectly for all teachers or all learners. These strategies and tips may be applied to any language-teaching method.

Maintain the Target Language

As much as possible, create an immersion environment by using German to *teach* German. Encourage the exclusive use of the target language in your classroom, employing visual aids, mnemonics, circumlocution, or gestures to complement what you say. Encourage students to perceive meaning directly through careful listening and observation, and by using cognates and familiar structures and patterns to deduce meaning.

Cultivate Critical Thinking

Prompt students to reflect, observe, reason, and form judgments in German. Engaging students in activities that require them to compare, contrast, predict, criticize, and estimate will help them to internalize the language structures they have learned.

Encourage Use of Circumlocution

Prompt students to discover various ways of expressing ideas and of overcoming potential blocks to communication through the use of circumlocution and paraphrasing.

Assessment

As you use the **Mosaik** program, you can employ a variety of assessments to evaluate progress. The program provides comprehensive, discrete answer assessments as well as more communicative assessments that elicit open-ended, personalized responses.

Diagnostic Testing

The **Wiederholung** section in each lesson provides you with an informal opportunity to assess students' readiness for the listening, reading, and writing activities in the **Weiter geht's** section. If some students need additional practice or instruction in a particular area, you can identify this before students move on.

Writing Assessment

At the end of each chapter, the **Weiter geht's** section includes a **Schreiben** page that introduces a writing strategy, which students apply as they complete the writing activity. These activities include suggestions that will focus students' attention on what is important for attaining clarity in written communication.

Testing Program

The **Mosaik** Testing Program offers two quizzes for each **Lektion**, one test per chapter, one cumulative exam per level, IPAs with rubrics for every chapter, oral testing suggestions with grading rubrics, audioscripts for listening comprehension activities, and all answer keys. The quizzes, tests, and exams may administered online, and may be customized by adding, eliminating, or moving items according to your classroom and student needs. Editable RTFs are also available in the Resources area of the Supersite and on the Teacher Resources DVD.

Portfolio Assessment

Portfolios can provide further valuable evidence of your students' learning. They are useful tools for evaluating students' progress in German and also suggest to students how they are likely to be assessed in the real world. Since portfolio activities often comprise classroom tasks that you would assign as part of a lesson or as homework, you should think of the planning, selecting, recording, and interpreting of information about individual performance as a way of blending assessment with instruction.

You may find it helpful to refer to portfolio contents, such as drafts, essays, and samples of presentations when writing student reports and conveying the status of a student's progress to his or her parents.

Ask students regularly to consider which pieces of their own work they would like to share with family and friends, and help them develop criteria for selecting representative samples of essays, stories, poems, recordings of plays or interviews, mock documentaries, and so on. Prompt students to choose a variety of media in their activities wherever possible to demonstrate development in all four language skills. Encourage them to seek peer and parental input as they generate and refine criteria to help them organize and reflect on their own work.

Strategies for Differentiating Assessment

Here are some strategies for modifying tests and other forms of assessment according to your students' needs and your own purposes for administering the assessment.

Adjust Questions Direct complex or higher-level questions to students who are equipped to answer them adequately and modify questions for students with greater needs. Always ask questions that elicit thinking, but keep in mind the students' abilities.

Provide Tiered Assignments Assign tasks of varying complexity depending on individual student needs.

Promote Flexible Grouping Encourage movement among groups of students so that all learners are appropriately challenged. Group students according to interest, oral proficiency levels, or learning styles.

Adjust Pacing Pace the sequence and speed of assessments to suit your students' learning needs. Time advanced learners to challenge them and allow slower-paced learners more time to complete tasks or answer questions.

Integrated Performance Assessment

Integrated Performance Assessments (IPA) begin with a real-life task that engages students' interest. To complete the task, students progress through the three modes of communication: they read, view, and listen for information (interpretive mode); they talk and write with classmates about what they have experienced (interpersonal mode); and they share formally what they have learned (presentational mode).

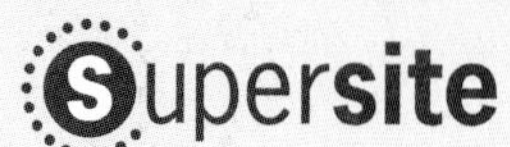

Editable worksheets in the **Content > Resources** area of the Supersite

Integrated Performance Activity — Kapitel 4

Context
Your county is holding a bilingual research symposium. They are sponsoring a contest open to all students: you must present a prominent field of research, as well as the implications of advances in this field. First, you will read a text about research institutions in Germany. Next, you will choose one field and discuss its implications with a partner. Finally, you will prepare a presentation for the symposium.

Interpretive Task
Read the **Kultur** spread on pages 180–181 of your textbook. As you read, write down at least three research fields mentioned in the articles.

Interpersonal Task
With a partner, discuss the research fields you noted from the articles and decide on one that you would like to present. Then, working together, come up with at least three details you could present at the county research symposium, and think of a couple implications of advances in the chosen field.

Presentational Task
Prepare a brief oral presentation in which you describe your field. Give at least three facts about it and two implications for advances within the field. Be prepared to answer any questions your audience may have.

	5 points	3 points	1 point
Interpretive	The student can easily identify three fields mentioned in the articles.	The student can identify several fields mentioned in the articles.	The student has difficulty identifying fields mentioned in the articles.
Interpersonal	The student can complete a basic conversation demonstrating mutual understanding. The result of the conversation is a clear list of details about the field.	The student can complete a basic conversation with only some difficulty in mutual understanding. The result of the conversation is a list of details about the field.	The student can complete a basic conversation but does not reach mutual understanding. The student is not able to prepare a list for his/her presentation.
Presentational	The student can provide clear, relevant information about his/her field of research, and several implications of its advances.	The student can provide some information about a field of research, as well as an implication of its advances.	Presentation lacks detail, and the information about the field is unclear.

"I Can" Statements

Students can assess their own progress by using "I Can" (or "Can-Do") Statements. Use customizable "I Can" Worksheets provided for each chapter of **Mosaik** to guide student learning, and to train students to assess their progress.

Editable worksheets in the **Content > Resources** area of the Supersite

"I Can" Statements

STUDENT OBJECTIVES
Lektion 4A Mosaik 2

Name ______________________ Datum ______________

Ziele: Kontext	Datum	Was kann ich schon?
1. I can talk about cars and driving.		
2. I can name various means of public transportation.		

Was kann ich schon?

4 *Ausgezeichnet!* I know this well enough to teach it to someone.
3 *Sehr gut!* I can do this with almost no mistakes.
2 *Mehr oder weniger!* I can do much of this but I have questions.
1 *Nicht so gut:* I can do this only with help.
0 *Hilfe!* I do not understand this, even with help.

Notizen: ______________________

Engage all students

Learning German isn't all about grammar and memorization. **Mosaik** provides multiple ways to get students excited about the language and culture of German-speaking people.

Make It Personal

- Find out why students decided to learn German. Is it to speak to relatives? To interact with German-speaking friends on social media? To learn more about a particular element of German culture, film, or literature? Keep students motivated by helping them see how individual tasks lead to the larger goal of communicating with German-speaking people. Take the time to explore (and expand on) the **Kultur** and **Panorama** sections to engage students with daily life and geography, as well as fine and performing arts.
- Have students talk about themselves! The Teacher's Edition interpersonal communication annotations point out activities where students ask each other questions about their own lives. Personalizing the discussion helps keep students engaged with the material they are practicing in German.

Get Students Talking

Look for icons calling out pair and group work. Some great speaking activities include:

Supersite Virtual and Partner Chat activities:

- Offer opportunities for spoken production beyond the face-to-face classroom
- Help reduce students' affective filter and build confidence
- Provide a recorded portfolio of students' spoken work that can be easily graded

Info Gap activities: Give students these worksheets either electronically or in print, and have them work to get information from a partner.

Textbook Activity Worksheets: Get the whole class on their feet to participate in activities, such as surveys, using the language they have just been learning.

Take Advantage of Multimedia

For students:

- Are your students on YouTube every minute of their free time? Engage them with the TV advertisements in **Zapping**.
- Do your students want to study abroad in a German-speaking area of Europe? Get them engaged with the **Fotoroman** series featuring George, an American studying abroad in Berlin. Younger students are fascinated by what older students are doing, so the situations with university students should hold their interest.
- Make learning vocabulary engaging and effective for students with the My Vocabulary on the Supersite. They can focus on the vocabulary for each lesson or customize flashcard banks to study only those words they need to learn for an upcoming quiz. The flashcard tool is ideal for student self-study of vocabulary.

For teachers:

- Assign or use the audio-enabled Vocabulary Presentations on the Supersite to give students an interactive experience while they hear the new terms spoken by a native speaker of German.
- Use the Digital Image Bank to enliven your own digital or print activities.
- Have students follow along in their text as the selections in **Lesen** are read aloud by a native German speaker.
- Keep grammar instruction focused by using the Grammar Slides. Breaking up the instructional points into slides helps make the lesson more digestible.
- Don't forget to use the summaries of the **Fotoroman** to reinforce grammar instruction.

Addressing the Modes of Communication

Interpretive Skills

One of **Mosaik**'s greatest strengths is in fostering students' interpretive communication skills. The **Lesen** sections provide various types of authentic written texts and the **Zapping** videos feature German spoken at a natural pace. Encourage students to interact with as much authentic language as possible, as this will lead to long-term success.

- Audio activities
- **Fotoroman**
- **Kultur**
- **Zapping**
- **Panorama**
- **Lesen**
- **Hören**

Presentational Skills

Scaffolded writing tasks help students build solid writing skills in German. Many activities can be turned into either spoken or written presentations to create additional opportunities for students to practice in this mode.

- **Schreiben**
- **Wiederholung**

Interpersonal Skills

With the inclusion of abundant activities for classroom interaction as well as Partner and Virtual Chats online, students can practice their speaking skills by sharing personal information throughout each lesson.

- Pair and group activities
- Partner and Virtual Chats

General Suggestions for Using the *Fotoroman* Video Episodes

The **Fotoroman** section in each lesson and the **Fotoroman** video were created as interlocking pieces. All photos in **Fotoroman** are actual video stills from the corresponding video episode, while the printed conversations are abbreviated versions of the dramatic segment. Both the **Fotoroman** conversations and their expanded video versions represent comprehensible input at the discourse level; they were purposely written to use language from the corresponding lesson's **Kontext** and **Strukturen** sections. Thus, they recycle known language, preview grammar points students will study later in the lesson, and, in keeping with Krashen's concept of "i + 1," contain some amount of unknown language.

Because the **Fotoroman** textbook sections and the dramatic episodes of the **Fotoroman** video are so closely connected, you may use them in many different ways. For instance, you can use **Fotoroman** as a preview, presenting it before showing the video episode. You can also show the video episode first and follow up with **Fotoroman**. You can even use **Fotoroman** as a stand-alone, video-independent section.

Depending on your teaching preferences and school facilities, you might decide to show all video episodes in class or to assign them solely for viewing outside the classroom. You could begin by showing the first one or two episodes in class to familiarize yourself and students with the characters, storyline, style, and **Summary** sections. After that, you could work in class only with **Fotoroman** and have students view the remaining video episodes outside of class. No matter which approach you choose, students have ample materials to support viewing the video independently and processing it in a meaningful way. For each video episode, there are activities in the **Fotoroman** section of the corresponding textbook lesson, as well as additional activities in the **Mosaik** Video Manual section of the Student Activities Manual.

You might also want to use the **Fotoroman** video in class when working with the **Strukturen** sections. You could play the parts of the dramatic episode that correspond to the video stills in the grammar explanations or show selected scenes and ask students to identify certain grammar points.

You could also focus on the **Zusammenfassung** sections that appear at the end of each episode to summarize the key language functions and grammar points used. In class, you could play the parts of the **Zusammenfassung** section that exemplify individual grammar points as you progress through each **Strukturen** section. You could also wait until you complete a **Strukturen** section and review it and the lesson's **Kontext** section by showing the corresponding **Summary** section in its entirety.

On the **Mosaik** Supersite, teachers can control what, if any, subtitles students can see. They are available in German or in English, and in transcript format.

About **Zapping TV Clips and Short Films**

A TV clip or a short film from the German-speaking world appears in the first **Lektion** of each **Kapitel**. The purpose of this feature is to expose students to the language and culture contained in authentic media pieces. The following list of the television commercials and short films is organized by **Kapitel**.

MOSAIK 1

Kapitel 1
Deutsche Bahn
(29 seconds)

Kapitel 2
TU Berlin
(1 minute, 15 seconds)

Kapitel 3
Bauer Joghurt
(33 seconds)

Kapitel 4
Yello Strom
(39 seconds)

MOSAIK 2

Kapitel 1
Penny
(35 seconds)

Kapitel 2
Hausarbeit
(1 minute, 13 seconds)

Kapitel 3
Urlaub im grünen Binnenland
(3 minutes, 41 seconds)

Kapitel 4
Mercedes Benz
(35 seconds)

MOSAIK 3

Kapitel 1
Central Krankenversicherung
(23 seconds)

Kurzfilm

Kapitel 2
Fanny
(13 minutes, 45 seconds)

Kapitel 3
Die Berliner Mauer
(15 minutes)

Kapitel 4
Bienenstich ist aus
(15 minutes)

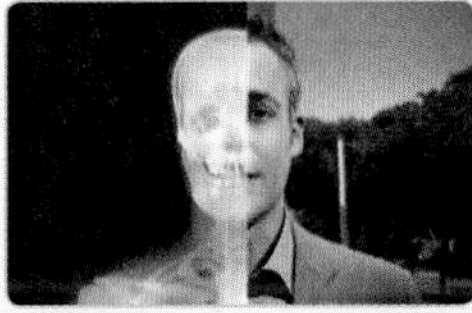

MOSAIK 2 Pacing Guides

DAY	WARM-UP / ACTIVATE	PRESENT / PRACTICE / COMMUNICATE	REFLECT / CONCLUDE / CONNECT
1 Context for Communication	• Evoke student experiences and vocabulary for context; orient to **Kontext** **5 minutes**	• Present vocabulary through illustrations, Digital Image Bank (**Supersite**), phrases, categories, association [15] • Student pairs begin **Anwendung** [15] **30 minutes**	• Students restate context for vocabulary [5] • Introduce homework: select **Anwendung** (text/**Supersite**) [5] **10 minutes**
2 Vocabulary as a Tool	• Student groups review **Anwendung** from previous day and homework **5 minutes**	• Students complete **Anwendung** [15] • Students begin **Kommunikation** [15] **30 minutes**	• Introduce homework: **Supersite** flashcards, context illustrations and audio; end-of-chapter list with audio; remaining **Supersite** activities (as applicable) [5] • Students do select **Kommunikation** activities [5] **10 minutes**
3 Vocabulary as a Tool	• Student groups review **Anwendung** and **Kommunikation** activities **5 minutes**	• Students complete **Kommunikation** activities and/or do select **Info Gap** activities (**Supersite**: **Resources**) [15] • Present **Aussprache und Rechtschreibung** (**Supersite**) [15] **30 minutes**	• Students review vocabulary for assessment preparation [5] • Introduce homework: select **Aussprache und Rechtschreibung** (**Supersite**) activities [5] **10 minutes**
4 Media as a Bridge	• Reflection and preparation: **Kontext** assessment **5 minutes**	• Assessment: **Kontext** [20] • Clarity check on **Aussprache und Rechtschreibung** [5] • Orient students to **Fotoroman** through video stills [10] **35 minutes**	• Introduce homework: review stills for **Fotoroman** (text/**Supersite**) **5 minutes**
5 Media as a Bridge	• Review results of Assessment: **Kontext** **10 minutes**	• Orient students to **Nützliche Ausdrücke** [10] • View and discuss **Fotoroman** [20] **30 minutes**	• Introduce homework: select **Fotoroman** (text/**Supersite**) **Übungen** **5 minutes**
6 Media as a Bridge	• Review **Fotoroman Übungen**, as applicable **10 minutes**	• Use **Fotoroman** and **Nützliche Ausdrücke** for communication practice [20] • Pair/group work with **Fotoroman Übungen** [10] **30 minutes**	• Introduce homework: complete **Fotoroman** (text/**Supersite**) **Übungen** **5 minutes**
7 Culture for Communication	• Review **Fotoroman Übungen**, as applicable **5 minutes**	• Present select **Kultur** features in whole class or small groups, jigsaw, numbered heads together, etc. **35 minutes**	• Introduce homework: select **Kultur** (text/**Supersite**) **Übungen** **5 minutes**
8 Culture for Communication	• Student pairs/groups review **Kultur Übungen** **5 minutes**	• Focus on select **Kultur** items to confirm understanding [10] • Class, group, pair or individual research using **Im Internet** (**Supersite**) [25] **35 minutes**	• Introduce homework: complete **Im Internet** (**Supersite**) **5 minutes**
9 Structure as a Tool	• Whole class review of **Im Internet** research **10 minutes**	• Present grammar point A.1 using text, **Supersite** (presentations, grammar slides in **Resources**), and corresponding **Fotoroman** segments [15] • Student pairs/groups do A.1 **Jetzt sind Sie dran**, begin **Anwendung** [15] **30 minutes**	• Introduce homework: select **Anwendung** (text/**Supersite**) **5 minutes**
10 Structure as a Tool	• Student pairs share results of completed items in **Anwendung** **5 minutes**	• Students complete and/or review **Anwendung** [15] • Students begin A.1 **Kommunikation** [20] **35 minutes**	• Introduce homework: complete and/or review **Kommunikation** (text/**Supersite**) **5 minutes**

DAY	WARM-UP / ACTIVATE	PRESENT / PRACTICE / COMMUNICATE	REFLECT / CONCLUDE / CONNECT
11 Structure as a Tool	• Student pairs/groups review and/or present select **Kommunikation** **10 minutes**	• Lead discussion, review, or practice of grammar point A.1 [5] • Present grammar point A.2 using text, **Supersite** (presentations, grammar slides in **Resources**), and corresponding **Fotoroman** segments [15] • Student pairs/groups do A.2 **Jetzt sind Sie dran**, begin **Anwendung** [10] **30 minutes**	• Introduce homework: select **Anwendung** (text/**Supersite**) **5 minutes**
12 Structure as a Tool	• Student pairs share results of completed items in **Anwendung** **5 minutes**	• Students complete and/or review **Anwendung** [15] • Students begin A.2 **Kommunikation** [20] **35 minutes**	• Introduce homework: complete and/or review **Kommunikation** (text/**Supersite**) **5 minutes**
13 Structure as a Tool	• Student pairs/groups review and/or present select **Kommunikation** **10 minutes**	• Lead discussion, review, or practice of grammar point A.2 [5] • Present grammar point A.3 using text, **Supersite** (presentations, grammar slides in **Resources**), and corresponding **Fotoroman** segments [15] • Student pairs/groups do A.3 **Jetzt sind Sie dran**, begin **Anwendung** [10] **30 minutes**	• Introduce homework: select **Anwendung** (text/**Supersite**) **5 minutes**
14 Structure as a Tool	• Student pairs share results of completed items in **Anwendung** **5 minutes**	• Students complete and/or review **Anwendung** [15] • Students begin A.3 **Kommunikation** [20] **35 minutes**	• Introduce homework: complete and/or review **Kommunikation** (text/**Supersite**) **5 minutes**
15 Structure as a Tool	• Student pairs/groups review and/or present select **Kommunikation** **10 minutes**	• Student pairs/groups do **Wiederholung** **30 minutes**	• Introduce homework: prepare for assessment on **Strukturen** **5 minutes**
16 Authentic Media	• Students reflect in preparation for assessment on **Strukturen** **5 minutes**	• Assessment on grammar points [20] • Introduce and guide discussion of **Zapping** show clip via **Supersite**; do **Verständnis** as a class [15] **35 minutes**	• Introduce homework: prepare for **Diskussion** from **Zapping** **5 minutes**
17 Context for Communication	• Class/groups/pairs engage in **Diskussion** from **Zapping** **5 minutes**	• Present vocabulary through illustrations, Digital Image Bank (**Supersite**), phrases, categories, association [15] • Student pairs begin **Anwendung** [15] **30 minutes**	• Students restate context of vocabulary [5] • Introduce homework: select **Anwendung** (text/**Supersite**) [5] **10 minutes**
18 Vocabulary as a Tool	• Student groups review **Anwendung** from previous day and homework **5 minutes**	• Students complete **Anwendung** **30 minutes**	• Students review and personalize key vocabulary in context [5] • Introduce homework: **Supersite** flashcards, context illustrations and audio; end-of-chapter list with audio; remaining **Supersite** activities (as applicable) [5] **10 minutes**
19 Vocabulary as a Tool	• Student groups review **Anwendung** from previous day and homework **5 minutes**	• Students do select **Kommunikation** activities [20] • Students do select **Info Gap** activities (**Supersite: Resources**) [10] **30 minutes**	• Students review and personalize key vocabulary in context [5] • Introduce homework: **Supersite** flashcards, context illustrations and audio; end-of-chapter list with audio; select **Kommunikation** activities (as applicable) [5] **10 minutes**

DAY	WARM-UP / ACTIVATE	PRESENT / PRACTICE / COMMUNICATE	REFLECT / CONCLUDE / CONNECT
20 Vocabulary as a Tool	• Student groups review **Kommunikation** from previous day and homework **5 minutes**	• Present **Aussprache und Rechtschreibung** (**Supersite**) [10] • Invite students to reflect on their pronunciation accuracy in preceding activities [15] **25 minutes**	• Students review vocabulary for assessment preparation [10] • Introduce homework: select **Aussprache und Rechtschreibung** (**Supersite**) activities [5] **15 minutes**
21 Media as a Bridge	• Reflection and preparation: **Kontext** assessment **5 minutes**	• Assessment: **Kontext** [20] • Clarity check on **Aussprache und Rechtschreibung** [5] • Orient students to **Fotoroman** through video stills [10] **35 minutes**	• Introduce homework: review stills for **Fotoroman** (text/**Supersite**) **5 minutes**
22 Media as a Bridge	• Review results of Assessment: **Kontext** **10 minutes**	• Orient students to **Nützliche Ausdrücke** [10] • View and discuss **Fotoroman** [20] **30 minutes**	• Introduce homework: select **Fotoroman** (text/**Supersite**) **Übungen** **5 minutes**
23 Media as a Bridge	• Review **Fotoroman Übungen**, as applicable **10 minutes**	• Use **Fotoroman** and **Nützliche Ausdrücke** for communication practice [20] • Pair/group work with **Fotoroman Übungen** [10] **30 minutes**	• Introduce homework: complete **Fotoroman** (text/**Supersite**) **Übungen** **5 minutes**
24 Culture for Communication	• Review **Fotoroman Übungen**, as applicable **5 minutes**	• Present select **Kultur** features in whole class or small groups, jigsaw, numbered heads together, etc. **35 minutes**	• Introduce homework: select **Kultur** (text/**Supersite**) **Übungen** **5 minutes**
25 Culture for Communication	• Student pairs/groups review **Kultur Übungen** **5 minutes**	• Focus on select **Kultur** items to confirm understanding [10] • Class, group, pair or individual research using **Im Internet** (**Supersite**) [25] **35 minutes**	• Introduce homework: complete **Im Internet** (**Supersite**) **5 minutes**
26 Structure as a Tool	• Whole class review of **Im Internet** research **10 minutes**	• Present grammar point B.1 using text, **Supersite** (presentations, grammar slides in **Resources**), and corresponding **Fotoroman** segments [15] • Student pairs/groups do B.1 **Jetzt sind Sie dran**, begin **Anwendung** [15] **30 minutes**	• Introduce homework: select **Anwendung** (text/**Supersite**) **5 minutes**
27 Structure as a Tool	• Student pairs share results of completed items in **Anwendung** **5 minutes**	• Students complete and/or review **Anwendung** [15] • Students begin B.1 **Kommunikation** [20] **35 minutes**	• Introduce homework: complete and/or review **Kommunikation** (text/**Supersite**) **5 minutes**
28 Structure as a Tool	• Student pairs/groups review and/or present select **Kommunikation** **10 minutes**	• Lead discussion, review, or practice of grammar point B.1 [5] • Present grammar point B.2 using text, **Supersite** (presentations, grammar slides in **Resources**), and corresponding **Fotoroman** segments [15] • Student pairs/groups do B.2 **Jetzt sind Sie dran**, begin **Anwendung** [10] **30 minutes**	• Introduce homework: select **Anwendung** (text/**Supersite**) **5 minutes**
29 Structure as a Tool	• Student pairs share results of completed items in **Anwendung** **5 minutes**	• Students complete and/or review **Anwendung** [15] • Students begin B.2 **Kommunikation** [20] **35 minutes**	• Introduce homework: complete and/or review **Kommunikation** (text/**Supersite**) **5 minutes**

DAY	WARM-UP / ACTIVATE	PRESENT / PRACTICE / COMMUNICATE	REFLECT / CONCLUDE / CONNECT
30 Structure as a Tool	• Student pairs/groups review and/or present select **Kommunikation** **10 minutes**	• Lead discussion, review, or practice of grammar point B.2 [5] • Present grammar point B.3 using text, **Supersite** (presentations, grammar slides in **Resources**), and corresponding **Fotoroman** segments [15] • Student pairs/groups do B.3 **Jetzt sind Sie dran**, begin **Anwendung** [10] **30 minutes**	• Introduce homework: select **Anwendung** (text/**Supersite**) **5 minutes**
31 Structure as a Tool	• Student pairs share results of completed items in **Anwendung** **5 minutes**	• Students complete and/or review **Anwendung** [15] • Students begin B.3 **Kommunikation** [20] **35 minutes**	• Introduce homework: complete and/or review **Kommunikation** (text/**Supersite**) **5 minutes**
32 Structure as a Tool	• Student pairs/groups review and/or present select **Kommunikation** **10 minutes**	• Student pairs/groups do **Wiederholung** **30 minutes**	• Introduce homework: prepare for assessment on **Strukturen** **5 minutes**
33 Skill Synthesis: Culture and Geography	• Students reflect in preparation for assessment on **Strukturen** **5 minutes**	• Assessment on **Strukturen** [20] • Present select **Weiter geht's** - **Panorama** features in whole class or small groups, jigsaw, numbered heads together, etc. [15] **35 minutes**	• Introduce homework: **Panorama - Was haben Sie gelernt?** activity/activities and/or initial research using **Im Internet** **5 minutes**
34 Skill Synthesis: Interpretive (Reading)	• Student pairs review homework from **Panorama** **10 minutes**	• Class review and discussion from **Panorama** [15] • Guide students through **Vor dem Lesen**, including **Strategien** [15] **30 minutes**	• Introduce homework: select **Vor dem Lesen** activities (text/**Supersite**) **5 minutes**
35 Skill Synthesis: Interpretive (Reading)	• Student pairs review homework from **Vor dem Lesen** **5 minutes**	• Students read **Lesen** (whole class or small groups) [25] • Students begin **Nach dem Lesen** [10] **35 minutes**	• Introduce homework: complete **Nach dem Lesen** activities (text/**Supersite**) **5 minutes**
36 Skill Synthesis: Interpretive (Listening)	• Share and discuss results from **Nach dem Lesen** **10 minutes**	• Guide students through **Strategien** and **Vorbereitung** in **Hören**; present selection [20] • Students (individuals, pairs, or small groups) do select **Verständnis** activities [10] **30 minutes**	• Introduce homework: complete **Verständnis** from **Hören** (text or **Supersite**) **5 minutes**
37 Skill Synthesis: Presentational (Writing)	• Student pairs check results from **Verständnis** **10 minutes**	• Guide students through **Schreiben**, including **Strategien** and **Thema** [15] • Review and preparation through use of communication activities, additional Partner Chat or Virtual Chat activities (**Supersite**) and **Wortschatz** (text/**Supersite**) [10] **25 minutes**	• Introduce homework: first draft of **Schreiben - Thema** • Review content and concepts for chapter assessment **10 minutes**
38 Skill Synthesis and Review	• Student pairs/groups do initial peer review of drafts of **Schreiben** - **Thema** **15 minutes**	• Review and preparation through use of communication activities, additional Partner Chat or Virtual Chat activities (**Supersite**) and **Wortschatz** (text/**Supersite**) and/or begin **IPA** (**Supersite**: **Resources**) **25 minutes**	• Confirm understanding of assessment content (and/or grading rubric if using **IPA**) • **Schreiben - Thema** due **5 minutes**
39 Assessment	• Confirm all students submitted **Schreiben - Thema** (text/**Supersite**) **5 minutes**	• Written or digital chapter assessment (from **Resources** section or **Assessment** section of **Supersite**, respectively) and/or complete **IPA**	**40 minutes**

MOSAIK 2 Pacing Guides

DAY	WARM-UP / ACTIVATE	PRESENT / PRACTICE / COMMUNICATE
1 Context for Communication	• Present and practice first half of review section 1 (of 4) **25 minutes**	• Evoke student experiences and vocabulary for context; orient to **Kontext** [10] • Present vocabulary through illustrations, Digital Image Bank (**Supersite**), phrases, categories, association [15] **25 minutes**
2 Vocabulary as a Tool	• Present and practice second half of review section 1 (of 4) **15 minutes**	• Student pairs/groups review **Anwendung** from previous day and homework [10] • Students do **Kommunikation** activities [10] **20 minutes**
3 Media as a Bridge	• Present and practice first half of review section 2 (of 4) **20 minutes**	• Reflection and preparation: **Kontext** assessment [5] • Assessment: **Kontext** [20] **25 minutes**
4 Media as a Bridge	• Present and practice second half of review section 2 (of 4) **15 minutes**	• Review **Fotoroman** [5] • Second viewing and discussion/communication using **Fotoroman** [10] • Student pairs/groups complete **Fotoroman Übungen** [10] **25 minutes**
5 Culture for Communication	• Present and practice first half of review section 3 (of 4) **20 minutes**	• Student pairs/groups review **Kultur Übungen** [5] • Class, group, pair or individual research using **Im Internet** (**Supersite**) [20] **25 minutes**
6 Structure as a Tool	• Present and practice second half of review section 3 (of 4) **15 minutes**	• Student pairs share results of completed items in A.1 **Anwendung** [5] • Students complete A.1 **Anwendung** and **Kommunikation** [20] **25 minutes**
7 Structure as a Tool	• Present and practice first half of review section 4 (of 4) **20 minutes**	• Student pairs share results of completed items in A.2 **Anwendung** [5] • Students complete A.2 **Anwendung** and **Kommunikation** [15] **20 minutes**
8 Structure as a Tool	• Present and practice second half of review section 4 (of 4) **15 minutes**	• Student pairs share results of completed items in A.3 **Anwendung** [5] • Students complete A.3 **Anwendung** and **Kommunikation** [20] **25 minutes**
9 Authentic Media	• Students reflect in preparation for assessment on **Strukturen** **10 minutes**	• Assessment on **Strukturen** **35 minutes**
10 Context for Communication	• Evoke student experiences and vocabulary for context **5 minutes**	• Present vocabulary through illustrations, Digital Image Bank (**Supersite**), phrases, categories, association **35 minutes**

REFLECT	PRESENT / PRACTICE / COMMUNICATE	REFLECT / CONCLUDE / CONNECT
• Student pairs restate context of vocabulary **5 minutes**	• Students do **Anwendung** (individual, pairs, small groups) **25 minutes**	• Introduce homework: **Supersite** flashcards, context illustrations and audio; end-of-chapter list with audio; remaining **Supersite** activities (as applicable) **5 minutes**
• Students reflect on and take note of personal areas of strength and challenge **5 minutes**	• Students do select **Info Gap** activities (**Supersite**: **Resources**) [25] • Present **Aussprache und Rechtschreibung** (**Supersite**) [15] **40 minutes**	• Students review vocabulary for assessment preparation • Introduce homework: select **Aussprache und Rechtschreibung** (**Supersite**) activities **5 minutes**
• Students individually review points in **Aussprache und Rechtschreibung** **5 minutes**	• Orient students to **Fotoroman** through video stills [5] • Orient students to **Nützliche Ausdrücke** [15] • First viewing of **Fotoroman** [10] **30 minutes**	• Introduce homework: select **Fotoroman** (text/**Supersite**) **Übungen** **5 minutes**
• Students individually review and consolidate **Nützliche Ausdrücke** **5 minutes**	• Present select **Kultur** features in whole class or small groups, jigsaw, numbered heads together, etc. **35 minutes**	• Introduce homework: select **Kultur** (text/**Supersite**) **Übungen** **5 minutes**
• Students individually review and consolidate understanding of cultural information **5 minutes**	• Present grammar point A.1 using text, **Supersite** (presentations, grammar slides in **Resources**), and corresponding **Fotoroman** segments [15] • Student pairs/groups do A.1 **Jetzt sind Sie dran**, begin **Anwendung** [15] **30 minutes**	• Introduce homework: select A.1 **Anwendung** (text/**Supersite**) **5 minutes**
• Students individually reflect on and take note of personal areas of strength and challenge with regard to the grammar point and its use **5 minutes**	• Present grammar point A.2 using text, **Supersite** (presentations, grammar slides in **Resources**), and corresponding **Fotoroman** segments [25] • Student pairs/groups do A.2 **Jetzt sind Sie dran**, begin **Anwendung** [10] **35 minutes**	• Introduce homework: select A.2 **Anwendung** (text/**Supersite**) **5 minutes**
• Students individually reflect on and take note of personal areas of strength and challenge with regard to the grammar point and its use **5 minutes**	• Present grammar point A.3 using text, **Supersite** (presentations, grammar slides in **Resources**), and corresponding **Fotoroman** segments [25] • Student pairs/groups do A.3 **Jetzt sind Sie dran**, begin **Anwendung** [10] **35 minutes**	• Introduce homework: select A.3 **Anwendung** (text/**Supersite**) **5 minutes**
• Students individually reflect on and take note of personal areas of strength and challenge with regard to the grammar point and its use **5 minutes**	• Student pairs/groups do **Wiederholung** **35 minutes**	• Introduce homework: prepare for assessment on **Strukturen** **5 minutes**
	• Introduce and guide discussion of **Zapping** show clip via **Supersite**; do **Verständnis** and **Diskussion** as a class **35 minutes**	• Introduce homework: preview **Kontext B** through pictures and word lists (text/**Supersite**) **5 minutes**
• Student pairs restate context of vocabulary **5 minutes**	• Students do **Anwendung** (individual, pairs, small groups) **35 minutes**	• Introduce homework: **Supersite** flashcards, context illustrations and audio; end-of-chapter list with audio; remaining **Supersite** activities (as applicable) **5 minutes**

DAY	WARM-UP / ACTIVATE	PRESENT / PRACTICE / COMMUNICATE
11 Vocabulary as a Tool	• Student pairs/groups review **Anwendung** from previous day and homework **5 minutes**	• Students do **Kommunikation** activities **30 minutes**
12 Media as a Bridge	• Reflection and preparation: **Kontext** assessment **5 minutes**	• Assessment: **Kontext** **35 minutes**
13 Media as a Bridge	• Review **Fotoroman Übungen** **10 minutes**	• Second viewing and discussion/communication using **Fotoroman** [15] • Student pairs/groups complete **Fotoroman Übungen** [15] **30 minutes**
14 Culture for Communication	• Student pairs/groups review **Kultur Übungen** **10 minutes**	• Focus on select **Kultur** items to confirm understanding [10] • Class, group, pair or individual research using **Im Internet** (**Supersite**) [25] **35 minutes**
15 Structure as a Tool	• Student pairs share results of completed items in B.1 **Anwendung** **5 minutes**	• Students complete B.1 **Anwendung** and **Kommunikation** **35 minutes**
16 Structure as a Tool	• Student pairs share results of completed items in B.2 **Anwendung** **5 minutes**	• Students complete B.2 **Anwendung** and **Kommunikation** **35 minutes**
17 Structure as a Tool	• Student pairs share results of completed items in B.3 **Anwendung** **5 minutes**	• Students complete B.3 **Anwendung** and **Kommunikation** **35 minutes**
18 Skill Synthesis: Culture and Geography	• Assessment on **Strukturen** **25 minutes**	• Present select **Weiter geht's** - **Panorama** features in whole class or small groups, jigsaw, numbered heads together, etc. [25] • Class review and discussion from **Panorama** [10] **35 minutes**
19 Skill Synthesis: Interpretive (Reading and Listening)	• Student pairs review homework from **Vor dem Lesen** **5 minutes**	• Students read **Lesen** (whole class or small groups) [25] • Students do **Nach dem Lesen** [15] **40 minutes**
20 Skill Synthesis: Presentational (Writing)	• Student pairs check results from **Verständnis** **10 minutes**	• Guide students through **Schreiben**, including **Strategien** and **Thema**, and connect to chapter context [10] • Students prepare writing plan in discussion with partner [15] **25 minutes**
21 Assessment	• Peer review of **Schreiben** - **Thema** **5 minutes**	

REFLECT	PRESENT / PRACTICE / COMMUNICATE	REFLECT / CONCLUDE / CONNECT
• Students reflect on and take note of personal areas of strength and challenge **5 minutes**	• Students do select **Info Gap** activities (**Supersite**: **Resources**) [25] • Present **Aussprache und Rechtschreibung** (**Supersite**) [15] **40 minutes**	• Students review vocabulary for assessment preparation • Introduce homework: select **Aussprache und Rechtschreibung** (**Supersite**) activities **5 minutes**
• Students individually review points in **Aussprache und Rechtschreibung** **5 minutes**	• Orient students to **Fotoroman** through video stills [10] • Orient students to **Nützliche Ausdrücke** [15] • First viewing of **Fotoroman** [10] **35 minutes**	• Introduce homework: select **Fotoroman** (text/**Supersite**) **Übungen** **5 minutes**
• Students individually review and consolidate **Nützliche Ausdrücke** **5 minutes**	• Present select **Kultur** features in whole class or small groups, jigsaw, numbered heads together, etc. **35 minutes**	• Introduce homework: select **Kultur** (text/**Supersite**) **Übungen** **5 minutes**
• Students individually review and consolidate understanding of cultural information **5 minutes**	• Present grammar point B.1 using text, **Supersite** (presentations, grammar slides in **Resources**), and corresponding **Fotoroman** segments [15] • Student pairs/groups do B.1 **Jetzt sind Sie dran**, begin **Anwendung** [15] **30 minutes**	• Introduce homework: select **Anwendung** (text/**Supersite**) **5 minutes**
• Students individually reflect on and take note of personal areas of strength and challenge with regard to the grammar point and its use **5 minutes**	• Present grammar point B.2 using text, **Supersite** (presentations, grammar slides in **Resources**), and corresponding **Fotoroman** segments [25] • Student pairs/groups do B.2 **Jetzt sind Sie dran**, begin **Anwendung** [10] **35 minutes**	• Introduce homework: select **Anwendung** activities **5 minutes**
• Students individually reflect on and take note of personal areas of strength and challenge with regard to the grammar point and its use **5 minutes**	• Present grammar point B.3 using text, **Supersite** (presentations, grammar slides in **Resources**), and corresponding **Fotoroman** segments [25] • Student pairs/groups do B.3 **Jetzt sind Sie dran**, begin **Anwendung** [10] **35 minutes**	• Introduce homework: select **Anwendung** (text/**Supersite**) **5 minutes**
• Students individually reflect on and take note of personal areas of strength and challenge with regard to the grammar point and its use **5 minutes**	• Student pairs/groups do **Wiederholung** **35 minutes**	• Introduce homework: prepare for assessment on **Strukturen** **5 minutes**
• Each student reviews what has just been presented from **Panorama** **5 minutes**	• Guide students through **Vor dem Lesen**, including **Strategien** **15 minutes**	• Introduce homework: **Panorama - Was haben Sie gelernt** activity/activities and/or initial research using **Im Internet**; and/or **Vor dem Lesen** activities (text/**Supersite**) **5 minutes**
• Students individually reflect on understanding of **Lesen** **5 minutes**	• Guide students through **Strategien** and **Vorbereitung** in **Hören**; present selection [20] • Students (individuals, pairs, or small groups) do **Verständnis** activities [10] **30 minutes**	• Introduce homework: complete **Verständnis** from **Hören** (text/**Supersite**) **5 minutes**
• Confirm understanding of assessment content and/or grading rubric if using **IPA** (**Supersite**: **Resources**) [5] **10 minutes**	• Students work on **Schreiben - Thema** and/or review chapter content **35 minutes**	• Introduce homework: prepare for chapter assessment and/or complete **Thema** (text/**Supersite**) **5 minutes**
• Written or digital chapter assessment (from **Resources** section or **Assessment** section of **Supersite**, respectively) and/or complete **IPA** **40 minutes**		

AP® German Themes & Contexts

Long-term success in language learning starts in the first year of instruction. **Mosaik** incorporates AP® themes and contexts into all **Kultur**, **Zapping**, **Kurzfilm**, and **Weiter geht's** sections. **Mosaik** exposes students to the themes early in their language learning career. This will allow them to build the broad background they need to succeed on the AP® German Language and Culture Exam.

The numbers following each entry can be understood as follows:

(2)115 = **(Volume)** page
As shown, the entry above would be found in Volume 2, page 115.

Beauty & Aesthetics

Contemporary Life

Families & Communities

Global Challenges

Personal & Public Identities

Science & Technology

MOSAIK 2

German Language and Culture

Boston, Massachusetts

On the cover: Houses by Friedensreich Hundertwasser, Vienna, Austria

Publisher: José A. Blanco
Professional Development Director: Norah Lulich Jones
Editorial Development: Brian Contreras, Sharla Zwirek
Project Management: Sally Giangrande
Rights Management: Ashley Dos Santos, Annie Pickert Fuller
Technology Production: Fabián Montoya, Paola Ríos Schaaf, Erica Solari
Design: Radoslav Mateev, Gabriel Noreña, Andrés Vanegas
Production: Manuela Arango, Oscar Díez, Adriana Jaramillo Ch.

Student Text ISBN: 978-1-68005-094-3
Library of Congress Control Number: 2016947899

1 2 3 4 5 6 7 8 9 WC 21 20 19 18 17 16

MOSAIK 2

German Language and Culture

Überblick

KONTEXT / FOTOROMAN

KAPITEL 1

Feiern

LEKTION 1A

LEKTION 1B

KAPITEL 2

Trautes Heim

LEKTION 2A

LEKTION 2B

KULTUR

STRUKTUREN

WEITER GEHT'S

		KONTEXT	FOTOROMAN
KAPITEL 3 Urlaub und Ferien	LEKTION 3A	Kontext Jahreszeiten ... 112 Aussprache und Rechtschreibung Long and short vowels ... 115	Folge 5 Berlin von oben ... 116
	LEKTION 3B	Kontext Reisen ... 130 Aussprache und Rechtschreibung Pure vowels versus diphthongs ... 133	Folge 6 Ein Sommer in der Türkei? ... 134
KAPITEL 4 Verkehrsmittel und Technologie	LEKTION 4A	Kontext Auto und Rad fahren ... 156 Aussprache und Rechtschreibung Long and short vowels with an Umlaut ... 159	Folge 7 Ein Ende mit Schrecken ... 160
	LEKTION 4B	Kontext Technik und Medien ... 174 Aussprache und Rechtschreibung The German l ... 177	Folge 8 Ein Spaziergang durch Spandau ... 178

APPENDICES

KULTUR	STRUKTUREN	WEITER GEHT'S
Im Fokus Windenergie .... 118 Porträt Klima in Deutschland 119	3A.1 Separable and inseparable prefix verbs (Präteritum) .... 120 3A.2 Prepositions of location; Prepositions in set phrases .... 124 Wiederholung .... 128 Zapping *Urlaub im grünen Binnenland* .. 129	Panorama: Schleswig-Holstein, Hamburg und Bremen .... 148 Lesen: Die Nordseeküste Schleswig-Holsteins in 6 Tagen........ 150 Hören .... 152 Schreiben .... 153 Wortschatz 154
Im Fokus Flughafen Frankfurt .... 136 Porträt Der ICE 137	3B.1 Infinitive expressions and clauses .... 138 3B.2 Time expressions .... 142 3B.3 Indefinite pronouns .... 144 Wiederholung 146	
Im Fokus Die deutsche Autobahn .... 162 Porträt Clärenore Stinnes 163	4A.1 Das Plusquamperfekt .... 164 4A.2 Comparatives and superlatives .. 168 Wiederholung .... 172 Zapping *Mercedes Benz* 173	Panorama: Hessen und Thüringen .... 192 Lesen: Vierfarbdrucker Installationsanleitung .... 194 Hören .... 196 Schreiben .... 197 Wortschatz 198
Im Fokus Max-Planck-Gesellschaft .... 180 Porträt Darmstadt 181	4B.1 The genitive case .... 182 4B.2 Demonstratives .... 186 Wiederholung 190	

The *Fotoroman* Episodes

Fully integrated with your textbook, the **Mosaik Fotoroman** contains 8 dramatic episodes—one for each lesson of the text. The episodes relate the adventures of four students who are studying in Berlin.

The **Fotoroman** dialogues in the printed textbook lesson are an abbreviated version of the dramatic episode featured in the video. Therefore, each **Fotoroman** section can be used as preparation before you view the corresponding video episode, as post-viewing reinforcement, or as a stand-alone section.

As you watch the video, you will see the characters interact using the vocabulary and grammar you are studying. Their conversations incorporate new vocabulary and grammar with previously taught language. At the conclusion of each episode, the **Zusammenfassung** segment summarizes the key language functions and grammar points used in the episode.

The Cast

Learn more about each of the characters you'll meet in **Mosaik Fotoroman**:

George
is from Milwaukee, Wisconsin.
He is studying Architecture.

Meline
is from Vienna.
She is studying Business.

Hans
is from Straubing, in Bavaria.
He studies Political Science and History.

Sabite
is from Berlin.
She studies Art.

About **Zapping TV Clips**

A TV clip from the German-speaking world appears in the first **Lektion** of each **Kapitel**. The purpose of this feature is to expose students to the language and culture contained in authentic media pieces. The following list of the television commercials is organized by **Kapitel.**

Kapitel 1

Penny: Shopping im Discounter

(35 seconds)

Kapitel 2

Hausarbeit

(1 minute, 13 seconds)

Kapitel 3

Urlaub im grünen Binnenland

(3 minutes, 41 seconds)

Kapitel 4

Mercedes Benz

(35 seconds)

Ancillaries

- **Student Activities Manual (SAM)**

  The Student Activities Manual consists of three sections: the Workbook, the Video Manual, and the Lab Manual. The Workbook activities provide additional practice of the vocabulary and grammar for each textbook lesson. The Video Manual section includes activities for the **Mosaik Fotoroman**, and the Lab Manual activities focus on building your listening comprehension, speaking, and pronunciation skills in German.

- **Lab Audio MP3s**

  The Lab Audio MP3 files on the Supersite contain the recordings needed to complete the Lab Manual activities in the Student Activities Manual.

- **Textbook Audio MP3s**

  The Textbook Audio MP3 files contain the recordings needed to complete the listening activities in **Kontext**, **Aussprache und Rechtschreibung**, **Hören**, and **Wortschatz** sections. The files are available on the **Mosaik** Supersite.

- **Fotoroman Video**

  All episodes of the **Fotoroman** are available for streaming on the **Mosaik** Supersite.

- **Online Student Activities Manual (WebSAM)**

  Completely integrated with the **Mosaik** Supersite, the WebSAM provides online access to the SAM activities with instant feedback and grading. The complete audio program is online and features record-submit functionality for select activities.

- **Mosaik Supersite**

  The Supersite (**vhlcentral.com**) gives you access to a wide variety of interactive activities for each section of every lesson of the student text, including: auto-graded activities for extra practice with vocabulary, grammar, video, and cultural content; teacher-graded Partner Chat, Virtual Chat, and composition activities; reference tools; the **Zapping** TV commercials; the **Fotoroman** episodic videos; the Textbook Audio MP3 files, the Lab Program MP3 files, and more.

Each section of your textbook comes with activities on the **Mosaik** Supersite, many of which are auto-graded with immediate feedback. Plus, the Supersite is iPad®-friendly*, so it can be accessed on the go! Visit **vhlcentral.com** to explore the wealth of exciting resources.

KONTEXT	• Image-based vocabulary activities with audio • Additional activities for extra practice • **Aussprache und Rechtschreibung** presentation followed by record-compare activities	• Textbook activities • Chat activities for conversational skill-building and oral practice
FOTOROMAN	• Streaming video for all episodes of the **Fotoroman** with teacher-controlled options for subtitles • Textbook activities	• **Zusammenfassung** section with key vocabulary and grammar from the episode • Additional activities for extra practice
KULTUR	• Culture reading • Internet search activity	• Textbook activities • Additional activities for extra practice
STRUKTUREN	• Grammar presentations • Chat activities for conversational skill-building and oral practice • Streaming video of **Zapping** TV clip	• Textbook activities • Additional activities for extra practice
WEITER GEHT'S	**Panorama** • Interactive map with statistics and cultural notes • Additional activity for extra practice **Im Internet** • Internet search activity • Textbook activity with auto-grading **Lesen** • Audio-sync reading • Additional activities for extra practice • Textbook activities	**Hören** • Textbook activities • Additional activities for extra practice **Schreiben** • Submit your writing assignment online
WORTSCHATZ	• Audio recordings of all vocabulary items	• My Vocabulary to create lists and flashcards

Plus! Also found on the Supersite:

- All textbook and lab audio MP3 files
- Communication center for teacher notifications and feedback
- A single gradebook for all Supersite activities
- WebSAM online Workbook/Video Manual and Lab Manual
- vText online, interactive student edition with access to Supersite activities, audio, and video

*Students must use a computer for audio-recording.

Icons

Familiarize yourself with these icons that appear throughout **Mosaik**.

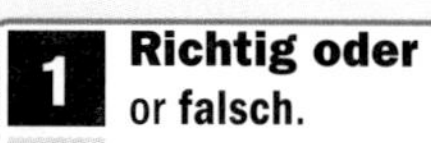

Online Activities
The mouse icon indicates when an activity is also available on the Supersite.

Pair Activities
Two heads indicate a pair activity.

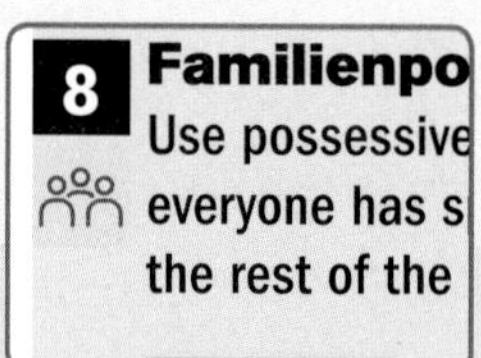

Group Activities
Three heads indicate a group activity.

Recycle
The recycling icon indicates that you will need to use vocabulary and grammar learned in previous lessons.

Partner and Virtual Chat Activities
Two heads with a speech bubble indicate that the activity may be assigned as a Partner Chat or a Virtual Chat activity on the Supersite.

Listening
The listening icon indicates that audio is available on the Supersite.

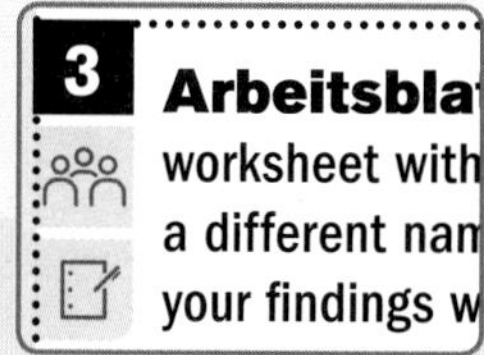

Worksheets
The activities marked with these icons require worksheets that your teacher will provide for you to complete the activity in a group.

Info Gap Activities
Two heads with a puzzle piece indicate an activity which will be done with a partner using a handout your teacher will provide.

Ressourcen

Ressourcen boxes tell you exactly what print and digital resources you can use to reinforce and expand on every section of the textbook lesson with page numbers where applicable.

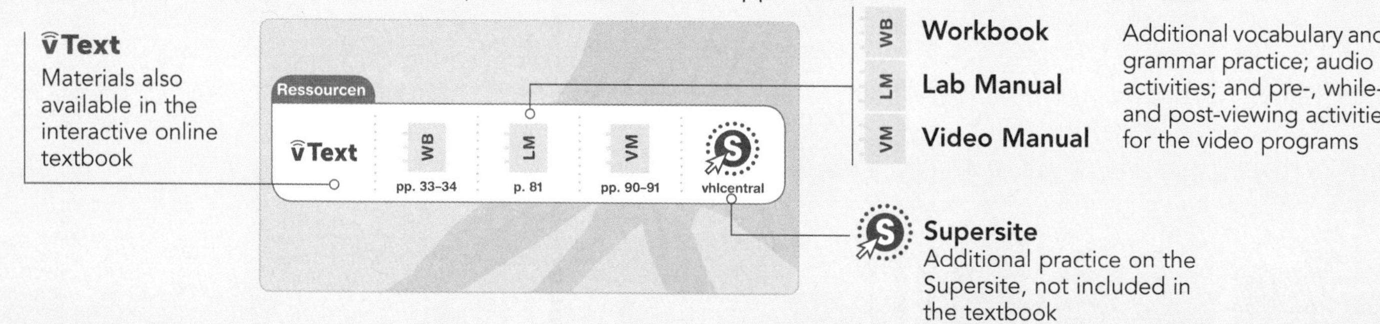

Why Learn German?

The German-Speaking World

The German language is spoken primarily in Germany, Austria, and Switzerland and holds official status in Belgium, Liechtenstein, Luxembourg, and the European Union. The United States has the largest German-speaking population outside of Europe. After English and Spanish, German is the third most commonly spoken language in over a dozen states in the nation. After Hispanics, German descendants are the largest ethnic group in the U.S., making up about one third of the German diaspora worldwide.

German culture has a broad historical past dating back more than two thousand years. From Goethe to Mozart and from Gutenberg to Einstein, German language and culture has influenced the spheres of arts and sciences. Today, the German-speaking population has major economic and political importance in the European Union and beyond.

Explore Your Future

Are you already planning your future career? Employers in today's global economy look for workers who know different languages and understand other cultures. Your knowledge of German will make you a valuable job candidate, especially if you want to work abroad in the European Union.

In addition, studying a foreign language can improve your ability to analyze and interpret information and help you succeed in many other subject areas. When you first begin learning German, your studies will focus mainly on reading, writing, grammar, listening, and speaking skills. Many people who study a foreign language claim that they gained a better understanding of English. German can even help you understand the origins of many English words and expand your own vocabulary in English. Then, when you travel to a German-speaking country, you'll be able to converse freely with the people you meet. You'll find that speaking to people in their native language is the best way to bridge any culture gap.

How to Learn German

Start with the Basics

As with anything you want to learn, start with the basics and remember that learning takes time! The basics are vocabulary, grammar, and culture.

Vocabulary | Every new word you learn in German will expand your vocabulary and ability to communicate. The more words you know, the better you can express yourself. Focus on sounds and think about ways to remember words. Use your knowledge of English and other languages to figure out the meaning of and memorize words like **Wasser, Apfel, Buch, Karte,** and **Fisch.**

Grammar | Grammar helps you put your new vocabulary together. By learning the rules of grammar, you can use new words correctly and speak in complete sentences. As you learn verbs and tenses, you will be able to speak about the past, present, or future, express yourself with clarity, and be able to persuade others with your opinions. Pay attention to structures and use your knowledge of English grammar to make connections with German grammar.

Culture | Culture provides you with a framework for what you may say or do. As you learn about the culture of German-speaking communities, you'll improve your knowledge of German. Think about a word like **Kindergarten**, and how it relates to the level of education and who attends it. Think about and explore customs like **die Sternsinger** ("Star Singers" who dress up in costume on Epiphany) and how they are similar to celebrations with which you're familiar. Observe customs—watch people greet each other or say good-bye. Listen for idioms and sayings that capture the spirit of what you want to communicate.

Die Sternsinger in traditional costumes.

Listen, Speak, Read, and Write

Listening | Listen for sounds and for words you can recognize. Listen for inflections and watch for key words that signal a question such as **wie** (*how*), **wo** (*where*), or **was** (*what*). Get used to the sound of German. Play German pop songs or watch German movies. Borrow audiobooks from your local library. Don't worry if you don't understand every single word. If you focus on key words and phrases, you'll get the main idea. The more you listen, the more you'll understand!

Speaking | Practice speaking German as often as you can. As you talk, work on your pronunciation, and read aloud texts so that words and sentences flow more easily. Don't worry if you don't sound like a native speaker, or if you make some mistakes. Time and practice will help you get there. Participate actively in German class. Try to speak German with classmates, especially native speakers (if you know any), as often as you can.

Reading | Read the lyrics of a song as you listen to it, or read books you've already read in English translated into German. Use reading strategies that you know to understand the meaning of a text that looks unfamiliar. Look for cognates, or words that are related in English and German, to guess the meaning of some words. Read as often as you can, and remember to read for fun.

Writing | German has standardized and largely phonetic rules for spelling. You'll need to learn how to interpret the sounds of the German language, but once you do, you can become a proficient speller. Write for fun—make up poems or songs, write e-mails or instant messages to friends, or start a journal or blog in German.

Tips for Learning German

Practice, practice, practice!

Seize every opportunity you find to listen, speak, read, or write German. Think of it like a sport or learning a musical instrument—the more you practice, the more you will become comfortable with the language and how it works. You'll marvel at how quickly you can begin speaking German and how the world that it transports you to can change your life forever.

- Listen to German radio shows. Write down words that you can't recognize or don't know and look up the meaning.
- Watch German TV shows or movies. Read subtitles to help you grasp the content.
- Read German-language newspapers, magazines, or blogs.
- Listen to German songs that you like —anything from contemporary pop music to traditional **Volksmusik**. Sing along and concentrate on your pronunciation.

Beatrice Egli, Swiss pop singer

- Seek out German speakers. Look for cultural centers where German might be spoken in your community. Order from a menu at a Viennese restaurant in German.
- Pursue language exchange opportunities (**Schüleraustausch**) in your school or community. Join language clubs or cultural societies, and explore opportunities for studying abroad or hosting a student from a German-speaking country in your home or school.
- Connect your learning to everyday experiences. Research naming the ingredients of your favorite dish in German. Research the origins of German place names in the U.S., like Anaheim, California and Bismarck, North Dakota, or of common English words like *pretzel, hamster, pumpernickel, rucksack, waltz, dachshund, glitz,* and *strudel.*
- Use mnemonics, or a memorizing device, to help you remember words. Make up a saying in English to remember the order of the days of the week in German by using their abbreviations (Mo, Di, Mi, Do, Fr, Sa, So).
- Visualize words. Try to associate words with images to help you remember meanings. For example, think of different sorts of **Wurst** as you learn the names of different types of meat. Visualize a national park and create mental pictures of the landscape as you learn names of animals, plants, and habitats.
- Enjoy yourself! Try to have as much fun as you can learning German. Take your knowledge beyond the classroom and find ways to make the learning experience your own.

Überblick

INHALT

Hallo! Wie geht's? Seiten 2–5

- Gender, articles, and nouns
- Plurals
- Subject pronouns, **sein**, and the nominative case
- **Haben** and the accusative case
- Word order
- Numbers

Familie und Freunde Seiten 10–13

- Possessive adjectives
- Descriptive adjectives and adjective agreement
- Modals
- Prepositions with the accusative
- The imperative

Schule und Studium Seiten 6–9

- Regular verbs
- Interrogative words
- Talking about time and dates
- Stem-changing verbs
- Present tense used as future
- Negation

Essen Seiten 14–18

- Adverbs
- The modal **mögen**
- Separable and inseparable prefix verbs
- The dative
- Prepositions with the dative

KOMMUNIKATIONSZIELE

I will be able to:

- Identify myself and others
- Discuss everyday activities
- Make plans and invitations

1A.1 Gender, articles, and nouns

	MASCULINE	FEMININE	NEUTER
DEFINITE ARTICLES	**der Tisch**	**die Tür**	**das Fenster**
INDEFINITE ARTICLES	**ein Tisch**	**eine Tür**	**ein Fenster**

Remind students that the nouns ending with *-in* that refer to people are always feminine; die Freun**din**

- The definite article **die** is used with all plural nouns, regardless of gender.

die Tische **die Türen** **die Fenster**

- There is no plural form of the indefinite article.

Er ist **ein Mann.** ⟶ Sie sind **Männer.**

- Two or more simple nouns can be combined to form a compound noun.

die Nacht + **das Hemd** ⟶ **das Nachthemd**

1A.2 Plurals

ACHTUNG

The gender and number of a compound noun is determined by the last noun in the compound; das Haus + die Aufgabe ⟶ **die** Hausaufgabe

- There are five main patterns for forming plural nouns in German.

notation	singular	plural
-	**das Fenster** ⟶	**die Fenster**
¨	**die Mutter** ⟶	**die Mütter**
-e	**der Freund** ⟶	**die Freunde**
¨e	**der Stuhl** ⟶	**die Stühle**
-er	**das Kind** ⟶	**die Kinder**
¨er	**der Mann** ⟶	**die Männer**
-n	**der Junge** ⟶	**die Jungen**
-en	**die Frau** ⟶	**die Frauen**
-nen	**die Freundin** ⟶	**die Freundinnen**
-s	**der Park** ⟶	**die Parks**

1A.3 Subject pronouns, *sein*, and the nominative case

sein (*to be*)			
singular		plural	
ich **bin**	*I am*	wir **sind**	*we are*
du **bist**	*you are* (inf.)	ihr **seid**	*you are* (inf.)
Sie **sind**	*you are* (form.)	Sie **sind**	*you are* (form.)
er/sie/es **ist**	*he/she/it is*	sie **sind**	*they are*

- The grammatical subject of a sentence is always in the nominative case (**der Nominativ**). The nominative case is also used for nouns that follow a form of **sein**, **werden**, or **bleiben**.

Das ist **eine gute Idee**. Wir bleiben **Freunde**.

1 Was ist das? Ergänzen Sie die Tabelle. Schauen Sie sich das Beispiel an.

der Computer *ein Computer*	das Problem ein Problem	die Frage eine Frage
das Hemd ein Hemd	der Junge ein Junge	der Tisch ein Tisch
die Note eine Note	die Prüfung eine Prüfung	das Zeugnis ein Zeugnis
der Taschenrechner ein Taschenrechner	das Lehrbuch ein Lehrbuch	die Frau eine Frau
der Rucksack ein Rucksack	die Stunde eine Stunde	das Mädchen ein Mädchen
das Fenster ein Fenster	der Bleistift ein Bleistift	die Tafel eine Tafel

2 Wer ist das? Wählen Sie das Pronomen, das am besten passt.

1. 
2. 
3. 

4. 
5. 
6. 

1. Sie (Sie / Du) sind froh.
2. Wir (Wir / Du) sind Tänzer.
3. Es (Sie / Es) ist ein Fahrrad.
4. Ihr (Ihr / Ich) seid in der Bibliothek.
5. Er (Du / Er) ist mein Onkel.
6. Du (Du / Sie) bist müde.

3 Freunde in Deutschland Sie sprechen mit Freunden in Deutschland. Ergänzen Sie die Sätze mit dem richtigen bestimmten Artikel (der/die/das).

1. Wann ist die Prüfung? Sie ist am Montag.
2. Wo ist der Student? Er ist hier.
3. Wie ist das Ergebnis? Nicht schlecht.
4. Was ist das Problem?
5. Wo ist der Stuhl?
6. Hier ist das Wörterbuch.
7. Das Foto ist prima!
8. Der Computer ist ziemlich gut.

4 Das Verb sein Ergänzen Sie die Sätze mit der richtigen Form von „sein".

1. Das Wörterbuch ist neu.
2. Wir sind Freunde.
3. Ich bin Amerikaner.
4. Sie sind Studenten.
5. Valeria ist in der Schule.

5 Der Nominativ Ergänzen Sie die Sätze mit der richtigen Form vom unbestimmten Artikel (ein/eine/ein).

1. Das ist ein Lehrbuch.
2. Eine Prüfung ist im Dezember.
3. Entschuldigung, wo ist ein Papierkorb?
4. Das ist ein großes Fenster.
5. Ein Mann im Hotel spricht etwas Englisch.

6 Wo sind sie? Klara sucht ihre Mitstudenten. Sie fragt Herrn Koch. Ergänzen Sie das Gespräch mit der richtigen Form von „sein".

KLARA Guten Tag, Herr Koch. Entschuldigen Sie, wo (1) sind Herr Wagner und meine Klassenkameraden?

HERR KOCH Herr Wagner (2) ist zu Hause. Die Studenten (3) sind in der Bibliothek.

KLARA Dankeschön!

HERR KOCH (4) Bist du Klara?

KLARA Ja, ich (5) bin Klara.

7 Fragen Beantworten Sie die Fragen schriftlich. Suchen Sie dann einen Partner, um das Gespräch zu führen. Stellen Sie Suggestivfragen. Präsentieren Sie der Klasse Ihre Resultate. Answers will vary.

BEISPIEL

S1: *Ist deine Mutter New Yorkerin?*
S2: *Nein, sie ist Schweizerin.*

1. Ist deine Mutter/Vater (*from another city/state*)?
2. Wo sind deine Bücher?
3. Bist du in einer Sportmannschaft?

8 Beschreibungen Schreiben Sie eine kurze Beschreibung von Ihnen und ihrer Deutschklasse. Wie heißen Sie? Wo sind Sie zu Hause? Wer ist Ihr Deutschlehrer? Wie ist der Unterricht? Answers will vary.

1B.1 *Haben* and the accusative case

haben (*to have*)			
ich **habe**	*I have*	wir **haben**	*we have*
du **hast**	*you have* (inf.)	ihr **habt**	*you have* (inf.)
Sie **haben**	*you have* (form.)	Sie **haben**	*you have* (form.)
er/sie/es **hat**	*he/she/it has*	sie **haben**	*they have*

- A noun that functions as a direct object is in the accusative case.

definite and indefinite articles				
	masculine	**feminine**	**neuter**	**plural**
nominative	der/ein Stuhl	die/eine Tür	das/ein Fenster	die/- Notizen
accusative	den/einen Stuhl	die/eine Tür	das/ein Fenster	die/- Notizen

1B.2 Word order

- In German, the verb is always the second element in a sentence. The first element is often the subject, but it can also be a time expression or a prepositional phrase.

Ich **habe** heute Abend viele Hausaufgaben.
Viele Hausaufgaben **habe** ich heute Abend.

- To turn a statement into a yes-or-no question, move the verb to the first position.

Die Lehrerin **ist** nett. ⟶ **Ist die Lehrerin** nett?
Jetzt **habt** ihr einen Computer. ⟶ **Habt ihr jetzt** einen Computer?

1B.3 Numbers

numbers 0–99							
0	null	**10**	zehn	**20**	zwanzig	**30**	dreißig
1	eins	**11**	elf	**21**	einundzwanzig	**31**	einunddreißig
2	zwei	**12**	zwölf	**22**	zweiundzwanzig	**40**	vierzig
3	drei	**13**	dreizehn	**23**	dreiundzwanzig	**45**	fünfundvierzig
4	vier	**14**	vierzehn	**24**	vierundzwanzig	**50**	fünfzig
5	fünf	**15**	fünfzehn	**25**	fünfundzwanzig	**60**	sechzig
6	sechs	**16**	sechzehn	**26**	sechsundzwanzig	**70**	siebzig
7	sieben	**17**	siebzehn	**27**	siebenundzwanzig	**80**	achtzig
8	acht	**18**	achtzehn	**28**	achtundzwanzig	**90**	neunzig
9	neun	**19**	neunzehn	**29**	neunundzwanzig	**99**	neunundneunzig

mathematical expressions					
+	**plus**	×	**mal**	=	**ist (gleich)**
–	**minus**	÷ or :	**geteilt durch**	%	**Prozent**

25,4 **fünfundzwanzig Komma vier**
4,99 € **vier Euro neunundneunzig**
1.960.000 **eine Million neunhundertsechzigtausend**

3 · 3 = 9 **Drei mal drei ist gleich neun.**
20 : 5 = 4 **Zwanzig geteilt durch fünf ist vier.**

1 Wer hat was? Ergänzen Sie die Sätze mit der richtigen Form von „haben".

1. Er hat ein Lehrbuch.
2. Wir haben eine Deutschstunde.
3. Ich habe eine Frage.
4. Die Universität hat eine Mensa.
5. Habt ihr heute eine Prüfung?
6. Du hast ein schönes Foto.
7. Frau Müller hat ein Lehrbuch für Mathematik.
8. Monika und Sabine haben Freunde in Berlin.

2 Was haben sie? Ergänzen Sie „haben" in der richtigen Form und den unbestimmten Artikel im Akkusativ.

1. Wir haben einen Lehrer aus Deutschland.
2. Die Lehrerin hat einen Taschenrechner.
3. Die Klasse hat eine Hausaufgabe.
4. Du hast eine Uhr.
5. Die Ergebnisse haben ein Problem.
6. Der Bleistift hat einen Radiergummi.

3 Ein paar Fragen Verändern Sie die Sätze in Entscheidungsfragen.

1. Ich habe viele Hausaufgaben.
   Hast du viele Hausaufgaben?
2. Die Lehrerinnen haben viele Fragen.
   Haben die Lehrerinnen viele Fragen?
3. Die Schülerin hat einen neuen Lehrer.
   Hat die Schülerin einen neuen Lehrer?
4. Die Bibliothek hat eine schöne Tür.
   Hat die Bibliothek eine schöne Tür?
5. Du hast den Rucksack.
   Hast du den Rucksack?

4 Im Klassenzimmer Bilden Sie Fragen. Achten Sie auf den richtigen Satzbau.

BEISPIEL

die Schüler / die Bücher / haben
Haben die Schüler die Bücher?

1. Tische / die Schüler / haben Haben die Schüler Tische?
2. der Lehrer / hat / eine Klasse Hat der Lehrer eine Klasse?
3. Computer / die Schüler / haben Haben die Schüler Computer?
4. die Lehrerin / eine Karte / hat Hat die Lehrerin eine Karte?
5. einen Terminkalender / die Lehrerin / hat Hat die Lehrerin einen Terminkalender?
6. die Schüler / haben / Bleistifte Haben die Schüler Bleistifte?

5 Zum Besprechen Stellen Sie Ihrem Partner / Ihrer Partnerin die Fragen in Aufgabe 4. Beantworten Sie die Fragen mit **Ja** oder **Nein**. Präsentieren Sie der Klasse Ihren Dialog.

BEISPIEL

S1: *Haben die Schüler die Bücher?*
S2: *Ja, die Schüler haben die Bücher.*

6 Expansion Ask students to write out their own numbers and equations. Have them take turns reading their numbers and equations and figuring out the answers.

6 Mathespaß Bitte ergänzen Sie die Sätze.

1. Siebzehn minus drei ist vierzehn.
2. Neunundzwanzig plus vierzehn ist dreiundvierzig.
3. Sechzig plus zwanzig ist achtzig.
4. Neunhundert geteilt durch zehn ist neunzig.
5. Fünfundzwanzig mal vier ist einhundert.
6. Vierundfünfzig minus achtzehn ist sechsunddreißig.
7. Achtundneunzig minus sechzehn ist zweiundachtzig.
8. Zwölf geteilt durch drei ist vier.

7 Die Zahlen Bitte schreiben Sie die Zahlen und mathematischen Gleichungen (*math equations*).

1. 1949
   neunzehnhundertneunundvierzig
2. 317
   dreihundertsiebzehn
3. 2.013
   zweitausenddreizehn
4. 0,8
   null Komma acht
5. 67 + 4 = 71
   Siebenundsechzig plus vier ist (gleich) einundsiebzig.
6. 213 · 3 = 639
   Zweihundertdreizehn mal drei ist (gleich) sechshundertneununddreißig
7. 24 : 4 = 6
   Vierundzwanzig geteilt durch vier ist (gleich) sechs
8. 91 – 6 = 85
   Einundneunzig minus sechs ist (gleich) fünfundachtzig

8 Was ist da drin? Diskutieren Sie mit einem Partner / einer Partnerin, was im Klassenzimmer ist. Präsentieren Sie der Klasse Ihren Dialog. Answers will vary.

BEISPIEL

S1: *Was hat das Klassenzimmer?*
S2: *Das Klassenzimmer hat eine Karte und viele Bücher.*
S1: *Haben wir Computer?*
S2: *Ja, wir haben Computer.*

2A.1 Regular Verbs

	studieren (*to study*)		wandern (*to hike*)	
ich	studiere	*I study*	wandere	*I hike*
du	studierst	*you study*	wanderst	*you hike*
Sie	studieren	*you study*	wandern	*you hike*
er/sie/es	studiert	*he/she studies*	wandert	*he/she hikes*
wir	studieren	*we study*	wandern	*we hike*
ihr	studiert	*you study*	wandert	*you hike*
Sie	studieren	*you study*	wandern	*you hike*
sie	studieren	*they study*	wandern	*they hike*

- Regular verbs whose stems end in *-d* or *-t* add an e before the endings *-st* or *-t* for ease of pronunciation.

finden ⟶ du findest; er/sie/es findet; ihr findet
arbeiten ⟶ du arbeitest; er/sie/es arbeitet; ihr arbeitet

- Verbs whose stems end in *-gn* or *-fn* also add an *-e* before the endings *-st* and *-t*.

Es **regnet** morgen. **Öffnest** du das Fenster?

- If a verb stem ends in *-s*, *-ß*, *-x*, or *-z*, the *-s* is dropped from the second person singular ending.

Er **reist** oft in die Schweiz. Du **heißt** Sabine.

2A.2 Interrogative words

ACHTUNG

The form of **welcher** depends on the gender and number of the noun it modifies.
Welche Lehrerin unterrichtet Mathematik?
Welches Fach macht Spaß?

interrogatives			
wann?	*when?*	wie?	*how?*
warum?	*why?*	wie viel?	*how much?*
was?	*what?*	wie viele?	*how many?*
welcher/welche/welches?	*which?*	wo?	*where?*
wen?/wem?	*whom?*	woher?	*where (from)?*
wer?	*who?*	wohin?	*where (to)?*

2A.3 Talking about time and dates

ACHTUNG

Use the 24-hour clock when talking about train schedules, movie listings, and official timetables.
18.45 Uhr = **achtzehn Uhr fünfundvierzig**

- To ask *What time is it?*, say **Wie spät ist es?** or **Wie viel Uhr ist es?**

Es ist **zwanzig nach** vier. Es ist **halb zehn**.
Es ist **Viertel vor** elf. Es ist **Mitternacht**.

ordinal numbers					
1.	erste	**8.**	achte	**31.**	einunddreißigste
2.	zweite	**9.**	neunte	**55.**	fünfundfünfzigste
3.	dritte	**10.**	zehnte	**69.**	neunundsechzigste
4.	vierte	**11.**	elfte	**93.**	dreiundneunzigste
5.	fünfte	**12.**	zwölfte	**100.**	hundertste
6.	sechste	**19.**	neunzehnte	**1000.**	tausendste
7.	siebte	**20.**	zwanzigste		

1 **Alle studieren die Konjugation.** Bitte ergänzen Sie „studieren" mit der richtigen Endung.

1. Wir studieren online.
2. Peter studiert in Magdeburg.
3. Maria und Sebastian studieren Mathematik.
4. Ich studiere in Potsdam.
5. Du studierst doch in Wien, oder?
6. Ihr studiert Physik.
7. Annabelle studiert in Wittenberg.

2 **Konjugation** Bitte ergänzen Sie die Verben in Klammern mit der richtigen Endung.

1. Wir brauchen (brauchen) Fahrräder.
2. Die Professorin korrigiert (korrigieren) die Prüfung.
3. Die Klasse spielt (spielen) Fußball.
4. Findest (finden) du Biologie interessant?
5. Das Restaurant öffnet (öffnen) um 11 Uhr.
6. Ich wohne (wohnen) in Weimar.
7. Wann antwortest (antworten) du auf meine E-Mail?
8. Hört (hören) ihr gern deutsche Musik?

3 **Wortschatz** Wählen Sie das richtige Verb.

1. Angelika und Rosa (wandern / spielen) Volleyball.
2. Du (kaufst / wartest) die Bücher.
3. Ihr (geht / macht) jetzt die Hausaufgaben.
4. Jürgen (belegt / reist) Architektur.
5. Wir (bedeuten / verstehen) nicht alle Fragen.
6. Meine Freundin (träumt / grüßt) von Bayern.
7. Ich (baue / liebe) deutsche Filme.
8. Die Lehrer (wiederholen / warten) das Thema.

4 **Fragen Sie!** Wählen Sie das richtige Fragewort.

1. –Woher (Woher / Welche) kommst du?
   –Ich komme aus Nürnberg.
2. –Warum (Warum / Wo) belegst du Informatik?
   –Ich denke, das ist interessant.
3. –Wann (Wie / Wann) hast du die Prüfung?
   –Am Montag.
4. –Wie viele (Wie viele / Welche) Schüler sind hier?
   –Achtzehn.
5. –Wen (Wen / Wie) kennst du?
   –Ich kenne einen Professor für Chemie.
6. –Wer (Wer / Wo) ist der Lehrer?
   –Dr. Bebel ist der Lehrer.

5 **Wie spät ist es?** Bitte schreiben Sie diese Uhrzeiten.

1. 5.30 Es ist halb sechs. / Es ist fünf Uhr dreißig.
2. 7.10 Es ist zehn nach sieben. / Es ist sieben Uhr zehn.
3. 5.45 Es ist Viertel vor sechs. / Es ist Dreiviertel sechs.
4. 19.40 Es ist zwanzig vor acht. / Es ist neunzehn Uhr vierzig.
5. 23.30 Es ist halb zwölf. / Es ist dreiundzwanzig Uhr dreißig.
6. 15.15 Es ist Viertel nach drei. / Es ist Viertel vier.

6 **Welcher Tag ist es?** Bitte ergänzen Sie die Sätze mit den richtigen Informationen.

1. Der Valentinstag ist am (14.) vierzehnten Februar.
2. Heilige Drei Könige ist am (6.) sechsten Januar.
3. Der St.-Patricks-Tag ist am (17.) siebzehnten März.
4. Weihnachten ist am (25.) fünfundzwanzigsten Dezember.
5. Der Neujahrstag ist am (1.) ersten Januar.

7 **Mein Geburtstagskalender** Notieren Sie die Geburtstage von sechs Klassenkameraden und Mitgliedern Ihrer Familie. Schreiben Sie dann Sätze wie die Beispiele. Answers will vary.

BEISPIEL

Mein Geburtstag ist am dritten März.
Susis Geburtstag ist am achtzehnten Oktober.

8 **Fragen im Dialog** Stellen Sie Ihrem deutschen Gesprächspartner sechs Fragen mit verschiedenen Fragewörtern. Answers will vary.

BEISPIEL

S1: *Wohin reist ihr?*
S2: *Wir reisen an die Ostsee.*
S1: *Wie viel kostet die Karte?*
S2: *Die Karte kostet zwölf Euro.*

1. Welcher Tag ist heute?
2. Wann hast du Geburtstag?
3. Wann ist dein Lieblingsfeiertag (*favorite holiday*)?
4. Wie spät ist es?
5. Um wie viel Uhr ist der Deutschunterricht vorbei?
6. Wann hast du die Veranstaltung?

2B.1 Stem-changing verbs

- Certain irregular verbs use the regular endings but have changes to their stem vowels in the **du** and **er/sie/es** forms. Most stem-changing verbs follow one of four patterns in the present tense.

	schlafen a → ä	**laufen** au → äu	**sprechen** e → i	**lesen** e → ie
ich	schlafe	laufe	spreche	lese
du	schläfst	läufst	sprichst	liest
er/sie/es	schläft	läuft	spricht	liest
wir	schlafen	laufen	sprechen	lesen
ihr	schlaft	lauft	sprecht	lest
Sie/sie	schlafen	laufen	sprechen	lesen

- Besides an **e → i** vowel change, **nehmen** (*to take*) and **werden** (*to become*) have additional changes in the **du** and **er/sie/es** forms.

nehmen → du n**immst**; er/sie/es n**immt**
werden → du w**irst**; er/sie/es w**ird**

2B.2 Present tense used as future

- The adverbs **heute** (*today*), **morgen** (*tomorrow*), and **übermorgen** (*the day after tomorrow*) are commonly used with the present tense to express future ideas.

Morgen gehen wir einkaufen. **Heute Nachmittag** gehe ich schwimmen.

- Use **am** with **Morgen**, **Vormittag**, **Mittag**, **Nachmittag**, **Abend**, **Wochenende**, or the days of the week to specify when something will occur.

Am Sonntag gehen wir angeln. **Am Freitagnachmittag** gehe ich zum Arzt.

- Use **im** with months and seasons (**Frühling**, **Sommer**, **Herbst**, **Winter**).

Im Frühling gehe ich wandern. **Im Februar** fahre ich Ski.

- When both the day of the week and the time of day are specified, they form a compound noun: **Dienstagmittag**, **Mittwochabend**.

2B.3 Negation

- In negative statements or questions, place **nicht** after the subject, conjugated verb, direct object, and definite time expressions, but before other sentence elements.

Ich gehe heute **nicht** in die Sporthalle. Brauchst du den Fußball **nicht**?

- **Kein** is the negative form of the indefinite article **ein**. Use **kein** to negate a noun preceded by an indefinite article or by no article.

–Spielen Sie Tennis? → –Nein, wir spielen **kein** Tennis.
–Hat er Hobbys? → –Nein, er hat **keine** Hobbys.

- The conjunction **doch** has no exact equivalent in English. Use it to contradict a negative question or statement.

–Ich habe **keine** Freunde. → –**Doch**, du hast viele Freunde!

1 Ich und du
Bitte ersetzen Sie in den folgenden Sätzen „ich" durch „du".

1. Ich esse gern Bratwurst. Du isst gern Bratwurst.
2. Ich nehme das Fahrrad. Du nimmst das Fahrrad.
3. Ich fahre im Winter oft Ski. Du fährst im Winter oft Ski.
4. Ich werde Chemiker. Du wirst Chemiker.
5. Ich laufe in die Bibliothek. Du läufst in die Bibliothek.
6. Ich schlafe nie in der Deutschstunde. Du schläfst nie in der Deutschstunde.

2 Was fehlt?
Bitte ergänzen Sie die Verben in Klammern in der richtigen Form.

1. Renate liest (lesen) ein Buch über Tennis.
2. Frank sieht (sehen) einen Film über Berlin.
3. Die Klasse fährt (fahren) im Sommer nach München.
4. Hilfst (Helfen) du deiner Mutter?
5. Der Lehrer vergisst (vergessen) die Hausaufgaben.
6. Gibst (Geben) du mir deine Telefonnummer?
7. Monika trifft (treffen) Theresa im Stadion.
8. Fängt (Fangen) Michael den Ball?

3 Wortschatz
Wählen Sie das richtige Verb.

1. Sophie (trägt / hilft) dir.
2. Du (nimmst / wirfst) ein Taxi.
3. (Lauft / Gebt) ihr mir die Hausaufgaben?
4. Die Kinder (fahren / treffen) gern Fahrrad.
5. Wir (braten / empfehlen) den Film.
6. Mein Freund (wird / fängt) Lehrer.
7. Ich (empfehle / vergesse) den Ball.
8. Die Schüler (lesen / lassen) viele Bücher.

4 Zeitangaben
Bitte schreiben Sie die richtige Zeitangabe für die Antwort. Suchen Sie dann einen Partner um das Gespräch zu führen. Präsentieren Sie Ihre Resultate der Klasse.

1. —Wann klettert ihr? (*weekend*)
   —Wir klettern am Wochenende.
2. —Wann regnet es viel? (*fall*)
   —Im Herbst regnet es viel.
3. —Wann beginnt der Unterricht? (*midmorning*)
   —Der Unterricht beginnt am Vormittag.
4. —Wann siehst du den Film? (*evening*)
   —Ich sehe den Film am Abend.
5. —Wann besuchen die Schüler Berlin? (*next week*)
   Die Schüler besuchen nächste Woche Berlin.
6. —Wann gehst du zum Arzt? (*this afternoon*)
   —Ich gehe heute Nachmittag zum Arzt.

5 Präsens als Zeitform der Zukunft
Bitte bilden Sie Sätze.

1. du / gehen / heute Nachmittag / Ski fahren
   Du gehst heute Nachmittag Ski fahren.
2. nächste Woche / Volleyball / spielen / die Mannschaft
   Die Mannschaft spielt nächste Woche Volleyball.
3. reisen / übermorgen / Antje / nach Österreich
   Antje reist übermorgen nach Österreich.
4. ihr / im Frühling / Fahrrad / fahren
   Ihr fahrt im Frühling Fahrrad.
5. Karin / kochen / heute Abend / Schnitzel
   Karin kocht heute Abend Schnitzel.
6. mehr / ich / schreiben / morgen
   Ich schreibe morgen mehr.
7. nächsten Freitag / wir / im Wald / wandern
   Wir wandern nächsten Freitag im Wald.
8. fahren / Ursula / Ski / im Februar
   Ursula fährt im Februar Ski.

6 „Kein" oder „nicht"?
Bitte verneinen Sie richtig.

1. Das sind Schülerinnen.
   Das sind keine Schülerinnen.
2. Ich verstehe dich.
   Ich verstehe dich nicht.
3. Manuela trainiert im Stadion.
   Manuela trainiert nicht im Stadion.
4. Hast du Freizeit?
   Hast du keine Freizeit?
5. Am Wochenende fahren Thomas und Ute in die Berge.
   Am Wochenende fahren Thomas und Ute nicht in die Berge.
6. Nächste Woche haben wir Prüfung.
   Nächste Woche haben wir keine Prüfung.

7 Was ist nur mit Holger los?
Finden Sie mindestens fünf Gründe, warum Holger unglücklich ist. Schreiben Sie Sätze mit „kein" oder „nicht". Answers will vary.

3A.1 Possessive adjectives

personal pronouns and possessive adjectives		
personal pronouns	**possessive adjectives**	
ich	mein	*my*
du	dein	*your* (sing., inf.)
er	sein	*his*
sie	ihr	*her*
es	sein	*its*
wir	unser	*our*
ihr	euer	*your* (pl., inf.)
Sie	Ihr	*your* (sing./pl., form.)
sie	ihr	*their*

- The endings of the possessive adjectives change according to the gender, case, and number of the object possessed.

Mein Großvater liebt **seine** Schwester. Tobias liebt **seinen** Bruder.

3A.2 Descriptive adjectives and adjective agreement

- Adjectives can describe people, places, or things. Here are some adjectives commonly used to describe people and their physical attributes.

physical description			
alt	*old*	hübsch	*pretty*
blond	*blond*	jung	*young*
braunhaarig	*brown-haired*	klein	*small; short (stature)*
dick	*fat; thick*	kurz	*short (hair)*
dunkelhaarig	*dark-haired*	lang	*long (hair)*
dünn	*thin*	lockig	*curly*
glatt	*straight (hair)*	rothaarig	*red-headed*
groß	*big; tall*	schlank	*slim*
großartig	*terrific*	schön	*pretty; beautiful*
gut aussehend	*handsome*	schwarzhaarig	*black-haired*
hässlich	*ugly*	sportlich	*athletic*

- Use an adjective with no added endings after the verbs **sein**, **werden**, and **bleiben**.

Mein Bruder ist **klein**. Seine Mutter bleibt **sportlich**. Deine Schwester wird **groß**.

- Adjective endings depend on the case, number, and gender of the noun they modify, and whether they are preceded by a **der**-word, an **ein**-word, or neither.

Sie lieben ihren **jungen** Sohn. Das **kleine** Baby hat **blaue** Augen.
Gudrun ist ein **junges** Kind. **Altes** Brot schmeckt nicht so gut.

- If multiple adjectives precede the same noun, they all take the same ending.

Ist das **kleine, rothaarige** Mädchen deine Schwester? Sie hat einen **großen, gut aussehenden** Bruder.

Suggestion You may want to explain to students that **gut** has no endings here because it is used as an adverb modifying **aussehenden**.

- Some adjectives ending in **-er** or **-el**, such as **teuer** and **dunkel**, drop the **e** in the stem when an ending is added. Dropping the e in **teuer** is optional.

Das ist ein **teu(e)res** Buch. Das ist ein **dunkles** Foto.

1 **Possessivpronomen** Bitte ergänzen Sie die deutschen Possessivpronomen im Nominativ.

1. ___Deine___ (*Your* - informal) Idee ist ziemlich gut.
2. ___Unsere___ (*Our*) Schule hat eine neue Website.
3. ___Mein___ (*My*) Freund studiert Geschichte.
4. ___Seine___ (*His*) Freundin kommt aus Potsdam.
5. ___Ihr___ (*Her*) Hobby ist Klettern.
6. Wo ist ___eure___ (*your, pl.*) Lehrerin?
7. Wer ist ___Ihr___ (*your, formal*) Lehrer für Biologie?
8. Was ist ___seine___ (*its - when talking about* das Schwimmbad) Adresse?

2 **Mein or meine?** Bitte ergänzen Sie die richtige Form des Possessivpronomens „mein" im Nominativ.

1. ___Meine___ Großmutter kommt aus Leipzig, ___mein___ Großvater aus Berlin.
2. ___Meine___ Verwandten besuchen sie oft, denn ___meine___ Großeltern sind schon über achtzig Jahre alt.
3. ___Mein___ Onkel ist Rechtsanswalt, ___meine___ Tante ist Journalistin.

3 **unser / unsere** Bitte ergänzen Sie die richtige Form des Possessivpronomens „unser" im Nominativ.

1. ___Unsere___ Eltern sind seit zwanzig Jahren verheiratet.
2. Sie sind stolz auf ___unser___ tolles Haus.
3. ___Unser___ Hund heißt Max.
4. ___Unsere___ Katze ist sehr intelligent und dynamisch.
5. Morgen spielt ___unsere___ Mannschaft in Stuttgart.
6. Ich glaube, ___unser___ Lehrer ist krank.
7. ___Unsere___ Hausaufgaben sind wirklich schwierig.

4 **euer / eur...** Jetzt sprechen Sie mit Ute und Rosi. Benutzen Sie die richtige Form des Possessivpronomens „euer".

1. Wo wohnt ___eure___ Familie?
2. Kennt ihr ___euren___ Architekten gut?
3. Braucht ihr ___euer___ Wörterbuch im Moment?
4. Spielt ___eure___ Fußballmannschaft am Wochenende?
5. Nehmt ihr ___euren___ Hund mit zum Wandern?
6. Kocht ___eure___ Oma morgen Schnitzel?

5 **Was braucht Matthias?** Matthias ist der Assistent für Mathematik. Bitte schreiben Sie, was er braucht. Benutzen Sie das Possessivpronomen „sein" im Akkusativ.

1. Matthias braucht ___seinen Computer___.
2. Matthias braucht ___sein Fahrrad___.
3. Matthias braucht ___seine Bleistifte___.
4. Matthias braucht ___seine Tafel___.

6 **Adjektive** Bitte ergänzen Sie das Adjektiv im Nominativ.

1. Die ___schlanke___ (schlank) Frau dort ist meine Professorin für Geschichte.
2. Der ___ledige___ (ledig) Mann heißt Müller.
3. Ein ___freundlicher___ (freundlich) Schüler hilft gern.
4. Der ___interessante___ (interessant) Vortrag ist heute langweilig.
5. Das ist wirklich ein ___lustiger___ (lustig) Film!
6. Du bist ein ___fleißiges___ (fleißig) Mädchen.
7. Das ___helle___ (hell) Zimmer ist unser Klassenzimmer.
8. Josefine ist eine ___tolle___ (toll) Musikerin.

7 **Meine Verwandten und Freunde** Beschreiben Sie, was Ihre Verwandten oder Freunde gern oder nicht gern machen. Schreiben Sie mindestens sechs Sätze. Answers will vary.

BEISPIEL *Mein Onkel und meine Tante tanzen gern, aber sie reisen nicht gern.*

3B.1 Modals

- Modals express an attitude towards an action, such as permission, obligation, ability, desire, or necessity. *May*, *can*, and *must* are examples of English modals.

modals in the present tense					
	dürfen	**können**	**müssen**	**sollen**	**wollen**
ich	darf	kann	muss	soll	will
du	darfst	kannst	musst	sollst	willst
er/sie/es	darf	kann	muss	soll	will
wir	dürfen	können	müssen	sollen	wollen
ihr	dürft	könnt	müsst	sollt	wollt
Sie/sie	dürfen	können	müssen	sollen	wollen

- When you use a modal to modify the meaning of another verb, put the conjugated form of the modal in second position. Put the infinitive of the other verb at the end of the sentence.

Ich **muss** Französisch **lernen**. **Willst** du Wasser **trinken**?

3B.2 Prepositions with the accusative

prepositions with the accusative					
bis	*until, to*	**für**	*for*	**ohne**	*without*
durch	*through*	**gegen**	*against*	**um**	*around; at (time)*

Der Besitzer kommt **durch die Tür**. Was hast du **gegen meinen Freund**?

- **Pro** is also an accusative preposition. The object it precedes takes no article.

Der Kellner verdient 300 Euro **pro Woche**. Das Auto fährt 130 Kilometer **pro Stunde**.

- The accusative is also used with objects that precede **entlang**.

Wir gehen **den Fluss entlang.** Ich fahre **die Straße entlang.**

3B.3 The imperative

ACHTUNG

The verb **sein** has irregular imperative forms.

Sei lieb!
Seid diskret!
Seien Sie mutig!
Seien wir realistisch!

the *Imperativ* conjugation	
Indikativ	**Imperativ**
du kaufst	kauf(e)
ihr kauft	kauft
Sie kaufen	kaufen Sie
wir kaufen	kaufen wir

Mach deine Hausaugaben!
Fahren Sie nicht so schnell!
Öffnen Sie bitte Ihren Rucksack!
Esst das Gemüse, Kinder!

Antworte auf die Frage!
Hör keine laute Musik!
Gehe nach Hause, bitte!
Lernt für dir Prüfung!

1 Satzbau mit Modalverben

Bitte bilden Sie Sätze, achten Sie auf den richtigen Satzbau.

1. müssen / wir / machen / viele Hausaufgaben
   Wir müssen viele Hausaufgaben machen.
2. heute / nicht schwimmen / darf / Sybille
   Sybille darf heute nicht schwimmen.
3. will / helfen / meiner Schwester / ich
   Ich will meiner Schwester helfen.
4. können / wir / empfehlen / den Fisch
   Wir können den Fisch empfehlen.
5. sollt / ihr / spielen / leise
   Ihr sollt leise spielen.
6. lernen / musst / du / für die Prüfung
   Du musst für die Prüfung lernen.

2 Konjugation der Modalverben

Bitte ergänzen Sie die Verben in Klammern mit der richtigen Endung.

1. Wir ___können___ (können) Thomas am Stadion treffen.
2. Die Mannschaft ___muss___ (müssen) noch viel trainieren.
3. Die Klasse ___will___ (wollen) an die Nordsee reisen.
4. ___Darf___ (dürfen) ich etwas fragen?
5. Du ___darfst___ (dürfen) die Hausaufgaben nicht vergessen.
6. Hans ___kann___ (können) sehr gut Ski fahren.
7. ___Wollt___ (wollen) ihr in die Bibliothek gehen?
8. ___Soll___ (sollen) ich einen Arzt rufen?

3 Fragen mit Modalverb

Bilden Sie Fragen mit Modalverb.

1. 2.

3. 4.

1. Kuchen essen / wollen / ihr
   Wollt ihr Kuchen essen?
2. lernen / jetzt / müssen / du
   Musst du jetzt lernen?
3. Sabine / dürfen / Fußball spielen
   Darf Sabine Fußball spielen?
4. Musik hören / dürfen / wir
   Dürfen wir Musik hören?

4 Einladungen

Beantworten Sie die Fragen schriftlich. Suchen Sie dann einen Partner, um das Gespräch zu führen. Präsentieren Sie Ihre Resultate der Klasse. Answers will vary.

BEISPIEL

S1: *Willst du morgen Tennis spielen?*
S2: *Ich kann morgen nicht Tennis spielen, ich muss in die Bibliothek gehen.*

1. Willst du morgen Schach spielen? (ich / Französisch lernen)
2. Wollen wir Karten spielen? (wir / für unsere Bekannten kochen)
3. Wollt ihr übermorgen in die Bibliothek gehen? (wir / Vorlesung besuchen)

5 Präpositionen

Wählen Sie die richtige Präposition.

1. (Ohne / Bis) meinen Freund gehe ich nicht in das Kino. [Ohne]
2. Meine Freunde spielen (durch / bis) 19 Uhr Volleyball. [bis]
3. Jürgen braucht ein Geschenk (um / für) seine Bekannten. [für]
4. Der Sportler muss (gegen / entlang) den Wind laufen. [gegen]
5. Sie geht immer (für / durch) den Park zur Schule. [durch]
6. Die Journalistin arbeitet heute (durch / bis) Mitternacht. [bis]

6 Präpositionen mit dem Akkusativ

Benutzen Sie die richtige Präposition mit dem Akkusativ.

1. Das Geschenk ist ___für den___ Freund aus Trier. (*for the*)
2. Am Abend gehen wir oft ___den Fluss entlang___. (*along the river*)
3. Ich bin ___bis nächsten___ Monat in Österreich. (*until next*)
4. Wir dürfen jetzt nicht ___durch die___ Bibliothek gehen. (*through the*)
5. Der Architekt läuft ___um unser___ Haus. (*around our*)
6. Die Kellnerin verdient 8 Euro ___pro Stunde___. (*per hour*)

7 Was sollen wir machen?

Bilden Sie Sätze im Imperativ.

1. Du öffnest dein Buch. ___Öffne dein Buch!___
2. Ihr geht in die Bibliothek. ___Geht in die Bibliothek!___
3. Du nimmst ein Schnitzel. ___Nimm ein Schnitzel!___
4. Sie sprechen mit der Journalistin. ___Sprechen Sie mit der Journalistin!___
5. Ihr schreibt an die Tafel. ___Schreibt an die Tafel!___
6. Du bist nicht gierig. ___Sei nicht gierig!___

8 Der neue Schüler

Ein neuer Schüler kommt in Ihre Klasse. Bitte schreiben Sie ihm/ihr auf, was wichtig ist. Benutzen Sie Sätze im Imperativ. Präsentieren Sie die Liste dann der Klasse. Answers will vary.

BEISPIEL

Sei pünktlich! Arbeite leise!

4A.1 Adverbs

- When an adverb modifies a verb, it generally comes immediately after the verb it modifies. Adverbs of time or place can also come directly before the verb.

Ich esse **täglich** Gemüse. **Morgens** trinken wir **immer** Kaffee.

- If there is more than one time expression in a sentence, general time references are placed before adverbs of specific time.

Samstag morgens um 11 Uhr esse ich Frühstück mit meinem Vater.

- When there is more than one adverbial expression in a sentence, adverbs of time come first, followed by adverbs of manner, then adverbs of place.

Ihr kocht **am Wochenende zusammen zu Hause**. Sie essen **morgen Abend bestimmt woanders**.

- In sentences with adverbial expressions, the negation **nicht** usually *precedes* general expressions of time, manner, and place, but *follows* adverbs of specific time.

Wir kaufen Fleisch **nicht oft** im Supermarket. Ich möchte **am Montag nicht** in die Schule gehen.

4A.2 The modal *mögen*

4A.2: Remind students that **möchten** is the subjunctive form of **mögen**. It is used for polite requests and to say what one *would like* to have or do.

Remind students that while most modals modify another verb, **mögen** almost always appears on its own. It is used to say what one usually likes to have or do.

mögen (*to like*)			
ich mag	*I like*	wir mögen	*we like*
du magst	*you like*	ihr mögt	*you like*
er/sie/es mag	*he/she/it likes*	Sie/sie mögen	*you/they like*

Die Kinder **mögen** diesen Joghurt. **Magst** du Zwiebeln und Knoblauch?

möchten			
ich möchte	*I would like*	wir möchten	*we would like*
du möchtest	*you would like*	ihr möchtet	*you would like*
er/sie/es möchte	*he/she/it would like*	Sie/sie möchten	*you/they would like*

Ich **möchte** Fußball spielen. **Möchten Sie** Pasta oder Reis?

4A.3 Separable and inseparable prefix verbs

ACHTUNG

Move the infinitive of the separate prefix verb to the end of the sentence when using a modal with a separable prefix verb.

Die Mädchen **möchten** morgen Abend **ausgehen.**

Ich **soll** mit meinen Hausaufgaben **anfangen.**

separable prefix verbs	
anfangen	mitbringen
ankommen	mitkommen
anrufen	vorbereiten
aufstehen	vorstellen
ausgehen	zuschauen
einkaufen	zurückkommen
einschlafen	

inseparable prefix verbs	
bestellen	verkaufen
besuchen	überlegen
bezahlen	wiederholen
erklären	

Jakob **verkauft** sein Fahrrad. Wir **bezahlen** die Rechnung.
Ich **kaufe** im Supermarket **ein.** Ich **komme** nicht **zurück.**

1 Im Restaurant

Bitte schreiben Sie die richtige Form von „möchten".

1. Was möchten Sie essen?
2. Möchtest du Eis mit Himbeeren?
3. Ich möchte bitte bezahlen.
4. Wir möchten einen Tisch am Fenster.
5. Möchtet ihr vielleicht zuerst eine Suppe?
6. Meine Freundin möchte noch ein Stück Kuchen.

2 Zum Abendessen gehen

Bitte bilden Sie Sätze mit der richtigen Form von „möchten". Answers will vary.

Wir Meine Freunde Ich Du Ihr Meine Eltern Ihre Großmutter	möchten	*(the menu)* *(a napkin)* *(desserts)* *(a fork)* *(no appetizer)* *(the check)* *(beef with rice)*

3 mögen

Bitte wählen Sie die richtige Form von „mögen".

1. Wir (mögen / magst) Knoblauch.
2. Sie (mag / mögt) Schweinefleisch.
3. Sie (mögt / mögen) Pilze.
4. Ich (mag / mögt) Brötchen.
5. Er (magst / mag) Hähnchen.
6. (Mögt / Magst) du Würstchen?

4 Adverbien

Bitte bilden Sie Sätze. Achten Sie auf den korrekten Satzbau.

1. schmeckt / wirklich / Schnitzel / ausgezeichnet
   Schnitzel schmeckt wirklich ausgezeichnet.
2. er / selten / kauft / Thunfisch
   Er kauft selten Thunfisch.
3. scharf / immer / kocht / seine Mutter
   Seine Mutter kocht immer scharf.
4. wir / jetzt / zusammen / zum Lebensmittelgeschäft / fahren
   Wir fahren jetzt zusammen zum Lebensmittelgeschäft.

5 Trennbare Verben

Bitte kombinieren Sie immer den zweiten Satz in der richtigen Form.

1. der Unterricht / anfangen / um 7 Uhr
   Wir müssen uns beeilen! *Der Unterricht fängt um 7 Uhr an.*
2. Frau Müller / einkaufen / jeden Donnerstag / Lebensmittel
   Sie ist nicht zu Hause. Frau Müller kauft jeden Donnerstag Lebensmittel ein.
3. ich / einschlafen / fast
   Es ist so langweilig! Ich schlafe fast ein.
4. mitkommen / ihr?
   Wir gehen ins Restaurant. Kommt ihr mit?
5. morgen / aufstehen / er / schon / um 5.30 Uhr
   Er geht schon ins Bett. Morgen steht er schon um 5.30 Uhr auf.

6 Trennbare und untrennbare Verben

Bitte beenden Sie die Sätze in der richtigen Form.

1. (vorstellen / uns seine Freunde)
   Der Schüler stellt uns seine Freunde vor.
2. (erklären / den Gästen die Rechnung)
   Die Kellnerin erklärt den Gästen die Rechnung.
3. (verkaufen / unser Auto)
   Meine Eltern verkaufen unser Auto.
4. (mitkommen / nach Dresden)
   Mein Bruder kommt nach Dresden mit.
5. (ausgehen / fast jedes Wochenende)
   Unsere Klassenkameraden gehen fast jedes Wochenende aus.
6. (zuschauen / beim Fußballspiel)
   Die Gäste schauen beim Fußballspiel zu.

7 Was magst du so?

Suchen Sie einen Partner. Erzählen Sie Ihrem Gesprächspartner unter anderem, was Sie mögen, sehr gern mögen, nicht so sehr mögen und gar nicht gern mögen. Präsentieren Sie der Klasse Ihre Resultate. Answers will vary.

Hey! Ich **mag** das! Danke.

BEISPIEL

S1: *Was magst Du zum Frühstück?*
S2: *Ich mag Brötchen mit Marmelade.*
S1: *Mögen deine Freunde Kaffee?*
S2: *Nein, meine Freunde mögen keinen Kaffee.*

4B.1 The dative

- An object in the dative case indicates to whom or for whom an action is performed.

Ich bringe **dem Lehrer** einen Apfel. Zeig **der Lehrerin** deine Arbeit.

dative				
	masculine	**feminine**	**neuter**	**plural**
definite articles	dem Kellner	der Kellnerin	dem Kind	den Kindern
indefinite articles	**einem** Kellner	**einer** Kellnerin	**einem** Kind	**keinen** Kindern
possessive adjectives	**meinem** Koch	**meiner** Köchin	**meinem** Kind	**meinen** Kindern

- The endings for possessive adjectives are the same as the endings for the indefinite articles.

Der Kellner bringt **meiner Frau** einen Salat.
Peter empfiehlt **seinen Freunden** das Restaurant.

- When using plural nouns in the dative case, add **-n** to any noun whose plural form does not already end in **-n** or **-s**.

die Teller ⟶ den Teller**n** die Esslöffel ⟶ den Esslöffel**n**

- In the dative case, an adjective preceded by an **ein**-word or an **der**-word always ends in **-en**.

Anna kauft **dem kleinen** Jungen ein Eis. Ich gebe **meiner kleinen** Schwester eine Banane.

- Adjectives in the dative that are not preceded by an article have endings similar to the definite article endings.

Ich biete **guten** Freunde**n** immer gutes Essen an.
Die Lehrerin hilft **neuen** Schülern gern.

- Use the dative question word **wem** to ask *to whom*?

Wem gehört diese Tasse? Sie gehört **meinem** Opa.

4B.2 Prepositions with the dative

prepositions with the dative			
aus	*from*	nach	*after; to*
außer	*except for*	seit	*since; for*
bei	*at; near; with*	von	*from*
mit	*with*	zu	*to; for; at*

- The prepositions **bei**, **von**, and **zu** can combine with the definite article **dem** to form contractions. The preposition **zu** also forms a contraction with the definite article **der**.

Wir kaufen oft **beim** Supermarkt ein. Tina fährt **zur** Schule.

1 Dativ von weiblichen Substantiven Bitte ergänzen Sie im Dativ.

1. Mein Vater spricht mit _der_ (die) Kellnerin.
2. Peter, kannst du bitte _der_ (die) Lehrerin meine Hausaufgaben geben?
3. Melanie dankt _einer_ (eine) Schülerin aus Kanada.
4. Ich schreibe _meiner_ (meine) Mutter eine E-Mail.
5. Der Kellner empfiehlt _deiner_ (deine) Schwester bestimmt das Hähnchen.
6. Helft ihr _unserer_ (unsere) Nachbarin?
7. Anja zeigt _ihrer_ (ihre) Ärztin den Arm.

2 Nettigkeiten Bitte ergänzen Sie im Dativ.

1. Wir zeigen _dem_ (das) Kind das Schwimmbad.
2. Die Lehrerin gibt _meinem_ (mein) Freund das Zeugnis.
3. Kannst du _unserem_ (unser) Sohn einen Ball bringen?
4. Meine Mutter dankt _dem_ (der) Kellner und gibt ihm ein Trinkgeld.
5. Ich kaufe _meinem_ (mein) Großvater das Buch.
6. Die Studenten helfen _dem_ (der) Verkäufer im Lebensmittelgeschäft.
7. Die Köchin bringt _dem_ (der) Gast das Rezept (*recipe*).

3 Dativ in Singular und Plural Bitte beantworten Sie die folgenden Fragen.

1. Wem antwortet Angelika? Sie antwortet _ihrem Lehrer_. (ihr Lehrer)
2. Wem helfen die Nachbarn? Sie helfen _meinen Verwandten_. (meine Verwandten)
3. Wem schickst du die Fotos? Ich schicke sie _meiner Oma_. (meine Oma)
4. Wem kauft Jürgen die Blumen? Er kauft sie _seiner Freundin_. (seine Freundin)
5. Wem bringen wir die Wörterbücher? Wir bringen sie _den Schülern_. (die Schüler)
6. Wem zeigt die Journalistin ihren Artikel? Sie zeigt den Artikel _der Köchin_. (die Köchin)

4 Geburtstagsgeschenke Bitte beschreiben Sie, was Sie Ihren Verwandten und Freunden zum Geburtstag schenken, kaufen, geben oder schicken. Achten Sie auf den Dativ. Schreiben Sie mindestens acht Sätze. Answers will vary.

BEISPIEL

*Ich schicke **meiner** Tante eine Karte. Ich gebe **meinem** Opa einen Fußball. Ich schenke **meiner** Freundin ein Fahrrad. Ich kaufe **meiner** Mutter einen Kuchen.*

5 Adjektive im Dativ Bitte beantworten Sie. Achten Sie auf den Dativ.

1. Wem schenkst du das Auto? (der kleine Junge)
   Ich schenke dem kleinen Jungen das Auto.
2. Wem schreibst du eine E-Mail? (meine gute Freundin)
   Ich schreibe meiner guten Freundin eine E-Mail.
3. Wem empfiehlt der Kellner die Suppe? (eine alte Dame)
   Er empfiehlt einer alten Dame die Suppe.
4. Wem gehört der Rucksack? (die schlanke Frau dort hinten)
   Er gehört der schlanken Frau dort hinten.
5. Wem hilft die Rechtsanwältin? (der spanische Musiker)
   Sie hilft dem spanischen Musiker.
6. Wem zeigen wir unsere Stadt? (die österreichischen Geschäftsleute)
   Wir zeigen den österreichischen Geschäftsleuten unsere Stadt.

6 Wer, wen oder wem? Schreiben Sie die richtigen Fragewörter.

1. _Wer_ kommt aus Hamburg?
2. _Wen_ kennen Sie gut?
3. _Wem_ hilft die Köchin?
4. _Wem_ gehört dieses Messer?
5. _Wen_ fotografiert die Journalistin?
6. _Wer_ interessiert sich für die Speisekarte?
7. _Wen_ besucht ihr morgen?
8. _Wem_ gibst du das Geburtstagsgeschenk?

7 Ortsangaben: Präpositionen mit dem Dativ Ergänzen Sie die Sätze mit der richtigen Form des Dativ.

1. Ich komme jeden Tag um 15 Uhr aus _der Schule_. (die Schule)
2. Morgen fährt er mit _dem Fahrrad_ (das Fahrrad) in die Schule.
3. Er kommt aber erst um 17 Uhr von _seinem Training_. (sein Training)
4. Der Lehrer ist heute bei _seinen Kindern_. (seine Kinder)
5. Dieser Schinken ist aus _dem Schwarzwald_. (der Schwarzwald)
6. Ich mag diese Vorlesung seit _dem ersten Tag_. (der erste Tag)

8 Meine Freizeit Beantworten Sie die Fragen schriftlich. Suchen Sie dann einen Partner um das Gespräch zu führen. Answers will vary.

1. Wo sind Sie gern?
2. Mit wem sind Sie am Wochenende zusammen?
3. Wohin gehen Sie?
4. Woher kommen Sie um 15 Uhr?

9 Kurze Gespräche Bitte ergänzen Sie den Dialog.

1. —Was (Was / Welches) ist da drin?
   —Lehrbücher. Sie sind (sind / ist) von Torsten.
2. —Wo (Wem / Wo) sind Ulrich und Sabine?
   —Sabine kommt aus der (aus der / auf die) Bibliothek. Ulrich hat eine (eine / einen) Prüfung.
3. —Wie viele (Wohin / Wie viele) Touristen sind dort?
   —Hmm... Da sind einundzwanzig (einundzwanzig / dritte) Touristen.
4. —Woher (Woher / Was) kommt Gudrun?
   —Gudrun kommt aus den (die / den) Vereinigten Staaten.

10 Fragewörter Bitte vervollständigen Sie.

1. —Wie heißt die Lehrerin?
   —Die Lehrerin heißt Schneider.
2. —Warum lernst du so viel?
   —Ich habe eine Prüfung.
3. —Welche Fächer sind einfach?
   —Biologie und Chemie sind einfach.
4. —Wann ist Mathematik?
   —Mathematik ist um 10 Uhr.
5. —Woher kommst du?
   —Ich komme aus Bern in der Schweiz.
6. —Was studiert Hugo?
   —Hugo studiert Medizin.

11 Wie spät ist es? Bitte schreiben Sie diese Uhrzeiten.

1. 3.40 Es ist zwanzig vor vier. / Es ist drei Uhr vierzig.
2. 8.30 Es ist halb neun. / Es ist acht Uhr dreißig.
3. 21.17 Es ist siebzehn nach neun. / Es ist einundzwanzig Uhr siebzehn.

12 Befehle Geben Sie Befehle in der **Sie**-Form.

BEISPIEL anfangen
Fangen Sie an.

1. überlegen — Überlegen Sie.
2. nicht mitkommen — Kommen Sie nicht mit.
3. zurückkommen — Kommen Sie zurück.
4. einkaufen — Kaufen Sie ein.
5. zuschauen — Schauen Sie zu.
6. anrufen — Rufen Sie an.
7. nicht ausgehen — Gehen Sie nicht aus.
8. aufstehen — Stehen Sie auf.
9. bezahlen — Bezahlen Sie.
10. nicht einschlafen — Schlafen Sie nicht ein.

13 Was fehlt? Ergänzen Sie die Sätze.

1. Ich habe einen großen (groß) Bruder.
2. Mein großer (groß) Bruder spielt Fußball.
3. Er hat einen kleinen (klein) Hund.
4. Der kleine (klein) Hund hat sehr kurze (kurz) Beine.
5. Seine kurzen (kurz) Beine sind auch sehr dünn (dünn).
6. Hast du auch so einen kleinen (klein), schönen (schön) Hund?

14 Was machen diese Leute? Bilden Sie Sätze und achten Sie auf den korrekten Satzbau.

1. in die Konditorei / gehen / morgen / wir
   Wir gehen morgen in die Konditorei.
2. immer / Brötchen / zum Frühstück / möchten / meine deutschen Freunde Meine deutschen Freunde möchten zum Frühstück immer Brötchen. / Meine deutschen Freunde möchten immer Brötchen zum Frühstück.
3. kann / ich / dir / nicht / leider / helfen
   Ich kann dir leider nicht helfen.
4. lesen / Klara / am Wochenende / möchten / gern
   Klara möchte gern am Wochenende lesen. / Klara möchte am Wochenende lesen.

15 Was ist richtig? Bitte wählen Sie den richtigen Satz.

1. (A.) Ich wünsche dir einen guten Rutsch ins neue Jahr.
   B. Ich wünsche dir ins neue Jahr einen guten Rutsch.
2. A. Meine Freundin überall sucht roten Paprika.
   (B.) Meine Freundin sucht überall roten Paprika.
3. (A.) Der Ober spricht viel zu schnell.
   B. Der Ober spricht zu schnell viel.
4. A. Ich bestelle in diesem Restaurant eine Nachspeise immer.
   (B.) Ich bestelle in diesem Restaurant immer eine Nachspeise.

16 Der Wochenplan Entscheiden Sie, was Sie diese Woche machen wollen. Suchen Sie andere Schüler in der Gruppe, die das Gleiche machen wollen, und finden Sie eine Zeit, wann Sie das machen können. Answers will vary.

16 Suggestion Have students brainstorm activities before they begin the exercise.

BEISPIEL

S1: *Willst du diese Woche einkaufen gehen?*
S2: *Ja, ich will diese Woche einkaufen gehen.*
S1: *Können wir zusammen einkaufen gehen?*
S2: *Ja, gern.*
S1: *Hast du am Mittwoch Zeit?*
S2: *Nein, am Mittwoch habe ich keine Zeit.*

16 Expansion Instead of working in small groups, have students stand up and circulate throughout the entire class.

Feiern

KAPITEL
1

Suggestion Have students guess the meaning of the unit title **Feiern** based on the image shown. Ask: **Was feiern Meline, Hans und Sabite?**

Teaching Tip Look for icons indicating activities that address the modes of communication. Follow this key:

→ᴖ←	Interpretive communication
←ᴖ→	Presentational communication
ᴖ↔ᴖ	Interpersonal communication

Communicative Goals

You will learn how to:

- talk about celebrations
- talk about life events

Feste feiern

AP* Theme: Contemporary Life
Context: Social Customs & Values

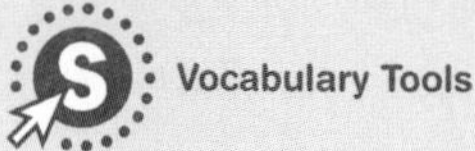

Vocabulary Tools

Suggestion Tell students that because of the influence of English, one often sees the plural form **Parties** on blogs and in advertising. Remind them that the correct plural form is still **Partys**.

Wortschatz

Feste	***celebrations***
der Feiertag, -e	*holiday*
die Karte, -n	*card*
die Party, -s	*party*
das Zimmer, -	*room*
anstoßen (stößt... an)	*to toast*
bekommen	*to receive*
einladen (lädt... ein)	*to invite*
feiern	*to celebrate*
eine Party geben	*to throw a party*
(keinen) Spaß haben	*(not) to have fun*
schenken	*to give (a gift)*
überraschen	*to surprise*
Herzlichen Glückwunsch!	*Congratulations!*
besondere Anlässe	***special occasions***
die Ehe, -n	*marriage*
der/die Frischvermählte, -n	*newlywed*
die Geburt, -en	*birth*
der Geburtstag, -e	*birthday*
die Hochzeit, -en	*wedding*
der Jahrestag, -e	*anniversary*
(das) Silvester	*New Year's Eve*
(das) Weihnachten	*Christmas*
in Rente gehen	*to retire*
einen Abschluss machen	*to graduate*
Ausdrücke	***expressions***
die Freundschaft, -en	*friendship*
das Glück	*happiness*
der Kuss, ¨e	*kiss*
die Liebe	*love*

Suggestion Point out to students that **Anlässe** is the plural form of **der Anlass**.

Suggestion Tell students that many German speakers also treat **Silvester** as a masculine noun.

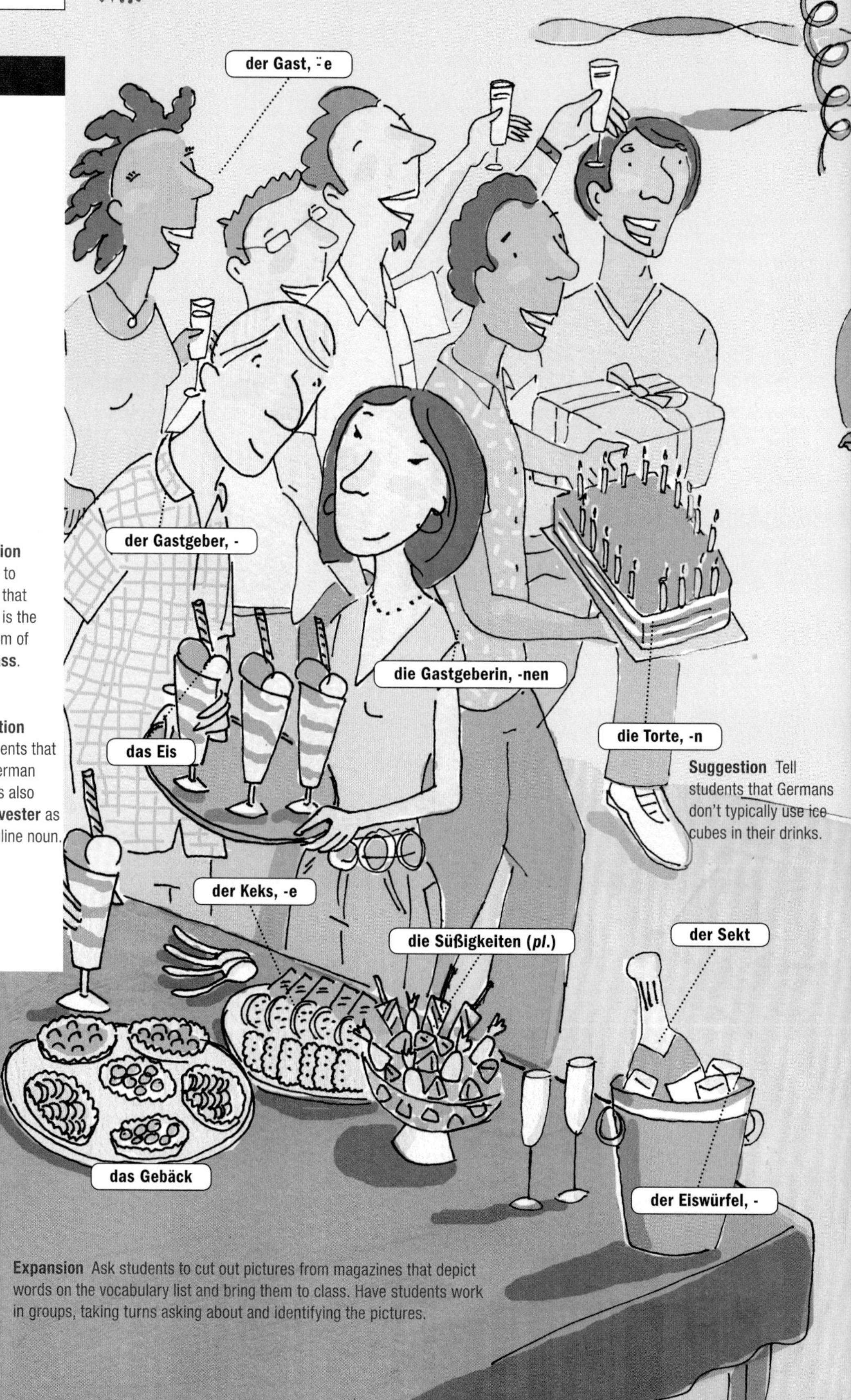

der Gast, ¨e
der Gastgeber, -
die Gastgeberin, -nen
die Torte, -n
das Eis
der Keks, -e
die Süßigkeiten (*pl.*)
der Sekt
das Gebäck
der Eiswürfel, -

Suggestion Tell students that Germans don't typically use ice cubes in their drinks.

Suggestion Tell students that the phrase **Ich lade dich ein** can also mean *It's my treat.*

Suggestion Teach students the verb form **küssen**.

Ressourcen
vText | WB pp. 1–2 | LM p. 57 | vhlcentral

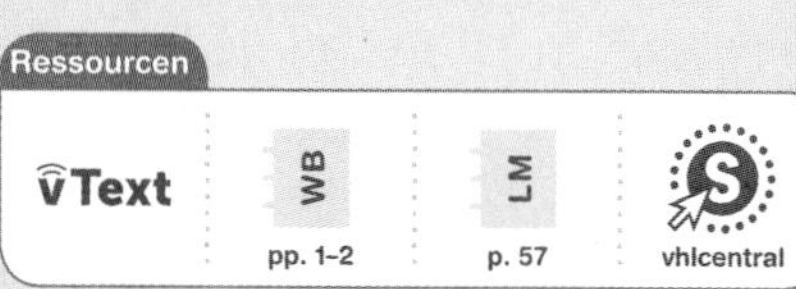

Expansion Ask students to cut out pictures from magazines that depict words on the vocabulary list and bring them to class. Have students work in groups, taking turns asking about and identifying the pictures.

Suggestion Tell students that the plural form **die Ballone** is also used, especially in Southern Germany, Austria, and Switzerland.

Anwendung

1 Suggestion Go over the first few items together, as a class.

1 Was passt zusammen?

Welche Wörter in der linken Spalte (*column*) passen am besten zu den Wörtern in der rechten Spalte?

a/b	1. der Geburtstag	a. der Kuchen
d	2. der Gast	b. die Karte
f/e	3. die Ehe	c. das Silvester
a	4. die Torte	d. die Gastgeberin
c	5. das Weihnachten	e. die Liebe
e/f	6. der Kuss	f. die Frischvermählten

2 Feste und Feiertage

Ergänzen Sie die Sätze.

1. An nationalen _Feiertagen_ muss man nicht arbeiten.
2. An Halloween kommen Kinder an die Haustür und man gibt ihnen _Süßigkeiten_.
3. Zum Geburtstag bekommt man _Geschenke/Karten_.
4. An Silvester stößt man um Mitternacht mit _Sekt_ an.
5. Nach 50 Ehejahren feiert man die goldene _Hochzeit_.
6. In Deutschland geht man normalerweise mit 67 Jahren in _Rente_.

3 Eine Party für Max

Hören Sie sich den Dialog an und markieren Sie dann die richtigen Aussagen.

3 Expansion Have students write a second dialogue that takes place at Max's surprise party, then act it out for the class.

	richtig	falsch
1. Max hat nächsten Monat Geburtstag.	☐	☑
2. Max braucht ein bisschen Spaß.	☑	☐
3. Max plant seine Geburtstagsparty selbst.	☐	☑
4. Max spielt in der Basketballmannschaft.	☑	☐
5. Zum Geburtstag kommen zehn Personen.	☐	☑
6. Die Party ist bei Emil.	☑	☐
7. Die Freunde kaufen das Geschenk zusammen.	☑	☐
8. Zum Geburtstag bekommt Max einen Baseball.	☐	☑

4 Satzsalat

Bilden Sie Sätze mit den diversen Elementen.

Answers will vary. Sample answers are provided.

BEISPIEL *Die Eltern bereiten eine Geburtstagsparty vor.*

die Eltern	anstoßen	die Kinder
die Gäste	bekommen	eine Geburtstagsparty
der Gastgeber	einladen	eine Geburtstagstorte
das Geburtstagskind	mitbringen	ein Geschenk
die Verwandten	vorbereiten	mit einem Getränk

1. Die Verwandten bringen ein Geschenk mit.
2. Das Geburtstagskind bekommt eine Geburtstagstorte.
3. Die Gastgeber laden die Kinder ein.
4. Die Gäste stoßen mit einem Getränk an.

4 Suggestion Have students identify the separable prefix verbs before they complete this activity.

ACHTUNG

Use the preposition **zu** to say *on Christmas* or *on New Year's Eve*: **Zu Silvester feiern wir bei meinem Bruder.**

Expansion Bring in a box with one or more objects inside and tell students it is an **Überraschung**. Have them ask yes-or-no questions to figure out what the object is.

Practice more at vhlcentral.com.

7 Suggestion Write the following useful phrases on the board: **Auf meinem Bild sind ..., Mein Bild hat ...,** and **Hast du das auch auf deinem Bild?** Make sure students understand that they should not show each other their pictures. Model this by protectively holding your sheet of paper and saying: **Mein Partner darf mein Bild nicht sehen.**

Kommunikation

5 Besondere Anlässe

Was feiern die Personen auf den Bildern? Bilden Sie mit Ihrem Partner / Ihrer Partnerin zusammen einen Satz zu jedem Bild. Answers will vary. Sample answers are provided.

BEISPIEL

Matthias hat heute Geburtstag.

5 Suggestion Encourage students to be inventive and detailed in their descriptions.

Matthias

1. Lena
Lena macht ihren Abschluss.

2. Kerstin und Simon
Kerstin und Simon feiern ihre Hochzeit.

3. die Familie Hartmann
Die Familie Hartmann feiert Weihnachten.

4. Andreas und seine Freunde
Andreas gibt eine Silvesterparty für seine Freunde.

5. Herr Aydin
Herr Aydin ist jetzt in Rente.

6. Martin
Martin gibt seiner Freundin einen Kuss.

6 Eine Einladung

Lesen Sie Kiaras Einladung an ihre Verwandten und beantworten Sie mit Ihrem Partner / Ihrer Partnerin die Fragen zum Text. Answers will vary. Sample answers are provided.

Von:	Kiara Gökda
An:	Familie Özer; Familie Celik; Murat Gökda; Familie Gökda; Ela Cengiz; Kenan Cengiz; Alik Aymaz; Familie Yilmaz
Betreff:	Feier für meine Eltern

Hallo an alle,

im Mai feiern unsere Eltern ihre silberne Hochzeit. 25 Jahre – unglaublich! Mein Bruder Murat und ich planen eine Feier für sie am Samstag, dem 5. Mai, im Restaurant „Zum Alten Markt" hier in München. Unsere Idee ist, dass wir alle, wir beide und ihr, ihnen eine Reise nach Marokko schenken. Die Reise ist für eine Woche und kostet 520 Euro pro Person.

Wir hoffen, ihr könnt kommen und macht bei dem Geschenk mit.

Kiara

1. Warum schreibt Kiara die E-Mail? Sie plant eine Feier für ihre Eltern.
2. Wie lange sind die Eltern verheiratet? Sie sind 25 Jahre verheiratet.
3. Was wollen sie den Eltern schenken? Sie wollen den Eltern eine Reise nach Marokko schenken.
4. Von wem ist das Geschenk? Das Geschenk ist von Kiara und Murat und den Verwandten.
5. Wie viel Geld braucht Kiara für das Geschenk? Sie braucht 1.040 Euro für das Geschenk.
6. Wann und wo ist die Feier? Sie ist am 5. Mai im Restaurant „Zum Alten Markt" in München.

6 Virtual Chat You can also assign activity 6 on the Supersite. Students record individual responses that appear in your gradebook.

7 Diskutieren und kombinieren

Finden Sie die sieben kleinen Unterschiede auf den Bildern, die Sie von Ihrem Lehrer / Ihrer Lehrerin bekommen. Answers will vary.

BEISPIEL

S1: *Auf meinem Bild sind fünf Personen. Wie viele Personen sind auf deinem Bild?*
S2: *Auf meinem Bild sind sechs Personen.*

8 Feiern wir!

Sie planen eine Party für nächstes Wochenende. Beraten Sie (*Discuss*), wo Sie die Party machen wollen, wen Sie einladen, was Sie alles brauchen, wer Essen macht, wer die Getränke kauft, welche Musik Sie hören möchten und so weiter. Answers will vary.

BEISPIEL

S1: *Bei wem wollen wir die Party machen?*
S2: *Bei Hanna? Sie wohnt bei ihren Eltern, und ihr Haus ist ziemlich groß. Und wen wollen wir einladen?*
S3: *Wir können unsere Freunde vom Basketball einladen.*

8 Expansion Have students plan an actual party as the culmination of this unit. Make sure students use German to discuss the plans.

Aussprache und Rechtschreibung

The consonantal *r*

To pronounce the German consonant **r**, start by placing the tip of your tongue against your lower front teeth. Then, raise the back of your tongue toward the roof of your mouth. Let air flow from the back of your throat over your tongue creating a soft vibrating sound from the roof of your mouth.

Rock **rot** **Brille** **Freund** **Jahrestag**

Note that the consonant **r** sound always precedes a vowel.

Orange **frisch** **fahren** **Rucksack** **Paprika**

When the German **r** comes at the end of a word or a syllable, it sounds more like a vowel than a consonant.

Suggestion Tell students that in some parts of Bavaria and Austria, the **r** sound is produced with the tongue at the front of the mouth, and sounds similar to the Spanish r.

1 **Aussprechen** Wiederholen Sie die Wörter, die Sie hören.

1. Rente
2. rosa
3. reden
4. Schrank
5. schreiben
6. sprechen
7. Sprudel
8. Straße
9. gestreift
10. frisch
11. Bruder
12. tragen
13. grau
14. Haare
15. Amerika
16. studieren

2 **Nachsprechen** Wiederholen Sie die Sätze, die Sie hören.

1. Veronika trägt einen roten Rock.
2. Mein Bruder schreibt einen Brief.
3. Rolf reist mit Rucksack nach Rosenheim.
4. Regensburg und Bayreuth liegen in Bayern.
5. Warum fahren Sie nicht am Freitag?
6. Marie und Robert sprechen Russisch.
7. Drei Krokodile fressen frische Frösche.
8. Im Restaurant bestellt die Frau Roggenbrot mit Radieschen.

3 **Sprichwörter** Wiederholen Sie die Sprichwörter, die Sie hören.

[1] You learn how to do something by doing it. (lit. *Speak, if you want to learn how to speak.*)

[2] If you overdo it, you'll wear yourself out. (lit. *The pitcher goes to the well until it breaks.*)

Ressourcen: vText | LM p. 58 | vhlcentral

Frohes neues Jahr!

Video

Vorbereitung Have students preview the scenes and write down one adjective to describe each scene.

Meline und Sabite wollen Silvester feiern, aber Torsten und Lorenzo haben andere Pläne. Da klingelt es plötzlich an der Tür...

1

SABITE Torsten! Es ist Silvester! Aber es sind Weihnachtsferien! Die Uni fängt erst wieder in zwei Wochen an. Warte mal.

2

MELINE Niemand lernt an Silvester. Man geht auf Partys und hat Spaß. Du hast eine wunderschöne Freundin, Torsten. Verlange nicht von ihr, das neue Jahr ohne dich zu beginnen. Bist du ihr immer noch böse?

3

SABITE Torsten? Dir auch ein frohes neues Jahr!

4

MELINE Lorenzo ist in der Stadt. Wir gehen später am Abend essen und danach gehen wir zu einer Party am Brandenburger Tor.
SABITE Schön, dass du Silvester mit ihm feierst.
MELINE Wir haben Spaß zusammen. Wieso kommst du nicht mit uns mit? Es sind bestimmt eine Million Leute da.
SABITE Ich mag keine Menschenmassen. Danke für die Einladung.

5

MELINE Sind Hans und George schon aus Bayern zurück? Wo ist Lorenzo?
SABITE Er ist nicht da! Es wird langsam spät.
MELINE Voicemail.
SABITE Nur die Ruhe, Meline.
MELINE Lorenzo!

6

GEORGE UND HANS Frohes neues Jahr!!!!
GEORGE Wir haben die Party einfach zu euch gebracht!
HANS George hat das Licht in eurer Wohnung gesehen.
GEORGE Hans hat Meline schreien gehört.
MELINE Ich habe nicht geschrien.
HANS Wo ist Lorenzo?
MELINE Ha, ha, ha, Hans. Wo ist denn deine neue Freundin?

ÜBUNGEN

1 Richtig oder falsch? Entscheiden Sie, ob die folgenden Sätze richtig oder falsch sind.

1. Torsten will Silvester lernen. Richtig.
2. Lorenzo ist in der Stadt. Richtig.
3. Meline und Lorenzo wollen ins Kino gehen. Falsch.
4. Es sind eine Million Leute am Fernsehturm. Falsch.
5. George und Hans haben Licht in der Wohnung gesehen. Richtig.
6. Hans hat Meline singen gehört. Falsch.
7. George und Hans sind auf einer Party in Kreuzberg gewesen. Richtig.
8. Meline möchte, dass Hans und George zurück zur Party gehen. Falsch.
9. Hans hat Kekse gebacken. Falsch.
10. George möchte mit seinen Freunden anstoßen. Richtig.

PERSONEN

George

Hans

Meline

Sabite

7

HANS Gut, dann gehen wir eben zurück zur Party in Kreuzberg.
SABITE Ah, ah! Geht nicht. Ich bin so froh, dass ihr hier seid. Frohes neues Jahr, Hans, George.
MELINE Bitte geht nicht. Ich habe Sekt.

8

HANS Ich habe einen Stollen für uns gebacken.
SABITE Oh, sieht lecker aus. Bitte schön.
HANS Danke. Hier, reich mal rüber.
MELINE Oh, Hans, er schmeckt genau wie der von meiner Mutter!

9

MELINE Es ist Mitternacht! Frohes neues Jahr!

10

GEORGE Ich möchte gern mit euch anstoßen, meine neuen Freunde. *Happy New Year!*
SABITE *Mutlu yillar.*

Nützliche Ausdrücke

- **Silvester**
  New Year's Eve
- **die Weihnachtsferien**
  winter break
- **Die Uni fängt erst wieder in zwei Wochen an.**
  Classes don't begin for two weeks.
- **wunderschön**
  gorgeous
- **Bist du ihr immer noch böse?**
  Are you still mad at her?
- **Frohes neues Jahr!**
  Happy New Year!
- **die Menschenmassen**
  crowds
- **Nur die Ruhe!**
  Relax!
- **Hans hat Meline schreien gehört.**
  Hans heard Meline yelling.
- **Reich mal rüber!**
  Hand it over!

1A.1

- **Ich habe einen Stollen für uns gebacken.**
  I baked a stollen for us.

1A.2

- **Verlange nicht von ihr, das neue Jahr ohne dich zu beginnen.**
  Don't make her start the new year without you.

1A.3

- **Schön, dass du Silvester mit ihm feierst.**
  It's great that you're celebrating New Year's with him.

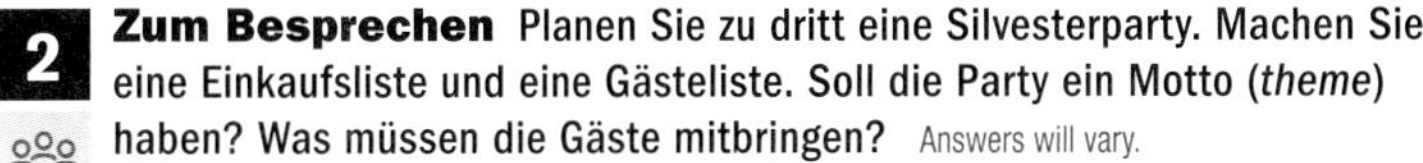

2 **Zum Besprechen** Planen Sie zu dritt eine Silvesterparty. Machen Sie eine Einkaufsliste und eine Gästeliste. Soll die Party ein Motto (*theme*) haben? Was müssen die Gäste mitbringen? Answers will vary.

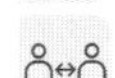

Suggestion Explain to students that Hans speaks in Bavarian at the end of this episode: **Is' scho' recht. A guat's Nei's!** (**Ist schon recht. Ein gutes Neues!**)

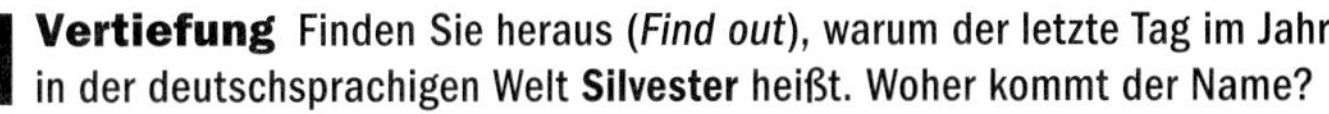

3 **Vertiefung** Finden Sie heraus (*Find out*), warum der letzte Tag im Jahr in der deutschsprachigen Welt **Silvester** heißt. Woher kommt der Name? Seit wann heißt der Tag so? Possible answer: Seit 1582 heißt der letzte Tag des Jahres Silvester, benannt nach dem Todestag von Papst Silvester I. (31. Dezember).

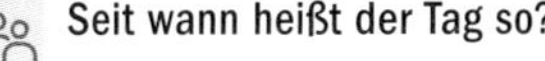

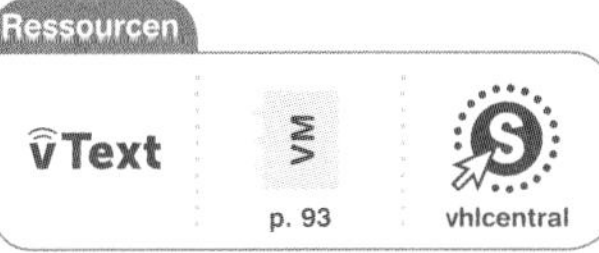

Expansion As a post-reading exercise, show students pictures of the places or things mentioned (ex., **Prinzessin Therese, Bierzelte, ein Karussell, eine Brille**), and ask them to explain what each picture has to do with **Oktoberfest**, as described in the text.

IM FOKUS

AP* Theme: Contemporary Life
Context: Entertainment, Travel, & Leisure

Das Oktoberfest

Suggestion Before they read the text, ask students what they know about **Oktoberfest**. Create a mind-map by writing the word **Oktoberfest** on the board and asking students what they associate with the event.

Am 12. Oktober 1810 heiratet Kronprinz Ludwig (der spätere König Ludwig I. von Bayern) Prinzessin Therese. Vor den Toren Münchens° feiern Menschen aus ganz Bayern die königliche Hochzeit auf einem Feld. Dieses Feld heißt heute noch Theresienwiese. Viele Menschen nennen es einfach die Wiesn, ein Wort aus der bayerischen Umgangssprache°. 1810 kann man Pferderennen° auf der Theresienwiese sehen und in den nächsten Jahren wiederholt man diese Pferderennen. Das ist der Anfang des Oktoberfests.

Im Jahr 1818 gibt es das erste Karussell° beim Oktoberfest. Heute findet man neben Karussells und Festzelten° auch Willenborgs Riesenrad° und einen Flohzirkus° für Kinder. Aus Wettergründen° beginnt das Oktoberfest bereits im September. Traditionell ist der erste Tag immer der erste Samstag nach dem 15. September. Der Oberbürgermeister° Münchens zapft° das erste Bierfass° an und sagt dann: „O'zapft is!" Das ist Bayerisch und bedeutet „Es ist angezapft!" Der letzte Tag ist der erste Sonntag im Oktober. In über 200 Jahren findet das Oktoberfest 24-mal wegen° Cholera oder Kriegen° nicht statt°.

Das Oktoberfest

Erstes Oktoberfest:	1810
Ort:	Theresienwiese
Fläche:	0,42 km² (Quadratkilometer)
Besucher:	mehr als 6 Millionen Gäste
Festzelte:	14 große und 20 kleine
Schweinswürste:	112.772 Paar
Schweinshaxen°:	78.216
Abfall°:	935 Tonnen
Verlorene Gegenstände°:	275 Brillen° und 380 Handys

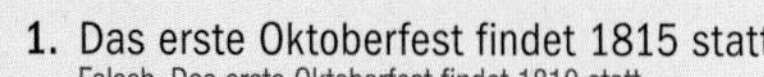
QUELLE: offizielles Stadtportal für München

den Toren Münchens *the gates of Munich* **bayerischen Umgangssprache** *Bavarian vernacular* **Pferderennen** *horse races* **Karussell** *merry-go-round* **Festzelten** *pavilions* **Riesenrad** *Ferris wheel* **Flohzirkus** *flea circus* **aus Wettergründen** *due to weather concerns* **Oberbürgermeister** *mayor* **zapft... an** *taps* **Bierfass** *beer barrel* **wegen** *due to* **Kriegen** *wars* **findet... statt** *takes place* **Schweinshaxen** *pork knuckles* **Abfall** *garbage* **Verlorene Gegenstände** *Lost items* **Brillen** *eyeglasses*

Suggestion To help students process the information in the statistics box, give them a series of sentence fragments to complete. Ex.: **Das erste Oktoberfest war... Die Besucher essen... Die Besucher verlieren jedes Jahr...**

ÜBUNGEN

1 **Richtig oder falsch?** Sind die Aussagen **richtig** oder **falsch**? Korrigieren Sie die falschen Aussagen.

1. Das erste Oktoberfest findet 1815 statt.
   Falsch. Das erste Oktoberfest findet 1810 statt.
2. Die Menschen feiern die Hochzeit von Kronprinz Ludwig und Prinzessin Therese in Nürnberg.
   Falsch. Die Menschen feiern die Hochzeit in München.
3. In der bayerischen Umgangssprache heißt die Theresienwiese „Wiesn".
   Richtig.
4. Das erste Karussell gibt es 1815. Falsch. Das erste Karussell gibt es 1816.
5. Für Kinder gibt es heute auch einen Flohzirkus. Richtig.
6. Der erste Tag des Oktoberfests ist immer der erste Sonntag nach dem 15. September.
   Falsch. Der erste Tag des Oktoberfests ist der erste Samstag nach dem 15. September.
7. Der Münchener Oberbürgermeister zapft das erste Bierfass an. Richtig.
8. In über 200 Jahren findet das Oktoberfest 20-mal nicht statt.
   Falsch. Es findet 24-mal nicht statt.
9. Mehr als 10 Millionen Gäste besuchen das Oktoberfest jedes Jahr.
   Falsch. Mehr als 6 Millionen Gäste besuchen das Oktoberfest jedes Jahr.
10. Zu den verlorenen Gegenständen gehören 275 Brillen und 380 Handys. Richtig.

Practice more at **vhlcentral.com.**

Suggestion Have students highlight key words before reading each paragraph. Ex.: **heiratet, Prinzessin Therese, feiern, Hochzeit, Feld, München, Pferderennen.** Then ask simple comprehension questions built around the key words and have them scan the paragraph to find answers: **Wer heiratet? Wann? Wo ist die Hochzeit?**

Expansion Teach students to sing a German Christmas carol, such as "**O Tannenbaum**". Explain that Christmas is a major holiday in German-speaking countries, but be culturally sensitive toward students who don't celebrate Christmas.

DEUTSCH IM ALLTAG

Herzlichen Glückwunsch

Alles Gute zum Geburtstag!	*Happy birthday!*
Ein gutes neues Jahr!	*Happy New Year!*
Frohe Ostern!	*Happy Easter!*
Frohe Weihnachten!	*Merry Christmas!*
Gute Besserung!	*Get well!*
Hals- und Beinbruch!	*Break a leg!*
Viel Glück!	*Good luck!*

DIE DEUTSCHSPRACHIGE WELT

Weihnachten

Am 6. Dezember besucht Sankt Nikolaus Kinder in vielen Gegenden° Deutschlands, Österreichs und der Schweiz. Brave° Kinder bekommen Schokolade, Nüsse° und andere Süßigkeiten. Manchmal bringt der Sankt Nikolaus einen Partner mit. Diese zweite Person heißt Krampus im Süden und Knecht Ruprecht im Norden. Er soll böse° Kinder erschrecken°.

Die Weihnachtsfeiertage sind der 25. und 26. Dezember. Geschenke bekommen Kinder aber schon am 24. Dezember, dem Heiligen Abend. Das Christkind, ein blonder Engel°, bringt Geschenke, und Familien öffnen sie am gleichen Abend.

AP* Theme: Contemporary Life
Context: Social Customs & Values

in vielen Gegenden *in many areas* **Brave** *Well-behaved* **Nüsse** *nuts* **böse** *naughty* **erschrecken** *scare* **Engel** *angel*

PORTRÄT

Die Sternsinger

Suggestion Ask students what differences they've noticed between Christmas as it is celebrated in their country and Christmas in German-speaking countries.

Vor allem in Bayern und Österreich sind die Sternsinger ein sehr bekanntes Brauchtum°. Drei Kinder oder junge Leute verkleiden sich° als die Heiligen Drei Könige° Caspar, Melchior und Balthasar. Sie gehen zwischen dem 27. Dezember und dem 6. Januar, dem Tag des Dreikönigsfestes, von Haus zu Haus. Sie singen Lieder in den Häusern, sprechen ein Gebet° und sagen ein Gedicht° auf. Dann schreiben sie mit Kreide° einen Segen° über° die Haustür. In Deutschland sammeln° die Sternsinger seit dem 16. Jahrhundert Geld für wohltätige Zwecke°, vor allem für Kinder in Not°. Die Aktion Dreikönigssingen ist weltweit° die größte organisierte Hilfsaktion von Kindern für Kinder. Alleine im Jahr 2013 sammeln die Sternsinger fast 70 Millionen Euro.

AP* Theme: Contemporary Life
Context: Social Customs & Values

Brauchtum *tradition* **verkleiden sich** *dress up* **Könige** *kings* **Gebet** *prayer* **Gedicht** *poem* **Kreide** *chalk* **Segen** *blessing* **über** *over* **sammeln** *collect* **wohltätige Zwecke** *charitable causes* **in Not** *in need* **weltweit** *worldwide*

IM INTERNET

Welche anderen Feste und Festivals werden in Deutschland, Österreich und der Schweiz gefeiert?

Find out more at **vhlcentral.com**.

Expansion Have students research more details about **Nikolaustag** and **Weihnachten**. Ask them: **Was macht man mit seinen Schuhen am Nikolaustag? Was trägt der Ruprecht mit sich? Wer ist der Weihnachtsmann?**

2 Was fehlt? Ergänzen Sie die Sätze.

1. Sankt Nikolaus besucht Kinder am 6. Dezember.
2. Brave Kinder bekommen Schokolade, Nüsse und andere Süßigkeiten.
3. Weihnachtsgeschenke bringt in Deutschland, Österreich und der Schweiz das Christkind.
4. Zwischen dem 27. Dezember und dem 6. Januar gehen Sternsinger von Haus zu Haus.

3 Wie feiern Sie zu Hause? Wählen Sie mit einem Partner / einer Partnerin einen Feiertag in Ihrem Land. Was feiert man an diesem Tag, wie feiert man den Tag, wann feiert man und welche regionalen Variationen gibt es? Präsentieren Sie Ihre Beschreibung Ihren Mitschülern/ Mitschülerinnen Ihre Beschreibung. Sie erraten (*guess*) den Feiertag.

3 Suggestion Give students a model to help them understand how to approach this activity. Ex.: **Ich denke an einen Feiertag. Mein Feiertag ist im Herbst. An diesem Tag muss man nicht arbeiten. Der Tag ehrt den Arbeiter. Das ist ein amerikanischer Feiertag. Die Deutschen haben auch so einen Feiertag, aber dort feiert man ihn am ersten Mai. Welcher Feiertag ist das?** (Labor Day)

Ressourcen

1A.1 The *Perfekt* (Part 1)

Presentation

Startblock In English, there are several ways of talking about events in the past: *I ate, I have eaten, I was eating.* In German, all of these meanings can be expressed with the **Perfekt** tense.

QUERVERWEIS

In **2A.1** and **2B.1**, you will learn about the **Präteritum**, a past tense used mainly in writing.

The *Perfekt* tense

QUERVERWEIS

Most verbs form the **Perfekt** with **haben**. You will learn about forming the **Perfekt** with **sein** in **1B.1**.

- To form the **Perfekt**, use a present tense form of **haben** or **sein** with the *past participle* of the verb that expresses the action.

Ich **habe** zu viel Kuchen **gegessen**.
*I **ate** too much cake.*

Wir **haben** den Kindern Geschenke **gekauft**.
*We **bought** the kids presents.*

Forming past participles

- German verbs can be grouped into three main categories, based on the way their past participles are formed.

Ich **habe** eine Torte **gemacht**.
*I **made** a cake.*

Wir **haben** Kekse **gegessen**.
*We **ate** cookies.*

Er **hat** eine CD **gebrannt**.
*He **burned** a CD.*

ACHTUNG

The **-et** ending is added to verb stems ending in **-d**, **-t**, or a consonant cluster, to make pronunciation easier: **Es hat geregnet**.

- Most German verbs are *weak*. Form the past participle of a weak verb by adding **ge-** before the verb stem and **-t** or **-et** after the stem.

common weak verbs			
infinitive	**past participle**	**infinitive**	**past participle**
arbeiten	gearbeitet	lernen	gelernt
feiern	gefeiert	öffnen	geöffnet
hören	gehört	sagen	gesagt
kaufen	gekauft	spielen	gespielt
lachen	gelacht	tanzen	getanzt

Suggestion Write on the board: **ge-** + stem + **-t** and have students copy it down in their notes. Give students the infinitives of other weak verbs, and have them figure out the past participles, based on the pattern. Ex.: **kochen, machen**.

Haben Sie eine Flasche Wasser **gekauft**?
***Did** you **buy** a bottle of water?*

Ich **habe** mit den Gästen **geredet**.
*I **chatted** with the guests.*

- Verbs ending in **-ieren** are almost always weak. Their past participles end in **-t**, but omit the **ge-** prefix.

Der Lehrer **hat** die Hausaufgaben **korrigiert**.
*The teacher **corrected** the homework.*

Wie lange **habt** ihr in Deutschland **studiert**?
*How long **did** you **study** in Germany?*

Suggestion Point out that the past participle of **verlieren** is an exception: **Ich habe *verloren*.**

- To form the past participle of a *strong* verb, add **ge-** before the verb stem and **-en** after. Strong verbs may be regular or irregular in the present, but verbs that have a stem change in the present tense are almost always strong verbs in the **Perfekt**.

Wir **haben** unsere Freunde **gesehen**.
*We **saw** our friends.*

Ich **habe** meinen Eltern **geholfen**.
*I **helped** my parents.*

- Note that many strong verbs have a stem change in the past participle.

common strong verbs			
infinitive	**past participle**	**infinitive**	**past participle**
essen	gegessen	schlafen	geschlafen
finden	gefunden	schreiben	geschrieben
geben	gegeben	sprechen	gesprochen
heißen	geheißen	tragen	getragen
helfen	geholfen	treffen	getroffen
lesen	gelesen	trinken	getrunken
nehmen	genommen	waschen	gewaschen

Habt Ihr den Bus nach Hause **genommen**?
***Did** you **take** the bus home?*

Sie **hat** viele Bücher **geschrieben**.
*She**'s written** a lot of books.*

Hast du gut **geschlafen**?
***Did** you **sleep** well?*

Was **habt** ihr auf der Party **getragen**?
*What **did** you **wear** to the party?*

- There is a small group of verbs called *mixed* verbs. The past participles of mixed verbs have a **ge-** prefix and end in **-t** like weak verbs, but they have irregular stems like many strong verbs.

common mixed verbs	
infinitive	**past participle**
brennen (*to burn*)	gebrannt
bringen	gebracht
denken (*to think*)	gedacht
nennen (*to name*)	genannt
rennen (*to run*)	gerannt

Habt ihr an die Hochzeit **gedacht**?
***Were** you **thinking** about the wedding?*

Sie **haben** ihr Kind Johanna **genannt**.
*They **named** their child Johanna.*

Suggestion Show students the verb list in **Appendix A**. Give them the infinitive of a strong or mixed verb, and have them check the appendix to find the past participle.

Suggestion Tell students that there are 10 vowel change patterns for the past forms of strong verbs, which will become more apparent when they learn the **Präteritum** in **Kapitel 2**: **ei-e-ie**, **ei-i-i**, **i-a-u**, **i-a-o**, **ie-o-o**, **e-a-o**, **e-a-e**, **e-o-o**, **a-u-a**, **a-ie-a**. Emphasize that while it is useful to be aware of these patterns, they still need to memorize which verbs are strong or mixed and what if any stem changes they have.

ACHTUNG

You cannot tell which category a verb belongs to by looking at the infinitive. You must learn the past participle of a verb along with its present tense forms.

QUERVERWEIS

See **Appendix A** for a complete list of past participles for all strong and mixed verbs taught in this book.

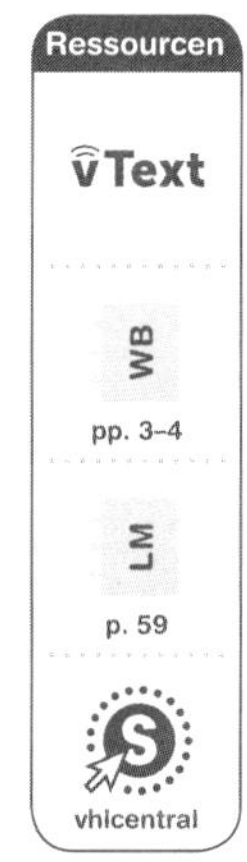

Jetzt sind Sie dran! **Ergänzen Sie die Sätze mit den richtigen Formen der Hilfsverben und der Partizipien.**

1. Wir ___haben___ Monikas Geburtstag ___gefeiert___. (feiern)
2. Die Katzen ___haben___ viel Milch ___getrunken___. (trinken)
3. Unsere Freunde ___haben___ viel Spaß ___gehabt___. (haben)
4. Jens ___hat___ mit seinen Geschenken ___gespielt___. (spielen)
5. Ich ___habe___ am Montag ___gearbeitet___. (arbeiten)
6. Peter ___hat___ vier Jahre an der Uni ___studiert___. (studieren)
7. Die Gäste ___haben___ dem Geburtstagskind viele Geschenke ___gegeben___. (geben)
8. ___Habt___ ihr die Bücher ___gelesen___? (lesen)
9. ___Hast___ du an die Pläne ___gedacht___? (denken)
10. Wir ___haben___ sehr viel ___gelacht___. (lachen)
11. ___Habt___ ihr Süßigkeiten ___gegessen___? (essen)
12. Meine Freundin ___hat___ einen Hund ___adoptiert___. (adoptieren)

1 Suggestion Make sure students understand the meaning of these verbs before you begin. Practice pronunciation of **schreiben/geschrieben** and tell students to highlight the "vowel swap" in their books.

1 Expansion Mime *correcting, reading, eating,* and *finding* and ask students **Was habe ich gemacht?** They must produce sentences in the perfect to describe the action you mimed. Ex.: **Sie haben Hausaufgaben korrigiert. Sie haben Ihr Handy gefunden.**

2 Suggestion Ask students to identify the mixed verb (**denken**) before doing this activity. Also, practice pronunciation of **gearbeitet** by having students repeat after you.

3 Suggestion Remind students that when they learn a new verb, there is usually no way to know if it is strong or weak, and that while there are some patterns, they still need to learn participles on a verb-by-verb basis.

Anwendung

1 Was passt zusammen? Welche Verben in Spalte 1 entsprechen (*match*) den Partizipien in Spalte 2?

c 1. essen	a. gebracht
f 2. finden	b. geholfen
b 3. helfen	c. gegessen
e 4. schreiben	d. genommen
a 5. bringen	e. geschrieben
d 6. nehmen	f. gefunden

2 Das Perfekt Setzen Sie die Verben ins Perfekt.

BEISPIEL tanzen (ich)
ich habe getanzt

1. kaufen (du) du hast gekauft
2. lernen (wir) wir haben gelernt
3. feiern (er) er hat gefeiert
4. arbeiten (Sie) Sie haben gearbeitet
5. hören (ihr) ihr habt gehört
6. regnen (es) es hat geregnet
7. kochen (sie, *sing.*) sie hat gekocht
8. denken (ich) ich habe gedacht

3 Was haben sie gemacht? Ergänzen Sie die Sätze mit der richtigen Form von **haben** und dem passenden Partizip.

1. Ich ___habe___ einen neuen Rucksack ___gekauft___. (kaufen)
2. Julius ___hat___ seine Freunde ___getroffen___. (treffen)
3. ___Habt___ ihr das Fußballspiel mit Paul ___diskutiert___? (diskutieren)
4. Der Koch ___hat___ die Zwiebeln ___gewaschen___. (waschen)
5. ___Hast___ du mit deinem Bruder ___gesprochen___? (sprechen)
6. Anna ___hat___ ihre Tochter zum Friseur ___gebracht___. (bringen)
7. Kiara ___hat___ eine Party ___gegeben___. (geben)
8. Professor Schulz, ___haben___ Sie meine Arbeit ___korrigiert___? (korrigieren)

4 Am Wochenende Was haben diese Personen am Wochenende gemacht? Schreiben Sie zu jedem Foto einen Satz im Perfekt. Answers will vary. Sample answers are provided.

BEISPIEL
meine Eltern und ich
Meine Eltern und ich haben Karten gespielt.

1. Herr Peters
Herr Peters hat gelesen.

2. Erik und Emil
Erik und Emil haben Tee getrunken.

3. Jessica
Jessica hat geschlafen.

4. Nina
Nina hat getanzt.

5. Hasan
Hasan hat sein Auto gewaschen.

6. Sara und Max
Sara und Max haben im Restaurant gegessen.

Practice more at **vhlcentral.com.**

Kommunikation

5 **Letzten Sommer** Fragen Sie Ihren Partner / Ihre Partnerin, was er/sie letzten Sommer gemacht hat. Answers will vary.

1. Hast du viel geschlafen?
2. Hast du viel gegessen?
3. Hast du gearbeitet? Wo?
4. Hast du Deutsch gelernt?
5. Hast du Sport gemacht?
6. Hast du oft Freunde getroffen?
7. Hast du etwas gekauft? Was?
8. Hast du viele Filme gesehen? Welche?

5 **Virtual Chat** You can also assign activity 5 on the Supersite. Students record individual responses that appear in your gradebook.

6 **Auf Dieters Geburtstagsparty** Sehen Sie mit einem Partner / einer Partnerin das Bild (*picture*) an. Was haben die Personen auf Dieters Geburtstagsparty gemacht?

BEISPIEL

S1: *Jutta hat Karaoke gesungen.*
S2: *Ja, und ihre Freunde haben viel gelacht.*

7 **Im Deutschkurs** Fragen Sie Ihre Mitschüler/Mitschülerinnen, was man heute im Deutschkurs gemacht hat. Vergleichen Sie die Antworten in Ihrer Gruppe.

BEISPIEL

S1: *Habt ihr gelesen?*
S2: *Ja, wir haben gelesen.*
S3: *Wer hat gelacht?*
S1: *Ben hat gelacht!*

antworten	schlafen
diskutieren	schreiben
essen	singen
lachen	spielen
lernen	sprechen
lesen	trinken

7 **Suggestion** Divide students into small groups and ask each group to come up with their own sample question, using verbs from the word bank. Write their suggestions on the board.

8 **Meine Großeltern** Erzählen Sie den Schülern/Schülerinnen in Ihrer Gruppe, was Ihre Großeltern gemacht haben, als sie jünger waren (*when they were younger*).

BEISPIEL

S1: *Mein Großvater hat immer viele Geschenke für seine Kinder gekauft.*
S2: *Meine Großmutter hat jeden Tag Kuchen oder Kekse gebacken.*
S3: *Meine Großeltern haben oft Karten gespielt.*

8 **Suggestion** Smaller groups are recommended for this activity. Tell students that if they don't know much about their grandparents, they can be creative and make something up.

1A.2

Suggestion You might want to direct students to **Vol. 1, 1A.3** to review the nominative pronouns.

Suggestion Give students a moment to read through the list of accusative pronouns. Then, with their books closed, have them provide the accusative form of each nominative pronoun you give them.

Suggestion Remind students that a noun following the verb **sein** is *not* a direct object and is in the nominative case.

Suggestion The song **"Ich will"** by Rammstein is full of pronouns and features ample repetition. Give students a fill-in-the-blanks worksheet containing the song lyrics, with the pronouns omitted. Have students listen to the song and fill in the missing pronouns.

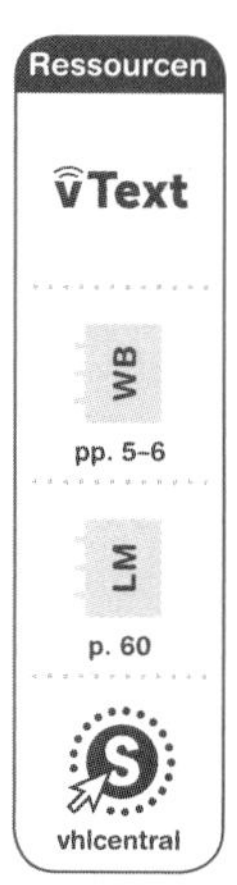

Accusative pronouns

Startblock Just as nouns in the nominative case can be replaced by nominative pronouns, nouns in the accusative case can be replaced by accusative pronouns.

personal pronouns				
	nominative		accusative	
singular	ich	*I*	**mich**	*me*
	du	*you (inf.)*	**dich**	*you (inf.)*
	Sie	*you (form.)*	**Sie**	*you (form.)*
	er/sie/es	*he/she/it*	**ihn/sie/es**	*him/her/it*
plural	wir	*we*	**uns**	*us*
	ihr	*you (inf.)*	**euch**	*you (inf.)*
	Sie	*you (form.)*	**Sie**	*you (form.)*
	sie	*they*	**sie**	*them*

Wer hat **die Torte** gebacken?
*Who baked **the cake**?*

Ich habe **sie** gebacken.
*I baked **it**.*

- Direct objects are always in the accusative case. An accusative pronoun replaces a noun that functions as a direct object.

Er hat **mich** überrascht.
*He surprised **me**.*

Hast du **ihn** geküsst?
*Did you kiss **him**?*

- Certain prepositions are always followed by the accusative. A pronoun that follows an accusative preposition must be in the accusative case.

Wir haben eine Überraschung **für dich**.
*We have a surprise **for you**.*

Ihr fahrt **ohne mich** zur Hochzeit.
*You're going to the wedding **without me**.*

- In simple sentences, accusative pronouns go directly after the conjugated verb. If the sentence has a modal verb, the accusative pronoun goes after the conjugated modal verb.

Ich sehe **euch** jeden Tag.
*I see **you** every day.*

Ich muss **es** heute machen.
*I have to do **it** today.*

- In the **Perfekt**, place the accusative pronoun directly after the conjugated helping verb.

Sie haben **uns** zur Party eingeladen.
*They invited **us** to the party.*

Wir haben **sie** mit einer Torte überrascht.
*We surprised **them** with a cake.*

- In sentences with inverted word order, such as yes-or-no questions, place the accusative pronoun after the subject.

Siehst du **sie** oft?
*Do you see **her** often?*

Morgen rufe ich **dich** an.
*I'll call **you** tomorrow.*

Jetzt sind Sie dran! **Wählen Sie die richtigen Pronomen.**

1. Das Buch? Du sollst (es / ihn) lesen.
2. Da sind die Ballons. Siehst du (sie / uns) nicht?
3. Ihr müsst ohne (uns / euch) ins Kino gehen.
4. Ich finde Paul süß und habe (uns / ihn) geküsst.
5. Jana und dich? Wir finden (euch / sie) nett.
6. Sophia, warte! Ich habe eine Karte für (dich / ihn).
7. Die große Liebe? Gibt es (uns / sie)?
8. Nina, liebst du (mich / dich)?

Anwendung und Kommunikation

1 **Bei meinen Eltern** Ersetzen Sie (*Substitute*) die unterstrichenen Wörter mit Akkusativpronomen.

BEISPIEL Ich sehe Peter.
Ich sehe ihn.

1. Ich rufe meinen Freund an.
Ich rufe ihn an.
2. Mein Freund besucht mich und meine Familie.
Mein Freund besucht uns.
3. Mein Bruder kocht das Essen für uns.
Mein Bruder kocht es für uns.
4. Mein Vater isst die Suppe gern.
Mein Vater isst sie gern.
5. Meine Schwester kauft die Erdbeeren auf dem Markt.
Meine Schwester kauft sie auf dem Markt.
6. Mein Freund sagt: „Ich besuche dich und deine Eltern gern."
Mein Freund sagt: „Ich besuche euch gern."

2 **Sätze bilden** Bilden Sie logische Sätze mit den angegebenen Wörtern. Ersetzen Sie die Wörter in Klammern (*parentheses*) mit Akkusativpronomen.
Answers may vary. Sample answers are provided.

BEISPIEL (die Erdbeeren) essen wollen
Ich will sie essen.

1. (das Buch) lesen müssen
Ich muss es lesen.

2. (Lisa) einladen wollen
Ich will sie einladen.

3. (der Film) sehen möchten
Ich möchte ihn sehen.

4. (das Auto) kaufen sollen
Ich soll es kaufen.

5. (Hausaufgaben) machen müssen
Ich muss sie machen.

3 **Die Überraschungsparty** Ihr Partner / Ihre Partnerin fragt Sie über die Party am Samstag bei Max. Beantworten Sie die Fragen und benutzen Sie Akkusativpronomen. Answers may vary. Sample answers are provided.

BEISPIEL **S1:** *Ruft ihr Emil und Maria an?*
S2: *Ja, wir rufen sie an.*

1. Ist es eine Party für Max?
Ja, es ist eine Party für ihn.
2. Lädst du Erik ein?
Ja, ich lade ihn ein.
3. Kommt Erik ohne seine Freundin?
Ja, er kommt ohne sie.
4. Hast du das Geschenk schon gekauft?
Ja, ich habe es schon gekauft.
5. Bringst du deine Cousins mit?
Nein, ich bringe sie nicht mit.
6. Soll ich den Kuchen mitbringen?
Ja, du sollst ihn mitbringen.
7. Können wir dort laute Musik hören?
Ja, ihr könnt sie dort hören.
8. Überraschen wir Max?
Ja, wir überraschen ihn.

3 **Suggestion** Students are sometimes confused when answering **wir** questions with **ihr**. You may wish to do item 7 together as a class.

3 **Virtual Chat** You can also assign activity 3 on the Supersite. Students record individual responses that appear in your gradebook.

4 **Der Computer** Erstellen Sie ein Gespräch mit den angegebenen Wörtern. Benutzen Sie Akkusativpronomen. Answers will vary.

BEISPIEL der Computer
S1: *Meine Eltern haben ihn für mich gekauft.*
S2: *Ohne ihn kann ich nicht lernen.*
S3: *Ich finde ihn schlecht.*

das Eis	das Geschenk
der Gastgeber	die Karten
der Geburtstag	die Kekse

Practice more at **vhlcentral.com.**

1A.3 Dative pronouns

ACHTUNG

Be careful when deciding whether the pronoun you need is a direct or an indirect object.

Ich sehe <u>ihn</u>.
[direct object]

Ich gebe <u>ihm</u> das Buch.
[indirect object]

Suggestion You might want to direct students to **Vol. 1, 2B** and **Vol. 1, 4A.2** to review the use of **gern** and **mögen** to express liking and the use of **gefallen** to say that you like the way something looks or sounds.

Die Musik gefällt mir.

Der Film hat mir gefallen.

Startblock Use dative pronouns in place of dative nouns to indicate *to whom* or *for whom* an action is done.

- Indirect objects are always in the dative case. When the indirect object is a pronoun rather than a noun, use a dative pronoun.

Suggestion Give students two or three simple sentences that feature pronouns, and have them identify the subjects, the direct objects, the indirect objects, and any objects of prepositions. Use humorous or dramatic sentences to keep students engaged.

personal pronouns			
	nominative	accusative	dative
singular	ich du Sie er/sie/es	mich dich Sie ihn/sie/es	**mir** **dir** **Ihnen** **ihm/ihr/ihm**
plural	wir ihr Sie sie	uns euch Sie sie	**uns** **euch** **Ihnen** **ihnen**

Musst du **ihr** eine E-Mail schreiben?
*Do you have to write **her** an e-mail?*

Wir wollen **euch** die Stadt zeigen.
*We want to show **you** the city.*

ACHTUNG

Certain prepositions are always followed by the dative case. If a dative preposition is followed by a pronoun, use a dative pronoun: **mit mir**, **von ihnen**, **bei uns**

- The verbs **helfen**, **danken**, and **gehören** always take an object in the dative case. Here are some other verbs that always take a dative object.

antworten	*to answer*	glauben	*to believe*
folgen	*to follow*	gratulieren	*to congratulate*
gefallen (gefällt)	*to please*	passen	*to fit*

Das gefällt **mir** sehr gut.
***I** like that a lot.*

Ich glaube **dir** nicht.
*I don't believe **you**.*

Gehört das **euch**?
*Does this belong to **you**?*

Antworte **mir**!
*Answer **me**!*

- When one object is a noun and the other is a pronoun, place the pronoun first.

Gib **mir** einen Kuss!
*Give **me** a kiss!*

Zeig **es** dem Lehrer!
*Show **it** to the teacher!*

- When a sentence has both a direct and an indirect object and both are pronouns, place the dative pronoun after the accusative pronoun.

Ich habe **dem Gastgeber das Geschenk** gegeben.
*I gave **the present** to **the host**.*

Ich habe **es ihm** gegeben.
*I gave **it** to **him**.*

Ressourcen

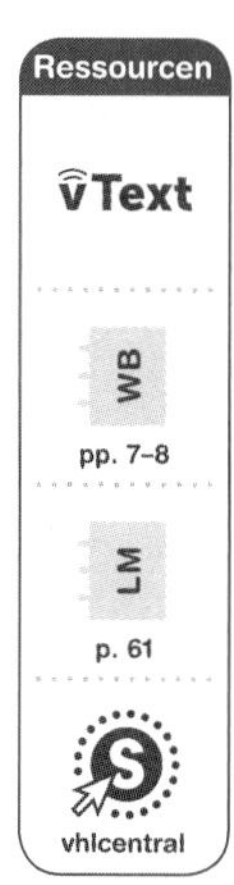

Jetzt sind Sie dran!

Wählen Sie den richtigen Fall (*case*) für die unterstrichenen Wörter: Nominativ (N), Akkusativ (A), oder Dativ (D).

__D__ 1. Er hat <u>ihr</u> eine Blume gegeben.
__N__ 2. <u>Wir</u> bringen Wein und Käse zur Party mit.
__A__ 3. Hast du <u>sie</u> zu Weihnachten besucht?
__D__ 4. Kannst du <u>mir</u> beim Backen helfen?
__D__ 5. Ich danke <u>euch</u> für die Fotos von der Hochzeit.
__N__ 6. Vielleicht glaubt <u>seine Mutter</u> ihm nicht.
__A__ 7. Gabi besucht <u>dich</u> am Wochenende, nicht?
__D__ 8. Das Geschenk ist von <u>ihr</u>.

Suggestion Point out to students that in item 4, **Backen** is used as a noun. Explain that in this context, **beim Backen** means *with the baking*.

Anwendung und Kommunikation

1 Meine Tante Ersetzen Sie die Dativobjekte mit Dativpronomen.

BEISPIEL Meine Tante hat mit meiner Mutter telefoniert.
Meine Tante hat mit ihr telefoniert.

1. Ich habe viel von meiner Tante Marie gelernt. Ich habe viel von ihr gelernt.
2. Ich habe oft bei Tante Marie und Onkel Hans geschlafen. Ich habe oft bei ihnen geschlafen.
3. Sie haben immer mit mir und meinem Bruder gespielt. Sie haben immer mit uns gespielt.
4. Mein Onkel hat meinem Bruder oft geholfen. Mein Onkel hat ihm oft geholfen.
5. „Tante Marie, kann ich bei dir und Onkel Hans wohnen?" „Tante Marie, kann ich bei euch wohnen?"

2 Was ist richtig? Wählen Sie in jedem Satz das richtige Pronomen.

1. Wir haben (ihr / sie) das Geschenk gegeben.
2. Gehören (euch / ihn) die Karten?
3. Hast du (ihn / ihm) zum Geburtstag gratuliert?
4. Haben die Gäste mit (sie / ihnen) angestoßen?
5. Wer hat außer (dir / dich) Kuchen gegessen?
6. Und das Baby? Habt ihr (ihm / es) auch gesehen?
7. Wann feiert ihr die Hochzeit? Feiert ihr (sie / ihr) im Sommer?
8. Lädst du (mich / mir) auch ein?

3 Alles Gute zum Geburtstag! Erzählen Sie Ihrem Partner / Ihrer Partnerin, was Sie diesen Personen zum Geburtstag schenken. Answers will vary.

BEISPIEL

Ihre Mutter

S1: *Was schenkst du deiner Mutter zum Geburtstag?*
S2: *Ich schenke ihr einen kleinen Hund! Und deiner Mutter?*
S1: *Meine Mutter mag Hunde nicht. Ich schenke ihr einen Computer.*

1. Ihr Bruder
2. Ihre Großeltern
3. Ihre Schwester
4. Ihre Katze
5. Ihr Vater
6. Ihr Professor / Ihre Professorin

4 Danke schön! Erfinden Sie mit Ihren Kommilitonen eine Geschichte (*story*) über die Personen auf dem Bild. Answers will vary.

BEISPIEL

S1: *Die junge Frau ruft ihre Schwester an.*
S2: *Sie dankt ihr für das Geburtstagsgeschenk.*
S3: *Nein! Sie gratuliert ihr zu ihrem Abschluss…*

anrufen	einladen	gratulieren (zu)
antworten (auf)	gefallen	helfen
danken (für)	gehören	kaufen
einkaufen	glauben	schreiben

Practice more at vhlcentral.com.

3 Partner Chat You can also assign activity 3 on the Supersite. Students work in pairs to record the activity online. The pair's recorded conversation will appear in your gradebook.

4 Suggestion Circulate among groups and provide vocabulary as needed. Allow students to focus on content and comprehensibility rather than on accuracy.

4 Expansion Have students write their stories down, this time paying closer attention to grammatical correctness. Have them read their stories out loud to the class.

Wiederholung

1 Auf der Party

Wer hat dieses Essen gemacht und diese Geschenke gekauft? Answers will vary.

BEISPIEL

S1: *Wer hat den Apfelsaft gekauft?*
S2: *Anja hat ihn gekauft.*

backen	kaufen
bringen	machen
gehören	schenken

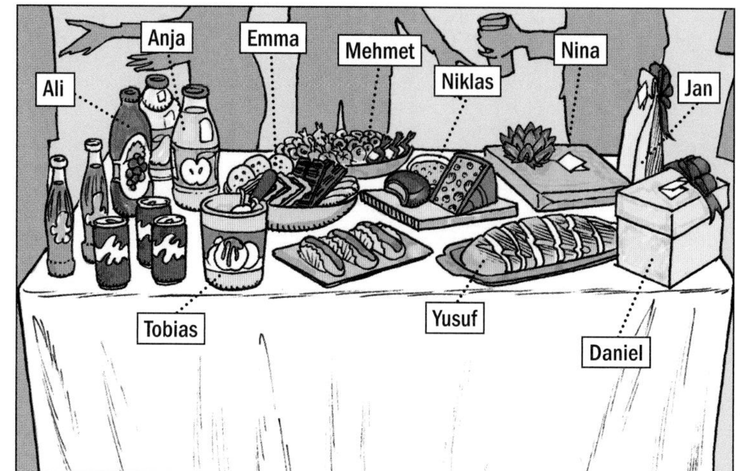

1 Partner Chat You can also assign activity 1 on the Supersite.

2 Suggestion Before beginning this activity, have students review the gender of each food item listed, to make sure they apply the appropriate pronouns in the accusative.

2 Was isst du gern?

Was isst Ihr Partner / Ihre Partnerin gern? Benutzen Sie Wörter aus der Liste in den Fragen und Akkusativpronomen in den Antworten. Answers will vary.

BEISPIEL

S1: *Isst du gern Garnelen?*
S2: *Nein, ich esse sie nicht gern.*

2 Expansion Have students jot down which foods their partner likes and report back to the class.

2 Virtual Chat You can also assign activity 2 on the Supersite.

Auberginen	Pilze
Eis	Schinken
Gebäck	Schweinefleisch
Kekse	Süßigkeiten
Knoblauch	Torten
Meeresfrüchte	Trauben
Pfirsiche	Würstchen

3 Arbeitsblatt

Wer hat in Ihrer Klasse diese Aktivitäten gemacht? Schreiben Sie die Namen der Mitschüler/Mitschülerinnen auf. Fragen Sie dann weiter nach mehr Informationen. Answers will vary.

3 Suggestion You may wish to set a time limit for this activity, or encourage students to go as quickly as possible, to help them stay on task.

BEISPIEL

S1: *Hast du zu viel gegessen? Wann?*
S2: *Ich habe an Thanksgiving zu viel gegessen.*

4 Geschenke

Was haben Sie und Ihr Partner / Ihre Partnerin Freunden und Familie zum Geburtstag oder zu Weihnachten geschenkt? Answers will vary.

4 Partner Chat You can also assign activity 4 on the Supersite.

BEISPIEL

S1: *Was hast du deiner Mutter zum Geburtstag geschenkt?*
S2: *Ich habe ihr einen schönen Terminkalender geschenkt.*

5 Diskutieren und kombinieren

Sie und Ihr Partner / Ihre Partnerin bekommen unterschiedliche Blätter mit Bildern von einer Party. Beschreiben Sie mit Ihrem Partner / Ihrer Partnerin Laras Aktivitäten. Answers will vary.

BEISPIEL

S1: *Um halb acht hat Lara mit einem Freund gesprochen. Was hat sie um acht Uhr gemacht?*
S2: *Um acht Uhr hat sie gesungen.*

6 Und Sie?

Was haben Sie auf der letzten Party gemacht? Was haben die anderen in der Gruppe gemacht? Answers will vary.

BEISPIEL

S1: *Auf der Party am Freitagabend habe ich getanzt. Und du? Hast du auf der letzten Party getanzt?*
S2: *Nein, ich habe nicht getanzt. Aber ich habe auf der Party am Samstagabend Musik gehört. Das mache ich gern.*

Geschenke kaufen
essen
(keinen) Spaß haben
Musik hören
kochen
lachen
mit Freunden reden
tanzen

4 Suggestion Emphasize correct use of case. Students may need a moment to formulate their questions in writing before they speak with their partners.

Video

AP* Theme: Personal & Public Identities
Context: Stereotypes

Penny: Shopping im Discounter

Lebensmittel-Discounter, wo alles günstig ist, liegen im Trend. Dazu gehören beispielsweise Aldi, Lidl oder Penny. Diese Märkte machen es für den Verbraucher° leicht, denn man kann viel Geld sparen° und schnell einkaufen. Man findet sie an fast jeder Ecke°: Penny-Markt hat in Deutschland über 2.200 Filialen°, Aldi über 4.000. Die Auswahl° ist nicht immer so groß wie bei größeren Supermärkten, dafür° aber bieten Discounter immer sehr günstige Preise und tolle Schnäppchen°. Mit Couponing wird alles noch billiger°, ob man Spar-Coupons in Papierform oder eine Mobile-Couponing-App auf dem Handy benutzt.

Was soll das denn jetzt werden?°

Mit der Penny-App.

Have students identify all the English words in the ad.
You may wish to ask students to compare discount grocery stores such as Penny with full-service ***Supermärkte*** and farmers' markets (***Wochenmärkte***). Ask ***Wo hat man mehr Auswahl? Wo ist alles immer frisch? Was sind die Vorteile und Nachteile von Discountern und Supermärkten?***

Anfänger°!

Verbraucher *customer* **sparen** *save* **Ecke** *corner* **Filialen** *chain stores* **Auswahl** *selection* **dafür** *instead* **Schnäppchen** *bargains* **noch billiger** *even cheaper*
Was soll das denn jetzt werden? *Now what's up with that?* **Anfänger** *rookie*

Verständnis Beantworten Sie die Fragen mit den Informationen aus dem Video.

1. Warum ist der junge Mann irritiert? Er ...
   a. findet den Orangensaft nicht. b. hat kein Geld. c. hat nicht viel Zeit.
2. Warum ist er überrascht? Die alte Frau ...
   a. will nicht zahlen. b. benutzt neue Technik.
   c. ist eigentlich seine Nachbarin.

Diskussion Besprechen Sie die folgenden Fragen mit einem Partner/einer Partnerin. Answers will vary.

1. Gehen Sie gern im Discounter einkaufen? Warum oder warum nicht?
2. Sie planen eine Party mit Freunden. Sie haben nicht viel Zeit und wenig Geld. Was wollen Sie alles im Discounter finden?

Kontext

Communicative Goals

You will learn how to:

- describe clothing
- talk about shopping

Wortschatz

Kleidung	*clothing*
die Bluse, -n	blouse
die Brille, -n	glasses
der Handschuh, -e	glove
die Jeans, -	jeans
der Mantel, ¨	coat
der Pullover, -	sweater
die Socke, -n	sock
der Stiefel, -	boot
das Sweatshirt, -s	sweatshirt
das Trägerhemd, -en	tank top
das T-Shirt, -s	T-shirt
die Unterwäsche	underwear
Einkaufen	***shopping***
die Baumwolle	cotton
die Farbe, -n	color
die Kleidergröße, -n	size
das Leder	leather
der Kunde, -n / die Kundin, -nen	customer
die Seide	silk
der Verkäufer, - / die Verkäuferin, -nen	salesperson
die Wolle	wool
im Angebot	on sale
einfarbig	solid colored
eng	tight
gestreift	striped
kurzärmlig	short-sleeved
langärmlig	long-sleeved
weit	loose; big
anziehen (zieht... an)	to put on

Suggestion Tell students that **Jeans** may be used in the singular (**Ich trage eine Jeans**) or plural (**Meine Jeans sind alt**).

Suggestion Tell students that **Kleider** can also mean clothing, in general. Ex: **Hast du neue Kleider gekauft?**

Suggestion Give students sample sentences using the verb anziehen. Ex.: **Ich ziehe eine Jacke an.**

ACHTUNG

You can add the prefix **hell** (*light; bright*) or **dunkel** (*dark*) to any color word, to form a compound adjective: **dunkelbraun**, **hellblau**.

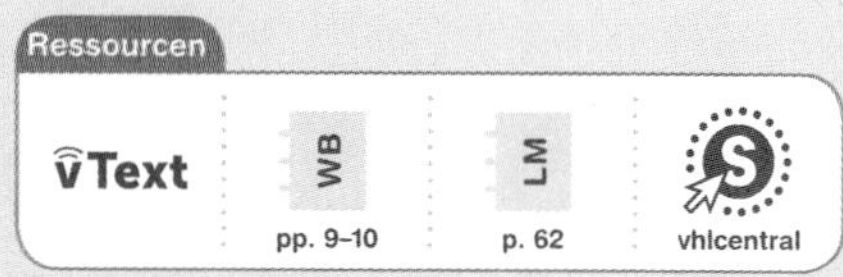

Kleidung

Vocabulary Tools

AP* Theme: Beauty & Aesthetics
Context: Fashion & Design

der Hut, ¨e
der Badeanzug, ¨e
Er ist teuer.
die Krawatte, -n
der Gürtel, -
das Kleid, -er
das Hemd, -en
die kurze Hose (*pl.* die kurzen Hosen)
Er trägt einen Anzug (*pl.* ¨e). (tragen)
die Turnschuhe (*sing.* der Turnschuh)
die Handtasche, -n
gelb
grün
lila
rosa
grau
orange
blau
schwarz
braun
weiß
rot

Suggestion Use items in the classroom to practice color, or bring a bag of assorted colorful objects and ask students to name the colors they see. Ask: **Welche Farbe hat der Tisch? Welche Farbe hat die Tafel? Welche Farbe hat Jakes Sweatshirt?**

ACHTUNG

Note that the adjectives **lila** and **rosa** are invariable: they do not vary in case, number, or gender to match the noun they modify. **Ich mag den lila Hut.**

Suggestion Point out to students that while English uses the plural to talk about *pants*, the German word **Hose** is singular.

Expansion Write the conjugation of **tragen** on the board and practice pronunciation. Describe what you are wearing and ask questions about what students are wearing. Ex.: **Wer trägt ein blaues T-Shirt? Wie viele Leute tragen heute eine Jeans? Welche Farbe hat Leslies Jacke? Was trägt Molly?**

Anwendung

2 Expansion Ask students additional questions to practice colors. Ex: **Welche Farbe hat die Sonne? Welche Farbe hat ein Ei? Welche Farbe hat Spinat? Welche Farbe hat ein Panther? Welche Farbe haben deine Augen?**

1 Was passt nicht? Welches Wort passt nicht zu den anderen?

BEISPIEL lila, grün, (hell)

1. (die Unterwäsche), der Mantel, die Jacke
2. teuer, günstig, (langärmlig)
3. das Leder, die Seide, (die Farbe)
4. die Schuhe, (die Halsketten), die Stiefel
5. (die Verkäuferin), die Mütze, der Schal
6. das Kleid, der Rock, (die Krawatte)

2 Farben bezeichnen Nennen Sie die Farben von den Dingen, die Sie auf den Fotos sehen.

1. gelb

2. weiß

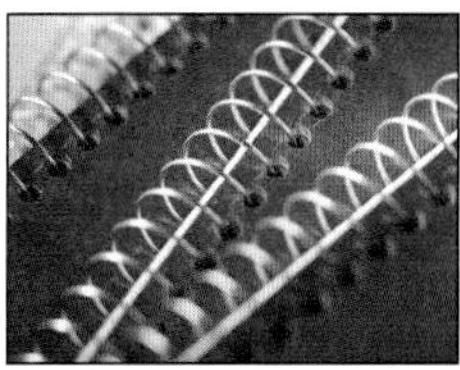

3. rot

4. rosa

5. braun

6. schwarz/dunkelgrau

3 Semesterferien Manfred plant eine kurze Reise in die Schweizer Alpen. Hören Sie an, was Manfred sagt, und markieren Sie am Ende die Kleidungsstücke, die er kaufen will.

	ja	nein		ja	nein
1. einen Pullover	☐	☑	5. eine Lederjacke	☐	☑
2. Skistiefel	☑	☐	6. eine Skihose	☑	☐
3. eine Jeans	☑	☐	7. eine Skijacke	☐	☑
4. ein Hemd	☐	☑	8. einen Mantel	☑	☐

4 Passende Kleidungsstücke Welche Kleidungsstücke trägt man in diesen Situationen? Answers will vary. Sample answers are provided.

1. Hasan trägt am Strand seine Sonnenbrille.
2. Zum Wandern in den Alpen soll man gute Schuhe tragen.
3. Im Winter trägt Alexandra ihren Mantel und ihren Pullover.
4. Zum Schwimmen trägt Lena ihren Badeanzug.
5. Für ihren Abschlussball kauft Emma ein schönes Kleid.

3 Suggestion Prepare students for the listening task by asking what kind of clothing one needs in specific situations. Ex: **Es ist ein sehr heißer Tag. Was trage ich am besten? Ich gehe schwimmen. Was brauche ich? Was packe ich für einen Skiurlaub?**

Practice more at **vhlcentral.com**.

Kommunikation

5 Was tragen die Leute?

Was tragen die Leute? Beschreiben Sie mit Ihrem Partner / Ihrer Partnerin die Kleidungsstücke von den Personen auf den Fotos. Answers will vary. Sample answers are provided.

die Tennisspielerin

BEISPIEL

Die Tennisspielerin trägt ein weißes Trägerhemd und einen weißen Tennisrock.

5 Suggestion Give students sample adjective phrases that model correct endings for all genders in the accusative. Ex.: *masculine:* **einen roten Rock;** *feminine:* **eine gelbe Bluse;** *neuter:* **ein weißes Hemd;** *plural:* **grüne Socken.**

5 Virtual Chat You can also assign activity 5 on the Supersite.

1. Thomas
Thomas trägt einen grauen Mantel, Jeans und einen schwarzen Pullover.

2. der Geschäftsmann
Der Geschäftsmann trägt ein blaues Hemd und eine schwarze Hose.

3. die Studentin Die Studentin trägt einen roten Pullover, eine dunkle Hose und einen braunen Rucksack.

4. die Kinder Die Kinder tragen weiße T-Shirts, grüne kurze Hosen, weiße Socken und Turnschuhe.

5. Frau Walter Frau Walter trägt einen hellbraunen Mantel, einen hellbraunen Schal und eine schwarze Handtasche.

6. Herr Huber Herr Huber trägt einen hellen Anzug und einen dunklen Hut.

6 Diskutieren und kombinieren

Diskutieren und kombinieren Finden Sie die sieben kleinen Unterschiede auf den Bildern, die Sie von Ihrem Professor / Ihrer Professorin bekommen. Answers will vary.

BEISPIEL

S1: *Trägt die Person auf deinem Bild (picture) eine Jeans?*
S2: *Nein, sie trägt einen Rock.*

6 Expansion Draw a **Strichmännchen** wearing assorted items of clothing, but do not show students the picture. Ask them to draw a stick figure and clothe him or her according to your oral description. Then, reveal your drawing so students can compare it to their own.

7 Wir gehen auf eine Party!

Wir gehen auf eine Party! Annika lädt Ihren Deutschkurs zu einer Party ein. Besprechen Sie mit Ihren Mitschülern/Mitschülerinnen, was für eine Party es wird und was Sie für die Fete anziehen wollen. Answers will vary.

BEISPIEL

S1: *Annikas Fete ist morgen Abend. Was soll ich anziehen? Vielleicht meine enge, schwarze Jeans und ein schwarzes T-Shirt.*
S2: *Hmm, ganz in schwarz? Ich bringe auch einen Badeanzug mit. Sie hat ein Schwimmbad im Garten.*
S3: *Soll ich dann auch einen Hut und eine Sonnenbrille mitnehmen?*

7 Suggestion Have each group report back to the class about who will be wearing what to the party.

8 Im Kaufhaus

Im Kaufhaus Schreiben Sie in kleinen Gruppen einen Dialog im Kaufhaus. Sprechen Sie mit dem Verkäufer / der Verkäuferin über die Kleider, die Sie brauchen, aus welchem Material sie sein sollen, für welchen Anlass Sie einkaufen und so weiter. Answers will vary.

BEISPIEL

S1: *Guten Tag. Kann ich Ihnen helfen?*
S2: *Ja, ich brauche für eine Hochzeitsfeier ein passendes Kleid.*
S3: *Und ich brauche einen Anzug. Schwarz oder dunkelgrau.*

ein baumwollenes Nachthemd
ein dunkelblaues Abendkleid
gute Wanderschuhe
einen rot gestreiften Badeanzug
eine flexible Skibrille
traditionelle Lederhosen
warme Stiefel
weiße Tenniskleidung

Aussprache und Rechtschreibung

The letter combination *ch* (Part 1)

The letter combination **ch** has two distinct pronunciations, which depend on its placement within a word. To pronounce **ch** after the vowels **a**, **o**, **u**, and **au**, start by pressing the tip of your tongue against your lower front teeth and raising the back of the tongue to the roof of the mouth. Then blow out air through the small space between the back of the tongue and the roof of the mouth.

Nachname **Tochter** **Buch** **brauchen** **acht**

In loanwords, **ch** may appear at the beginning of a word. In these words, the **ch** is sometimes pronounced like the *k* in the English word *king*. It may also be pronounced like the *sh* in the English word *ship*.

Chaos **Chor** **Christ** **Chance** **Chef**

Expansion Have students come up with a class motto including as many **ch**-sounds following a back vowel as possible.

1 Aussprechen Wiederholen Sie die Wörter, die Sie hören.

1. lachen
2. nach
3. auch
4. gesprochen
5. geflochten
6. brauchen
7. fluchen
8. Tuch
9. flache

2 Nachsprechen Wiederholen Sie die Sätze, die Sie hören.

1. Wir haben schon wieder Krach mit den Nachbarn.
2. Christians Tochter macht die Nachspeise.
3. Die Kinder waren nass bis auf die Knochen.
4. Hast du Bauchweh?
5. Der Schüler sucht ein Buch über Fremdsprachen.
6. Jochen kocht eine Suppe mit Lauch.

3 Sprichwörter Wiederholen Sie die Sprichwörter, die Sie hören.

Wo Rauch ist, da ist auch Feuer.[1]

[1] Where there's smoke, there's fire.
[2] Look before you leap. (*lit.* Doing before thinking has brought great suffering to many.)

Ressourcen
vText | LM p. 63 | vhlcentral

Sehr attraktiv, George!

Video

Meline findet Georges Stil nicht sehr attraktiv. Kann sie ihm helfen, attraktive Kleidung zu finden?

Vorbereitung Ask students to describe what George and Meline are wearing in each scene.

GEORGE Hallo, Meline.
MELINE Hallo, George.
GEORGE Wer ist das gewesen?
MELINE Esteban Aurelio Gómez de la Garza. Kommt aus Madrid. Langweilig.
GEORGE Hast du seit Silvester mit Lorenzo gesprochen?
MELINE Lorenzo ist unhöflich gewesen. Ich habe ihn gelöscht.

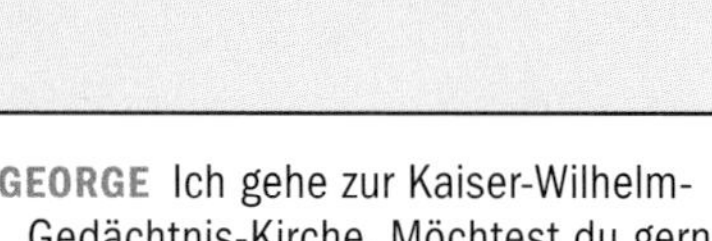

GEORGE Ich gehe zur Kaiser-Wilhelm-Gedächtnis-Kirche. Möchtest du gern mitkommen?
MELINE Ja.

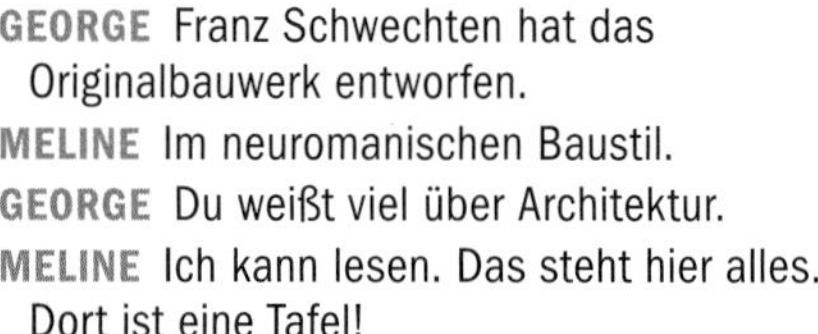

GEORGE Franz Schwechten hat das Originalbauwerk entworfen.
MELINE Im neuromanischen Baustil.
GEORGE Du weißt viel über Architektur.
MELINE Ich kann lesen. Das steht hier alles. Dort ist eine Tafel!

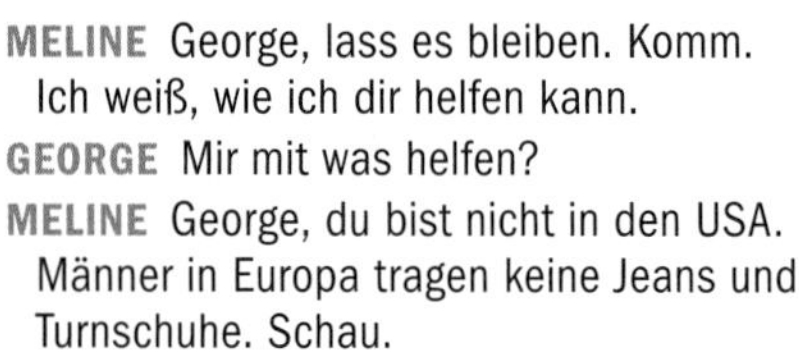

MELINE George, lass es bleiben. Komm. Ich weiß, wie ich dir helfen kann.
GEORGE Mir mit was helfen?
MELINE George, du bist nicht in den USA. Männer in Europa tragen keine Jeans und Turnschuhe. Schau.

GEORGE Woher hast du gewusst, dass das passiert?
MELINE Du kennst deine Architektur. Und ich kenne die Menschen. Gehen wir.

MELINE Wie sieht's aus da drin, George? George?
GEORGE Okay?
MELINE Komm, lass mich mal sehen!

ÜBUNGEN

1 Was fehlt? Ergänzen Sie die Sätze mit den richtigen Informationen.

1. Esteban Aurelio Gómez de la Garza kommt aus (Madrid / Barcelona).
2. George möchte zur (Berliner Mauer / Kaiser-Wilhelm-Gedächtnis-Kirche) gehen.
3. (Franz Beckenbauer / Franz Schwechten) hat das Originalbauwerk entworfen.
4. George weiß viel über (Kleidung / Architektur).
5. Meline kann George mit seiner (Kleidung / Hausaufgabe) helfen.
6. Männer in Europa tragen keine (Jeans und Turnschuhe / Seidenkrawatten).
7. Meline findet die Kleidung im Geschäft zu (teuer / hässlich).
8. George empfiehlt Meline einen Freund aus einem anderen (Land / Beruf).
9. Mit dem Hut und der (Sonnenbrille / Jacke) sieht George sehr europäisch aus.
10. Meline hat eine schöne (Halskette / Handtasche) gesehen.

PERSONEN

George

Meline

MELINE Dieser Pullover ist zu eng. Die Hosen sind zu lang. Du musst ein gestreiftes Hemd unter dem Pullover anziehen, kein einfarbiges. Was meinst du?
GEORGE Mir gefallen die Stiefel?
MELINE Das ist alles falsch. Zu teuer, zu teuer. Diese sind ein Schnäppchen. Wo ist der Verkäufer?
GEORGE Warum bin ich in diesen Laden gekommen? Ich sehe lächerlich aus.

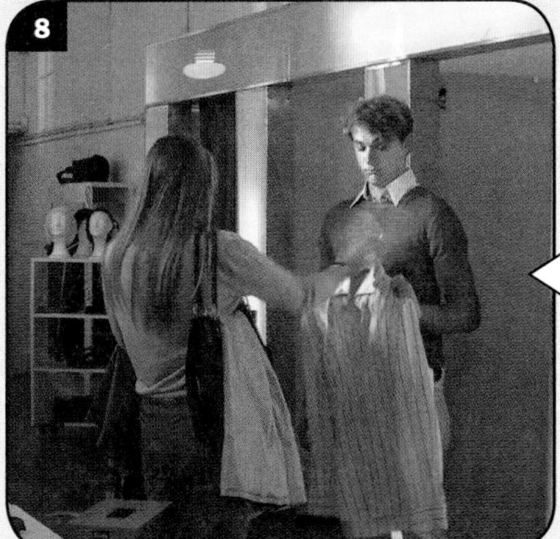

MELINE Blau? Nein. Schwarz? Nein. Grün? Nein. Okay. Zieh dieses Hemd... und diese Hose an... mit... dieser Seidenkrawatte. Komm schon! Wir haben nicht den ganzen Tag Zeit.

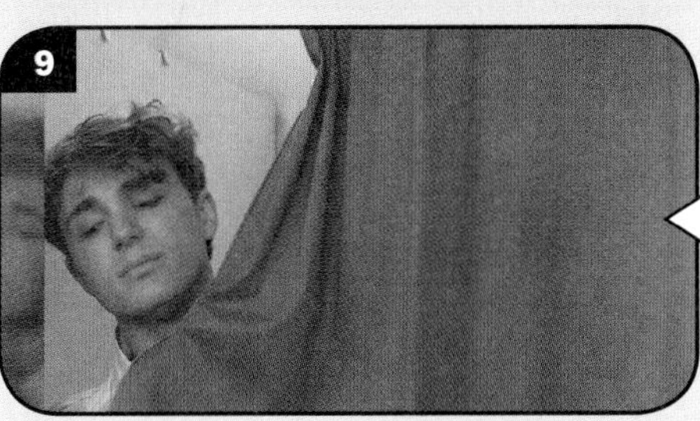

GEORGE Wie wäre es du denn mal mit einer Person aus einem anderen Beruf?
MELINE Wie Architektur?
GEORGE Ähmm... nein. Literatur oder Philosophie. Informatik oder Geschichte? Wie Hans.

MELINE Sehr attraktiv, George. Setz diese Sonnenbrille auf. Hut. So sieht ein europäischer Mann aus.
GEORGE Hast du gehört, was ich gesagt habe?
MELINE Zieh schnell deine Jeans wieder an. Ich habe eine Handtasche gesehen. Die muss ich unbedingt kaufen. Hans. Also wirklich.

Nützliche Ausdrücke

- **die Kirche**
  church
- **Franz Schwechten hat das Originalbauwerk entworfen.**
  Franz Schwechten designed the original structure.
- **Im neuromanischen Baustil.**
  In the neo-Romanesque style.
- **die Tafel**
  plaque
- **George, lass es bleiben.**
  George, don't even try.
- **Mir mit was helfen?**
  Help me with what?
- **Woher hast du gewusst, dass das passiert?**
  How did you know that was going to happen?
- **Wie sieht's aus da drin, George?**
  How's it going in there, George?
- **lächerlich**
  ridiculous
- **Wir haben nicht den ganzen Tag Zeit.**
  We don't have all day.
- **unbedingt**
  at all costs

1B.1

- **Wer ist das gewesen?**
  Who was that?

1B.2

- **Du weißt viel über Architektur.**
  You know a lot about architecture.
- **Und ich kenne die Menschen.**
  And I know people.

1B.3

- **George, du bist nicht in den USA.**
  George, you're not in the U.S.
- **Warum bin ich in diesen Laden gekommen?**
  Why did I come into this store?

2 **Zum Besprechen** Bilden Sie Gruppen zu dritt und diskutieren Sie: Was denken Sie über Mode? Ist sie Ihnen wichtig? Was ist Ihre Lieblingskleidung? Answers will vary.

3 **Vertiefung** Suchen Sie einen bekannten Designer oder eine bekannte Designerin aus Deutschland, Österreich, der Schweiz oder Liechtenstein und finden Sie Informationen zu ihm/ihr im Internet. Geben Sie vor Ihrer Klasse eine kurze Präsentation. Research possibilities include: Karl Lagerfeld, Wolfgang Joop, Jil Sander, Helmut Lang

3 Suggestion Encourage students to bring photos of their chosen designer and his/her fashions to share with the class.

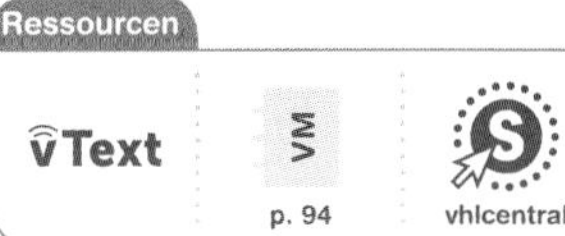

Kultur

Suggestion Ask students if they have a favorite designer. Also ask them which countries they associate with fashion. Are they familiar with any German clothing brands, department stores or designers?

IM FOKUS

Deutsche Modewelt°

Reading

AP* Theme: Beauty & Aesthetics
Context: Fashion & Design

FRANKREICH UND ITALIEN SIND klassische Modeländer. Aber in Deutschland entwirft° und produziert man auch viel Mode und Kleidung. Ähnlich wie° in Frankreich und Italien gibt es berühmte Modedesigner: Karl Lagerfeld, Wolfgang Joop und Jil Sander sind internationale Stars. Deutsche Marken° wie Hugo Boss, Bogner und Escada sind weltweit° bekannt.

Kleidergrößen

Frauenkleider		Männerhosen	
Deutschland	USA	Deutschland	USA (Bundweite/Länge in Zoll°)
30	2	44	30/32
32	4	46	32/32
34	6	48	33/32
36	8	50	34/32
38	10	52	36/34
40	12	54	38/34
42	14	56	40/34
44	16		

Mode spielt in Deutschland eine große Rolle für die Wirtschaft. Deutschland gehört heute zu den führenden° Mode-Exporteuren. Jedes Jahr importieren deutsche Firmen aber auch Kleidung im Wert von 36,2 Milliarden Euro nach Deutschland: Deutschland ist einer der größten internationalen Kleiderimporteure. Im Bereich° der Sportmode sind deutsche Firmen wie Adidas und Puma überall bekannt. Diese beiden Firmen haben ihren Hauptsitz° in Herzogenaurach, einer kleinen Stadt in Bayern. In Berlin findet man das größte Warenhaus° auf dem europäischen Kontinent: das Kaufhaus des Westens (KaDeWe), mit rund 60.000 m² Verkaufsfläche°. Die wichtigsten Modestädte in Deutschland sind Berlin und Düsseldorf. Auch München wird für Mode immer wichtiger.

TIPP

The symbol **m²** stands for **Quadratmeter** (*square meters*).

Deutschland ist ein Magnet für Modeexperten aus der ganzen Welt. In Düsseldorf findet zweimal pro Jahr die CPD (Collections Premieren Düsseldorf) statt°. Das ist die größte Modemesse° weltweit. In München kommen Fachbesucher° aus über 100 Ländern zweimal pro Jahr zur ISPO (Internationale Fachmesse für Sportartikel und Sportmode), wo rund 2.500 Aussteller° neue Sportkleidung und Accessoires präsentieren. Die PREMIUM Internationale Fachmesse für Mode findet in Berlin auch zweimal pro Jahr statt. Hier findet man viele junge Modeschöpfer°.

Modewelt *world of fashion* **entwirft** *designs* **Ähnlich wie** *Similar to* **Marken** *brands* **weltweit** *worldwide* **führenden** *leading* **Bereich** *area* **Hauptsitz** *headquarters* **Warenhaus** *department store* **Verkaufsfläche** *sales floor* **findet... statt** *takes place* **Modemesse** *fashion trade fair* **Fachbesucher** *trade visitors* **Aussteller** *exhibitors* **Modeschöpfer** *fashion designers* **Zoll** *inches*

ÜBUNGEN

1 Richtig oder falsch? Sind die Aussagen **richtig** oder **falsch**? Korrigieren Sie die falschen Sätze.

1. Frankreich und Italien sind die klassischen Modeländer. Richtig.
2. Mode spielt in Deutschland keine große Rolle. Falsch. Mode spielt in Deutschland eine große Rolle.
3. Karl Lagerfeld und Jil Sander sind internationale Modestars. Richtig.
4. Deutschland ist ein großer Mode-Exporteur. Richtig.
5. Puma und Adidas sind Sportmodefirmen aus Bayern. Richtig.
6. Das größte Warenhaus auf dem europäischen Kontinent ist in Frankreich. Falsch. Das größte Warenhaus auf dem europäischen Kontinent ist das KaDeWe in Berlin.
7. In Deutschland gibt es viele internationale Modemessen. Richtig.
8. Die Herren-Mode-Woche/Inter-Jeans ISPO kann man zweimal pro Jahr in Berlin besuchen. Falsch. Die ISPO kann man zweimal pro Jahr in München besuchen.
9. Das KaDeWe ist die größte Modemesse der Welt. Falsch. Die CPD ist die größte Modemesse der Welt.
10. Jil Sander und Wolfgang Joop sind bekannte deutsche Designer. Richtig.

Practice more at **vhlcentral.com**.

Suggestion Remind students that when dealing with long sentences, identifying the subject and verb can help them to figure out the gist.

DEUTSCH IM ALLTAG

Modevokabeln

der letzte Schrei	*the latest thing*
der Stil	*style*
angesagt	*trendy*
ausgefallen	*offbeat*
elegant	*elegant*
gut gekleidet	*well-dressed*
modisch	*fashionable*
schlecht gekleidet	*badly dressed*

DIE DEUTSCHSPRACHIGE WELT

Die Tracht

Das Wort „Tracht" bezeichnet° oft traditionelle oder historische Kleidung. In der Alpenregion, genauer gesagt° in Bayern und in Österreich, bezieht sich° das Wort heute auf Lederhosen für Männer und Dirndl für Frauen. Männer tragen neben° Lederhosen Hosenträger°, Haferlschuhe° und Bundhosenstrümpfe°. Frauen in Dirndl tragen eine weiße Bluse mit Puffärmeln° und ein Kropfband°. Ursprünglich° waren Lederhosen und Dirndl Arbeitskleidung, aber heute sieht man sie bei Umzügen° wie dem Oktoberfest.

AP* Theme: Personal & Public Identities
Context: National Identity

bezeichnet *denotes* **genauer gesagt** *more precisely* **bezieht sich** *refers to* **neben** *in addition to* **Hosenträger** *suspenders* **Haferlschuhe** *brogue shoes* **Bundhosenstrümpfe** *long socks* **Puffärmeln** *puffed sleeves* **Kropfband** *choker* **Ursprünglich** *originally* **Umzügen** *parades*

PORTRÄT

Rudolf Moshammer

AP* Theme: Beauty & Aesthetics
Context: Fashion & Design

Rudolf Moshammer war ein bekannter bayerischer Modedesigner. International war er nicht so bekannt wie Karl Lagerfeld oder Jil Sander. Aber namhafte° Kunden wie zum Beispiel Arnold Schwarzenegger, Siegfried und Roy, José Carreras und Carl XVI. Gustaf von Schweden kauften seine Mode. Moshammer verkaufte seine Designs in der Münchner Boutique Carneval de Venise, einem Geschäft an der Maximilianstraße im Herzen Münchens. Neben seiner Mode war Moshammer berühmt für seine Yorkshire-Hündin Daisy, seine aufwendige° schwarze Frisur° mit zwei Locken im Gesicht° und sein soziales Engagement für Obdachlose°. Im Januar 2005 wurde Moshammer in seiner Münchner Villa ermordet°.

Suggestion Tell students that nowadays one rarely sees Germans dressed **in Tracht**, even in Bavaria--except, as mentioned in the article, **bei Festen und Umzügen.**

namhafte *famous* **aufwendige** *lavish* **Frisur** *hairstyle* **Gesicht** *face* **Obdachlose** *homeless people* **wurde... ermordet** *was murdered*

IM INTERNET

Suchen Sie Namen bekannter Designer in Deutschland, Österreich und der Schweiz.

Find out more at **vhlcentral.com**.

2 Mode in Bayern Ergänzen Sie die Sätze.

1. Eine Tracht ist traditionelle und historische Kleidung.
2. Ursprünglich waren Lederhosen und Dirndl Arbeitskleidung.
3. Arnold Schwarzenegger und José Carreras waren zwei namhafte Kunden von Rudolf Moshammer.
4. Rudolf Moshammers Boutique war in München.
5. Moshammers Yorkshire-Hündin heißt Daisy.

3 Campusmode Besprechen Sie mit einem Partner / einer Partnerin, was die Schüler Ihrer Schule tragen: Gibt es eine Jugendmode? Tragen Sie diese Kleidung auch gern? Welche Kleidung sollen junge Leute tragen?

3 Partner Chat You can also assign activity 3 on the Supersite.

BEISPIEL

S1: *Viele junge Leute tragen gern Jeans mit Sweatshirt in der Schule. Wie findest du das?*

S2: *Das gefällt mir. Blaue Jeans und einfarbige Sweatshirts passen gut zusammen.*

Ressourcen

1B.1 The *Perfekt* (Part 2)

Presentation

Startblock Most verbs form the **Perfekt** with **haben**. However, certain types of verbs form the **Perfekt** with **sein**.

Suggestion You might want to direct the students to **Vol. 1, 1B.1** to review the function of direct objects.

The *Perfekt* with *sein*

- Only a few verbs form the **Perfekt** with **sein**. They are all verbs that indicate a change of condition or location. These verbs never take a direct object.

  Die Pflanzen **sind** schnell **gewachsen**.
  *The plants **grew** quickly.*

  Wir **sind** zusammen nach Innsbruck **gefahren**.
  *We **drove** to Innsbruck together.*

  Peter **ist** krank **gewesen**.
  *Peter **got** sick.*

  Ich **bin** vom Fahrrad **gefallen**.
  *I **fell** off my bike.*

ACHTUNG

Use the adverb **gestern** to say that something happened *yesterday*.

Gestern sind wir zum Park gelaufen.
Paul ist gestern Abend auf eine Party gegangen.

- To form the **Perfekt** tense of a verb with **sein**, use a conjugated form of **sein** plus the past participle of the verb that expresses the action.

  Amira **ist** schon nach Hause **gegangen**.
  *Amira already **went** home.*

  Sie **sind** gestern Abend **gekommen**.
  *They **came** last night.*

  Mein Opa **ist** gestern nach München **gefahren**.
  *My grandpa **went** to Munich yesterday.*

  Letzten Sommer **sind** wir nach Italien **gereist**.
  *Last summer we **traveled** to Italy.*

Suggestion Remind students that this rule is helpful as a general guideline, but that ultimately, they will need to memorize the correct participles and auxiliaries on a verb-by-verb basis.

- Both **sein** and **bleiben** are conjugated with **sein** in the **Perfekt**. Note that the past participle of **sein** is **gewesen**.

  Ich **bin** in der Bibliothek **geblieben**.
  *I **stayed** in the library.*

  Vor zwei Jahren **bin** ich in Istanbul **gewesen**.
  *Two years ago I **was** in Istanbul.*

Suggestion Point out to students that **bleiben** and **sein** are an exception to the "change of condition or location" rule.

- Here is a list of common verbs that take **sein** in the **Perfekt**. Note that most are strong verbs.

verbs that form the *Perfekt* with *sein*			
infinitive	**past participle**	**infinitive**	**past participle**
bleiben	geblieben	reisen	gereist
fahren	gefahren	sein	gewesen
fallen	gefallen	steigen (*to climb*)	gestiegen
gehen	gegangen	sterben (*to die*)	gestorben
kommen	gekommen	wachsen (*to grow*)	gewachsen
laufen	gelaufen	wandern	gewandert
passieren (*to happen*)	passiert	werden	geworden

Was **ist passiert**?
*What **happened**?*

Ich **bin** gerade zwanzig **geworden**.
*I just **turned** twenty.*

Suggestion Have students identify whether each verb listed describes a "change of location" or a "change of state".

Word order in the *Perfekt*

- The conjugated verb is always in second position in a statement and in first position in a yes-or-no question. In the **Perfekt**, the conjugated form of **haben** or **sein** is always in second position for statements and first in yes-or-no questions.

Suggestion You might want to direct the students to **Vol. 1, 1B.2** and **2A.2** to to review word order in simple sentences.

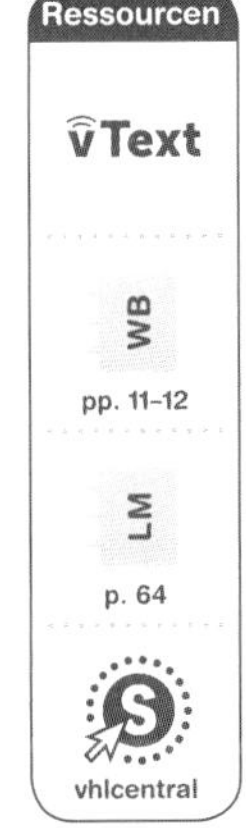

Die roten Schuhe **haben** nicht viel **gekostet**.
*The red shoes **didn't cost** very much.*

Seid ihr im Sommer viel **gereist**?
*Did you **travel** a lot over the summer?*

- In statements and questions, always place the past participle at the end of the sentence or clause.

Ich **habe** gestern ein neues Kleid **gekauft**.
*I **bought** a new dress yesterday.*

Wo **hast** du die tollen Stiefel **gekauft**?
*Where **did** you **buy** those awesome boots?*

Jetzt sind Sie dran! **Wählen Sie das passende Hilfsverb.**

1. Wir (sind / haben) den ganzen Abend bei unseren Eltern gewesen.
2. Ich (bin / habe) nicht lange auf der Party geblieben.
3. (Ist / Hat) Philip eine teure Sonnenbrille gekauft?
4. Leider (ist / hat) Jasmins Katze letzte Woche gestorben.
5. Wann (seid / habt) ihr nach Italien gereist?
6. Ich (bin / habe) einen schicken Rock aus Seide getragen.
7. (Bist / Hast) du die Kleider gewaschen?
8. Michael (ist / hat) zum Kaufhof gefahren.
9. Meine Eltern (sind / haben) mir Handschuhe geschenkt.
10. Leider (ist / hat) mein Bleistift ins Wasser gefallen.
11. Ihr (seid / habt) nicht viel gelaufen.
12. (Bist / Hast) du ohne Brille ins Theater gegangen?

Anwendung

1 Perfektformen Ergänzen Sie die Sätze mit den richtigen Formen von **sein** und den Partizipien.

1. Ich ___bin___ am Samstag zu Michaela ___gegangen___. (gehen)
2. Meine Mutter ___ist___ fünf Kilometer ___gelaufen___. (laufen)
3. Die Wintermonate ___sind___ sehr warm ___gewesen___. (sein)
4. Wann ___ist___ Sigmund Freud ___gestorben___? (sterben)
5. Jan und Klara, ihr ___seid___ zu spät ___gekommen___. (kommen)
6. Zu Silvester ___sind___ wir zu Hause ___geblieben___. (bleiben)
7. ___Bist___ du letzten Sommer durch Europa ___gereist___? (reisen)
8. Professor Schmidt, wann ___sind___ Sie nach Hause ___gefahren___? (fahren)

2 Expansion Have students play pictionary using sentences in the **Perfekt**. Choose sentences with verbs that are easy to depict in a drawing. Ex.: **Mein Hund ist geschwommen**.

2 Letzten Juli Beschreiben Sie, was diese Personen letzten Juli gemacht haben. Answers may vary. Sample answers are provided.

nach Nürnberg fahren	am Strand laufen
von einem Stuhl fallen	nach Europa reisen
nach Hause kommen	schwimmen gehen

▶ **BEISPIEL** Mein Bruder Max
ist am Strand gelaufen.

1. Anja ___ist nach Hause gekommen___.

2. Mein Neffe Emil ___ist von einem Stuhl gefallen___.

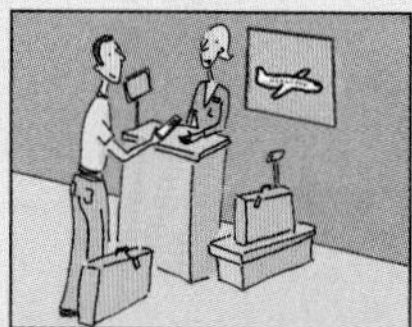

3. Professor Aydin ___ist nach Europa gereist___.

4. Frau Weber ___ist nach Nürnberg gefahren___.

5. Meine Cousins ___sind schwimmen gegangen___.

3 In letzter Zeit Bilden Sie Sätze im Perfekt. Benutzen Sie **sein** als Hilfsverb. Answers may vary. Sample answers are provided.

BEISPIEL meine Oma / kommen / zu meiner Abschlussfeier
Meine Oma ist zu meiner Abschlussfeier gekommen.

1. fahren / du / nach Hause
   Bist du nach Hause gefahren?
2. meine Eltern und ich / reisen / im Januar / nach Österreich
   Meine Eltern und ich sind im Januar nach Österreich gereist.
3. mein Freund / bleiben / bei seinen Eltern / in Berlin
   Mein Freund ist bei seinen Eltern in Berlin geblieben.
4. ich / werden / nach der Party / sehr müde
   Ich bin nach der Party sehr müde geworden.
5. dein Baby / wachsen / so schnell
   Dein Baby ist so schnell gewachsen!
6. gehen / ihr / auf die Hochzeit / von Nils und Julia
   Seid ihr auf die Hochzeit von Nils und Julia gegangen?

Practice more at **vhlcentral.com**.

Kommunikation

4 Bilden Sie Sätze Was hat Ihrer Partner / Ihre Partnerin zu Silvester gemacht? Stellen Sie ihm/ihr sechs logische Fragen darüber. Benutzen Sie das Perfekt und verwenden Sie Wörter aus jeder Spalte. Answers will vary.

BEISPIEL

S1: *Bist du mit deinen Freunden auf eine Party gegangen?*
S2: *Ja, wir sind zusammen auf eine Party gegangen!*

A	B	C
ich	bleiben	mit dem Auto
du	fahren	nicht
das Wetter	gehen	neue Kleider
der/die Gastgeber(in)	kommen	bei deine Eltern
ihr	passieren	mit deinen Freunden
deine Freunde	sein	warm
was?	tragen	zu spät

5 Historische Personen Erraten Sie mit Ihrer Gruppe, was jede von diesen historischen Personen in ihrem Leben gemacht hat. Answers will vary. Sample answers are provided.

BEISPIEL George Washington
Er ist Präsident von Amerika gewesen.

fallen	laufen	sein
gehen	reisen	spielen
helfen	schreiben	werden

1. Julia Child / Kochbücher
   Sie hat Kochbücher geschrieben.
2. Babe Ruth / Baseball
   Er hat Baseball gespielt.
3. Angela Merkel / Kanzlerin von Deutschland
   Sie ist Kanzlerin von Deutschland geworden.
4. Humpty Dumpty / die Mauer
   Er ist von der Mauer gefallen.
5. Mutter Teresa / arme Leute
   Sie hat armen Leuten geholfen.
6. Marco Polo / nach China
   Er ist nach China gereist.

6 Semesterferien Fragen Sie Ihren Partner / Ihre Partnerin, was er/sie in den Schulferien (*school break*) gemacht hat. Answers will vary.

BEISPIEL

S1: *Bist du in den Schulferien gereist?*
S2: *Nein, ich bin hier geblieben. Ich habe in einer Pizzeria gearbeitet. Und du?*
S1: *Meine Familie und ich sind nach Deutschland gefahren.*

arbeiten	spazieren gehen
bleiben	kommen
fahren	reisen
einkaufen gehen	sein
schwimmen gehen	wandern

7 Als Kind Machen Sie ein Interview über Ihre Kindheit (*childhood*) in der Grundschule (*elementary school*). Wenn Sie fertig sind, tauschen Sie die Rollen.

BEISPIEL gern zur Schule gehen

S1: *Bist du gern zur Schule gegangen?*
S2: *Ja, ich bin gern zur Schule gegangen. Aber meine Hausaufgaben habe ich nicht immer gern gemacht!*

1. ein guter Schüler / eine gute Schülerin sein
2. nach der Schule mit Freunden spielen
3. oft zu spät zur Schule kommen
4. Fahrrad fahren
5. im Sommer mit den Eltern reisen
6. gern ins Schwimmbad gehen
7. am Wochenende zu Hause bleiben
8. einen Hund oder eine Katze haben

5 Expansion For homework, have students research biographical information about a famous person of their choice and write ten simple sentences about that person in the **Perfekt**. In class, students must present their sentences and have classmates guess who the person is.

6 Partner Chat You can also assign activity 6 on the Supersite. Students work in pairs to record the activity online. The pair's recorded conversation will appear in your gradebook.

7 Suggestion If you hear many mistakes in the formation of participles or use of the correct auxiliary, interrupt this activity to form some sample questions together with the class.

7 Partner Chat You can also assign activity 7 on the Supersite.

Students will learn about dependent clauses in **Vol. 3, 2A.3**.

QUERVERWEIS

The verb **wissen** is often used with dependent clauses.

ACHTUNG

The verb **wissen** is used in many common idiomatic expressions:

Weißt du was?
You know what?

Weißt du das bestimmt?
Are you sure about that?

Woher soll ich das wissen?
How should I know?

QUERVERWEIS

To review the formation of mixed verbs, see **1A.1**.

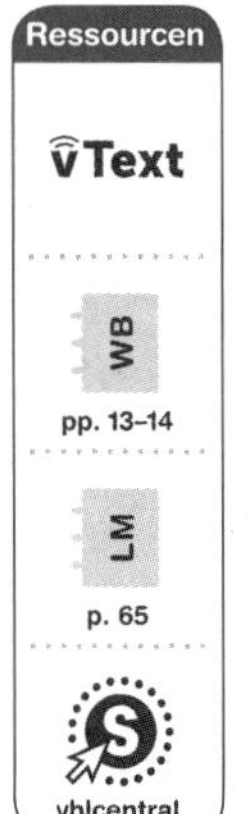

1B.2 Wissen and kennen

Presentation

Startblock In German, the verbs **wissen** and **kennen** are used to express different types of knowledge.

- Use **wissen** to express the idea of *knowing a fact* or piece of information. **Wissen** is irregular in its present-tense singular forms.

wissen (*to know information*)			
ich weiß	*I know*	wir wissen	*we know*
du weißt	*you know*	ihr wisst	*you know*
er/sie/es weiß	*he/she/it knows*	Sie/sie wissen	*you/they know*

Michael **weiß** die Antwort nicht.
*Michael doesn't **know** the answer.*

Weißt du Saras Telefonnummer?
*Do you **know** Sara's phone number?*

- Use **kennen** to express the idea of *being familiar with* someone or something. **Kennen** always takes a direct object, usually a person or place. It is regular in the present tense.

kennen (*to know, to be familiar with*)			
ich kenne	*I know*	wir kennen	*we know*
du kennst	*you know*	ihr kennt	*you know*
er/sie/es kennt	*he/she/it knows*	Sie/sie kennen	*you/they know*

Ich **kenne** viele Leute.
*I **know** a lot of people.*

Du **kennst** Jana schon seit zwei Jahren.
*You've **known** Jana for two years.*

- In the **Perfekt**, both **kennen** and **wissen** are mixed verbs; their past participles end in **-t**, but their stems are irregular.

Jan **hat** den Professor sehr gut **gekannt**.
*Jan **knew** the professor very well.*

Mein Opa **hat** viel über Kunst **gewusst**.
*My grandpa **knew** a lot about art.*

Das **habe** ich nicht **gewusst**.
*I **didn't know** that.*

Hast du deine Urgroßeltern **gekannt**?
***Did** you **know** your great grandparents?*

Jetzt sind Sie dran! Wählen Sie das richtige Verb.

1. (Wisst / Kennt) ihr was?
2. Wir (wissen / kennen) die Musik von Mozart.
3. (Wisst / Kennt) ihr die neue Schülerin?
4. (Weiß / Kennt) er das bestimmt?
5. Woher sollen wir das (wissen / kennen)?
6. Du (weißt / kennst) die Antwort nicht.
7. Ich habe ihn nicht gut (gewusst / gekannt).
8. Ich habe das nicht (gewusst / gekannt).

Anwendung und Kommunikation

1 Wissen und kennen Ergänzen Sie die richtigen Formen von **kennen** und **wissen.**

Präsens	**Perfekt**
1. sie (*sing.*) kennt (kennen)	7. Sie haben gewusst (wissen)
2. ihr wisst (wissen)	8. du hast gekannt (kennen)
3. wir kennen (kennen)	9. ihr habt gekannt (kennen)
4. du weißt (wissen)	10. er hat gewusst (wissen)
5. er weiß (wissen)	11. ich habe gekannt (kennen)
6. ich kenne (kennen)	12. wir haben gewusst (wissen)

2 Wissen oder kennen? Wählen Sie das passende Verb und ergänzen Sie die Sätze mit den richtigen Formen von **wissen** oder **kennen.**

1. Weißt du die Telefonnummer von Marie?
2. Wir kennen ihren Freund, aber wir wissen nicht viel über ihn.
3. Wisst ihr das bestimmt?
4. Meine Freundin kennt Berlin sehr gut.
5. Habt ihr euch schon letztes Semester gekannt? (Perfekt)
6. Einstein hat sehr viel über Physik gewusst! (Perfekt)

3 Die Stadt und das Schulgelände Fragen Sie Ihren Partner / Ihre Partnerin nach Ihrer Stadt (*city*) und Ihrem das Schulgelände. Wen oder was kennen Sie dort? Was wissen Sie darüber? Answers will vary.

BEISPIEL

S1: *Kennst du ein schönes Café?*
S2: *Ja, ich kenne ein sehr schönes Café!*
S1: *Weißt du auch die Adresse?*
S2: *Natürlich weiß ich die: Schillerstraße 5.*

unsere Stadt
die Telefonnummer von dem Lehrer / der Lehrerin
ein gutes und nicht so teures Restaurant
die E-mail-Adressen von deinen Kommilitonen
einen guten Friseur

3 Suggestion Formulate the first few questions and answers together as a class.

3 Partner Chat You can also assign activity 3 on the Supersite. Students work in pairs to record the activity online. The pair's recorded conversation will appear in your gradebook.

4 Ihre Kommilitonen Finden Sie ein paar Informationen über die Personen in Ihrer Gruppe.

BEISPIEL

S1: *Wo wohnst du?*
S2: *Ich wohne in Brooklyn.*
S1: *Kennst du Herrn Schmidt?*
S2: *Nein, ich kenne ihn nicht.*

Name: Caroline

Ich weiß:	1. ihren Namen. (Caroline) 2. ihre Adresse. (24 Kennedy Avenue) 3. ihre Telefonnummer.
Ich kenne:	4. ihre Freundin Katia. 5. ihren Freund Jeffrey. (Sie spielen Tennis zusammen.) 6. ihr Lieblingsrestaurant. (Blue Moon)

Practice more at **vhlcentral.com.**

1B.3 Two-way prepositions

Suggestion Before starting with the **Wechselpräpositionen**, help students solidify their existing knowledge of prepositions. Ask them what prepositions are and have them give some examples in both English and German. Remind them that some prepositions always take the accusative, **(Vol. 1, 3B.2)**, and some always take the dative **(Vol. 1, 4B.2)**. Review these prepositions to ensure that students remember their meaning and usage.

Startblock Certain prepositions are always followed by the accusative case, while others are always followed by the dative case. A small number of prepositions can be followed by either the dative or the accusative, depending on the situation.

- Prepositions that can be followed by either the dative or the accusative are called *two-way prepositions.*

two-way prepositions			
an	*at, on*	**über**	*above, over*
auf	*on, on top of*	**unter**	*under*
hinter	*behind*	**vor**	*in front of*
in	*in, into*	**zwischen**	*between*
neben	*next to*		

Ich trage ein T-Shirt **unter dem Pullover**.
I'm wearing a T-shirt ***under my sweater****.*

Stell deine Schuhe nicht **auf den Tisch!**
Don't put your shoes ***on the table!***

ACHTUNG

Remember that dative prepositions *always* take a dative object, even if the verb in the sentence indicates movement: **Ich fahre <u>mit meinem Onkel</u>**.

- Whether you choose a dative or an accusative object to follow a two-way preposition depends on the meaning of the sentence. If the verb indicates *movement toward* a destination, use an object in the accusative.

Ich **fahre** das Auto **in die Garage**.
I'm driving *the car* ***into the garage****.*

Der Hund **geht in die Küche**.
The dog ***is going into the kitchen****.*

- If the verb does *not* indicate movement toward a destination, use an object in the dative case.

Suggestion Teach students the rhyme *Where at? Dat! Where to? Accu!* and the German equivalent **Wo? Dativ! Wohin? Akkusativ!** to help them remember this rule. Emphasize that the deciding factor is not just movement, but movement *towards* a destination.

Expansion Use objects in the classroom to demonstrate two-way prepositions. Ex: **Ich lege mein Buch <u>auf den Tisch</u>. Das Buch liegt <u>auf dem Tisch</u>.** In each sentence, emphasize the distinction between *destination* and *location*.

Das Auto **ist in der Garage**.
The car ***is in the garage****.*

Der Hund **isst in der Küche**.
The dog ***eats in the kitchen****.*

- When you use a two-way preposition with a pronoun, make sure to select a pronoun in the appropriate case.

Ich sitze **neben dem alten Mann**. *I'm sitting **next to the old man**.*	Ich sitze **neben ihm**. *I'm sitting **next to him**.*
Er hat den Teller **vor seinen Sohn** gestellt. *He put the plate **in front of his son**.*	Er hat den Teller **vor ihn** gestellt. *He put the plate **in front of him**.*

- Here are some common contractions of two-way prepositions and definite articles.

an	+	das	→	**ans**
auf	+	das	→	**aufs**
in	+	das	→	**ins**
an	+	dem	→	**am**
in	+	dem	→	**im**

- The question **wohin?** (*where to?*) asks about movement. When you answer this question with a two-way preposition, always use an object in the accusative case.

Wohin fahren wir morgen? ***Where** are we going tomorrow?*	Wir fahren morgen **in die Stadt**. *We're going **to the city** tomorrow.*
Wohin gehen die Leute? ***Where** are the people going?*	Sie gehen **ins Konzert**. *They're going **to the concert**.*

- The question **wo?** (*where?*) asks about location. When you answer this question with a two-way preposition, always use an object in the dative case.

Wo ist mein Schal? ***Where** is my scarf?*	Dein Schal liegt **auf dem Tisch**. *Your scarf is lying **on the table**.*

- Use the dative after a two-way preposition with a verb that indicates where something is located. Use the accusative with a verb that indicates where something is being placed.

wo?	
hängen	*to hang, to be hanging*
liegen	*to lie*
sitzen	*to sit*
stehen	*to stand*

wohin?	
hängen	*to hang (something)*
legen	*to lay (down)*
setzen	*to set (down)*
stellen	*to put (down)*

Das Bild **hängt an der** Wand. *The picture **is hanging on the** wall.*	Ich **hänge** das Bild **an die** Wand. ***I'm hanging** the picture **on the** wall.*

QUERVERWEIS

To review the forms of dative and accusative pronouns, see **1A.2** and **1A.3**.

Suggestion You might want to direct the students to **Vol. 1, 3B.2** to review contractions with accusative prepositions and **Vol. 1, 4B.2** to review contractions with dative prepositions.

Suggestion Make sure students understand that the "**wo**" verbs all describe location (place) and the "**wohin**" verbs all describe the process of placing something somewhere (placement).

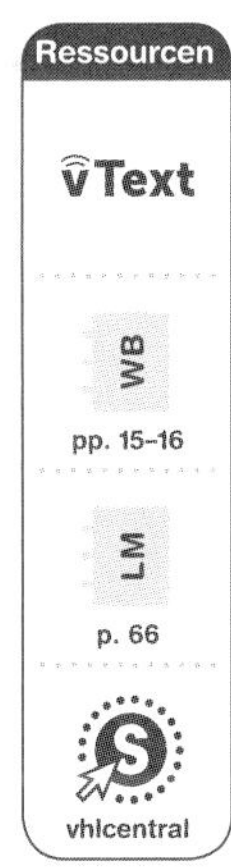

Jetzt sind Sie dran! **Wählen Sie den richtigen Artikel.**

Suggestion Remind students that they need to look at the verb in order to make a decision about case. Students may have difficulty with item 7 because of the motion verb **fahren**. Point out that the car is your *location*, not your *destination*. You are *in the car*, not moving *towards the car.*

1. Wir wohnen über (einer / eine) Bäckerei.
2. Ich lege den gestreiften Hut auf (den / dem) Tisch.
3. Aha! Unter (den / dem) Tisch liegt meine Mütze.
4. Die Verkäuferin hängt das kurzärmlige Kleid zwischen (die / den) langärmligen Kleider und die Blusen.
5. Matthias trägt selten ein Sweatshirt über (sein / seinem) T-Shirt.
6. Dein Schal hängt neben (die / der) Tür.
7. Ich bin in (meinem / mein) Auto gefahren.
8. Frau Vögele braucht Unterwäsche und geht in (ein / einem) Geschäft.
9. Die Katze sitzt gern auf (meine / meiner) Jacke.
10. Seid ihr am Montag wieder in (ein / einem) Konzert gegangen?

1 Suggestion Point out that not all of these sentences use two-way prepositions. You might want to direct students to review the accusative and dative prepositions taught in **Vol. 1, 3B.2** and **4B.2**.

2 Suggestion Emphasize the distinction between *movement and movement towards.* **Ski fahren**, for example, of course entails movement, but the skiers are skiing in the mountains, not into the mountains. Hence the dative case is used, not the accusative.

2 Expansion Have students write two sentences for each photo, one using the dative with the verb given and one using a different verb with the accusative. Ex: **Wir lesen in der Bibliothek. Wir gehen in die Bibliothek**.

Anwendung

1 Präpositionen Ergänzen Sie die Sätze mit den richtigen bestimmten (*definite*) Artikeln.

BEISPIEL Die neue Bäckerei ist zwischen *der* Metzgerei und *dem* Supermarkt.

1. Die warme Jacke hängt an ___der___ Tür.
2. Hast du dein Fahrrad hinter ___das___ Haus gestellt?
3. Der Kellner geht um ___den___ Tisch.
4. Trägst du ein Trägerhemd unter ___dem___ T-Shirt?
5. Ich gehe in ___die___ Bibliothek.
6. Sophia und Hans laufen morgens durch ___den___ Park.
7. Die Katze liegt gern neben ___dem___ Fenster.
8. Der Hund ist hinter ___das___ Auto gelaufen.

2 Wo macht man das? Schreiben Sie zu jedem Foto, wo man diese Aktivitäten machen kann.

die Berge	ein altes Haus	das Restaurant
die Bibliothek	der Park	das Stadion

BEISPIEL lesen
in der Bibliothek

1. Fußball spielen
im Stadion

2. essen
im Restaurant

3. Ski fahren
in den Bergen

4. spazieren gehen
im Park

5. wohnen
in einem alten Haus

3 Überraschung beim Abendessen Bilden Sie Sätze. Sample answers are provided.

BEISPIEL das Trinkgeld / liegen / auf / der Tisch
Das Trinkgeld liegt auf dem Tisch.

1. der Pizzaservice / bringen / die Pizza / an / die Haustür
Der Pizzaservice bringt die Pizza an die Haustür.
2. die Großmutter / stellen / Teller und Gläser / auf / der Tisch
Die Großmutter stellt Teller und Gläser auf den Tisch.
3. die Kinder / sitzen / zwischen / die Eltern
Die Kinder sitzen zwischen den Eltern.
4. die kleine Lisa / setzen / ihre neue Barbie / neben / ihr großer Bruder
Die kleine Lisa setzt ihre neue Barbie neben ihren großen Bruder.
5. die leckere Pizza / sein / schon / auf / der Tisch
Die leckere Pizza ist schon auf dem Tisch.
6. eine kleine Maus / laufen / über / die Teller
Eine kleine Maus ist über die Teller gelaufen.
7. der Vater / bringen / schnell / die Katze / in / das Zimmer
Der Vater hat schnell die Katze ins Zimmer gebracht.
8. was / finden / die Familie / später / unter / der Tisch
Was hat die Familie später unter dem Tisch gefunden?

Kommunikation

4 Auf dem und das Schulgelände Beantworten Sie die Fragen von Ihrem Partner / Ihrer Partnerin. Answers will vary.

BEISPIEL

S1: *Wohin hast du deinen Rucksack gelegt?*
S2: *Ich habe ihn unter den Tisch gelegt.*

1. Wohin können wir zum Kaffee trinken gehen?
2. Wo lernen die Schülern Fremdsprachen?
3. Wohin gehen die Schülern zum Mittagessen?
4. Wo kann ich ein leckeres Eis kaufen?
5. Wohin sollen die Schülern ihre Fahrräder stellen?
6. Wo wanderst du gern?

4 Suggestion Make sure partners take turns asking and answering questions.

4 Virtual Chat You can also assign activity 4 on the Supersite. Students record individual responses that appear in your gradebook.

5 Wohin gehst du? Sie wollen diese Aktivitäten machen. Fragen Sie die Schüler / die Schülerinnen in Ihrer Gruppe, wohin Sie gehen müssen. Answers will vary.

BEISPIEL frühstücken

S1: *Ich will frühstücken. Wohin muss ich gehen?*
S2: *Du musst in die Cafeteria gehen.*
S3: *Ja, in der Cafeteria kannst du Mittag essen.*

1. Deutsch lernen
2. Basketball spielen
3. ein Fußballspiel sehen
4. schwimmen
5. Lebensmittel kaufen
6. Bücher lesen
7. Gebäck kaufen
8. mit Freunden zum Essen ausgehen

6 Hier auf dem Schulgelände Sarah ist neu an Ihrer Schule. Erfinden Sie mit Ihrem Partner / Ihrer Partnerin zusammen sechs Ratschläge (*pieces of advice*) für sie. Sie können auch andere Verben benutzen. Answers will vary.

BEISPIEL Die Mensa is nicht sehr gut. (essen)
Iss nicht in der Mensa. Geh ins Café!

1. Das Café ist leider teuer. (bestellen)
2. Dein Zimmer ist sehr warm. (öffnen)
3. Der Deutschkurs ist nicht einfach. (lernen)
4. Parken ist ein Problem. (stellen)
5. Der Park ist abends sehr dunkel. (laufen)

6 Suggestion Briefly review formation of the **du**-imperative for each verb.

7 Was passiert alles im Restaurant? Erfinden Sie eine Geschichte (*story*) mit den Schülern / die Schülerinnen in Ihrer Gruppe über die Personen auf dem Bild. Benutzen Sie Präpositionen. Answers will vary.

BEISPIEL

S1: *Die junge Frau ist mit ihrem Mann ins Restaurant gekommen.*
S2: *Sie sitzt am Tisch neben ihrem Mann.*
S3: *Ein Kellner stellt einen Teller auf den Tisch...*

7 Suggestion Make sure students understand that they need to use a preposition in each sentence. You may wish to set a time limit and have groups compete to create the most correct sentences.

Wiederholung

1 Kleidung zu jedem Anlass

Kleidung zu jedem Anlass Beschreiben Sie mit einem Partner / einer Partnerin, was Tobias und Anna zu jedem (*each*) Anlass tragen. Answers will vary.

1 Virtual Chat You can also assign activity 1 on the Supersite.

BEISPIEL

S1: *Was trägt Tobias zur Geburtstagsfeier im Restaurant?*
S2: *Zur Geburtstagsfeier im Restaurant trägt er eine grüne Hose und ein oranges T-shirt. Und was trägt Anna?*

im Regen (*rain*)
im Rockkonzert
in den Bergen, zum Ski fahren
ins Schwimmbad
zur Geburtstagsfeier im Restaurant
zur Sporthalle

2 Arbeitsblatt

Arbeitsblatt Ihr Lehrer / Ihre Lehrerin gibt Ihnen ein Blatt mit einigen Fragen und Fakten. Finden Sie eine Person, die die Antwort weiß.

BEISPIEL

S1: *Wie heißt der längste (longest) Fluss in Österreich?*
S2: *Ich weiß es nicht. / Ich weiß es. Das ist die Donau.*

3 Diskutieren und kombinieren

Diskutieren und kombinieren Sie und ein Partner / eine Partnerin bekommen zwei verschiedene Blätter. Sehen Sie die Bilder an und antworten Sie auf die Fragen von Ihrem Partner / Ihrer Partnerin.

BEISPIEL

S1: *Wohin ist Jasmin gegangen?*
S2: *Sie ist ins Stadion gegangen.*
S1: *Was macht sie in dem Stadion?*
S2: *Sie sieht ein Fußballspiel an.*

4 Lenas Großeltern

Lenas Großeltern Erzählen Sie mit einem Partner / einer Partnerin von Lenas Großeltern. Benutzen Sie die angegebenen Daten und erfinden Sie (*invent*) weitere (*additional*) Informationen.

BEISPIEL

S1: *Lenas Großeltern sind 1967 auf die Uni gegangen.*
S2: *Im Deutschseminar hat die Oma den Opa gesehen.*
S1: *Sie hat gedacht: „Er ist der Mann für mich!"*

1967	1973	1975	1976	2012
Die Oma sieht den Opa im Deutschseminar.	Oma und Opa machen den Abschluss.	Oma und Opa heiraten.	Die Frischvermählten reisen nach Indien.	Beide gehen in Rente.

5 Unsere Woche

Unsere Woche Schreiben Sie auf, was Sie in der letzten Woche gemacht haben. Fragen Sie Ihren Partner / Ihre Partnerin, was er/sie gemacht hat.

BEISPIEL

S1: *Am Montag bin ich in die Bibliothek gegangen. Und du, Monika, was hast du gemacht?*
S2: *Ich bin auf meinem Zimmer geblieben.*

	meine Woche	
	ich	mein Partner / meine Partnerin
Montag	Ich bin in die Bibliothek gegangen.	Monika ist auf ihrem Zimmer geblieben.
Dienstag		
Mittwoch		
Donnerstag		
Freitag		
Samstag		
Sonntag		

6 Kennst du diese Person?

Kennst du diese Person? Beschreiben Sie eine bekannte Person. Die Gruppe soll erraten, wer es ist.

BEISPIEL

S1: *Er hat 2015 einen Oscar gewonnen. Kennt ihr ihn?*
S2: *Ja, ich kenne ihn. Das ist Eddie Redmayne.*

7 Im Kleidergeschäft

Im Kleidergeschäft Spielen Sie mit einem Partner / einer Partnerin die Rollen von Verkäufer / Verkäuferin und Kunden / Kundin im Kleidergeschäft. Der Kunde / Die Kundin sucht Kleider für einen besonderen Anlass. Benutzen Sie Wörter aus der Liste.

BEISPIEL

S1: *Kann ich Ihnen helfen?*
S2: *Ja, bitte. Ich suche ein schönes Hemd für eine Party.*

danken	kaufen
glauben	kennen
helfen	passen

7 Partner Chat You can also assign activity 7 on the Supersite. Students work in pairs to record the activity online. The pair's recorded conversation will appear in your gradebook.

8 Das Klassenzimmer

Das Klassenzimmer Beschreiben Sie, wo die Gegenstände (*objects*) und Personen in Ihrem Klassenzimmer sind.

BEISPIEL

S1: *Vor der Tafel steht der Lehrer.*
S2: *Unter dem Tisch...*

Mein Wör | ter | buch

Schreiben Sie noch fünf weitere Wörter in Ihr persönliches Wörterbuch zu den Themen **Feste feiern** und **Kleidung**.

das Bekleidungsgeschäft, -e

Übersetzung
clothing store

Wortart
ein Substantiv

Gebrauch
Der Verkäufer im Bekleidungsgeschäft hat mir eine neue Bluse verkauft.

Synonyme
der Klamottenladen

Antonyme
—

KAPITEL 1

Weiter geht's

Panorama

Interactive Map
AP* Theme: Global Challenges
Context: Geography

Bayern

Bayern in Zahlen

- **Fläche:** *70.549 km² (größtes deutsches Bundesland)*
- **Bevölkerung:** *12,4 Millionen Menschen (zweite Stelle° hinter Nordrhein-Westfalen)*
- **Religion:** *römisch-katholisch 67,2 %, evangelisch-lutherisch 24,1%*
- **Städte:** *München (1,3 Mio. Einwohner), Nürnberg (503.500), Augsburg (263.600), Würzburg (133.100) und Regensburg (134.600)*
- **Berge:** *die Zugspitze (2.962 m) (höchster Berg Deutschlands), Hochfrottspitze (2.649 m), Großer Arber (1.456 m)*
- **Niedrigster Punkt:** *Kahl am Main (107 m)*
- **Flüsse:** *die Donau, der Inn*
- **Wichtige Industriezweige:** *Automobil, IT, Medien und Verlage°, Tourismus*
- **Touristenattraktionen:** *Befreiungshalle (Kelheim), Fuggerei (Augsburg), Marienplatz (München), Schloss Neuschwanstein (Füssen), Steinerne Brücke (Regensburg), Walhalla (Donaustauf)*
  Touristen können in Städten wie München, Augsburg und Regensburg viel Kultur genießen. In den Alpen oder dem Bayerischen Wald können sie Berg- und Wintersport treiben. Wirtschaftlich entwickelt sich° Bayern in den letzten Jahrzehnten von einem Agrar- zu einem Technologieland.

QUELLE: Bayerisches Landesportal

Berühmte Bayern

- **Adam Ries,** *Mathematiker (1492/93–1559)*
- **Levi Strauss,** *Erfinder° der Jeans (1829–1902)*
- **Elizabeth „Sisi",** *Kaiserin° von Österreich und Ungarn (1837–1898)*
- **Ludwig II.,** *König von Bayern (1845–1886)*
- **Lena Christ,** *Autorin (1881–1920)*
- **Franz Josef Strauß,** *Politiker (1915–1988)*
- **Dirk Nowitzki,** *Basketballspieler (1978–)*
- **Magdalena Neuner,** *Biathletin (1987–)*

Stelle *position* **Verlage** *publishing companies* **entwickelt sich** *evolves* **Erfinder** *inventor* **Kaiserin** *empress* **Weltkulturerbe** *World Heritage Site* **herrscht** *exists* **Dialektpfleger** *dialect conservator* **Ortseingängen** *city limit* **Verbotsschilder** *ban signs*

Suggestion Tell students that in many regions of Germany, only the older generation still speaks the dialect and many dialects are dying out. In Bavaria, however, the dialect is still alive and well, and it is closely intertwined with the Bavarian identity.

HESSEN · SACHSEN · BAYERN · BADEN-WÜRTTEMBERG · Bayreuth · Würzburg · Main · Nürnberg · Regensburg · Straubing · Ingolstadt · Donau · Isar · Passau · Augsburg · München · Inn · Ammersee · Starnberger See · Chiemsee · Bodensee · Garmisch-Partenkirchen · Zugspitze · NATIONALPARK BAYERISCHER WALD · BAYERISCHER WALD · NATIONALPARK BERCHTESGADEN

Landesgrenzen · Stadt · Landeshauptstadt

0 25 Meilen · 0 25 Kilometer

Steinerne Brücke in Regensburg, ein UNESCO-Weltkulturerbe°

Im Bayerischen Wald

Das Alte Rathaus, München

AP* Theme: Global Challenges **Context:** Communication

Unglaublich, aber wahr!

„Auf Wiedersehen" heißt im bayerischen Dialekt „Servus". In Norddeutschland kann man „Tschüss" (oder „Tschüß") sagen. In dem bayerischen Dorf Gotzing herrscht° ein Tschüss-Verbot oder eine „Tschüss-freie Zone". Hans Triebel, ein Dialektpfleger°, installiert deshalb an den Ortseingängen° „Tschüss"-Verbotsschilder°.

Expansion Ask students if they think the **Verbot** rule will work, and whether or not they agree with imposing that kind of rule. Teach students a few phrases of the Bavarian dialect, such as: **I mog di (Ich mag dich), a Gaudi (ein Riesenspass),** and **Schleich di (Hau ab).**

Suggestion Before they read the **Kunst** article, play students the beginning of **Ritt der Walküren**. Ask them if they like it, if they've heard it before, and who composed it. Have them find Bayreuth on the map.

Kunst

AP* Theme: Beauty & Aesthetics
Context: Performing Arts

Bayreuther Festspiele

Die Bayreuther Festspiele heißen auch Richard-Wagner-Festspiele. Sie finden jedes Jahr in der Stadt Bayreuth im Festspielhaus auf dem Grünen Hügel statt. Die Werke von Richard Wagner, einem berühmten deutschen Komponisten°, kann man während dieses weltberühmten Events seit 1876 sehen. Bei den ersten Festspielen inszeniert Richard Wagner seine Oper° „Der Ring des Nibelungen". Jedes Jahr besuchen 58.000 Zuschauer eine von dreißig Aufführungen° in Bayreuth. Allerdings versuchen° jedes Jahr 500.000 Menschen Karten zu kaufen. Deshalb dauert es bis zu zehn Jahre, bis man eine Karte bekommt.

Städte

AP* Theme: Beauty & Aesthetics
Context: Architecture

Die sieben Hügel° von Bamberg

Bamberg ist eine Stadt in Franken, einer Region in Bayern. Seit 1993 ist sie ein UNESCO-Weltkulturerbe wegen des größten unversehrt erhaltenen° historischen Stadtzentrums in Deutschland. Genauso wie° Rom ist Bamberg auf sieben Hügeln gebaut. Deshalb trägt es auch den Namen „das Fränkische Rom". Die sieben Hügel Bambergs sind der Altenburger Berg, der Domberg, der Michaelsberg, der Abtsberg, der Jakobsberg, der Kaulberg und der Stephansberg. Auf dem Domberg kann man den mächtigen°, viertürmigen Dom° aus dem 13. Jahrhundert° finden.

Industrie

Suggestion Ask students which other German car brands they are familiar with.

AP* Theme: Science & Technology
Context: Transportation

Audi

Die Autofirma Audi hat ihren Hauptsitz° in Ingolstadt, Oberbayern. Neben VW, Porsche, BMW und Opel ist Audi einer der wichtigsten Autoproduzenten Deutschlands. Audi baut besonders sportliche Autos. Die Audi-Quattro-Modelle zum Beispiel gibt es seit 1980. Diese Modelle haben permanenten Vierradantrieb°. Zwischen 2000 und 2014 haben Audis das Autosport Rennen dreizehn Mal° gewonnen. Im Jahr 2013 arbeiten 67.000 Mitarbeiter bei Audi. Im gleichen Jahr macht die Firma 49 Milliarden € Umsatz° und baut 1,5 Millionen Autos.

Komponisten *composer* **Oper** *opera* **Aufführungen** *performances* **versuchen** *try* **Hügel** *hills* **unversehrt erhaltenen** *preserved undamaged* **Genauso wie** *Just like* **mächtigen** *mighty* **viertürmigen Dom** *cathedral with four towers* **Jahrhundert** *century* **Hauptsitz** *headquarters* **Vierradantrieb** *four-wheel drive* **Mal** *times* **Umsatz** *sales* **Schlösser** *castles* **verantwortlich** *responsible* **wichtig** *important* **Stahlbau** *steel construction* **Licht** *light*

Suggestion Tell students that because of "Mad King Ludwig's" extravagant building projects, he ended his life deeply in debt.

Architektur

AP* Theme: Beauty & Aesthetics
Context: Architecture

Die Schlösser° von Ludwig II.

Ludwig II. ist der bekannteste König Bayerns. Er ist in erster Linie für seine Schlösser weltberühmt. Neben dem bekanntesten Schloss, Schloss Neuschwanstein, ist er auch für das Königshaus am Schachen und Schloss Linderhof verantwortlich°. Auf der Herreninsel im Chiemsee steht der Anfang von Schloss Herrenchiemsee. Dieses Schloss ist aber nicht fertig gebaut. Ludwigs Schlossbauten sind wegen neuer Technologien wichtig°: Stahlbau° und elektrisches Licht° sind integriert. Die Schlösser sind heute die bedeutendsten touristischen Attraktionen Bayerns.

IM INTERNET

1. Wie viele Touristen besuchen jedes Jahr die Schlösser Ludwigs II.? Wo sind die Schlösser?
2. Was bedeutet der Name *Audi*? Warum gibt es vier Ringe im Unternehmenslogo (*company logo*) von Audi?

Find out more at **vhlcentral.com**.

Was haben Sie gelernt? Ergänzen Sie die Sätze.

1. „Auf Wiedersehen" heißt im bayerischen Dialekt „__Servus__".
2. In Gotzing, einem Dorf in Bayern, darf man nicht __Tschüss/Tschüß__ sagen.
3. Bei den ersten Bayreuther Festspielen inszeniert __Richard Wagner__ seine Oper „Der Ring des Nibelungen".
4. Jedes Jahr versuchen __500.000__ Menschen, Karten für die Bayreuther Festspiele zu kaufen.
5. Seit __1993__ ist Bamberg ein UNESCO-Weltkulturerbe.
6. Genauso wie Rom ist Bamberg auf __sieben__ Hügeln gebaut.
7. Der Hauptsitz der Firma Audi ist in __Ingolstadt__.
8. Audis haben __dreizehn Mal__ das Rennen „24 Stunden von Le Mans" gewonnen.
9. Das bekannteste Schloss von König Ludwig II. ist __Schloss Neuschwanstein__.
10. Ludwigs Schlossbauten integrieren neue Technologien wie Stahlbau und __elektrisches Licht__.

Practice more at **vhlcentral.com**.

Lesen

Audio: Reading

National Standards: communication, cultures

Vor dem Lesen

AP* Theme: Families & Communities
Context: Urban, Suburban, & Rural Life

Strategien

Skimming

Skimming involves quickly reading through a document to absorb its general meaning. This allows you to understand the main ideas without having to read word for word. When you skim a text, look at its title and subtitles and read the first sentence of each paragraph.

Untersuchen Sie den Text Lesen Sie den Text schnell. Was ist der Titel des Texts? Wie viele Teile hat der Text? Wie heißen die Teile? Sehen Sie sich jetzt die Fotos an. Was ist das Thema des Texts?

Lehnwörter Sehen Sie sich mit einem Partner / einer Partnerin den Text an und machen Sie eine Liste mit englischen Lehnwörtern (*loanwords*) und Kognaten. Sample answers are provided. Trend, Internet, Web, traditionell, Millionen, Accessoires, hier, Alternative, Probleme, Internetpräsenz, coole

Suchen Sehen Sie sich mit einem Partner / einer Partnerin den Text an. Stehen die Informationen im Text oder nicht? Markieren Sie **ja** oder **nein**.

	ja	nein
1. wo Deutsche Kleider kaufen	☑	☐
2. das Internet	☑	☐
3. Modenschauen	☐	☑
4. Designer	☐	☑
5. Warenhäuser	☑	☐
6. Boutiquen	☐	☑
7. Modeketten	☑	☐
8. Flohmärkte	☑	☐

Deutschland heute

Hauptseite | Politik | Wirtschaft

WO KAUFEN DEUTSCHE HEUTE IHRE KLEIDUNG?

In den letzten Jahren gibt es einen neuen Trend: Deutsche kaufen ihre Kleider immer öfter im Internet. Neben dem Web besuchen Deutsche aber auch weiterhin° traditionelle Geschäfte wie Warenhäuser° und Kleidergeschäfte. Nur noch wenige° Deutsche finden ihre Kleidung auf Flohmärkten°.

INTERNET, DAS GROSSE GESCHÄFT

Im Jahr 2014 sind 51 Millionen Deutsche online shoppen gegangen. Mehr als 65 Prozent dieser Internetkäufer haben Bekleidung und Accessoires im Web gekauft. Vor allem Frauen kaufen hier gerne ein; im Jahr 2013 haben mehr als siebzig Prozent aller Frauen Kleidung oder Sportartikel im Internet gekauft. Bei den Männern sind es fast sechzig Prozent.

WARENHÄUSER WERDEN IMMER WENIGER

Warenhäuser wie Karstadt und Galeria Kaufhof sind immer noch eine Alternative für den Kleiderkauf. In den letzten Jahren haben Warenhäuser aber immer größere wirtschaftliche Probleme und viele Warenhäuser schließen°. Zwischen 2009 und 2015 hat Kaufhof mehr als zehn Warenhäuser in Deutschland geschlossen und dieser Trend geht weiter°.

MODEKETTEN° HABEN ERFOLG°

Kleidergeschäfte wie H&M, Zara, Esprit und Orsay kann man heute in allen großen deutschen Städten finden. Diese Ketten sind bei jungen Menschen besonders beliebt. H&M ist der Marktführer° in Deutschland. Alle Modeketten haben immer mehr Internetpräsenz.

AUF DEM FLOHMARKT

Es gibt immer noch eine kleine Gruppe Deutscher, die am Samstagmorgen früh aufsteht°, um Flohmärkte zu besuchen. Hier kann man unter anderem gebrauchte° Kleidung günstig kaufen. Es gibt sie in jeder Stadt besonders im Sommer. Vor allem coole Klamotten° aus den 60er und 70er Jahren findet man hier für wenig Geld.

weiterhin *still* **Warenhäuser** *department stores* **wenige** *few* **Flohmärkten** *flea markets* **schließen** *close* **geht weiter** *continues* **Modeketten** *Fashion chains* **Erfolg** *success* **Marktführer** *market leader* **gemeinsam** *in common* **aufsteht** *gets up* **gebrauchte** *used* **Klamotten** *clothes (colloquial)*

Nach dem Lesen

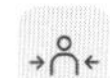

Was fehlt? Ergänzen Sie die Sätze.

1. Deutsche kaufen Kleider vor allem __im Internet__, in Warenhäusern und in Kleidergeschäften.
2. __51 Millionen__ Deutsche sind 2014 im Internet einkaufen gegangen.
3. Mehr __Frauen__ als Männer kaufen Kleider im Internet.
4. Kaufhof hat mehr als __zehn__ Warenhäuser geschlossen.
5. Der Marktführer der Modeketten in Deutschland ist __H&M__.
6. Flohmärkte gibt es besonders im __Sommer__.

Richtig oder falsch? Sind die Aussagen **richtig** oder **falsch**? Korrigieren Sie die falschen Sätze. Sample answers are provided.

	richtig	falsch
1. Deutsche kaufen Mode immer öfter im Internet.	☑	☐
2. Fast 60 Prozent aller Frauen haben Kleidung oder Sportartikel im Internet gekauft. *Fast 60 Prozent aller Männer haben Kleidung oder Sportartikel im Internet gekauft.*	☐	☑
3. Karstadt und Galeria Kaufhof sind deutsche Warenhäuser.	☑	☐
4. Junge Menschen kaufen nicht gern bei H&M ein. *Diese Kette ist bei jungen Menschen beliebt.*	☐	☑
5. Alle Modeketten verkaufen Kleidung auch im Internet.	☑	☐
6. Auf dem Flohmarkt ist Kleidung teuer. *Auf dem Flohmarkt ist Kleidung günstig.*	☐	☑

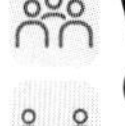

Was tragen Sie? Besprechen Sie in einer Gruppe: Was tragen Sie gern zu verschiedenen Anlässen (in der Schule, bei einer Party, zu Hause)? Wo kaufen Sie Ihre Kleider?

BEISPIEL

S1: *Zu Hause trage ich gerne Jeans und T-Shirts.*
S2: *Wo kaufst du deine Jeans?*
S1: *Meine Jeans kaufe ich im Internet.*
S3: *Ich trage im Sommer gern Kleider.*

Hören

Strategien

Listening for key words

By listening for key words (**Schlüsselwörter**) or phrases, you can identify the subject and main ideas of a conversation or speech, as well as some of the details.

To practice this strategy, you will listen to a short radio spot. Jot down the key words that help you identify the subject of the radio spot and its main ideas.

Vorbereitung

Schauen Sie sich das Foto an. Wer ist in dem Foto? Wo sind sie? Was machen sie?

Zuhören

Hören Sie sich an, wie Marion Scholz ihre neue Mode beschreibt. Lesen Sie dann die Liste. Hören Sie sich die Beschreibung ein zweites Mal an. Welche Kleidungsartikel tragen die Models?

1. ___ Mütze	7. ___ Rock
2. ✓ Anzug	8. ✓ Gürtel
3. ✓ Hemd	9. ___ Bluse
4. ✓ Kleid	10. ✓ Hut
5. ___ Stiefel	11. ___ Badeanzug
6. ___ Jacke	12. ✓ Socken

Verständnis

Was fehlt? Ergänzen Sie die Sätze mit den richtigen Informationen.

braun Handtasche	hellblau kurz	lange orange	Sandalen schwarz	Seide weiten

1. Robert trägt einen weiten Anzug.
2. Die Farbe des Anzugs ist hellblau.
3. Die Sandalen sind schwarz.
4. Elizabeth trägt ein Kleid aus Seide.
5. Am Arm trägt sie eine Handtasche.
6. Ihre Sandalen sind braun.
7. Carolas Hose und T-Shirt sind kurz.
8. Ihre Hose und ihr T-Shirt sind orange und gelb.
9. Thomas trägt lange Socken zu seiner kurzen Hose.
10. Die Kleidung von Thomas ist braun.

Ein Star, ein Fest Wählen Sie einen Star und einen besonderen Anlass. Was trägt der Star zu diesem Anlass? Beschreiben Sie den Star einem Partner / einer Partnerin.

Expansion Show students pictures of celebrities at a **Preisverleihung** such as the Grammy Awards. Have students describe what the celebrities are wearing and then have them vote on the best and worst outfits.

Schreiben

Strategien

Using a dictionary

The dictionary is a useful tool that can provide valuable information about vocabulary. However, in order to use the dictionary correctly, you must understand the elements of each entry.

If you glance at an English-German dictionary, you will notice that its format is similar to that of an English dictionary. Most words are listed with several different definitions, organized by part of speech. The most frequently used meanings are usually listed first.

To find the best word for your needs, refer to the abbreviations and explanatory notes that appear next to each entry. For example, imagine that you are writing about fashion. You want to write *The man is wearing a suit*, but you don't know the German word for *suit*. In the dictionary, you might find an entry like this one:

> **suit** *n.* 1. der Anzug, Anzüge; (*woman's*) das Kostüm, -e 2. der Prozess, -e (*Jur*); 3. die Farbe, -n (*Cards*)

The abbreviation key at the front of the dictionary says that *n.* corresponds to **Substantiv** (*noun*). The second translation is **der Prozess** followed by the abbreviation *Jur*, indicating that it's a law term, and thus that **der Prozess** is a *law suit*. The third word is **die Farbe**, followed by the word *Cards*, indicating that **die Farbe** is a *suit* in a card game. Since **der Anzug** is listed first, you can assume that this is the main translation of the word. The first definition also specifies the difference between a suit for a man, **der Anzug**, and a suit for a woman, **das Kostüm**. Since the other two meanings do not apply to clothing, these details tell you that **der Anzug** is the best choice for your needs.

Thema

Beschreiben Sie

Sehen Sie sich das Bild an. Beschreiben Sie dann in einem Absatz (*paragraph*) den Mann oder die Frau für einen Artikel in einem Modejournal.

Beschreiben Sie das Aussehen (*look*) im Detail. Aus welchem Material sind die Kleider? Wie sind die Kleider geschnitten (*cut*)? Welche Muster (*patterns*) und Farben haben die Kleider? Wo kann man diese Kleider tragen? Sagen Sie auch etwas über den Designer und darüber, wo man die Kleider kaufen kann. Am Ende schreiben Sie Ihre Meinung über die Kleidung. Geben Sie dem Artikel einen Titel.

Bevor Sie den Artikel schreiben, machen Sie sich Notizen. Suchen Sie Vokabeln, die Sie brauchen, in einem Wörterbuch.

- Material
- Schnitt
- Muster
- Farben
- Wo kann man es tragen?
- Wo kann man es kaufen?

Neueste Mode

Lederjacken sind wieder in. Dieser Mann trägt eine schwarze Lederjacke mit einem weißen Trägerhemd. Der Schnitt ist…

Lektion 1A

Feste

der Ballon, -s *balloon*
der Feiertag, -e *holiday*
der Gast, ¨-e *guest*
der Gastgeber, - / die Gastgeberin, -nen *host / hostess*
das Geschenk, -e *gift*
die Karte, -n *card*
die Party, -s *party*
die Überraschung, -en *surprise*
das Zimmer, - *room*
anstoßen (stößt... an) *to toast*
bekommen *to receive*
einladen (lädt... ein) *to invite*
feiern *to celebrate*
eine Party geben *to throw a party*
(keinen) Spaß haben *(not) to have fun*
schenken *to give (a gift)*
überraschen *to surprise*
Herzlichen Glückwunsch! *Congratulations!*

besondere Anlässe

die Ehe, -n *marriage*
der / die Frischvermählte, -n *newlywed*
die Geburt, -en *birth*
der Geburtstag, -e *birthday*
die Hochzeit, -en *wedding*
der Jahrestag, -e *anniversary*
(das) Silvester *New Year's Eve*
(das) Weihnachten *Christmas*
in Rente gehen *to retire*
einen Abschluss machen *to graduate*

Essen und Trinken

das Eis *ice cream*
der Eiswürfel, - *ice cube*
das Gebäck *pastries; baked goods*
der Keks, -e *cookie*
der Sekt *champagne*
die Süßigkeiten (*pl.*) *candy*
die Torte, -n *cake*

Ausdrücke

die Freundschaft, -en *friendship*
das Glück *happiness*
der Kuss, ¨-e *kiss*
die Liebe *love*

Past participles with *haben* *See pp. 28–29.*
Accusative pronouns *See p. 32.*
Dative pronouns *See p. 34.*

Lektion 1B

Kleidung

der Anzug, ¨-e *suit*
der Badeanzug, ¨-e *bathing suit*
die Bluse, -n *blouse*
die Brille, -n *glasses*
der Gürtel, - *belt*
die Halskette, -n *necklace*
der Handschuh, -e *glove*
die Handtasche, -n *purse*
das Hemd, -en *shirt*
die Hose, -n *pants*
die kurze Hose (*pl.* die kurzen Hosen) *shorts*
der Hut, ¨-e *hat*
die Jacke, -n *jacket*
die Jeans, - *jeans*
das Kleid, -er *dress*
die Krawatte, -n *tie*
der Mantel, ¨- *coat*
die Mütze, -n *cap*
der Pullover, - *sweater*
der Rock, ¨-e *skirt*
der Schal, -s *scarf*
der Schuh, -e *shoe*
die Socke, -n *sock*
die Sonnenbrille, -n *sunglasses*
der Stiefel, - *boot*
das Sweatshirt, -s *sweatshirt*
das Trägerhemd, -en *tank top*
das T-Shirt, -s *T-shirt*
der Turnschuh, -e *sneakers*
die Unterwäsche *underwear*

Farben

blau *blue*
braun *brown*
gelb *yellow*
grau *gray*
grün *green*
lila *purple*
orange *orange*
rosa *pink*
rot *red*
schwarz *black*
weiß *white*

Einkaufen

die Baumwolle *cotton*
die Farbe, -n *color*
die Kleidergröße, -n *size*
der Kunde, -n / die Kundin, -nen *customer*
das Leder *leather*
die Seide *silk*
der Verkäufer, - / die Verkäuferin, -nen *salesperson*
die Wolle *wool*
im Angebot *on sale*
günstig *inexpensive*
einfarbig *solid colored*
eng *tight*
gestreift *striped*
kurzärmlig *short-sleeved*
langärmlig *long-sleeved*
teuer *expensive*
weit *loose; big*
anziehen (zieht... an) *to put on*
tragen (trägt) *to wear*

Past participles with *sein* *See p. 47.*
Wissen* and *kennen *See p. 50.*
Two-way prepositions *See p. 52.*

Ressourcen

Trautes Heim

KAPITEL 2

Suggestion Ask students: **Wo ist George? Was kocht er?**

Teaching Tip Look for icons indicating activities that address the modes of communication. Follow this key:

→ᐱ←	Interpretive communication
←ᐱ→	Presentational communication
ᐱ↔ᐱ	Interpersonal communication

LEKTION 2A

Kontext

Communicative Goals

You will learn how to:

- describe your home
- talk about living arrangements

Zu Hause

AP* Theme: Families & Communities
Context: Urban, Suburban, & Rural Life
Vocabulary Tools

Suggestion Point out that **das Möbel,-** is a countable noun in German, but that *furniture* is a non-count noun in English. Explain that German speakers typically use **Möbel** to refer to furniture in general and **Möbelstück** to refer to a piece of furniture .

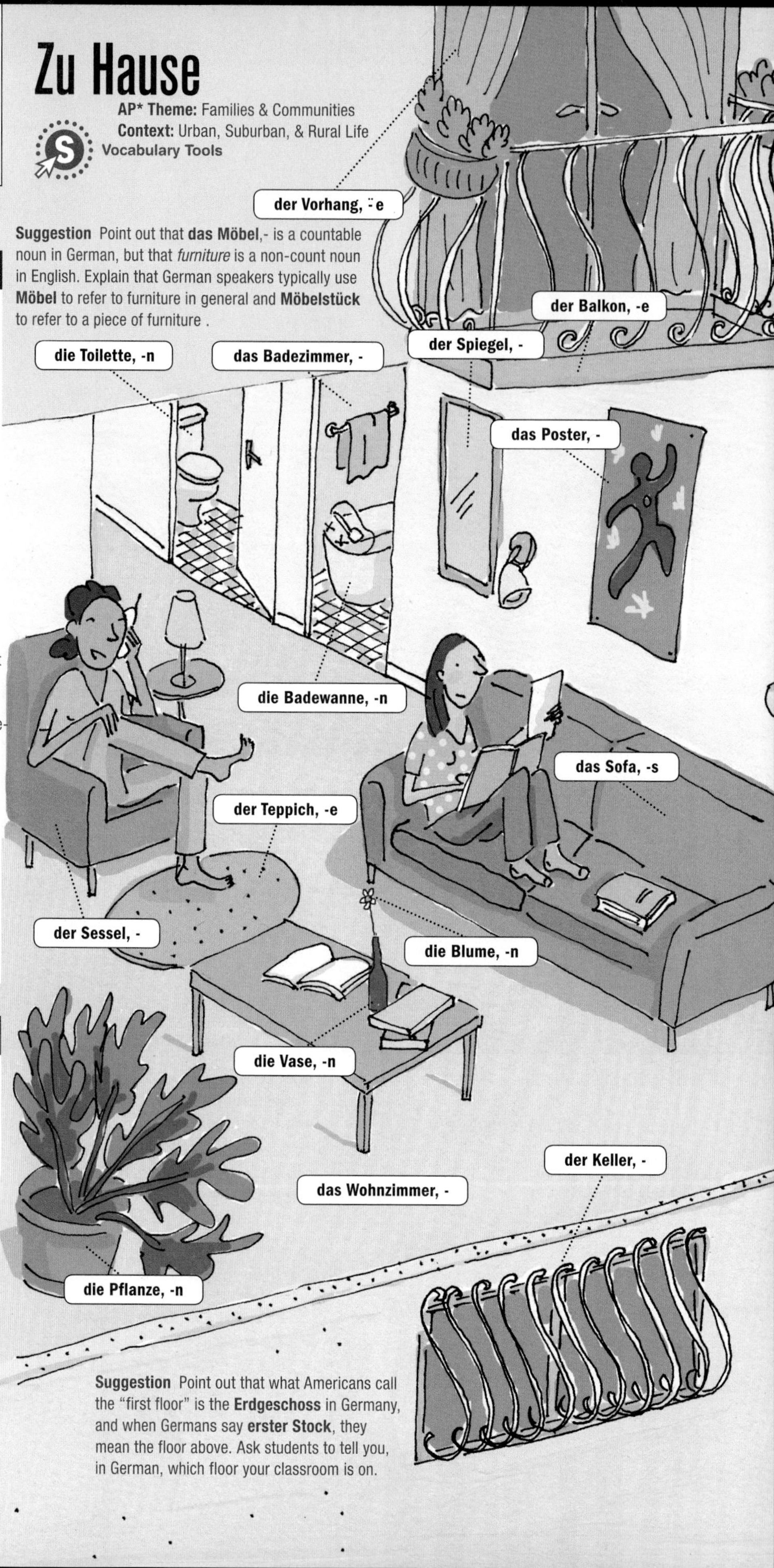

der Vorhang, ¨-e
der Balkon, -e
der Spiegel, -
das Badezimmer, -
die Toilette, -n
das Poster, -
die Badewanne, -n
das Sofa, -s
der Teppich, -e
der Sessel, -
die Blume, -n
die Vase, -n
der Keller, -
das Wohnzimmer, -
die Pflanze, -n

Wortschatz

Zimmer	***rooms***
das Arbeitszimmer, -	*home office*
der Dachboden, ¨-	*attic*
das Erdgeschoss, -e	*ground floor*
das Esszimmer, -	*dining room*
der Flur, -e	*hall*
die Küche, -n	*kitchen*
der erste/zweite Stock	*second/third floor*
Möbel	***furniture***
das Bild, -er	*picture*
das Möbelstück, -e	*piece of furniture*
der Nachttisch, -e	*night table*
der Schrank, ¨-e	*cabinet; closet*
die Schublade, -n	*drawer*
die Treppe, -n	*stairway*
Orte	***places***
das Haus, ¨-er	*house*
das Wohnheim, -e	*dorm*
die Wohnung, -en	*apartment*
nach rechts/links	*to the right/left*
Ausdrücke	***expressions***
mieten	*to rent*
umziehen (zieht... um)	*to move*
wohnen	*to live*

Suggestion Point out that many Germans in big cities live in apartments, not single-family homes.

ACHTUNG

Note that **mieten** means to rent *from* someone, while **vermieten** means to rent *to* someone. **Ich miete eine kleine Wohnung in der Stadt. Die Familie vermietet ein Zimmer in ihrem Haus.**

Expansion Have students play a memory game to internalize the new vocabulary. The first student starts with **In meiner Wohnung gibt es...** and names an item of furniture. The next student repeats the previous item(s) and adds one. If a student can't repeat the entire sequence, he or she is eliminated. Remind students to use the accusative with **Es gibt.**

Suggestion Point out that what Americans call the "first floor" is the **Erdgeschoss** in Germany, and when Germans say **erster Stock**, they mean the floor above. Ask students to tell you, in German, which floor your classroom is on.

Ressourcen

vText | WB pp. 17–18 | LM p. 67 | vhlcentral

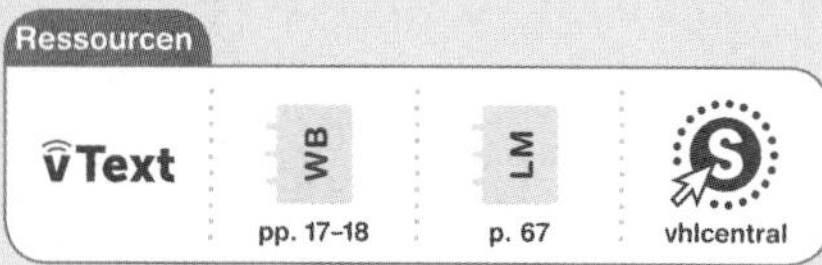

Suggestion Make sure that students understand the difference between **der Stock** and **der Boden**. Point out that **der Dachboden** is a compound of **das Dach** (*roof*) and **der Boden**.

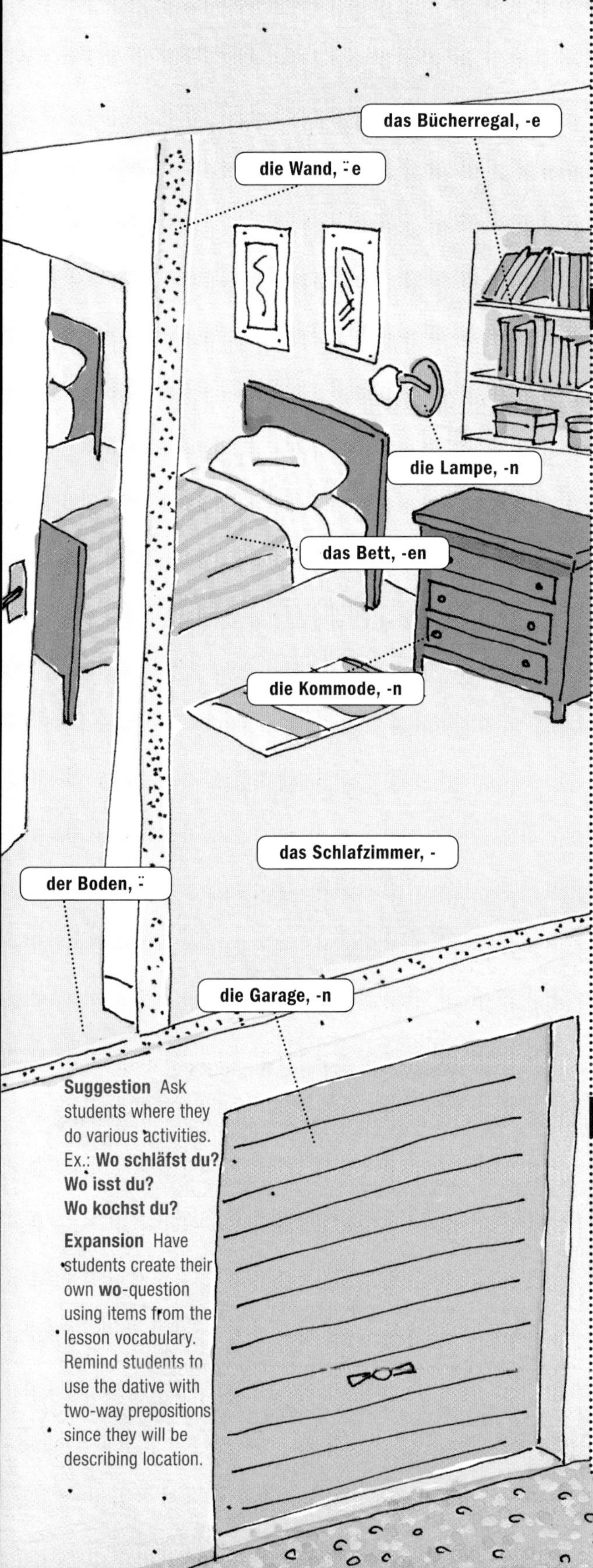

das Bücherregal, -e

die Wand, ¨-e

die Lampe, -n

das Bett, -en

die Kommode, -n

das Schlafzimmer, -

der Boden, ¨

die Garage, -n

Suggestion Ask students where they do various activities. Ex.: **Wo schläfst du? Wo isst du? Wo kochst du?**

Expansion Have students create their own **wo**-question using items from the lesson vocabulary. Remind students to use the dative with two-way prepositions since they will be describing location.

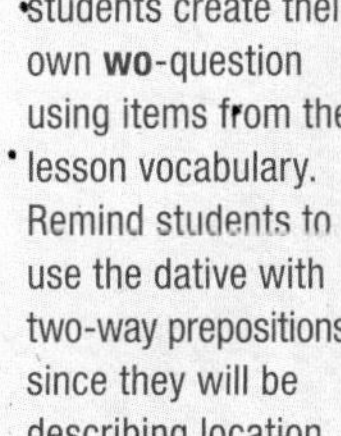

Anwendung

1 Expansion Give students a description of a mixed-up apartment and ask them to tell you where things ought to be. Ex.: **Mein Sofa ist in der Garage. Wo sollte es sein? Mein Bett ist in der Küche. Wo sollte es sein? Meine Bücher sind unter dem Bett. Wo sollten sie sein?**

1 Paare finden Welche Objekte assoziieren Sie mit den Zimmern in einem Haus?

d	1. die Küche	a. das Bücherregal
b	2. das Wohnzimmer	b. das Sofa
f	3. das Esszimmer	c. das Auto
c	4. die Garage	d. die Lebensmittel
h	5. das Badezimmer	e. die Kommode
e	6. das Schlafzimmer	f. der Esstisch
g	7. der Balkon	g. die Blumen
a	8. das Arbeitszimmer	h. die Toilette

2 Expansion Have students compile a list of what they have, don't have, or would like to have in their rooms and share it with the class or a partner. Provide a model to demonstrate correct use of the accusative and of **kein**.

2 Bilder beschriften Wie heißen die verschiedenen Bereiche (*parts*) in einem Haus?

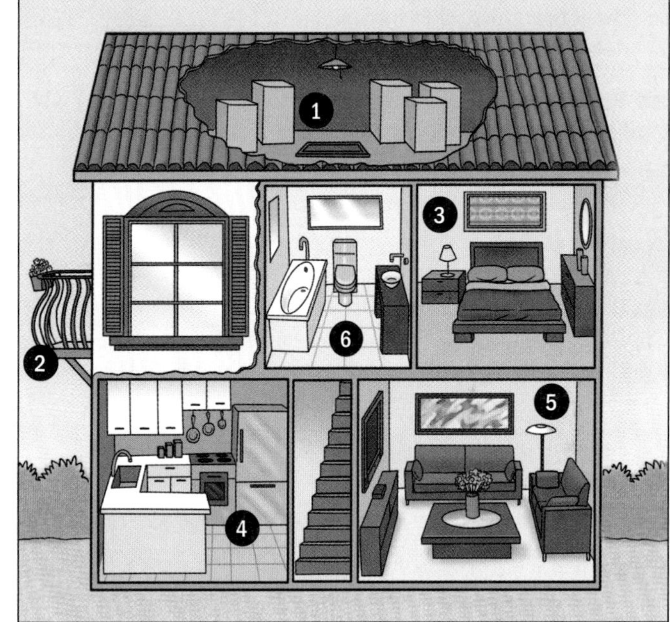

1. der Dachboden
2. der Balkon
3. das Schlafzimmer
4. die Küche
5. das Wohnzimmer
6. das Badezimmer

3 Was ist richtig? Hören Sie die Definitionen und wählen Sie das Wort, das am besten passt.

1. Flur / **Küche**
2. Wand / **Vorhang**
3. **Badezimmer** / Wohnzimmer
4. **Garage** / Dachboden
5. Rucksack / **Vase**
6. **Bild** / Kommode
7. **Haus** / Esszimmer
8. Bücherregal / **Lampe**

3 Expansion Play a guessing game using vocabulary items not mentioned in the recording. Give students clues and have them guess which word you are thinking of. Ex.: **Ich denke an ein Möbelstück. Da schlafe ich. Was ist das? Das steht in meinem Wohnzimmer. Ich sitze darauf. Was ist das?**

Practice more at **vhlcentral.com**.

Kommunikation

4 **Wo ich wohne** Arbeiten Sie mit einem Partner / einer Partnerin. Benutzen Sie die Wörter aus den drei Spalten und beschreiben Sie Ihr Zimmer, Ihre Wohnung oder Ihr Haus. Answers will vary.

BEISPIEL

S1: *Meine Wohnung ist ziemlich groß und hat einen kleinen Balkon.*
S2: *Mein Zimmer ist klein. Aber alle meine Möbel sind neu.*

A	B	C
mein Haus mein Zimmer meine Wohnung	ist (nicht) hat (kein)	Badezimmer Balkon Fenster Garage Küche Schlafzimmer Schreibtisch groß/klein alt/neu modern/unmodern

4 Partner Chat You can also assign activity 4 on the Supersite. Students work in pairs to record the activity online. The pair's recorded conversation will appear in your gradebook.

5 Expansion After students have put the dialogue in the correct order, have two volunteers read it aloud.

5 **Janas Haus** Klara besucht Jana in ihrem neuen Haus. Bringen Sie den Dialog in eine logische Reihenfolge (*order*). Wenn Sie fertig sind, vergleichen Sie Ihr Haus oder Ihre Wohnung mit Janas Haus.

_4_ **JANA** Sechs Zimmer. Das hier ist das Wohnzimmer und dann hier links die Küche und das Esszimmer.
_1_ **KLARA** Jana, dein neues Haus ist wirklich schön.
_6_ **JANA** Ja, die Küche gefällt meinem Mann sehr gut. Er kocht so gern! So, und hier rechts siehst du den Flur zu den drei Schlafzimmern und den zwei Badezimmern. Es gibt nur den einen Stock.
_3_ **KLARA** Das stimmt. Wie viele Zimmer hat es?
_7_ **KLARA** Ihr braucht ja auch nicht noch mehr Zimmer. Also, ich muss sagen, du hast ein ganz tolles Haus gefunden.
_2_ **JANA** Danke schön! Es ist ziemlich groß. Die alte Wohnung in der Stadt war einfach zu klein.
_5_ **KLARA** Die Küche ist auch super. Da kann dein Mann leckeres Essen kochen.

7 Expansion Review the differences between **stellen**, **legen**, and **hängen**. Place a classroom eraser horizontally on the desk and say: **Ich legen den Schwamm auf den Tisch.** Then stand the eraser on one end and say: **Ich stelle den Schwamm auf den Tisch.** Finally, tape the **Schwamm** to the wall and say: **Ich hänge den Schwamm an die Wand.**

6 **Mein Zimmer** Beschreiben Sie zwei Mitschülern Ihr Zimmer. Answers will vary.

BEISPIEL

S1: *In meinem Zimmer habe ich ein Bett und einen Schreibtisch.*
S2: *Ich habe auch ein Bett, aber ich habe keinen Schreibtisch.*
S3: *Ich habe in meinem Zimmer einen grünen Teppich...*

7 **Diskutieren und kombinieren** Arbeiten Sie mit einem Partner / einer Partnerin. Ihr Lehrer / Ihre Lehrerin gibt Ihnen zwei verschiedene Blätter mit dem Grundriss (*floor plan*) von Ihrer neuen Wohnung. Sagen Sie Ihrem Partner / Ihrer Partnerin, was Sie alles mitgebracht haben. Er/Sie wird Ihnen sagen, in welche Zimmer Sie die Sachen stellen sollen. Answers will vary.

BEISPIEL

S1: *Ich habe Balkonpflanzen mitgebracht.*
S2: *Stell sie auf den Balkon. Er ist rechts von der Küche. Ich habe...*

7 Suggestion Remind students to use the accusative with two-way prepositions when they tell each other where to place an item.

Aussprache und Rechtschreibung

The letter combination *ch* (Part 2)

To pronounce the soft **ch** after the vowel sounds **i/ie**, **e**, **ä**, **ö**, **ü**, or **ei**, start by placing the tip of your tongue behind your lower teeth. Then pronounce the *h* sound while breathing out forcefully.

Chemie **rechts** **Teppich** **Küche** **leicht**

Use the same soft **ch** sound when pronouncing the **g** in the suffix **-ig** at the end of a word. However, when there is an adjective ending after the **-ig**, the **g** is pronounced like the hard *g* in the word *garden*. In the combination **-iglich**, the **g** is pronounced like the *k* in the word *kind*. The soft **ch** is also used in the suffix **-lich**, whether or not there is an ending after it.

dreckig **schmutzig** **billige** **königlich** **freundlichen**

When **ch** appears before an **s**, the letter combination is pronounced like the *x* in the word *fox*. Do not confuse **chs** with the combination **sch**, which is pronounced like the *sh* in the word *shade*.

sechs **wachsen** **schlafen** **waschen** **Dachs**

When **ch** appears at the beginning of loanwords, its pronunciation varies.

Charakter **Chip** **Chef** **Charterflug** **Chronik**

1 Aussprechen Wiederholen Sie die Wörter, die Sie hören.

1. Bücher
2. freundlich
3. China
4. zwanzig
5. braunhaarige
6. lediglich
7. höchste
8. Achsel
9. Ochse
10. Chaos
11. checken
12. Charme

2 Nachsprechen Wiederholen Sie die Sätze, die Sie hören.

1. Die königliche Köchin schläft wieder in der Küche.
2. Mein neugieriger Nachbar will täglich mit mir sprechen.
3. Den Rechtsanwalt finden wir freundlich und zuverlässig.
4. Der Chef schickt mich nächstes Jahr nach China.
5. Der Dachs hat einen schlechten Charakter.

2 Suggestion Have students take turns reading the sentences aloud. Explain the meaning of any unfamiliar words.

3 Sprichwörter Wiederholen Sie die Sprichwörter, die Sie hören.

[1] Love thy neighbor as thyself.
[2] To each his/her own. (lit. *For every creature its own pleasure.*)

Ressourcen
vText
LM p. 68
vhlcentral

Fotoroman

Besuch von Max

Vorbereitung Have students read the title of the episode and discuss in pairs what they expect to happen in the episode.

Hans' kleiner Bruder Max kommt ihn in Berlin besuchen. Meline ist froh, Max kennen zu lernen. Zu froh, in den Augen von Hans.

GEORGE Max!
MAX Hallo, George!
GEORGE Schön, dich wiederzusehen! Wie viele Nächte schläfst du auf unserem Sofa?
MAX Zwei. Ich bin übers Wochenende in Berlin. Doch bis Sonntagabend muss ich wieder in Straubing sein.

HANS Warum lernst du eigentlich nicht an deinem Schreibtisch in deinem Zimmer?
GEORGE Es ist bequemer im Wohnzimmer, denn die Küche ist gleich nebenan. Und es ist schön hell hier.
HANS Da ist was dran.
MAX Wir gehen in den Biergarten. Komm doch mit.

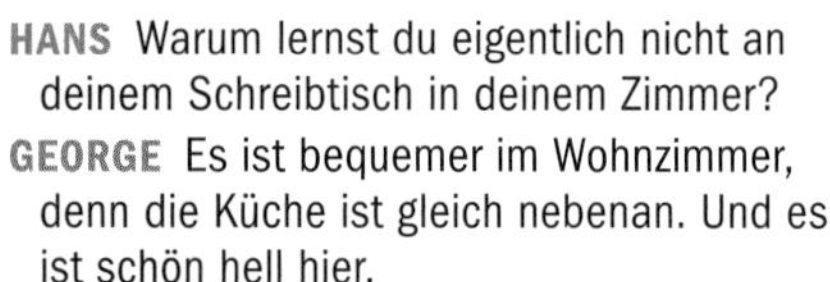

Suggestion Explain to students that **Servus!** means both *Hello!* and *Goodbye!* in Bavaria and Austria.

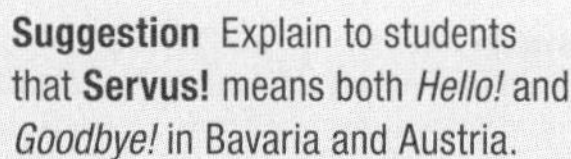

MAX Wir bleiben bestimmt lange dort.
GEORGE Nach dieser Lektion komme ich herunter.
HANS Alles klar! Okay! Servus!

MAX Das tut mir leid.
MELINE Es ist schon okay. Kein Problem.
HANS Meline, das ist mein kleiner Bruder Max.
MELINE Hallo.
MAX Wir gehen in den Biergarten. Komm doch mit uns.
MELINE Ich muss nur noch schnell die Lebensmittel in die Küche bringen.

MELINE Max, ich kann das Regalbrett nicht erreichen. Kannst du mir das dort oben hinstellen?
MAX Deine Wohnung gefällt mir.
MELINE Ja. Die Lampen und Vorhänge gehören Sabite. Und die ganzen Gemälde.

MAX Du bist aus Wien?
MELINE Ja. Hast du das an meinem Akzent erkannt?
MAX Ja. Als Hans zu Weihnachten nach Hause kam, sprach er übrigens von dir.
MELINE Wirklich? Was hat er gesagt?

ÜBUNGEN

1 **Wer ist das?** Welche Person(en) beschreiben die folgenden Sätze: George, Hans, Max, Meline oder Sabite?

1. Er/Sie ist übers Wochenende in Berlin. Max
2. Er/Sie lernt im Wohnzimmer, denn die Küche ist gleich nebenan. George
3. Sie wollen in den Biergarten gehen. Hans und Max
4. Nach einer Lektion kommt er/sie herunter. George
5. Er/Sie muss Lebensmittel in die Küche bringen. Meline
6. Die Wohnung gefällt ihm/ihr. Max
7. Ihm/Ihr gehören die Vorhänge, die Lampen und die Gemälde. Sabite
8. Weihnachten sprach er/sie von Meline. Hans
9. Er/Sie war satt und konnte nicht schlafen. George
10. Er/Sie überlegt, ob (*whether*) Hans und Max wirklich Brüder sind. Meline

PERSONEN

George

Hans

Meline

Max

7

GEORGE Wir hatten Heiligabend ein riesiges Essen.
HANS Es war drei Uhr früh, am Weihnachtsmorgen.
GEORGE Ich war ja noch total satt und konnte nicht einschlafen.
HANS Es war ja noch total dunkel im Haus.

8

GEORGE Ich ging den Gang hinunter und hörte ein Geräusch.
HANS Max, meine Familie und ich, wir schliefen in unseren Zimmern.
GEORGE Ich ging in die Küche, und am Herd stand ihr Großvater.
HANS Opa Otto bereitete die Weihnachtsgans zu. George überraschte ihn und... „Ja! Wo kommst du denn her?"

9

GEORGE Sie war köstlich! Wo ist Sabite heute Abend?
MELINE Mit Torsten weg.
GEORGE Sind sie immer noch zusammen?
MELINE Ja, aber es ist schwierig seit den Feiertagen.

10

MELINE Ich mag Torsten, aber man sagt an Silvester keine Verabredung ab.
HANS So wie Lorenzo?
MELINE Wer?
HANS Na, Lorenzo. Der Italiener.
MELINE Seid ihr wirklich Brüder?

Nützliche Ausdrücke

- **Doch bis Sonntagabend muss ich wieder in Straubing sein.**
  But by Sunday evening I have to be back in Straubing.
- **Da ist was dran.**
  You have a point there.
- **Servus!**
  So long!
- **Ich kann das Regalbrett nicht erreichen.**
  I can't reach the shelf.
- **Kannst du mir das dort oben hinstellen?**
  Can you put this up there for me?
- **das Gemälde**
  painting
- **Hast du das an meinem Akzent erkannt?**
  Could you tell from my accent?
- **riesig**
  huge
- **satt**
  full (of food)
- **das Geräusch**
  noise
- **der Herd**
  stove
- **Opa Otto bereitete die Weihnachtsgans zu.**
  Grandpa Otto was preparing the Christmas goose.

2A.1

- **Als Hans zu Weihnachten nach Hause kam, sprach er übrigens von dir.**
  When Hans was home for Christmas, he talked about you, by the way.

2A.2

- **Nach dieser Lektion komme ich herunter.**
  After this lesson, I'll come down.

2A.3

- **Es ist bequemer im Wohnzimmer, denn die Küche ist gleich nebenan.**
  The living room is more convenient, because it's right next to the kitchen.

2 **Zum Besprechen** George trifft Opa Otto an Heiligabend in der Küche. Bereiten Sie mit einem Partner / einer Partnerin einen kurzen Dialog zwischen George und Opa Otto vor. Präsentieren Sie Ihren Dialog der Klasse. Answers will vary.

Suggestion After each pair has presented their role play, have the class vote on the most interesting, realistic, and convincing performances.

3 **Vertiefung** Suchen Sie im Internet Informationen über die Weihnachtsgans. Woher kommt diese Tradition? In welchen Ländern isst man Weihnachtsgans? Was isst man als Beilage? Schreiben Sie einen kurzen Absatz mit Ihren Ergebnissen. Answers will vary.

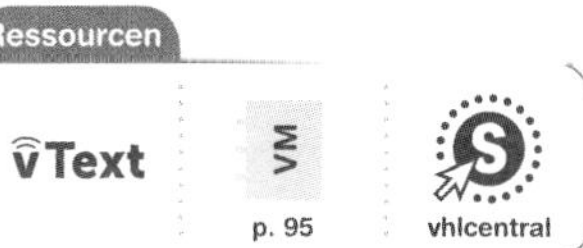

IM FOKUS

AP* Theme: Beauty & Aesthetics
Context: Architecture

Fribourg

Reading

Suggestion Before students read the article, ask them **Welche Sprachen spricht man in der Schweiz?** Have students locate Fribourg on a map of Switzerland. Have them guess what languages are spoken there, based on its location.

FRIBOURG LIEGT GENAU AN DER Grenze° zwischen deutschsprachiger und französischsprachiger Schweiz. Die Saane fließt° durch die Stadt und trennt sie in zwei Teile°. Im westlichen Teil spricht man Französisch und im östlichen Teil Deutsch. Etwa 63% der Bevölkerung spricht Französisch und 21% spricht Deutsch. Studenten können hier in beiden Sprachen studieren und machen einen großen Teil der über 40.000 Einwohner aus. Die Stadt ist sehr alt und existiert bereits seit 1157. Damals war Fribourg noch deutschsprachig.

Wohnen in der Schweiz

- **Wohnungen:** 4,2 Millionen (2013)
- **durchschnittliche° Größe:** 99 m^2
- **durchschnittlicher Kaufpreis für Wohnungen**
  - **Bern:** SFr (Schweizer Franken) 750.000
  - **Zürich:** SFr 1,4 Millionen
  - **durchschnittlicher Mietpreis:** SFr 1.332
  - **Mieteranteil°:** 55,8%

QUELLEN: Schweizerisches Bundesamt für Statistik

TIPP

The abbreviation **St.** stands for **Sankt**, meaning *Saint*.

Die Architektur Fribourgs bietet° Beispiele vieler historischer Epochen. Die Altstadt im Zentrum ist eines der größten geschlossenen Ortsbilder° des mittelalterlichen° Europa. Die St.-Niklaus-Kathedrale, gebaut zwischen 1283 und 1490, ist das Symbol Fribourgs. Es ist ein Beispiel gotischer Architektur. Die Stadt hat über 200 gotische Gebäude. Den Renaissancestil kann man im Ratzéhof sehen, gebaut zwischen 1581 und 1585. Heute ist dieses Gebäude die Heimat° des Museums für Kunst und Geschichte. Neben den vielen alten Teilen der Stadt kann man auch neue Gebäude finden wie zum Beispiel die Universität (1889) oder die Villenviertel° im Gembachquartier. Viele Villen sind Jugendstil-Bauten°. Bekannt sind in Fribourg auch die alten Brücken° und seine zwölf historischen Brunnen°.

Expansion Give students numbers and ask them to explain what each number has to do with Fribourg. Ex.: **21%, 1157, 12,** etc.

Grenze *border* **fließt** *flows* **Teile** *parts* **bietet** *offers* **geschlossenen Ortsbilder** *complete townscapes* **mittelalterlichen** *medieval* **Heimat** *home* **Villenviertel** *mansion district* **Jugendstil-Bauten** *Art Nouveau buildings* **Brücken** *bridges* **Brunnen** *wells* **durchschnittliche** *average* **Mieteranteil** *percentage of renters*

Expansion Have students take turns reading aloud from the article. Ask questions to check comprehension and keep the class engaged. Ex.: **Wie heißt der Fluss von Fribourg? Wo spricht man Französisch? Wie viel Prozent der Bevölkerung spricht Französisch?**

Expansion Have students use an online currency converter to find out how Swiss apartment prices compare to prices in other countries.

ÜBUNGEN

1 Richtig oder falsch? Sind die Aussagen richtig oder falsch? Korrigieren Sie die falschen Aussagen. Answers will vary.

1. Fribourg liegt an der Grenze zwischen der Schweiz und Frankreich.
   Falsch. Fribourg liegt an der Grenze zwischen deutschsprachiger und französischsprachiger Schweiz.
2. Mehr als 60% der Bevölkerung spricht Französisch. Richtig.
3. In Fribourg kann man auf Deutsch oder Französisch studieren. Richtig.
4. Das Symbol Fribourgs ist der Ratzéhof.
   Falsch. Das Symbol Fribourgs ist die St. Niklaus Kathedrale.
5. Der Ratzéhof ist im gotischen Stil gebaut.
   Falsch. Der Ratzéhof ist im Renaissancestil gebaut.
6. Brücken gibt es in Fribourg nicht.
   Falsch. Die alten Brücken in Fribourg sind bekannt.
7. Eine durchschnittliche Wohnung in Zürich kostet SFr 750.000.
   Falsch. Eine durchschnittliche Wohnung in Zürich kostet SFr 1,4 Millionen.
8. Über 50% der Schweizer mieten eine Wohnung. Richtig.

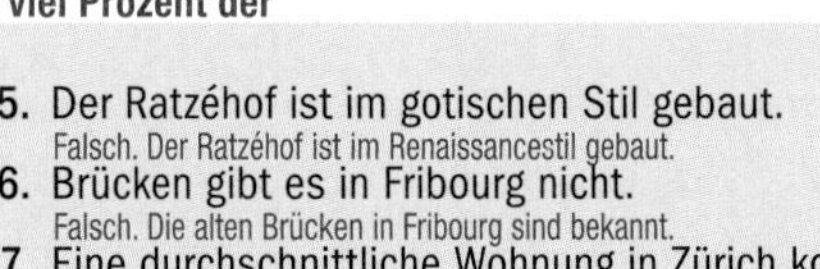

Suggestion Remind students that Switzerland is a neutral country, has not joined the EU, and has also kept its own currency, **der Schweizer Franken.**

Practice more at **vhlcentral.com**.

DEUTSCH IM ALLTAG

Studentenzimmer

der Gemeinschaftsraum	*common room*
die Kaution	*security deposit*
die Miete	*rent*
die Nebenkosten	*additional charges*
die Wohngemeinschaft (WG)	*apartment share*
(un)möbliert	*(un)furnished*
Zimmer frei	*vacancy*

DIE DEUTSCHSPRACHIGE WELT

Chalets

AP* Theme: Beauty & Aesthetics
Context: Architecture

Chalets sind ein Häusertyp. Es ist ursprünglich ein französisches Wort und bedeutet Sennhütte°. Man kann diese Häuser im Alpenbereich allgemein, insbesondere° aber in der Schweiz finden. Früher haben Hirten° in Chalets gewohnt. Traditionell sind sie aus Holz° gebaut. In den Schweizer Gemeinden° Lenk, Grindelwald, Saanen und Zermatt darf man nur Chalets bauen. Moderne Architektur will man so in den Alpen verhindern°. Heute nennt man oft auch Ferienhäuser° aus Holz Chalets. Sie müssen nicht in einer Bergregion stehen, und man findet sie überall auf der Welt.

Sennhütte *herdsman's hut* **insbesondere** *especially* **Hirten** *shepherds* **Holz** *wood* **Gemeinden** *townships* **verhindern** *prevent* **Ferienhäuser** *vacation homes*

PORTRÄT

César Ritz

3 Expansion For homework, have students draw their dream apartments and prepare a written description to present in class.

César Ritz war ein berühmter Schweizer Hotelier. Er wurde am 23. Februar 1850 als dreizehntes Kind einer armen Familie in Niederwald im Goms geboren. Die Schule beendete er nicht. Anfangs arbeitete er als Schuhputzer°, Träger° und Kellner in verschiedenen Hotels. Im Rigi-Kulm-Hotel in der Schweiz wurde er schließlich° Hoteldirektor. 1888 heiratete er die Hotelierstochter Marie-Louise Beck. Er hatte großen Erfolg als Direktor und eröffnete° 1898 das Grandhotel Le Ritz in Paris, 1906 das Hotel Ritz in London und 1910 das Hotel Ritz in Madrid. Alle Hotels gelten° als absolute Luxushotels. Wegen seines großen Erfolgs nannte König Edward VII. César Ritz den „König der Hoteliers und Hotelier der Könige".

AP* Theme: Families and Communities
Context: Urban, Suburban, & Rural Life

Schuhputzer *shoeshine boy* **Träger** *porter* **schließlich** *eventually* **eröffnete** *opened* **gelten** *count*

IM INTERNET

Finden Sie ein Zimmer zum Mieten in einer deutschsprachigen Stadt. Wie groß ist es? Wie viel kostet es? Was ist im Preis inbegriffen (*included*)?

Find out more at **vhlcentral.com**.

3 Suggestion Provide a simple model for this activity describing your own dream apartment. Then ask students about their own preferences. Ex.: **Möchten Sie lieber eine Wohnung mit einem Schwimmbad oder mit einem Atelier? Möchten Sie lieber ein Chalet in den Alpen oder eine Villa am Strand? Möchten Sie lieber ein Schloss in der Schweiz oder eine große Wohnung in Manhattan?**

2 Was fehlt? Ergänzen Sie die Sätze.

1. Chalets sind ein Schweizer ___Häusertyp___.
2. In den Schweizer Alpen sind Chalets aus ___Holz___ gebaut.
3. In Lenk und Grindelwald, darf man nur ___Chalets___ bauen.
4. César Ritz ist ein berühmter ___Schweizer___ Hotelier.
5. Er ist das ___dreizehnte___ Kind seiner Eltern.
6. Die Ritz-Hotels in Paris und London sind absolute ___Luxushotels___.

3 Eine gute Wohnung Diskutieren Sie mit einem Partner / einer Partnerin über die Wohnung, in der Sie wohnen möchten. Reden Sie über Größe, Preis, und Lage (*location*).

Suggestion Before students read the article on César Ritz, preview the relevant vocabulary and concepts. Show the class a picture of a Swiss **Schule**, a **Schuhputzer**, and a fancy hotel. While showing the pictures say: **Dieser Mann kommt aus einer armen Familie. Er beendet die Schule nicht. Er arbeitet als Schuhputzer. Später eröffnet er ein neues großes Hotel.**, etc.

3 Partner Chat You can also assign activity 3 on the Supersite.

Ressourcen

2A.1 The *Präteritum*

QUERVERWEIS

The **Präteritum** appears most often in writing. You will learn more about the uses of the **Präteritum** in **2B.1**.

ACHTUNG

The **ich** form and the **er/sie/es** form are always identical in the **Präteritum**.

Suggestion Tell students that the **Präteritum** is also frequently called the "simple past". Point out that whereas the perfect tense has two parts --the auxiliary and the participle--, the **Präteritum** only has one.

Suggestion Give students a series of weak verbs and have them guess the simple past forms, based on the pattern shown. Ex: **tanzen, machen, leben, kaufen, mieten, vermieten.**

QUERVERWEIS

See **1A.1** to review mixed verbs in the **Perfekt**.

You might want to use **Vol. 1, 4A.1** to review the uses of **mögen**.

Suggestion Emphasize to students that the past tense forms of mixed and strong verbs must be memorized on a verb-by-verb basis.

Startblock In **1A.1**, you learned to use the **Perfekt** to talk about past events. Another tense, the **Präteritum**, is also used to refer to past events.

- To form the **Präteritum** of weak verbs, add **-te**, **-test**, **-ten**, or **-tet** to the infinitive stem. Add an **-e** before these endings if the stem ends in **-d**, **-t**, or a consonant cluster.

Präteritum of weak verbs			
	sagen	**wohnen**	**arbeiten**
ich	**sagte**	**wohnte**	**arbeitete**
du	**sagtest**	**wohntest**	**arbeitetest**
er/sie/es	**sagte**	**wohnte**	**arbeitete**
wir	**sagten**	**wohnten**	**arbeiteten**
ihr	**sagtet**	**wohntet**	**arbeitetet**
Sie/sie	**sagten**	**wohnten**	**arbeiteten**

Die Kinder **spielten** in ihren Zimmern.
*The children **played** in their rooms.*

Ich **mietete** eine kleine Wohnung.
*I **rented** a small apartment.*

- Modal verbs have the same endings as weak verbs in the **Präteritum**. If the modal stem has an **Umlaut**, the **Umlaut** is dropped.

sollen		dürfen	
ich sollte	**wir sollten**	**ich durfte**	**wir durften**
du solltest	**ihr solltet**	**du durftest**	**ihr durftet**
er/sie/es sollte	**Sie/sie sollten**	**er/sie/es durfte**	**Sie/sie durften**

Warum **wolltet** ihr einen neuen Teppich kaufen?
*Why **did** you **want** to buy a new rug?*

Bianca **musste** ihre Großeltern besuchen.
*Bianca **had** to visit her grandparents.*

- The modal **mögen** has an additional stem change in the **Präteritum**. Be careful not to confuse the **Präteritum** form **mochte** with the polite form **möchte**.

Anna **möchte** eine neue Lampe für ihr Schlafzimmer.
*Anna **would like** a new lamp for her bedroom.*

Als Junge **mochte** Peter das Zimmer auf dem Dachboden.
*As a boy, Peter **liked** the room in the attic.*

- The **Präteritum** stem of a mixed verb is the same as the stem of its past participle.

Perfekt and *Präteritum* of mixed verbs		
Infinitiv	**Perfekt**	**Präteritum**
bringen	**er hat gebracht**	**er brachte**
denken	**er hat gedacht**	**er dachte**
kennen	**er hat gekannt**	**er kannte**
wissen	**er hat gewusst**	**er wusste**

Wir **brachten** die Tischlampe ins Arbeitszimmer.
*We **brought** the desk lamp into the office.*

Wusste Daniel Emmas Adresse?
***Did** Daniel **know** Emma's address?*

- Strong verbs in the **Präteritum** have irregular stems and add different endings from those of weak verbs.

beginnen	gefallen	liegen
ich begann	ich gefiel	ich lag
du begannst	du gefielst	du lagst
er/sie/es begann	er/sie/es gefiel	er/sie/es lag
wir begannen	wir gefielen	wir lagen
ihr begannt	ihr gefielt	ihr lagt
Sie/sie begannen	Sie/sie gefielen	Sie/sie lagen

irregular verb stems in the *Präteritum*					
bleiben	**blieb**	helfen	**half**	sehen	**sah**
essen	**aß**	kommen	**kam**	sprechen	**sprach**
fahren	**fuhr**	lesen	**las**	sterben	**starb**
finden	**fand**	nehmen	**nahm**	tragen	**trug**
geben	**gab**	schlafen	**schlief**	trinken	**trank**
gehen	**ging**	schreiben	**schrieb**	verstehen	**verstand**

Wir **blieben** gestern zu Hause.
*We **stayed** home yesterday.*

Ich **aß** ein kleines Stück Kuchen.
*I **ate** a little piece of cake.*

Er **sah** mir in die Augen.
*He **looked** me in the eyes.*

Sie **fuhren** nach Frankfurt.
*They **drove** to Frankfurt.*

- The verbs **sein**, **haben**, and **werden** do not follow the pattern of other irregular verbs.

Suggestion Some students may incorrectly add the **-te** ending to the preterite form of strong verbs, creating nonsense forms such as **begannte** or **gefielte**. Explain that adding **-te** to a strong verb in its simple past form is like adding the -ed ending to an irregular verb like *sang* or *swam* in English.

sein	haben	werden
ich war	ich hatte	ich wurde
du warst	du hattest	du wurdest
er/sie/es war	er/sie/es hatte	er/sie/es wurde
wir waren	wir hatten	wir wurden
ihr wart	ihr hattet	ihr wurdet
Sie/sie waren	Sie/sie hatten	Sie/sie wurden

Es **wurde** schnell dunkel.
*It **got** dark quickly.*

Als Kinder **hatten** wir viele Haustiere.
*We **had** a lot of pets when we were kids.*

Suggestion Have students review the meanings of these verbs before having them practice the simple past forms. Emphasize the vowel change from **bleiben** to **blieb** and **schreiben** to **schrieb**. It may be helpful to remind them that "E-I" says "I" and "I-E" says "E."

ACHTUNG

Note that the **Präteritum** endings for strong verbs follow the same pattern as those of weak and mixed verbs, but without the addition of **-te-** as a past-tense marker.
Also note that the **ich** and **er/sie/es** forms of strong verbs have no added endings in the **Präteritum**.

QUERVERWEIS

See **Appendix A** for a complete list of strong verbs and their **Präteritum** forms.

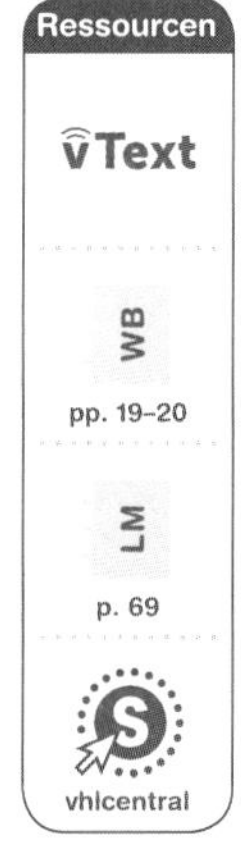

Jetzt sind Sie dran! **Ergänzen Sie die Sätze mit den richtigen Formen der Verben im Präteritum.**

1. Wir ___machten___ (machen) zusammen unsere Hausaufgaben.
2. Die alten Möbel ___waren___ (sein) hässlich.
3. Mein Bruder ___wollte___ (wollen) ein Motorrad zu Weihnachten.
4. Das Mathebuch ___lag___ (liegen) auf dem Schreibtisch.
5. ___Hattet___ (Haben) ihr als Kinder einen Hund?
6. Wolfgang ___trank___ (trinken) Tee zum Frühstück.
7. In der 8. Klasse ___schrieben___ (schreiben) wir jede Woche eine Prüfung.
8. Jan ___kaufte___ (kaufen) die Bluse für seine Freundin.
9. ___Musstest___ (Müssen) du am Donnerstag lange arbeiten?
10. Unsere Eltern ___fuhren___ (fahren) ohne uns in die Türkei.
11. Gestern ___gab___ (geben) es Knödel in der Mensa.
12. Ich ___fand___ (finden) diese Präsentation interessant.

Anwendung

1 **Zeitformen** Wählen Sie für jeden Satz die richtige Zeitform (*tense*).

	Präsens	Perfekt	Präteritum
1. Er ist nach Berlin gereist.	☐	☑	☐
2. Sie arbeitete mit seiner Freundin.	☐	☐	☑
3. Mietet ihr ein Haus am Strand?	☑	☐	☐
4. Hast du schon zu Abend gegessen?	☐	☑	☐
5. Sie hatten viel Spaß auf der Party.	☐	☐	☑
6. Wir kaufen die Möbel bei Ikea.	☑	☐	☐
7. Wie fandest du den Film?	☐	☐	☑
8. Ich konnte gestern nicht kommen.	☐	☐	☑

2 **Sätze umformen** Formen Sie die Sätze vom **Präsens** ins **Präteritum** um.

BEISPIEL **Der Fußballspieler geht nach Europa.**
Der Fußballspieler ging nach Europa.

1. Die Schülerin wohnt bei ihren Eltern.
   Die Schülerin wohnte bei ihren Eltern.
2. Seid ihr verheiratet?
   Wart ihr verheiratet?
3. Ich bringe ihnen eine Zimmerpflanze.
   Ich brachte ihnen eine Zimmerpflanze.
4. Die Schüler bauen Legohäuser.
   Die Schüler bauten Legohäuser.
5. Du gibst ihr ein Hochzeitsgeschenk.
   Du gabst ihr ein Hochzeitsgeschenk.
6. Das Haus hat keinen Keller.
   Das Haus hatte keinen Keller.
7. Wir ziehen nach Hamburg um.
   Wir zogen nach Hamburg um.
8. Sie bleiben eine Woche in Paris.
   Sie blieben eine Woche in Paris.

3 **Der gestrige Tag** Erzählen Sie, was gestern alles passierte. Benutzen Sie das Präteritum.

BEISPIEL **ich / wollen / ins Feinkostgeschäft gehen**
Ich wollte ins Feinkostgeschäft gehen.

1. die Kinder / dürfen / auf die Geburtstagsfeier gehen Die Kinder durften auf die Geburtstagsfeier gehen.
2. wir / müssen / neue Möbel für das Wohnzimmer kaufen Wir mussten neue Möbel für das Wohnzimmer kaufen.
3. Papa / sollen / seine Hemden in die Schublade legen Papa sollte seine Hemden in die Schublade legen.
4. du / wollen / Blumen für den Balkon kaufen Du wolltest Blumen für den Balkon kaufen.
5. ihr / können / leider nicht lange bei uns bleiben Ihr konntet leider nicht lange bei uns bleiben.
6. Sophia / mögen / die Gemüsesuppe nicht Sophia mochte die Gemüsesuppe nicht.

4 **Ein Märchen** Ergänzen Sie die Sätze mit den richtigen Präteritumsformen.

Es (1) ___war___ (sein) einmal ein kleines Mädchen. Ihr Name war Aschenputtel. Ihre Mutter (2) ___starb___ (sterben), als sie jung war. Ihr Vater (3) ___fand___ (finden) bald eine neue Frau. Seine neue Frau (4) ___hatte___ (haben) zwei hässliche Töchter. Die Stiefschwestern und die Stiefmutter (5) ___mochten___ (mögen) Aschenputtel nicht. Aschenputtel (6) ___musste___ (müssen) den Boden wischen, die Wäsche waschen und alle Betten machen. Die bösen Stiefschwestern (7) ___trugen___ (tragen) selber schöne Kleider, aber sie (8) ___gaben___ (geben) Aschenputtel nur ein altes, dreckiges Kleid. Eines Tages (*One day*) (9) ___besuchte___ (besuchen) Aschenputtel das Grab (*grave*) ihrer Mutter. Sie (10) ___sprach___ (sprechen) über ihr Unglück (*misfortune*)...

Practice more at **vhlcentral.com**.

4 Suggestion Ask students if they can guess which famous fairy tale this is. You may want to share the original version of the **Aschenputtel** (*Cinderella*) story with students, and point out how it differs from modern retellings.

4 Expansion For homework, have students write an ending for the story, based on their knowledge of the fairy tale, or from their imaginations.

Kommunikation

5 **Das Leben vor hundert Jahren** Wie war das Leben vor hundert Jahren? Arbeiten Sie mit einem Partner / einer Partnerin und bilden Sie logische Sätze mit Wörtern aus jeder Spalte. Answers will vary.

BEISPIEL

S1: *Jungen konnten allein in den Wald gehen.*
S2: *Frauen konnten nicht an einer Universität studieren.*

Frauen	dürfen	im Garten schlafen
Hunde	können	nicht so viele Prüfungen korrigieren
Jungen	müssen	an einer Universität studieren
Kinder	sollen	allein in den Wald gehen
Mädchen	wollen	viel arbeiten
Männer		in einem großen Kaufhaus einkaufen
Lehrer		Brot backen
Schüler		mit dem Auto fahren

6 **Meine Familie** Erzählen Sie Ihrem Partner / Ihrer Partnerin von Ihrem Familienleben als junges Kind. Benutzen Sie das Präteritum. Answers will vary.

BEISPIEL

S1: *Meine Familie wohnte in New York. Mein Vater war Musiker. Er arbeitete auch in einer Bibliothek. Wir gingen oft am Wochenende zu meinen Großeltern...*
S2: *Ich wohnte zusammen mit meinen Eltern, meinem kleinen Bruder und meiner Oma...*

7 **Ein schöner Tag** Erzählen Sie Ihrem Partner / Ihrer Partnerin von einem sehr schönen Tag in Ihrem Leben. Benutzen Sie das Präteritum. Answers will vary.

BEISPIEL

S1: *Es war ein Samstag. Das Wetter war schön und ich hatte keine Hausaufgaben. Ich ging in die Stadt...*
S2: *Ein sehr schöner Tag war mein 16. Geburtstag. Meine Eltern hatten ein großes Geschenk für mich und es stand vor der Haustür...*

8 **Ein trauriger Tag** Gestern war ein sehr trauriger Tag für Erik. Schreiben Sie mit zwei Mitschülern zusammen eine Geschichte über Eriks Tag. Benutzen Sie das Präteritum. Answers will vary.

BEISPIEL

Erik ging in die Küche. Er fand ein Blatt Papier. Es war von seiner Freundin...

8 Expansion Collect the stories, read them out loud, and have the class guess which group wrote which story. You may want to have students vote for their favorite.

7 Suggestion Before having students work with a partner, give them time to take notes and prepare. You might want to give them a list of verbs in the simple past. Ex.: **aß, gab, bekam, ging, fand, trank, machte, sagte, arbeitete, besuchte, spielte, schlief, lag, hatte, war, wohnte, kaufte, verlor.**

7 Partner Chat You can also assign activity 7 on the Supersite. Students work in pairs to record the activity online. The pair's recorded conversation will appear in your gradebook.

2A.2 *Da-, wo-, hin-,* and *her-* compounds

Suggestion Write some common **da**-compounds on the board, along with their English equivalents. Ex.: **darüber** (*about that*), **darunter** (*under that*). Give concrete examples for each, such as: **Hier ist mein Rucksack. Darunter ist der Stuhl und darunter ist der Boden.** Have students guess the meanings of other **da**-compounds. Ex.: **dazwischen, danach, daneben, davor, darauf, dahinter**.

QUERVERWEIS

See **1B.3** to review two-way prepositions.

Many German verbs are used idiomatically with certain prepositions. You will learn more about these verbs in **3A.2**.

You might want to use **Vol. 1, 3B.2** to review accusative prepositions; **Vol. 1, 4B.2** to review dative prepositions; and **Vol. 1, 4B.1** to review the use of **wen** and **wem**.

Expansion Give students clues using **da**-compounds and have them guess which item in the classroom you're referring to. Ex.: **Damit schreibt man. Darauf sitzen die Studenten. Darunter sind wir alle. Damit lernen wir Deutsch. Max sitzt daneben**. Have students write their own **da**-compound riddles to share with the class.

ACHTUNG

Note that **warten auf** (*to wait for*), **denken an** (*to think about*), and **sprechen über** (*to talk about*) always take accusative objects.

Startblock In German, personal pronouns following a preposition can only refer to people. Special forms are used when the object of the preposition refers to a thing or an idea.

Als Hans zu Weihnachten nach Hause kam, sprach er übrigens **von dir**.

Davon nehme ich einen Teller, bitte.

- Use personal pronouns to refer to the object of a preposition. When the object is a thing or an idea, use a **da**-compound instead.

Kennst du Alex? Wir sind am Samstag **mit ihm** essen gegangen.
*Do you know Alex? We went out to eat **with him** on Saturday.*

Wo ist der Teddybär? Das Baby will **damit** spielen.
*Where's the teddy bear? The baby wants to play **with it**.*

- Form a **da**-compound by adding **da-** to a preposition. If the preposition begins with a vowel, insert an **-r-** after **da-**.

common da-compounds	
dafür davon davor	daran darauf darin

Wo ist der Bus? Wir warten seit einer halben Stunde **darauf**.
*Where's the bus? We've been waiting **for it** for half an hour.*

—Hat Max dir ein Geschenk gegeben?
—Ja, und ich habe ihm **dafür** gedankt.
Did Max give you a present?
*—Yes, and I thanked him **for it**.*

- German speakers often drop the **-a-** in **da**-compounds that begin with **dar-**.

Wer ist da **drin**?
*Who's **in** there?*

Denk mal **drüber** nach.
*Think it **over**.*

- Use **wen** or **wem** to ask about the object of a preposition when it refers to a person. When you ask about a thing or idea, use a **wo**-compound.

Mit wem seid ihr ins Restaurant gegangen?
***Who** did you go to the restaurant **with**?*

Womit spielt die Katze?
***What** is the cat playing **with**?*

- Form a **wo**-compound by combining **wo(r)-** with a preposition.

common wo-compounds	
wofür wovon wovor	woran worauf worin

Wofür braucht sie den Spiegel?
***What** does she need the mirror **for**?*

Woran denkst du jetzt?
***What** are you thinking **about** now?*

Worüber sprecht ihr?
***What** are you talking **about**?*

- Use **wohin** to ask *where to*? and **woher** to ask *from where*? In conversation, **hin** and **her** can be separated from **wo**, moving to the end of the sentence.

Wohin soll ich den Spiegel hängen? *Where should I hang the mirror?*	**Woher** hast du diese Möbel bekommen? *Where did you get this furniture?*
Wo gehst du jetzt **hin**? *Where are you going **to** now?*	**Wo** kommst du **her**? *Where are you **from**?*

- Use the adverb **dahin** or **daher** to replace a prepositional phrase expressing motion.

Reist ihr **in die Schweiz**? *Are you going **to Switzerland**?*	Ja, wir reisen **dahin**. *Yes, we're going **there**.*

- **Hin** or **her** can also be combined with the prefix of a separable prefix verb, to indicate motion. Note that **hin** generally indicates motion *away* from the speaker, while **her** indicates motion *toward* the speaker.

Birgit **geht** die Treppe **hinauf**. *Birgit **is going up** the stairs.*	Paul **kommt** die Treppe **herunter**. *Paul **is coming down** the stairs.*
Komm **herein** oder geh **hinaus**! *Either come **in** or go **out**!*	Rapunzel, lass dein Haar **herunter**! *Rapunzel, let **down** your hair!*

Suggestion The **Jetzt sind Sie dran!** activity helps to underscore the fact that **da**- and **wo**-compounds are not used when the pronoun refers to a person. Go over the answers as a class, and emphasize that since items 2, 4, and 7 refer to people, they must use the preposition with a personal pronoun.

- Compound prefixes like **herauf**-, **herein**-, **herunter**-, or **heraus**- are often shortened in spoken German to **rauf**-, **rein**-, **runter**-, **raus**-, and so on.

Lässt du mich bitte ins Badezimmer **rein**? *Will you please **let** me **into** the bathroom?*	Papa soll die alte Kommode in den Keller **runterbringen**. *Dad is supposed to **bring** the old dresser **down** to the basement.*

QUERVERWEIS

See **1B.3** to review the difference between **wo** and **wohin**.

ACHTUNG

The phrase **hin und her** means *back and forth:* **Warum laufen die Kinder hin und her?**

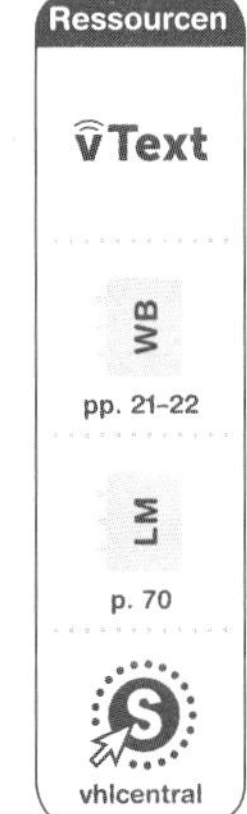

Jetzt sind Sie dran! **Wählen Sie die richtigen Formen.**

1. (Woher / Wohin) kommt das Sprichwort „Zeit ist Geld"?
2. (Womit / Mit wem) hast du auf der Party getanzt?
3. (Womit / Mit wem) sollen wir anfangen?
4. Hast du Herrn Schulz gesehen? Ich denke oft (an ihn / daran).
5. (Wohin / Woher) soll ich die Lampe stellen?
6. (Wofür / Für wen) brauchst du so viele Bleistifte?
7. Marie ist wirklich unangenehm. Ich will nicht (damit / mit ihr) sprechen.
8. So eine schöne Vase! Wir danken euch sehr (für sie / dafür).
9. Die neue Wohnung ist wunderschön! Paul und Fabian haben viel (über sie / darüber) geredet.
10. (Woher / Wohin) bekomme ich das Geld für die Miete?

2 Suggestion Before they complete the activity, have students identify which noun is being replaced in each sentence.

Anwendung

1 Ersetzungen Ersetzen Sie die Satzteile mit den entsprechenden **wo-** oder **da-Komposita.**

1. **wo-**: vor dem Kaufhaus wovor
2. **wo-**: unter dem Teppich worunter
3. **da-**: über das Buch darüber
4. **da-**: gegen die Wand dagegen
5. **wo-**: aus Baumwolle woraus
6. **da-**: für das Geschenk dafür
7. **wo-**: mit dem Fahrrad womit
8. **da-**: hinter der Schule dahinter

2 Was ist richtig? Wählen Sie die passenden Präposition + Pronomen-Verbindungen oder die passenden **da-Komposita.**

1. Mias Cousinen wohnen in Wels. Letzten Sommer hat sie (bei ihnen / dabei) gewohnt.
2. Laura gab mir ein Geburtstagsgeschenk und ich dankte ihr (für es / dafür).
3. Frank ist gegen diese Idee und seine Freunde sind auch alle (gegen ihn / dagegen).
4. Meine große Schwester hat mir immer bei den Hausaufgaben geholfen. Ich habe sie täglich (mit ihr / damit) zusammen gemacht.
5. Simon spricht selten über Politik. Seine Freundin diskutiert aber gern (über sie / darüber).

3 Was fehlt? Ergänzen Sie die Sätze mit den passenden Wörtern. Bilden Sie Kombinationen mit **hin** oder **her.**

BEISPIEL

Jasmin *geht* die Treppe *hinauf* (hinaufgehen).

1. Der Junge klettert den Baum hinauf (hinaufklettern).

2. Der Kellner kommt mit der Speisekarte heraus (herauskommen).

3. Herr Scholz geht in die Metzgerei hinein (hineingehen).

4. Die Blätter (*leaves*) fallen von den Bäumen herunter (herunterfallen).

4 Fragen bilden Was sind die Fragen zu den Antworten?

BEISPIEL Zur Schule fahre ich mit dem Bus.
Womit fährst du zur Schule?

1. Lukas geht mit seiner Schwester ins Theater. Mit wem geht Lukas ins Theater?
2. Sarah ist gegen die Gartentür gefahren. Wogegen ist Sarah gefahren?
3. Das neue Sofa ist aus Leder gemacht. Woraus ist das neue Sofa gemacht?
4. Die Vorlesung war über Neurobiologie. Worüber war die Vorlesung?

Practice more at **vhlcentral.com.**

Kommunikation

5 **Hin oder her?** **Entscheiden Sie mit Ihrem Partner / Ihrer Partnerin, welches Verb zu jedem Bild passt, und beantworten Sie die Fragen.** Sample answers are provided.

herauskommen | hinausgehen | hineingehen | hinfallen | hinstellen

BEISPIEL **Was macht der Kellner?**
Er stellt das Essen hin.

1. Was ist der Frau passiert? Sie ist hingefallen.

2. Papa kommt gerade von der Arbeit. Was macht er? Er geht hinein.

3. Was will das Kind machen? Es will hinausgehen.

4. Herr und Frau Koch waren im Konzert. Was machen sie jetzt? Sie kommen heraus.

6 **So bin ich** **Stellen Sie Ihrem Partner / Ihrer Partnerin die Fragen.** Answers will vary.

BEISPIEL **Worüber lachst du oft?**
Ich lache oft über meine Katze. Sie ist immer so lustig.

1. Woher kommt deine Familie?
2. Worüber sprichst du gern?
3. Wohin gehst du gern?
4. An wen denkst du oft?

7 **Mein bester Freund** **Wie ist der beste Freund / die beste Freundin von Ihrem Partner / Ihrer Partnerin? Stellen Sie Fragen und benutzen Sie wo-Komposita oder Präposition + wen/wem.** Answers will vary.

BEISPIEL **sehr viel wissen / über**
S1: *Worüber weiß dein bester Freund sehr viel?*
S2: *Er weiß sehr viel über Rockmusik.*

1. oft denken / an
2. selten Probleme haben / mit
3. gern ausgehen / mit
4. mit dir sprechen / über

8 **Mein Zimmer** **Beschreiben Sie Ihr Zimmer. Benutzen Sie da-Komposita. Ihr Partner / Ihre Partnerin versucht dann, ein Bild von Ihrem Zimmer zu zeichnen. Dann tauschen Sie die Rollen.** Answers will vary.

BEISPIEL *Da ist mein Bett. Darauf liegt eine Bettdecke von meiner Oma, und darüber hängt ein Poster. Mein Nachttisch steht neben dem Bett. Darauf liegt…*

hängen	links davon	an	über	hinter
liegen	rechts davon	auf	unter	vor
stehen	zwischen	in	neben	

5 Expansion TPR (total physical response) exercises can be useful for demonstrating the difference between **hin** and **her**. Give students a list of commands and have them take turns giving and following the commands Ex.: **Geh zur Tür hin! Komm wieder zu mir her! Geh aus dem Klassenzimmer hinaus! Komm herauf zu mir! Gehen wir beide die Treppe hinunter!**

5 Virtual Chat You can also assign activity 5 on the Supersite. Students record individual responses that appear in your gradebook.

6 Suggestion Have students ask you the questions, so that they can hear more sample answers. Remind them that they can give creative or humorous responses when answering the questions.

6 Virtual Chat You can also assign activity 6 on the Supersite.

7 Suggestion Introduce the activity by bringing a picture of your own best friend and modeling questions and answers. Ex.: **Das ist ein guter Freund von mir, Todd. Worüber spricht er mit mir? Er spricht gern über sein Hobby, Radfahren. An wen denkt er oft? Er denkt oft an seine Freundin Mary.**

7 Partner Chat You can also assign activity 7 on the Supersite. Students work in pairs to record the activity online. The pair's recorded conversation will appear in your gradebook.

2A.3 Coordinating conjunctions

You might want to direct the students to **Vol.1, 1B.2** to review conjunctions **und, oder,** and **aber.**

Suggestion Remind students what conjunctions are, and have them give you examples in English. Tell them that German has three kinds — adverbial, coordinating, and subordinating. Explain that coordinating conjunctions have no impact on word order, and are simply inserted between two clauses like a plus sign.

Suggestion Tell students that whenever *but* can be replaced with *rather* in English, the equivalent German conjunction will be **sondern**.

Startblock Use coordinating conjunctions to combine two related sentences, words, or phrases into a single sentence.

Ich ging in die Küche, **und** am Herd stand ihr Großvater.

Es ist bequemer hier, **denn** die Küche ist gleich nebenan.

- The most common coordinating conjunctions are **aber, denn** (*for, because*), **oder, sondern** (*but rather/instead*), and **und.**

Ich habe eine Wohnung mit großer Küche gemietet, **denn** ich koche gern.
*I rented an apartment with a big kitchen, **because** I like to cook.*

Lina braucht einen Schrank **oder** eine Kommode für ihre Kleider.
*Lina needs a closet **or** a dresser for her clothes.*

- Both **aber** and **sondern** correspond to the English word *but*. **Sondern** is used after a negated clause and indicates that the two ideas being coordinated are mutually exclusive.

Erik hat ein großes Sofa, **aber** er sitzt gern auf dem Boden.
*Erik has a big sofa, **but** he likes to sit on the floor.*

Meine Wohnung ist nicht im Erdgeschoss, **sondern** im ersten Stock.
*My apartment is not on the ground floor, **but rather** on the second floor.*

- When two clauses are connected by a coordinating conjunction, both follow normal subject-verb word order. Always use a comma before **aber, denn,** and **sondern.**

Die Katze sitzt auf dem Balkon **und der Hund liegt** auf dem Teppich.
*The cat is sitting on the balcony **and the dog is lying** on the carpet.*

Ihr esst immer im Esszimmer, **aber wir essen** gern in der Küche.
*You always eat in the dining room, **but we** like to **eat** in the kitchen.*

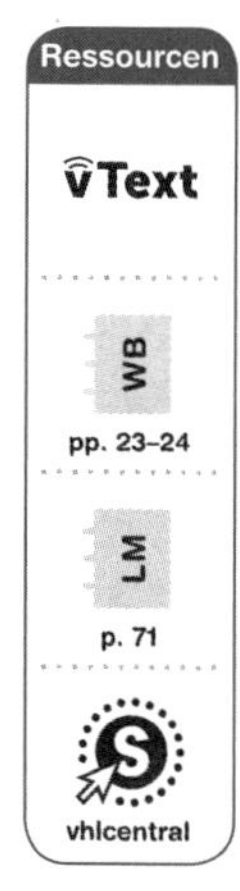

Jetzt sind Sie dran! **Wählen Sie die passende Konjunktion.**

1. Seine Schwester hat einen braunen Sessel (und / sondern) ein blaues Sofa im Wohnzimmer.
2. Im Keller ist es nicht warm, (sondern / aber) kalt.
3. Wir haben ein Haus mit einer großen Garage gekauft, (und / denn) wir haben zwei Autos.
4. Ich liebe Schokolade, (denn / aber) ich bin leider auf Diät.
5. Annika kauft gern Pflanzen für ihr Arbeitszimmer, (aber / denn) sie liebt die Natur.
6. Die Kinder wollen spielen, (sondern / aber) sie müssen ihre Hausaufgaben machen.
7. Wohnst du in einem Haus (oder / sondern) mietest du eine Wohnung?
8. Auf meinem Schreibtisch habe ich eine Lampe (und / denn) ein hübsches Bild von meiner Freundin.
9. Ich parke mein Auto nicht auf der Straße, (sondern / aber) in der Garage.
10. Zieht ihr im Januar (denn / oder) im Februar um?

Anwendung und Kommunikation

1 **Aber oder sondern?** Ergänzen Sie die Sätze mit **aber** oder **sondern**.

1. Nils ist intelligent, ___aber___ ein bisschen schüchtern.
2. Er und seine Frau wohnen in Deutschland, ___aber___ sie kommen aus den USA.
3. Anna studiert nicht mehr an der Universität, ___sondern___ arbeitet jetzt als Architektin.
4. Sie wollten letztes Jahr in ein neues Haus umziehen, ___aber___ es war zu teuer.
5. Ihre Kinder sind nicht in der Schule, ___sondern___ im Kindergarten.

1 Suggestion Remind students that **sondern** follows negative statements, so if the first clause contains the word **nicht**, the correct "but" will be probably be **sondern**.

2 **Was und warum** Bilden Sie logische Sätze aus Spalte A und B und verbinden Sie sie mit **aber**, **oder**, **denn**, **und** oder **sondern**. Sample answers are provided.

BEISPIEL

Ich arbeitete gerne mit Antonia, denn sie war sehr fleißig.

A	B
Ich arbeitete immer gerne mit Antonia.	*Sie fanden dort einen günstigen Kleiderschrank.*
Sie waren beim Möbelhaus Fischer.	*Sie war fleißig.*
Hannes wollte das gestreifte Hemd kaufen.	*Er wollte nicht im Erdgeschoss wohnen.*
Sie kauften kein zweites Auto.	*Sie kauften ein Fahrrad.*
Er wollte ein Zimmer bei einer Familie mieten.	*Es war zu eng.*
Ich bin heute Abend zu Hause geblieben.	*Ich war sehr müde.*

2 Sample answers: Sie waren beim Möbelhaus Fischer und sie fanden dort einen günstigen Kleiderschrank. / Hannes wollte das gestreifte Hemd kaufen, aber es war zu eng. / Sie kauften kein zweites Auto, sondern ein Fahrrad. / Er wollte ein Zimmer bei einer Familie mieten, aber er wollte nicht im Erdgeschoss wohnen. / Ich bin heute Abend zu Hause geblieben, denn ich war sehr müde.

3 **Lara und ihre Familie** Erfinden Sie einen passenden Satz zu jedem Bild, und benutzen Sie dabei die angegebenen Konjunktionen. Answers will vary.

BEISPIEL sondern

Lara hat keinen Hund, sondern eine Katze.

1. oder

2. und

3. und

4. oder

3 Expansion Invite students to draw their own simple pictures. Then have them share their pictures in small groups and generate captions together using coordinating conjunctions.

Practice more at vhlcentral.com.

Wiederholung

1 Umzug Lena reist viel. Sprechen Sie mit einem Partner / einer Partnerin darüber, wo Lena war und was sie machte. Sample answers are provided.

1 Virtual Chat You can also assign activity 1 on the Supersite.

BEISPIEL München / Oktoberfest besuchen

S1: *In München besuchte Lena das Oktoberfest.*
S2: *In Berlin…*

1. Berlin / das Brandenburger Tor sehen In Berlin sah sie das Brandenburger Tor.
2. Hamburg / ein Konzert hören In Hamburg hörte sie ein Konzert.
3. Düsseldorf / in der Königsallee wohnen In Düsseldorf wohnte sie in der Königsallee.
4. Köln / ein Fahrrad kaufen In Köln kaufte sie ein Fahrrad.
5. Heidelberg / Chemie studieren In Heidelberg studierte sie Chemie.

2 Eine laute Party Sie sind auf einer Party, aber die Musik ist sehr laut, und Sie können nicht gut hören. Fragen Sie Ihren Partner / Ihre Partnerin, was er/sie gesagt hat. Answers may vary. Sample answers are provided.

BEISPIEL Am Montag / ins Musikgeschäft gehen möchten

S1: *Am Montag möchte ich ins Musikgeschäft gehen.*
S2: *Wie bitte? Wohin möchtest du gehen?*

1. am Dienstag / in der Mensa essen wollen Wo willst du essen?
2. im Sommer / nach Österreich reisen möchten Wohin möchtest du reisen?
3. am Freitag / im Schwimmbad schwimmen können Wo kannst du schwimmen?
4. am Wochenende / für die Physikprüfung lernen sollen Wofür sollst du lernen?
5. nächste Woche / einen Essay über München schreiben müssen Worüber musst du schreiben?
6. morgen Abend / mit den Eltern im Restaurant essen können Mit wem kannst du essen?/Wo kannst du essen?
7. morgen Nachmittag / lange in der Bibliothek bleiben müssen Wo musst du lange bleiben?
8. im Winter / in den Alpen Ski fahren wollen Wo willst du Ski fahren?

2 Virtual Chat You can also assign activity 2 on the Supersite.

3 Expansion Before beginning the info-gap activity, show students a picture of a room and ask true or false questions about the picture using **da**-compounds. Ex.: **Richtig oder falsch? Das Zimmer hat keine Lampe. Es gibt ein Bett. Daneben ist ein Nachttisch. Darauf liegt ein Buch. Darüber hängt ein Poster.**

3 Diskutieren und kombinieren Sie und Ihr Partner / Ihre Partnerin bekommen zwei Blätter mit verschiedenen Bildern. Vergleichen Sie die Bilder, und machen Sie eine Liste mit den sieben Unterschieden auf den Bildern. Answers will vary.

BEISPIEL

S1: *Es gibt nur ein Bett und eine Lampe rechts daneben, vor dem Fenster.*
S2: *Ich habe auch ein Bett, aber ich habe keine Lampe, …*

4 Im Stadtzentrum Erzählen Sie Ihrem Partner / Ihrer Partnerin, was Sie am Dienstag im Stadtzentrum machten. Wählen Sie ein Wort aus jeder Spalte und bilden Sie logische Sätze. Answers will vary.

BEISPIEL

S1: *Am Dienstag lasen wir Bücher in der Bibliothek.*
S2: *An der Uni sprach ich mit…*

A	B	C
Bücher	mit Freunden	essen
Meeresfrüchte	Kaffee	fahren
an der Uni	Kleider	finden
im Café	Steak	kaufen
im Modegeschäft	auf dem Markt	kommen
im Restaurant „Tivoli“	durch die Stadt	lesen
mit dem Fahrrad	in der Bibliothek	spazieren
langsam	in die Stadt	sprechen
spät	nach Hause	trinken

5 Arbeitsblatt Fragen Sie Ihre Klassenkameraden, ob Sie die Aktivitäten in der Liste gern machen. Finden Sie eine Person für jede Aktivität. Answers will vary.

BEISPIEL

S1: *Fährst du gern mit dem Fahrrad?*
S2: *Ja, ich fahre gern damit.*

6 Das Wochenende Erzählen Sie sich gegenseitig, was sie am Wochenende gemacht haben. Nennen Sie mindestens sechs Dinge und auch einen Grund für jede Aktivität. Answers will vary.

6 Partner Chat You can also assign activity 6 on the Supersite.

BEISPIEL

S1: *Am Samstagmorgen war ich drei Stunden in der Bibliothek, denn ich musste einen Essay für mein Literaturseminar schreiben.*
S2: *Am Samstagmorgen war ich nicht in der Bibliothek, sondern ich sollte mit meiner Mannschaft Fußball spielen…*

Video

AP* Theme: Personal & Public Identities
Context: Gender Identity

Hausarbeit

Das Schweizer Fernsehen° produziert deutschsprachige Fernsehsendungen für das Schweizer Publikum. Die Sendung „Tagesschau" ist das Programm, das täglich die meisten Zuschauer hat. Die folgende TV-Reportage aus der Tagesschau berichtet, wie viel Hausarbeit Schweizer Männer heute machen. Die Reportage basiert auf einer Studie der Schweizer Regierung°. Die Art der Arbeit, die Männer und Frauen zu Hause machen, ist unterschiedlich°.

Immer mehr Frauen mit Kindern sind berufstätig°.

Väter mit kleinen Kindern helfen mehr im Haushalt.

Dass beide Geschlechter zu Hause gleich viel° arbeiten, davon sind wir noch weit weg°.

Fernsehen *television* **Regierung** *government* **unterschiedlich** *different* **Geschlecht** *gender* **berufstätig** *working* **gleich viel** *the same amount* **weit weg** *far away*

Verständnis Beantworten Sie die Fragen mit den Informationen aus dem Video.

1. Laut (*according to*) des Videos, welche Aktivität machen normalerweise die Männer zu Hause?

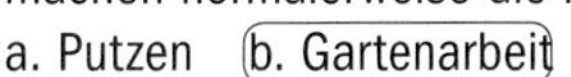

a. Putzen (b. Gartenarbeit) c. Bügeln

2. Welche Aktivität machen Frauen *und* Männer?

a. Aufräumen b. Waschen (c. Kochen)

Diskussion. Besprechen Sie die folgenden Fragen mit einem Partner / einer Partnerin. Answers will vary.

1. Wer macht was in Ihrem Haushalt? Arbeiten die Männer und die Frauen in Ihre Familie gleich viel zu Hause?
2. Schreiben Sie eine kurze Szene über ein berufstätiges Paar. Die beiden Partner diskutieren, wie die Hausarbeit aufgeteilt sein soll.

Kontext

Communicative Goals

You will learn how to:

- talk about household chores
- talk about appliances

Hausarbeit

Vocabulary Tools

AP* Theme: Families & Communities
Context: Urban, Suburban, & Rural Life

Expansion Play "vocabulary bingo" with your students. Give students a list of 16 words from **2A** and **2B** and have them fill in a 4 X 4 grid with the words in mixed-up order. Then given an oral definition for each word. Ex: **Das ist grün. Es lebt. Es ist in einem Topf in meinem Wohnzimmer. (Die Pflanze.) Das ist wie ein Besen mit einem Motor. Damit mache ich meine Teppiche sauber. (Der Staubsauger)** As you define a word, students call out the answer and everyone gets to put an 'X' in the corresponding box. The first student to complete a row or column calls out **Ich gewinne**.

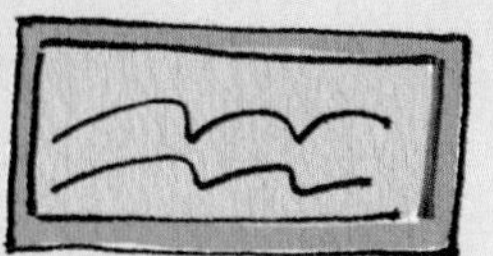

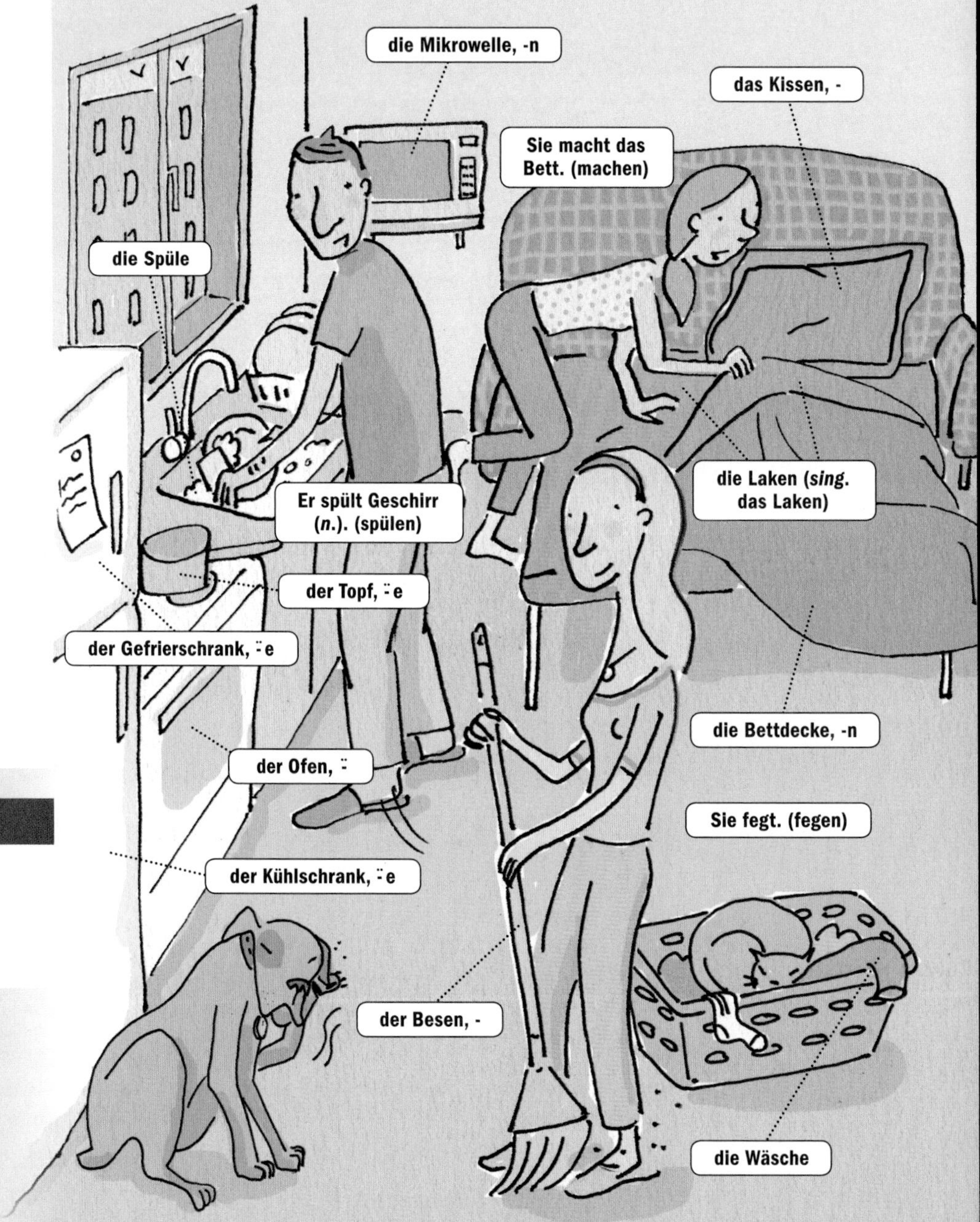

die Mikrowelle, -n
das Kissen, -
Sie macht das Bett. (machen)
die Spüle
die Laken (*sing.* das Laken)
Er spült Geschirr (*n.*). (spülen)
der Topf, ¨-e
der Gefrierschrank, ¨-e
die Bettdecke, -n
der Ofen, ¨
Sie fegt. (fegen)
der Kühlschrank, ¨-e
der Besen, -
die Wäsche

Wortschatz

die Hausarbeit	***housework***
den Tisch decken	*to set the table*
staubsaugen	*to vacuum*
Wäsche waschen	*to do laundry*
Haushaltsartikel	***household items***
die Decke, -n	*blanket*
der Herd, -e	*stove*
die Kaffeemaschine, -n	*coffeemaker*
die Pfanne, -n	*pan*
die Spülmaschine, -n	*dishwasher*
der Staubsauger, -	*vacuum cleaner*
der Toaster, -	*toaster*
der Wäschetrockner, -	*dryer*
die Waschmaschine, -n	*washing machine*
zum Beschreiben	***to describe***
dreckig	*filthy*
ordentlich	*tidy*
sauber	*clean*
schmutzig	*dirty*
Es ist ein Saustall!	*It's a pigsty!*
Verben	***verbs***
aufräumen (räumt... auf)	*to clean up*
putzen	*to clean*
waschen	*to wash*
wischen	*to wipe; to mop*

ACHTUNG

German speakers often shorten a compound when the context is clear:
Anja wirft die Wäsche in den Trockner.
But: **Der Wäschetrockner ist kaputt.**

Suggestion Ask students to describe their house, apartment, or dorm room using three adjectives, including at least one from the **zum Beschreiben** list.

Ressourcen

vText

WB pp. 25–26

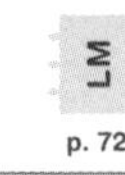
LM p. 72

vhlcentral

Expansion Have students write **wo**-compound questions related to the lesson vocabulary and share them with the class. **Womit mache ich mir einen Toast? Womit fegt man den Boden?**

Anwendung

3 Expansion Divide the class into small groups. Assign each group one of the sentences from this activity, and have them turn the sentence into a short dialogue. Have each group perform their dialogue for the class.

1 Was passt nicht? Welches Wort passt nicht zu den anderen?

BEISPIEL Topf, Pfanne, Ofen, (Müll)

1. Spülmaschine, Geschirr, (Besen), Spüle
2. schmutzig, (sauber), unordentlich, dreckig
3. (Herd), Kissen, Decke, Laken
4. spülen, waschen, bügeln, (mieten)
5. fegen, (wohnen), wischen, staubsaugen
6. putzen, (umziehen), wischen, aufräumen
7. Mikrowelle, Toaster, (Staubsauger), Ofen
8. (Saustall), Bügeleisen, Wäsche, Bügelbrett

2 Vergleiche Ergänzen Sie die Analogien mit einem Wort aus der Liste.

faul	staubsaugen
fegen	schmutzig
Gefrierschrank	Spülmaschine
Laken	Teppich

1. Hose ⟶ Waschmaschine // Messer ⟶ Spülmaschine
2. Bügeleisen ⟶ bügeln // Besen ⟶ fegen
3. weiß ⟶ schwarz // sauber ⟶ schmutzig/dreckig
4. Wäsche ⟶ waschen // Teppich ⟶ staubsaugen
5. Mantel ⟶ Kleid // Decke ⟶ Laken
6. Ofen ⟶ Herd // Kühlschrank ⟶ Gefrierschrank

3 Was fehlt? Ergänzen Sie die Sätze mit dem richtigen Wort.

1. In der Küche ist das pure Chaos! Wir müssen sie wirklich heute noch (dreckig / (sauber)) machen.
2. Ich spüle das Geschirr und du (fegst / (bügelst)) die Hemden.
3. Wir können die Kleider nicht waschen. Die (Spülmaschine / (Waschmaschine)) ist kaputt.
4. Die Lasagne backt schon seit zwei Stunden im ((Ofen) / Topf), aber sie braucht nur 50 Minuten. Weißt du das?
5. Die Sonne brennt heute richtig! Gib bitte den ((Pflanzen) / Decken) auf dem Balkon mehr Wasser.
6. Diese Töpfe sind dreckig! Wir müssen (Wäsche waschen / (Geschirr spülen))!

4 Der Besuch Im Haus von Familie Fuchs ist es noch ein bisschen unordentlich. Hören Sie zu und markieren Sie, welche Hausarbeiten Frau Fuchs den Familienmitgliedern gibt.

4 Suggestion Ask students guiding questions to keep in mind as they listen to the recording. Ex.: **Diese Familie muss das Haus aufräumen. Warum? Wer kommt zu Besuch? Was müssen sie alles machen?**

b 1. Claudia
e 2. Erik
f 3. Frau Fuchs
b/d 4. Lukas
c 5. Nina
a 6. Peter

a. Bad putzen
b. Betten machen
c. Geschirr spülen
d. Hund waschen
e. Müll rausbringen
f. staubsaugen

Kommunikation

5 Räumen wir auf! Die Wohnung ist mal wieder ein Saustall! Diskutieren Sie mit zwei Mitschülern, welche Hausarbeiten jeder von Ihnen heute noch macht. Machen Sie dann auch einen Wochenplan, worin steht, wer in der Woche was machen muss, damit (*so that*) die Wohnung sauber bleibt. Answers will vary.

BEISPIEL

S1: *Wer spült das Geschirr?*
S2: *Ich spüle das Geschirr. Und wer...?*

5 Expansion After students have completed their partner conversations, ask them whether they think the housework is divided up fairly in their own families.

6 Hausarbeiten Besprechen Sie mit Ihrem Partner / Ihrer Partnerin, wer in Ihrer Familie die angegebenen (*indicated*) Hausarbeiten macht. Answers will vary.

BEISPIEL

Betten machen
S1: *Bei uns in der Familie macht meine Mutter die Betten.*
S2: *Ich mache mein Bett jeden Morgen.*

1. Geschirr spülen
2. Kleider bügeln
3. Müll rausbringen
4. Staub wischen
5. Toilette putzen
6. Wäsche waschen

6 Virtual Chat You can also assign activity 6 on the Supersite.

7 Expansion Have students write about their own experiences from the day before, using modals in the simple past: What did they have to do yesterday? (**Ich musste...**) What did they want to do? (**Ich wollte...**) What could they or could they not do? (**Ich konnte...**) What did they enjoy doing? (**Ich mochte...**)

7 Diskutieren und kombinieren Gestern Abend haben Tim und Lara eine große Party gegeben, aber heute müssen sie alles aufräumen. Ihr Lehrer / Ihre Lehrerin gibt Ihnen und Ihrem Partner / Ihrer Partnerin zwei verschiedene Blätter mit Informationen über Tim und Laras Tag. Erzählen Sie einander, was Tim und Lara heute machen. Schreiben Sie dann einen kurzen Absatz über ihren Tag.

BEISPIEL

S1: *Um Viertel nach zehn räumt Lara den Tisch auf. Was macht Tim um Viertel nach zehn?*
S2: *Um Viertel nach zehn macht Tim das Bett.*

8 Mein Traumhaus Beschreiben Sie Ihrem Partner / Ihrer Partnerin Ihr Traumhaus: wo ist es, wie groß ist es, wie viele Stockwerke und Zimmer hat es, welche Möbel und Haushaltsartikel haben Sie, und wer macht die diversen Hausarbeiten?

8 Virtual Chat You can also assign activity 8 on the Supersite.

BEISPIEL

S1: *Mein Traumhaus ist am Strand und es hat fünf Schlafzimmer, vier Badezimmer, ein Studierzimmer und auch eine große Garage für drei Autos. Im Garten ist ein Schwimmbad und ein zweites, kleines Haus für meine acht Hunde.*
S2: *Mein Traumhaus ist in der Stadt. Es hat...*

8 Suggestion Give students a few minutes to make notes about their dream house before they work with a partner. Encourage them to be creative and to include lots of detail.

Aussprache und Rechtschreibung

The German *k* sound

The German **k** is pronounced like the *k* in the English word *kind*. At the end of a syllable, this sound may be written as **ck**.

Kaffee **Laken** **Decke** **Frack** **Kreide**

In a few loanwords, the **c** at the beginning of a word is pronounced like a **k**. In other loanwords, the initial **c** may be pronounced similarly to the *ts* in *cats* or the *c* in *cello*.

Computer **Caravan** **Couch** **Celsius** **Cello**

When the consonant combination **kn** appears at the beginning of a word, both letters are pronounced. In the combination **nk**, the sound is very similar to the *nk* in the English word *thank*.

Knie **knusprig** **Knödel** **danken** **Schrank**

Remember that the **ch** sound and the **k/ck** sound are pronounced differently.

dich **dick** **Bach** **Back**

Suggestion Tell students that a distinctive feature of Swiss German is the pronunciation of the initial **k** sound, as in the word **Kirche**. It is pronounced as a **k** immediately followed by the back **ch** sound (IPA [*kx*]).

1 Aussprechen Wiederholen Sie die Wörter, die Sie hören.

1. Keller
2. Keramik
3. Stock
4. Container
5. Cola
6. Celsius
7. knackig
8. Knallfrosch
9. Bank
10. Hockey
11. lach
12. Lack

2 Nachsprechen Wiederholen Sie die Sätze, die Sie hören.

1. In der Küche backt man Kekse.
2. Deine Kleider hängen im Kleiderschrank.
3. In Frankfurt essen glückliche Kinder knackige Bockwürste.
4. Mein Lieblingsmöbelstück ist diese knallrote Couch.
5. Wir kaufen das Cabriolet in Köln.
6. Kann Klaus Knödel kochen?

3 Sprichwörter Wiederholen Sie die Sprichwörter, die Sie hören.

[1] Talking it up is part of the trade. (lit. *Rattling is part of the trade.*)

[2] We'll figure it out with time. (lit. *With time comes counsel.*)

Ich putze gern!

Meline und Sabite wollen die Wohnung aufräumen, doch plötzlich hat Meline eine wichtige Verabredung. Muss Sabite jetzt alleine putzen?

Vorbereitung In preparation for this episode, have students list in German all the chores they typically do around the house.

NATIONAL STANDARDS communication cultures

MELINE Super. Ich treffe dich dann dort in einer halben Stunde.
SABITE Wohin gehst du?
MELINE Meine Freundin Beatrice besucht ihre Großmutter in Wilmersdorf und sie haben mich zum Tee zu sich eingeladen.
SABITE Wir haben darüber gesprochen, die Wohnung zu putzen. Sie ist ein Saustall.

MELINE Das können wir doch später machen.
SABITE Meline, seit wir hier eingezogen sind, hast du nicht ein Mal bei der Hausarbeit geholfen. Du hast kein Geschirr gewaschen, den Boden nicht gefegt und auch die Möbel nicht abgestaubt.

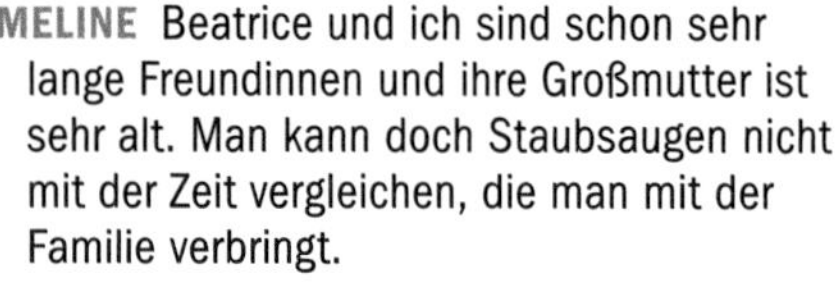

MELINE Beatrice und ich sind schon sehr lange Freundinnen und ihre Großmutter ist sehr alt. Man kann doch Staubsaugen nicht mit der Zeit vergleichen, die man mit der Familie verbringt.
SABITE Warte. Nimm den Abfall mit raus.

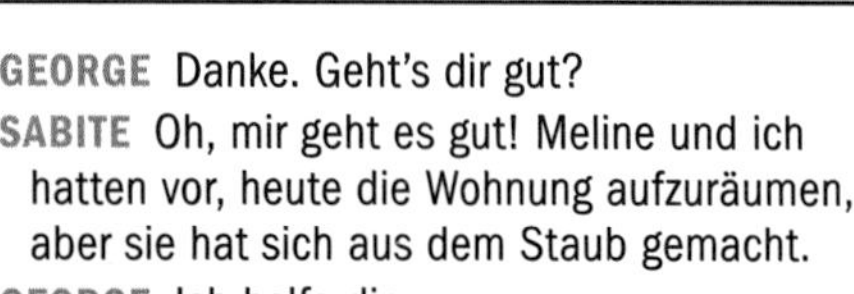

GEORGE Danke. Geht's dir gut?
SABITE Oh, mir geht es gut! Meline und ich hatten vor, heute die Wohnung aufzuräumen, aber sie hat sich aus dem Staub gemacht.
GEORGE Ich helfe dir.

GEORGE Ich wusste nicht, dass Mädchen so...
SABITE Unordentlich sein können?
GEORGE Letzte Woche sah es hier tadellos aus. Was ist passiert?
SABITE Es ist so stressig an der Uni. Wir haben keine Zeit zum Putzen. Und Meline macht keine Hausarbeiten.

SABITE Das kann ich von dir nicht verlangen. Es ist schmutzig hier drin.
GEORGE Ich hatte als Kind ein Zimmer mit meinem Bruder zusammen. Er war superfaul. Ich habe die Betten gemacht und die Wäsche gewaschen.

Suggestion Have students do this activity with their books closed. Divide the class into groups and see how many questions each group can answer correctly.

ÜBUNGEN

1 Richtig oder falsch? Entscheiden Sie, ob die folgenden Sätze richtig oder falsch sind.

1. Meline besucht eine Freundin in Wilmersdorf. Richtig.
2. Sabite und Meline wollten die Wohnung putzen. Richtig.
3. Meline hilft oft bei der Hausarbeit. Falsch.
4. Meline muss den Abfall mit rausnehmen. Richtig.
5. Sabite ist glücklich darüber, dass Meline nicht hilft. Falsch.
6. George hatte als Kind ein Zimmer allein. Falsch.
7. Er hat die Betten gemacht und die Wäsche gewaschen. Richtig.
8. Sabite und Meline haben keine Zeit zum Putzen. Richtig.
9. George und Sabite haben Melines Wäsche gefaltet. Falsch.
10. Meline muss ihre Bluse bügeln. Falsch.

PERSONEN

George

Meline

Sabite

7

Suggestion Explain to students that although there is no official progressive verb form in German, the so-called **am-Progressiv** (or **Rheinische Verlaufsform**) is increasingly common in standard German: **Da du gerade am Bügeln bist...** (*Since you're ironing...*).

SABITE Vielen Dank für deine Hilfe, George.
GEORGE Ich putze gern. Aber sag das bitte nicht Hans.
MELINE Oh, George. Ich dachte, dass du Torsten bist. Beatrices Großmutter hat einen Mandelkuchen gebacken. Das wird euch aufheitern.

Suggestion Tell students that the expression **sich aus dem Staub machen** originally referred to soldiers who, wanting to escape from their compulsory military service, would take advantage of the large amounts of dust kicked up during battles to sneak away without being detected.

8

SABITE Wir haben die Böden gefegt, das Geschirr gewaschen, den Herd geputzt, Staub gesaugt und abgestaubt.
GEORGE Wir haben die Töpfe und Pfannen weggeräumt und eklige Dinge aus dem Kühlschrank und dem Spülbecken entfernt.

9

SABITE Deine Wäsche haben wir *nicht* gefaltet.

10

MELINE Ach, dieses Kleid möchte ich heute Abend anziehen. Jetzt muss ich bügeln.
SABITE Oh, Meline, da du gerade am Bügeln bist... Danke!

Nützliche Ausdrücke

- **Sie haben mich zum Tee zu sich eingeladen.**
  They invited me over for tea.
- **einziehen**
  to move in
- **nicht ein Mal**
  not even once
- **Man kann doch Staubsaugen nicht mit der Zeit vergleichen, die man mit der Familie verbringt.**
  You can't compare vacuuming to spending time with family.
- **Sie hat sich aus dem Staub gemacht.**
  She ran away.
- **tadellos**
  spotless
- **der Mandelkuchen**
  almond cake
- **aufheitern**
  to cheer up
- **eklig**
  disgusting
- **Da du gerade am Bügeln bist...**
  Since you're ironing...

2B.1

- **Ich habe die Betten gemacht und die Wäsche gewaschen.**
  I made the beds and did the laundry.
- **Ich hatte als Kind ein Zimmer mit meinem Bruder zusammen.**
  I shared a bedroom with my brother when I was a kid.

2B.2

- **Wir haben die Töpfe und Pfannen weggeräumt und eklige Dinge aus dem Kühlschrank und dem Spülbecken entfernt.**
  We put away all the pots and pans, and got rid of disgusting things from the refrigerator and the kitchen sink.

2 **Zum Besprechen** Stellen Sie sich vor (*Imagine*), Ihre Wohnung ist so ein „Saustall" wie die von Sabite und Meline. Machen Sie zu dritt einen Plan, um die Wohnung aufzuräumen. Wer macht was? Arbeiten Sie zusammen oder alleine? Was machen Sie zuerst? Answers will vary.

3 **Vertiefung** Sabites Professor hat das Gedicht „Kenner und Enthusiast" von Goethe zitiert, um ihr Kunstprojekt zu kommentieren. Suchen Sie das Gedicht im Internet. Finden Sie heraus, wie die Strophe (*stanza*) weitergeht. Um ihn versammelten Männer sich, Die ihn einen Kenner nannten.

3 Expansion In class, discuss the meaning of the Goethe poem "**Kenner und Enthusiast**". For homework, have students find out more about Goethe and prepare a brief report to present to the class.

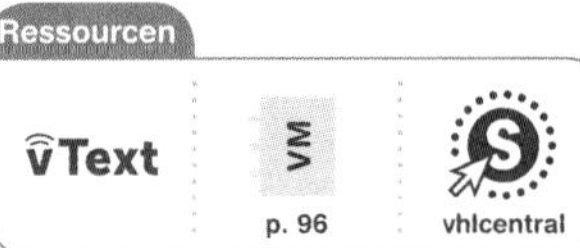

IM FOKUS

AP* Theme: Science & Technology
Context: Social Impacts

Suggestion Before they read the text, ask students what appliances they have in their home or dorm and which ones they use the most. Ex.: **Hast du einen Kühlschrank? Eine Mikrowelle? Eine Kaffeemaschine? Welche von diesen Geräten gebrauchst du jeden Tag?**

Haushaltsgeräte°

Reading

Einige wichtige Haushaltsgeräte wurden von Technikern deutschsprachiger Länder erfunden°.

Thermoskannen

In einer Thermoskanne bleiben Getränke länger warm. Der Chemnitzer Professor Adolf Ferdinand Weinhold entdeckte° 1881 ein Prinzip, damit Glasgefäße° weniger Wärme verlieren. Reinhold Burger, ein anderer Deutscher, forschte° an einer Nutzung° dieses Prinzips. 1903 registrierte er sein Patent. Die Flaschen hatten eine Silberbeschichtung° und ein schützendes Metallgehäuse°. 1909 verkaufte Burger sein Patent an die Charlottenburger Thermos AG. Deshalb heißen diese Flaschen heute Thermosflaschen. Die erste Serienproduktion fand 1920 statt.

Kaffeefilter

Für das Kaffeekochen braucht man Kaffeefilter. Ein sehr bekannter Name bei Kaffeefiltern ist Melitta. Der Firmenname geht zurück auf Melitta Bentz aus Dresden. 1908 revolutionierte sie das Kaffeekochen. Sie verwendete° ein Stück Filterpapier und einen durchlöchterten Messingtopf°. Damit filterte sie den bitteren Kaffeesatz°. Aus dieser Idee entstand das Kaffeefiltern mit Kaffeefilter und Filterpapier. Das Patent erhielt Melitta Bentz am 20. Juni 1908 vom Kaiserlichen Patentamt in Berlin.

Nähmaschinen°

Eine Nähmaschine ist eine Maschine für die Kleiderproduktion. Die erste Nähmaschinenfirma, Bernina International AG, wurde von Karl Friedrich Gegauf gegründet°. Gegauf wusste, dass Nähen kompliziert und arbeitsaufwendig° sein kann. 1893 erfand er die erste Hohlsaum°-Nähmaschine der Welt. Damit konnte man 100 Stiche pro Minute nähen. 1885 zerstörte ein Großbrand° die Werkstatt der Gebrüder Gegauf komplett; lediglich der Prototyp der Hohlsaum-Nähmaschine konnte gerettet werden°. Heute ist Bernina eine sehr erfolgreiche Firma in der Schweiz.

Haushaltsgerätehersteller in Deutschland	
Bauknecht: Küchengeräte	1.917 Mitarbeiter in Deutschland
Bosch/Siemens: Haushaltsgeräte	14.642 Mitarbeiter in Deutschland
Liebherr: Kühlschränke und Gefriertruhen°	1.775 Mitarbeiter in Deutschland
Miele: Elektro-Haushaltsgeräte	11.000 Mitarbeiter in Deutschland
Rowenta: Küchen- und Haushaltsgeräte	1.100 Mitarbeiter in Deutschland

QUELLE: Statistisches Bundesamt Deutschland

Haushaltsgeräte *appliances* **wurden... erfunden** *were invented* **entdeckte** *discovered* **Glasgefäße** *glass containers* **forschte** *researched* **Nutzung** *use* **Silberbeschichtung** *silver coating* **schützendes Metallgehäuse** *protective metal casing* **verwendete** *used* **durchlöchterten Messingtopf** *perforated brass pot* **Kaffeesatz** *coffee grounds* **Nähmaschinen** *sewing machines* **wurde... gegründet** *was founded* **arbeitsaufwendig** *labor-intensive* **Hohlsaum** *hemstitch seam* **Großbrand** *large fire* **gerettet werden** *be saved* **Gefriertruhen** *freezers*

Suggestion Remind students that they don't have to understand every word and should focus instead on key words and main themes. Give them targeted pre-reading questions to help them pick out key information. Ex.: **Seit wann gibt es Kühlschränke? Was braucht man für das Kaffeekochen? Wer erfand die erste Hohlsaum-Nähmaschine?**

ÜBUNGEN

1 Richtig oder falsch? Sind die Aussagen richtig oder falsch? Korrigieren Sie die falschen Aussagen. Answers will vary.

1. In Thermoskannen bleiben Getränke länger warm. Richtig.
2. Adolf Ferdinand Weinhold registrierte 1903 ein Patent für Thermoskannen. Falsch. Reinhold Burger registrierte das Patent für Thermoskannen.
3. Melitta ist ein bekannter Name bei Kaffeefiltern. Richtig.
4. 1904 revolutionierte Melitta Bentz das Kaffeekochen. Falsch. 1908 revolutionierte Melitta Bentz das Kaffeekochen.
5. Melitta Bentz kommt aus Österreich. Falsch. Melitta Bentz kommt aus Deutschland.
6. Karl Friedrich Gegauf erfand in der Schweiz eine Nähmaschine. Richtig.
7. Seine Nähmaschine nähte 50 Stiche pro Minute. Falsch. Seine Nähmaschine nähte 100 Stiche pro Minute.
8. Der Prototyp der Hohlsaum-Nähmaschine wurde 1885 von einem Großbrand zerstört. Falsch. Der Großbrand zerstörte die Werkstatt der Gebrüder Gegauf, aber nicht den Prototyp der Hohlsaum-Nähmaschine.
9. Miele produziert Elektro-Haushaltsgeräte und hat in Deutschland 11.000 Mitarbeiter. Richtig.
10. Rowenta produziert nur Küchengeräte. Falsch. Rowenta produziert Küchen- und Haushaltsgeräte.

Practice more at vhlcentral.com.

DEUTSCH IM ALLTAG

Materialien

die Fliesen (*pl.*)	*tiles*
der Granit	*granite*
das Holz	*wood*
die Keramik	*ceramic*
der Kunststoff	*plastic*
das Leder	*leather*
der Marmor	*marble*
der Stahl	*steel*

DIE DEUTSCHSPRACHIGE WELT

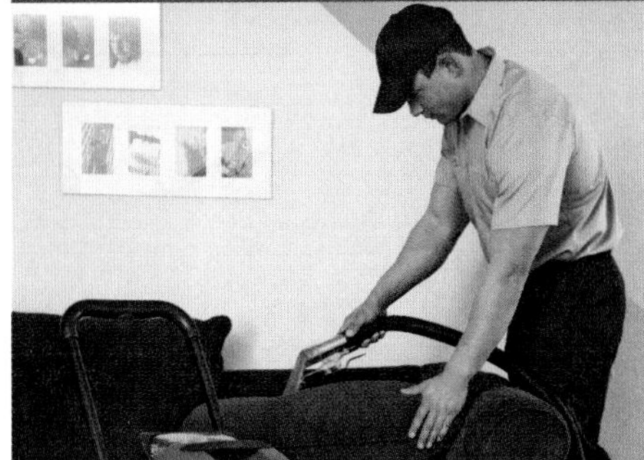

Fachleute Hauswirtschaft°

Ein offizieller Beruf in der Schweiz ist Fachmann/Fachfrau Hauswirtschaft. Personen mit diesem Beruf sind Experten für Hausarbeit. Das Berufsziel°: Menschen fühlen sich in ihrer Wohnung wohl°. Deshalb putzen sie Zimmer schnell, gründlich° und umweltschonend°. Bei Schäden° in Zimmern reparieren sie diese Schäden. Fachleute Hauswirtschaft arbeiten in Heimen°, Krankenhäusern°, Hotels und Restaurants. Die Ausbildung° dauert drei Jahre. Man muss in einem Betrieb° arbeiten, jede Woche einen Tag in die Schule gehen und am Ende Prüfungen machen.

Fachleute Hauswirtschaft *home economics specialists* **Berufsziel** *professional aim* **fühlen sich... wohl** *feel comfortable* **gründlich** *thoroughly* **umweltschonend** *environmentally friendly* **Schäden** *damages* **Heimen** *(nursing) homes* **Krankenhäusern** *hospitals* **Ausbildung** *training* **Betrieb** *firm*

AP* Theme: Contemporary Life
Context: Education & Career

PORTRÄT

Johanna Spyri

Johanna Spyri (1827-1901), geborene Heusser, war eine sehr erfolgreiche° Schweizer Autorin. Sie war das vierte von sechs Kindern. Bis sie 25 Jahre alt war, unterrichtete sie ihre jüngeren Geschwister und half ihrer Mutter im Haushalt. 1852 heiratete sie den Rechtsberater Johann Bernhard Spyri. Ihr Mann war nicht oft zu Hause und Johanna Spyri mochte Hausarbeit nicht. Deshalb animierte° sie ein Freund, der Pastor Cornelius Rudolph Vietor, zum Schreiben. 1871 veröffentlichte° sie ihre erste Geschichte „Ein Blatt auf Vronys Grab". Es war ein großer Erfolg. Später schrieb sie ihr berühmtestes Buch „Heidis Lehr- und Wanderjahre" über das Waisenmädchen° Heidi. Es ist ein Roman° über die romantische Idylle der Schweizer Alpen. Dieser Roman alleine existiert in mehr als 50 Sprachen. Insgesamt schrieb Spyri 31 Bücher, 27 Erzählbände° und 48 Erzählungen°.

AP* Theme: Beauty & Aesthetics
Context: Language & Literature

erfolgreich *successful* **animierte** *encouraged* **veröffentlichte** *published* **Waisenmädchen** *orphan girl* **Roman** *novel* **Erzählbände** *anthologies* **Erzählungen** *stories*

IM INTERNET

Suchen Sie Stellenangebote als Fachmann/frau Hauswirtschaft in der Schweiz. Was muss man machen? Schreiben Sie Beispiele auf.

Find out more at **vhlcentral.com**.

Suggestion Before they read the article on Johanna Spyri, have students scan the text and underline all the **Präteritum** forms they can find.

2 **Was fehlt?** Ergänzen Sie die Sätze.

1. Ein Fachmann / Eine Fachfrau Hauswirtschaft ist ein Experte für _Hausarbeit_.
2. Fachleute Hauswirtschaft reparieren _Schäden_ in Zimmern.
3. Die Ausbildung für Fachleute Hauswirtschaft dauert _3 Jahre_.
4. Johanna Spyri fing mit dem Schreiben an, denn sie mochte _Hausarbeit_ nicht.
5. Das bekannteste Buch Spyris ist über das Waisenmädchen _Heidi_.
6. Dieses Buch existiert in mehr als 50 _Sprachen_.

3 **Ihre Traumküche** Diskutieren Sie mit einem Partner / einer Partnerin Ihre Traumküche. Welche Geräte sind in der Küche? Aus welchen Materialien ist die Küche? Ist die Traumküche klein, groß, hell, etc.? Wie sieht die Küche Ihres Partners aus?

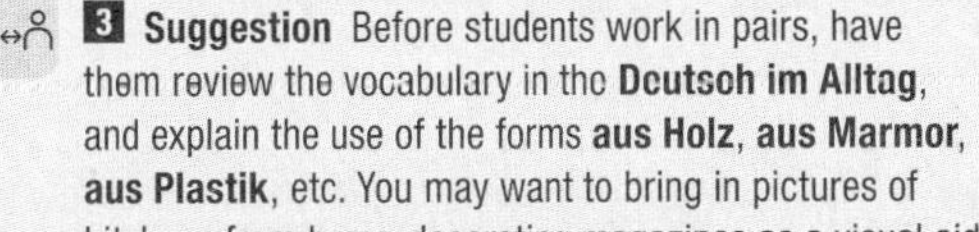

3 Suggestion Before students work in pairs, have them review the vocabulary in the **Deutsch im Alltag**, and explain the use of the forms **aus Holz**, **aus Marmor**, **aus Plastik**, etc. You may want to bring in pictures of kitchens from home-decorating magazines as a visual aid.

Ressourcen

Strukturen

2B.1 *Perfekt versus Präteritum*

Suggestion Tell students that the use of the **Präteritum** in speech varies regionally. Although rarely used in Southern Germany or Austria, it is somewhat more common in parts of Northern Germany.

Startblock You have learned to use both the **Perfekt** and the **Präteritum** to talk about past events. However, these two tenses are not used interchangeably.

QUERVERWEIS

See **1A.1** and **1B.1** to review the formation of the **Perfekt**.

See **2A.1** to review the formation of the **Präteritum**.

- The **Perfekt** tense is most often used in conversation and in informal writing, such as e-mails, blog entries, personal letters, or diaries.

Habt ihr den Tisch **gedeckt**?
*Did you **set** the table?*

Nein, aber wir **haben** den Boden **gewischt**.
*No, but we **mopped** the floor.*

- The **Präteritum** is generally used in formal or literary writing, such as novels or newspaper articles, or in other formal contexts, such as news reports or speeches. It is sometimes called the *narrative past*, since it is often used to narrate a series of related past events.

Suggestion Tell students that German speakers sometimes use the **Präteritum** in speech when narrating a long string of events.

Es **war** einmal eine junge Frau mit dem Namen Aschenputtel.
*Once upon a time, there **was** a young woman named Cinderella.*

Jeden Tag **fegte** sie den Boden, **machte** sie die Betten und **spülte** sie das Geschirr.
*Every day, she **swept** the floors, **made** the beds, and **washed** the dishes.*

- A few specific verbs are commonly used in the **Präteritum**, even in informal contexts. In conversation, German speakers typically use the **Präteritum** of **sein**, **haben**, and modal verbs, rather than the **Perfekt**.

Hattet ihr am Mittwoch keine Hausaufgaben?
*Didn't you **have** any homework on Wednesday?*

Meine alte Wohnung **war** ein Saustall.
*My old apartment **was** a pigsty.*

Die Kinder **wollten** das Gemüse nicht essen.
*The kids **didn't want** to eat their vegetables.*

Solltet ihr gestern nicht staubsaugen?
***Weren't** you **supposed** to vacuum yesterday?*

Students will learn more about subordinating conjunctions in **Vol. 3, 2A.1**.

QUERVERWEIS

You will learn more about **als** and other subordinating conjunctions in **4A.1**.

- The **Präteritum** is also preferred by most speakers after the subordinating conjunction **als**.

Als wir Kinder **waren**, haben wir viel Hausarbeit gemacht.
***When** we **were** kids, we did a lot of housework.*

Als ich die Garage **aufräumte**, habe ich viele alte Bücher gefunden.
***When** I **cleaned up** the garage, I found lots of old books.*

Suggestion Have students orally review the coordinating conjunctions they learned in **2A.3**. Tell them that **als** is a subordinating conjunction. Have them look at the examples with **als**, and point out its effect on word order.

- German verbs are usually listed in dictionaries and vocabulary lists by their *principal parts* (**Stammformen**): the infinitive, the third-person singular form of the **Präteritum**, and the past participle. For verbs with stem changes in the **Präsens**, the third-person singular form is given in parentheses. For completely regular verbs, only the infinitive is listed.

geben (gibt)	**gab**	**gegeben**
to give (gives)	*gave*	*given*

- Knowing the principal parts of a verb allows you to produce all of its conjugations in any tense. Here are the principal parts of some of the verbs you've learned so far.

infinitive	*Präteritum*	past participle
bringen	brachte	gebracht
denken	dachte	gedacht
essen (isst)	aß	gegessen
helfen (hilft)	half	geholfen
laufen (läuft)	lief	ist gelaufen
nehmen (nimmt)	nahm	genommen
schlafen (schläft)	schlief	geschlafen
sehen (sieht)	sah	gesehen
sitzen	saß	gesessen
verstehen	verstand	verstanden
waschen (wäscht)	wusch	gewaschen
wissen (weiß)	wusste	gewusst

Sie **nahm** einen Besen und **gab** ihrem Bruder den Staubsauger.
*She **took** a broom and **gave** her brother the vacuum cleaner.*

Ich **habe** nur einen Keks **genommen** und habe Peter die anderen **gegeben**.
*I only **took** one cookie and **gave** the rest to Peter.*

Suggestion Go over the verbs in this list and make sure students remember their meanings. Then have them close their books and quiz them on the past tense forms. Give them infinitives from the list and have them call out the preterite and perfect forms.

Expansion Give students the first sentence of a story using the preterite. One at a time, have students add a sentence to the story, on a piece of paper folded so that only the previous sentence is visible. When everyone has contributed, unfold the paper and share the story with the class.

QUERVERWEIS

See **Appendix A** for a complete list of strong verbs with their principal parts.

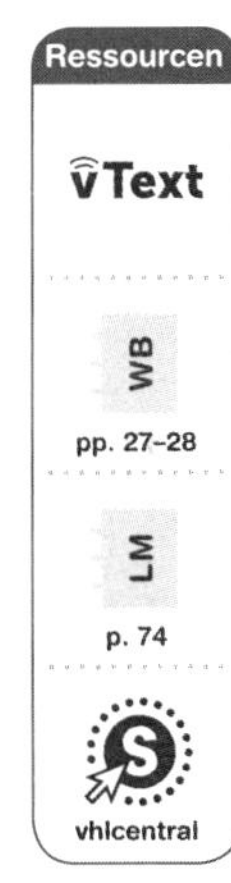

Jetzt sind Sie dran! **Wählen Sie die richtige Zeitform (*tense*) für die folgenden Sätze.**

1. Es war einmal ein Mädchen mit dem Namen Rapunzel. (Perfekt / (Präteritum))
2. Der Junge saß allein in seinem Zimmer und weinte. (Perfekt / (Präteritum))
3. Donnerstags wusch ich die Wäsche. (Perfekt / (Präteritum))
4. Was hast du an der Universität studiert? ((Perfekt) / Präteritum)
5. Meine Eltern haben ein Haus in München gemietet. ((Perfekt) / Präteritum)
6. Sie wollten schon immer in Bayern wohnen. (Perfekt / (Präteritum))
7. Hast du schon den Balkon gefegt? ((Perfekt) / Präteritum)
8. Heute Morgen war die Mikrowelle noch sauber. (Perfekt / (Präteritum))
9. In meiner alten Wohnung hatte ich eine Spülmaschine. (Perfekt / (Präteritum))
10. Die ganze Familie hat Alex bei seinem Umzug geholfen. ((Perfekt) / Präteritum)
11. In seiner neuen Wohnung konnte er sehr gut schlafen. (Perfekt / (Präteritum))
12. Er hat wirklich Glück gehabt. ((Perfekt) / Präteritum)

1 Suggestion Remind students that postcards, although written, tend to be informal and chatty and reflect spoken language.

Anwendung

1 Perfekt oder Präteritum? Welche Zeitform benutzt man gewöhnlich (*generally*) in diesen Situationen?

▶ **BEISPIEL** Perfekt

1. Präteritum

2. Perfekt

3. Perfekt

4. Präteritum

2 Was fehlt? Ergänzen Sie die Tabelle mit den fehlenden Informationen.

	Infinitiv	Präteritum	Perfekt
1.	dürfen	durfte	hat gedurft
2.	gehen	ging	ist gegangen
3.	fahren	fuhr	ist gefahren
4.	nehmen	nahm	hat genommen
5.	kommen	kam	ist gekommen
6.	sehen	sah	hat gesehen
7.	bringen	brachte	hat gebracht
8.	mögen	mochte	hat gemocht

3 Suggestion Use this activity to verify that students understand the basic guidelines regarding when to use the **Präteritum** as opposed to the **Perfekt**.

3 Ein kurzes Gespräch Ergänzen Sie die Sätze mit den fehlenden Verbformen im Perfekt oder im Präteritum.

BEISPIEL **SARA** Was ___hast___ du gestern Abend ___gemacht___? (*machen*)

ANNA Ich (1) ___sollte___ in die Bibliothek gehen, aber Michael (2) ___wollte___ mit mir spazieren gehen. Es (3) ___war___ langweilig. (sollen, wollen, sein)

SARA Ach ja? (4) ___Musste___ er nicht mit Mira einkaufen gehen? (müssen)

ANNA Mira (5) ___konnte___ nicht, denn ihre Eltern (6) ___sind___ zum Abendessen (7) ___gekommen___. (können, kommen)

SARA Haha! Das (8) ___hat___ sie bestimmt toll (9) ___gefunden___. (finden)

ANNA Das weiß ich nicht. Ich (10) ___habe___ heute nicht mit ihr (11) ___gesprochen___. (sprechen)

Practice more at vhlcentral.com.

Kommunikation

4 **Ein bisschen Geschichte** Erraten Sie zusammen mit Ihrem Partner / Ihrer Partnerin, welches Ereignis (*event*) zu welchem historischen Datum passt.

BEISPIEL

S1: *Was ist im Jahr 2005 passiert?*
S2: *2005 ist Angela Merkel als erste Frau Bundeskanzlerin von Deutschland geworden.*

Historisches Datum	Ereignis
b **1.** 1295	**a.** Die Berliner Mauer fiel.
d **2.** 1492	**b.** Marco Polo brachte chinesische Nudeln nach Italien.
c **3.** 1824	**c.** Ludwig van Beethoven komponierte seine 9. Sinfonie.
e **4.** 1918	**d.** Christoph Kolumbus reiste nach Amerika.
a **5.** 1989	**e.** Deutschland verlor den Ersten Weltkrieg (*World War*).
f **6.** 2005	**f.** Angela Merkel wurde als erste Frau Bundeskanzlerin von Deutschland.

5 **Julians Kalender** Erzählen Sie zusammen mit Ihrem Partner / Ihrer Partnerin, was Julian im April alles gemacht hat. Benutzen Sie das Perfekt und/oder Präteritum. Sample answers are provided.

BEISPIEL

S1: *Am 6. April hat er einen Film gesehen.*
S2: *Und am 7. April war er beim Friseur.*

Am 2. April hat er ein Basketballspiel gehabt. / Am 4. April musste er ein Geschenk kaufen. / Am 6. April ist er ins Kino gegangen. / Am 11. April hatte seine Mutter Geburtstag. / Am 15. April ist er auf die Party bei Tom gegangen. / Am 19. April war er auf dem Coldplay-Konzert. / Am 23. April ist er mit Lara im Restaurant gewesen. / Am 27. April hatte er einen Deutschtest.

APRIL

MO	DI	MI	DO	FR	SA	SO
					1	Basketballspiel 2
3	Geschenk kaufen 4	5	Film „Sophie Scholl" 6	Friseur 7	8	9
10	Mama Geburtstag 11	12	13	14	Party bei Tom 15	16
17	18	Coldplay-Konzert 19	20	21	22	Essen mit Lara 23
24	25	26	Deutschtest 27	28	29	30

6 **Ein Märchen** Schreiben Sie mit Ihrem Partner / Ihrer Partnerin das Märchen zu Ende. Sie dürfen auch Ihr eigenes Märchen erfinden (*make up*). Schreiben Sie sechs bis acht Sätze im Präteritum. Answers will vary.

1. Es war einmal ein junges Mädchen. Sie hatte einen gemeinen Stiefbruder. Eines Tages...

2. Es waren einmal ein Hund, eine Katze, ein Hamster und ein Vogel. Sie wohnten alle bei einer alten Frau. Eines Tages...

3. Es war einmal ein kleiner Hund. Er wohnte allein im Wald und wollte so gern eine Familie haben. Eines Tages...

5 Suggestion Verify that students remember how to read dates out loud. Ex.: **am zweiten April, am fünften April, am siebten April.**

5 Expansion Have students create their own calendar (real or fictional) for the last month and have them share their activities with the class, using complete sentences in the present perfect.

5 Virtual Chat You can also assign activity 5 on the Supersite. Students record individual responses that appear in your gradebook.

Suggestion Tell students that **Es war einmal...** is a standard fairy tale beginning in German. Provide them with a standard ending that they can use for their fairy tales, such as: **Und wenn sie nicht gestorben sind, dann leben sie noch heute.**

2B.2 Separable and inseparable prefix verbs in the *Perfekt*

Startblock You previously learned about separable and inseparable prefix verbs in the present tense. In the **Perfekt**, the past participles of verbs with prefixes are formed slightly differently than those of other verbs.

Suggestion For these two examples, have students provide the present tense forms of the verbs in the **Perfekt**. Then have them identify which verb has no prefix **(fegen)**, which verbs have separable prefixes (**abstauben** and **wegräumen**) and which verb has an inseparable prefix (**entfernen**).

- Verbs with prefixes can be either strong, weak, or mixed.

Ihr **habt** das Zimmer **aufgeräumt**.
*You **cleaned up** the room.*

Wir **haben** Kuchen **mitgebracht**.
*We **brought** cake.*

Sie **sind** nach Berlin **umgezogen.**
*They **moved** to Berlin.*

- To form the past participle of a separable prefix verb, add the separable prefix to the past participle of the root verb, before the **-ge-** prefix.

infinitive	participle	infinitive	participle
anrufen	angerufen	rausbringen	rausgebracht
aufräumen	aufgeräumt	umtauschen	umgetauscht
ausgehen	(ist) ausgegangen	umziehen	(ist) umgezogen
einkaufen	eingekauft	vorstellen	vorgestellt
mitbringen	mitgebracht	wegräumen	weggeräumt

Suggestion Explain that the expressions **Staub saugen** and **staubsaugen** are equivalent in meaning. Point out that, when written as a single word, **staubsaugen** has the past participle form **gestaubsaugt**.

Wir **haben** das Geschirr **weggeräumt**.
*We **put away** the dishes.*

Ich **habe** den kaputten Staubsauger **umgetauscht**.
*I **exchanged** the broken vacuum cleaner.*

- The past participles of inseparable prefix verbs are formed like those of separable prefix verbs, but without the **-ge-** prefix.

infinitive	participle	infinitive	participle
bedeuten	bedeutet	erklären	erklärt
beginnen	begonnen	gehören	gehört
besuchen	besucht	verkaufen	verkauft
bezahlen	bezahlt	verschmutzen	verschmutzt
entdecken	entdeckt	verstehen	verstanden

Herr Koch **hat** uns einen neuen Gefrierschrank **verkauft**.
Mr. Koch ***sold*** *us a new freezer.*

Sarahs Bruder **hat** uns einmal **besucht**.
Sarah's brother ***came to visit*** *us once.*

Der Vermieter **hat** das Loch in der Wand **entdeckt**.
The landlord ***discovered*** *the hole in the wall.*

Ich **habe** die Frage nicht **verstanden**.
I ***didn't understand*** *the question.*

- Remember that the prefixes of inseparable prefix verbs are never stressed, while the prefixes of separable prefix verbs are always stressed.

Wie viel hast du für den Toaster be**zahlt**?
How much did you pay for the toaster?

Wir haben viele Gäste **ein**geladen.
We invited a lot of guests.

- Most separable and inseparable prefix verbs are conjugated with **haben**. However, prefixed verbs that indicate a change in condition or location and do not take a direct object are conjugated with **sein**.

Der Hund **hat** den sauberen Boden **verschmutzt**.
The dog ***got*** *the clean floor* ***dirty***.

Du **hast** den dreckigen Teppich **rausgebracht**.
You ***took out*** *the dirty rug.*

Wir **sind** mit unseren Großeltern in die Schweiz **mitgefahren**.
We ***went*** *to Switzerland with our grandparents.*

Tobias **ist** gestern Abend **ausgegangen**.
Tobias ***went out*** *last night.*

- Since prefixes change the meaning of a verb, in some cases a prefixed verb is conjugated with **sein**, while its base form is conjugated with **haben**.

Sie **sind** vor einem Jahr **umgezogen**.
They ***moved*** *a year ago.*

Die Hunde **haben** den Schlitten **gezogen**.
The dogs ***pulled*** *the sled.*

Expansion Have students write a fictional journal entry using the following verbs in the present perfect tense: **aufräumen, verkaufen, einkaufen, anrufen, bekommen, bestellen, verlieren, vergessen.**

QUERVERWEIS

See **1B.1** to review the formation of the **Perfekt** with **sein**.

Ressourcen
vText
WB pp. 29–30
LM p. 75
vhlcentral

Jetzt sind Sie dran! **Ergänzen Sie die Sätze mit den richtigen Formen der Verben im Perfekt.**

Suggestion Before they begin this **Jetzt sind Sie dran!** activity, have students identify the verbs with inseparable prefixes.

1. Paul _hat_ den Müll nicht _rausgebracht_. (rausbringen)
2. Liebe Kinder, _habt_ ihr eure Zimmer schon _aufgeräumt_? (aufräumen)
3. Frau Schulz _hat_ den Wäschetrockner _verkauft_. (verkaufen)
4. David _hat_ seine Freundin _angerufen_. (anrufen)
5. Anna, _habe_ ich dir meinen neuen Freund _vorgestellt_? (vorstellen)
6. Mama _hat_ eine schöne Vase zu Weihnachten _bekommen_. (bekommen)
7. Du _hast_ den Ring in der Waschmaschine _entdeckt_. (entdecken)
8. Ich _bin_ mit meinem Freund _ausgegangen_. (ausgehen)
9. Wir _haben_ eine Kaffeemaschine im Internet _bestellt_. (bestellen)
10. Wie viel _habt_ ihr für den Wäschetrockner _bezahlt_? (bezahlen)
11. Maria, _hast_ du das Geschirr _weggeräumt_? (wegräumen)
12. Ich _habe_ die Hausaufgaben zu Hause _vergessen_! (vergessen)

Anwendung

1 Perfektformen Formen Sie die Sätze vom Präsens ins Perfekt um.

BEISPIEL Er ruft seine Schwester an.
Er hat seine Schwester angerufen.

1. Mein Bruder kommt mit.
   Mein Bruder ist mitgekommen.
2. Ich stelle meine Eltern vor.
   Ich habe meine Eltern vorgestellt.
3. Georg kommt in Zürich an.
   Georg ist in Zürich angekommen.
4. Du besuchst das Museum.
   Du hast das Museum besucht.
5. Wir bringen ein Geschenk mit.
   Wir haben ein Geschenk mitgebracht.
6. Sara vergisst ihre Handtasche.
   Sara hat ihre Handtasche vergessen.
7. Der Lehrer wiederholt die Grammatik.
   Der Lehrer hat die Grammatik wiederholt.
8. Ihr schaut bei dem Fußballmatch zu.
   Ihr habt bei dem Fußballmatch zugeschaut.

2 Letzten Freitag Was haben diese Leute letzten Freitag gemacht? Bilden Sie Sätze im Perfekt.

BEISPIEL Paula / ihre Schwester anrufen
Paula hat ihre Schwester angerufen.

1. Klara / nicht früh aufstehen
   Klara ist nicht früh aufgestanden.

2. Moritz / sein Fahrrad verkaufen
   Moritz hat sein Fahrrad verkauft.

3. Herr Huber / neue Schuhe anziehen
   Herr Huber hat neue Schuhe angezogen.

4. Ali / sein Zimmer aufräumen
   Ali hat sein Zimmer aufgeräumt.

5. Marie und ihre Freundin / ausgehen
   Marie und ihre Freundin sind ausgegangen.

3 Das war früher anders Sarah ist heutzutage (*nowadays*) sehr fleißig und nett, aber das war nicht immer so. Erzählen Sie, was Sarah alles gemacht hat, als sie jünger war. Answers will vary. Sample answers are provided.

BEISPIEL Heutzutage ruft sie ihre Mutter oft an.
Früher (Before) hat sie ihre Mutter selten angerufen.

1. Heutzutage steht sie immer früh auf.
   Früher ist sie immer spät aufgestanden.
2. Heutzutage geht sie oft einkaufen.
   Früher ist sie selten einkaufen gegangen.
3. Heutzutage bereitet sie täglich Essen vor.
   Früher hat sie selten Essen vorbereitet.
4. Heutzutage bringt sie immer den Müll raus.
   Früher hat sie selten den Müll rausgebracht.
5. Heutzutage geht sie nur selten aus.
   Früher ist sie oft ausgegangen.
6. Heutzutage schläft sie immer früh ein.
   Früher ist sie selten früh eingeschlafen.

4 Was ist passiert? Was hat Georg letztes Wochenende in Zürich gemacht? Schreiben Sie acht Sätze im Perfekt. Answers will vary.

BEISPIEL *Georg ist am frühen Morgen in Zürich angekommen.*

ankommen	ausgehen	bezahlen	mitkommen
anrufen	bekommen	einkaufen	vergessen
aufstehen	besuchen	mitbringen	zurückkommen

Practice more at vhlcentral.com.

Kommunikation

5 **Kindheitserinnerungen** Stellen Sie Ihrem Partner / Ihrer Partnerin acht logische Fragen über seine/ihre Kindheit. Benutzen Sie das Perfekt und verwenden Sie Wörter aus jeder Spalte. Sie dürfen auch andere Elemente hinzufügen (*add*). Answers will vary.

BEISPIEL

S1: *Wie oft hast du dein Zimmer aufgeräumt?*
S2: *Ich habe es einmal in der Woche aufgeräumt.*

A	B	C
Mit wem?	einmal in der Woche	aufhängen
Wen?	immer sehr spät	aufräumen
Wann?	in ein neues Haus	aufstehen
Was?	Poster von Rockstars	ausgehen
Wie oft?	deine Verwandten	bekommen
Wer?	mit Freunden	besuchen
deine Eltern	immer dein Zimmer	einschlafen
deine Geschwister	im Unterricht	umziehen
du	zum Geburtstag	vorbereiten

5 Suggestion Before students begin writing, have them review the past participle of each verb and identify which ones will have **sein** as the auxiliary.

6 **Nicht nur Hausarbeiten** Was haben diese Personen am Wochenende gemacht? Schreiben Sie mit Ihrem Partner / Ihrer Partnerin zu jedem Bild einen Satz im Perfekt. Sample answers are provided.

▶ **BEISPIEL** Greta und Jan
Greta und Jan sind ausgegangen.

1. Martin
Martin hat seine Schwester angerufen.

2. Jonas
Jonas ist spät aufgestanden.

3. Nils und Max
Nils und Max haben den Müll rausgebracht.

4. Frau Lange
Frau Lange hat das Wohnzimmer aufgeräumt.

5. Yusuf
Yusuf hat seine Freundin besucht.

7 **Die neugierige Oma** Ihre Oma will wissen, was Sie dieses Schuljahr schon alles gemacht haben. Spielen Sie mit Ihrem Partner / Ihrer Partnerin einen Dialog und benutzen Sie die Perfektformen. Answers will vary.

BEISPIEL

Kaffee trinken

S1: *Hast du viel Kaffee getrunken?*
S2: *Ja, Oma, ich habe viel Kaffee getrunken.*

oft die Eltern anrufen	immer das Bett machen
früh aufstehen	die Badewanne putzen
oft ausgehen	den Müll rausbringen
oft Freunde einladen	die Hausaufgaben vorbereiten
fleißig lernen	die Kleider waschen

7 Partner Chat You can also assign activity 7 on the Supersite. Students work in pairs to record the activity online. The pair's recorded conversation will appear in your gradebook.

8 **Die Haushaltsführung** Schreiben Sie zu zweit einen Dialog. Ein Hotelbesitzer / Eine Hotelbesitzerin spricht mit einem Fachmann / einer Fachfrau Hauswirtschaft über die Haushaltsführung (*housekeeping*). Answers will vary.

BEISPIEL **S1:** *Haben Sie den Dachboden aufgeräumt?*
S2: *Ja, ich habe ihn aufgeräumt und habe auch die Wäsche gewaschen.*

Wiederholung

1 Expansion Take survey of the class, based on this activity. Ex.: **Haben wir saubere Zimmer? Wie viele von uns haben diese Woche Staub gewischt? Wer hat gestaubsaugt?**, etc.

1 Suggestion Before they begin the activity, have students review the past participles of the verbs listed.

1 Hausarbeit

Fragen Sie Ihren Partner / Ihre Partnerin, was für Hausarbeit er/sie diese Woche gemacht hat.

1 Partner Chat You can also assign activity 1 on the Supersite.

BEISPIEL

S1: *Hast du diese Woche den Boden gewischt?*
S2: *Ja, ich habe den Boden gewischt. Du auch?*

Kleider bügeln	den Müll rausbringen
den Tisch decken	Geschirr spülen
die Küche fegen	staubsaugen
das Bett machen	Wäsche waschen
Hausarbeit machen	den Boden wischen

2 Arbeitsblatt

Sie bekommen von Ihrem Lehrer / Ihrer Lehrerin eine Liste mit Aktivitäten. Fragen Sie Ihre Klassenkameraden, ob sie die Aktivitäten letzten Monat gemacht haben. Finden Sie eine Person für jede Aktivität.

BEISPIEL

S1: *Hast du letzten Monat deine Eltern angerufen?*
S2: *Ja, ich habe sie angerufen.*

3 Die neue Küche

Machen Sie zu dritt ein Rollenspiel. Eine Person spielt einen Hausbesitzer / eine Hausbesitzerin. Die anderen zwei spielen Lieferanten (*delivery people*) von Haushaltgeräten. Die Lieferanten fragen, wohin sie die Geräte stellen sollen.

BEISPIEL

S1: *Wohin sollen wir die Waschmaschine stellen?*
S2: *Stellen Sie sie links neben die Tür.*
S3: *Und die Kaffeemaschine?*

der Gefrierschrank	die Mikrowelle
der Herd	der Ofen
die Kaffeemaschine	die Spülmaschine
der Kühlschrank	der Wäschetrockner

4 Diskutieren und kombinieren

Sie und Ihr Partner / Ihre Partnerin bekommen zwei verschiedene Blätter mit Alexandras Aktivitäten. Ergänzen Sie Alexandras Tageslauf. Schreiben Sie dann eine Erzählung darüber.

BEISPIEL

S1: *Um halb fünf ist Alexandra im Park gelaufen.*
S2: *Danach, um fünf Uhr…*

5 Ein Luxushotel

Erstellen Sie (*Create*) mit einem Partner / einer Partnerin einen Text für die Website von einem Luxushotel in der Schweiz. Beschreiben Sie das Hotel, die Zimmer und Aktivitäten im Hotel und in der Gegend (*area*).

BEISPIEL

6 Die Mitbewohner

Schreiben Sie mit Ihrem Partner / Ihrer Partnerin eine Geschichte (*story*) über zwei Mitbewohner. Ein Mitbewohner ist sehr fleißig, aber der andere ist ganz anders (*completely different*). Benutzen Sie das Präteritum.

BEISPIEL

Es waren einmal zwei Mitbewohner, Daniel und Fabian. Daniel war sehr fleißig. Er lernte viel, machte jeden Abend seine Hausaufgaben, und machte jedes Wochenende die Hausarbeit. Aber Fabian…

2 Suggestion Have students compete to see who can be the first to get a positive answer for all eight questions. Circulate around the classroom, monitoring production and keeping students on task.

7 **Ein Festessen** Sie und Ihre Klassenkameraden wollen Gäste zum Essen einladen. Besprechen Sie mit zwei Partnern/Partnerinnen die Vorbereitungen für den Abend. Schreiben Sie auf, wer was macht.

BEISPIEL

S1: *Das Wohnzimmer ist ein Saustall! Wir müssen es putzen. Wer will staubsaugen?*
S2: *Ich kann staubsaugen. Und du? Kannst du…*

8 **Was ist passiert?** Fragen Sie Ihren Partner / Ihre Partnerin, was er/sie letzte Woche gemacht hat. Schreiben Sie dann einen Bericht (*report*) über seine/ihre Aktivitäten. Benutzen Sie das Präteritum. Answers will vary.

BEISPIEL

S1: *Hast du letzte Woche den Boden gefegt?*
S2: *Nein, aber ich habe mein Bett gemacht.*
S1: *(Schreibt) Sie fegte den Boden nicht, aber sie machte ihr Bett.*

9 **Eine Lebensgeschichte** Wählen Sie eine berühmte Person, und schreiben Sie mit einem Partner / einer Partnerin eine kurze Biographie über diese Person. Sie dürfen auch eine Person erfinden (*invent*).

BEISPIEL

Brad Pitt (1963–)

Mit zwei musste er mit seiner Familie nach Springfield Missouri umziehen, denn sein Vater hatte da einen Job. Im Gymnasium hat er…

Mein Wör | ter | buch

Schreiben Sie noch fünf weitere Wörter in Ihr persönliches Wörterbuch zu den Themen **zu Hause** und **Hausarbeit**.

Übersetzung
dust

Wortart
Substantiv

Gebrauch
Ich putze mein Zimmer, denn es liegt zu viel Staub unterm Bett.

Synonyme
—

Antonyme
—

Vocabulary Tools

Weiter geht's

Panorama

AP* Theme: Global Challenges
Context: Geography
Interactive Map

Die Schweiz und Liechtenstein

Die Schweiz in Zahlen

- **Fläche:** *41,277 km²*
- **Offizielle Sprachen:** *Deutsch (64,9%), Französisch (22,6%), Italienisch (8,3%), Rätoromanisch° (0,5%)*
- **Bevölkerung:** *8,1 Millionen*
- **Religion:** *römisch-katholisch 38,2%, evangelisch 26,9%*
- **Hauptstadt:** *Bern*
- **Städte:** *Zürich (390.000 Einwohner), Genf (192.000), Basel (193.000) und Bern (134.000)*
- **Berge:** *Hohe Dufourspitze (4.634 m), Dom (4.545 m), Matterhorn (4.478 m)*
- **Flüsse:** *der Rhein, die Aare, die Rhone*
- **Wichtige Industriezweige:** *Uhrenindustrie°, Maschinenbau, Banken und Versicherungen°*
- **Touristenattraktionen:** *St.-Gotthard-Pass, Burgen von Bellinzona, Schweizerischer Nationalpark, Jungfraujoch bei Grindelwald.*

QUELLE: Offizielles Informationsportal der Schweiz

Liechtenstein in Zahlen

- **Offizieller Name:** *Fürstentum° Liechtenstein*
- **Fläche:** *160 km²*
- **Bevölkerung:** *37.313*
- **Religion:** *römisch-katholisch 76%, evangelisch 8%*
- **Hauptstadt:** *Vaduz (5.372 Einwohner)*
- **Berge:** *Vorderer Grauspitz (2.599 m), Naafkopf (2.570 m)*
- **Niedrigster Punkt:** *Ruggeller Riet (430 m)*
- **Flüsse:** *der Rhein, die Samina*
- **Wichtige Industriezweige:** *Maschinenbau, Nahrungsmittel°*
- **Touristenattraktionen:** *Schloss Vaduz, Kathedrale St. Florin, Kunstmuseum Liechtenstein.*

QUELLE: Portal des Fürstentums Liechtenstein

Expansion For homework, have students find online pictures of the people and places mentioned on this page. Depending on the size of your class, each student could be responsible for one or two pictures.

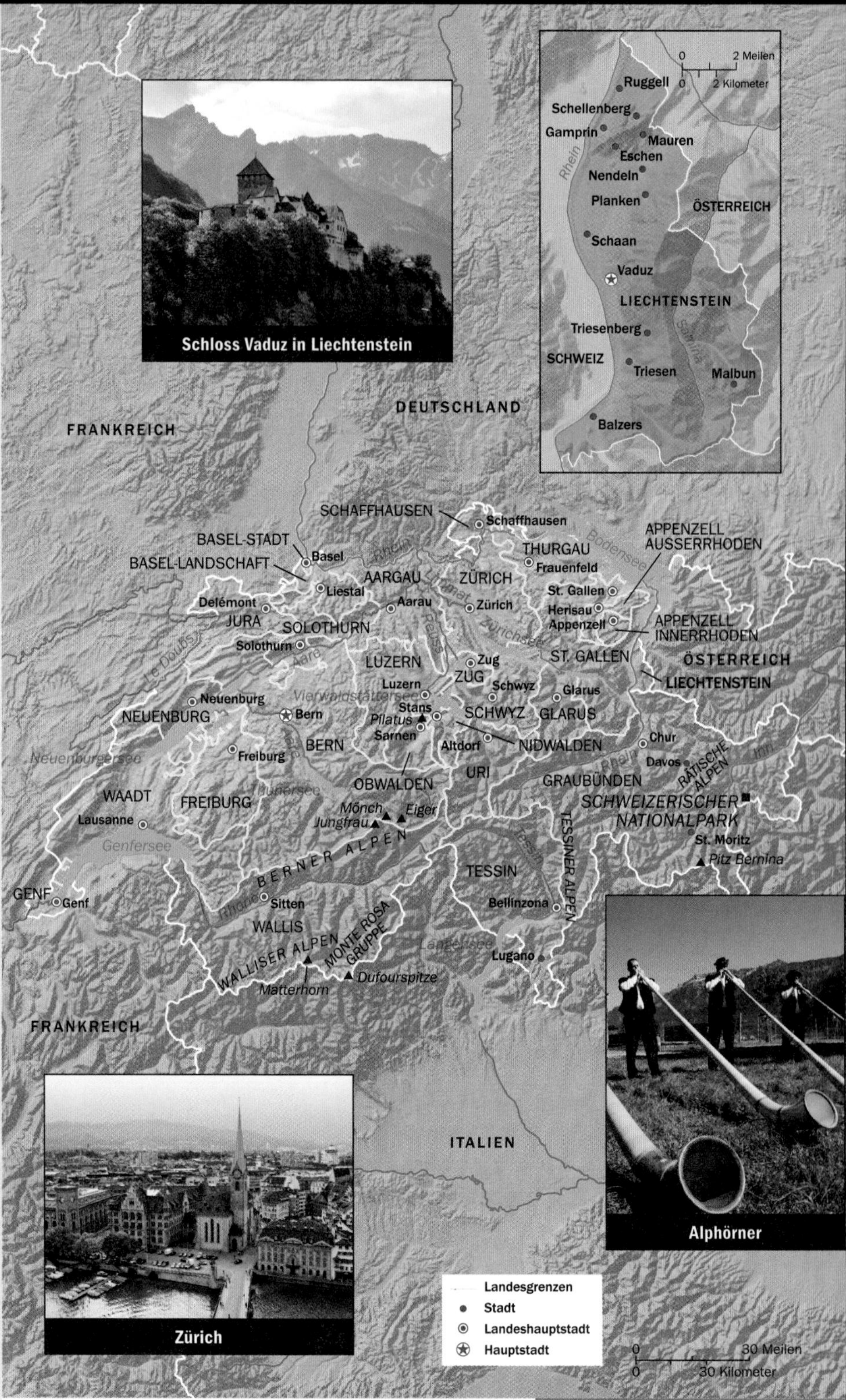

Schloss Vaduz in Liechtenstein

Alphörner

Zürich

Landesgrenzen
Stadt
Landeshauptstadt
Hauptstadt

Unglaublich, aber wahr!

In Liechtenstein ist die Kriminalitätsrate° extrem niedrig°. In den Gefängnissen° sitzen nur wenige Häftlinge°. Die Kollaboration zwischen Liechtenstein, Österreich und der Schweiz ist sehr eng. Zum Beispiel kommen alle Liechtensteiner Häftlinge mit Haftstrafen° über zwei Jahren in österreichische Gefängnisse.

AP* Theme: Families & Communities
Context: Citizenship

Rätoromanisch *Romansch* **Uhrenindustrie** *clock and watch industry* **Versicherungen** *insurance companies* **Fürstentum** *principality* **Nahrungsmittel** *food products* **Kriminalitätsrate** *crime rate* **niedrig** *low* **Gefängnissen** *prisons* **Häftlinge** *inmates* **Haftstrafen** *sentences*

Suggestion Tell students that **Schweizerdeutsch** can be difficult for Germans to understand, so much so that when Swiss speakers are interviewed for German news, subtitles are often added.

Politik

Fürstentum Liechtenstein

AP* Theme: Global Challenges
Context: Political Issues

Liechtenstein ist ein Binnenland° in Mitteleuropa. Es liegt in den Alpen zwischen Österreich und der Schweiz. Unabhängig° ist das Land seit 1806. Liechtenstein ist ein Fürstentum. Fürst Hans-Adam II. von und zu Liechtenstein ist das Staatsoberhaupt°, aber Adrian Hasler ist seit 2013 der demokratisch gewählte Regierungschef°. Das Land hat keine Armee. Liechtenstein ist das kleinste deutschsprachige Land. Allerdings ist Deutsch nur in Liechtenstein die alleinige Amts- und Landessprache°.

Menschen

AP* Theme: Contemporary Life
Context: Current Events

Roger Federer

Roger Federer ist ein Schweizer Tennisspieler. Viele Experten halten° ihn für den besten Tennisspieler aller Zeiten. Er gewann 17 Grand-Slam-Turniere (Australian Open, French Open, Wimbledon, US Open) und stand 237 Wochen lang auf Platz 1 der Tennisweltrangliste. Er ist einer von sieben Spielern, die in ihrer Karriere alle Grand-Slam-Turniere gewannen. 2008 gewann er zusammen mit Stanislas Wawrinka in Beijing eine olympische Goldmedaille im Doppel. In den Jahren 2005–2008 war er Weltsportler des Jahres.

Kultur

AP* Theme: Personal & Public Identity
Context: National Identity

Vier Amtssprachen

In der Schweiz gibt es vier offizielle Sprachen: Deutsch, Französisch, Italienisch und Rätoromanisch. Kantone haben aber meistens nur eine Amtssprache. Im Westen, an der Grenze zu Frankreich, dominiert Französisch und im Südosten, an der Grenze zu Italien, Italienisch. Im Norden, Zentrum und Osten dominiert Deutsch. Nur im Kanton Graubünden gibt es drei Amtssprachen: Deutsch, Rätoromanisch und Italienisch. Die meisten Schweizer sprechen nur eine Sprache als Muttersprache. Dafür lernen viele Schweizer mindestens eine weitere° Sprache. Einige sind auch dreisprachig.

Industrie

AP* Theme: Science & Technology
Context: Personal Technologies

Präzisionszeitmessgeräte°

In der Schweiz gibt es eine sehr lange Tradition für die Produktion von Präzisionszeitmessgeräten. Ein Beispiel ist das Marinechronometer. Auf einem Schiff° kann man mit diesem Gerät Längengrade bestimmen° und es für astronomische Ortsbestimmungen benutzen. Der Schweizer Uhrmacher° Louis Berthoud (1753–1813) stellte ein Präzisions-Taschenchronometer her°, das Alexander von Humboldt 1799 auf seinen Schiffsreisen testete. Heute müssen Chronometer extrem exakt sein. Nur eine Organisation weltweit, das unabhängige Schweizer Observatorium *Contrôle officiel suisse des chronomètres* (COSC) darf die Präzision von Chronometern prüfen° und zertifizieren.

IM INTERNET

1. Suchen Sie Informationen über andere berühmte Schweizer Sportler. Welchen Sport machen sie? Was haben sie gewonnen?
2. Suchen Sie weitere Informationen über Schweizer Uhren: Was können Sie über die Uhrenproduktion in der Schweiz finden? Was sind bekannte Marken? Warum sind sie bekannt?

Find out more at **vhlcentral.com**.

Binnenland *land-locked country* **Unabhängig** *Independent* **Staatsoberhaupt** *head of state* **Regierungschef** *head of government* **Amts- und Landessprache** *official and national language* **halten** *consider* **weitere** *more* **Präzisionszeitmessgeräte** *precision time measuring instruments* **Schiff** *ship* **Längengrade bestimmen** *determine longitude* **Uhrmacher** *watchmaker* **stellte... her** *produced* **prüfen** *test*

Expansion Teach students a few Swiss German phrases, such as **Uf Widerleuge (Auf Wiedersehen)** or **Merci villmool (vielen Dank)**.

Was haben Sie gelernt? Ergänzen Sie die Sätze.

1. In Liechtenstein ist die Kriminalitätsrate extrem ___niedrig___.
2. Ein Häftling mit über zwei Jahren Haft sitzt in ___Österreich___ im Gefängnis.
3. Liechtenstein liegt zwischen Österreich und ___der Schweiz___.
4. Liechtenstein hat ein Staatsoberhaupt sowie einen ___Regierungschef___.
5. Roger Federer stand ___237___ Wochen lang an der Spitze der Tennisweltrangliste.
6. In den Jahren 2005–2008 war Federer ___Weltsportler___ des Jahres.
7. Die vier Amtssprachen der Schweiz sind Deutsch, ___Französisch___, Italienisch und Rätoromanisch.
8. Die meisten Schweizer sprechen eine Sprache als ___Muttersprache___.
9. Alexander von Humboldt testete ___1799___ ein Schweizer Präzisions-Taschenchronometer auf seinen Schiffsreisen.
10. Nur eine ___Organisation___ weltweit darf Chronometer prüfen.

Practice more at **vhlcentral.com**.

Audio: Reading

Vor dem Lesen

AP* Theme: Families & Communities
Context: Urban, Suburban, & Rural Life

Strategien

Recognizing word families

Recognizing related words can help you guess the meaning of words in context. Using this strategy will improve your reading comprehension and enrich your German vocabulary.

Text untersuchen

Suchen Sie im Text ein anderes Wort aus der gleichen Wortfamilie. Answers will vary. Sample answers are provided.

BEISPIEL

Zimmer *Zweizimmerwohnung*

1. Möbel — Möblierung
2. Küche — Einbauküche
3. Monat — monatlich
4. Garage — Tiefgarage
5. Miete — Kaltmiete
6. Wohnung — Luxuswohnung
7. Internet — Internetanschluss
8. Bett — Bettwäsche

Präfixe

Suchen Sie mit einem Partner / einer Partnerin im Text ein neues Verb für jede Wortfamilie.

1. mieten	*vermieten*	untermieten
2. kaufen	verkaufen	einkaufen
3. fangen	anfangen	verfangen
4. stehen	aufstehen	verstehen
5. lassen	verlassen	entlassen
6. bieten	anbieten	verbieten

Suggestion Learning to break down long compound words and identify their roots is an important reading strategy. For homework, have students find long German words online or in a dictionary. Have students write their words on the board, then break them down together into their component words.

IEN +41 56 5559990 SCHWEIZER IMMOBILIEN +41 56 5559990 SCHWE

Wohnung im historischen Fribourg

SIE SUCHEN eine kuschelige° Wohnung für zwei? Sie möchten das Leben in der historischen Innenstadt Fribourgs nicht verlassen°? Dann ist diese Zweizimmerwohnung ideal!

Die Schlafzimmer sind mit Einbauschränken ausgestattet°. Die Wohnung hat eine moderne Einbauküche mit Gasherd und Backofen. Sie bietet° ein modernes Bad, ein großes Wohn- und Esszimmer mit direktem Zugang° zur Küche. Einkaufen können Sie natürlich bequem° in einem Umkreis von fünf Minuten. Sie haben ein Auto? Kein Problem! Sie können Ihr Auto für monatlich SFr 75 auf einen Parkplatz in der Tiefgarage stellen. Zu vermieten ab Juli für SFr 1.100 Kaltmiete.

SIE SUCHEN FÜR IHRE FAMILIE ein neues Zuhause im Kanton Tessin? Ihnen gefällt die Kombination von Kultur und Natur? Sie lieben traditionelle Architektur, viel Holz und warmes Wetter? Dann ist dieses Einfamilienhaus perfekt!

Das Chalet liegt direkt am Lago Maggiore in der Nähe° von Locarno. Es ist als typisches Chalet mit Holzfassaden gebaut. Für eine Familie bieten Esszimmer, Wohnzimmer, zwei Badezimmer plus drei Schlafzimmer viel Platz. Die Küche mit Einbauküche und Frühstücksecke° ist familienfreundlich. Im Keller stehen Waschmaschine und Trockner. Im Garten können Kinder spielen, Hunde herumlaufen und Eltern Grillpartys feiern. Das Haus liegt fünf Minuten entfernt von Locarnos Innenstadt und in 20 Minuten ist man in den Bergen. Zu vermieten ab August. Die Miete beträgt monatlich SFr 2.000 ohne Nebenkosten°.

Expansion Give students a fictional profile of someone looking for an apartment and have them decide which of the three dwellings would be best for that person. Ex: **Bettina: ledig, ist eine 29-jährige Rechtsberaterin, die von Fribourg nach Zürich umziehen möchte. Sie ist ambitiös und perfektionistisch. Am liebsten mag sie alles schlicht und modern. Sie arbeitet viel und hat keine Zeit zu putzen. Welche Wohnung ist am besten für sie?**

BILIEN +41 56 5559990 SCHWEIZER IMMOBILIEN +41 56 5559990

SIE LEBEN ALLEIN? Nur das Beste ist gut genug? Sie arbeiten in Zürich bei einer Bank oder einer Versicherung? Dann ist diese Luxuswohnung genau das Richtige! Top gestylte, neu renovierte Zweizimmerwohnung in der Nähe des Züricher Bankenviertels ab sofort zu vermieten. Moderne Möblierung. Nur das Beste! Küche mit Espressomaschine und Mikrowelle vorhanden. Im Wohnzimmer stehen ein Fernseher° und eine Bar. Internetanschluss in allen Zimmern. Die wöchentliche Apartmentreinigung und das Wechseln° der Bettwäsche sind im Mietpreis inklusive. Mietverträge° können sofort anfangen. Die Miete beträgt SFr 2.100 pro Monat.

kuschelig *cozy* **verlassen** *leave* **mit Einbauschränken ausgestattet** *equipped with built-in cabinets* **bietet** *offers* **Zugang** *access* **bequem** *conveniently* **in der Nähe** *in the vicinity* **Frühstücksecke** *breakfast nook* **Nebenkosten** *additional charges* **Fernseher** *television* **Wechseln** *changing* **Mietverträge** *rental agreements*

Nach dem Lesen 

Was fehlt? Ergänzen Sie die Sätze.

1. Die Wohnung in Fribourg hat eine Einbauküche mit Gasherd und Backofen.
2. Im Schlafzimmer gibt es Einbauschränke.
3. Die Miete für die Wohnung in Fribourg kostet SFr 1.100 inklusive Parkplatz.
4. Das Chalet liegt im Tessin.
5. Im Chalet stehen im Keller Waschmaschine und Trockner.
6. Beim Chalet können Kinder im Garten spielen.
7. In der Wohnung in Zürich stehen ein Fernseher und eine Bar im Wohnzimmer.
8. Die Miete der Züricher Wohnung beträgt SFr 2.100 pro Monat.

Richtig oder falsch? Sind die Sätze richtig oder falsch? Korrigieren Sie die falschen Sätze.

Sample answers are provided.

	richtig	falsch
1. Die Wohnung in Fribourg ist ideal für eine Familie.	☐	☑
Falsch. Die Wohnung ist ideal für zwei Personen.		
2. Einkaufen ist in der Nähe der Fribourger Wohnung sehr schwierig.	☐	☑
Falsch. Man kann hier bequem einkaufen.		
3. Das Chalet ist ein sehr modernes Haus.	☐	☑
Falsch. Das Chalet hat traditionelle Architektur.		
4. Die Tessiner Wohnung hat viel Platz.	☑	☐
5. Natur und Stadtleben sind dem Chalet sehr nah.	☑	☐
6. Die Züricher Zweizimmerwohnung ist nicht sehr modern.	☐	☑
Falsch. Sie ist top gestylt und neu renoviert.		
7. In allen Zimmern der Züricher Wohnung ist ein Internetanschluss.	☑	☐
8. Die Wohnung in Zürich reinigt (*cleans*) man jede Woche.	☑	☐

Die beste Wohnung Diskutieren Sie in einer kleinen Gruppe: Welche ist die beste Wohnung?

Answers will vary.

BEISPIEL

S1: *Die Zweizimmerwohnung in Zürich ist klein, aber sie liegt in der Innenstadt. Man braucht kein Auto.*

S2: *Leider ist sie auch sehr teuer! Ich mag das Haus im Tessin.*

S3: *Ja, es ist ideal für eine Familie!*

Hören

Strategien

Using background knowledge

If you know the topic being discussed, using knowledge you already have about the subject can help you to predict the kind of information you might hear.

To help you practice this strategy, you will listen to a commercial for a cleaning product. Before you listen, jot down some key words related to the topic of cleaning that you might expect to hear in the commercial.

Vorbereitung

Sehen Sie sich das Foto an. Wer sind die Menschen auf dem Foto? Was machen sie? Könnte das eine Werbung (*advertisement*) sein?

Zuhören

Hören Sie der Sprecherin der Firma *Zauber* (*Magic*) *bis sauber* zu. Hören Sie die Werbung ein zweites Mal und wählen Sie die Dienstleistungen (*services*), die die Firma anbietet (*offers*).

1. (staubsaugen)
2. Wäsche waschen
3. bügeln
4. Geschirr spülen
5. (Kühlschränke putzen)
6. den Müll rausbringen
7. (Böden putzen)
8. (Fenster sauber machen)

Suggestion Before students listen to the recording, teach them the words **reinigen** and **Zauber**. Have students practice pronouncing **sauber** and **Zauber**, and make sure they can hear the difference.

Verständnis

Was fehlt? Welche Wörter oder Ausdrücke fehlen?

arbeiten	Experten	neu
Bad	Fenster	putzen
Böden	kostenloses	sauber
bügeln	Kühlschränke	schnell

1. Die Reinigungsfirma (*cleaning company*) heißt Zauber bis __sauber__.
2. Die Kunden der Reinigungsfirma __arbeiten__ oft viel und haben keine Zeit zum Putzen.
3. Andere Kunden __putzen__ einfach nicht gern.
4. Die Reinigungsfirma ist Experte für Küche, __Bad__ und Wohnzimmer.
5. Sie staubsaugen und reinigen die __Böden__.
6. Sie putzen auch __Kühlschränke__ und Herde.
7. Die Leute der Reinigungsfirma sind __Experten__ beim Saubermachen.
8. Diese Leute sind __schnell__ und gründlich (*thorough*).
9. Die Zimmer sehen am Ende immer wie __neu__ aus.
10. Die Reinigungsfirma gibt Kunden ein __kostenloses__ Angebot (*offer*).

Die Reinigungsfirma Machen Sie mit zwei Mitschülern/Mitschülerinnen eine Werbung für ein neues Produkt oder eine Dienstleistung.

BEISPIEL

S1: *Mit Sauberküche können Sie Ihre Küche einfach reinigen!*
S2: *Sie brauchen keine anderen Produkte! Mit Sauberküche können Sie putzen, waschen, wischen…*

Schreiben

Strategien

Reporting on an interview

When you transcribe a conversation in German, you should pay careful attention to format and punctuation. You can indicate a dialogue format by including the names of the speakers, or by using a dash (**der Gedankenstrich**) to indicate a new speaker. Compare these two formats.

MARIA Nina, was hast du gestern Abend gemacht?
NINA Ich war zu Hause.
MARIA Oh, schade! Wolltest du nicht zu Davids Party?
NINA Ja, aber ich musste noch putzen.

—Hallo, Jonas!
—Hallo, Sarah!
—Wie geht's?
—Gut. Und dir?

Whichever format you choose, your interview should begin with a brief introduction of the person you're interviewing, answering the six W-questions (**Wer?**, **Was?**, **Wann?**, **Wo?**, **Warum?**, and **Wie?**) about the topic of the interview.

Thema

Schreiben Sie ein Interview

Anton Krüger ist Architekt. Er hat ein neues Buch über energiesparendes (*energy-efficient*) Wohnen geschrieben. Diese Woche gibt er an der Universität eine Präsentation darüber. Sie arbeiten für die Studentenzeitung (*student newspaper*) und interviewen Herrn Krüger.

- Schreiben Sie zuerst 2-3 Sätze über den Autor.
- Schreiben Sie ein erfundenes Gespräch (etwa 10-12 Zeilen) zwischen Ihnen und Anton Krüger. Geben Sie mit einem Gedankenstrich oder mit dem Namen der Person an, wer spricht.

BEISPIEL

Anton Krügers Buch kann man in Buchläden und im Internet kaufen. Er hielt diese Woche einen Vortrag...

Journalistin Guten Tag, Herr Krüger! Herzlichen Glückwunsch! Ihr neues Buch ist sehr interessant. Ich habe es wirklich toll gefunden.

Krüger Vielen Dank!

Journalistin Unsere Leser interessiert: Warum haben Sie dieses Buch geschrieben?

Wortschatz

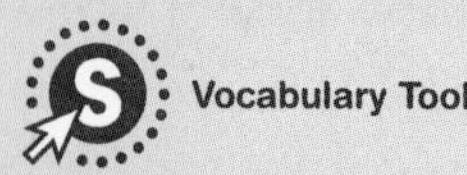

Lektion 2A

Zimmer

das Arbeitszimmer, - *home office*
das Badezimmer, - *bathroom*
der Balkon, -e *balcony*
der Dachboden, ¨ *attic*
das Erdgeschoss, -e *ground floor*
das Esszimmer, - *dining room*
der Flur, -e *hall*
die Garage, -n *garage*
der Keller, - *cellar*
die Küche, -n *kitchen*
das Schlafzimmer, - *bedroom*
der erste/zweite Stock *second/third floor*
die Toilette, -n *toilet*
das Wohnzimmer, - *living room*

Orte

das Haus, ¨er *house*
das Wohnheim, -e *dorm*
die Wohnung, -en *apartment*
nach rechts/links *to the right/left*

Verben

mieten *to rent*
umziehen (zieht... um) *to move*
wohnen *to live*

Möbel

die Badewanne, -n *bathtub*
das Bett, -en *bed*
das Bild, -er *picture*
die Blume, -n *flower*
der Boden, ¨ *floor*
das Bücherregal, -e *bookshelf*
die Kommode, -n *dresser*
die Lampe, -n *lamp*
das Möbelstück, -e *piece of furniture*
der Nachttisch, -e *night table*
die Pflanze, -n *plant*
das Poster, - *poster*
der Schrank, ¨e *cabinet; closet*
die Schublade, -n *drawer*
der Sessel, - *armchair*
das Sofa, -s *sofa*
der Spiegel, - *mirror*
der Teppich, -e *rug*
die Treppe, -n *stairway*
die Vase, -n *vase*
der Vorhang, ¨e *curtain*
die Wand, ¨e *wall*

The *Präteritum* *See pp. 74–75.*
***Da-*, *wo-*, *hin-*, and *her-* compounds** *See pp. 78–79.*
Coordinating conjunctions of verbs *See p. 82.*

Lektion 2B

die Hausarbeit

den Tisch decken *to set the table*
das Bett machen *to make the bed*
den Müll rausbringen *to take out the trash*
Geschirr (*n.*) spülen *to do the dishes*
staubsaugen *to vacuum*
Wäsche waschen *to do laundry*

Haushaltsartikel

der Besen, - *broom*
die Bettdecke, - n *duvet*
das Bügelbrett, -er *ironing board*
das Bügeleisen, - *iron*
die Decke, -n *blanket*
der Gefrierschrank, ¨e *freezer*
der Herd, -e *stove*
die Kaffeemaschine, -n *coffeemaker*
das Kissen, - *pillow*
der Kühlschrank, ¨e *refrigerator*
das Laken, - *sheet*
die Mikrowelle, -n *microwave*
der Ofen, ¨ *oven*
die Pfanne, -n *pan*
die Spüle, -n *kitchen sink*
die Spülmaschine, -n *dishwasher*
der Staubsauger, - *vacuum cleaner*
der Toaster, - *toaster*
der Topf, ¨e *pot*
die Wäsche *laundry*
der Wäschetrockner, - *dryer*
die Waschmaschine, -n *washing machine*

zum Beschreiben

dreckig *filthy*
ordentlich *tidy*
sauber *clean*
schmutzig *dirty*
Es ist ein Saustall! *It's a pigsty!*

Verben

aufräumen (räumt... auf) *to clean up*
bügeln *to iron*
fegen *to sweep*
putzen *to clean*
waschen *to wash*
wischen *to wipe; to mop*

Principal parts of verbs *See p. 95.*
***Perfekt* of verbs with prefixes** *See pp. 98–99.*

Ressourcen

Urlaub und Ferien

KAPITEL
3

LEKTION 3A

LEKTION 3B

WEITER GEHT'S

Suggestion Ask students where they think George and Meline are, and what they might be doing.

Teaching Tip Look for icons indicating activities that address the modes of communication. Follow this key:

→웃←	Interpretive communication
←웃→	Presentational communication
웃↔웃	Interpersonal communication

Kontext

Communicative Goals

You will learn how to:

- discuss the weather and seasons
- talk about the months of the year

Jahreszeiten 

Vocabulary Tools **AP* Theme:** Contemporary Life
Context: Current Events

Suggestion Point out that all months and seasons are masculine. Remind students to use **im** to talk about what happens during specific months and seasons. Ex., **im Winter**, **im März**, etc.

Expansion Mime various weather conditions, (ex., fanning yourself to indicate **Es ist heiß.**), and ask students: **Wie ist das Wetter?**

Wortschatz

das Datum	*date*
das Jahr, -e	*year*
die Jahreszeit, -en	*season*
der Monat, -e	*month*
der Tag, -e	*day*
die Woche, -n	*week*
Wann hast du Geburtstag?	*When is your birthday?*
Am 23. Mai.	*May 23rd.*
das Wetter	*weather*
Wie ist das Wetter?	*What's the weather like?*
Es ist schön draußen.	*It's nice out.*
Das Wetter ist gut/schlecht.	*The weather is nice/bad.*
Das Wetter ist furchtbar.	*The weather is awful.*
Wie warm/kalt ist es?	*How warm/cold is it?*
Es sind 18 Grad draußen.	*It's 18 degrees out.*
der Blitz, -e	*lightning*
der Donner, -	*thunder*
das Gewitter, -	*thunderstorm*
der Hagel	*hail*
der Nebel, -	*fog; mist*
der Regen	*rain*
der Schnee	*snow*
der Sturm, ¨-e	*storm*
der Wetterbericht, -e	*weather report*
die Wolke, -n	*cloud*

Suggestion Remind students that they first learned to talk about dates and birthdays in **Vol. 1, 2A.3**. Point out that they can say either **Ich habe am 23. Mai Geburtstag** or **Mein Geburtstag ist am 23. Mai.**

Suggestion Ask students to describe today's weather, using vocabulary from this section.

ACHTUNG

You have already learned to ask **Der Wievielte ist heute?** to find out the date. You can also use the question **Was ist heute?** to ask about the date or the day of the week.

Suggestion Have students review the use of ordinal numbers, taught in **Vol. 1, 2A.3**.

Suggestion Teach students the song **Immse wimmse Spinne** (the German version of "Eensy Weensy Spider"), which includes references to rain and sun. Lyrics can be found online.

Es schneit. (schneien)

Es ist kalt.

0°C

der Winter: Dezember, Januar, Februar

Es ist sonnig.

Sommerfest

29°C

Es ist heiß.

– Welcher Tag ist heute?
– Der 15. August.

der Sommer: Juni, Juli, August

Ressourcen

vText | WB pp. 31–32 | LM p. 76 |  vhlcentral

Expansion Have students create a "word chain." The first student names a word from the vocabulary list, such as **Sommer**. The next student names a related word, such as **sonnig** or **heiß**, etc. When a student can't think of a word, the chain is "broken," and he or she must start a new "chain."

Anwendung

1 Was fehlt? Ergänzen Sie die Sätze.

1 Suggestion Students may not be familiar with the Celsius scale. Explain that **8° C** is 46.4° F; **17° C** is 62.6° F; and **25° C** is 77° F. Tell students that the conversion formula is: F = (C x 9/5) + 32; C = (F - 32) x 5/9.

regnet	warm
schneit	windig
Sturm	wolkig

BEISPIEL **Nürnberg: 25° C** In Nürnberg ist es sehr warm und _sonnig_. 

1. **Wien: 8° C** In Wien ist es kühl und _wolkig_.  
2. **Genf: 17° C** In Genf ist es _windig_.
3. **Konstanz: 32° C** In Konstanz kommt am Abend ein _Sturm/Gewitter_. 
4. **Innsbruck -5° C** In Innsbruck ist es kalt und es _schneit_.
5. **Basel: 12° C** In Basel ist es wolkig und es _regnet_. 
6. **Hamburg: 21° C** In Hamburg ist es windig, aber _warm_. 

2 Was ist richtig? Entscheiden Sie, welche Aussage zu welchem Bild passt.

a. Es ist heute wieder furchtbar heiß!
b. Wenn es regnet, braucht man einen Regenschirm.
c. Es kommt ein starker Sturm!
d. Auf dicke Wolken folgt schlechtes Wetter.

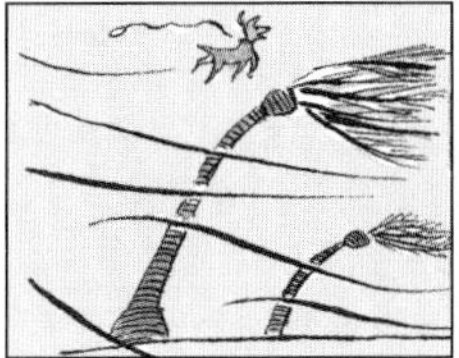

1. _c_

2. _a_

3. _b_

4. _d_

3 Der Wetterbericht Hören Sie den Wetterbericht an und entscheiden Sie danach, ob (whether) die Aussagen richtig oder falsch sind.

3 Suggestion Have students correct the false statements.

	richtig	falsch
1. Der Wetterbericht ist für die ganze Woche.	☐	☑
2. Am Freitag beginnt der Winter.	☑	☐
3. Im Norden ist es sonnig.	☐	☑
4. Die Wetterfront im Norden kommt aus Skandinavien.	☑	☐
5. In Stuttgart regnet es am Freitag.	☐	☑
6. Am Wochenende schneit es in ganz Deutschland.	☑	☐

3 Expansion Have students work in small groups to predict the weather for the coming days, using simple sentences. Ex.: **Unsere Wettervorhersage: Am Montag schneit es. Am Dienstag gibt es Regen. Am Mittwoch ist es 18 Grad.**

Practice more at vhlcentral.com.

Kommunikation

4 Suggestion To get students started, find the first statement for each dialogue together as a class.

4 Vom Wetter und den Jahreszeiten

Arbeiten Sie mit einem Partner / einer Partnerin und bringen Sie die Sätze in jedem Dialog in eine logische Reihenfolge (*order*).

4 Expansion After the dialogues have been put in order, have volunteers read them out loud to the class.

Dialog 1

2 Schön. Die Sonne scheint und es ist ziemlich warm für die Jahreszeit.
4 Es regnet oft und die Sonne kommt selten durch die Wolkendecke hervor.
1 Paul, wie ist das Wetter heute in Köln?
3 Ja? Wie ist das typische Herbstwetter?

Dialog 2

3 April? Da ist es noch kühl und Schnee gibt es auch oft.
2 Der Monat, in dem ich Geburtstag habe. Der April.
1 Was ist dein Lieblingsmonat?
4 Ja, aber die Natur ist grün, die Vögel singen, alles beginnt neu.

5 Gute Ratschläge

Schreiben Sie mit einem Partner / einer Partnerin eine E-Mail an eine Austauschschülerin aus Deutschland. Sie will im Herbst Ihre Schule besuchen und möchte etwas über das Wetter und passende (*appropriate*) Kleidung wissen. Answers will vary.

5 Suggestion Have students peer-edit each other's e-mails.

BEISPIEL

Wetter und Kleidung
Von: Anna Webber [anna.webber@students.uni.edu]
An: Jasmin Peters [peterchen@gigglepost.de]
Datum: 26. Juni
Betreff: Wetter und Kleidung

Hallo Jasmin,
wie geht es dir? Wie läuft es mit deinen Prüfungen?
In deiner letzten E-Mail hast du mich nach dem Wetter hier in Atlanta gefragt. Also, du kommst im August an und da ist es hier einfach nur heiß und sonnig! Ab Mitte September…

7 Expansion Encourage students to choose a German-speaking city and use the Internet to find an actual weather report (in German) for that city.

6 Arbeitsblatt

Fragen Sie acht Personen in der Gruppe, wann sie Geburtstag haben, und schreiben Sie das Datum auf.

BEISPIEL

S1: *Sarah, in welcher Jahreszeit hast du Geburtstag?*
S2: *Ich habe im Frühling Geburtstag. Mein Geburtstag ist am achten April.*

6 Suggestion Before they start the activity, give students a moment to write down their birthdays and to practice pronouncing the date. Provide a model by writing your own birthday on the board.

6 Expansion Teach your class a short and simple birthday song, such as **Hoch soll er/sie leben** or **Zum Geburtstag viel Glück**. Lyrics can be found online.

7 Ein Wetterbericht

Schreiben Sie mit einem Partner / einer Partnerin einen Wetterbericht.

- Sagen Sie, welches Datum und welche Jahreszeit es ist.
- Berichten Sie über das Wetter für die nächsten sieben Tage.
- Illustrieren Sie Ihren Wetterbericht mit Hilfe von einem Poster.
- Sagen Sie, was man an den einzelnen (*individual*) Tagen machen kann oder soll.

Der Wetterbericht für Juli: Hamburg

Mittwoch, der 14. Juli	Donnerstag, der 15. Juli	Freitag, der 16. Juli
25° C	32° C	30° C
sonnig	sehr wolkig	stürmisch

Heute ist Mittwoch, der 14. Juli. Der Sommer zeigt seine schöne Seite. Die Sonne scheint den ganzen Tag und es ist das perfekte Wetter für das Schwimmbad…

7 Expansion Have students create short videos of their own **Wetterbericht**.

Aussprache und Rechtschreibung

Long and short vowels

German vowels can be either long or short. Long vowels are longer in duration and typically occur before a single consonant, before the letter **h**, or when the vowel is doubled. Short vowels are shorter in duration and usually occur before two consonants.

Meter **mehr** **Meer** **Messer** **melden**

The long **a** is pronounced like the *a* in the English word *calm*, but with the mouth wide open. The short **a** sounds almost like the long **a**, but it is held for a shorter period of time and pronounced with the mouth more closed.

mahnen **Mann** **lasen** **lassen**

The long **e** sounds like the *a* in the English word *late*. The short **e** sounds like the *e* in *pet*. The long **i** may be written as **i** or **ie**. It is pronounced like the *e* in *be*. The short **i** is pronounced like the *i* in *mitt*.

wen **wenn** **Visum** **fliegen** **Zimmer**

The long **o** is pronounced like the *o* in *hope*, but with the lips firmly rounded. The short **o** is pronounced like the *o* in *moth*, but with the lips rounded. The long **u** is pronounced like the *u* in *tuna*, but with the lips firmly rounded. The short **u** is pronounced like the *u* in *put*, but with the lips rounded.

Zoo **Zoll** **Flug** **Hund**

Suggestion Model the mouth position needed to produce the **o** and **u** sounds, with lips rounded and pushed forward.

1 Aussprechen Wiederholen Sie die Wörter, die Sie hören.

1. Haken / hacken
2. den / denn
3. Bienen / binnen
4. Sohn / Sonne
5. buchen / Bucht
6. Nase / nass
7. fehl / Fell
8. Miete / Mitte
9. wohne / Wonne
10. Humor / Hummer
11. Wagen / Wangen
12. Zehner / Zentner
13. Linie / Linde
14. Lot / Lotto
15. Mus / muss

1 Expansion Conduct a dictation based on these word pairs. For each pair, read only one of the words out loud and tell students to circle the word they hear.

2 Nachsprechen Wiederholen Sie die Sätze, die Sie hören.

1. Viele machen im Sommer Urlaub am Strand.
2. Wolf und Monika wollen den ganzen Tag in der Sonne liegen.
3. Sabine und Michael schwimmen lieber im Meer.
4. Alle sieben Studenten übernachten in einer Jugendherberge.
5. Hast du den Flug schon gebucht?
6. Wenn das Wetter schlecht ist, gehen wir ins Museum.

3 Sprichwörter Wiederholen Sie die Sprichwörter, die Sie hören.

[1] The way to the heart is through the stomach. (lit. *Love goes through the stomach.*)
[2] All's well that ends well.

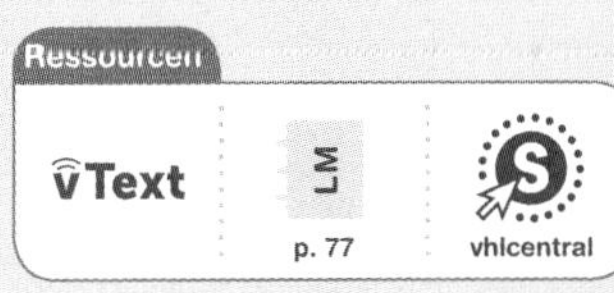

Fotoroman

Berlin von oben

Video

Sabites Kunst gefällt Meline nicht, aber sie sind trotzdem Freundinnen. George und Hans sprechen über ihre Nachbarinnen und wollen hoch hinaus.

Vorbereitung Have students look closely at scenes 1, 2, 9, and 10 and describe the weather in each one.

SABITE Meline! Hallo.
MELINE Hallo.
SABITE Wie findest du es? Gut, es gefällt dir nicht.
MELINE Wie bitte?
SABITE Ich weiß, dass dir meine Kunst nicht gefällt. Ich mag VWL auch nicht, aber wir sind dennoch Freundinnen.

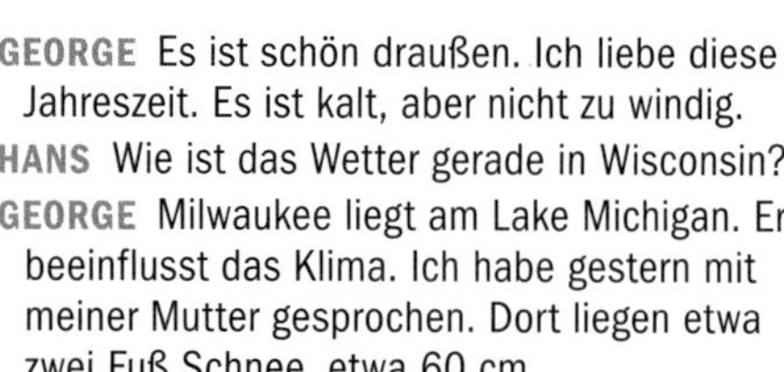

GEORGE Es ist schön draußen. Ich liebe diese Jahreszeit. Es ist kalt, aber nicht zu windig.
HANS Wie ist das Wetter gerade in Wisconsin?
GEORGE Milwaukee liegt am Lake Michigan. Er beeinflusst das Klima. Ich habe gestern mit meiner Mutter gesprochen. Dort liegen etwa zwei Fuß Schnee, etwa 60 cm.

HANS Wie ist das Wetter im Sommer?
GEORGE Im August ist es heiß und feucht. Es regnet, donnert und hagelt. Ich mag alle vier Jahreszeiten, aber der Frühling ist meine Lieblingsjahreszeit.
HANS Warum?
GEORGE Mein Geburtstag ist am 26. April. Und deiner?
HANS Am 17. Juli.

GEORGE Hey, was meinst du zu dieser Krawatte?
HANS Sie ist ganz okay. Warum?
GEORGE Ich habe mit Meline eingekauft. Sie hat sie ausgewählt. Ich war „zu amerikanisch" angezogen, also probiere ich neue Kleidung aus.

HANS Meline. Magst du sie?
GEORGE Ja. Nein, also nicht auf diese Weise. Zu Hause bin ich nicht mit Frauen befreundet. Wir haben Spaß zusammen. Ich habe gesehen, wie du mit ihr gelacht hast, also magst du sie doch.

SABITE Istanbul ist nicht weit von Berlin. Etwa 2.200 Kilometer. George ist 8.000 Kilometer von zu Hause entfernt.
MELINE George hat auch keine Freundin. Wann hast du zum ersten Mal über die Idee gesprochen?

ÜBUNGEN

1 Richtig oder falsch? **Entscheiden Sie, ob die folgenden Sätze richtig oder falsch sind.**

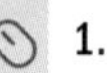

1. Meline und Sabite mögen dieselbe (*the same*) Kunst. Falsch.
2. In Milwaukee gibt es keinen Schnee. Falsch.
3. Im August ist es dort heiß und feucht. Richtig.
4. Der Frühling ist Georges Lieblingsjahreszeit. Richtig.
5. Der Geburtstag von Hans ist im Herbst. Falsch.
6. Hans findet Georges Krawatte hässlich. Falsch.
7. Istanbul ist etwa 8.000 Kilometer von Berlin entfernt. Falsch.
8. Sabite hat mit Lorenzo über Istanbul gesprochen. Richtig.
9. Der Berliner Fernsehturm ist das höchste Gebäude in Deutschland. Richtig.
10. Von dort kann man den Reichstag und das Brandenburger Tor sehen. Richtig.

PERSONEN

George

Hans

Meline

Sabite

7

SABITE An dem Abend, als wir dich und Lorenzo im Restaurant gesehen haben. Ich stand auf, ging Richtung Toilette und kam an deinem Tisch vorbei.
MELINE Torsten war also überrascht?
SABITE Ja.
MELINE Das ist das Problem! Du hast es ihm nicht zuerst gesagt.

8

SABITE Das ist doch dumm.
MELINE Sabite. Männer können manchmal dumm sein. Liebst du ihn? Sabite?
SABITE Ich weiß nicht.

9

GEORGE Der Fernsehturm ist 365 Meter hoch! Von dort kann man den Reichstag und das Brandenburger Tor sehen! Hans, ist alles in Ordnung?
HANS Ja. Mir geht's gut.
GEORGE Dies ist das höchste Gebäude in ganz Deutschland.
HANS Ich weiß.

10

HANS Mir geht's gut. Genieß den Ausblick. Ich bleibe solange hier stehen. Weit weg vom Rand.
GEORGE Hey, ist das Sabite?
HANS Wo?
GEORGE Fühlst du dich besser, Kumpel? Lass uns auf den Turm gehen und von dort oben Berlin sehen.
HANS Wow.

Nützliche Ausdrücke

- **Wie bitte?**
  Excuse me?
- **dennoch**
  nevertheless
- **beeinflussen**
  to influence
- **feucht**
  moist
- **auswählen**
  to choose
- **ausprobieren**
  to try
- **Nein, also nicht auf diese Weise.**
  No, not like that.
- **weit**
  far
- **Du hast es ihm nicht zuerst gesagt.**
  You didn't tell him first.
- **Dies ist das höchste Gebäude in ganz Deutschland.**
  This is the tallest building in all of Germany.
- **genießen**
  to enjoy
- **Fühlst du dich besser, Kumpel?**
  Are you feeling better, buddy?

3A.1

- **Ich stand auf, ging Richtung Toilette und kam an deinem Tisch vorbei.**
  I got up, went towards the restroom, and stopped by your table.

3A.2

- **Milwaukee liegt am Lake Michigan.**
  Milwaukee is on Lake Michigan.
- **Wann hast du zum ersten Mal über die Idee gesprochen?**
  When was the first time you mentioned the idea?

2  **Zum Besprechen** Sprechen Sie mit Ihren Klassenkameraden und finden Sie heraus, wer im gleichen Monat Geburtstag hat. Wie ist das Wetter in diesem Monat? Besprechen Sie es mit einem Partner. Answers will vary.

Suggestion Tell students that in 1961, West Germany and Turkey signed a labor recruitment agreement which allowed Turkish citizens to move to Germany as guest workers (**Gastarbeiter**). Today, there are approximately 3 million people of Turkish descent living in Germany.

3  **Vertiefung** Sabite möchte ein Semester lang in Istanbul studieren. Es ist das Heimatland (*country of origin*) von Faik, Sabites Vater. Finden Sie Informationen über Türken in Deutschland. Wie viele Türken leben in Deutschland? Wann sind sie nach Deutschland gekommen? Answers may vary.

Expansion Tell students that Berlin is home to the largest Turkish community outside of Turkey. There are some 300,000 people with Turkish roots living in Berlin.

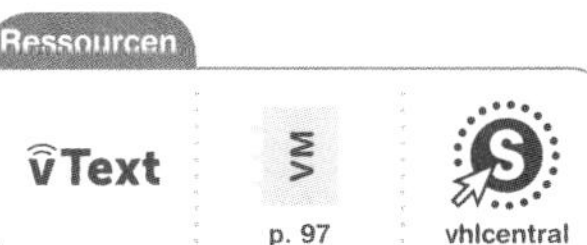

IM FOKUS

Windenergie

Reading

Suggestion Prepare students for the reading by asking them to describe what they see in the picture, including what the weather is like.

AP* Theme: Global Challenges
Context: Environmental Issues

TIPP

The **Deutsche Mark** (**DM** or **D-Mark**) was Germany's currency prior to the adoption of the **Euro** in 2002.

SCHLESWIG-HOLSTEIN LIEGT ZWISCHEN zwei Meeren, der Nordsee und der Ostsee. Dieses Bundesland ist relativ flach° und wegen der Nähe° zum Meer gibt es viel Wind. Schon seit 1982 investiert man hier immer mehr Geld in diese erneuerbare Energiequelle°.

Am Anfang waren es noch fünfzehn Windturbinen in einem Windpark in Braderup. Dreiunddreißig Privatbürger° finanzierten das Projekt mit einem Darlehen° von 12 Millionen DM (etwa 6 Millionen Euro).

Heute gibt es in Schleswig-Holstein über 2.400 Windturbinen. Bis zu ein Drittel des Strombedarfs° produziert man durch Windenergie in dem Bundesland. Aber Windturbinen stehen nicht nur auf dem Land. Seit 2009 kann man die Turbinen auch im Meer° finden. Hier, wo der Wind sehr stark bläst°, installiert man Turbinen in 30 Meter tiefem Wasser. Zwölf Turbinen produzieren bereits den Strom für etwa 50.000 Haushalte.

In Deutschland will man bis zum Jahr 2025 mit Windenergie 25% des Strombedarfs produzieren. 2014 gab es bereits 24.867 Windkraftanlagen in ganz Deutschland. Die Produktion von Strom mit Wind – aber auch mit Sonne, Wasser, Geothermie und Bioenergie – produziert weniger Stickstoff° im Vergleich° mit Atom-, Kohle- und Gaskraftwerken. Man braucht weniger Öl aus anderen Ländern. Und es gibt neue Arbeitsplätze° in Regionen wie Schleswig-Holstein.

Windenergie

	Deutschland	Österreich	Schweiz
Windkraftanlagen°:	24.867	1.016	37
Stromproduktion:	4.750 MW (Megawatt)	2.095 MW	60 MW
Anteil am Strombedarf:	5,8%	7,2%	0,5%

QUELLE: Bundesverband WindEnergie, IG Windkraft, Suisse Eole

Suggestion Ask students questions to check their understanding of the statistics. Ex.: **Welches Land hat die meisten Windkraftanlagen?**

flach *flat* **wegen der Nähe** *due to its closeness* **erneuerbare Energiequelle** *renewable energy source* **Privatbürger** *private citizens* **Darlehen** *loan* **ein Drittel des Strombedarfs** *one third of electricity requirements* **im Meer** *at sea* **bläst** *blows* **Stickstoff** *nitrogen* **Vergleich** *comparison* **Arbeitsplätze** *jobs* **Windkraftanlagen** *wind power plants*

ÜBUNGEN

1 **Richtig oder falsch?** Sind die Aussagen **richtig** oder **falsch**? Korrigieren Sie die falschen Aussagen.

1. Schleswig-Holstein liegt zwischen der Nord- und Ostsee. Richtig.
2. Seit 1982 investiert man in Schleswig-Holstein in Windenergie. Richtig.
3. Der Staat baute in Braderup 15 Windturbinen. Falsch. 33 Privatbürger bauten die Windturbinen.
4. In Schleswig-Holstein gibt es 24.867 Windturbinen. Falsch. In ganz Deutschland gibt es 24.867 Windturbinen.
5. Seit 2009 gibt es auch Windturbinen im Meer. Richtig.
6. Diese Turbinen sind in 30 Meter tiefem Wasser installiert. Richtig.
7. In Deutschland will man mit Windenergie ein Viertel des Stroms produzieren. Richtig.
8. In Schleswig-Holstein gibt es wegen der Windturbinen mehr Arbeit. Richtig.
9. In Österreich ist der Windenergie-Anteil am Strombedarf weniger als 1%. Falsch. In der Schweiz ist der Windenergie-Anteil am Strombedarf weniger als 1%.
10. In der Schweiz gibt es nur 37 Windkraftanlagen. Richtig.

Practice more at vhlcentral.com.

Deutsch im Alltag Ask students: **Welcher Ausdruck passt am besten zu dem heutigen Wetter?**

DEUTSCH IM ALLTAG

Wetterausdrücke

Hundewetter	*terrible weather*
Kaiserwetter	*beautiful, sunny weather*
Schmuddelwetter	*dreary, wet weather*
Es schüttet wie aus Eimern!	*It's raining cats and dogs!*
Petrus meint es gut!	*The weather's great!*

DIE DEUTSCHSPRACHIGE WELT

Planten un Blomen

Im Sommer kann man im Zentrum Hamburgs den berühmten Park Planten un Blomen besuchen. Hier gibt es einen alten Botanischen Garten. Außerdem finden Besucher den größten Japanischen Garten Europas in dem Park. Die einzelnen Gärten haben verschiedene Themen: der Rosengarten, der Apothekergarten° und die Tropengewächshäuser°. Im Musikpavillon finden im Sommer Konzerte statt° und man kann Wasserlichtkonzerte bewundern°. Kinder können auf Spielplätzen oder der Trampolinanlage spielen und auf Ponys reiten.

Suggestion Point out that the name of the park, **Planten un Blomen**, is **Plattdeutsch**. Have students translate the phrase into **Hochdeutsch**.

Apothekergarten *apothecary's garden* **Tropengewächshäuser** *tropical greenhouses* **finden... statt** *take place* **bewundern** *admire*

AP* Theme: Families & Communities
Context: Urban, Suburban, & Rural Life

PORTRÄT

Klima in Deutschland

AP* Theme: Families & Communities
Context: Urban, Suburban, & Rural Life

Das Wetter in Deutschland ist gemäßigt°: Im Winter ist es nicht sehr kalt und im Sommer nicht sehr warm. Im Durchschnitt° ist die Jahrestemperatur 8,1° C. Im Januar liegt die Durchschnittstemperatur bei -0,4° C und im Juli bei 16,9° C. Im Jahr fallen etwa 790 Millimeter Regen, besonders viel fällt im Juni. Die absolute Höchsttemperatur gab es 2003 in Karlsruhe und in Freiburg: 40,2° C. Freiburg liegt im Schwarzwald und gilt als° wärmste und sonnigste Stadt Deutschlands. Man kann hier jedes Jahr 1650 Sonnenstunden genießen. Die absolute Tiefsttemperatur gab es 2001 am Funtensee in den Bayrischen Alpen: -45,9° C.

Suggestion Point out that the German annual average of **8,1° C** is equivalent to 46.58° F, while the extreme temperatures of **-45,9° C** and **40,2° C** correspond to -50.62° F and 104.36° F, respectively.

gemäßigt *moderate* **Durchschnitt** *average* **gilt als** *is regarded as*

IM INTERNET

Finden Sie einen Plan von Planten un Blomen in Hamburg. Welche Gärten möchten Sie besuchen? Machen Sie eine Liste und planen Sie eine Tour.

Find out more at **vhlcentral.com**.

2 **Was fehlt?** Ergänzen Sie die Sätze.

1. Der Park Planten un Blomen liegt ___im Zentrum___ Hamburgs.
2. Besucher finden hier den größten ___Japanischen Garten___ Europas.
3. Es gibt einzelne Gärten wie zum Beispiel den Apothekergarten, ___den Rosengarten___ und die Tropengewächshäuser.
4. Der Winter in Deutschland ist nicht ___sehr kalt___.
5. In ___Freiburg___ kann man viel Sonne genießen.

3 **Lieblingsjahreszeit** Diskutieren Sie mit einem Partner / einer Partnerin Ihre Lieblingsjahreszeit. Warum lieben Sie diese Jahreszeit? Was machen Sie in der Jahreszeit? Welche Kleidung tragen Sie?

3 Virtual Chat You can also assign activity 3 on the Supersite. Students record individual responses that appear in your gradebook.

Resources

3A.1 Separable and inseparable prefix verbs (*Präteritum*)

You might want to direct students to **Vol. 1, 4A.3** to review the **Präsens** of separable and inseparable prefix verbs.

QUERVERWEIS

See **2B.2** to review the **Perfekt** of verbs with prefixes. To review the difference between **Perfekt** and **Präteritum**, see **2B.1**.

Suggestion Have students brainstorm a list of separable and inseparable prefix verbs they've already learned. Have them write sentences to demonstrate how each type of verb functions in the present and perfect tenses.

Startblock Both separable and inseparable prefix verbs can be used in the **Präteritum** to describe past events.

Ich **stand auf**, ging Richtung Toilette und **kam** an deinem Tisch **vorbei**.

Opa Otto **bereitete** die Weihnachtsgans **zu**. George **überraschte** ihn und...

- In the **Präteritum**, just like the **Präsens**, some prefixes are always attached to the verb, and others can be separated from it. When using a separable prefix verb in the **Präteritum**, move the prefix to the end of the sentence or clause.

Jan **verbrachte** den Sommer in der Schweiz.
*Jan **spent** the summer in Switzerland.*

Einmal **brachten** wir unseren Hund zur Schule **mit**.
*Once we **brought** our dog to school.*

Der Lehrer **erklärte** die Aufgabe.
*The teacher **explained** the assignment.*

Jans Schwester **rief** ihn zu seinem Geburtstag **an**.
*Jan's sister **called** him on his birthday.*

QUERVERWEIS

To review the formation of the **Präteritum**, see **2A.1**. See **Appendix A** for a complete list of strong verbs with their principal parts.

Suggestion Review the meaning of these verbs, making sure students recall which prefixes are separable and which are not.

- You learned in **2B.2** that verbs with prefixes can be either strong, weak, or mixed. The **Präteritum** of a verb with a prefix is the same as the **Präteritum** of its base verb, but with the prefix added to the front of the conjugated verb, if it is inseparable, or to the end of the clause, if it is separable.

Präteritum of separable and inseparable prefix verbs					
weak verbs					
kaufen	→	**kaufte**	**verkaufen**	→	**verkaufte**
schauen (*to look*)	→	**schaute**	**anschauen** (*to watch, look at*)	→	**schaute an**
strong verbs					
finden	→	**fand**	**erfinden** (*to invent*)	→	**erfand**
sprechen	→	**sprach**	**besprechen** (*to discuss*)	→	**besprach**
sehen	→	**sah**	**fernsehen** (*to watch TV*)	→	**sah fern**
mixed verbs					
bringen	→	**brachte**	**mitbringen**	→	**brachte mit**
			verbringen (*to spend (time)*)	→	**verbrachte**
kennen	→	**kannte**	**erkennen** (*to recognize*)	→	**erkannte**

Die Lehrerin **schaute** die Schüler **an**.
*The teacher **looked at** the students.*

Ich **erkannte** meine Tante nicht auf dem alten Foto.
*I didn't **recognize** my aunt in the old photo.*

Wir **sahen** als Kinder immer am Samstagmorgen **fern**.
*When we were kids, we always **watched TV** on Saturday mornings.*

Wer **erfand** das Internet?
*Who **invented** the Internet?*

- Remember that the prefix of a separable prefix verb is always stressed, while the prefix of an inseparable prefix verb is never stressed.

Als wir am Freitag **ausgingen**, regnete es noch nicht.
*When we **went out** on Friday, it wasn't raining yet.*

Wir **bestellten** zwei Pizzas zum Abendessen.
*We **ordered** two pizzas for dinner.*

- In a negative sentence, put **nicht** before the separable prefix.

Erik **rief** mich gestern **nicht an**.
*Erik **didn't** call me yesterday.*

Meine Mitbewohnerin **räumte** ihre Sachen **nicht auf**.
*My roommate **didn't** pick up her things.*

- When you talk about past events using a modal and a verb with a prefix, put the modal verb in the **Präteritum**. The prefixed verb goes at the end of the sentence in the infinitive form.

Frau Müller **musste** den kaputten Regenschirm **umtauschen**.
*Mrs. Müller **had to exchange** the broken umbrella.*

Niklas **wollte** sein altes Fahrrad **verkaufen**.
*Niklas **wanted to sell** his old bicycle.*

Suggestion Before they begin the **Jetzt sind Sie dran!** activity, verify that students know the meanings of each of the verbs, and have them identify which verbs have separable prefixes and which do not. Do the first few items as a class.

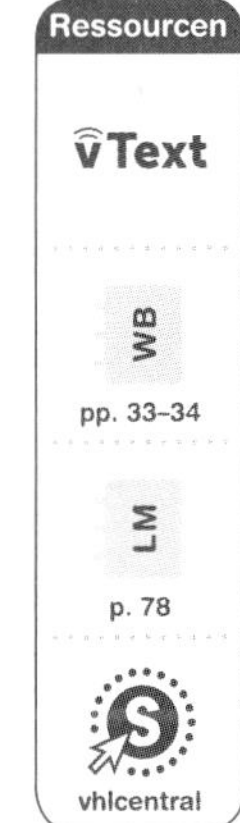

Jetzt sind Sie dran!

Ergänzen Sie die Tabelle mit den Verben im Präteritum.

	Infinitiv	Präteritum		Infinitiv	Präteritum
1.	bedeuten	*bedeutete*	7.	wegräumen	räumte weg
2.	einschlafen	schlief ein	8.	wiederholen	wiederholte
3.	beschreiben	beschrieb	9.	besuchen	besuchte
4.	zurückkommen	kam zurück	10.	entdecken	entdeckte
5.	umziehen	zog um	11.	mitbringen	brachte mit
6.	erkennen	erkannte	12.	verstehen	verstand

Anwendung

1 **Was fehlt?** Ergänzen Sie die Sätze mit den richtigen Formen der Verben im Präteritum.

BEISPIEL Frau Behrens _rief_ ihre Tochter jeden Tag _an_. (anrufen)

1. Im Sand _entdeckten_ wir eine alte Halskette. (entdecken)
2. Wann _fing_ der Regen _an_? (anfangen)
3. Ich _verkaufte_ mein Auto vor einem Monat. (verkaufen)
4. Meine Großeltern _sahen_ immer nach dem Essen _fern_. (fernsehen)
5. Wir _besuchten_ unsere Cousinen oft im Sommer. (besuchen)
6. Markus _verstand_ als Schüler nichts von Mathematik. (verstehen)

2 **Was für ein Tag** Ergänzen Sie die Sätze mit den richtigen Verben aus der Liste im Präteritum.

aufräumen	besuchen	erklären
aufwachen	einkaufen	verkaufen

▶ **BEISPIEL** Tobias _wachte_ um acht Uhr _auf_.

1. Michael _kaufte_ fürs Abendessen _ein_.

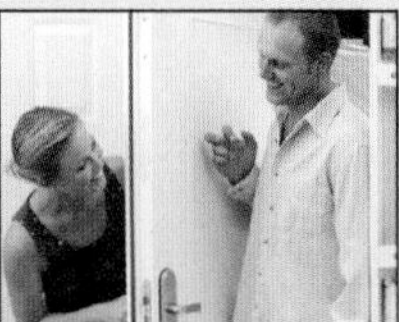

2. Am Samstag _besuchte_ Julian seine Schwester in Heidelberg.

3. Frau Hölzel _erklärte_ den Schülern die Aufgabe.

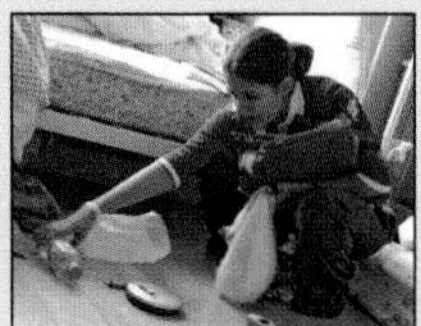

4. Ich _räumte_ mein Zimmer _auf_.

5. Wir _verkauften_ gestern viel Currywurst.

3 **Noch einmal** Schreiben Sie die Sätze im Präteritum. Benutzen Sie dabei das Modalverb in Klammern.

BEISPIEL Wir tauschten unser Geld auf der Bank um. (wollen)
Wir wollten unser Geld auf der Bank umtauschen.

1. Thomas sah den ganzen Morgen fern. (wollen)
   Thomas wollte den ganzen Morgen fernsehen.
2. Wir bereiteten ein schönes Essen vor. (wollen) Wir wollten ein schönes Essen vorbereiten.
3. Erik rief seine Freundin nicht an. (dürfen)
   Erik durfte seine Freundin nicht anrufen.
4. Herr Roth verkaufte sein Auto nicht. (können) Herr Roth konnte sein Auto nicht verkaufen.
5. Die Lehrerin wiederholte den Satz. (müssen)
   Die Lehrerin musste den Satz wiederholen.
6. Ich brachte meinen Computer in den Urlaub mit. (dürfen)
   Ich durfte meinen Computer in den Urlaub mitbringen.

Practice more at **vhlcentral.com.**

Kommunikation

4 **Eine Überraschungsfeier** Lukas und Lena planten letzten Herbst eine Überraschungsfeier für ihre Eltern. Bilden Sie mit einem Partner / einer Partnerin zu jedem Bild einen Satz im Präteritum. Answers may vary.

▶ **BEISPIEL** Lukas und Lena *bereiteten eine Überraschungsfeier für ihre Eltern vor.*

1. Lukas und Lena kauften Sachen für die Feier ein.

2. Lena lud viele Verwandte und Freunde ein.

3. Die Gäste kamen am Nachmittag an.

4. Frau Braun brachte eine Schokoladentorte mit.

5. Die Großeltern überraschten Svens und Lenas Eltern mit einer Reise nach Amerika.

5 **Historische Personen** Bilden Sie mit einem Partner / einer Partnerin logische Fragen im Präteritum. Wechseln Sie sich bei den Fragen und Antworten ab.

BEISPIEL

S1: *Wer entdeckte die Stadt Troja?*
S2: *Heinrich Schliemann.*

Wer...
entdecken / die Allgemeine (*General*) Relativitätstheorie
erklären / die genetischen Regeln (*rules*)
erfinden / den Buchdruck (*printing press*)
bekommen / einen Nobelpreis für Literatur

Gregor Johann Mendel
Günter Grass
Heinrich Schliemann
Albert Einstein
Johannes Gutenberg

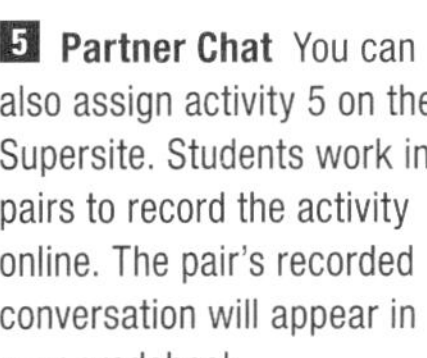

5 **Partner Chat** You can also assign activity 5 on the Supersite. Students work in pairs to record the activity online. The pair's recorded conversation will appear in your gradebook.

Sample answers:
Wer entdeckte die Allgemeine Relativitätstheorie? Albert Einstein
Wer erklärte die genetischen Regeln? Gregor Johann Mendel
Wer erfand den Buchdruck? Johannes Gutenberg
Wer bekam einen Nobelpreis für Literatur? Günter Grass

6 **Eine spannende Geschichte** Schreiben Sie mit einem Partner / einer Partnerin eine Geschichte. Benutzen Sie das Präteritum und mindestens (*at least*) drei Elemente aus der Liste. Answers will vary.

BEISPIEL Es war eine dunkle und stürmische Nacht.
Ich schlief schlecht und stand um drei Uhr nachts wieder auf. Ich sah aus dem Fenster hinaus...

den Regenmantel anziehen	hinausgehen
aufräumen	weggehen
aufstehen	das Handy vergessen
Angst bekommen	die Orientierung verlieren
wieder einschlafen	(nicht) verstehen

3A.2 Prepositions of location / Prepositions in set phrases

Presentation

Startblock When describing locations, and in certain fixed expressions, many German prepositions are used in ways that differ from their English counterparts.

Suggestion English speakers may find phrases like **auf der Post**, **auf der Bank**, and **auf dem Markt** counter-intuitive. Encourage students to simply memorize these phrases as "sound bites."

Prepositions of location

- In **1B.3** you learned to use two-way prepositions with the dative to indicate location and with the accusative to show movement toward a destination.

Neben dem Schreibtisch steht ein großes Bücherregal.
*There's a big bookcase **next to the desk**.*

Stell den Stuhl bitte **neben den Tisch**.
*Please put the chair **next to the table**.*

QUERVERWEIS

See **1B.3** to review two-way prepositions.

- Use **auf** with the dative to indicate that something is located on a horizontal surface or to describe a location in a public building or open space.

Deine Bücher liegen **auf dem Tisch**.
*Your books are **on the table**.*

Ich war gestern **auf der Bank**.
*I was **at the bank** yesterday.*

Greta hat schöne Blumen **auf dem Markt** gekauft.
*Greta bought beautiful flowers **at the market**.*

Suggestion Remind students that the expression **zu Hause**, which they learned in **Vol 1.**, **4B.2**, is an exception to the general rule of using **in** with enclosed spaces.

Suggestion Point out that most masculine and neuter country names are directly preceded by **in** with no article, but there are a few that always take a definite article, and are thus preceded by **im** in the dative, ex. **Er lebt im Libanon**.

- Use **an** with the dative to indicate a location *on* or *at* a border, wall, or body of water.

An der Wand hängt ein schöner Kalender.
*There's a nice calendar hanging **on the wall**.*

Am Strand war es heute kühl und windig.
*It was cool and windy **at the beach** today.*

- Use **in** with the dative to indicate a location *on* or *in* an enclosed space.

Die Sonnenbrille ist **in meiner Handtasche**.
*The sunglasses are **in my purse**.*

Die Kinder spielen gern **im Park**.
*The kids like to play **in the park**.*

Ich wohne **in der Joachimstraße**.
*I live **on Joachim Street**.*

ACHTUNG

Note that the idea of an enclosed space includes the radio, television, or Internet: **Das habe ich im Radio gehört; Das können wir im Internet finden.**

- To indicate location in a country whose name is feminine or plural, use **in** with the dative form of the definite article, plus the country name.

Wagner wohnte **in der Schweiz**.
*Wagner lived **in Switzerland**.*

Meine Mutter ist jetzt **in den USA**.
*My mother is **in the U.S.** right now.*

Suggestion Remind students that they have already seen the phrase **Im Internet** in the activity boxes at the end of each **Kultur** section.

You will learn more about using prepositions with geographical locations in **Vol. 3, 2B.1**.

- In **1B.3** you learned that **bei** is always used with the dative case. Use **bei** with a noun referring to a person or business to indicate a location at that person's home or at that place of business.

Ich kaufe gern **bei Aldi** ein.
*I like shopping **at Aldi's**.*

Anna war gestern **beim Friseur**.
*Anna was **at the hairdresser's** yesterday.*

Als Student wohnte Nils im Sommer **bei seinen Eltern**.
*When he was a student, Nils lived **with his parents** during the summer.*

Heute Abend spielen wir **bei mir** Karten.
*We're playing cards **at my place** tonight.*

- You can also use **bei** to mean *near* a location or *in the presence of* a condition.

Das Restaurant liegt **bei Wilhelmshaven**.
*The restaurant is **near Wilhelmshaven**.*

Bei schönem Wetter gehen wir gern spazieren.
*We like to go for walks **when the weather is nice**.*

Prepositions in set phrases

- Certain combinations of verbs and prepositions have specific, idiomatic meanings. The prepositions in these fixed expressions are always followed by the same case, regardless of whether the verb they are associated with indicates location or movement.

Jasmin **erzählte** uns **von ihren Problemen**.
*Jasmin **told** us **about her problems**.*

Max muss einen Brief **an seine Tante schreiben**.
*Max has to **write** a letter **to his aunt**.*

- Use the *dative* after the following set phrases.

Verb phrases with the dative	
Angst haben vor	*to be afraid of*
arbeiten an	*to work on*
erzählen von	*to talk about; to tell a story about*
fragen nach	*to ask about*
handeln von	*to be about; to have to do with*
helfen bei	*to help with*
träumen von	*to dream of*

Meine Nichte **hat Angst vor** Hunden.
*My niece **is afraid of** dogs.*

Herr Weiss **arbeitet an** einem neuen Buch.
*Mister Weiss **is working on** a new book.*

- Use the *accusative* after the following expressions.

Verb phrases with the accusative	
antworten auf	*to answer*
denken an	*to think about*
schreiben an	*to write to*
sprechen/reden über	*to talk about*
warten auf	*to wait for*

Wir haben lange **auf** den Bus **gewartet**.
*We **waited** a long time **for** the bus.*

Antworte bitte **auf** die Frage.
*Please **answer** the question.*

Suggestion Remind students that they can also use **bei** with a person's name to refer to that person's home. Ex.: **Wir waren *bei Jonas*.**

Suggestion Point out that **bei** + dative can also be used to "set the scene" for the action in a sentence. Ex.: **Beim Abendessen haben wir über die Ferien geredet**.

Suggestion Students may have difficulty with these German verb/preposition combinations. Point out that English also has specific verb/preposition combinations with specific, idiomatic meanings. Ex: "to wait for" *vs.* "to wait on".

Expansion Have students ask each other **Wovor hast du Angst?** Provide humorous model answers.

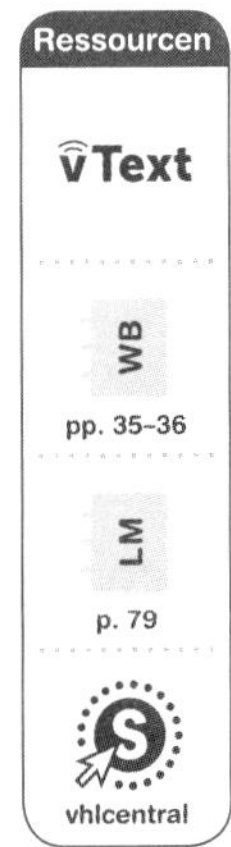

Jetzt sind Sie dran! **Wählen Sie die passenden Präpositionen.**

1. Wir haben (mit / (auf) / über) dem Markt Obst gekauft.
2. Mein Hund hat Angst (über / von / (vor)) Donner und Blitz.
3. Nach dem Sturm lag viel Hagel ((auf) / an / in) der Straße.
4. Sara verbringt ihren Sommer (mit / aus / (in)) der Türkei.
5. Wir helfen unserer Mutter ((bei) / vor / in) der Hausarbeit.
6. ((An) / Mit / Unter) der Berliner Mauer gibt es viel Graffiti.
7. Du hast nicht (über / bei / (auf)) meine Frage geantwortet.
8. Wohnt dein Bruder immer noch (an / (bei) / auf) dir?
9. Hast du schon (bei / (an) / nach) Oma geschrieben?
10. Sophia hat mir (mit / nach / (von)) ihrem Wochenende erzählt.

Anwendung

1 Präpositionen Ergänzen Sie die passenden Präpositionen.

BEISPIEL ___Bei___ schlechtem Wetter werde ich oft müde.

1. Wir campen jeden Sommer ___auf___ dem Campingplatz.
2. Maria reitet oft ihr Pferd ___im___ Park.
3. Gehst du oft ___bei___ Aldi einkaufen?
4. Cuxhaven liegt ___an___ der Nordsee.
5. Unsere Katze sitzt gern ___auf___ dem Balkon und schaut den Vögeln zu.

2 Was fehlt? Ergänzen Sie die Lücken mit den richtigen Präpositionen.

BEISPIEL Meine Schlüssel sind nicht ___in___ meiner Tasche.

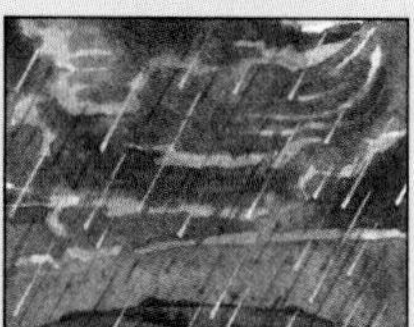

1. Meine Hunde haben immer Angst ___vor___ einem Sturm.

2. Der Film handelt ___von___ einer Naturkatastrophe.

3. Im Sommer mieten wir ein kleines Haus ___an___ einem Strand.

4. Die Frau fragt den Verkäufer ___nach___ dem Preis.

5. Elias arbeitet ___an___ seiner Hausaufgabe.

3 Kombinieren Ergänzen Sie die passenden Präpositionen und wählen Sie dann die beste Antwort auf jede Frage.

___a___ 1. Hast du das ___im___ Internet gefunden?
___d___ 2. Warum hat deine Mutter Angst ___vor___ Hunden?
___b___ 3. Oma, erzähl mir bitte ___von___ deiner Kindheit.
___e___ 4. Bleibt Daniel die ganzen Semesterferien ___bei___ seinen Eltern?
___c___ 5. Arbeitet Greta schon ___an___ ihrem Referat?

a. Nein, ich habe es im Radio gehört.
b. Ach Kindchen, das war vor so langer Zeit.
c. Ja, sie hat schon damit angefangen.
d. Ich weiß nicht, aber sie mag Katzen.
e. Nein, er macht einen Sprachkurs in Spanien für vier Wochen.

4 Fragen Stellen Sie einem Partner / einer Partnerin diese Fragen. Answers will vary.

1. An wen schreibst du oft E-Mails?
2. Worüber redest du mit deinen Freunden?
3. Wo verbringst du deine Semesterferien?
4. Wo kaufst du deine Lebensmittel ein?
5. Wovon träumst du?
6. Wovor hast du Angst?

Practice more at **vhlcentral.com.**

4 Virtual Chat You can also assign activity 4 on the Supersite. Students record individual responses that appear in your gradebook.

NATIONAL communication STANDARDS

Kommunikation

5 Kettenreaktion Sagen Sie abwechselnd, wo diese Dinge in Ihrem Klassenzimmer sind. Answers will vary.

BEISPIEL

S1: *die Uhr*
S2: *Die Uhr hängt an der Wand.*
S3: *der Stuhl*
S4: *Oliver sitzt auf dem Stuhl.*

der Boden	die Lampen	die Tafel
das Buch	das Poster	die Uhr
der Computer	der Stuhl	die Wand

6 Was und wo ist das? Wählen Sie ein Objekt aus dem Bild und beschreiben Sie seine Lage (*location*). Ihr Partner / Ihre Partnerin muss erraten, welchen Ort oder Objekt Sie beschreiben. Answers will vary.

BEISPIEL

S1: *Ein blaues Auto steht davor.*
S2: *Ist es der Supermarkt?*
S1: *Ja.*

6 Partner Chat You can also assign activity 6 on the Supersite. Students work in pairs to record the activity online. The pair's recorded conversation will appear in your gradebook.

7 Was kann man wo machen? Entscheiden Sie (*Decide*) mit einem Partner / einer Partnerin, wo Sie die folgenden Aktivitäten machen können. Answers will vary.

BEISPIEL

S1: *Wo kann ich ein Buch kaufen?*
S2: *Das kannst du im Buchgeschäft machen.*

Wo kann ich... ?	*Das kannst du... machen.*
eine Tasse Kaffee bestellen	*beim Bäcker*
Obst und Gemüse kaufen	*auf der Bank*
leckere Brötchen kaufen	*in der Bibliothek*
in der Sonne liegen	*im Café*
ein Bild von Picasso sehen	*im Internetcafé*
ein Wörterbuch finden	*im Museum*
Geld bekommen	*am Strand*
im Internet surfen	*im Supermarkt*

7 Virtual Chat You can also assign activity 7 on the Supersite. Students record individual responses that appear in your gradebook.

8 Persönliche Fragen Machen Sie ein Interview mit einem Partner / einer Partnerin und finden Sie ein paar persönliche Informationen heraus. Answers will vary.

1. Hast du Angst vor:	___ Gewitter	___ Hunden?	___ schlechten Noten?
2. Redest du gern über:	___ Politik?	___ Musik?	___ Sport?
3. Arbeitest du heute an:	___ einem Referat?	___ deinen Hausaufgaben?	___ nichts?
4. Denkst du oft an:	___ deine Freunde?	___ deine Kurse?	___ deine Familie?
5. Handeln deine Träume von:	___ deiner Kindheit?	___ deinem Leben jetzt?	___ anderen Situationen?

8 Virtual Chat You can also assign activity 8 on the Supersite.

Wiederholung

1 **In der Stadt** Wechseln Sie sich mit einem Partner / einer Partnerin ab: Beschreiben Sie, wo Yusuf gestern in der Stadt war. Sample answers are provided.

1 Suggestion Do the first few sentences together as a class. Remind students that since they will be talking about Yusuf's *location*, they will use the dative with any two-way prepositions.

▶ **BEISPIEL** *Zuerst war Yusuf auf der Post. Dann war er...*

2 Suggestion Remind students that in sentences beginning with a time expression, the conjugated verb will appear in 2nd position, *before* the subject. Provide model answers that say what you like to do.

1. Dann war er auf der Bank.

2. Dann hat er im Restaurant gegessen.

3. Im Park hat er in der Sonne gelegen.

4. In der Metzgerei hat er Wurst gekauft.

5. In der Bäckerei hat er frisches Brot gekauft.

2 **Bei so einem Wetter** Fragen Sie Ihren Partner / Ihre Partnerin, was er/sie bei verschiedenem Wetter macht. Answers may vary.

2 Virtual Chat You can also assign activity 2 on the Supersite.

BEISPIEL

S1: *Was machst du bei windigem Wetter?*
S2: *Bei windigem Wetter gehe ich spazieren.*

1. windig
2. sonnig
3. schlecht
4. kalt
5. heiß
6. schön

3 **Hausarbeit** Beschreiben Sie mit einem Partner / einer Partnerin, wie Sie und Ihre Geschwister (*siblings*) am Wochenende die Wohnung putzten. Benutzen Sie Vokabeln aus der Liste. Answers will vary.

BEISPIEL

S1: *Am Wochenende mussten wir viel Hausarbeit machen.*
S2: *Im Bad putzte Eric die Toilette und die Badewanne.*

abstauben	Müll rausbringen
aufräumen	Geschirr spülen
fegen	staubsaugen
Bett machen	Wäsche waschen
putzen	wischen

3 Partner Chat You can also assign activity 3 on the Supersite. Students work in pairs to record the activity online. The pair's recorded conversation will appear in your gradebook.

4 **Arbeitsblatt** Sie bekommen ein Arbeitsblatt von Ihrem Lehrer / Ihrer Lehrerin mit verschiedenen Aktivitäten. Wer in der Gruppe hat diese Aktivitäten gemacht? Answers will vary.

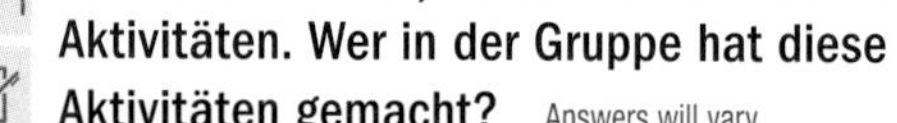

BEISPIEL

S1: *Hast du deinen Freunden von einem guten Buch erzählt?*
S2: *Ja, ich habe meinen Freunden von einem guten Buch erzählt.*

5 **Diskutieren und kombinieren** Tauschen Sie mit Ihrem Partner / Ihrer Partnerin Informationen aus: Was machten Paul und Sara gestern? Füllen Sie die Tabelle für Ihren Partner / Ihre Partnerin und sich selber (*yourself*) aus. Answers will vary.

BEISPIEL

S1: *Was hat Sara am Donnerstag gemacht?*
S2: *Sie hat bei A&P eingekauft.*

6 **Als ich zehn war** Erzählen Sie Ihrem Partner / Ihrer Partnerin, was Sie machten, als Sie zehn Jahre alt waren. Was machten Sie im Frühling, im Sommer, im Herbst und im Winter?

6 Virtual Chat You can also assign activity 6 on the Supersite.

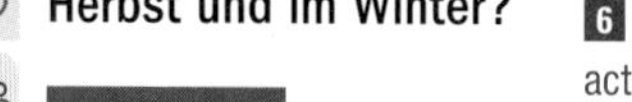

BEISPIEL

S1: *Was hast du mit zehn im Herbst gemacht?*
S2: *Im Herbst bin ich Fahrrad gefahren. Im Winter...*

Zapping

Video

AP* Theme: Contemporary Life
Context: Entertainment, Travel, & Leisure

Expansion Pause the video on the image of the map at the beginning. Ask:

- **Wo liegt „das grüne Binnenland"?**
- **Welches Land liegt nördlich von Schleswig-Holstein?**
- **Schleswig-Holstein liegt zwischen zwei Meeren. Wie heißen die zwei Meere?**

Urlaub im grünen Binnenland

Im Norden Schleswig-Holsteins, zwischen Nord- und Ostsee, an der Grenze zu Dänemark, liegt das grüne Binnenland. In dieser Gegend können Touristen Wiesen°, Flüsse und zwei sehr unterschiedliche° Meere° finden. Die wunderschöne Fluss- und Seenlandschaft° ist sehr flach und hat nur sanfte Hügel°. Zu den Hauptattraktionen gehört der Nationalpark Wattenmeer mit tollen Stränden, Schlössern und Wikingerdörfern. Neben der Natur gibt es viel Kultur in Städten wie Flensburg und Schleswig zu sehen.

Suggestion After showing students the scene in the tourist center, ask:

- **Wie begrüßt die Frau die Touristen? Warum?**
- **Wie lange will das Paar hier Urlaub machen?**

Reetdachdecker° bei ihrer Arbeit

Sie sind im Land der Wikinger!

Badeurlaub° genießen Sie im Seebad°, an Sandstränden oder Naturbadestellen.

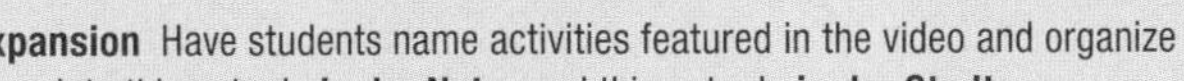

Expansion Have students name activities featured in the video and organize them into things to do **in der Natur** and things to do **in der Stadt**.

Wiesen *meadows* **unterschiedliche** *different* **Meere** *seas* **Seenlandschaft** *lake landscape* **sanfte Hügel** *gentle hills*
Reetdachdecker *roof thatchers* **Badeurlaub** *beach vacation* **Seebad** *beach resort*

Verständnis Markieren Sie alle richtigen Antworten.

1. Was kann man in der Region Grünes Binnenland Schleswig-Holstein *nicht* sehen?
   a. Meere (b. hohe Berge) c. Flüsse d. Strände
2. Welche Aktivitäten kann man in dieser Region *nicht* machen?
   a. Rad fahren b. einkaufen (c. Ski fahren) d. schwimmen

Diskussion Diskutieren Sie die folgenden Fragen mit einem Partner / einer Partnerin. Answers will vary.

1. Was möchten Sie gerne im grünen Binnenland Schleswig-Holsteins sehen und machen? Warum?
2. Sie sind die Touristen am Anfang des Videos und besuchen die Touristeninformation: Welche Fragen wollen Sie der Frau stellen?

Partner Chat You can also assign this activity on the Supersite.

Kontext

Communicative Goals

You will learn how to:

- talk about travel
- talk about vacations and tourism

Reisen

Vocabulary Tools

AP* Theme: Contemporary Life
Context: Entertainment, Travel, & Leisure

Suggestion Model correct pronunciation of **Passagier**. Point out that the **g** is soft.

der Ausgang, -¨e
Er liest eine Karte.
Sonne und Meer
der Strand, -¨e
das Meer, -e
die Reisenden (*pl.*)
(*sing.* der Reisende)
Sport
die Bordkarte, -n
die Zeitung, -en
das Handgepäck

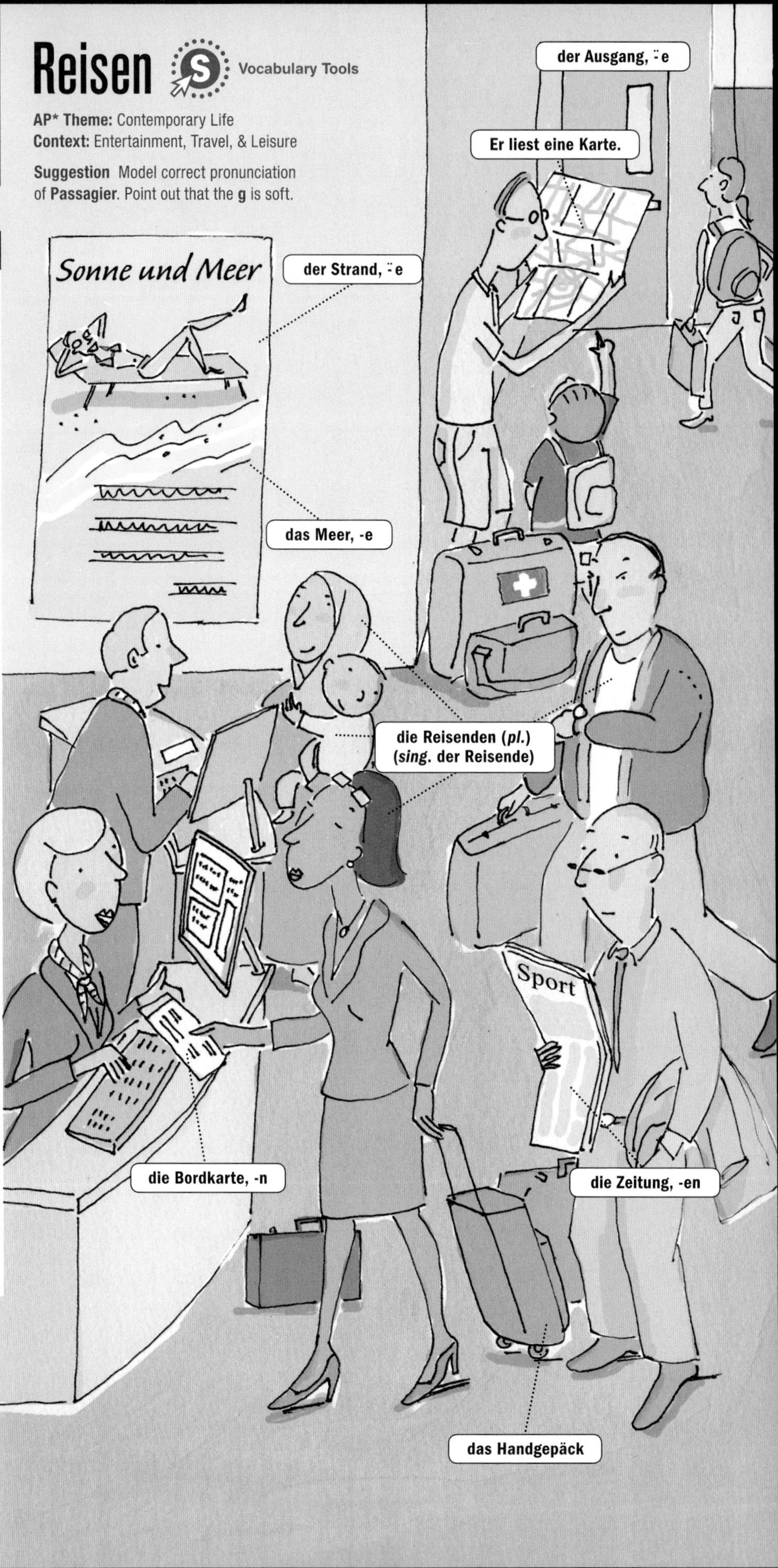

Wortschatz

am Flughafen	***at the airport***
der Abflug	*departure*
die Ankunft	*arrival*
die Businessklasse	*business class*
der Flug, -¨e	*flight*
das Flugticket, -s	*ticket*
das Gepäck	*luggage*
der Koffer, -	*suitcase*
der Passagier, -e	*passenger*
die Passkontrolle, -n	*passport control*
der Personalausweis, -e	*ID card*
die Reise, -n	*trip*
das Reisebüro, -s	*travel agency*
die Touristenklasse	*economy class*
die Verspätung, -en	*delay*
das Visum (*pl.* die Visa)	*visa*
der Zoll	*customs*
fliegen	*to fly*
das Ausland	*abroad*
pünktlich	*on time*
die Ferien	***vacation***
die Kreuzfahrt, -en	*cruise*
der Skiurlaub, -e	*ski vacation*
packen	*to pack*
übernachten	*to spend the night*
Unterkünfte	***accommodations***
der Fahrstuhl, -¨e	*elevator*
der Gast, -¨e	*(hotel) guest*
das (Fünf-Sterne-)Hotel	*(five-star) hotel*
die Jugendherberge, -n	*youth hostel*
der Schlüssel, -	*key*
der Zimmerservice	*room service*
abbrechen (bricht... ab)	*to cancel*
buchen	*to make a (hotel) reservation*
voll besetzt	*fully occupied*

Expansion Ask students: **Fliegen Sie gerne? Warum? Warum nicht?** Have them brainstorm a list of things they associate with flying.

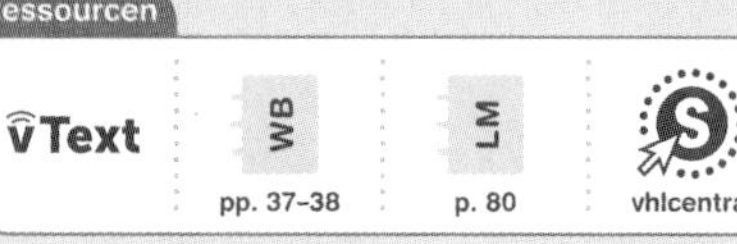

Ressourcen

vText | WB pp. 37–38 | LM p. 80 | vhlcentral

Es landet. (landen)

Es fliegt ab. (abfliegen)

das Flugzeug, -e

Sie machen Urlaub.

Sie stehen Schlange.

Die Welt

Anwendung

Expansion Have students write and act out short dialogues that take place at an airport, using at least six vocabulary words from this lesson.

1 Vergleiche Ergänzen Sie die Vergleiche mit dem richtigen Wort.

1. das Hotel : der Gast :: das Flugzeug : (der Passagier / der Familienstand)
2. heimkommen : ausgehen :: ankommen : (abfliegen / aufstehen)
3. früh : spät :: frei : (besorgt / besetzt)
4. buchen : die Reise :: packen : (der Koffer / der Keller)
5. das Zimmer : der Schlüssel :: das Ausland : (das Seminar / das Visum)
6. der Skiurlaub : die Alpen :: die Kreuzfahrt : (das Meer / der Park)

2 Kategorien Schreiben Sie die Wörter aus der Liste in die passenden Kategorien. Answers may vary slightly.

die Bordkarte	die Kreuzfahrt	das Reisebüro
das Hotel	die Passkontrolle	der Tourist
die Jugendherberge	der Personalausweis	der Zimmerservice

Unterkunft	Flughafen	Urlaub
die Jugendherberge	die Bordkarte	das Hotel
das Hotel	der Personalausweis	die Kreuzfahrt
der Zimmerservice	der Tourist	der Tourist
der Personalausweis	die Passkontrolle	das Reisebüro

2 Expansion Have students add at least one additional word to each category.

3 Kombinationen Kombinieren Sie die Wörter mit ihren Definitionen.

c 1. der Reisende
d 2. der Zoll
f 3. die Verspätung
e 4. die Businessklasse
b 5. die Jugendherberge
a 6. der Pass

a. den braucht man für eine Reise ins Ausland
b. hier kann man billig übernachten
c. eine Person macht eine Reise
d. hier kontrolliert man Importe aus dem Ausland
e. hier sitzt man im Flugzeug mit allem Komfort
f. nicht pünktlich ankommen

4 Ansagen Hören Sie die Ansagen (*announcements*) an und entscheiden Sie, welche Ansage am besten zu welchem Satz passt.

Ansage 4 1. Die Passagiere fliegen nach Russland.
Ansage 5 2. Das Flugzeug ist gerade gelandet.
Ansage 1 3. Der Check-in für Air France ist im Terminal 1.
Ansage 3 4. Der Flug nach Hamburg fliegt bald ab.
Ansage 2 5. Die Passagiere kommen mit Verspätung in Rom an.

4 Suggestion Students may need to hear the recording several times in order to complete the exercise.

ACHTUNG

To say *highway map* in German, use **die Landkarte**; for *city map* use **der Stadtplan**. A GPS system is called **das Navi**.

Kommunikation

5 **Reisen** **Beantworten Sie die Fragen mit ganzen Sätzen. Vergleichen Sie dann Ihre Antworten mit den Antworten Ihres Partners / Ihrer Partnerin.** Answers will vary.

1. In welcher Jahreszeit machen Sie gern Urlaub? Warum?
2. Mit wem reisen Sie nicht gern? Warum?
3. Was bringen Sie mit auf eine Kreuzfahrt nach Europa?
4. Was packen Sie normalerweise in Ihr Handgepäck?
5. Wo haben Sie schon Urlaub gemacht?
6. Wohin möchten Sie gern reisen? Warum?

5 Suggestion Have students share their answers to items 5 and 6 with the class.

5 Virtual Chat You can also assign activity 5 on the Supersite. Students record individual responses that appear in your gradebook.

6 **Diskutieren und kombinieren** **Ihr Lehrer / Ihre Lehrerin gibt Ihnen verschiedene Blätter mit Durchsagen. Fragen Sie Ihren Partner / Ihre Partnerin nach den fehlenden Informationen und wechseln Sie sich dabei ab.** Answers will vary.

BEISPIEL

S1: *Wer kann zum Ausgang gehen?*
S2: *Nur Passagiere mit Bordkarten.*

6 Suggestion Before beginning the activity, clarify the meaning of any unfamiliar vocabulary and practice pronunciation of the longer words.

7 **Beschreibungen** **Schreiben Sie mit einem Partner / einer Partnerin eine Beschreibung (*description*) von jedem (*each*) Bild. Lesen Sie danach einem anderen Paar Ihre Beschreibung vor. Das andere Paar soll erraten, welches Bild zu welcher Beschreibung passt.** Answers will vary.

BEISPIEL

S1: *Es ist Abend. Ein Mädchen sitzt auf einem Koffer.*
S1: *Sie liest Zeitung.*
S3: *Das ist Bild 1.*

7 Suggestion Point out that in the expression **Zeitung lesen** the article is not used.

1. 

2. 

3. 

4. 

5. 

6. 

Aussprache und Rechtschreibung

Pure vowels versus diphthongs

German has three diphthongs: **au**, **ai/ei**, and **eu/äu**. In these vowel combinations, two vowel sounds are pronounced together in the same syllable.

Haus **Mai** **meine** **scheu** **läuft**

All other German vowel sounds are pure vowels. Whether long or short, they never glide into another vowel sound.

kalt **Schnee** **Spiel** **Monat** **Schule**

Be sure to pronounce the vowels in German words as pure vowel sounds, even when they resemble English words with similar pronunciations.

kann **Stereo** **Apfel** **Boot** **Schuh**

Suggestion Have students pronounce each German word alongside its English counterpart, to help them hear the difference in the vowel sounds: "**kann**, *can*", "**Stereo**, *stereo*", etc.

1 Aussprechen Wiederholen Sie die Wörter, die Sie hören.

1. Hagel
2. wann
3. Regen
4. Wetter
5. minus
6. Winter
7. Oktober
8. Sommer
9. Januar
10. Geburtstag
11. August
12. Mai
13. Zeit
14. heute
15. Häuser
16. Gasthaus

2 Nachsprechen Wiederholen Sie die Sätze, die Sie hören.

1. Es hat fast den ganzen Tag geregnet.
2. Im Juli ist es am Nachmittag zu heiß.
3. Im Winter gehe ich gern langlaufen.
4. Trink eine Tasse Tee, damit du wieder wach wirst!
5. Im Mai wird es schön warm und sonnig.
6. Im Sommer schwimmen die Kinder im See.
7. Im Herbst muss Max sein Segelboot reparieren lassen.
8. Meine Freundin besucht mich heute.

3 Sprichwörter Wiederholen Sie die Sprichwörter, die Sie hören.

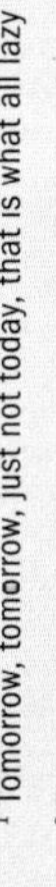

[1] Tomorrow, tomorrow, just not today, that is what all lazy people say.

[2] Things will look brighter tomorrow. (lit. *After the rain comes sunshine.*)

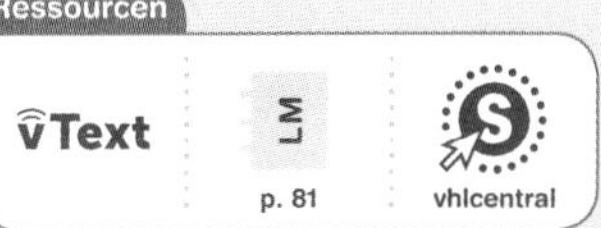

Fotoroman

Ein Sommer in der Türkei?

Anke hat Pläne für den Sommer: Die ganze Familie soll den Sommer in der Türkei verbringen.

Vorbereitung Have students look at scene 10, and discuss with a partner why they think Sabite is sad. After they have watched the episode, have students get together with their partners again and check their predictions.

ANKE Ich habe eine Überraschung für euch.
ZEYNEP Ich weiß schon, was es ist!
ANKE Zeynep, psst!
SABITE Was ist es denn?
ANKE Wir verbringen den Sommer in der Türkei.
SABITE Warum?
ZEYNEP Ja, warum wohl!

ANKE Es ist das Heimatland von deinem Vater. Und du und deine Schwester wart nicht mehr im Ausland seit... unseren Ferien in Frankreich vor drei Jahren. Wir wollen dort etwas über die Kunststudiengänge für dich erfahren, deshalb machen wir die Reise gemeinsam.

SABITE Ich kann es kaum erwarten, George, Hans und Meline davon zu erzählen.
ZEYNEP Und Torsten?

4

SABITE Mama, ich brauche deine Hilfe. Kann ich dich was fragen?
ANKE Du bittest mich doch sonst nie um Hilfe. Das muss ein großes Problem sein.

5

SABITE Torsten und ich haben uns gestritten. Ich habe ihm gesagt, dass ich überlege, in der Türkei Kunst zu studieren. Naja, ich habe es zuerst Meline gesagt. Ich habe mich mit Melines Freund über Kunst unterhalten und er stand daneben.

ANKE Du hast es ihm nicht zuerst gesagt. Und jetzt ist er unglücklich?
SABITE Ja. Und jetzt werden wir den Sommer nicht zusammen sein.
ANKE Wir müssen nicht in die Türkei fahren.
ZEYNEP Ähm, doch!
SABITE Oh, doch, das müssen wir. Aber ich will es ihm noch nicht sagen.

ÜBUNGEN

1 **Was fehlt?** Ergänzen Sie die Sätze mit den richtigen Informationen.

1. Anke möchte den (Sommer / Herbst) in der Türkei verbringen.
2. Die Türkei ist das Heimatland von (Anke / Faik).
3. Sabite und Zeynep waren schon in (Italien / Frankreich) im Urlaub.
4. Familie Yilmaz möchte etwas über (Jugendherbergen / Kunststudiengänge) in der Türkei erfahren.
5. Sabite bittet ihre Mutter um (Hilfe / Geld).
6. Sie hat Meline zuerst davon erzählt, in der Türkei (Kunst zu studieren / Urlaub zu machen).
7. Deshalb (*Therefore*) ist Torsten jetzt (unglücklich / unangenehm).
8. Anke glaubt, dass Beziehungen (einfach / kompliziert) sind.
9. Vor einem (Monat / Jahr) hat Sabite einige Arbeiten bei einer Galerie eingereicht.
10. Meline mag (Zeynep / Torsten) nicht.

PERSONEN

Anke

Sabite

Zeynep

ANKE Was noch? Bei Problemen zwischen zwei Partnern geht es nie nur um eine Sache. Beziehungen sind kompliziert.
SABITE Er versteht meine Kunst nicht.
ZEYNEP Niemand versteht deine Kunst, ohne dass er verrückt ist.
ANKE Hör auf, deine Schwester zu ärgern.

SABITE Er möchte meine Kunst nicht verstehen. Vor einem Monat habe ich einige Arbeiten bei einer Galerie in der Torstraße eingereicht. Torsten sagte... sie werden das niemals ausstellen.

ZEYNEP Das ist gemein.
ANKE Er darf so etwas nicht zu dir sagen.
SABITE Meline mag ihn nicht.
ZEYNEP Meline ist komisch.

SABITE Aber sie versteht, dass ich Künstlerin bin, ohne meine Kunst zu verstehen. Mama, was soll ich tun?
ANKE Liebst du ihn, Sabite?

Nützliche Ausdrücke

- **Heimatland**
  homeland, country of origin
- **der Kunststudiengang**
  art course
- **gemeinsam**
  together
- **erwarten**
  to expect
- **Du bittest mich doch sonst nie um Hilfe.**
  You never ask for my help.
- **Torsten und ich haben uns gestritten.**
  Torsten and I have been fighting.
- **zuerst**
  first
- **daneben**
  aside, on the side
- **zwischen**
  between
- **ausstellen**
  to exhibit
- **komisch**
  weird

3B.1
- **Aber sie versteht, dass ich Künstlerin bin, ohne meine Kunst zu verstehen.**
  But she understands that I'm an artist, without understanding my art.

3B.2
- **Vor einem Monat habe ich einige Arbeiten bei einer Galerie in der Torstraße eingereicht.**
  A month ago, I submitted some work to a gallery on Torstraße.

3B.3
- **Niemand versteht deine Kunst, ohne dass er verrückt ist.**
  Nobody can understand your art, unless they're crazy.

2 **Zum Besprechen** Familie Yilmaz möchte zusammen Urlaub in der Türkei machen. Planen Sie mit einem Partner/einer Partnerin die Reise. Besprechen Sie das Ziel (*destination*), die Dauer der Reise, die Transportmittel, die Unterkünfte und weitere Details. Answers will vary.

2 Expansion Instead of having them write a paragraph, ask students to act out a conversation about vacation planning.

3 **Vertiefung** Anke, Sabite und Zeynep sind im Bauhaus-Museum. Suchen Sie weitere Museen in Berlin und finden Sie heraus (*find out*), welche Ausstellungen zur Zeit dort zu sehen sind. Answers will vary.

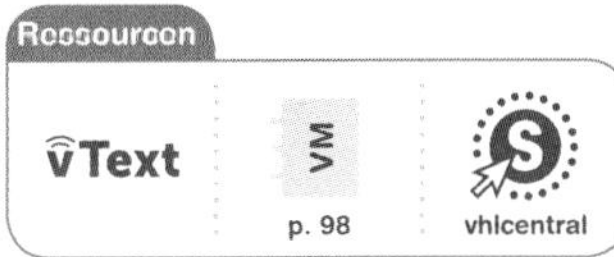

Suggestion Have students figure out the literal English translation of **Kofferwort**.

IM FOKUS

Flughafen Frankfurt

Reading

AP* Theme: Contemporary Life
Context: Entertainment, Travel, & Leisure

Der Frankfurt Airport (auch Rhein-Main-Flughafen) ist der größte Flughafen in Deutschland. Fast 60 Millionen Passagiere kamen hier 2014 an oder flogen von hier ab. In München waren es 2014 39,7 Millionen und in Düsseldorf 21,8 Millionen. In Europa fliegen Passagiere nur London-Heathrow und Paris-Charles de Gaulle öfter an.

Weltweit ist der Frankfurter Flughafen die Nummer 11. Der Flughafen ist sehr praktisch für Passagiere, weil es direkt im Flughafen einen Bahnhof° gibt. Man kann Flug und Zugreise bequem miteinander kombinieren. Über dem Bahnhof findet man auch „The Squaire", ein großes Gebäude mit Büros, zwei Hotels und Geschäften.

Neben dem Passagierverkehr° ist der Frankfurt Airport auch für den Cargoverkehr wichtig. Innerhalb Europas werden nur in Paris-Charles de Gaulle mehr Güter° transportiert. Wegen der vielen Passagiere und der Güter nennt man den Frankfurt Airport auch ein wichtiges Luftfahrtdrehkreuz°. Der Flughafen ist aber nicht nur für Passagiere und Cargotransport wichtig. Hier arbeiten insgesamt über 78.000 Menschen. Innerhalb Deutschlands gilt der Flughafen als größte lokale Arbeitsstätte°. Er ist so groß, dass er seine eigene Postleitzahl° hat!

Flughafen	Passagiere (2014)	Flüge (2014)	Fluggesellschaften°
Frankfurt Airport	59,6 Millionen	469.000	109
London-Heathrow (größter in Europa)	73,4 Millionen	471.000	80
Atlanta International Airport (größter weltweit)	96,2 Millionen	868.000	58

QUELLE: Frankfurt Airport, Heathrow Airport, Atlanta International Airport

TIPP

The Squaire comes from a combination of the English words *square* and *air*. This type of word combination is called a **Kofferwort** in German.

Bahnhof *train station* **Passagierverkehr** *passenger traffic* **Güter** *freight* **Luftfahrtdrehkreuz** *aviation hub* **Arbeitsstätte** *place of employment* **Postleitzahl** *zip code* **Fluggesellschaften** *airline companies*

Suggestion Before they begin the reading, have students describe the picture to you, using as many vocabulary words as possible.

ÜBUNGEN

1 Richtig oder falsch? Sind die Aussagen richtig oder falsch? Korrigieren Sie die falschen Aussagen.

1. Frankfurt Airport ist der größte Flughafen in Deutschland. Richtig.
2. Der Flughafen Nummer 2 in Deutschland ist Düsseldorf. Falsch. Der Flughafen Nummer 2 ist München.
3. Leider gibt es am Frankfurt Airport keinen Bahnhof. Falsch. Direkt im Flughafen gibt es einen Bahnhof.
4. Am Frankfurt Airport können Reisende übernachten. Richtig.
5. In London-Heathrow transportiert man mehr Güter als in Frankfurt. Falsch. Nur in Paris-Charles de Gaulle transportiert man an einem europäischen Flughafen mehr Güter.
6. Am Frankfurt Airport arbeiten 74.000 Menschen. Falsch. Am Frankfurt Airport arbeiten über 78.000 Menschen.
7. Der Frankfurt Airport ist die größte lokale Arbeitsstätte in Deutschland. Richtig.
8. Frankfurt Airport hat seine eigene Postleitzahl. Richtig.
9. Der Frankfurt Airport hat mehr Fluggesellschaften als London. Richtig.
10. Am größten Flughafen Europas flogen 2014 96,2 Millionen Passagiere ab. Falsch. In London-Heathrow flogen 2014 73,4 Millionen Passagiere ab.

Practice more at vhlcentral.com.

Deutsch im Alltag You may want to teach the verb **zelten**. Ask the class: **Wer zeltet gern?**

DEUTSCH IM ALLTAG

Urlaub für Studenten

die Pension, -en	*guesthouse*
das Zelt, -e	*tent*
der Zeltplatz, ¨-e	*camping area*
der Zug, ¨-e	*train*
Sofa-surfen	*to couch surf*
Zimmer frei	*vacancy*

DIE DEUTSCHSPRACHIGE WELT

Sylt

AP* Theme: Global Challenges
Context: Environmental Issues

Sylt ist die größte deutsche Insel in der Nordsee. Sie heißt auch „die Hamburger Badewanne". Jedes Jahr machen hier über 800.000 Menschen Urlaub. Berühmt ist Sylt für seine langen Strände (mehr als 40 Kilometer) und die Wanderdünen° in List. Sie sind bis zu 1.000 Meter lang und 35 Meter hoch. Sie „wandern" jedes Jahr bis zu 4 Meter. Interessant ist auch das Wattenmeer, wo viele Fische und Vögel leben. Auf Sylt findet man auch seltene° Pflanzen, Tiere und Schmetterlinge°. Die Heide° ist auch eine bekannte Landschaft° der Insel.

Wanderdünen *hiking dunes* **seltene** *rare* **Schmetterlinge** *butterflies* **Heide** *heath* **Landschaft** *landscape*

PORTRÄT

Der ICE

AP* Theme: Science & Technology
Context: Transportation

Der ICE, oder Intercity-Express, ist die schnellste Zugart° in Deutschland. Dieser Zug fährt in Deutschland und 6 Nachbarländern (Belgien, Dänemark, Frankreich, Niederlande, Österreich und der Schweiz) 180 ICE-Bahnhöfe an. Für Passagiere ist der ICE interessant, weil die Züge nicht nur extrem schnell fahren, sondern auch sehr bequem sind. Passagiere haben viel Platz. Alle Wagen haben Klimaanlagen°. Es gibt auch ein Bordrestaurant im Zug und oft ein Abteil° für Kinder. Mit Kopfhörern° kann man Musik- und Sprachprogramme hören und für Computer gibt es Steckdosen°.

Zugart *type of train* **Klimaanlagen** *air conditioning* **Abteil** *section* **Kopfhörern** *headphones* **Steckdosen** *electrical outlets*

IM INTERNET

Suchen Sie Informationen über die Vogelfluglinie: Was ist die Vogelfluglinie? Wo liegt sie? Ist sie nur für Vögel?

Find out more at **vhlcentral.com**.

2 Was fehlt? Ergänzen Sie die Sätze.

1. Die Insel Sylt liegt in der <u>Nordsee</u>.
2. Die Insel Sylt hat lange <u>Strände</u> und Wanderdünen.
3. Eine Attraktion ist das <u>Wattenmeer</u>, wo viele Fische und Vögel leben.
4. Die schnellste Zugart in Deutschland ist der <u>ICE</u>.
5. Der ICE ist extrem schnell und auch <u>(sehr) bequem</u>.
6. Es gibt Bordrestaurants und Abteile für <u>Kinder</u>.

3 Urlaub Diskutieren Sie mit einem Partner / einer Partnerin, wo Sie in Deutschland, Österreich oder der Schweiz Urlaub machen wollen. Wählen Sie ein Urlaubziel (*destination*). Warum wollen Sie diese Orte besuchen? Was möchten Sie hier gerne sehen? Was möchten Sie hier gerne machen? Mit wem möchten Sie diese Orte besuchen?

Suggestion After reading the article about Sylt, have students search the text for words that describe the island. Ask comprehension questions, ex.: **Wo ist die Insel Sylt? Warum heißt sie wohl die „Hamburger Badewanne"?**

Ressourcen

3 Virtual Chat You can also assign activity 3 on the Supersite.

Suggestion Emphasize that **zu** is not used with modals. Write an example of an incorrect sentence on the board, such as **Ich will zu schlafen**, and have students identify the error. Have a volunteer come to the board to cross out the **zu**.

3B.1 Infinitive expressions and clauses

Startblock When you use a non-modal verb with an infinitive clause, add the preposition **zu** before the infinitive.

Ich habe Sabite letzte Woche geholfen, ihre Wohnung **zu putzen**.

Ich habe ihm gesagt, dass ich überlege, ein Semester in der Türkei Kunst **zu studieren**.

- When a conjugated modal verb modifies the meaning of another verb, the infinitive moves to the end of the sentence. The preposition **zu** is not needed in this case.

  Ich möchte Checkpoint Charlie **besuchen**.
  *I want **to visit** Checkpoint Charlie.*

  Es regnet. Wir müssen unsere Regenmäntel **anziehen**.
  *It's raining. We need **to put on** our raincoats.*

- After most other verbs, however, you need to put **zu** before the infinitive clause. Place **zu** plus the infinitive at the end of the sentence.

  Es macht viel Spaß **zu reisen**!
  ***Travelling** is so much fun!*

  Ich hatte keine Zeit, Postkarten **zu schreiben**.
  *I didn't have time **to write** postcards.*

- When using a double verb expression like **spazieren gehen**, put the preposition **zu** between the two verbs.

  Philip hat Angst, **schwimmen zu gehen**.
  *Philip is afraid **to go swimming**.*

  Es ist uns zu teuer, jeden Abend **essen zu gehen**.
  ***Going out to eat** every night is too expensive for us.*

- If the verb in the infinitive clause is a separable prefix verb, place **zu** between the prefix and the main part of the verb.

  Es macht keinen Spaß, die Küche **aufzuräumen**.
  ***Cleaning** the kitchen is no fun.*

  Vergiss bitte nicht, den Müll **rauszubringen**.
  *Please don't forget **to take out** the trash.*

- Infinitive constructions with **zu** often occur after the verbs **anfangen**, **beginnen**, **helfen**, **vergessen**, and **versuchen** (*to try*), the expressions **Lust haben** (*to be in the mood*), **Angst haben**, and **Spaß machen**, and the adjectives **einfach**, **wichtig** (*important*), and **schön**.

  Ich **habe vergessen**, meine Eltern **anzurufen**.
  *I **forgot to call** my parents.*

  Kannst du mir bitte **helfen**, meine Bordkarte **zu finden**?
  *Can you please **help** me **find** my boarding pass?*

  Wir **haben** keine **Lust**, heute Abend **auszugehen**.
  *We don't **feel like going out** this evening.*

  Ich finde es **wichtig**, pünktlich **zu sein**.
  *I think it's **important to be** on time.*

ACHTUNG

The comma before an infinitive clause is optional. Use it for clarity, especially in longer sentences. Any adverbs that modify the infinitive expression come after the comma: **Es ist schön, im Sommer Eis zu essen.**

- Impersonal expressions beginning with **Es ist/war...** are also frequently followed by an infinitive clause.

Es war so schön, in einem Fünf-Sterne-Hotel **zu übernachten**.
It ***was*** *so nice* ***to spend the night*** *at a five-star hotel.*

Es ist nicht gut, bei Nebel **zu fliegen**.
It's *not good* ***to fly*** *when it's foggy.*

- The expressions **um... zu** (*in order to*), **ohne... zu** (*without*), and **anstatt... zu** (*instead of*) are frequently used in infinitive clauses. **Anstatt** is often shortened to **statt**, especially in informal conversation.

Ich esse viel Gemüse und gehe jeden Tag schwimmen, **um** fit **zu bleiben**.
I eat lots of vegetables and swim every day ***to stay*** *fit.*

Man kann einen schönen Urlaub machen, **ohne** ins Ausland **zu fahren**.
You can have a nice vacation ***without going*** *abroad.*

Sie sind in die Schweiz gefahren, **anstatt** nach Rom **zu fliegen**.
Instead of flying *to Rome, they drove to Switzerland.*

Fahrt ihr nach Hamburg, **um** eure Freunde **zu besuchen**?
Are you driving to Hamburg ***to visit*** *your friends?*

- In sentences with **um... zu**, **ohne... zu**, or **(an)statt... zu**, the infinitive clause may be the first element in a sentence. When the infinitive clause is the first element, the conjugated verb becomes the second element, and the subject comes after the conjugated verb.

Statt zu schlafen, **hat Peter** die ganze Nacht gelesen.
Instead of sleeping, *Peter spent all night reading.*

Um ein Zimmer in diesem Hotel **zu bekommen**, **muss man** sehr früh buchen.
To get *a room at that hotel, you have to book early.*

Ohne vorher **zu fragen**, **haben sie** die Kekse gegessen.
They ate the cookies ***without asking*** *first.*

Anstatt meine Hausaufgaben **zu machen**, **bin ich** gestern Abend ausgegangen.
Instead of doing *my homework, I went out last night*

Expansion Ask students to explain why they are learning German and answer using the expression **um... zu**. Emphasize that **um** sets off the clause, while **zu** and the infinitive appear at the very end.

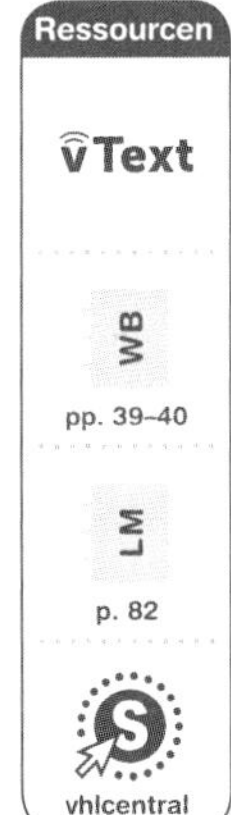

Jetzt sind Sie dran! **Wählen Sie das passende Wort.**

1. Ich bin rausgegangen, (um / ohne / anstatt) den Schlüssel mitzunehmen!
2. (Um / Ohne / Anstatt) einen Skiurlaub zu machen, fahren wir ans Meer.
3. Der Student hat eine gute Note in seiner Prüfung bekommen, (um / ohne / anstatt) dafür zu lernen.
4. (Um / Ohne / Anstatt) mit dem Auto zu fahren, fliegt Jana nach Italien.
5. Willst du Deutsch lernen, (um / ohne / anstatt) in Deutschland zu studieren?
6. Michael hat das Hotel gefunden, (um / ohne / anstatt) auf den Stadtplan zu schauen.
7. (Um / Ohne / Anstatt) Zeitung zu lesen, schlafe ich gern im Flugzeug.
8. Der Geschäftsmann bestellte Zimmerservice, (um / ohne / anstatt) nach dem Preis zu fragen.
9. Wir fahren zwei Stunden vor unserem Flug zum Flughafen, (um / ohne / anstatt) pünktlich zu sein.
10. Nina ist faul und fährt mit dem Fahrstuhl, (um / ohne / anstatt) die Treppe zu nehmen.
11. Ich trage einen Mantel bei schlechtem Wetter, (um / ohne / anstatt) warm zu bleiben.
12. Das Gute an Jugendherbergen ist, man kann dort übernachten, (um / ohne / anstatt) ein Bett zu reservieren.

Anwendung

1 Was fehlt? Ergänzen Sie die Sätze mit der richtigen Form des Verbs im Infinitiv.

1. Wir helfen unseren Eltern, die Koffer zu packen. (packen)
2. Mama fängt an, die Zimmer im Hotel zu reservieren. (reservieren)
3. Es macht Spaß, in Europa zu reisen. (reisen)
4. Papa hat vergessen, unsere Personalausweise mitzubringen. (mitbringen)
5. Der Taxifahrer hatte keine Zeit zurückzufahren. (zurückfahren)
6. Er musste sehr schnell fahren, um am Flughafen pünktlich anzukommen. (ankommen)

2 Ausdrücke Ergänzen Sie die Sätze mit dem passenden Ausdruck **um... zu, ohne... zu oder (an)statt... zu.**

BEISPIEL Im Flugzeug lese ich viel, (an)statt zu schlafen.

1. Wir gehen mit unseren Freunden am Abend vor unserer Reise aus, (an)statt unsere Koffer zu packen.
2. Die Studenten reisen viel, um verschiedene Länder kennen zu lernen.
3. Maria hat eine gute Note in Deutsch geschrieben, ohne viel dafür zu lernen.
4. Warum habt ihr stundenlang in der Sonne gestanden, ohne einen Hut zu tragen?
5. Am Freitag gehen wir ins Theater, um das neue Theaterstück anzusehen.
6. Anstatt / Statt ein Hotelzimmer zu buchen, werden wir in der Jugendherberge übernachten.

3 Suggestion Do the first few items as a class to make sure that students understand the activity.

3 Wozu braucht man das? Sagen Sie, wozu man die abgebildeten Dinge braucht. Sample answers are provided.

fit bleiben	tanzen gehen	E-Mails schreiben
im Regen trocken bleiben	Deutsch lernen	in den Bergen wandern

BEISPIEL Man braucht einen Badeanzug, um schwimmen zu gehen.

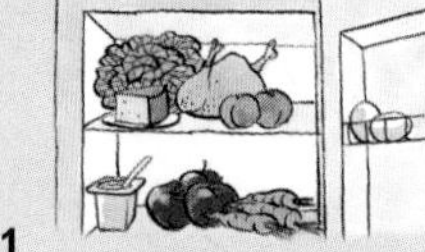

1. Man soll viel Gemüse essen, um fit zu bleiben.

2. Man braucht einen Regenschirm, um im Regen trocken zu bleiben.

3. Man braucht ein Wörterbuch, um Deutsch zu lernen.

4. Man braucht einen Rucksack, um in den Bergen zu wandern.

5. Man braucht einen Computer, um E-Mails zu schreiben.

6. Man braucht ein schönes Kleid, um tanzen zu gehen.

Practice more at vhlcentral.com.

Kommunikation

4 Viel gereist Sie waren im Sommer in Deutschland. Besprechen Sie mit einem Partner / einer Partnerin, wo Sie waren und warum Sie dort waren. Answers will vary.

BEISPIEL in München

S1: *Wo warst du im Sommer?*
S2: *Ich war in München, um meine Familie zu besuchen. Meine Schwester wohnt dort.*

in den Alpen	in Hamburg
in Berlin	in Heidelberg
an der Donau	in München
in Füssen	an der Ostseeküste

4 Expansion Review various cultural attractions unique to the cities and landmarks on the list. Encourage students to research points of interest on their own or in groups, and share what they have discovered with the class.

4 Partner Chat You can also assign activity 4 on the Supersite. Students work in pairs to record the activity online. The pair's recorded conversation will appear in your gradebook.

5 Ein schwerer Koffer Sie haben viel in den Urlaub mitgebracht. Erzählen Sie einem Partner / einer Partnerin, wieso Sie so viel im Gepäck haben. Answers will vary.

BEISPIEL

S1: *Warum hast du eine Gitarre mitgebracht?*
S2: *Um Musik zu machen. Und du? Warum hast du einen Badeanzug gepackt?*
S1: *Um schwimmen zu gehen.*

einen gestreiften Anzug	eine kurze Hose	einen Rucksack
einen Badeanzug	ein Kleid	viele Bücher
die Brille	eine Krawatte	eine Sonnenbrille
eine Gitarre	eine Mütze	ein langärmliges T-Shirt
eine schöne Halskette	einen Regenschirm	Turnschuhe

5 Virtual Chat You can also assign activity 5 on the Supersite. Students record individual responses that appear in your gradebook.

6 Wohin wollen wir reisen? Denken Sie an drei mögliche Urlaubsziele. Fragen Sie Ihren Partner / Ihre Partnerin, wohin er/sie reisen möchte, und besprechen Sie dabei die Sehenswürdigkeiten in jeder Stadt. Answers will vary.

BEISPIEL

S1: *Wo machen wir im Sommer Urlaub?*
S2: *Ich will nach Disneyland fahren, anstatt Museen zu besuchen.*
S1: *Warum?*
S2: *Um Mickey Mouse zu treffen. Ich finde ihn toll!*

6 Partner Chat You can also assign activity 6 on the Supersite.

7 Meiner Meinung nach Ergänzen Sie die folgenden Aussagen mit Ihrer Meinung. Vergleichen Sie die Antworten mit anderen Studenten.

1. Ich finde es schwer...
2. Es macht mir Spaß...
3. Ich habe keine Lust...
4. Ich versuche immer...
5. Ich finde es wichtig...
6. Es ist schön...

7 Suggestion Make sure students know to use a **zu** + infinitive clause in each answer.

3B.2 Time expressions Presentation

Suggestion You might want to direct students to **Vol. 1, 2A.3** and **2B.2** to review times and dates in German; and **Vol 1., 4A.2** to review word order with time expressions.

Suggestion Ask travel-related questions that can be answered with these expressions, such as: **Wie oft waren Sie in Europa? Wie oft waren Sie am Strand? Wie viele Male sind Sie geflogen?**

Startblock German has two main concepts related to expressions of time. **Zeit** describes a span of time, while **Mal** refers to specific occurrences and repetitions.

Ich habe noch **50 Minuten Zeit** vor meinem Flug.
*I still have **50 minutes** before my flight.*

Ich war nur **einmal** in Hamburg.
*I've only been to Hamburg **once**.*

- Many German time expressions use **Mal** or a compound word containing **-mal**:

diesmal	*this time*	**manchmal**	*sometimes*
das erste Mal	*the first time*	**niemals**	*never*
einmal	*once*	**zum ersten/letzten Mal**	*for the first/last time*

Expansion Write on the board: **0X, 1X, 2X, 3X, ...20X**, etc. and have students verbalize what these shorthand forms indicate: **niemals, einmal, zweimal, dreimal, ...zwanzigmal**, etc. You may also wish to introduce the colloquialism **zigmal**, "a zillion times".

- Use the accusative case to talk about a particular span of time or point in time. To describe how long something lasted, use **dauern** with the accusative.

Die Kreuzfahrt dauerte **einen Monat**.
*The cruise lasted **a month**.*

Letzten Montag haben meine Ferien angefangen.
*My break started **last Monday**.*

Nächsten Sommer fahren wir an den Strand.
***Next summer** we're going to the beach.*

Die Leute tanzten **die ganze Nacht**.
*The people danced **all night long**.*

Suggestion To practice the use of **seit** and **schon**, ask students how long they've been doing a particular activity and write their responses on the board. Ex.: **Carrie spielt seit einem Jahr Gitarre. Tom lernt seit Januar Deutsch.** Underline the verbs and emphasize that they are in the present tense.

- Use the present tense with **seit** plus a dative time expression or **schon** plus an accusative time expression to indicate how long something has been going on.

Seit einem Monat wohnt Patrick in Berlin.
*Patrick has been living in Berlin **for a month**.*

Er ist **schon zwei Jahre** in Deutschland.
*He's been in Germany **for two years**.*

- The two-way prepositions **an**, **in**, and **vor** can all be used to answer the question **wann?** Use the dative case with these time expressions.

Vor einem Jahr studierte ich im Ausland.
A year ago I was studying abroad.

Mein Geburtstag ist **am 18. Februar**.
*My birthday is **on February 18**.*

- Use the time expressions **zuerst** (*first*), **dann** (*then*), **danach** (*after that*), and **zuletzt** (*last*) or **schließlich** (*finally*) to narrate a series of events.

Zuerst musst du die wichtigen Papiere in das Handgepäck packen.
***First** you have to pack your important papers in the carry-on bag.*

Dann kannst du die anderen Sachen in den großen Koffer packen.
***Then** you can pack the other things in the big suitcase.*

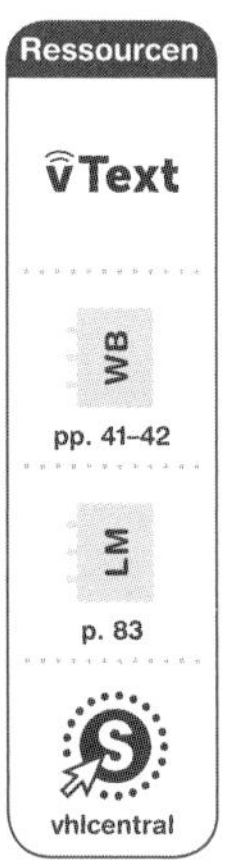

Jetzt sind Sie dran!

Wählen Sie die passenden Wörter.

1. (Im / In den) Frühling regnet es viel.
2. In (der / die) Nacht habe ich schlecht geträumt.
3. Laura reist für (ein / einen) Monat nach Österreich.
4. Vor (einer / eine) Woche haben wir unsere Flugtickets bekommen.
5. (Nächster / Nächsten) Sommer musst du in den Urlaub mitkommen.
6. (Am / An das) Wochenende fahre ich nach Zürich.
7. Herr Boas wartet schon (einer / eine) Stunde auf ein Taxi.
8. Wir waren (letzter / letzten) Dienstag nicht zu Hause.
9. Hugo arbeitet seit (ein / einem) Jahr an seinem neuen Buch.
10. In (einer / eine) Woche macht er eine Kreuzfahrt.

Expansion Have students work in small groups to write a short travel cartoon using **zuerst**, **dann**, **danach**, and **zuletzt**. Remind them of correct verb position.

Anwendung und Kommunikation

1 **Was fehlt?** Ergänzen Sie die Sätze mit den passenden Zeitergänzungen aus der Liste.

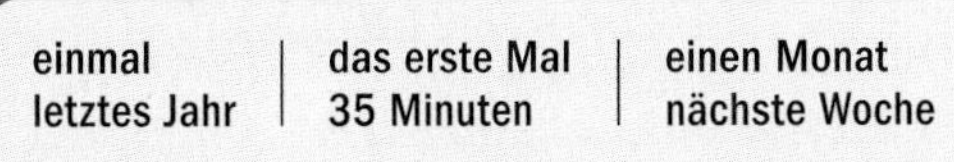

einmal	das erste Mal	einen Monat
letztes Jahr	35 Minuten	nächste Woche

1. Saras Geburtstag ist ___nächste Woche___ und dann wird sie zweiundzwanzig.
2. Mit 18 Jahren durfte ich ___das erste Mal___ allein in Urlaub fahren.
3. Silvester ist ___letztes Jahr___ auf einen Sonntag gefallen.
4. Der Flug von München nach Nürnberg dauert nur ___35 Minuten___.
5. Wir haben noch ___einen Monat___ bis zum Ende von unserem Semester.
6. Meine Großeltern planen eine Familienfeier, denn Goldene Hochzeit hat man nur ___einmal___ im Leben.

2 **Ein kleines Interview** Beantworten Sie die Fragen von Ihrem Partner / Ihrer Partnerin. Answers will vary.

BEISPIEL seit wann / Deutsch lernen

S1: *Seit wann lernst du Deutsch?*
S2: *Seit letztem Semester.*

1. wann / Geburtstag haben Wann hast du Geburtstag?
2. seit wann / hier studieren Seit wann studierst du hier?
3. was / zuerst machen nach dem Semesterende / Und danach? Was machst du zuerst nach dem Semesterende? Und danach?
4. wann und wo / zuletzt am Strand sein Wann und wo bist du zuletzt am Strand gewesen?
5. vor wie vielen Jahren / zum ersten Mal im Flugzeug fliegen Vor wie vielen Jahren bist du zum ersten Mal im Flugzeug geflogen?
6. wen / einmal kennen lernen möchten Wen möchtest du einmal kennen lernen?

2 Suggestion Give students some time to write out the questions before they conduct their interviews. Point out that they will need to use the past tense to construct logical questions for items 4 and 5.

2 Partner Chat You can also assign activity 2 on the Supersite. Students work in pairs to record the activity online. The pair's recorded conversation will appear in your gradebook.

3 **Reiselust** Erfinden Sie mit Ihren Mitschülern/Mitschülerinnen eine kurze Geschichte über eine Reise. Benutzen Sie Wörter aus der Liste oder Ihre eigenen.

BEISPIEL

Thomas und seine Familie wollten zum ersten Mal eine Kreuzfahrt von Marseille nach Palermo machen. Zuerst...

Zeitausdrücke	Hauptwörter	Verben
danach	die Crew	einkaufen
dann	das Gepäck	einpacken
niemals	das Meer	essen
seit	der Pass	regnen
vor	der Sandstrand	schwimmen
zuerst	das Souvenir	tanzen
zuletzt	das Wetter	vergessen

3 Suggestion Invite the groups to share their stories with the class.

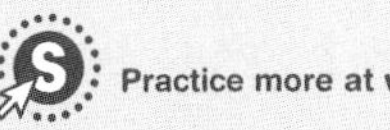
Practice more at **vhlcentral.com**.

3B.3 Indefinite pronouns

Presentation

QUERVERWEIS

To review the use of subject, accusative, and dative pronouns, see **1.A.2** and **1A.3**.

Suggestion Have students review the use of the subject, accusative, and dative pronouns, taught in **Vol. 1, 1.A.3**.

Suggestion Provide sample sentences that demonstrate the different case endings. Ex.: **Niemand war im Zimmer. Wir sahen niemanden im Zimmer. Wir gaben niemandem die Blumen.**

Expansion Provide your class with a list of travel destinations and have students find out who has been to those places. Then have them summarize their results. Ex.: **Niemand ist nach Wyoming gereist. Maria war schon in Kuba, aber niemand aus der Klasse ist in Ecuador gewesen.**

ACHTUNG

In conversation, **etwas** may be shortened to **was**. Ex.: **Kann ich dich was fragen?**

Remember that **man** is singular. When **man** is the subject, always use a verb in the third-person singular.

Suggestion Emphasize that the declension of **alles** parallels the declension of **das**: the nominative form is **alles**, the accusative form is **alles**, and the dative form is **allem**.

Startblock Pronouns that refer to an unknown or nonspecific person or thing are called indefinite pronouns.

- Two indefinite pronouns that refer to people are **jemand** (*someone*) and **niemand** (*no one*). Use the ending **-en** for the accusative case and **-em** for the dative.

Jemand hat seinen Personalausweis an der Passkontrolle vergessen.
***Someone** left his I.D. card at passport control.*

Herr Klein will mit **niemandem** sprechen.
*Mr. Klein does**n't** want to speak with **anyone**.*

- To talk about indefinite things, use **alles** (*everything*), **etwas** (*something*), or **nichts** (*nothing*). **Etwas** and **nichts** do not change in different cases; **alles** is declined like the neuter definite article **das**.

Wir haben noch **nichts** gegessen.
*We haven't eaten **anything** yet.*

Möchten Sie **etwas** zu trinken bestellen?
*Would you like to order **something** to drink?*

Ich habe **alles** ins Handgepäck gepackt.
*I packed **everything** in the carry-on.*

Meine Schwester kann dir mit **allem** helfen.
*My sister can help you with **everything**.*

- Use the pronoun **man** to talk about people in general.

Man darf im Flugzeug nicht rauchen.
***You're** not allowed to smoke on an airplane.*

In Hamburg ist **man** froh, wenn es im Winter nicht zu viel schneit.
*In Hamburg **we**'re happy if it doesn't snow too much in winter.*

In Liechtenstein spricht **man** Deutsch.
*In Liechtenstein **they** speak German.*

Man soll zwei Stunden vor dem Abflug am Flughafen sein.
***One** should be at the airport two hours before departure.*

Jetzt sind Sie dran! Wählen Sie das passende Wort.

1. Anna vergisst oft ihre Hausaufgaben, aber Emil vergisst (nichts / etwas).
2. (Etwas / Niemand) will arbeiten, wenn das Wetter draußen so schön ist.
3. Wenn (man / alles) nicht ins Ausland will, gibt es auch in Deutschland viele schöne Ferienorte (*vacation spots*).
4. (Nichts / Jemand) hat vergessen, das Fenster zu schließen.
5. Hast du (niemand / etwas) gesagt?
6. Ich möchte (alles / man) in dieser Stadt sehen!
7. Ich will im Urlaub (jemand / nichts) machen – nur schlafen und essen!
8. Sollen wir (man / jemanden) fragen, oder findest du die Antwort im Internet?
9. Jasmin ist sehr schüchtern – sie will mit (niemandem / etwas) reden.
10. (Nichts / Man) kann in diesem Geschäft viele schöne Sachen finden.

Suggestion Tell students that **man** cannot be replaced by **er**, and that in the accusative or dative it is replaced by **einen/einem**. Have students write down sample sentences; ex.: **Wenn man traurig ist, dann soll man spazieren gehen. Dann geht es einem besser.**

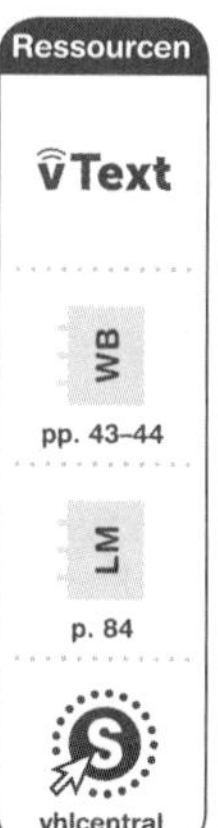

Anwendung und Kommunikation

1 Fragen zur Grammatik Ergänzen Sie die Sätze mit den passenden Wörtern aus der Liste.

alles	nichts
etwas	niemand
jemand	niemandem

1. Hat ___jemand___ noch Fragen zur Grammatik?
2. Herr Krause, können Sie uns ___alles___ noch einmal erklären?
3. ___Niemand___ hat die Grammatik verstanden.
4. Sie haben wirklich ___nichts___ verstanden?
5. Also kann ich leider ___niemandem___ helfen.
6. Sie können ___etwas___ lernen, liebe Schüler, aber nur wenn Sie Ihre Hausaufgaben machen!

2 Was macht man hier? Schreiben Sie zu jedem Foto einen Satz mit man. Benutzen Sie die angegebenen Wörter.

BEISPIEL

hier / können / Medikamente kaufen

Hier kann man Medikamente kaufen.

1. bei Rot / müssen / stoppen
   Bei Rot muss man stoppen.

2. hier / kommen / zum Marienplatz
   Hier kommt man zum Marienplatz.

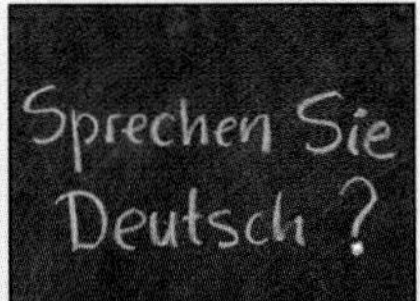

3. hier / sprechen / Deutsch
   Hier spricht man Deutsch.

4. hier / dürfen / parken
   Hier darf man parken.

5. hier / können / einkaufen
   Hier kann man einkaufen.

3 Armer Niklas Es geht Ihrem Freund Niklas wirklich schlecht. Besprechen Sie mit Ihrem Partner / Ihrer Partnerin, was Niklas machen muss oder was man machen soll, um Niklas zu helfen. Answers will vary. Suggested answers.

BEISPIEL

S1: *Niklas hat heute nichts gegessen.*
S2: *Er muss etwas essen!*

1. Niklas muss morgen ein Referat halten und hat noch nichts dazu vorbereitet.
   Er muss etwas dazu vorbereiten!
2. Die Lehrerin hat ihm nichts erklärt.
   Sie muss ihm alles erklären!
3. Im Unterricht hat er nichts zu sagen.
   Er soll im Unterricht etwas sagen.
4. Niemand hilft ihm.
   Jemand soll ihm helfen.
5. Er hat Angst vor allem.
   Er muss vor nichts Angst haben!
6. Er hat mit niemandem über seine Probleme gesprochen.
   Er muss mit jemandem über seine Probleme sprechen.

Practice more at **vhlcentral.com.**

3 Suggestion Make sure students take turns describing Niklas' problems and proposing solutions.

3 Virtual Chat You can also assign activity 3 on the Supersite. Students record individual responses that appear in your gradebook.

Wiederholung

1 **Die vergesslichen Schröders** Sehen Sie sich die Bilder an. Sagen Sie, was die Familie Schröder vergessen hat.
Sample answers are provided.

Jan

▶ **BEISPIEL** *Jan hat vergessen, das Geschirr zu spülen.*

1 Expansion Ask students: **Und Sie? Was haben Sie diese Woche vergessen?**

1. Opa
Opa hat vergessen, den Müll rauszutragen.

2. Tobias Tobias hat vergessen, das Schlafzimmer aufzuräumen.

3. Tante Ingrid Tante Ingrid hat vergessen, das Fenster zu schließen.

4. Onkel Paul Onkel Paul hat vergessen, im Wohnzimmer zu staubsaugen.

5. Greta Greta hat vergessen, ihre Hausaufgaben zu machen.

2 **Wie viel verstehst du?** Wie viel verstehen Sie und Ihr Partner / Ihre Partnerin von den Themen auf der Liste? Etwas? Nichts? Alles? Wechseln Sie sich ab.
Answers will vary.

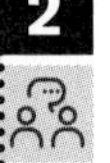

2 Partner Chat You can also assign activity 2 on the Supersite.

BEISPIEL

S1: *Wie viel verstehst du von Politik?*
S2: *Ich verstehe etwas von Politik. Und du?*

Chemie	Geographie	Popmusik
Fotographie	Geschichte	Skateboard fahren
Fußball spielen	Politik	Tanzen

3 **Diskutieren und kombinieren** Sie und Ihr Partner / Ihre Partnerin bekommen zwei verschiedene Arbeitsblätter von Ihrem Lehrer / Ihrer Lehrerin. Finden Sie heraus, warum die einzelnen Personen etwas tun.
Sample answers are provided.

BEISPIEL

S1: *Warum geht Kiara in die Bibliothek?*
S2: *Sie geht dahin, um ein Buch für ein Referat zu suchen.*

4 **Arbeitsblatt** Fragen Sie die anderen Schüler, wann sie die Dinge auf der Liste das letzte Mal gemacht haben. Finden Sie zu jedem Wochentag eine Person.
Answers will vary.

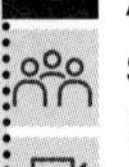
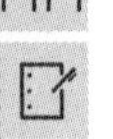

BEISPIEL in die Bibliothek gehen

S1: *Wann bist du das letzte Mal in die Bibliothek gegangen?*
S2: *Am Mittwoch bin ich dahin gegangen.*

5 **Wie lange?** Fragen Sie Ihren Partner / Ihre Partnerin, wie lange er/sie die Dinge auf der Liste schon macht. Answers will vary.

5 Virtual Chat You can also assign activity 5 on the Supersite.

BEISPIEL Deutsch lernen

S1: *Wie lange lernst du schon Deutsch?*
S2: *Seit 6 Monaten.*

Konzerte besuchen	schwimmen
Auto fahren	ein Musikinstrument spielen
Rad fahren	Videospiele spielen
Bücher lesen	an der Uni studieren

6 **Wie oft?** Arbeiten Sie mit einem Partner / einer Partnerin. Fragen Sie nach seinen/ihren Urlaubserfahrungen. Wie oft ist er/sie ins Ausland gereist oder in einem Hotel geblieben? Wie oft hat er/sie einen Nationalpark besucht? Wie oft hat er/sie Familie in einer anderen Stadt besucht? Answers will vary.

BEISPIEL

S1: *Wie oft bist du ins Ausland gereist?*
S2: *Ich bin zweimal ins Ausland gereist, einmal nach Mexiko und einmal nach Frankreich.*

6 Virtual Chat You can also assign activity 6 on the Supersite.

3 Suggestion In this activity, students will be practicing the **um… zu** + infinitive construction. To prepare them, ask a few **warum** questions and write student responses on the board, using **um… zu**.

7 **Beim Reisen** Diskutieren Sie mit Ihren Klassenkameraden, was man beim Reisen alles beachten (*consider*) muss. Benutzen Sie Wörter aus der Liste oder Ihre eigenen. Answers will vary.

BEISPIEL

S1: *Man braucht einen Pass für eine Reise nach Europa.*
S2: *Und man muss das Flugticket circa drei Monate vor der Reise kaufen.*
S3: *Man darf nicht zu spät am Flughafen ankommen.*

abfliegen	das Flugticket
ankommen	das Geld
bestellen	das Handy
buchen	die Kleidung
kaufen	die Kreditkarte
mitbringen	der Pass
packen	die Reservierung
vergessen	das Visum

8 Suggestion If students are having difficulty coming up with ideas for this role play, interrupt the activity to brainstorm ideas as a class.

8 **Rollenspiel** Spielen Sie mit einem Partner / einer Partnerin die Rollen von zwei älteren Menschen, die über ihr Leben nachdenken. Jede Person sagt etwas über einen anderen Abschnitt (*phase*) des Lebens. Answers will vary.

8 Partner Chat You can also assign activity 8 on the Supersite.

BEISPIEL

S1: *Mit 5 zog meine Familie in die USA.*
S2: *Mit 6 ging ich zum ersten Mal in die Schule.*

9 **Eine Geschichte** Schauen Sie sich das Bild an und schreiben Sie eine Geschichte dazu. Jede Person schreibt zwei Sätze der Geschichte und gibt sein Stück Papier an die nächste Person weiter. Der erste Satz beginnt mit „zuerst", der dritte mit „dann", der fünfte mit „danach" und so weiter. Answers will vary.

BEISPIEL *Zuerst spazierten zwei Freunde auf der Straße...*

Mein Wör | ter | buch

Schreiben Sie noch fünf weitere Wörter in Ihr persönliches Wörterbuch zu den Themen **Jahreszeiten** und **Reisen.**

der Altweibersommer

Übersetzung
Indian summer

Wortart
ein Substantiv

Gebrauch
Mitte September hatten wir den Altweibersommer. Das Wetter war warm und sonnig und wir haben alle Sommerkleidung getragen.

Synonyme
—

Antonyme
—

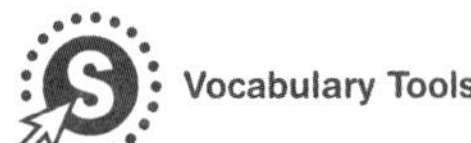

Weiter geht's

AP* Theme: Global Challenges
Context: Geography

Panorama

Interactive Map

Schleswig-Holstein, Hamburg und Bremen

Schleswig-Holstein in Zahlen

- **Fläche:** *15.800* km^2
- **Einwohner:** *2,8 Millionen*
- **Sprachen:** *Deutsch (2,7 Millionen), Plattdeutsch (1,3 Millionen), Dänisch (65.000), Friesisch (10.000)*
- **Städte:** *Kiel (240.000), Lübeck (212.000)*
- **Industrie:** *Landwirtschaft°, Seehandel°, Windenergie*
- **Touristenattraktionen:** *Danewerk und Haithabu (Wikingerstätten°), Karl-May-Festspiele° in Bad Segeberg*

Berühmte Schleswig-Holsteiner

- **Max Planck,** *Physiker (1858–1947)*
- **Thomas Mann,** *Literaturnobelpreisträger (1875–1955)*

Quelle: Landesportal Schleswig-Holstein

Suggestion Tell students that Hamburg is home to several German newspapers and magazines, including ***Der Spiegel***, ***Die Zeit***, and ***Stern***.

Hamburg in Zahlen

- **Fläche:** *755.000* km^2
- **Einwohner der Hansestadt Hamburg:** *1,7 Millionen*
- **Industrie:** *Flugzeugbau, Hafen, Schiffbau, Tourismus*
- **Touristenattraktionen:** *Altonaer Fischmarkt, Hamburger Michel, Museumsschiff Rickmer Rickmers*

Berühmte Hamburger

- **Johannes Brahms,** *Komponist (1833–1897)*
- **Jil Sander,** *Modedesignerin (1943–)*

Quelle: Landesportal Hamburg

Suggestion Ask students if they are familiar with any of Brahms' music. You may want to play them part of his **Wiegenlied**.

Bremen in Zahlen

- **Fläche:** *325* km^2 *(kleinstes deutsches Bundesland)*
- **Einwohner der Hansestadt Bremen:** *657.000*
- **Industrie:** *Außenhandel°, Automobilindustrie*
- **Touristenattraktionen:** *Böttcherstraße, Rathaus, Bremer Stadtmusikanten, Marktplatz, Schnoor*

Berühmte Bremer

- **Ernst Rowohlt,** *Verleger° (1887–1960)*
- **James Last,** *Komponist und Bandleader (1929–)*

Quelle: Landesportal Bremen

Landwirtschaft *agriculture* **Seehandel** *maritime trade* **Wikingerstätten** *Viking sites* **Festspiele** *festivals* **Außenhandel** *foreign trade* **Verleger** *publisher* **Brücken** *bridges* **überqueren** *cross* **Venedig** *Venice*

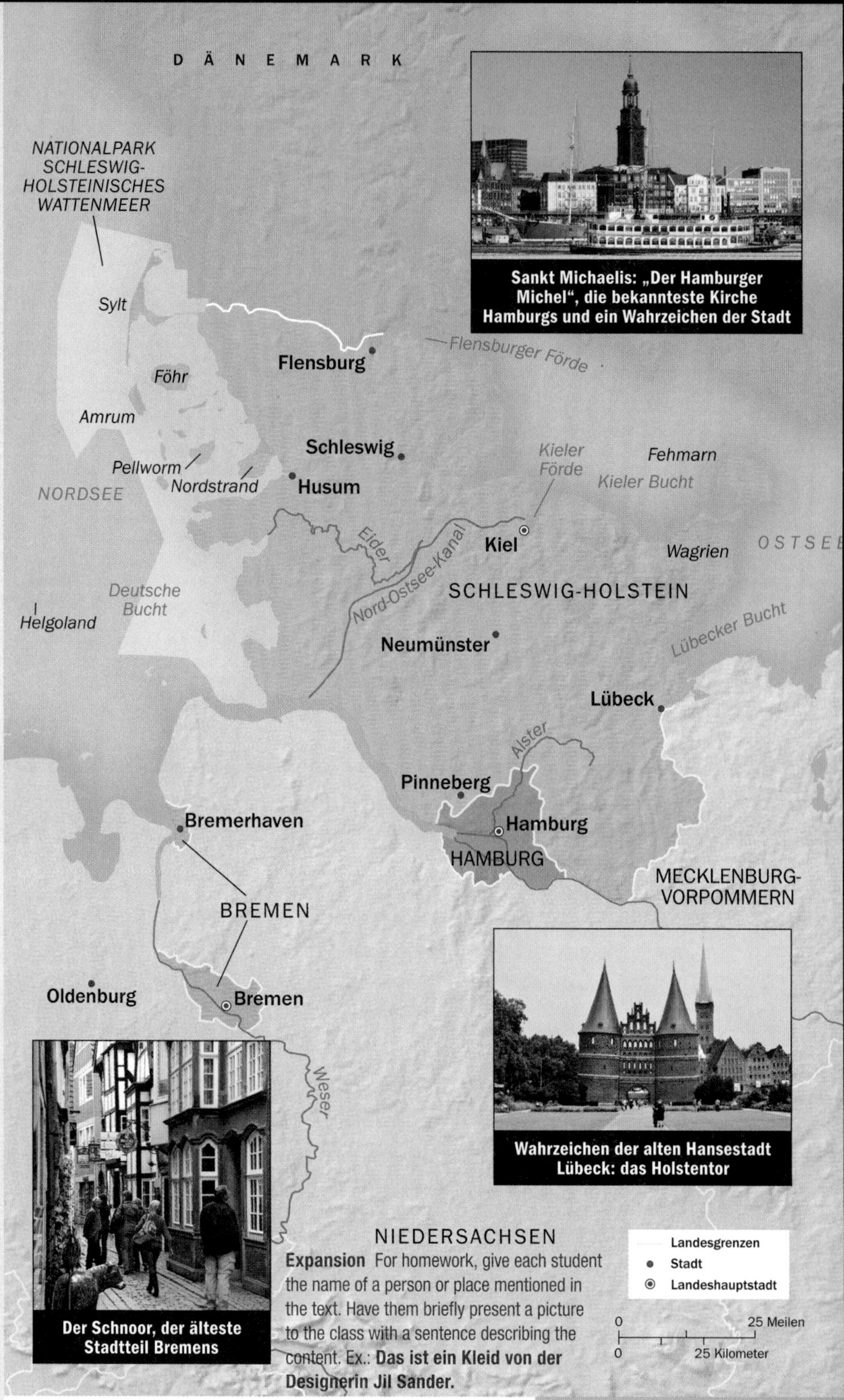

DÄNEMARK
NATIONALPARK SCHLESWIG-HOLSTEINISCHES WATTENMEER
Sylt
Föhr
Amrum
Pellworm
Nordstrand
Flensburg
Flensburger Förde
Schleswig
Husum
Kieler Förde
Fehmarn
Kieler Bucht
NORDSEE
Eider
Nord-Ostsee-Kanal
Kiel
Wagrien
OSTSEE
Helgoland
Deutsche Bucht
SCHLESWIG-HOLSTEIN
Neumünster
Lübecker Bucht
Lübeck
Alster
Pinneberg
Bremerhaven
Hamburg
HAMBURG
MECKLENBURG-VORPOMMERN
BREMEN
Oldenburg
Bremen
Weser
NIEDERSACHSEN

Sankt Michaelis: „Der Hamburger Michel", die bekannteste Kirche Hamburgs und ein Wahrzeichen der Stadt

Wahrzeichen der alten Hansestadt Lübeck: das Holstentor

Der Schnoor, der älteste Stadtteil Bremens

Landesgrenzen
Stadt
Landeshauptstadt
0 25 Meilen
0 25 Kilometer

Expansion For homework, give each student the name of a person or place mentioned in the text. Have them briefly present a picture to the class with a sentence describing the content. Ex.: **Das ist ein Kleid von der Designerin Jil Sander.**

Unglaublich, aber wahr!

In Hamburg gibt es mehr als 2.400 Brücken°. Die Brücken überqueren° die Alster, Süderelbe, Norderelbe und Kanäle der Stadt. Es gibt mehr Brücken in Hamburg als in Venedig°, Amsterdam und London zusammen.

AP* Theme: Science & Technology
Context: Transportation

Suggestion Tell students that the Beatles spent a few years in Hamburg in the early sixties. They also recorded German versions of "**Komm gib mir deine Hand**" and "**Sie liebt dich**"; videos for both can be found online.

Expansion A series of puppet shows called **Märchen der Welt** is available online, including a production of **Bremer Stadtmusikanten**. Show students the final five minutes, in which the thieves are driven away by the animals.

Märchen

Bremer Stadtmusikanten

Auf dem Marktplatz der Stadt Bremen gibt es eine Statue: Man kann einen Hahn° auf einer Katze auf einem Hund auf einem Esel° stehen sehen. Diese Tiere spielen die Hauptrollen eines Märchens der Gebrüder Grimm mit dem Namen „Die Bremer Stadtmusikanten". Es ist interessant, dass die Tiere in dem Märchen nie in Bremen ankamen. Zwar wollten sie am Anfang der Geschichte nach Bremen, hielten dann aber in einem Haus außerhalb der Stadt an. Trotzdem sind die Stadtmusikanten ein wichtiges Symbol der Stadt.

AP* Theme: Beauty & Aesthetics
Context: Language & Literature

Natur

AP* Theme: Global Challenges
Context: Environmental Issues

Nationalpark Schleswig-Holsteinsches Wattenmeer

Das Wattenmeer liegt in der Nordsee. Große Teile des Wattenmeers stehen unter Naturschutz°. Der Nationalpark Schleswig-Holsteinisches Wattenmeer hat eine Fläche von 4.410 Quadratkilometern und erstreckt sich von der deutsch-dänischen Seegrenze bis zur Elbmündung°. Er ist der größte deutsche Nationalpark. 70% des Nationalparks stehen permanent unter Wasser. Tiere und Pflanzen, die in diesem Nationalpark leben, sind Schweinswale°, Brandgänse° und diverse Seegräser. Seit 2009 ist das Wattenmeer ein UNESCO-Welterbe°.

Piraten

AP* Theme: Personal & Public Identities
Context: National Identity

Störtebeker

Klaus Störtebeker ist der berühmteste deutsche Pirat (wahrscheinlich 1360–1401). Viele Legenden existieren über ihn. Der Name Störtebeker (Stürz den Becher) kommt aus dem Niederdeutschen: angeblich konnte Störtebeker einen 4-Liter-Becher° in einem Schluck° austrinken. 1401 exekutierte man Störtebeker mit 30 Gefährten° in Hamburg. Laut einer Sage° durften alle Gefährten weiterleben°, an denen Störtebeker nach seiner Exekution ohne Kopf vorbeilief°. Er schaffte 11 Kameraden! Heute ist das Interesse an diesem Mann immer noch sehr groß. Einige Schiffe tragen seinen Namen und es gibt auch Filme und Festspiele über ihn.

Hahn *rooster* **Esel** *donkey* **Naturschutz** *conservation* **Elbmündung** *Elbe delta* **Schweinswale** *porpoises* **Brandgänse** *shelducks* **Welterbe** *world heritage site* **zweitgrößten Seehafen** *second largest seaport* **Zollfreiheit** *guaranteed duty exemption* **ausgedehnten** *extensive* **Bühnenprogramm** *stage program* **Becher** *mug* **Schluck** *gulp* **Gefährten** *companions* **Sage** *tale* **weiterleben** *be spared* **ohne Kopf vorbeilief** *ran by without his head*

Tradition

AP* Theme: Contemporary Life
Context: Social Customs & Values

Hafengeburtstag Hamburg

Ungefähr 13.000 Seeschiffe aus aller Welt laufen jährlich den zweitgrößten Seehafen° Europas an. Kaiser Friedrich Barbarossa hatte den Hamburgern am 7. Mai 1189 Zollfreiheit° für ihre Schiffe auf der Elbe von der Stadt bis an die Nordsee gewährt. Das Tor zur Welt war damit geöffnet, der Hamburger Hafen geboren. Seit 1977 feiert man Anfang Mai den Hafengeburtstag Hamburg. Mit vielen Attraktionen zu Wasser und in der Luft und einem ausgedehnten° Bühnenprogramm° zieht das Fest zahlreiche Touristen aus dem In- und Ausland an.

IM INTERNET

1. Suchen Sie Informationen über die Umwelthauptstadt Hamburg: Machen Sie eine Liste mit Aktionen, die es in Hamburg gab.
2. Suchen Sie Informationen über die Stadt Lübeck: Was kann man hier machen? Warum ist diese Stadt berühmt? Was kann man hier essen?

Find out more at **vhlcentral.com**.

Was haben Sie gelernt? Ergänzen Sie die Sätze.

1. Die Brücken Hamburgs überqueren die __Alster, Norderelbe, Süderelbe__ und Kanäle der Stadt.
2. In Hamburg gibt es mehr Brücken als in __Venedig, Amsterdam und London__ zusammen.
3. Auf dem Bremer Marktplatz gibt es eine Statue mit vier __Tieren__.
4. __Die Gebrüder Grimm__ haben das Märchen der Bremer Stadtmusikanten aufgeschrieben.
5. Der Hamburger Hafen wurde im Jahr __1189__ gegründet.
6. Jedes Jahr kommen ungefähr 13.000 __Seeschiffe__ in den Hamburger Hafen.
7. Der berühmteste Pirat Deutschlands heißt __Klaus Störtebeker__.
8. Er wurde __1401__ in Hamburg exekutiert.
9. Der Nationalpark Wattenmeer ist der größte deutsche __Nationalpark__.
10. Im Nationalpark leben Tiere wie Schweinswale und __Brandgänse__.

Practice more at **vhlcentral.com**.

Audio: Reading

Vor dem Lesen

AP* Theme: Contemporary Life
Context: Entertainment, Travel, & Leisure

Strategien

Predicting content from the title

You can often use titles and subheadings to predict the content of a text before you read it. For example, you can usually predict the content of a newspaper article from its headline. Predicting content from titles will help you increase your reading comprehension in German.

Untersuchen Sie den Text

Lesen Sie die Überschriften (*titles*) des Textes. Was für eine Textart ist das? Schreiben Sie mit einem Partner / einer Partnerin eine Liste: welche Informationen können Sie in jedem Teil des Textes finden? Answers will vary.

Überschriften

Lesen Sie die Überschriften: Was ist das Thema des Textes, der dieser Überschrift folgt (*follows*)? Wo kann man diese Überschriften finden (in einer Tageszeitung, einem Magazin, einer Broschüre, einem Reiseführer, etc.)? Sample answers are provided.

Regensburg entdecken
eine Broschüre, ein Reiseführer

Diese Woche in Berlin
eine Tageszeitung

Die Pyramiden Ägyptens in 8 Tagen!
eine Broschüre, ein Reiseführer

DFB-Team verliert Fußball-Länderspiel gegen Frankreich
eine Tageszeitung

Am Frankfurter Flughafen wird gestreikt
eine Tageszeitung

Die 15 besten Rezepte zum Grillen
ein Magazin

Gute Restaurants für Studenten in Kiel
eine Broschüre, ein Reiseführer

Suggestion Make sure students understand the difference between **Tageszeitung**, **Broschüre**, **Reiseführer**, etc. You may want to bring examples of each.

Die Nordseeküste° Schleswig-Holsteins in 6 Tagen

Nordfriesland, Schleswig-Flensburg, Dithmarschen, Rendsburg-Eckernförde, Plön, Ostholstein, Steinburg, Segeberg, Pinneberg, Stormarn, Herzogtum Lauenburg, 1, 2, 3, 4

6 Tage Naturerlebnis° für 450 Euro!

1. Tag: Hamburg-Büsum Mit dem Bus von Hamburg nach Brunsbüttel. Hier besichtigen° wir die Schleusen° des Nord-Ostsee-Kanals. Weiter geht es mit dem Bus nach Friedrichskoog. Wir besuchen die Seehundstation° Friedrichskoog, die einzige Seehundstation in Schleswig-Holstein. Per Bus geht es weiter nach Büsum, unserer Endstation heute. Am Nachmittag besuchen wir das „Museum am Meer“ mit Informationen über das Fischen an der Nordseeküste. Danach gibt es einen Besuch der 'Sturmflutenwelt° Blanker Hans' mit Demonstration der Flutkatastrophe von 1962.

2. Tag: Büsum-Tönning-St. Peter Ording-Husum Nach einer Busfahrt von Büsum nach Tönning besuchen wir das Multimar Wattforum. Hier kann man in Aquarien Wale und andere Tiere des Wattenmeers sehen. Mit dem Bus geht es weiter nach St. Peter Ording. Wir werden einen Spaziergang am Strand machen und dann den Westküstenpark mit Robbinarium° besuchen (bei schlechtem Wetter gehen wir in der Dünentherme im Freizeit- und Erlebnisbad schwimmen). Nach einer weiteren Busfahrt besuchen wir das Schloss° vor Husum und den Schlosspark mit seinen wunderschönen Blumen.

Nordseeküste *North Sea coast* **Naturerlebnis** *nature experience* **besichtigen** *tour* **Schleusen** *locks* **Seehundstation** *harbor seal ward* **Sturmflutwelt** *world of the storm tide* **Robbinarium** *seal zoo* **Schloss** *castle*

3. Tag: Husum-Insel Föhr
In Husum machen wir eine Stadtführung° mit dem Fahrrad: Wo hat der berühmte Autor Theodor Storm gelebt und gearbeitet? Mit dem Bus geht es dann nach Dagebüll und mit einer Fähre° auf die Insel° Föhr. Hier besuchen wir ein typisches friesisches Dorf°: Nieblum.

4. Tag: Insel Föhr-Insel Amrum
Mit der Fähre fahren wir von Föhr zu der Insel Amrum. Wir sehen uns die Stadt Wittdün an, besuchen den Amrumer Leuchtturm° (gebaut 1875) und gehen auf der Kniepsand-Sandbank spazieren.

5. Tag: Insel Amrum-Sylt
Mit der Fähre fahren wir von Amrum nach Sylt. Wir wandern zum Roten Kliff Kampen. Nachmittags besuchen wir eine Einkaufsarkade in Westerland und das Sylt Aquarium mit 2.000 verschiedenen Kreaturen aus dem Meer.

6. Tag: Sylt-Seebüll-Friedrichstadt-Hamburg Mit der Fähre geht es zurück zur Küste nach Niebüll und dann weiter nach Seebüll. Hier besuchen wir das Emil-Nolde-Museum. Mit dem Bus weiter nach Friedrichstadt. Diese Stadt heißt auch die „Holländerstadt".
Die Stadtführung ist inklusive einer Schiffsfahrt° auf den Grachten° und Kanälen der Stadt. Das Ende unserer Tour ist in Hamburg.

Stadtführung *tour of the town* **Fähre** *ferry* **Insel** *island* **friesisches Dorf** *Frisian village* **Leuchtturm** *lighthouse* **Schiffsfahrt** *boat tour* **Grachten** *town canals*

Nach dem Lesen

Richtig oder falsch? Korrigieren Sie die falschen Sätze. Sample answers are provided.

	richtig	falsch
1. Den Nord-Ostsee-Kanal kann man in Brunsbüttel besuchen.	☑	☐
2. In Schleswig-Holstein gibt es viele Seehundstationen. In Schleswig-Holstein gibt es nur in Friedrichskoog eine Seehundstation.	☐	☑
3. In der Nordsee gibt es keine Wale. In der Nordsee gibt es Wale.	☐	☑
4. Im Schlosspark in Husum kann man wunderschöne Blumen sehen.	☑	☐
5. Dagebüll ist ein typisches friesisches Dorf. Nieblum ist ein typisches friesisches Dorf.	☐	☑
6. Die Insel Amrum ist für ihre lange Sandbank aus Kniepsand bekannt.	☑	☐
7. Die Insel Amrum ist berühmt für das Rote Kliff. Die Insel Sylt ist berühmt für das Rote Kliff in Kampen.	☐	☑
8. In Seebüll, der „Holländerstadt", gibt es viele Grachten und Kanäle. In Friedrichstadt gibt es viele Grachten und Kanäle.	☐	☑

Kombinieren Sie Verbinden Sie jede Aktivität mit dem passenden Ort.

b 1. das Emil-Nolde-Museum besuchen
d 2. auf der Kniepsand-Sandbank spazieren gehen
a 3. eine Seehundstation besuchen
c 4. eine Stadtführung mit dem Fahrrad machen
e 5. das „Museum am Meer" besuchen

a. Friedrichskoog
b. Seebüll
c. Husum
d. Insel Amrum
e. Büsum

Suggestion Explain that **Kniepsand** is the name of a wandering sand dune that currently juts up against the western dunes of the island **Amrum**.

Urlaub in Schleswig-Holstein Führen Sie zu dritt eine Diskussion.

Sie werden Schleswig-Holstein drei Wochen lang besuchen. Sie wollen eine organisierte Tour machen, die in Hamburg beginnt. Sie besuchen das Reisebüro für weitere Informationen. Stellen Sie Fragen über Städte, Aktivitäten, Ausflüge, Hotels, den Transport, etc.

Suggestion Make sure students understand that the group activity is a role-play and that two people in the group will play tourists, while a third will play the travel agent.

Hören

Strategien

Using visual cues

Visual cues can provide useful context to help you make sense of information you hear.

To practice this strategy, you will listen to an advertisement.
As you listen, jot down information you hear that relates to the image below.

www.wilkommenimurlaub.de

Hauptseite | Angebote | Preise | Anfrage und Buchung

Teichhof Fehmarn. Direkt an der Nordsee. 2-Zimmer Wohnung mit Küche, Bad und Seeblick. 100 Euro pro Nacht.

Ferienwohnung Zugspitze. Gelegen in den Bayerischen Alpen. Wohnung für 2 Personen in traditionellem Haus mit Küche, Bad und Balkon. 50 Euro pro Nacht.

Ferienwohnung Schliemannstraße. Sehr zentral am Prenzlauer Berg in Berlin. Moderne Wohnung mit Küche und Bad. 36 Euro pro Person pro Nacht.

Vorbereitung

Schauen Sie sich das Foto rechts an. Worüber diskutieren Lisa und Martina?

Zuhören

Hören Sie sich das Gespräch an. Welchen Ort möchte Lisa besuchen und welchen Martina? Wo werden sie Urlaub machen?

Suggestion Before students listen to the conversation, pre-teach the words **gebongt** ("agreed") and **KaDeWe** (**Kaufhaus des Westens**, a large mall in Berlin).

Verständnis

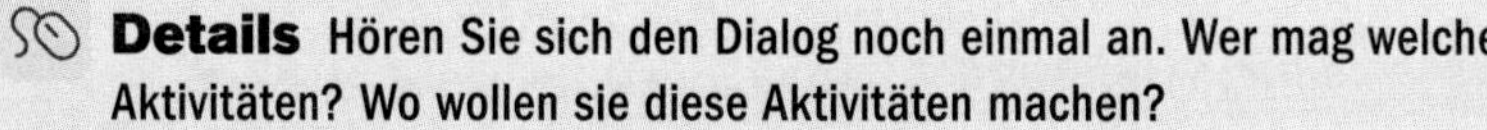

Details Hören Sie sich den Dialog noch einmal an. Wer mag welche Aktivitäten? Wo wollen sie diese Aktivitäten machen?

	wandern	Touristen-attraktionen besuchen	Fahrrad fahren	schwimmen	Theater besuchen	einkaufen
Fehmarn	Lisa		Lisa	Lisa		
Bayerische Alpen	Martina	Martina				
Berlin		Lisa	Martina		Lisa	Martina

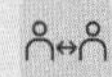

Urlaubsziele Besprechen Sie mit einem Partner / einer Partnerin, wo Sie gerne Urlaub machen und was Sie dort gerne machen. Fahren Sie gerne im Winter, Frühling, Sommer oder Herbst in Urlaub? Wohin fährt Ihr Partner / Ihre Partnerin gerne? Was macht er/sie gerne im Urlaub? Welchen Urlaub wollen Sie gerne zusammen machen?

BEISPIEL

S1: *Ich besuche jeden Sommer einen Nationalpark in den USA. Und du?*

S2: *Ich mag keine Nationalparks. Ich besuche Chicago mit meiner Familie.*

Expansion After they complete the chart, ask students why Lisa doesn't want to go to the Alps. Play the audio again, if necessary. (She says: **Ich habe Angst vor hohen Bergen! Und Schlösser finde ich langweilig.**)

Partner Chat You can also assign this activity on the Supersite. Students work in pairs to record the activity online. The pair's recorded conversation will appear in your gradebook.

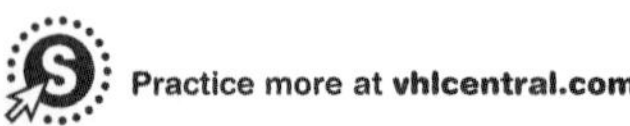

Schreiben

Strategien

Making an outline

Making an outline (**eine Gliederung**) before you write helps you to identify topics and subtopics, and provides a framework for presenting the information. Consider the following outline for a travel brochure.

I. Das Urlaubsziel
- **A.** Das Hotel
  - **1.** Die Lage (*location*)
  - **2.** Die Ausstattung (*facilities*)
  - **3.** Die Bewertung (*rating*)
- **B.** Die Landschaft
- **C.** Die Sehenswürdigkeiten

II. Die Reisezeit
- **A.** Das Klima
- **B.** Der Preis

Eine Mindmap

Idea maps provide a useful way to help you visualize information before you create an outline. The larger circles in an idea map correspond to the Roman numerals in an outline. The smaller circles correspond to the outline's capital letters, numbers, and so on. Consider the idea map that led to the outline above.

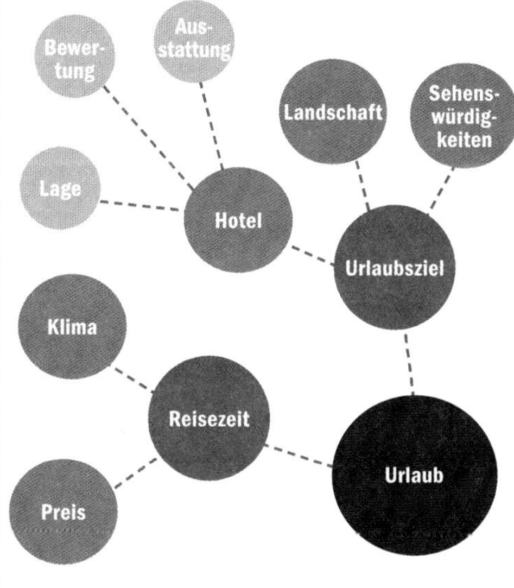

Thema

Schreiben Sie eine Broschüre

Schreiben Sie eine Tour-Broschüre für ein Reiseziel (*destination*) in einem deutschsprachigen Land.

Bevor Sie die Broschüre schreiben, schreiben Sie sich Ideen für die Broschüre auf. Hier ist eine Liste mit wichtigen Fragen:

- Welches Reiseziele wollen Sie beschreiben?
- Wie lange soll die Tour dauern?
- Wie ist das Wetter am Reiseziel?
- Welche Kleidung brauchen die Teilnehmer (*participants*)?
- Wo übernachten sie?
- Wo kann man essen gehen?
- Was soll man besuchen?
- Welche Aktivitäten gibt es (Sport, Einkaufen etc.)?
- Wie viel kostet der Urlaub pro Person?

Suggestion Tell students that they may use information from the articles in this unit, and/or do additional research online.

Organisieren Sie Ihre Ideen mit einer Mindmap. Schreiben Sie mit der fertigen Mindmap eine Gliederung. Jetzt können Sie eine Broschüre schreiben. Benutzen Sie Überschriften (*titles*), damit die Leser die Organisation der Broschüre verstehen können. In guten Broschüren sind oft Anschauungsmaterialien (*visual aids*) (Fotos, Tabellen etc.) integriert. Verwenden Sie Vokabeln und Grammatik, die Sie in diesem Kapitel gelernt haben.

Expansion Have students prepare a poster or short PowerPoint presentation in which they talk about a trip to Germany as though they have really taken it, using the past tense. Encourage them to be creative and to use real destinations featured in the unit.

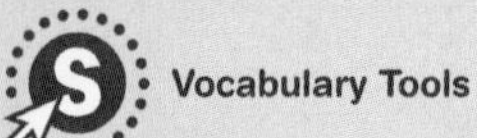

Lektion 3A

Jahreszeiten

der Winter, - *winter*
der Frühling, -e *spring*
der Sommer, - *summer*
der Herbst, -e *fall*

Monate

der Januar *January*
der Februar *February*
der März *March*
der April *April*
der Mai *May*
der Juni *June*
der Juli *July*
der August *August*
der September *September*
der Oktober *October*
der November *November*
der Dezember *December*

das Datum

Welcher Tag ist heute? *What day is it today?*
Der 15. August. *The 15th of August.*
Wann hast du Geburtstag? *When is your birthday?*
Am 23. Mai. *May 23rd.*
das Jahr, -e *year*
die Jahreszeit, -en *season*
der Monat, -e *month*
der Tag, -e *day*
die Woche, -n *week*

das Wetter

Wie ist das Wetter? *What's the weather like?*
Es ist schön draußen. *It's nice out.*
Das Wetter ist gut/schlecht. *The weather is nice/bad.*
Wie warm/kalt ist es? *How warm/cold is it?*
Es sind 18 Grad draußen. *It's 18 degrees out.*
Es ist heiß. *It's hot.*
Es ist kalt. *It's cold.*
Es ist kühl. *It's cool.*
Es ist sonnig. *It's sunny.*
Es ist windig. *It's windy.*
Es ist wolkig. *It's cloudy.*
Es regnet. *It's raining.*
Es schneit. *It's snowing.*
der Blitz, -e *lightning*
der Donner, - *thunder*
das Gewitter, - *thunderstorm*
der Hagel *hail*
der Nebel, - *fog; mist*
der Regen *rain*
der Regenmantel, ¨ *raincoat*
der Regenschirm, -e *umbrella*
der Schnee *snow*
der Sturm, ¨e *storm*
der Wetterbericht, -e *weather report*
die Wolke, -n *cloud*

***Präteritum* of verbs with prefixes** *See p. 120.*
Prepositions of location *See p. 124.*

Lektion 3B

am Flughafen

der Abflug *departure*
die Ankunft *arrival*
der Ausgang, ¨e *exit*
das Ausland *abroad*
die Bordkarte, -n *boarding pass*
die Businessklasse *business class*
der Flug, ¨e *flight*
das Flugticket, -s *ticket*
das Flugzeug, -e *airplane*
das Gepäck *luggage*
das Handgepäck *carry-on luggage*
der Koffer, - *suitcase*
der Passagier, -e *passenger*
die Passkontrolle, -n *passport control*
der Personalausweis, -e *ID card*
die Reise, -n *trip*
das Reisebüro, -s *travel agency*
der Reisende, -n *traveler*
die Touristenklasse *economy class*
die Verspätung, -en *delay*
das Visum (*pl.* die Visa) *visa*
die Zeitung, -en *newspaper*
der Zoll *customs*

die Ferien

die Kreuzfahrt, -en *cruise*
das Meer, -e *sea; ocean*
der Skiurlaub, -e *ski vacation*
der Strand, ¨e *beach*
eine Karte lesen *to read a map*
Urlaub machen *to go on vacation*

Unterkünfte

der Fahrstuhl, ¨e *elevator*
der Gast, ¨e *(hotel) guest*
das (Fünf-Sterne-) Hotel *(five-star) hotel*
die Jugendherberge, -n *youth hostel*
der Schlüssel, - *key*
der Zimmerservice *room service*

zum Beschreiben

voll besetzt *fully occupied*
pünktlich *on time*

Verben

abbrechen (bricht... ab) *to cancel*
abfliegen (fliegt... ab) *to take off*
buchen *to make a (hotel) reservation*
fliegen *to fly*
landen *to land*
packen *to pack*
Schlange stehen *to stand in line*
übernachten *to spend the night*

Infinitive expressions *See p. 138.*
Time expressions *See p. 142.*
Indefinite pronouns *See p. 144.*

Ressourcen

Verkehrsmittel und Technologie

KAPITEL
4

LEKTION 4A

LEKTION 4B

WEITER GEHT'S

Suggestion Ask students to identify who is in the picture and what type of transportation they are using.

Teaching Tip Look for icons indicating activities that address the modes of communication. Follow this key:

→Å←	Interpretive communication
←Å→	Presentational communication
Å↔Å	Interpersonal communication

Kontext

Communicative Goals

You will learn how to:

- talk about cars and driving
- talk about public transportation

Auto und Rad fahren

Vocabulary Tools

AP* Theme: Science & Technology
Context: Transportation

Suggestion Tell students that **Rad** means *wheel.* Ask them to guess the meaning of words like **Einrad**, **Dreirad**, and **Motorrad**.

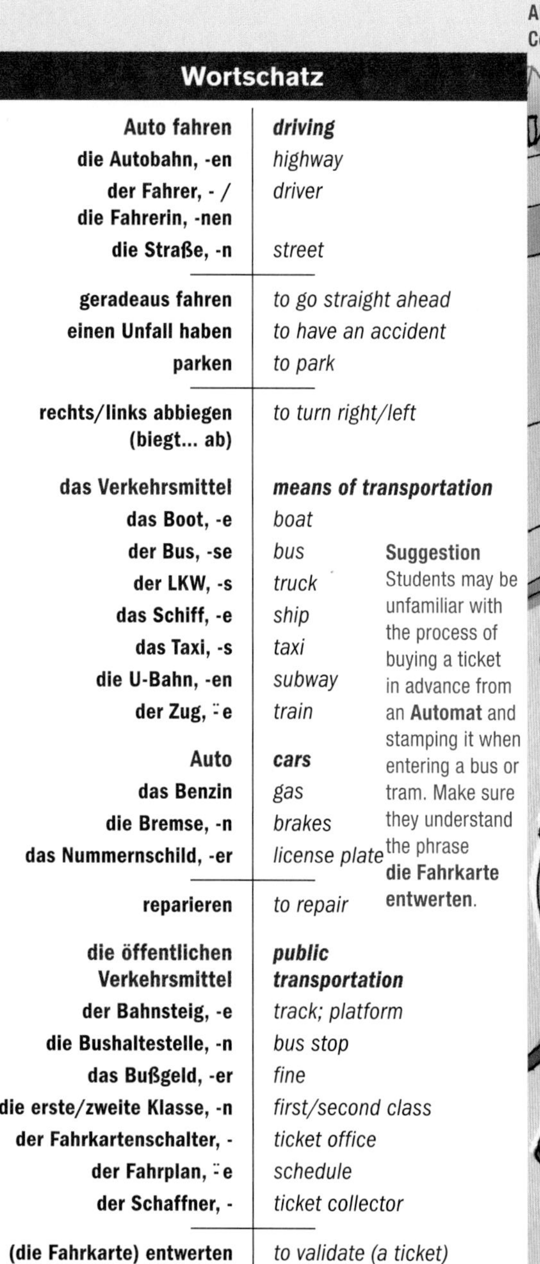

Wortschatz

Auto fahren	***driving***
die Autobahn, -en	*highway*
der Fahrer, - / die Fahrerin, -nen	*driver*
die Straße, -n	*street*
geradeaus fahren	*to go straight ahead*
einen Unfall haben	*to have an accident*
parken	*to park*
rechts/links abbiegen (biegt... ab)	*to turn right/left*
das Verkehrsmittel	***means of transportation***
das Boot, -e	*boat*
der Bus, -se	*bus*
der LKW, -s	*truck*
das Schiff, -e	*ship*
das Taxi, -s	*taxi*
die U-Bahn, -en	*subway*
der Zug, ¨-e	*train*
Auto	***cars***
das Benzin	*gas*
die Bremse, -n	*brakes*
das Nummernschild, -er	*license plate*
reparieren	*to repair*
die öffentlichen Verkehrsmittel	***public transportation***
der Bahnsteig, -e	*track; platform*
die Bushaltestelle, -n	*bus stop*
das Bußgeld, -er	*fine*
die erste/zweite Klasse, -n	*first/second class*
der Fahrkartenschalter, -	*ticket office*
der Fahrplan, ¨-e	*schedule*
der Schaffner, -	*ticket collector*
(die Fahrkarte) entwerten	*to validate (a ticket)*

Suggestion Students may be unfamiliar with the process of buying a ticket in advance from an **Automat** and stamping it when entering a bus or tram. Make sure they understand the phrase **die Fahrkarte entwerten**.

Suggestion Remind students that the **-in** suffix is often added to refer to female practitioners of a profession or activity. Say: **Ein Mann, der Autos repariert, ist *Mechaniker.* Wie heißt eine Frau, die Autos repariert?**

Ressourcen
vText | WB pp. 45–46 | LM p. 85 | vhlcentral

Benzin bleifrei
Diesel
die Tankstelle, -n
das Auto, -s
das Fahrrad, ¨-er
Er tankt. (tanken)
der Kofferraum, ¨-e
das Lenkrad, ¨-er
die Motorhaube, -n
der Sicherheitsgurt, -e
der Motor, -en
der Mechaniker, -
(die Mechanikerin, -nen f.)
Sie haben einen Platten.
das Öl, -e

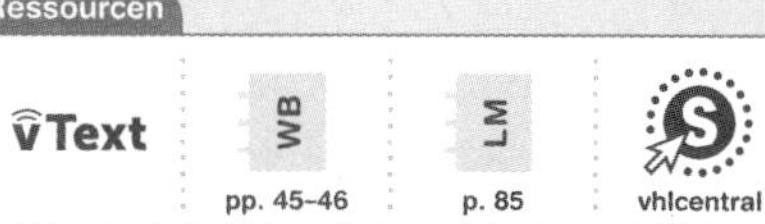

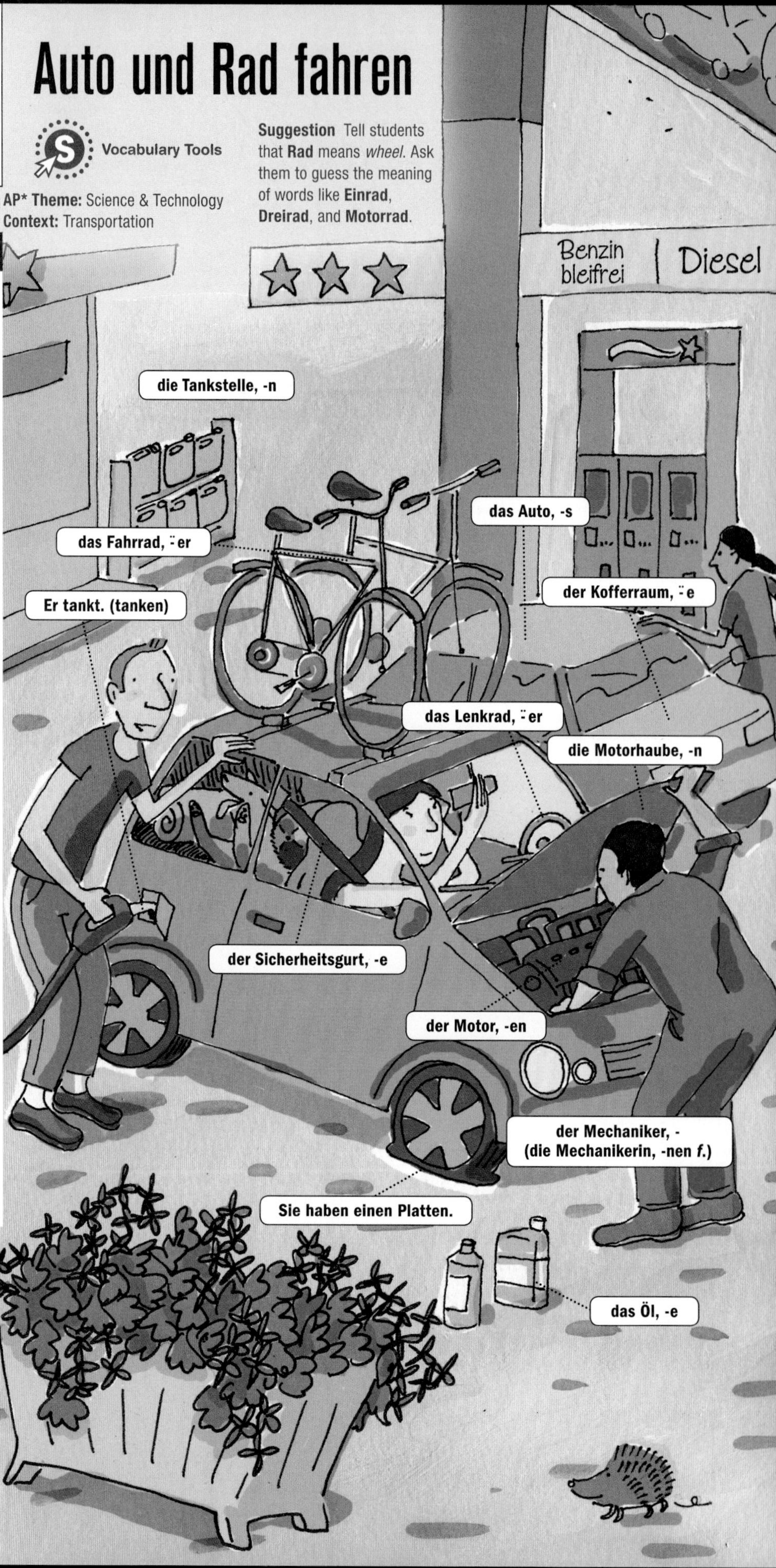

ACHTUNG

In German-speaking countries, distances are measured in kilometers (**Kilometer**). One kilometer is equal to 0.62 miles (**Meilen**).

Anwendung

Suggestion Have students look at a map of Germany. Give them the distance between two cities in kilometers. Have them convert the distance to miles. Ex.: **Ich fahre von Frankfurt nach Coburg. Das sind ungefähr 164 km. Wie viele Meilen sind das?**

1 Paare finden
Verbinden Sie das Verb mit dem richtigen Ausdruck (*expression*).

1 Suggestion Check comprehension by asking follow-up questions. Ex.: **Ich habe einen Platten. Was mache ich? Ich bin an der Tankstelle. Was mache ich da?**

d 1. entwerten
c 2. packen
f 3. reparieren
b 4. Schlange stehen
a 5. tanken
e 6. parken

a. die Tankstelle
b. die Bushaltestelle
c. der Kofferraum
d. die Fahrkarte
e. die Garage
f. der Mechaniker

2 Bilder beschriften
Wie heißen die verschiedenen Verkehrsmittel auf den Fotos?

1. der Zug

2. das Schiff

3. der Bus

4. das Fahrrad

5. die U-Bahn

6. der LKW

3 Achtung beim Autofahren
Bringen Sie die Sätze in eine logische Reihenfolge von 1 bis 6.

3 1. in die Straße einbiegen
1 2. die Tür öffnen und einsteigen
5 3. die Polizei anrufen
2 4. den Sicherheitsgurt anlegen (*fasten*)
6 5. ein Bußgeld bezahlen
4 6. einen Unfall haben

3 Suggestion To get students started on the right track, say: **Ich fahre mit dem Auto nach Koblenz. Ich stehe vor meinem Auto. Was mache ich zuerst?** (Mime opening the door.) **Gut, was mache ich dann?** (Mime putting on the seatbelt.) Have students complete the activity with a partner.

4 Wer, wen, was und wo
Hören Sie die sechs Aussagen an und wählen Sie das Wort, das am besten zu jeder Situation passt. Beantworten Sie danach die Fragen in ganzen Sätzen. Answers will vary.

1. (die Polizei) / den Schaffner
2. der Metzger / (der Mechaniker)
3. im Fahrstuhl / (am Fahrkartenschalter)
4. (ein Bußgeld) / eine Geldtasche
5. (an der Tankstelle) / am Bahnsteig
6. auf den Stadtplan / (auf den Fahrplan)

Kommunikation

5 **Aus dem Polizeibericht** Schauen Sie sich das Bild an und lesen Sie den kurzen Zeitungsartikel dazu. Beantworten Sie danach die Fragen. Arbeiten Sie mit einem Partner / einer Partnerin zusammen. Sample answers provided.

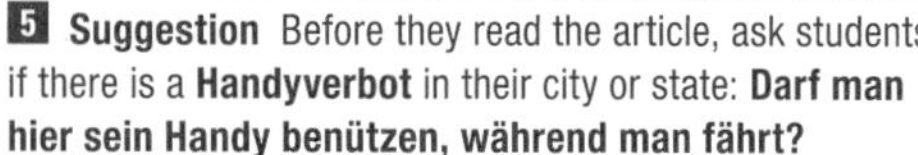

5 Suggestion Before they read the article, ask students if there is a **Handyverbot** in their city or state: **Darf man hier sein Handy benützen, während man fährt?**

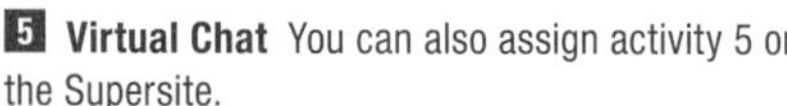

5 Virtual Chat You can also assign activity 5 on the Supersite.

Unfall in Frankfurter Innenstadt

Ein 23-jähriger Peugeotfahrer hat nicht aufgepasst und fuhr am Donnerstagabend bei Rot über die Kreuzung (*intersection*) Kaiserstraße und Friedensstraße. Ein LKW kam von links und die zwei Fahrzeuge sind zusammengestoßen (*collided*). Beim Unfall ist der Peugeotfahrer auch gegen ein geparktes Motorrad gestoßen. Beide Fahrer trugen Sicherheitsgurte und blieben unverletzt (*unhurt*). Der junge Mann sagte aus, er wollte nur schnell auf sein Handydisplay schauen und sah dann den LKW nicht. Der 23-Jährige bekam ein Bußgeld von 400 Euro. Seit 2001 gibt es ein Handyverbot am Steuer. Man darf nicht mit dem Auto fahren und dabei sein Handy benutzen.

1. Was ist am Donnerstagabend passiert? Ein Unfall zwischen einem Peugeot und einem LKW ist passiert.
2. Welche Fahrzeuge waren in den Unfall verwickelt (*involved*)? Ein Peugeot, ein LKW und ein Motorrad waren in den Unfall verwickelt.
3. Warum hat der Peugeotfahrer nicht bei Rot gehalten? Der Peugeotfahrer hat auf sein Handydisplay geschaut.
4. War jemand beim Unfall verletzt? Nein, niemand war verletzt.
5. Musste der Peugeotfahrer ein Bußgeld bezahlen? Ja, er musste 400 Euro Bußgeld bezahlen.
6. Was ist ein Handyverbot? Man darf nicht mit dem Auto fahren und dabei sein Handy benutzen.

7 Suggestion Before beginning the activity, ask students if public transportation is available in their hometowns. Explain that in Germany, the well-developed network of buses, trains, subways, and trams makes it easy to get around without a car.

6 **Diskutieren und kombinieren** Ihr Professor / Ihre Professorin gibt Ihnen zwei verschiedene Blätter. Finden Sie sieben Unterschiede zwischen Ihrem Bild und dem Bild Ihres Partner / Ihrer Partnerin. Answers will vary.

BEISPIEL

S1: *Ich sehe vier Fahrräder.*
S2: *Mein Bild hat zwei Fahrräder. Und es gibt eine Bushaltestelle.*
S1: *Ich sehe keine Bushaltestelle...*

7 **Verkehrsmittel** Diskutieren Sie in kleinen Gruppen, welche Verkehrsmittel Sie nehmen, um an die verschiedenen Orte zu kommen. Machen Sie danach eine Liste mit allen Verkehrsmitteln, die Sie normalerweise (*usually*) benutzen. Vergleichen Sie schließlich Ihre Liste mit der Liste einer anderen Gruppe. Answers will vary.

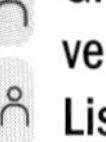

BEISPIEL

S1: *Um in die Innenstadt zu kommen, nehme ich die U-Bahn.*
S2: *Wirklich? Ich fahre mit meinem Fahrrad.*
S3: *Ich gehe zu Fuß, aber...*

Verkehrsmittel	Orte
das Auto	das Ausland
der Bus	das Haus von meinen Eltern
das Fahrrad	das Fußballstadion
das Flugzeug	der Supermarkt
zu Fuß	die Diskothek
das Taxi	die Innenstadt
die U-Bahn	die Unibibliothek
der Zug	?

Aussprache und Rechtschreibung

Long and short vowels with an *Umlaut*

You have already learned that adding an **Umlaut** to the vowels **a**, **o**, and **u** changes their pronunciation. Vowels with an **Umlaut** have both long and short forms.

Räder **Männer** **löhnen** **löschen** **Züge** **fünf**

The long **ä** is pronounced similarly to the *a* in the English word *bay*, without the final *y* sound. The short **ä** is pronounced like the *e* in *pet*.

Faxgerät **Unterwäsche** **Fahrpläne** **Spaziergänge**

To produce the long **ö** sound, start by saying the German long **e**, but round your lips as if you were about to whistle. To produce the short **ö** sound, start by saying the short **e**, but keep your lips rounded.

Öl **öffentlich** **schön** **Töchter**

To produce the long **ü** sound, start to say the German long **i**, but round your lips tightly. To produce the short **ü** sound, make the short **i** sound, but with tightly rounded lips. In some loanwords, the German **y** is pronounced like **ü**. In other loanwords, the German **y** is pronounced like the English consonant *y*.

Schüler **zurück** **Typ** **Physik**

Suggestion To help students pronounce the long **ü** sound, have them position their tongues behind the back of the lower front teeth and round their lips, as if they were about to whistle.

1 Aussprechen Wiederholen Sie die Wörter, die Sie hören.

1. Rad / Räder
2. Kopf / Köpfe
3. Zug / Züge
4. Käse / Kästchen
5. mögen / möchten
6. fühlen / füllen
7. kämen / kämmen
8. lösen / löschen
9. Dünen / dünn
10. typisch
11. MP3-Player
12. Handy

2 Nachsprechen Wiederholen Sie die Sätze, die Sie hören.

1. In der Küche kocht die Köchin mit einem großen Kochlöffel.
2. Sie ändern morgen alle Fahrpläne für die Züge in Österreich.
3. Lösch alles auf der Festplatte, bevor du deinen PC verkaufst.
4. Jürgen fährt mit den öffentlichen Verkehrsmitteln zur Universität.
5. Grüne Fahrräder sind schöner als rote oder schwarze Fahrräder.
6. Der blonde Typ da hat sein Handy verloren.

3 Sprichwörter Wiederholen Sie die Sprichwörter, die Sie hören.

Ein goldener Schlüssel öffnet alle Türen.[1]

Der Apfel fällt nicht weit vom Stamm.[2]

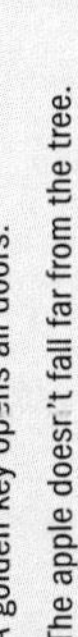
[1] A golden key opens all doors.
[2] The apple doesn't fall far from the tree.

Ressourcen: vText | LM p. 86 | vhlcentral

Fotoroman

Ein Ende mit Schrecken

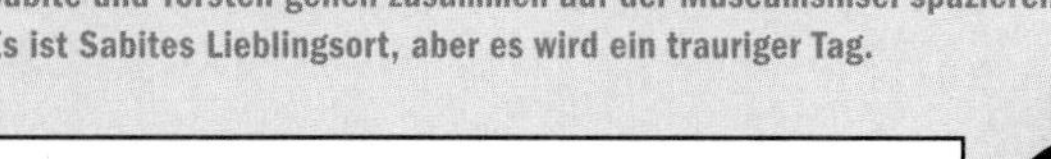
Sabite und Torsten gehen zusammen auf der Museumsinsel spazieren. Es ist Sabites Lieblingsort, aber es wird ein trauriger Tag.

NATIONAL STANDARDS communication cultures

Vorbereitung Have students read the episode title and try to predict what will happen in this episode. What do they think is going to end? Can they guess what **Schrecken** might mean? You may want to share with students the proverb **Besser ein Ende mit Schrecken als ein Schrecken ohne Ende.**

GEORGE Berlin hat die besten öffentlichen Verkehrsmittel! In Milwaukee haben wir nur Busse und kein S-Bahn-System.
HANS Hast du kein Auto?
GEORGE Doch, aber es ist alt und hat oft Pannen. Das Ölwarnlicht leuchtet ständig, und die Kupplung rutscht.
HANS Warum behältst du es?
GEORGE Es bringt mich zur Uni und zurück.

TORSTEN Sabite... es tut mir leid.
SABITE Wie bitte?
TORSTEN Es tut mir leid. An dem Abend im Restaurant, als ich von deinen Plänen erfahren habe...

SABITE Ich habe nicht darüber geredet, weil es nur eine Idee war. Ich hatte die Idee schon gehabt, bevor ich mit Lorenzo im Restaurant darüber gesprochen habe. Wir haben über Kunst geredet und da habe ich es zum ersten Mal laut ausgesprochen.
TORSTEN Ich habe das einfach nicht gewusst und bin wütend geworden.

SABITE Torsten, ich... ich glaube nicht...
TORSTEN Ich möchte nicht, dass du aus Berlin weggehst.
SABITE Warum?
TORSTEN Weil ich dich liebe.

SABITE Oh, Torsten, ich habe letzte Woche mit meiner Mutter zu Mittag gegessen. Wir haben etwas beschlossen. Meine ganze Familie verbringt den Sommer in der Türkei.

TORSTEN Ach so. Ich möchte nicht, dass du gehst, aber ich weiß, dass ich dich nicht davon abhalten kann. Du bist so stark, wie du schön bist. Was ich jetzt sagen muss, ist sehr schwer.
SABITE Torsten, machst du Schluss mit mir?
TORSTEN Liebst du mich?

ÜBUNGEN

1 Richtig oder falsch? Entscheiden Sie, ob die folgenden Sätze **richtig** oder **falsch** sind.

1. In Milwaukee gibt es Busse und ein S-Bahn-System. Falsch.
2. Georges Auto ist alt und hat oft Pannen. Richtig.
3. Sabite hat mit Lorenzo im Restaurant über Kunst gesprochen. Richtig.
4. Dort hat sie zum ersten Mal laut über die Türkei gesprochen Richtig.
5. Torsten war im Restaurant geduldig und ist ruhig geblieben. Falsch.
6. Sabite hat letzte Woche mit ihrer Mutter zu Abend gegessen. Falsch.
7. Torsten möchte, dass Sabite nach Istanbul geht. Falsch.
8. George und Hans fahren mit dem Bus in Berlin herum. Falsch.
9. Torsten hat mit Sabite auf der Museumsinsel Schluss gemacht. Richtig.
10. Sabite mag die Museumsinsel nicht. Falsch.

PERSONEN

George

Hans

Meline

Sabite

Torsten

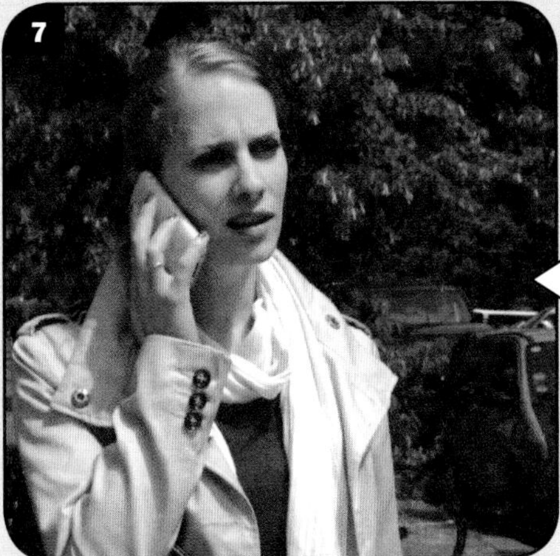
7

MELINE Hallo, Sabite. Wie geht's? Okay... Süße... es ist schon okay. Wo bist du? Bleib dort, ich bin gerade an einer U-Bahn-Station vorbeigekommen. Ich bin in einer Viertelstunde da. (*Zu sich selbst.*) Torsten. Er ist so dumm, wie er gemein ist.

8

GEORGE Sabite, hey. Hans und ich fahren mit der Bahn in der ganzen Stadt herum. Das ist die interessanteste Weise, Berlin zu sehen. Was? Jetzt mal ganz ruhig. Du bist wo? Er hat was? Wo sind wir?

HANS Spandau. Wir sind in der U-Bahn-Station Altstadt Spandau! Wo ist sie?

GEORGE Museumsinsel. Wir kommen so schnell wie möglich.

9

MELINE Er hat dich bis hierher zur Museumsinsel geschleppt, nur um mit dir Schluss zu machen?

SABITE Es war meine Idee, hierher zu kommen. Ich liebe diesen Ort. Ah, da kommen sie.

HANS Hey, Sabite, es tut mir so, so, so leid.

MELINE Hans. Hans!

10

HANS Also... du hast mit ihm Schluss gemacht?

SABITE Ich wollte mit ihm Schluss machen. Aber er... er war schneller als ich!

Nützliche Ausdrücke

- **die Panne**
  breakdown
- **Das Ölwarnlicht leuchtet ständig, und die Kupplung rutscht.**
  The oil warning light is always on, and the clutch slips.
- **erfahren (von)**
  to find out (about)
- **Wir haben über Kunst geredet und da habe ich es zum ersten Mal laut ausgesprochen.**
  We were talking about art, and that was the first time I said it out loud.
- **wütend**
  furious
- **Wir haben etwas beschlossen.**
  We decided something.
- **Ich möchte nicht, dass du gehst, aber ich weiß, dass ich dich nicht davon abhalten kann.**
  I don't want you to go, but I know I can't stop you.
- **vorbeikommen**
  to pass
- **herumfahren**
  to ride around
- **Wir kommen so schnell wie möglich.**
  We'll be there as soon as possible.
- **schleppen**
  to drag

4A.1

- **Berlin hat die besten öffentlichen Verkehrsmittel!**
  Berlin has the best public transportation!

4A.2

- **Ich hatte die Idee schon gehabt, bevor ich mit Lorenzo im Restaurant darüber gesprochen habe.**
  I'd already had the idea before Lorenzo and I discussed it at the restaurant.

2 **Zum Besprechen** Bilden Sie zu zweit einen Dialog zwischen Sabite und Torsten. Versuchen Sie, die Beziehung zu retten (*to save the relationship*). Answers will vary.

3 **Vertiefung** In Deutschland gibt es viele Autobahnen. Wie sind sie nummeriert? Welche haben eine, welche zwei und welche drei Ziffern (*digits*)? Welche haben gerade (*even*) und welche ungerade Nummern? Answers will vary.

3 **Expansion** Have students find out the speed limits for different types of vehicles on the German **Autobahnen**.

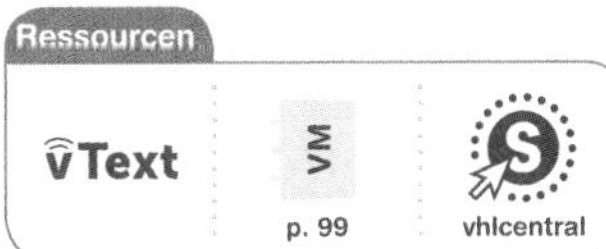

Kultur

Suggestion Before they begin the reading, ask students: **Welche Autos kommen aus Deutschland? Was wissen Sie über die Autobahn in Deutschland?**

IM FOKUS

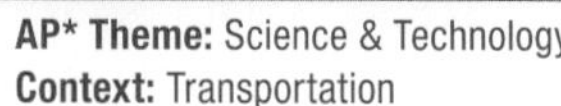

AP* Theme: Science & Technology
Context: Transportation

Die deutsche Autobahn

Reading

TIPP

The German **Autobahn** is toll-free for cars, but Austria and Switzerland charge a toll (**eine Maut**) for use of all limited-access highways. Cars in each country must display a toll sticker (**eine Mautvignette**) in their windshields to show that they have paid an annual fee to use the country's **Autobahnnetz**.

Die Geschichte der deutschen Autobahn geht mehr als 80 Jahre zurück. Die AVUS (Automobil-Verkehrs- und Übungs-Straße), heute Teil der Autobahn A115, war die erste nur für Autos zugelassene° Straße Europas. Schon seit 1921 erstreckte sie sich° zwischen den Berliner Stadtteilen Charlottenburg und Nikolassee. Um einmal darüber zu fahren, musste man zehn Mark bezahlen. Damals war das ziemlich teuer!

Am 6. August 1932 eröffnete der Kölner Oberbürgermeister Konrad Adenauer die erste so genannte „Autobahn". Ihr Bau hatte drei Jahre gedauert. Sie war 20 Kilometer lang und erstreckte sich zwischen Köln und Bonn. In beide Fahrtrichtungen war sie zweispurig° und kreuzungsfrei° Damit entsprach° sie einer Autobahn, wie wir sie heute kennen, mit einem Unterschied: Es gab keinen Mittelstreifen°. Deshalb bekam der Abschnitt erst 1958, nach weiterem Ausbau°, den offiziellen Status der Autobahn.

Heute hat Deutschland eines der dichtesten Autobahnnetze° der Welt und der Bau geht immer weiter. Es gilt zwar in Deutschland eine Richtgeschwindigkeit° von 130 Kilometern pro Stunde, ein generelles Tempolimit° gibt es aber nicht. Trotzdem haben 45 Prozent aller deutschen Autobahnkilometer Tempolimits. An fast allen Autobahnen gibt es mittlerweile komfortable Raststätten°, wo es neben Tankstellen, Hotels, Restaurants und Läden sogar Kinderspielplätze gibt.

Längste Autobahnnetze der Welt

Land	Strecke°
USA	97.355 km
China	75.932 km
Spanien	16.204 km
Deutschland	12.917 km

zugelassene *permitted* **erstreckte... sich** *extended* **zweispurig** *two-lane* **kreuzungsfrei** *intersection-free* **entsprach** *conformed to* **Mittelstreifen** *median strip* **Ausbau** *extension* **Autobahnnetze** *interstate highway networks* **Richtgeschwindigkeit** *target speed* **Tempolimit** *speed limit* **Raststätten** *service areas* **Strecke** *distance*

ÜBUNGEN

1 **Richtig oder falsch?** Sie die Aussagen richtig oder falsch? Korrigieren Sie die falschen Aussagen.

1. Die Geschichte der deutschen Autobahn geht 60 Jahre zurück.
   Falsch. Die Geschichte der deutschen Autobahn geht mehr als 80 Jahre zurück.
2. Konrad Adenauer eröffnete 1921 die erste so genannte „Autobahn".
   Falsch. Er eröffnete 1932 die erste so genannte „Autobahn".
3. Die AVUS erstreckte sich zwischen Köln und Bonn.
   Falsch. Die AVUS erstreckte sich zwischen Charlottenburg und Nikolassee.
4. Man baute die erste so genannte „Autobahn" in drei Jahren. Richtig
5. Eine Autobahn muss zweispurig und kreuzungsfrei sein. Richtig
6. Deuschland hat das dichteste Autobahnnetz der Welt.
   Falsch. Deuschland hat eines der dichtesten Autobahnnetze der Welt.
7. In Deutschland gibt es eine Richtgeschwindigkeit von 130 Kilometern pro Stunde. Richtig
8. Es gibt auf deutschen Autobahnen keine Tempolimits.
   Falsch. Etwa 45 Prozent aller deutschen Autobahnkilometer haben permanente Tempolimits
9. Heute umfasst das Autobahnnetz in Deutschland mehr als 75.000 Kilometer.
   Falsch. Heute umfasst das Autobahnnetz in Deutschland mehr als 12.000 Kilometer.
10. Nach Spanien hat Deutschland das längste Autobahnnetz Europas. Richtig

Practice more at **vhlcentral.com.**

DEUTSCH IM ALLTAG

Verkehrsschilder

die Kreuzung	*intersection*
das Stoppschild	*stop sign*
(die) Ausfahrt	*exit*
(die) Baustelle	*construction zone*
(die) Einbahnstraße	*one-way street*
(die) Umleitung	*detour*

DIE DEUTSCHSPRACHIGE WELT

Fahrrad fahren

In Deutschland besitzen mehr Haushalte° Fahrräder als ein Auto. Bei Familien haben sogar 96% der Haushalte Fahrräder. Deshalb gibt es in vielen Städten separate Fahrradwege°. Für das Fahrradfahren gibt es besondere Regeln°: Wenn es keinen Fahrradweg gibt, müssen Fahrradfahrer, die über 11 Jahre alt sind, auf der rechten Seite der Straße fahren. Besondere Schilder zeigen, wann Fahrradfahrer in Einbahnstraßen entgegen der Fahrtrichtung° fahren dürfen. In Fußgängerzonen° dürfen Radfahrer nur im Schritttempo° fahren. Außerdem muss jedes Fahrrad ein festes Fahrradlicht haben.

Haushalte *households* **Fahrradwege** *bike lanes* **Regeln** *rules* **entgegen der Fahrtrichtung** *against the flow of traffic* **Fußgängerzonen** *pedestrian zones* **Schritttempo** *walking speed*

AP* Theme: Science & Technology
Context: Transportation

PORTRÄT

Fräulein Stinnes' Weltreise°

AP* Theme: Contemporary Life
Context: Entertainment, Travel, & Leisure

Clärenore Stinnes kommt am 21. Januar 1901 als Tochter eines Großindustriellen zur Welt. Mit 24 Jahren nimmt sie zum ersten Mal an einem Autorennen° teil. Bis 1927 gewinnt sie 17 Rennen, darunter auch eine internationale Rallye in Russland. Sie ist die einzige Frau unter 53 Teilnehmern! Im Mai 1927 bricht Clärenore zu einer Weltreise auf. Sie finanziert die Reise mit Sponsoren wie Bosch und Aral. Auch das Außenministerium° und deutsche Auslandsvertretungen° unterstützen sie. Sie legt 47.000 Kilometer zurück und ist zwei Jahre und einen Monat unterwegs. Das Auto, ein Adler Standard 6, steht heute im Deutschen Museum in München.

Weltreise *world tour* **Autorennen** *car race* **Außenministerium** *Ministry of Foreign Affairs* **Auslandsvertretungen** *embassies*

IM INTERNET

Suchen Sie Informationen zu der Internationalen Automobil-Ausstellung (IAA). Wo und wann war die letzte Ausstellung?

Find out more at **vhlcentral.com**.

2 **Was fehlt?** Ergänzen Sie die Sätze.

1. In deutschen Haushalten gibt es öfter __Fahrräder__ als ein Auto.
2. In vielen Städten gibt es seperate __Fahrradwege__ für Fahrräder.
3. Jedes Fahrrad in Deutschland muss __ein Fahrradlicht__ haben.
4. Ihre Weltumrundung hat __zwei Jahre__ und einen Monat gedauert.
5. Das Auto, das Clärenore Stinnes bei ihrer Weltreise gefahren hat, kann man heute im __Deutschen Museum__ in München finden.

3 **Lieblingstransportmittel** Diskutieren Sie mit einem Partner / einer Partnerin Ihr Lieblingstransportmittel.
Wie bewegen Sie sich am liebsten fort? Sind Sie ein Fan von Fahrrad, Auto oder Bus? Gehen Sie am liebsten zu Fuß? Warum bewegen Sie sich gerne so fort? Was sind die Vorteile und Nachteile?

3 Partner Chat You can also assign activity 3 on the Supersite. Students work in pairs to record the activity online. The pair's recorded conversation will appear in your gradebook.

Ressourcen
vText

4A.1 Das Plusquamperfekt

Suggestion Explain that the **Plusquamperfekt** is used to talk about events that were "*already* in the past." Provide an example in English. Ex.: I had *already* eaten an entire pizza *by the time* the chocolate cake arrived."

Startblock Use the **Plusquamperfekt** tense to refer to a past event that occurred before another event in the past.

Das Plusquamperfekt

QUERVERWEIS

See **1A.1** and **1B.1** to review the formation of the **Perfekt** tense. See **2A.1** to review the formation of the **Präteritum**.

- To form the **Plusquamperfekt**, use the **Präteritum** form of **haben** or **sein** with the past participle of the verb that expresses the action.

Ich **hatte vergessen**, die Tür zu schließen.
*I **had forgotten** to close the door.*

Jasmin **war** noch nie nach Zürich **gefahren**.
*Jasmin **had** never **been** to Zurich.*

- Since the **Plusquamperfekt** refers to a past event that was completed prior to another past event, both events are often described in the same sentence.

Der Zug fährt ab. | Ich komme am Bahnsteig an.

14.45 Uhr — Plusquamperfekt | 14.47 Uhr — Perfekt/Präteritum

Suggestion The "formula" for the **Plusquamperfekt** can be expressed as: **hatte/war** (conjugated) + **Partizip** (at end of clause).

PRÄTERITUM	PLUSQUAMPERFEKT
Als ich am Bahnsteig **ankam**,	**war** der Zug schon **abgefahren**.
*When I **arrived** at the platform,*	*the train **had** already **left**.*

Expansion Have students look at the examples and underline both the helping verbs and the past participles. Ask a volunteer to restate the rule for verbs that require a form of **sein** as their helping verb.

Bevor Stefan in die Stadt gezogen ist, **hatte** er nie öffentliche Verkehrsmittel **benutzt**.
*Before Stefan moved to the city, he **had** never **used** public transportation.*

Nachdem der Mechaniker das Auto **repariert hatte**, **fuhr** er damit zur Tankstelle.
*After the mechanic **had fixed** the car, he **drove** it to the gas station.*

Bevor ich nach England **reiste, hatte** ich meinen Neffen noch nie **gesehen**.
***Before** I **went** to England, I **had** never **met** my nephew.*

Als wir im Kino **ankamen**, **hatte** der Film schon **angefangen**.
***When** we **got** to the movie theater, the film **had** already **started**.*

Suggestion Tell students that subordinating conjunctions like **bevor**, **nachdem**, and **als** "send" or "kick" the verb to the end of the clause.

Conjunctions *als, bevor, nachdem*

- Use the subordinating conjunctions **als** (*when*), **bevor** (*before*), and **nachdem** (*after*) to indicate the sequence in which two past events occurred.

Als Jan ins Restaurant **kam**, **hatte** seine Freundin schon **bestellt**.
*By the time Jan **got** to the restaurant, his girlfriend **had** already **ordered**.*

Unsere Eltern sind erst nach Hause gekommen, **nachdem** wir schon ins Bett **gegangen waren**.
*By the time our parents came home, we **had** already **gone** to bed.*

- When a clause begins with **als**, **bevor**, or **nachdem**, move the conjugated verb to the end of the clause.

Bevor ich in Deutschland **wohnte**...
*Before I **lived** in Germany...*

Als Hanna **anrief**...
*When Hanna **called**...*

- After **bevor** and **als**, use the **Perfekt** or **Präteritum** and put the main clause in the **Plusquamperfekt**.

Als Tom zur Bushaltestelle **kam**, **war** der Bus schon **abgefahren**.
*By the time Tom **got** to the bus stop, the bus **had** already **left**.*

Bevor ich Kalifornien **besucht habe**, **hatte** ich noch nie Artischocken **gegessen**.
*Before I **visited** California, I **had** never **eaten** artichokes.*

- After **nachdem**, use the **Plusquamperfekt** and put the main clause in the **Perfekt** or **Präteritum**.

Der Bus **ist** endlich **gekommen**, **nachdem** wir schon 30 Minuten **gewartet hatten**.
*The bus finally **came**, after we **had been waiting** for 30 minutes.*

Nachdem Sara ins Bett **gegangen war**, **hat** ihre Mutter **angerufen**.
*After Sara **had gone** to bed, her mother **called**.*

- If the clause with **bevor**, **nachdem**, or **als** is first in the sentence, the main clause after the comma begins with the verb. If that verb is in the **Plusquamperfekt** or **Perfekt**, put the helping verb first and the past participle at the end.

Als wir am Flughafen **ankamen**, **war das Flugzeug** schon **abgeflogen**.
*By the time we **got** to the airport, the plane **had** already **taken off**.*

Das Flugzeug **war** schon **abgeflogen**, als wir am Flughafen **ankamen**.
*The plane **had** already **taken off** by the time we **got** to the airport.*

Suggestion Point out to students that this word order is consistent with the "verb-in-second-position" rule. The dependent clause, set off by the comma, functions as the first sentence element, and the verb comes as the second element.

QUERVERWEIS

To review coordinating conjunctions, see **2A.3**.

Students will learn more about subordinating conjunctions in **Vol. 3, 2A.3.**

ACHTUNG

If the main clause comes first in the sentence, use the normal subject-verb word order.

Suggestion You may want to mention that in conversation, people often use the **Perfekt** tense instead of the **Plusquamperfekt** along with time expressions to help clarify the sequence of events: **Nachdem Ulrich einen Unfall gehabt hat, hat er sein Auto zum Mechaniker gebracht**.

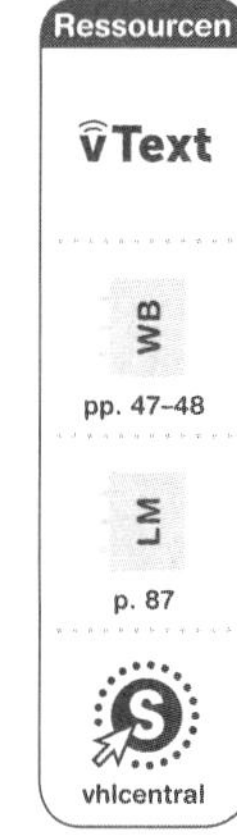

Jetzt sind Sie dran! **Schreiben Sie die Sätze ins Plusquamperfekt um.**

1. Haben Sie Ihre Freundin angerufen?
   Hatten Sie Ihre Freundin angerufen?
2. Ich habe das Auto zum Mechaniker gebracht.
   Ich hatte das Auto zum Mechaniker gebracht.
3. Bist du zu spät aufgestanden?
   Warst du zu spät aufgestanden?
4. Benjamin ist noch nie in Berlin gewesen.
   Benjamin war noch nie in Berlin gewesen.
5. Ihr habt die Fahrkarte schon entwertet, nicht?
   Ihr hattet die Fahrkarte schon entwertet, nicht?
6. Die Mechanikerin hat den LKW schon repariert.
   Die Mechanikerin hatte den LKW schon repariert.
7. Oma und Opa sind gerade zurückgekommen.
   Oma und Opa waren gerade zurückgekommen.
8. Wir haben falsch geparkt.
   Wir hatten falsch geparkt.
9. Papa hat das Auto letzte Woche verkauft.
   Papa hatte das Auto letzte Woche verkauft.
10. Wir haben das Buch noch nicht gelesen.
    Wir hatten das Buch noch nicht gelesen.
11. Seid ihr in die Stadt gefahren?
    Wart ihr in die Stadt gefahren?
12. Hast du das gewusst?
    Hattest du das gewusst?

Anwendung

1 **Was passt zusammen?** Welche Sätze in der rechten Spalte ergänzen die Sätze in der linken Spalte?

__d__ 1. Nachdem Paul seine Sachen gepackt hatte,
__b__ 2. Als Amila nach Hause kam,
__a__ 3. Wir haben noch lange geredet,
__f__ 4. Bevor du zurückkamst,
__c__ 5. Hattest du meinen Geburtstag vergessen,
__e__ 6. Ich war sehr traurig,

a. nachdem wir gegessen hatten.
b. hatte ihre Familie schon mit dem Essen angefangen.
c. oder wolltest du mich überraschen?
d. hat er eine Karte an Greta geschrieben.
e. nachdem du weggegangen warst.
f. hatte ich dich überall gesucht.

2 **Was fehlt?** Ergänzen Sie die Sätze mit den richtigen Plusquamperfektformen.

1. Vor meiner Reise nach Paris __hatte__ ich viel darüber __gelesen__. (lesen)
2. Nachdem wir __gelandet__ __waren__, sind wir zuerst ins Hotel gefahren. (landen)
3. Wir __hatten__ kein Auto __gemietet__, sondern sind immer mit der U-Bahn gefahren. (mieten)
4. Jasmin __hatte__ ihr Geld in den Hotelsafe __gelegt__, bevor sie ausgegangen ist. (legen)
5. Sie sind ins Museum gegangen, nachdem sie __getankt__ __hatten__. (tanken)
6. Als sie dort ankamen, __hatten__ ihre Freunde schon lange auf sie __gewartet__. (warten)

3 **Dornröschen** Im Jahr 2015 wacht Dornröschen auf (*Sleeping Beauty wakes up*). Erzählen Sie, was für sie alles neu ist. Bilden Sie Sätze im Plusquamperfekt.

BEISPIEL in einem Auto fahren
Sie war noch nie in einem Auto gefahren.

1. in einem Flugzeug sein
   Sie war (noch) nie in einem Flugzeug gewesen.
2. einen Film sehen
   Sie hatte (noch) nie einen Film gesehen.
3. mit dem Zug reisen
   Sie war (noch) nie mit dem Zug gereist.
4. ein Taxi nehmen
   Sie hatte (noch) nie ein Taxi genommen.
5. eine Fahrkarte entwerten
   Sie hatte (noch) nie eine Fahrkarte entwertet.
6. einen Sicherheitsgurt tragen
   Sie hatte (noch) nie einen Sicherheitsgurt getragen.

4 **Was hatten sie gemacht?** Schreiben Sie zu jedem Bild einen Satz im Plusquamperfekt und erzählen Sie, was diese Personen gemacht hatten, bevor sie jemand fotografiert hat. Benutzen Sie Wörter aus der Liste oder Ihre eigenen. Seien Sie kreativ. Sample answers are provided.

BEISPIEL
Manfred
war zur Tankstelle gefahren.

besuchen	kaufen
fahren	parken
gehen	warten (auf)

1. Herr Maier
hatte sein Auto geparkt.

2. Karl
hatte schon 15 Minuten auf Klara gewartet.

3. Birgit und Lara
hatten Fahrkarten gekauft.

4. Sebastian
war zur U-Bahn gegangen.

Practice more at vhlcentral.com.

Kommunikation

5 **Faul oder fleißig** Besprechen Sie mit Ihrem Partner / Ihrer Partnerin, was Jan und Maria gestern gemacht haben. Wechseln Sie sich ab. Answers will vary.

BEISPIEL

S1: *Maria hat um 8 Uhr gefrühstückt.*
S2: *Um 8 Uhr war Jan noch nicht aufgestanden.*

	Jan	Maria
8.00	--	frühstücken
9.00	aufstehen	mit dem Bus zur Uni fahren
10.00	Kaffee trinken	Chemieprüfung schreiben
11.00	mit Freunden chatten	mit der Professorin sprechen
12.00	Musik hören	ins Fitnessstudio gehen
13.00	mit Martin Videospiele spielen	--

5 Partner Chat You can also assign activity 5 on the Supersite. Students work in pairs to record the activity online. The pair's recorded conversation will appear in your gradebook.

6 **Warum wohl?** Stellen Sie Ihrem Partner / Ihrer Partnerin zu jedem Bild eine Frage und erfinden Sie eine Antwort. Answers will vary.

die Küche nicht aufräumen	im Regen dreckig werden	keine Brille tragen
eine gute Note bekommen	kein Hotelzimmer buchen	zu spät nach Hause kommen

Philip / einen Unfall haben

BEISPIEL

S1: *Warum hat Philip einen Unfall gehabt?*
S2: *Er war vielleicht zu schnell gefahren.*

1. Hasan und Greta / diskutieren

2. Sophia / Kopfschmerzen (*headache*) haben

3. Günther / laut singen

4. Paula und Rolf / Hund waschen

5. Ben und Hans / im Wald campen

6. Tom / einen Platten haben

6 Virtual Chat You can also assign activity 6 on the Supersite. Students record individual responses that appear in your gradebook.

7 **Wichtige Ereignisse** Sagen Sie Ihren Mitschuelern, in welchem Jahr Sie geboren sind. Ein anderer Schueler / eine andere Schuelerin nennt dann ein Ereignis (*event*), das schon vorher (*before that*) passiert war. Answers will vary.

BEISPIEL

S1: *Ich bin 1994 geboren.*
S2: *25 Jahre vorher waren Astronauten schon auf dem Mond gelandet.*

1946: man baut das erste Mobiltelefon	1984: Steve Jobs stellt den ersten Mac vor
1959: die Barbiepuppe kommt auf den Markt	1989: die Berliner Mauer fällt
1973: in Deutschland gibt es eine Ölkrise	

7 Suggestion To prepare students for this activity, have them convert the information provided into complete **Plusquamperfekt** sentences. Ex.: **Man hatte das erste Mobiltelefon gebaut.**

4A.2 Comparatives and superlatives

Presentation

Suggestion Have students review the use of adjectives, taught in **Vol. 1, 3A.2**; and the use of adverbs, taught in **Vol. 1, 4A.2**.

Startblock Use the comparative and superlative forms of adjectives and adverbs to compare two or more people or things.

Der Komparativ

Suggestion Model correct pronunciation of the **Grundformen** and comparative forms and have students repeat after you.

- There are three forms of adjectives and adverbs: **die Grundform** (**schnell**), **der Komparativ** (**schneller**), and **der Superlativ** (**am schnellsten**). When describing similarities between two people or things, use the expression **so... wie** (*as... as*) or **genauso... wie** (*just as... as*) with the **Grundform** of an adjective or adverb.

  Dieser LKW ist **so groß wie** ein Bus.
  *That truck is **as big as** a bus.*

  Der Zug fährt **genauso schnell wie** ein Auto.
  *The train goes **just as fast as** a car.*

- To describe differences between two people or things, you can use the expression **nicht so... wie** (*not as... as*), or you can use the **Komparativ**. Form the **Komparativ** by adding the ending **-er** to the **Grundform** of an adjective or adverb, followed by the word **als**.

  Lina fährt **nicht so langsam wie** Sara.
  *Lina **doesn't** drive **as slowly as** Sara.*

  Sara fährt **langsamer als** Lina.
  *Sara drives **more slowly than** Lina.*

- Common one-syllable words with the stem vowel **a**, **o**, or **u** often have an umlaut on the vowel in the comparative.

a → ä		o → ö		u → ü	
alt	**älter**	**groß**	**größer**	**dumm** (*dumb*)	**dümmer**
lang	**länger**	**oft**	**öfter**	**jung**	**jünger**
stark	**stärker**	**rot**	**röter**	**kurz**	**kürzer**

  Meine Geschwister sind alle **älter** als ich.
  *My siblings are all **older** than I am.*

  Die Fahrt nach Frankfurt dauert mit dem Auto **länger** als mit dem Zug.
  *The trip to Frankfurt takes **longer** by car than by train.*

ACHTUNG

The two-syllable word **gesund** (*healthy*) also has an umlaut on the **u** in the comparative form:
gesund → gesünder

For adjectives ending in **-el** or **-er**, German speakers usually drop the **-e-** before adding the comparative **-er** ending.
teuer → teurer
dunkel → dunkler

Expansion Provide additional examples for each adjective or adverb. Ex.: **Sarahs Haare sind länger als Bens. Lady Gaga ist jünger als Donald Trump.**

- A small number of adjectives and adverbs have irregular comparative forms.

GRUNDFORM		KOMPARATIV
gern	→	**lieber**
gut	→	**besser**

  Ich fahre **lieber** mit der U-Bahn als mit dem Bus.
  *I'd **rather** take the subway than the bus.*

GRUNDFORM		KOMPARATIV
hoch	→	**höher**
viel	→	**mehr**

  Benzin kostet in Deutschland **mehr** als in den USA.
  *Gasoline is **more expensive** in Germany than in the USA.*

- When a comparative adjective precedes a noun, add the appropriate case ending after the **-er** ending.

Leider kostet der **schnellere** Zug mehr.
*Unfortunately the **faster** train costs more.*

Ich brauche einen **größeren** Koffer.
*I need a **bigger** suitcase.*

Suggestion Have students review adjective agreement, taught in **Vol. 1, 3A.2**.

Der Superlativ

- Use the **Superlativ** form of an adjective or adverb to indicate that a person or thing has more of a particular quality than anyone or anything else.

Welches ist **das größte** Tier der Welt?
*What's **the biggest** animal in the world?*

Wie komme ich **am besten** zur Tankstelle?
*What's **the best** way to get to the gas station?*

Expansion Bring in a few items or pictures that lend themselves to comparison, and ask questions that model comparative and superlative forms. Ex.: **Was ist größer, dieser Roman oder das Deutschbuch? Welcher Hut ist lustiger, der oder der? Welcher steht mir besser?**

- To form the superlative of an adjective, add **-st** to the **Grundform**. If the **Grundform** ends in **-d**, **-t**, or an **s** sound, add **-est**. When an adjective in the superlative precedes a noun, use a definite article before the superlative and add the appropriate case ending.

Warum habt ihr **die teuersten** Fahrkarten gekauft?
*Why did you buy **the most expensive** tickets?*

Wir wollten mit **dem schnellsten** Zug fahren.
*We wanted to take **the fastest** train.*

ACHTUNG

The adjective **nah** (*near*) has a stem vowel change, as well as an additional spelling change in the superlative: **nah / näher / nächst-**

Most German speakers do not use the superlative form **öftest-**; instead, they use **(am) häufigst-** (*most often*).

- To form the superlative of adverbs and of adjectives that come after **sein**, **werden**, or **bleiben**, use the word **am** before the adverb or adjective and add **-(e)sten** as the superlative ending.

Wer fährt **am langsamsten**?
*Who drives **the slowest**?*

Welches Auto ist **am schnellsten**?
*Which car is **the fastest**?*

- If an adjective or adverb has an added umlaut in the comparative, it will also have an umlaut in the superlative.

a → ä			o → ö			u → ü		
alt	**älter**	**ältest-**	**rot**	**röter**	**rötest-**	**jung**	**jünger**	**jüngst-**

- If an adjective or adverb is irregular in the comparative form, the superlative form is also irregular.

GRUNDFORM	KOMPARATIV	SUPERLATIV
gern	**lieber**	**liebst-**
groß	**größer**	**größt-**
gut	**besser**	**best-**
hoch	**höher**	**höchst-**
viel	**mehr**	**meist-**

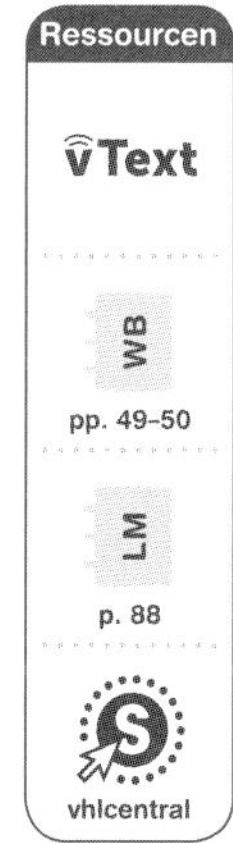

Jetzt sind Sie dran! **Ergänzen Sie die Lücken mit den richtigen Formen der Adjektive.**

	Base form	*Komparativ*	*Superlativ*		Base form	*Komparativ*	*Superlativ*
1.	groß	*größer*	am größten	7.	jung	jünger	am jüngsten
2.	gut	besser	am besten	8.	kurz	kürzer	am kürzesten
3.	lang	länger	am längsten	9.	gesund	gesünder	am gesündesten
4.	klein	kleiner	am kleinsten	10.	einfach	einfacher	am einfachsten
5.	hoch	höher	am höchsten	11.	viel	mehr	am meisten
6.	spät	später	am spätesten	12.	gern	lieber	am liebsten

Anwendung

1 **Meinungen** Ergänzen Sie die Sätze mit dem Adjektiv oder dem Adverb im Superlativ.

BEISPIEL Von allen Verkehrsmitteln benutzen wir die U-Bahn *am häufigsten*. (häufig)

1. Von allen Automodellen findet Ingrid einen Mercedes am schönsten. (schön)
2. Von allen meinen Kursen finde ich Chemie am schwierigsten. (schwierig)
3. Von allen Getränken trinkt Emil Tee am seltensten. (selten)
4. Von allen Obstsorten schmecken dir Bananen am besten? (gut)
5. Von allen meinen Kursen interessiert mich Mathematik am meisten. (viel)
6. Von allen meinen Freunden habe ich Peter am liebsten. (gern)

2 **Komparative** Bilden Sie Sätze im Komparativ. + bedeutet **-er als**, = bedeutet **(genau)so... wie** und ≠ bedeutet **nicht so... wie.**

BEISPIEL ein Auto / ist / ≠ groß / ein LKW
Ein Auto ist nicht so groß wie ein LKW.

1. die Mozartstraße / ist / + lang / die Beethovenstraße Die Mozartstraße ist länger als die Beethovenstraße.
2. Kiara / fährt / + gut / Dana Kiara fährt besser als Dana.
3. der Verkehr am Freitagabend / ist / = schlecht / der Verkehr am Montagmorgen Der Verkehr am Freitagabend ist (genau)so schlecht wie der Verkehr am Montagmorgen.
4. ich / reise / + gern / mit dem Zug / mit dem Flugzeug Ich reise lieber mit dem Zug als mit dem Flugzeug.
5. Die erste Klasse / ist / + teuer / die zweite Klasse Die erste Klasse ist teurer als die zweite Klasse.
6. heute / ist / es / ≠ warm / gestern Heute ist es nicht so warm wie gestern.

3 **Vergleichen Sie** Bilden Sie Sätze und benutzen Sie dabei die Komparativformen der angegebenen Adjektive. Sample answers are provided.

BEISPIEL ein Bus / ein Auto (klein)
Ein Auto ist kleiner als ein Bus.

1. eine U-Bahn / ein Flugzeug (schnell)
Ein Flugzeug ist schneller als eine U-Bahn.

2. Niklas / Lisa (alt)
Niklas ist nicht so alt wie Lisa.

3. Ben bezahlt 350 € Miete. / Jana bezahlt 320 € Miete. (viel)
Ben bezahlt mehr Miete als Jana.

4. Ihr esst Fisch einmal pro Monat. / Ihr esst Hähnchen einmal pro Woche. (gern)
Ihr esst lieber Hähnchen als Fisch.

Practice more at vhlcentral.com.

Kommunikation

4 Komparative Ergänzen Sie die Fragen mit den Komparativformen der angegebenen Adjektive und beantworten Sie die Fragen Ihres Partners. Answers will vary.

BEISPIEL Wer ist *schüchterner*, du oder dein bester Freund? (schüchtern)

S1: *Wer ist schüchterner, du oder dein bester Freund?*
S2: *Ich bin viel schüchterner!*

1. Was isst du ___lieber___, Joghurt oder Schokolade? (gern)
2. Womit fährst du ___seltener___, mit dem Fahrrad oder mit dem Auto? (selten)
3. Welche Sängerin findest du ___besser___, Rihanna oder Beyoncé? (gut)
4. Welches Fach findest du ___interessanter___, Marketing oder Anthropologie? (interessant)
5. Wovon verstehst du ___mehr___, von Mode oder von Sport? (viel)
6. Was machst du am Wochenende ___häufiger___, Hausaufgaben oder schlafen? (häufig)

5 Wie gut ist Ihr Allgemeinwissen? Finden Sie mit Ihrem Partner / Ihrer Partnerin zu jedem Begriff (*concept*) zwei Sachen, die man vergleichen kann, und stellen Sie einem anderen Paar Ihre Fragen. Answers will vary.

BEISPIEL welcher Kontinent / groß

S1: *Welcher Kontinent ist größer, Europa oder Asien*
S2: *Natürlich ist Asien größer!*

1. welches Land / klein
2. welche Stadt / alt
3. welcher Fluss / lang
4. welcher Flughafen / groß
5. welches Auto / schnell
6. welches Hotel / teuer
7. welche Person / reich
8. welche Schule / gut

6 Beschreiben Sie Besprechen Sie mit einem Partner / einer Partnerin die Leute im Bild. Machen Sie so viele Vergleiche wie möglich.

BEISPIEL

S1: *Sarah ist so groß wie Sabrina.*
S2: *Ja, aber David ist am größten.*

Sabrina · David · Lukas · Sarah · Emma

7 Ein kleines Interview Interviewen Sie zwei Mitstudenten und schreiben Sie ihre Antworten auf. Stellen Sie dann Ihre Informationen vor. Benutzen Sie dabei Komparativ- und Superlativformen. Answers will vary.

BEISPIEL

S1: *Wie alt bist du, Emily?*
S2: *Ich bin 18. Und du, Michael?*
S3: *Ich bin 21.*
S1: *Ich bin älter als Emily und jünger als Michael. Michael ist am ältesten.*

Name:	
Wie alt bist du?	
Wie groß bist du?	
Wie viele Geschwister hast du?	
Wie oft machst du Sport?	

4 Expansion After students have done this activity with comparatives, have them ask each other similar questions using superlatives.

6 Expansion Have pairs of students choose two very different celebrities and write sentences comparing the two. You may want to have them bring in photographs and present their comparisons to the class.

6 Partner Chat You can also assign activity 6 on the Supersite. Students work in pairs to record the activity online. The pair's recorded conversation will appear in your gradebook.

Wiederholung

4 Suggestion Remind students to "kick" the verb to the end of the clause when using conjunctions like **bevor** or **nachdem**.

1 **Vergleiche** Schreiben Sie mit einem Partner / einer Partnerin auf, was Sie auf den Fotos sehen. Benutzen Sie so viele Vergleiche wie möglich. Arbeiten Sie dann mit einem anderen Paar zusammen: Diskutieren Sie, was sie über die Bilder geschrieben haben. Answers will vary.

BEISPIEL

S1: *Taxis sind teurer als Busse.*
S2: *Aber Busse fahren nicht so schnell wie Taxis.*

1.  

2. 

2 **Diskutieren und kombinieren** Sie und Ihr Partner / Ihre Partnerin bekommen von Ihrem Professor / Ihrer Professorin verschiedene Autostatistiken. Sehen Sie sich die Statistiken der vier Autos an und vergleichen Sie dann, wie schnell, wie stark und wie teuer die Autos sind. Entscheiden Sie auch, welches Auto den größten Kofferraum hat. Answers will vary.

BEISPIEL

S1: *Wie schnell ist der Audi?*
S2: *Der Audi ist 247 Stundenkilometer schnell.*
S1: *Also ist der Audi am schnellsten.*

2 Suggestion Pre-teach the vocabulary **Marke**, **Geschwindigkeit**, and **Kraft**, and explain that **PS** is short for **Pferdestärken** (*horsepower*). Make sure students know how to pronounce **VW**. Explain that all car brands are masculine.

3 **Werbung** Entwerfen Sie (*Design*) in einer Dreiergruppe ein Zukunftsfahrzeug (*vehicle of the future*). Wie heißt das Fahrzeug? Machen Sie auch eine Liste mit der Ausstattung (*features*). Schreiben Sie dann eine Werbung, in der Sie das Zukunftsfahrzeug mit einem Auto von heute vergleichen. Answers will vary.

BEISPIEL

S1: *„Futura" – das Auto des 21. Jahrhunderts. Es kann CO_2 tanken.*
S2: *Unser Auto verbraucht viel weniger als die Autos von gestern.*

3 Suggestion You may wish to provide markers and paper so that students can make their ads more colorful. Set a time limit and make sure everyone stays on task.

4 **Arbeitsblatt** Fragen Sie andere im Unterricht, was sie gestern gemacht haben. Berichten Sie dann, wer was wann gemacht hat. Benutzen Sie das Plusquamperfekt. Answers will vary.

BEISPIEL

S1: *Bist du gestern zum Englischunterricht gegangen?*
S2: *Ja.*
S1: *Wann?*
S2: *Um 8.15 Uhr.*
S1 (schreibt): *Peter war schon zum Englischunterricht gegangen, bevor Julia Kaffee getrunken hat.*

5 **Die Party** Sie geben eine Party mit Ihren Freunden. Besprechen Sie, was Sie alle gemacht haben, um die Party vorzubereiten. Answers will vary.

BEISPIEL

S1: *Seid ihr einkaufen gegangen?*
S2: *Ja, aber bevor wir einkaufen gegangen sind, hatten wir die Küche geputzt.*

6 **Eine Reise nach Erfurt** Sie planen eine Zugfahrt von Marburg nach Erfurt. Spielen Sie mit Ihrem Partner / Ihrer Partnerin ein Gespräch im Reisebüro der Deutschen Bahn. Der Reiseberater (*travel agent*) hilft dem Reisenden, sich für eine Zugverbindung zu entscheiden. Answers will vary.

6 Partner Chat You can also assign activity 6 on the Supersite.

BEISPIEL

S1: *Wie kann ich Ihnen helfen?*
S2: *Ich möchte von Marburg nach Erfurt fahren und brauche eine Fahrkarte.*
S1: *Wann möchten Sie abfahren...?*

TIPP

Here are some abbreviations used in train schedules.

Umst. = Umsteigen (*transfer*)
RE = Regional-Express
IC = Intercity
ICE = Intercity-Express

ZUG Ihre Hinfahrtmöglichkeiten

Bahnhof	Zeit	Dauer	Umst	Produkte	Preis
MARBURG ERFURT	ab 8.21 an 12.40	4.19	2	RE, IC	51€
MARBURG ERFURT	ab 10.04 an 13.33	3.29	1	IC, ICE	65€
MARBURG ERFURT	ab 10.56 an 14.40	3.44	2	IC	51€
MARBURG ERFURT	ab 13.50 an 16.28	2.38	1	IC	51€

Video

AP* Theme: Science & Technology
Context: Transportation

Mercedes Benz

Im Jahr 1886 bekam der deutsche Ingenieur Carl Benz das Patent für das erste Automobil der Welt. 40 Jahren später fusionierte seine Firma mit der Daimler-Motoren-Gesellschaft und legte den Grundstein für eine schnelle Entwicklung der Autoindustrie in ganz Deutschland. Neben Volkswagen, Audi und BMW gilt Mercedes Benz als die bekannteste Automarke. Vor allem auf den Gebieten° Sicherheit und Komfort ist Mercedes Benz unschlagbar°. Laut einer Statistik, gesammelt über 30 Jahre vom Pannendienst° des ADAC (Allgemeiner Deutscher Automobilclub), hat Mercedes die wenigsten Pannen aller deutschen Automarken.

Suggestion Tell students that the ADAC is the German equivalent of the AAA service in the United States.

Entschuldigung. Welche deutschen Automarken kennen Sie?

Volkswagen, Opel, BMW, Audi, Porsche...

Klar, Mercedes Benz gibt's natürlich auch.

auf den Gebieten *in the area of* **unschlagbar** *unbeatable* **Pannendienst** *breakdown service*

Verständnis Beantworten Sie die Fragen mit den Informationen aus dem Video.

1. Wer ist der befragte Mann?
   a. ein Polizist
   b. ein Pannendienst-Mitarbeiter
   c. ein Autoverkäufer
2. Warum denkt der Mann nicht sofort an Mercedes Benz?
   a. Weil es eine unbekannte Automarke ist.
   b. Weil er nichts über Autos weiß.
   c. Weil Mercedes Benz selten Pannen hat.

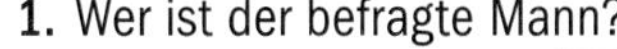

Diskussion Diskutieren Sie die folgenden Fragen mit einem Partner / einer Partnerin. Answers will vary.

1. Gibt es Automarken mit einer langen Tradition in Ihrem Land? Vergleichen Sie (*Compare*) diese Automarken mit Mercedes Benz.
2. Sind Sie oder Ihre Familie Mitglied in einem Automobilclub? Haben Sie den Pannendienst schon einmal zu Hilfe gerufen? Warum?

Kontext

Communicative Goals

You will learn how to:

- talk about electronic communication
- talk about computer technology

Technik und Medien

Expansion Teach students the phrases that refer to sending a text: **simsen** or **eine SMS schicken**.

AP* Theme: Science & Technology
Context: Personal Technologies

Wortschatz

Technik bedienen	***using technology***
anmachen (macht... an)	*to turn on*
aufnehmen (nimmt... auf)	*to record*
ausmachen (macht... aus)	*to turn off*
drucken	*to print*
fernsehen (sieht... fern)	*to watch television*
funktionieren	*to work, to function*
herunterladen (lädt... herunter)	*to download*
laden (lädt)	*to charge; to load*
löschen	*to delete*
online sein	*to be online*
schicken	*to send*
speichern	*to save*
starten	*to start*
im Internet surfen	*to surf the Web*
die Technik	***technology***
der Benutzername, -n	*screen name*
die CD, -s	*compact disc, CD*
die Datei, -en	*file*
die Digitalkamera, -s	*digital camera*
das Dokument, -e	*document*
die E-Mail, -s	*e-mail*
der Kopfhörer, -	*headphones*
das Ladegerät, -e	*battery charger*
der Laptop, -s	*laptop (computer)*
das Mikrofon, -e	*microphone*
das Passwort, ¨-er	*password*
das Programm, -e	*program*
der Sender, -	*channel*
das Smartphone, -s	*smartphone*
die SMS, -	*text message*
die Website, -s	*Web site*

die Stereoanlage, -n

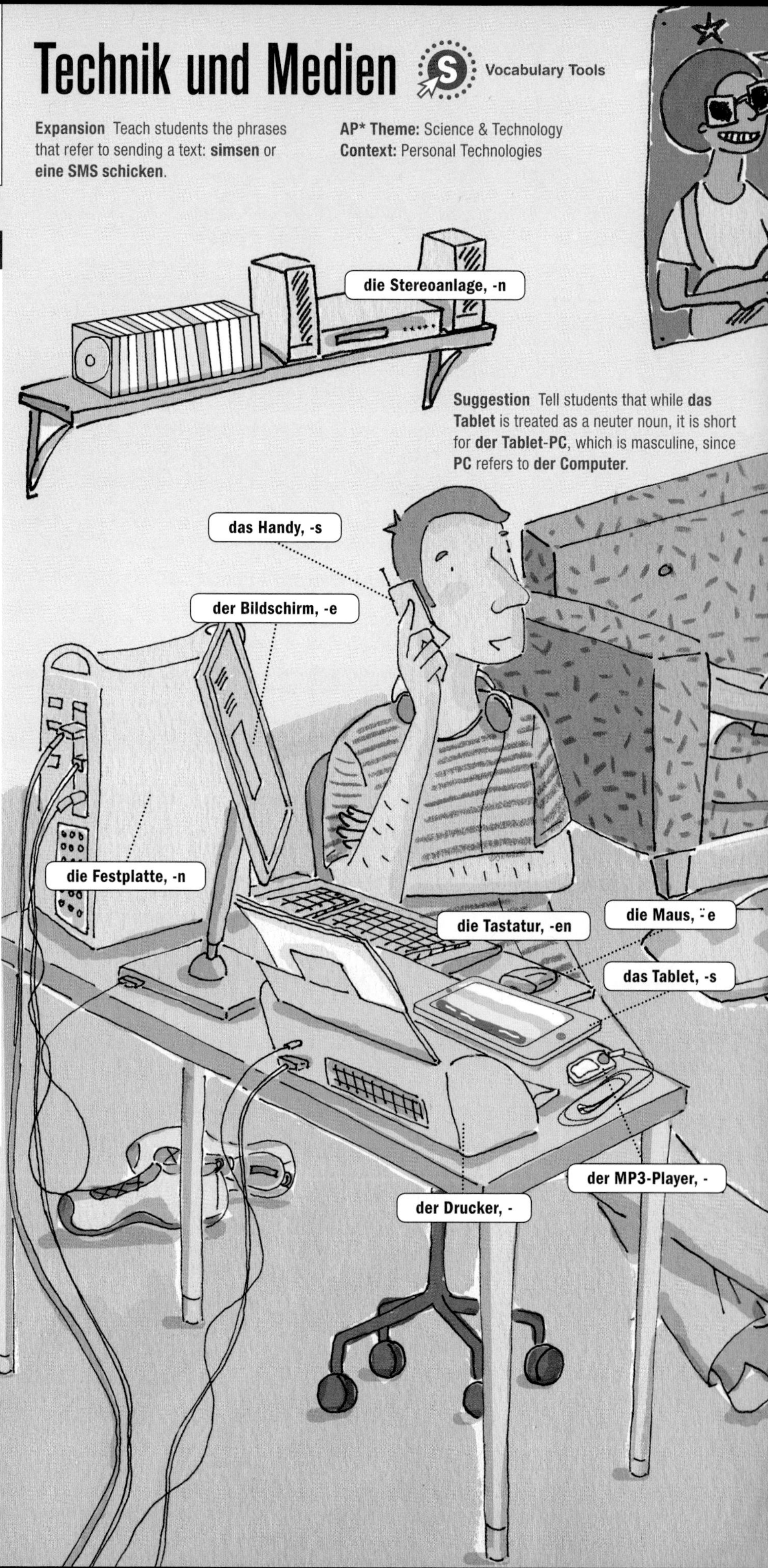

Suggestion Tell students that while **das Tablet** is treated as a neuter noun, it is short for **der Tablet-PC**, which is masculine, since **PC** refers to **der Computer**.

das Handy, -s

der Bildschirm, -e

die Festplatte, -n

die Tastatur, -en

die Maus, ¨-e

das Tablet, -s

der MP3-Player, -

der Drucker, -

ACHTUNG

The word **Gerät**, found in the compound noun **Ladegerät**, is used by itself to refer to any kind of device or appliance.

Ressourcen

pp. 51–52

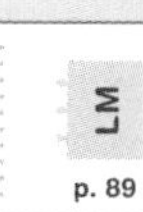

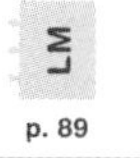
p. 89

vhlcentral

Suggestion To reinforce vocabulary acquisition, write a few words on the board with scrambled letters. Provide definitions, and have the class identify the scrambled words. Ex.: **L-N-E-I-G-L-N-K. Das macht mein Telefon, wenn jemand anruft.; L-P-T-O-A-P. (Das ist ein Computer, den ich leicht mit mir herumtragen kann.)**

Anwendung

1 Bilder beschriften Wie heißen die Geräte auf den Fotos?

a. der Drucker
b. die Fernbedienung
c. der Fernseher
d. die Kamera
e. der Laptop
f. das Mikrofon

1. c

2. d

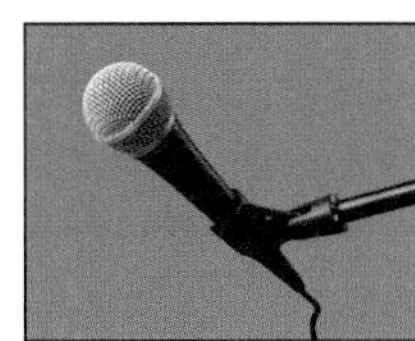

3. f

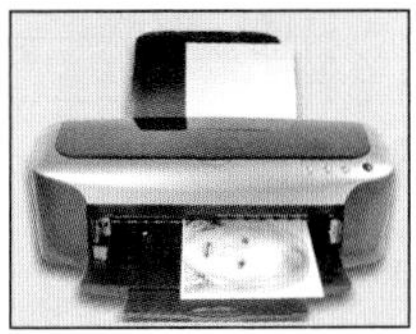

4. a

5. b

6. e

2 Was fehlt? Ergänzen Sie die Sätze mit einem passenden Wort aus der Vokabelliste.

1. Vergessen Sie nicht, Ihr Dokument zu __speichern__, bevor Sie den Computer ausmachen.
2. Um das Handy zu laden, braucht man ein __Ladegerät__.
3. Man soll nicht für jede Website dasselbe __Passwort__ benutzen.
4. Recyceln Sie Ihren Computer nicht, ohne alle Dokumente zu __löschen__.
5. Der Klingelton auf meinem __Handy__ ist ein Lied von Lady Gaga.
6. X-Box und Playstation sind __Spielkonsolen__.

3 Kategorien Finden Sie für jede Kategorie passende Wörter aus Ihrer Vokabelliste. Answers may vary slightly.

Computer	Telefon	Fernseher
die Maus	das Handy	fernsehen
die E-Mail	das Smartphone	die Fernbedienung
die Tastatur	klingeln	der Sender
speichern	die SMS	das Programm

4 Hören Sie zu Hören Sie sich die Dialoge 1-4 an und entscheiden Sie dann, welche Geräte die Personen brauchen. Schreiben Sie zu jedem Gerät die Nummer des passenden Dialogs. Answers will vary.

1. __4__ das Telefon
2. __1__ die Kamera
3. __2__ die Stereoanlage
4. __3__ die Fernbedienung

3 Suggestion Instead of filling in the answers in the book, have students write the words for each category on the board.

Practice more at **vhlcentral.com**.

Kommunikation

NATIONAL communication STANDARDS

5 Im Elektronikladen

Im Elektronikladen Was kann man hier im Elektronikladen (*electronics store*) alles kaufen? Fragen Sie Ihren Partner / Ihre Partnerin, wie er/sie die verschiedenen elektronischen Geräte findet. Answers will vary.

BEISPIEL

S1: *Wie findest du den Laptop?*
S2: *Er ist in Ordnung. Die Festplatte ist ziemlich groß.*

der Bildschirm	die Festplatte	die Tastatur
der Fernseher	der Drucker	die Videokamera

5 Suggestion Before beginning the activity, have the class look at the picture together. Ask students to tell you what they see, using as many vocabulary words as possible.

5 Virtual Chat You can also assign activity 5 on the Supersite. Students record individual responses that appear in your gradebook.

6 Diskutieren und kombinieren

Diskutieren und kombinieren Sie und Ihr Partner / Ihre Partnerin bekommen zwei verschiedene Versionen desselben Kreuzworträtsels (*crossword puzzle*). Lesen Sie sich gegenseitig die fehlenden Definitionen vor. Answers will vary.

BEISPIEL

S1: *Eins senkrecht: Man macht das mit einem neuen Programm.*
S2: *Das ist LADEN.*

6 Suggestion Before they begin this activity, have students prepare written definitions (in German) for the words in their **Kreuzworträtsel**, either in class or as homework.

7 Technische Geräte

Technische Geräte Erzählen Sie in Dreiergruppen, welche technischen Geräte Sie und die Mitglieder Ihrer Familie haben und auch oft benutzen. Answers will vary.

BEISPIEL

S1: *Meine Schwester kann ohne ihr Handy nicht leben. Sie schreibt bestimmt zweihundert SMS jeden Tag!*
S2: *Meine Eltern haben eine super Stereoanlage. Sie hören gern klassische Musik.*

8 Wie macht man das?

Wie macht man das? Beschreiben Sie mit einem Partner / einer Partnerin zusammen möglichst genau, was Sie tun müssen, um die folgenden Tätigkeiten auszuführen (*carry out*). Answers will vary.

BEISPIEL

S1: *Zuerst muss man die Fernbedienung finden.*
S2: *Dann macht man den Fernseher an und...*

- DVD ansehen
- Fotos drucken
- ein Buch herunterladen
- Informationen für ein Referat finden
- eine SMS schicken

8 Suggestion Tell students to describe each process in at least five steps. Give them time to prepare, and provide vocabulary as needed.

Aussprache und Rechtschreibung

The German *l*

To pronounce the German **l**, place your tongue firmly against the ridge behind your top front teeth and open your mouth wider than you would for the English *l*.

lang **Laptop** **Telefon** **normal** **stellen**

Unlike the English *l*, the German **l** is always produced with the tongue in the same position, no matter what sound comes before or after it. Practice saying **l** after the following consonants and consonant clusters.

Platten **schlafen** **Kleid** **pflegen** **fleißig**

Practice saying **l** at the end of words and before the consonants **d**, **m**, and **n**. Be sure to use the German **l**, even in words that are spelled the same in English and German.

Ball **Spiel** **Wald** **Film** **Zwiebeln**

Practice saying the German **l** in front of the consonant clusters **sch** and **ch**.

solch **falsch** **Milch** **Kölsch** **Elch**

Suggestion Pronounce German and English cognates side by side, and ask students if they can hear the difference in the articulation of the **l** sound. Ex.: **Ball** and *ball*; **Spiel** and *spiel*.

1 Aussprechen Wiederholen Sie die Wörter, die Sie hören.

1. Lenkrad
2. Fahrplan
3. Öl
4. Klasse
5. schlank
6. Geld
7. Köln
8. welch

2 Nachsprechen Wiederholen Sie die Sätze, die Sie hören.

1. Viele warten an der Bushaltestelle auf den letzten Bus nach Ludwigsfelde.
2. Luise, kannst du das Nummernschild von dem LKW lesen?
3. Lothar hatte leider einen Platten auf einer verlassenen Landstraße.
4. Man soll den Ölstand im Auto regelmäßig kontrollieren.
5. Natürlich hat der Laptop einen DVD-Player und eine Digitalkamera.
6. Klicken Sie auf das Bild, um den Film herunterzuladen.

3 Sprichwörter Wiederholen Sie die Sprichwörter, die Sie hören.

[1] People in glass houses shouldn't throw stones.

[2] It never rains, but it pours. (lit. *Misfortune seldom comes alone.*)

Fotoroman

Ein Spaziergang durch Spandau

Video

NATIONAL STANDARDS communication cultures

George und Sabite haben Spaß zusammen, doch ein älteres Paar sieht mehr in ihnen. Hans und Meline haben leider nicht so viel Spaß.

Vorbereitung Tell students to look at scene 2 and scene 4. Have them write a brief description of the relationship between George and Sabite, and between Meline and Hans. After they have watched the video episode, have them reconsider their descriptions.

1

GEORGE Unter uns sind zwei Flüsse. Dieser Fluss ist die Havel, und das da ist die Spree. Die Spandauer Zitadelle wurde im 16. Jahrhundert anstelle einer alten Burg erbaut. Endlich besuche ich sie mal. Viel besser, als nur darüber im Internet zu lesen. Die Architektur Deutschlands ist sagenhaft!

2

SABITE Er hat nicht angerufen, keine E-Mail und keine SMS geschickt. Ich habe seine Nummer von meinem Handy gelöscht. Doch trotz meiner Gefühle habe ich seinen Schal behalten.

GEORGE Die Farbe steht dir gut.

SABITE Danke. Sie steht dir besser.

3

HANS Ich habe mich aus meiner Wohnung ausgeschlossen. Darf ich hier warten, bis George zurückkommt?

MELINE Wieso gehst du nicht in ein Café oder in die Bibliothek? Oder... oder... machst einen Spaziergang im Viertel.

HANS Mein Mantel, mein Handy und mein Geldbeutel sind in meiner Wohnung.

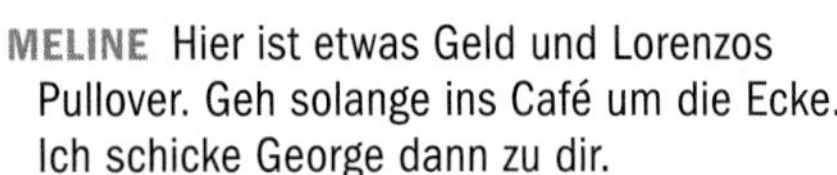

4

MELINE Hier ist etwas Geld und Lorenzos Pullover. Geh solange ins Café um die Ecke. Ich schicke George dann zu dir.

HANS Warum hast du den Pullover deines Ex-Freundes noch?

MELINE Tschüss, Hans.

5

GEORGE Wie nennst du es?

SABITE „Spandau... Spandau Ballet." Dein Handy klingelt.

GEORGE Es ist eine SMS von Meline. „Dein Mitbewohner, der Idiot, hat sich ausgeschlossen. Ich habe ihn ins Café geschickt. Bitte hol ihn dort ab. Lass dir Zeit."

MANN Berlin ist ein herrlicher Ort, um verliebt zu sein.

GEORGE Wie bitte?

FRAU Sie haben eine Verbindung. Wenn sie lacht, leuchten Ihre Augen.

MANN Katharinas Lächeln wärmt mein Herz noch immer.

FRAU Haben Sie noch viel Spaß.

6

ÜBUNGEN

1 **Wer ist das?** **Welche Personen beschreiben die folgenden Sätze: George, Hans, Meline oder Sabite?**

1. Er/Sie hat über die Spandauer Zitadelle im Internet gelesen. George
2. Er/Sie hat Torstens Nummer von seinem/ihrem Handy gelöscht. Sabite
3. Er/Sie hat sich aus seiner/ihrer Wohnung ausgeschlossen. Hans
4. Er/Sie hat Lorenzos Pullover behalten. Meline
5. Sein/Ihr Handy klingelt. George
6. Sein/Ihr Mitbewohner hat sich aus der Wohnung ausgeschlossen. George

7. Das ältere Paar glaubt, dass sie verliebt sind. George und Sabite
8. Er/Sie entschuldigt sich (*apologizes*) bei Hans. Meline
9. Er/Sie isst ein Stück Kuchen. Hans
10. Er/Sie hat ein Problem mit dem Computer. Meline

PERSONEN

George

Hans

Meline

Sabite

Frau

Mann

7

GEORGE Das ist verrückt. Wir sind Freunde. Gute Freunde.
SABITE Genau.

8

GEORGE Es tut mir leid, Sabite.
SABITE Es tut mir leid. Das war schrecklich.
GEORGE Ja, schrecklich. Die beiden waren trotz ihres Alters nicht wirklich weise.

9

MELINE Hans, es tut mir leid.
HANS Was willst du, Meline?
MELINE Ich? Nichts. Ich... ich bin unhöflich zu dir gewesen und bin hierher gekommen, um mich zu entschuldigen.
HANS Danke, ich nehme an. Setz dich doch. Kuchen?

10

MELINE Danke. Also, du kennst dich gut mit Computern aus?
HANS Ja...
MELINE Ich habe während eines Chats eine Datei runtergeladen, dann wurde mein Bildschirm plötzlich dunkel und die Festplatte hat angefangen, ein komisches Geräusch zu machen.
HANS Speichere deine Dateien ab und schalte den Computer aus.

Nützliche Ausdrücke

- **Die Spandauer Zitadelle wurde im 16. Jahrhundert anstelle einer alten Burg erbaut.**
  The Spandau Citadel was built during the 16th century, on the site of an old castle.
- **sagenhaft**
  legendary
- **das Gefühl**
  feeling
- **Die Farbe steht dir gut.**
  The color looks good on you.
- **Ich habe mich aus meiner Wohnung ausgeschlossen.**
  I'm locked out of my apartment.
- **das Viertel**
  neighborhood
- **der Geldbeutel**
  wallet
- **Berlin ist ein herrlicher Ort, um verliebt zu sein.**
  Berlin is a beautiful place to be in love.
- **Katharinas Lächeln wärmt mein Herz noch immer.**
  Katharina's smile still warms my heart.
- **schrecklich**
  terrible
- **unhöflich**
  rude

4B.1

- **Die beiden waren trotz ihres Alters nicht wirklich weise.**
  In spite of their age, those two weren't really wise.

4B.2

- **Dieser Fluss ist die Havel, und das da ist die Spree.**
  This river is the Havel and that one is the Spree.

2 **Zum Besprechen** Beschreiben Sie zu zweit, wie Sie Technologie täglich nutzen. Haben Sie einen Computer? Wofür benutzen Sie ihn? Schreiben Sie einen Blog? Was machen Sie, wenn Sie Probleme mit dem Computer haben? Answers will vary.

2 Expansion Have students write a blog entry about their reaction to George and Sabite's relationship.

2 Virtual Chat You can also assign activity 2 on the Supersite. Students record individual responses that appear in your gradebook.

3 **Vertiefung** Viele technische Erfindungen (*inventions*) kommen aus Deutschland, Österreich, Liechtenstein oder der Schweiz. Suchen Sie im Internet nach einer Erfindung und informieren Sie Ihre Klasse über den Erfinder, Ort und Zeit der Erfindung sowie den Zweck (*purpose*).

Answers may include: automobile, combustion engine, movable type, aspirin, MP3s, Swiss Army knife.

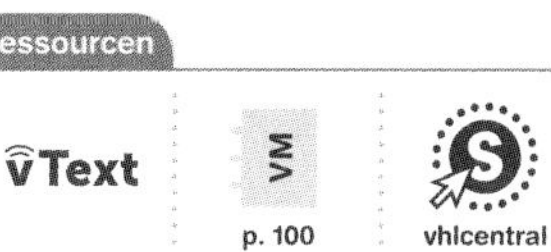

IM FOKUS

Suggestion Remind students that they are reading for the "gist." They should focus more on what they do understand than on what they do not.

Max-Planck-Gesellschaft°

Reading
AP* Theme: Personal & Public Identities
Context: Self-Image

connections cultures (National Standards)

Max Planck (1858–1947) war ein deutscher Physiker. Er entwickelte° die Quantentheorie und bekam dafür 1918 den Nobelpreis für Physik. Nach ihm ist die deutsche Max-Planck-Gesellschaft (MPG) benannt.

Diese Gesellschaft existiert seit 1948. Sie ist Nachfolgerin° der Kaiser-Wilhelm-Gesellschaft, die Kaiser Wilhelm II. 1911 in Berlin gegründet hatte. In beiden Gesellschaften bekamen und bekommen Spitzenforscher° weltweit beste Arbeitsbedingungen°, um sich voll auf ihre Forschungsinteressen konzentrieren zu können. Niemand sagt ihnen, was sie machen müssen, und die Forscher dürfen sich ihre Mitarbeiter selber aussuchen.

Heute besteht die MPG aus 80 Instituten in den Bereichen° Natur-, Sozial- und Geisteswissenschaften°. Immer wieder entstehen° neue Institute in neuen Forschungsbereichen und alte Institute schließen wieder. Zwischen 1948 und 2014 waren 18 Nobelpreisträger Mitglieder° der MPG, ein weiteres Zeichen für die herausragende° Arbeit dieser Gesellschaft. Bisher war Christiane Nüsslein-Volhard die einzige Frau unter ihnen, aber das könnte sich ändern°. Im Jahre 2015 waren immerhin 28% der Wissenschaftler an den Instituten Frauen.

TIPP

Note that the German words **die Forschung** (*research*), **ein Forscher / eine Forscherin** (*researcher*), and **forschen** (*to research*) are all closely related.

Nobelpreisträger der Max-Planck-Gesellschaft

Chemie	Medizin	Physik
Stefan W. Hell (2014)	Christiane Nüsslein-Volhard (1995)	Theodor Hänsch (2005)
Gerhard Ertl (2007)	Erwin Neher (1991)	Ernst Ruska (1986)
Paul Crutzen (1995)	Bert Sakmann (1991)	Klaus von Klitzing (1985)
Robert Huber (1988)	Georges Köhler (1984)	Walter Bothe (1954)
Hartmut Michel (1988)	Konrad Lorenz (1973)	
Johann Deisenhofer (1988)	Feodor Lynen (1964)	
Manfred Eigen (1967)		
Karl Zigler (1963)		

Gesellschaft *society* **entwickelte** *developed*
Nachfolgerin *successor* **Spitzenforscher** *top researchers*
Arbeitsbedingungen *work conditions* **Bereichen** *areas*
Geisteswissenschaften *humanities* **entstehen** *form*
Mitglieder *members* **herausragende** *outstanding*
sich ändern *to change*

ÜBUNGEN

1 **Richtig oder falsch?** Sind die Aussagen richtig oder falsch? Korrigieren Sie die falschen Aussagen.

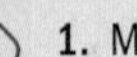

1. Max Planck war Chemiker. Falsch. Max Planck war Physiker.
2. Planck entwickelte die Quantentheorie. Richtig.
3. Die MPG entstand nach dem Zweiten Weltkrieg. Richtig.
4. Vor der MPG gab es in Deutschland die Kaiser-Wilhelm-Gesellschaft. Richtig.
5. In der MPG dürfen sich die Forscher ihre Mitarbeiter selber aussuchen. Richtig.
6. Die 80 Institute der MPG arbeiten im Bereich Naturwissenschaft. Falsch. Die Insitute arbeiten in den Bereichen Natur-, Sozial- und Geisteswissenschaften.
7. Siebzehn Forscher der MPG erhielten einen Nobelpreis. Richtig.
8. Nur ein Prozent aller Wissenschaftler der MPG sind Frauen. Falsch. Immerhin 28% der Wissenschaftler der MPG sind Frauen.
9. Der erste Nobelpreisträger der MPG war Feodor Lynen. Falsch. Der erste Nobelpreisträger der Gesellschaft war Walter Bothe.
10. Die meisten Nobelpreisträger der MPG waren Chemiker. Richtig.

Practice more at **vhlcentral.com**.

Suggestion Before they read the **Deutschsprachige Welt** article, ask students: **Welche Zeitungen, Zeitschriften oder Blogs lesen Sie? Kennen Sie auch deutsche Zeitungen?** If possible, bring a copy of ***Bild*** to show the class.

DEUTSCH IM ALLTAG

Wortfeld: machen

aufmachen	*to open*
durchmachen	*to experience*
mitmachen	*to participate*
nachmachen	*to imitate*
vormachen	*to fool somebody*
wettmachen	*to make up for something*
zumachen	*to close*

DIE DEUTSCHSPRACHIGE WELT

Deutsche Mediengiganten°

Die zwei deutschen Mediengiganten sind die Bertelsmann AG und die Axel Springer AG. Die Bertelsmann AG, ein 1835 in Gütersloh gegründetes deutsches Familienunternehmen°, ist das größte Medienhaus Europas. Weltweit arbeiten 104.000 Mitarbeiter für dieses Unternehmen. Neben Buchclubs sind auch Software-Entwicklung° und Fernsehsender Teil des Unternehmens. Die 1946 gegründete Axel Springer AG ist der zweite deutsche Mediengigant. Sie verlegt° mehr als 230 Zeitungen und Zeitschriften°. Die bekannteste ist die *Bild*, eine Zeitung mit täglich mehr als 12 Millionen Lesern.

AP* Theme: Contemporary Life
Context: Current Events

Mediengiganten *media giants* **Familienunternehmen** *family-owned company* **Entwicklung** *development* **verlegt** *publishes* **Zeitschriften** *magazines*

PORTRÄT

Darmstadt

AP* Theme: Science & Technology
Context: Social Impacts

Darmstadt, eine Stadt in Hessen, gilt als Wissenschaftsstadt°. Hier wohnen zwar nur 144.000 Einwohner, aber es gibt drei Universitäten mit insgesamt mehr als 35.000 Studenten. Neben den Universitäten gibt es auch Forschungseinrichtungen° wie zum Beispiel das Europäische Raumflugkontrollzentrum° (ESOC), die Europäische Organisation für die Nutzung° meteorologischer Satelliten (EUMETSAT) und drei Institute der Fraunhofer-Gesellschaft. Im GSI Helmholtzzentrum für Schwerionenforschung° entdeckten Forscher 1994 das chemische Element Darmstadtium, das man unter der Ordnungsnummer 110 im Periodensystem finden kann.

Wissenschaftsstadt *city of science* **Forschungseinrichtungen** *research institutions* **Raumflugkontrollzentrum** *space flight control center* **Nutzung** *use* **Schwerionenforschung** *heavy ion research*

IM INTERNET

Suchen Sie Informationen über digitale Medien in der deutschsprachigen Welt. Was sind die neuesten Trends?

Find out more at **vhlcentral.com**.

Expansion After reading about **Darmstadt**, have students suggest other examples of **Wissenschaftsstädte** or **-orte** like Silicon Valley. Ask them to list advantages and disadvantages of living in research and manufacturing centers such as these.

2 **Was fehlt?** Ergänzen Sie die Sätze.

1. Die Bertelsmann AG ist ein deutsches <u>Familienunternehmen</u> in Gütersloh.
2. Bertelsmann ist das <u>größte</u> Medienhaus Europas.
3. Die <u>Bild</u> ist die bekannteste Zeitung der Axel Springer AG.
4. Darmstadt gilt auch als <u>Wissenschaftsstadt</u>.
5. In Darmstadt studieren mehr als <u>35.000</u> Studenten.
6. Forscher entdeckten 1994 das chemische Element <u>Darmstadtium</u>.

3 **Technologie und digitale Medien** Diskutieren Sie mit einem Partner / einer Partnerin digitale Medien und Technologien, die Sie gerne benutzen. Warum mögen Sie sie? Gibt es ältere Technologien, die Sie bevorzugen? Warum? **3 Partner Chat** You can also assign activity 3 on the Supersite.

BEISPIEL

S1: *Welche digitalen Medien und Technologien benutzt du gerne?*
S2: *Ich schreibe gerne E-Mails. Und du?*

Ressourcen

4B.1 The genitive case

Startblock German speakers often use constructions with **von** to indicate a relationship of ownership or close connection between two nouns. To talk about these relationships in more formal speech or writing, use the genitive case (**der Genitiv**).

- In conversation, the preposition **von** is used with a noun in the dative case to indicate ownership or a close relationship.

Hast du den neuen Klingelton **von meinem Handy** schon gehört?
*Have you heard **my cell phone's** new ringtone?*

Um die Website **von Doktor Giese** zu sehen, braucht man ein Passwort.
*You need a password to access **Doctor Giese's** website.*

- Another way to indicate ownership or a close relationship, especially in more formal speech and writing, is to use the genitive case.

Tim hat die Rede **des Bundespräsidenten** heruntergeladen.
*Tim downloaded **the president's** speech.*

Das Mikrofon **der Reporterin** hat nicht funktioniert.
***The reporter's** microphone didn't work.*

Suggestion Have students review the nominative case, taught in **Vol. 1, 1B.1**; the accusative case, taught in **Vol. 1, 3B.2**; and the dative case, taught in **Vol. 1, 4B.1** and **4B.2**.

- The forms of definite articles, indefinite articles, and possessive adjectives used with genitive nouns differ from the nominative, accusative, and dative forms. Masculine and neuter nouns also change in the genitive case: those with more than one syllable add **-s**, and those with only one syllable add **-es**.

ACHTUNG

Possessive adjectives have the same genitive endings as the indefinite articles: **meines Druckers, meiner Festplatte, meines Handys, meiner E-Mails.**

definite articles				
	masculine	**feminine**	**neuter**	**plural**
nominative	**der** Drucker	**die** Festplatte	**das** Handy	**die** E-Mails
accusative	**den** Drucker	**die** Festplatte	**das** Handy	**die** E-Mails
dative	**dem** Drucker	**der** Festplatte	**dem** Handy	**den** E-Mails
genitive	**des** Druckers	**der** Festplatte	**des** Handys	**der** E-Mails

indefinite articles				
	masculine	**feminine**	**neuter**	**plural**
nominative	**ein** Drucker	**eine** Festplatte	**ein** Handy	**keine** E-Mails
accusative	**einen** Drucker	**eine** Festplatte	**ein** Handy	**keine** E-Mails
dative	**einem** Drucker	**einer** Festplatte	**einem** Handy	**keinen** E-Mails
genitive	**eines** Druckers	**einer** Festplatte	**eines** Handys	**keiner** E-Mails

Was ist der Preis **der Spielkonsole**?
*What is the price **of the game console**?*

Der Bildschirm **dieses Computers** ist sehr schmutzig.
***This computer's** screen is very dirty.*

Ich habe diese Fotos mit der Kamera **meines Vaters** gemacht.
*I took these photos with **my father's** camera.*

Ich kann die Telefonnummer **meiner Schwester** nicht finden.
*I can't find **my sister's** phone number.*

- Some masculine nouns add **-n** or **-en** in the accusative and dative cases: **der Herr, den Herrn, dem Herrn**. This is also true for the genitive case: **des Herrn**.

Ich habe **dem Polizisten** meinen Personalausweis gezeigt.
*I showed **the police officer** my ID card.*

Die Kamera **des Touristen** funktioniert nicht.
***The tourist's** camera isn't working.*

- In the genitive case, an adjective *preceded by* an **ein**-word or a **der**-word always ends in **-en**. *Unpreceded* adjectives in the genitive case have the endings: **-en**, **-er**, **-en**, and **-er**.

Ich mag das Aroma **schwarzen Kaffees.**
*I like the smell **of black coffee.***

Mögen Sie den Geschmack **grüner Paprikas**?
*Do you like the taste **of green peppers**?*

- When using the name of a person or place in the genitive, add **-s** to the end of the name. If the name already ends with an s sound, add an apostrophe instead.

Magst du **Laras** Website?
*Do you like **Lara's** website?*

Benjamin hat **Hans'** Ladegerät verloren.
*Benjamin lost **Hans's** charger.*

- Most nouns in the genitive case follow the noun they modify. However, the name of a person or place comes before the noun it modifies.

Die Eltern **meines Freundes** sind sehr nett.
***My boyfriend's** parents are really nice.*

Jans Digitalkamera ist sehr klein.
***Jan's** digital camera is really small.*

- Use the genitive question word **wessen** to ask *whose*?

nominative	accusative	dative	genitive
wer?	wen?	wem?	wessen?

Wessen Telefon klingelt?
***Whose** phone is ringing?*

Ich glaube, es ist **Josefs** Handy.
*I think it's **Josef's** cell phone.*

- The genitive case is also used after certain prepositions.

prepositions with the genitive			
(an)statt	*instead of*	trotz	*despite, in spite of*
außerhalb	*outside of*	während	*during*
innerhalb	*inside of, within*	wegen	*because of*

Anstatt einer Stereoanlage bekam mein Bruder ein Handy zum Geburtstag.
***Instead of a stereo,** my brother got a cell phone for his birthday.*

Trotz des Regens wollten unsere Freunde wandern gehen.
***Despite the rain,** our friends wanted to go hiking.*

QUERVERWEIS

You will learn more about **der**-words in **4B.2**.

See **1B.3** to review two-way prepositions.

Suggestion Have students review **ein**-words, taught in **Vol. 1, 2B.3, 3A.1, 3A.2**, and **4B.1**; **der**-words, taught in **Vol. 1, 3A.2** and **4B.1**; accusative prepositions, taught in **Vol. 1, 3B.2**; and dative prepositions, taught in **Vol. 1, 4B.2**.

ACHTUNG

Be careful not to confuse the genitive **-s** ending with the 's ending used in English. In German, the apostrophe is added instead of an **s**, never before it.

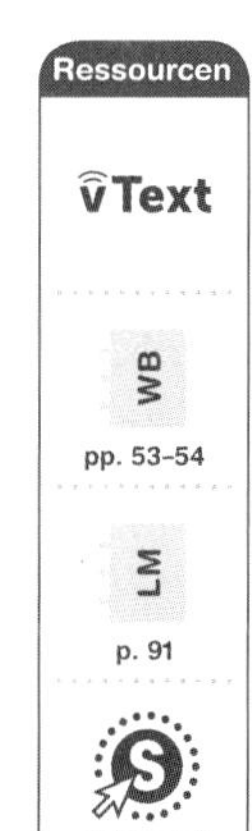

Suggestion Tell students that in colloquial German, people tend to use the dative instead of the genitive, especially with the prepositions **trotz** and **wegen**.

Jetzt sind Sie dran! **Wählen Sie die richtigen Genitivformen.**

1. Das ist der Computer (meines Bruders / meinen Bruder).
2. Wo ist der Kopfhörer (der Schüler / der Schülerin)?
3. Der Fernseher (eures Vaters / euren Vater) steht im Wohnzimmer.
4. Die Website (der neuen Lehrerin / die neue Lehrers) ist sehr interessant.
5. Ich darf den DVD-Player (meine ältere Schwester / meiner älteren Schwester) benutzen.
6. Der Bildschirm (unserem neuen Laptop / unseres neuen Laptops) ist kaputt.

3 Suggestion Remind students that **Neffe** (item 7) is an **n**-noun and does not take an **-s** in the genitive.

Anwendung

1 **Wessen?** Beantworten Sie die Fragen mit einem ganzen Satz und benutzen Sie dabei den Genitiv der angegebenen Substantive.

BEISPIEL Wessen Bücher sind das? (die Schülerin)
Das sind die Bücher der Schülerin.

1. Wessen Laptop ist das? (die Ingenieurin) Das ist der Laptop der Ingenieurin.
2. Wessen Fahrrad ist das? (das Kind) Das ist das Fahrrad des Kindes.
3. Wessen Auto war das? (Tobias) Das war Tobias' Auto.
4. Wessen Mikrofon ist das? (der Journalist) Das ist das Mikrofon des Journalisten.
5. Wessen Kamera ist das? (Johanna) Das ist Johannas Kamera.
6. Wessen Personalausweis ist das? (Julian) Das ist Julians Personalausweis.
7. Wessen Fahrplan ist das? (der Schaffner) Das ist der Fahrplan des Schaffners.
8. Wessen Abschlussparty war das? (die Deutschschüler) Das war die Abschlussparty der Deutschschüler.

2 **Was fehlt?** Ergänzen Sie die Sätze mit der Genitivform der Wörter in Klammern.

BEISPIEL

Das Auto *meiner kleinen Schwester* ist ein Mercedes. (meine kleine Schwester)

1. Gefällt dir die Farbe meines tollen Kleides? (mein tolles Kleid)
2. Der Blog der neuen Dozentin ist sehr interessant. (die neue Journalistin)
3. Wir müssen immer über die Eskapaden unserer jungen Hunde lachen. (unsere jungen Hunde)
4. Die Digitalkamera des amerikanischen Touristen ist kaputt. (der amerikanische Tourist)
5. Der Klingelton ihres billigen Handys ist sehr laut. (ihr billiges Handy)
6. Der Bildschirm des teuren Fernsehers ist größer als ein Fenster. (der teure Fernseher)
7. Der DVD-Player meines alten Computers funktioniert nicht mehr. (mein alter Computer)

3 **Dativ oder Genitiv?** Schreiben Sie die Sätze so um, dass Sie statt des Dativs den Genitiv benutzen.

BEISPIEL Der Benutzername von meinem Partner ist wirklich sehr lustig.
Der Benutzername meines Partners ist wirklich sehr lustig.

1. Die Vorlesungen von unserem Professor sind interessant.
   Die Vorlesungen unseres Professors sind interessant.
2. Die Website von der Schule ist nicht sehr schön.
   Die Website der Schule ist nicht sehr schön.
3. Die Stereoanlage von Alexander ist alt.
   Alexanders Stereoanlage ist alt.
4. Die Festplatte von deinem Computer ist nicht groß.
   Die Festplatte deines Computers ist nicht groß.
5. Meine Eltern verkaufen das Auto von meinen Großeltern.
   Meine Eltern verkaufen das Auto meiner Großeltern.
6. Der Fußball von dem Jungen ist zwischen die geparkten Autos gefallen.
   Der Fußball des Jungen ist zwischen die geparkten Autos gefallen.
7. Die Katze von meinem Neffen ist sehr aggressiv.
   Die Katze meines Neffen ist sehr aggressiv.
8. Die neue CD von Herbert Grönemeyer ist gerade (*just now*) auf den Markt gekommen.
   Herbert Grönemeyers neue CD ist gerade auf den Markt gekommen.

Practice more at **vhlcentral.com.**

Kommunikation

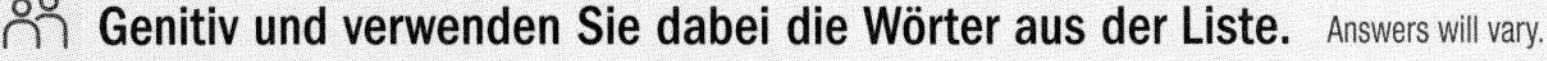

4 **Bilder beschreiben** Beschreiben Sie mit einem Partner / einer Partnerin zusammen, was man auf den Bilder sehen kann. Benutzen Sie den Genitiv und verwenden Sie dabei die Wörter aus der Liste. Answers will vary.

BEISPIEL

S1: *Was sieht man auf diesem Bild?*
S2: *Man sieht den Bildschirm eines Fernsehers.*

der Ausgang	der Motor	die Tastatur
der Bildschirm	der Seminarraum	

1. Man sieht die Tastatur eines Computers.

2. Man sieht den Seminarraum einer Schule.

3. Man sieht den Motor eines Autos.

4. Man sieht den Ausgang eines Flughafens.

5 **Bedeutende Erfinder** Finden Sie zusammen mit einem Partner / einer Partnerin heraus, was diese Personen erfunden (*invented*) haben. Verwenden Sie in Ihren Antworten den Genitiv und wechseln Sie sich ab. Answers will vary.

BEISPIEL

S1: *Wer war Melitta Bentz?*
S2: *Sie war die Erfinderin des Kaffeefilters.*

der Bunsenbrenner	das Luftschiff
der Dieselmotor	die Röntgenstrahlen (*X-rays*)
die Jeans	der Rorschachtest
der Kaffeefilter	der Sportschuh

1. Rudolf Diesel
2. Levi Strauss
3. Wilhelm Röntgen
4. Ferdinand von Zeppelin
5. Hermann Rorschach
6. Robert Bunsen
7. Adi Dassler
8. Melitta Bentz

6 **Wann machst du das?** Fragen Sie Ihren Partner / Ihre Partnerin, wann er/sie diese Aktivitäten macht. Verwenden Sie bei Ihren Antworten einen Zeitausdruck aus jeder (*each*) Spalte. Answers will vary.

BEISPIEL

S1: *Wann schreibst du die meisten Prüfungen?*
S2: *Am Ende des Semesters.*

Am Ende	das Semester
Am Anfang	die Woche
Während	der Tag
	das Jahr
	der Sommer
	die Ferien
	das Abendessen

1. Wann lernst du neue Mitschueler kennen?
2. Wann surfst du im Internet?
3. Wann fährst du mal für ein paar Tage weg?
4. Wann rufst du deine Familie an?
5. Wann bekommst du deine Noten?
6. Wann suchst du einen Ferienjob?

5 Suggestion Tell students that Adi Dassler's name provides a clue about his invention. Dassler is the founder of the sportswear company **Adidas.**

5 Suggested answers:
1. Wer war Rudolf Diesel? Er war der Erfinder des Dieselmotors.

2. Wer war Levi Strauss? Er war der Erfinder der Jeans.

3. Wer war Wilhelm Röntgen? Er war der Erfinder der Röntgenstrahlen.

4. Wer war Ferdinand von Zeppelin? Er war der Erfinder des Luftschiffes.

5. Wer war Hermann Rorschach? Er war der Erfinder des Rorschachtests.

6. Wer war Robert Bunsen? Er war der Erfinder des Bunsenbrenners.

7. Wer war Adi Dassler? Er war der Erfinder des Sportschuhs.

8. Wer war Melitta Bentz? Sie war die Erfinderin des Kaffeefilters.

5 Virtual Chat You can also assign activity 5 on the Supersite. Students record individual responses that appear in your gradebook.

6 Virtual Chat You can also assign activity 6 on the Supersite. Students record individual responses that appear in your gradebook.

4B.2 Demonstratives

Startblock Use demonstrative pronouns and adjectives to refer to something that has already been mentioned, or to point out a specific person or thing.

Demonstrative pronouns

Suggestion The humorous '90s song **Die Da!?!** by **Die Fantastischen Vier** can be found online and provides a good illustration of the use of demonstratives.

- Use demonstrative pronouns to refer to a person or thing that has already been mentioned or whose identity is clear, instead of repeating the noun.

Ist Greta online?
—Ja, **die** schreibt eine E-Mail.
Is Greta online?
*—Yes, **she**'s writing an e-mail.*

Gefällt dir dein neuer Drucker?
—Ja, **der** funktioniert sehr gut!
Do you like your new printer?
*—Yes, **it** works really well!*

ACHTUNG

When referring to people, the demonstrative pronoun is equivalent to *she, he, it,* or *they*. When referring to things, it is equivalent to *it*, *that*, or *those*.

A demonstrative pronoun usually appears at or near the beginning of a clause, even when it is an object.

Dem kann man nicht helfen.

Das will ich schnell löschen.

- The forms of the demonstrative pronoun are identical to the definite article, except for the genitive and dative plural forms. Use the demonstrative pronoun that agrees in gender and number with the noun it is replacing.

demonstrative pronouns				
	masculine	**feminine**	**neuter**	**plural**
nominative	der	die	das	die
accusative	den	die	das	die
dative	dem	der	dem	denen
genitive	dessen	deren	dessen	deren

Dieser Laptop ist wirklich alt. **Den** habe ich schon seit Jahren.
*This laptop is really old. I've had **it** for years.*

Lara ist sehr zuverlässig. **Die** wird nicht zu spät kommen.
*Lara is very reliable. **She** won't come too late.*

Was sagen deine Eltern? Hast du **denen** schon dein Zeugnis gezeigt?
*What do your parents say? Have you shown **them** your report card yet?*

Ich habe nur eine Fernbedienung, aber mit **der** kann man alles an- und ausmachen.
*I only have one remote, but you can turn everything on and off with **it**.*

- Use the genitive demonstrative pronouns **dessen** or **deren** in cases where the possessive adjectives **sein** or **ihr** might cause confusion.

Erik hat Daniel auf **seinem** neuen Boot gesehen.
*Erik saw Daniel on **his (Erik's? Daniel's?)** new boat.*

Erik hat Daniel auf **dessen** neuen Boot gesehen.
*Erik saw Daniel on **his (Daniel's)** new boat.*

- Use **hier** or **da** with a demonstrative to distinguish between *this one* or *that one*.

Der da gefällt Klara besser.
*Klara likes **that one** better.*

Vergiss nicht, **das hier** zu drucken!
*Don't forget to print **this one**!*

Der-words

- **Der**-words include **dieser** (*this; that*), **jeder** (*each, every*) and its plural counterpart **alle** (*all*), **mancher** (*some*), and **solcher** (*such*), as well as the question word **welcher** (*which*).

Nina, **welcher** Laptop gefällt dir am besten?
*Nina, **which** laptop do you like best?*

Ich finde **diesen** Laptop am schönsten.
*I think **this** laptop is the nicest.*

- **Der**-words are so called because they have the same endings as the definite articles. The chart below shows only **dieser**, but all the other **der**-words have the same endings.

der-words				
	masculine	**feminine**	**neuter**	**plural**
nominative	dieser Mann	diese Frau	dieses Kind	diese Kinder
accusative	diesen Mann	diese Frau	dieses Kind	diese Kinder
dative	diesem Mann	dieser Frau	diesem Kind	diesen Kindern
genitive	dieses Mannes	dieser Frau	dieses Kindes	dieser Kinder

Mit **dieser** Tastatur können Sie viel schneller tippen.
*With **this** keyboard, you can type much faster.*

Speichert dein neues Handy **jede** SMS?
*Does your new cellphone save **every** text message?*

Manche Sender haben keine guten Programme.
***Some** stations don't have any good programs.*

Solche Websites gefallen mir nicht.
*I don't like **those kinds of** websites.*

- Adjectives after **der**-words have the same endings as adjectives after definite articles.

Diese kleine Digitalkamera macht sehr schöne Fotos.
***That little** digital camera takes great photos.*

Welchen neuen Film wollt ihr heute Abend sehen?
***Which new** film do you want to see tonight?*

Suggestion Provide students with a few memorable **so ein** phrases to help them understand its idiomatic use. Ex.: **So ein Tag! So ein Zufall! So ein tolles Auto!**

ACHTUNG

Jeder is only used with singular nouns while **alle** is only used in the plural. The accusative forms of **jeder** appear in time expressions such as **jeden Tag/Monat**, **jede Woche**, and **jedes Jahr**.

Solcher is used mainly in the plural. Instead of using **solcher** in the singular, German speakers typically use **so ein** to mean *that kind of* or *such a*:
So einen Mann möchte ich heiraten.

QUERVERWEIS

To review adjective endings after **der**-words, see **4B.1**.

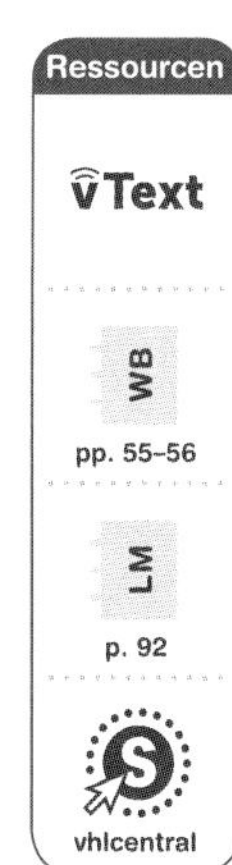

Suggestion Have students review adjective endings after **der**-words, taught in **Vol. 1, 3A.2** and **4B.1**.

Jetzt sind Sie dran! **Wählen Sie die passende Form.**

1. (Welches / Welcher) Mikrofon funktioniert am besten?
2. Simon speichert (jede / jedes) Dokument auf der Festplatte.
3. Frau Kaufmann hat einen neuen Laptop gekauft. (Die / Der) hat 700 € gekostet.
4. Von (welcher / welchem) Schwester hast du die Stereoanlage zum Geburtstag bekommen?
5. Danke für den guten Saft! (Den / Dem) trinken wir heute Abend.
6. Bringst du bitte das Ladegerät mit? (Das / Dem) brauche ich sofort (*right away*).
7. Mira speichert (manchen / manche) E-Mails und löscht den Rest.
8. Ich schreibe (jeder / jeden) Benutzernamen auf, um ihn nicht zu vergessen.
9. Mit (solche / solchen) Handys kann man E-Mails schreiben, SMS schicken und telefonieren.
10. Ihr wolltet den Fernseher mit der Fernbedienung anmachen, aber (die / das) war nirgendwo (*nowhere*) zu finden.
11. (Welches / Welcher) Freund hat dir mit deiner Website geholfen?
12. Antonia hat Nils und (dessen / deren) Frau das Dokument gezeigt.

3 **Sample answers:** 1. Ja, mit allen günstigen Smartphones kann man auch SMS schreiben. 2. Nein, so ein kleiner Laptop hat keinen DVD-Player. 3. Nein, diese amerikanische Tastatur kann man nicht in Deutschland benutzen. 4. Nein, ich möchte diese alte Videokamera nicht kaufen. 5. Nein, ich kann mit diesem nutzlosen Kopfhörer nichts hören.

3 **Suggestion** Do the first few items aloud and have students complete the rest in writing. Circulate around the classroom and check their answers.

Anwendung

1 **Was fehlt?** Ergänzen Sie die Sätze mit den richtigen Demonstrativpronomen.

1. Kennst du die Deutschlehrerin? Nein, ___die___ kenne ich nicht.
2. Welcher Computer ist der bessere? ___Der___ da für 1.200 €.
3. Welches Kleid ziehst du auf die Party an? ___Das___ da auf meinem Bett.
4. Welchem Kind gehört der Fußball? ___Dem___ dort auf dem Spielfeld.
5. Haben Schmidts dich schon angerufen? ___Deren___ Tochter hat letzte Woche ihren Abschluss gemacht.
6. Was machen deine Großeltern? Ach, ___denen___ geht's leider nicht sehr gut.
7. Bringt ihr euren Hund ins Hundehotel während eurer Reise? Nein, ___den___ nehmen wir natürlich mit.
8. Welcher Zug geht nach Kassel? ___Der___ fährt dort drüben auf Bahnsteig 7A.

2 **Was ist richtig?** Wählen Sie die passenden **der**-Wörter.

1. (Solches / **Welches**) Auto hast du denn jetzt gekauft?
2. (Jede / **Manche**) Modelle haben nur einen kleinen Kofferraum.
3. Heute kann man mit (**jedem** / welchem) Handy im Internet surfen.
4. Hast du (**diese** / jede) Website schon gesehen? Die ist wirklich interessant!
5. (Manche / **Solche**) Probleme möchte ich haben!
6. Mit (**solchen** / welchen) Leuten kann man leider nicht reden.

3 **Elektronische Geräte** Beantworten Sie die Fragen mit **ja** oder **nein**. Verwenden Sie die **der**-Wörter in Klammern und ein passendes Adjektiv aus der Liste. Achten Sie auf die Adjektivendungen. Sample answers are provided.

alt | amerikanisch | günstig | flach (*flat*) | kaputt | klein | nutzlos

BEISPIEL

Hat der Bildschirm des Fernsehers eine bessere Bildqualität? (so ein)

Ja, der Bildschirm so eines flachen Fernsehers hat wirklich eine bessere Bildqualität.

1. Kann man mit dem Smartphone auch SMS schreiben? (all-)

2. Hat der Laptop auch einen DVD-Player? (so ein)

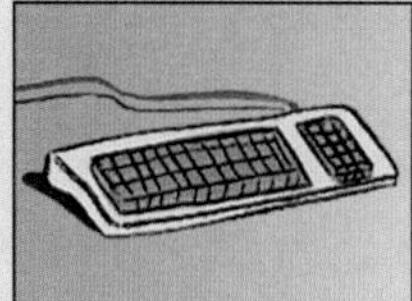

3. Kann man diese Tastatur auch in Deutschland benutzen? (dies-)

4. Möchtest du die Videokamera meiner Mutter kaufen? (dies-)

5. Kannst du mit deinem Kopfhörer alles hören? (dies-)

Practice more at **vhlcentral.com.**

Kommunikation

4 **Wie findest du das?** Fragen Sie Ihren Partner / Ihre Partnerin nach seiner/ihrer Meinung (*opinion*). Benutzen Sie Demonstrativpronomen und wechseln Sie sich ab. Answers will vary.

BEISPIEL

S1: *Wie findest du die Band Train?*
S2: *Die ist einfach fantastisch!*

Wie findest du...

1. die Musik von...?
2. die Kunst von...?
3. den Fernsehsender...?
4. den Film...?
5. die Kurse von Professor/Professorin...?
6. die Bücher von...?

egoistisch	langweilig
eingebildet	lustig
fade	romantisch
fantastisch	schlecht
hübsch	süß
intelligent	toll
interessant	

5 **Immer das Gleiche** Schreiben Sie, was Sie jeden Tag, jede Woche, jeden Monat und jedes Jahr machen, und dann interviewen Sie Ihre Mitstudenten. Answers will vary.

BEISPIEL

S1: *Was machst du jeden Tag?*
S2: *Ich esse jeden Tag in der Mensa. Und du, was machst du jeden Tag?*

jeden Tag:	
jede Woche:	
jeden Monat:	
jedes Jahr:	

6 **Rollenspiel: Im Modehaus** Sie sind Verkäufer / Verkäuferin in einem Modehaus. Leider hat der Kunde / die Kundin immer etwas auszusetzen (*criticize*). Erfinden Sie mit einem Partner / einer Partnerin einen Dialog. Answers will vary.

BEISPIEL

S1: *Wie finden Sie diesen Pullover?*
S2: *Der ist viel zu klein!*
S1: *Und wie gefällt Ihnen dieses rote Kleid?*
S2: *So ein hässliches Kleid habe ich noch nie gesehen!*

der Anzug	die Krawatte	billig	gestreift
die Baseballmütze	die Lederjacke	dunkel	hässlich
das Baumwollkleid	der Minirock	einfach	lang
die Halskette	die Sandalen	elegant	langweilig
die Handtasche	der Schal	eng	schmutzig
die Hose	das Trägerhemd	furchtbar	teuer

4 **Partner Chat** You can also assign activity 4 on the Supersite. Students work in pairs to record the activity online. The pair's recorded conversation will appear in your gradebook.

6 **Suggestion** Have students write their dialogues and perform them for the class.

6 **Partner Chat** You can also assign activity 6 on the Supersite. Students work in pairs to record the activity online. The pair's recorded conversation will appear in your gradebook.

Wiederholung

1 Logische Verbindungen

Sehen Sie sich mit einem Partner / einer Partnerin die Wortliste und die Bilder an. Welche Wörter passen zu welchen Bildern? Sample answers are provided.

BEISPIEL

Das ist die Schwimmerin des Jahres.

1 Suggestion Make sure students understand that each of their answers must contain a genitive construction.

das Jahr	die Schülerin
der Monat	der Tag
das Restaurant	

1. 

Das ist das Restaurant des Monats.

2. 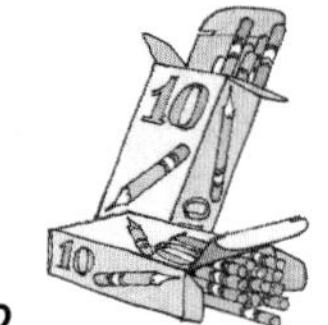

Das sind die Bleistifte der Schülerin.

3. 
Das ist das Auto des Jahres.

4. 
Das ist der Koch des Restaurants.

2 Diskutieren und kombinieren

Sehen Sie sich die Tabelle mit statistischen Informationen über Deutschland, Liechtenstein und die Schweiz an. Fragen Sie Ihren Partner / Ihre Partnerin nach den fehlenden Informationen.

2 Suggestion If you notice that students are having difficulty forming the questions, interrupt the activity to write the questions as a class.

BEISPIEL

S1: *Wie lang ist der längste Fluss der Schweiz?*
S2: *Das ist der Rhein. Er ist 375 Kilometer lang.*

3 Manche Leute

Viele Menschen machen komische Sachen (*strange things*). Was denken Sie und Ihr Partner / Ihre Partnerin darüber? Was sollen diese Menschen anders machen?

3 Suggestion Encourage students to be creative, and provide vocabulary help as needed. If your class is fairly small, invite students to share their answers on the board.

BEISPIEL

S1: *Manche Menschen tanzen im Regen.*
S2: *Solche Menschen sind dynamisch, aber sie sollen sich einen Regenschirm kaufen.*

3 Virtual Chat You can also assign activity 3 on the Supersite.

im Haus Rad fahren	draußen schlafen
unter dem Bett lesen	im Regen tanzen
auf dem Dach lesen	im Winter kurze Kleider tragen

4 Wem gehört's?

Sehen Sie sich die Bilder an. Fragen Sie einen Partner / eine Partnerin, wem die Dinge gehören. Wechseln Sie sich ab. Sample answers are provided.

4 Virtual Chat You can also assign activity 4 on the Supersite.

BEISPIEL

S1: *Wessen Stereoanlage ist das?*
S2: *Das ist die Stereoanlage des Studenten.*

meine Eltern	mein Opa
David	der Journalist
das Mädchen	der Student

1. 
Das ist der Drucker meines Opas.

2. 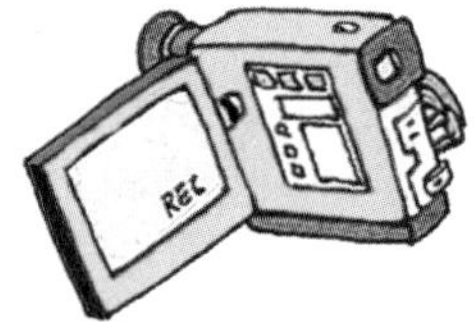

Das ist die Videokamera des Journalisten.

3. 
Das ist das Fotoalbum des Mädchens.

4. 
Das ist der Fernseher meiner Eltern.

5 Arbeitsblatt

Fragen Sie andere im Unterricht, was ihnen gefällt. Schreiben Sie sich die Antworten auf.

BEISPIEL Autor: Stephen King / Jane Austen

S1: *Wen liest du lieber, Stephen King oder Jane Austen?*
S2: *Mir ist Stephen King lieber.*

6 Technologie

Unterhalten Sie sich mit Ihrem Partner / Ihrer Partnerin, über die Geräte, die sie besitzen. Was halten Sie von solchen Geräten? Benutzen sie viele Menschen? Sind sie für jeden geeignet (*suitable*)?

BEISPIEL

S1: *Ich habe eine Spielkonsole.*
S2: *Ich habe auch eine Spielkonsole. Viele Studenten mögen sie.*
S1: *Was spielst du am liebsten?*
S2: *Am liebsten spiele ich…*

6 Partner Chat You can also assign activity 6 on the Supersite. Students work in pairs to record the activity online. The pair's recorded conversation will appear in your gradebook.

7 **Im Kleidergeschäft** Sehen Sie sich die Kleidung an und fragen Sie Ihren Partner / Ihre Partnerin nach seiner/ihrer Meinung.

BEISPIEL

S1: *Gefällt dir der blaue Rock?*
S2: *Der gefällt mir, aber diese grüne Hose gefällt mir nicht.*

7 Suggestion You may wish to briefly review adjective endings before having students begin this activity.

7 Partner Chat You can also assign activity 7 on the Supersite. Students work in pairs to record the activity online. The pair's recorded conversation will appear in your gradebook.

8 **Genitivpräpositionen** Schreiben Sie mit einem Partner / einer Partnerin ein Gedicht (*poem*) aus fünf Sätzen. Außer der letzten Zeile (*line*) muss jede Zeile mit einer Genitivpräposition beginnen.

BEISPIEL

Außerhalb der Stadt stürmt es.
Trotz des schlechten Wetters spielen wir Tennis.
Während des Spiels rollt der Ball in den Fluss.
Wegen des verlorenen Balls können wir nicht mehr spielen.
Das nächste Mal bleiben wir lieber mit der Spielkonsole zu Hause.

9 **Wahrheiten und Lügen** Schreiben Sie zwei Sätze darüber, was Sie schon vor Ihrem 14. Geburtstag gemacht haben. Eine der Aussagen ist wahr (*true*), eine Aussage ist eine Lüge (*lie*). Ihre Mitstudenten müssen erraten, welcher Satz die Lüge ist. Answers will vary.

BEISPIEL

Ich war schon zweimal nach Europa geflogen.
Ich hatte schon zwei Fremdsprachen gelernt.

9 Suggestion Provide a model with two truths and a lie about what you had already done before you turned 14. Have students guess which one is the lie.

Mein Wör|ter|buch

Schreiben Sie noch fünf weitere Wörter in Ihr persönliches Wörterbuch zu den Themen **Verkehrsmittel** und **Technologie**.

der Führerschein

Übersetzung
driver's license

Wortart
ein Substantiv

Gebrauch
In Amerika darf man den Führerschein mit 16 Jahren machen. In Deutschland muss man 18 Jahre alt sein und der Führerschein ist viel teurer.

Synonyme
die Fahrerlaubnis

Antonyme
—

Weiter geht's

Panorama

AP* Theme: Global Challenges
Context: Geography
Interactive Map

Hessen und Thüringen

Hessen in Zahlen

connections cultures — NATIONAL STANDARDS

- **Fläche:** *21.114 km²*
- **Bevölkerung:** *6 Millionen Menschen*
- **Religion:** *evangelisch-lutherisch 40,8%, römisch-katholisch 25,4%*
- **Städte:** *Frankfurt (701.000 Einwohner), Wiesbaden (274.000), Kassel (194.000)*
- **Flüsse:** *der Main, der Neckar, die Fulda*
- **Wichtige Industriezweige:** *chemische Industrie, Pharmaindustrie, Fahrzeugbau, Banken*
- **Touristenattraktionen:** *Römischer Grenzwall° Limes, Fossilienlagerstätte° Grube Messel, Benediktiner-Abtei° und Kloster° Lorsch*
  Touristen können in Marburg die Märchen der Gebrüder Grimm entdecken. Wirtschaftlich ist Hessen für die Banken in Frankfurt und die chemische und Pharmaindustrie bekannt.

QUELLE: Landesportal Hessen

Thüringen in Zahlen

- **Fläche:** *16.172 km²*
- **Bevölkerung:** *2,2 Millionen Menschen*
- **Religion:** *keine Religion 66%, evangelisch-lutherisch 26%*
- **Städte:** *Erfurt (205.000 Einwohner), Jena (108.000), Gera (95.000)*
- **Wichtige Industriezweige:** *Automobil, Metallverarbeitung, Lebensmittelindustrie, Tourismus*
- **Touristenattraktionen:** *Weimar, Wartburg (Eisenach), Schloss Friedenstein (Gotha)*
  Touristen können in Eisenach die Spuren berühmter Deutscher wie Luther und Bach entdecken. Wirtschaftlich ist Thüringen eines der erfolgreichsten° ostdeutschen Bundesländer.

QUELLE: Thüringen Tourismus

Berühmte Hessen und Thüringer

- **Johann Sebastian Bach,** *Komponist (1685–1750)*
- **Johann Wolfgang von Goethe,** *Autor (1749–1832)*
- **Anne Frank,** *Autorin und Opfer° des Nationalsozialismus (1929–1945)*

römischer Grenzwall *Roman boundary wall* **Fossilienlagerstätte** *natural fossil deposit* **Abtei** *abbey* **Kloster** *monastery* **erfolgreichsten** *most successful* **Opfer** *victim* **Karfreitag** *Good Friday* **Tanzverbot** *ban on dancing* **drohen** *threaten* **Geldstrafen** *fines*

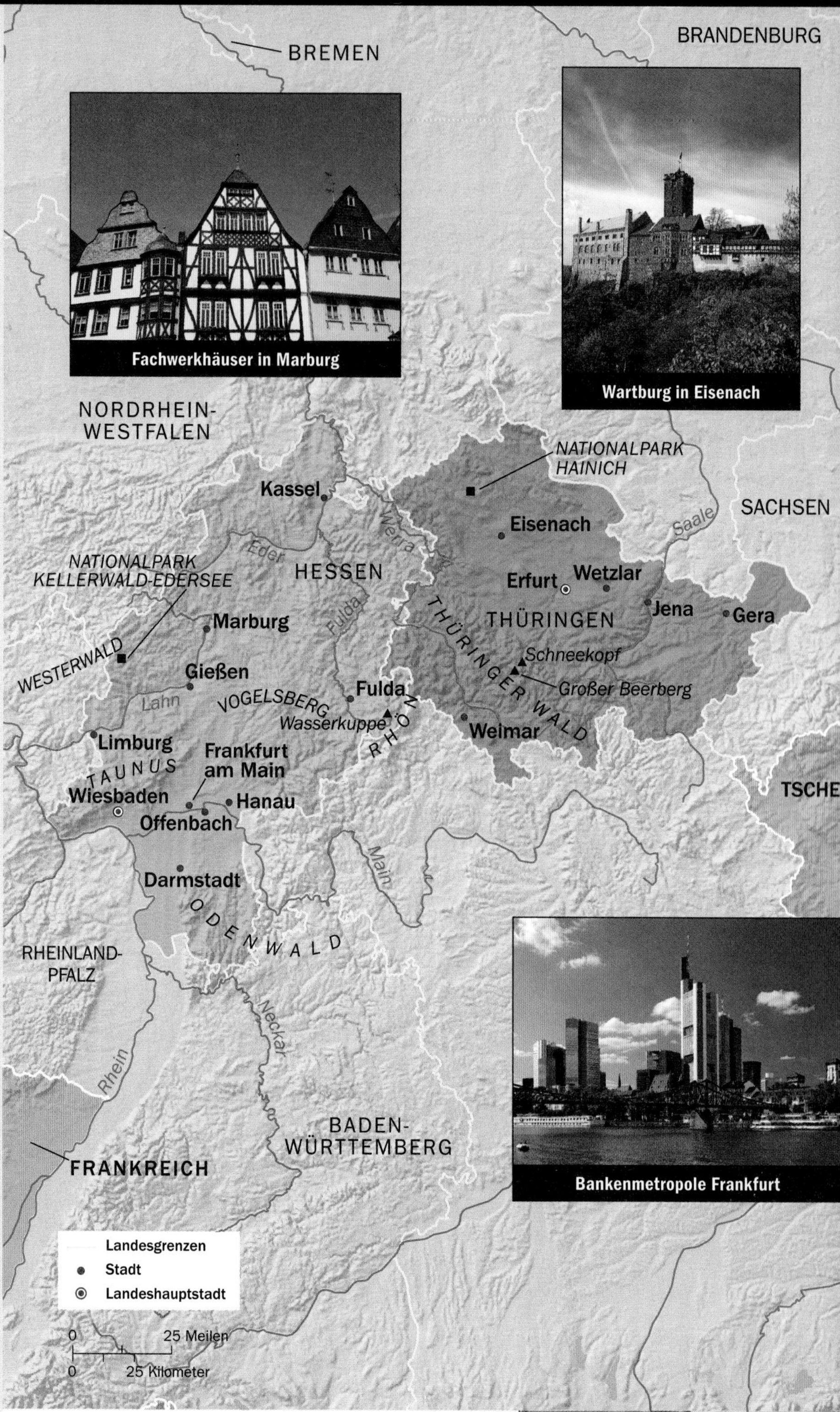

Fachwerkhäuser in Marburg

Wartburg in Eisenach

Bankenmetropole Frankfurt

BREMEN
BRANDENBURG
NORDRHEIN-WESTFALEN
NATIONALPARK HAINICH
SACHSEN
Kassel
Eisenach
Saale
Werra
Eder
NATIONALPARK KELLERWALD-EDERSEE
HESSEN
Erfurt
Wetzlar
Fulda
THÜRINGEN
Jena
Gera
Marburg
THÜRINGER WALD
Schneekopf
WESTERWALD
Gießen
Großer Beerberg
Lahn
VOGELSBERG
Fulda
Wasserkuppe
RHÖN
Weimar
Limburg
Frankfurt am Main
TAUNUS
Wiesbaden
Hanau
Offenbach
TSCHE
Main
Darmstadt
ODENWALD
RHEINLAND-PFALZ
Neckar
Rhein
BADEN-WÜRTTEMBERG
FRANKREICH

Landesgrenzen
Stadt
Landeshauptstadt

0 — 25 Meilen
0 — 25 Kilometer

AP* Theme: Contemporary Life **Context:** Social Customs & Values

Unglaublich, aber wahr!

Am Karfreitag° und an anderen religiösen Feiertagen darf man in vielen Bundesländern nicht tanzen. Hessen und Thüringen sind zwei von dreizehn Bundesländern, in denen das Tanzverbot° am Karfreitag 24 Stunden dauert. Seit 1952 dürfen Diskotheken an diesem Tag keine Tanzveranstaltungen organisieren oder es drohen° hohe Geldstrafen°.

Suggestion Point out that the term **Bußgeld** typically refers to fines incurred for parking violations, speeding, or fare evasion, while **Geldstrafe** is a more general term for a fine or legal penalty.

AP* Theme: Beauty & Aesthetics
Context: Architecture

Städte

Suggestion Have students read a short poem by Goethe, such as ***Wanderers Nachtlied II*** or ***Heidenröslein***.

Weimar

Weimar ist die viertgrößte Stadt in Thüringen. Im Jahre 1919 beschloss die Nationalversammlung° hier die deutsche Verfassung°. Deshalb nennt man die erste deutsche Demokratie auch „Weimarer Republik“. Für die Literatur ist Weimar wichtig, weil Autoren wie Goethe, Schiller und Nietzsche hier lebten. Berühmte Musiker, die in Weimar komponierten, waren Johann Sebastian Bach und Franz Liszt. Im Bereich der Architektur entwickelte° der Architekt Walter Gropius die Bauhaus-Schule in Weimar.

Kultur

AP* Theme: Contemporary Life
Context: Entertainment, Travel, & Leisure

Skat

Skat ist eines der beliebtesten Kartenspiele in Deutschland. Manche Menschen nennen es auch „das Spiel der Deutschen“. Etwa 20 Millionen Deutsche spielen Skat. Das Spiel wurde circa 1810 in der thüringischen Stadt Altenburg erfunden°. Seit 1938 gibt es deutsche Meisterschaften°. Altenburg ist immer noch die Skathauptstadt der Welt, in welcher der Deutsche Skatverband seine Geschäftsstelle° hat. Hier gibt es auch die berühmte Kartenfabrik Altenburger Spielkarten. 2007 feierte die Firma ihr 175-jähriges Jubiläum.

Geographie

AP* Theme: Contemporary Life
Context: Entertainment, Travel, & Leisure

Wald und Jagd° in Deutschland

In Hessen und Thüringen bestehen große Landesflächen aus Wäldern. In Hessen gibt es 8.472 Quadratkilometer Wald, etwa 40% der Landesfläche, mehr als in jedem anderen deutschen Bundesland. Der Nationalpark Thüringer Wald bietet ein sehr beliebtes Urlaubsziel für Wanderer, Fahrradfahrer und Skifahrer an. Seit dem 19. Jahrhundert nennt man Thüringen „das grüne Herz Deutschlands“. Auch Jäger° besuchen diese Region gerne zur Jagd von Rehen und Hirschen°.

Menschen

AP* Theme: Families & Communities
Context: Community Service

Heilige Elisabeth

Die heilige° Elisabeth, auch bekannt als Landgräfin Elisabeth von Thüringen, lebte zwischen 1207 und 1231. Sie war die Tochter des ungarischen° Königs Andreas II. und lebte die meiste Zeit ihres Lebens im hessischen Marburg. Sie starb im Alter von 24 Jahren, aber die Menschen liebten sie, weil sie sehr vielen Menschen während ihres Lebens geholfen hatte. Nur vier Jahre nach ihrem Tod sprach Papst Gregor IX. Elisabeth heilig°. In Marburg kann man heute ihr Grab° in der Elisabethkirche besuchen.

Nationalversammlung *national assembly* **Verfassung** *constitution* **entwickelte** *developed* **erfunden** *invented* **Meisterschaften** *championships* **Geschäftsstelle** *office* **Wald und Jagd** *forest and hunting* **Jäger** *hunters* **Rehen und Hirschen** *deer and stags* **heilige** *saint* **ungarischen** *Hungarian* **sprach... heilig** *canonized* **Grab** *grave*

IM INTERNET

1. Suchen Sie im Internet Informationen über Weimar: Was sind die berühmtesten Gebäude Weimars? Machen Sie eine Liste. Wie viele Touristen besuchen Weimar jedes Jahr?
2. Suchen Sie im Internet andere Spiele, die man in Deutschland spielt. Wo spielt man diese Spiele?

Find out more at **vhlcentral.com**.

Was haben Sie gelernt? Ergänzen Sie die Sätze.

1. In vielen deutschen Bundesländern darf man an religiösen Feiertagen nicht ___tanzen___.
2. Seit ___1952___ gibt es Karfreitag ein Tanzverbot.
3. Die erste deutsche ___Demokratie___ nennt man auch die „Weimarer Republik“.
4. Autoren, die in Weimar gelebt haben, sind ___Goethe___, Schiller und Nietzsche.
5. Skat wurde circa ___1810___ in Altenburg in Thüringen erfunden.
6. Etwa ___20 Millionen___ Deutsche spielen heute Skat.
7. In Hessen sind ___40%___ der Landesfläche Wald.
8. Der Nationalpark ___Thüringer Wald___ ist ein beliebtes Urlaubsziel in Thüringen.
9. Die heilige Elisabeth starb schon mit ___24___ Jahren.
10. In der Elisabethkirche in ___Marburg___ ist das Grab von Elisabeth.

Practice more at **vhlcentral.com**.

Lesen

Audio: Reading

Vor dem Lesen

AP* Theme: Science & Technology
Context: Personal Technologies

Strategien

Guessing meaning from context

As you read in German, you will often see words you have not learned. You can guess their meaning by looking at surrounding words. Read this e-mail and guess what **erleichtert** means.

> Hallo Sylvia! Ich habe heute meinen Führerschein gemacht. Zuerst musste ich durch die Stadt fahren. Das war ziemlich schwer, denn alle Ampeln waren rot. Danach ging es auf die Autobahn. Ich war sehr nervös und wollte keinen Fehler machen. Am Ende war ich sehr erleichtert, als ich die Prüfung bestanden hatte, weil es sehr stressig war. Jetzt darf ich endlich Auto fahren.
> Liebe Grüße,
> Lina

If you guessed *relieved*, you are correct. You can conclude that Lina is feeling happy about the outcome of the test.

Untersuchen Sie den Text Sehen Sie sich mit einem Partner / einer Partnerin den Text an und beschreiben Sie das Format. Um was geht es in dem Text Ihrer Meinung nach (*in your opinion*)? Suchen Sie die folgenden Wörter und Ausdrücke im Text. Benutzten Sie den Kontext, um die Bedeutung zu erraten.

- Zubehör (components)
- Luftfeuchtigkeit (humidity)
- Tintenpatrone (ink cartridge)
- Steckdose (electric outlet)
- Papiergröße (paper size)
- Laufwerk (drive)

Inhalt erraten Sie wissen schon etwas über das Format des Texts und einige Wörter: sagen Sie, was Sie wahrscheinlich in dem Text lernen werden.

- wie man eine Internetverbindung einrichtet
- wie man eine CD brennt
- wie man einen Drucker anschließt
- wie man ein Dokument druckt
- wie man Tintenpatronen recycelt

Drucker MI6-0070

Vierfarbdrucker Installationsanleitung

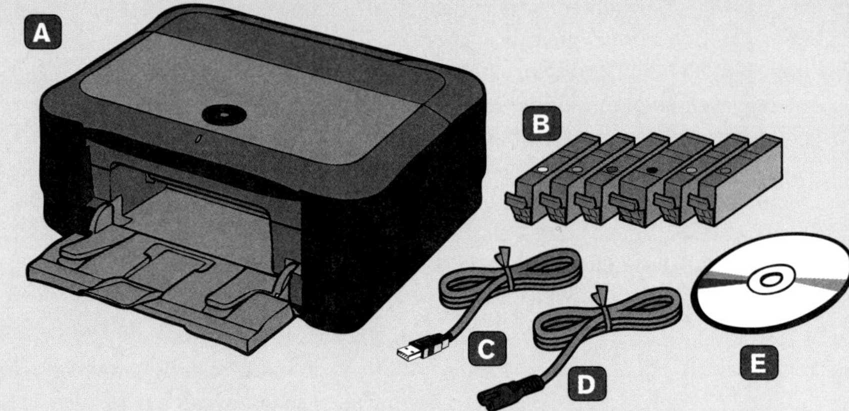

A. Drucker **B.** Tintenpatronen **C.** USB-Kabel **D.** Netzkabel **E.** CD

Schritt 1 Auspacken

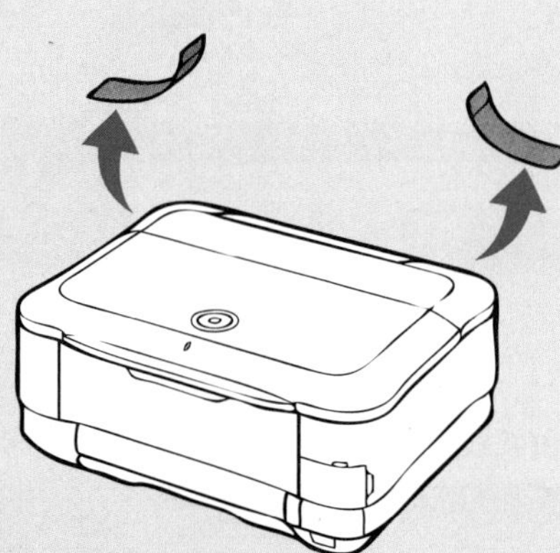

Heben Sie den Drucker und das Zubehör vorsichtig aus dem Karton. Prüfen Sie°, ob Sie alle Komponenten haben. Entfernen Sie° das Klebeband° vom Drucker. Entfernen Sie auch das Klebeband an der Rückseite des Druckers.

Schritt 2 Aufstellen des Druckers

Der Drucker darf nicht zu nahe an anderen Geräten stehen. Es muss genügend Platz um den Drucker herum sein, damit er nicht zu heiß wird. Die ideale Zimmertemperatur für den Drucker ist 23°C. Die Zimmertemperatur darf aber zwischen 10°C und 32°C variieren. Die Luftfeuchtigkeit darf zwischen 20% und 80% variieren. Die ideale Luftfeuchtigkeit beträgt 60%.

Schritt 3 Tintenpatrone einsetzen

Vor der ersten Verwendung° des Druckers müssen Sie die Tintenpatrone einsetzen. Öffnen Sie zuerst die obere Abdeckung° des Druckers. Nehmen Sie die Tintenpatronen aus der Verpackung°. Ziehen Sie den Schutzstreifen vorsichtig ab. Setzen Sie die Tintenpatrone in den Drucker ein. Drücken Sie fest auf die mit *PUSH HERE* gekennzeichneten° Stellen. Schließen Sie jetzt den Drucker.

Schritt 4 Drucker an den Computer anschließen

Schließen Sie ein Ende des USB-Kabels an der Rückseite des Druckers an. Schließen Sie das andere Ende des USB-Kabels an den USB-Anschluss des Computers an.

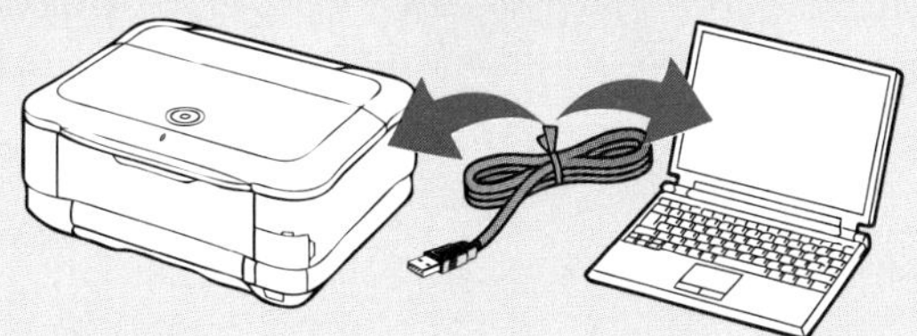

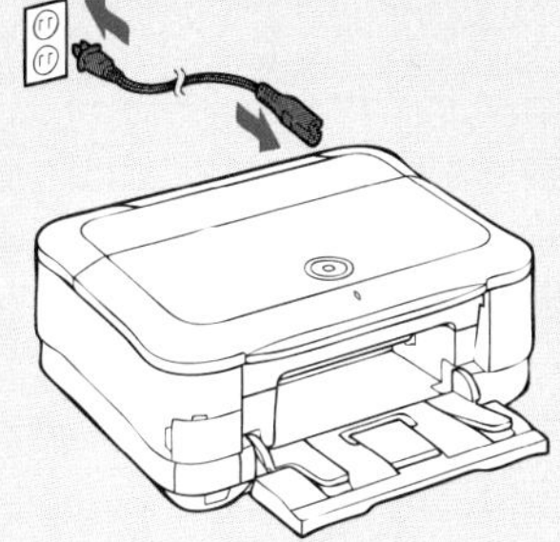

Schritt 5 Netzkabel anschließen

Verwenden Sie nur das Kabel, das mit dem Drucker geliefert wurde. Wenn der Drucker ausgeschaltet ist, schließen Sie das Netzkabel an den Anschluss° auf der Rückseite des Druckers an. Schließen Sie dann das andere Ende des Netzkabels an eine Steckdose an.

Schritt 6 Papier in Kassette einlegen

Sie können 250 Blatt Papier in die Papierkassette einlegen. Ziehen Sie zuerst die Papierkassette aus dem Drucker heraus. Legen Sie jetzt das Papier in die Kassette ein und schließen Sie den Drucker wieder.

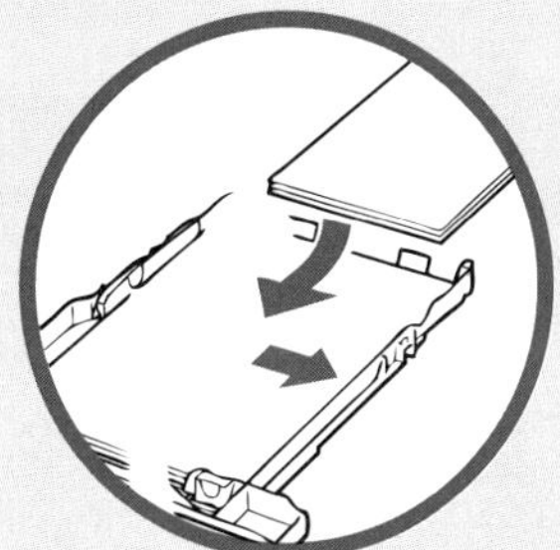

Schritt 7 Installation der Treiber

Schalten Sie den Drucker ein und schieben Sie die CD in das CD-Laufwerk. Installieren Sie das Programm „Drucker.exe" auf Ihrem Computer. Wenn Sie mit der Installation fertig sind, öffnet sich automatisch ein neues Fenster. Jetzt ist Ihr Drucker fertig installiert.

Schritt 8 Statusseite drucken

Testen Sie den Drucker, indem Sie eine Statusseite drucken. Schalten Sie den Drucker ein. Drücken Sie mindestens 3 Sekunden auf den EIN/AUS Knopf. Der Drucker sollte jetzt eine Statusseite drucken.

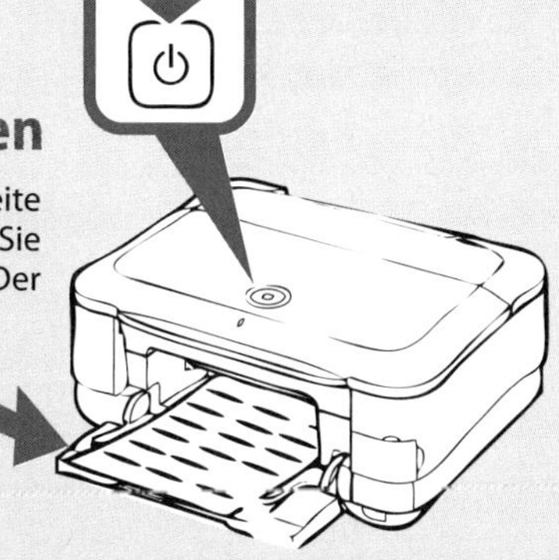

Prüfen Sie *Check* **Entfernen Sie** *Remove* **Klebeband** *adhesive tape* **Verwendung** *use* **Abdeckung** *cover* **Verpackung** *packaging* **gekennzeichneten** *marked* **Anschluss** *connection*

Nach dem Lesen

Richtig oder falsch Sind die Sätze **richtig** oder **falsch**? Korrigieren Sie die falschen Sätze.

Sample answers are provided.

	richtig	falsch
1. In dem Karton ist nur der Drucker. *Im Karton sind der Drucker und die Komponenten.*	☐	☑
2. Die Zimmertemperatur muss immer 23°C sein. *Die ideale Zimmertemperatur ist 23°C.*	☐	☑
3. Man muss erst die Tintenpatrone einsetzen, bevor man das erste Mal drucken kann.	☑	☐
4. Den Drucker muss man mit einem USB-Kabel an den Computer anschließen.	☑	☐
5. Das Netzkabel schließt man auf der Vorderseite des Druckers an. *Das Netzkabel schließt man auf der Rückseite des Druckers an.*	☐	☑
6. Man kann nur 150 Blatt Papier in die Kassette einlegen. *Man kann 250 Blatt Papier in die Kassette einlegen.*	☐	☑
7. Den Treiber für den Drucker installiert man mit einer CD auf dem Computer.	☑	☐
8. Am Ende kann man eine Statusseite drucken.	☑	☐

Druckerprobleme Arbeiten Sie mit einem Partner / einer Partnerin. Einer von Ihnen hat ein Problem mit dem Drucker. Beschreiben Sie das Problem. Versuchen Sie dann mit Ihrem Partner / Ihrer Partnerin, das Problem zu lösen.

BEISPIEL

S1: *Ich habe meinen Drucker gerade installiert. Aber ich kann die Statusseite nicht drucken.*
S2: *Hast du den Drucker eingeschaltet?*

Suggestion Make sure students understand that they should refer back to the text to solve their **Druckerprobleme**.

Hören

Strategien

Recognizing the genre of spoken discourse

You will encounter many different types of speech in German. For example, you may hear a political speech, a radio interview, a commercial, a voicemail message, or a news broadcast. Try to identify the context of the speech you hear, so that you can activate your background knowledge about that type of discourse and identify the speakers' motives and intentions.

 To practice this strategy, you will listen to two short selections. Identify the genre of each one.

Vorbereitung

Über was sollte man nachdenken, bevor man ein neues Handy kauft? Machen Sie eine Liste. Welche Funktionen sind Ihnen bei einem neuen Handy wichtig?

Zuhören

Hören Sie Rolf und Karin zu, wie sie den Kauf eines neuen Handys diskutieren. Welche Funktionen von Ihrer Liste diskutieren Rolf und Karin? Kreisen Sie die richtigen Antworten ein. Hören Sie sich dann das Gespräch nochmal an. Schreiben Sie jetzt die anderen Antworten in die Tabelle. Answers may vary slightly.

Name + Kosten	Anbieter	Beschreibung	andere Merkmale
1. Samsung Galaxy (235 Euro)	T-Mobile	silbern	unbegrenztes Datenvolumen
2. Apple iPhone (450 Euro)	Vodafone	einfach zu benutzen	bis zu 8 Stunden Gesprächszeit
3. Doro PhoneEasy (129 Euro)	O2	rot	extra große Tasten
4. LG P700 (259 Euro)	E-Plus	dünn	Surf-Flatrate

Verständnis

Suggestion Point out to students that cell phone brand names are neuter: **das iPhone, das Samsung,** etc.

Welches Handy? Empfehlen Sie das passende Handy. Sample answers provided.

1. Ich will lange telefonieren.
   Kauf dir das iPhone.
2. Ich brauche nur ein einfaches Telefon.
   Kauf dir das Doro.
3. Ich will ein dünnes Telefon.
   Kauf dir das LG.
4. Ich habe nicht viel Geld für ein Handy.
   Kauf dir das Doro.
5. Ich will ein Telefon, damit ich viel im Internet surfen kann.
   Kauf dir das LG.
6. Ich will ein Telefon, das nicht sehr kompliziert ist.
   Kauf dir das iPhone.
7. Ich will viele Videos sehen und viel Musik hören.
   Kauf dir das Samsung.

Das beste Telefon **Sie haben gehört, wie Rolf und Karin den Kauf eines neuen Handys diskutieren. Sprechen Sie mit einem Partner / einer Partnerin über die Vorteile der Handys. Entscheiden Sie, welches Handy das beste für Sie und Ihren Partner / Ihre Partnerin ist.**

Suggestion Have students present their partner's preferences using **denn: Das LG ist am besten für meinen Partner, denn er surft viel im Internet mit seinem Handy.**

Expansion Use this listening activity as a lead-in to a discussion of the pros and cons of cell phones. Ask students how often they use their cell phones. Could they imagine giving up their phones? Do they ever see people use cell phones in a rude manner?

 Practice more at **vhlcentral.com.**

Schreiben

Strategien

Expressing and supporting opinions

Written reviews are one of the many kinds of writing that require you to state your opinions. In order to convince your reader to take your opinions seriously, it is important to support them as thoroughly as possible, using details, facts, examples, and other forms of evidence. In a car review, for example, readers will want details about size, speed, fuel consumption, comfort, extra features, etc.

It is easier to include details that support your opinions if you plan ahead. Before trying out a product or going to an event that you are planning to review, write a list of questions that your readers might ask. Decide which aspects of the experience you are going to rate, and list the details that will help you decide upon a rating. You can then organize these lists into a questionnaire and a rating sheet. Bring these with you to remind you of the kind of information you need to gather in order to support your opinions. Later, the information you wrote down will help you organize your review into logical categories. It can also provide the details and evidence you need to convince your readers of your opinions.

Suggestion Assign this writing task as homework. Give students clear guidelines for word count, typing expectations, deadline, etc., and remind them to include a brief introduction and conclusion. Mark up the first version they submit and have them rewrite the paper to turn in as a final draft.

Thema

Schreiben Sie einen Bericht

Schreiben Sie einen Bericht (*review*) über ein Auto. Nennen Sie zuerst den Namen des Autos und sprechen Sie dann die folgenden Kategorien an. Bilden Sie sich zum Schluss eine eigene Meinung. Ist das ein gutes Auto?

- **Beschreibung**
  Wie groß ist das Auto? Wie viel wiegt (*weighs*) das Auto? Was für einen Motor hat es? Wie viele Liter verbraucht es je 100 Kilometer? Wie viele Gänge (*gears*) hat es? Was ist die Höchstgeschwindigkeit (*top speed*)? Wie viel Platz (*room*) haben die Passagiere? Wie groß ist der Kofferraum?
- **Ausstattung**
  Welche Farbe hat das Auto? Wie sieht es im Innenraum aus? Hat es hinten ein Kamerasystem zum Ein- und Ausparken? Kann es automatisch parken? Wie viele Türen hat das Auto? Hat es ein Sonnenfenster? Ist es ein Kombi (*station wagon*)?
- **Fahrzeugtyp**
  Ist es ein Familienauto? Ist es ein Sportauto? Ist es ein Geländewagen (*SUV*)?
- **Andere Funktionen**
  Welche Art von Elektronik hat das Auto? Wie bequem ist das Auto? Hat das Auto ein gutes Image? Wie viel kostet das Auto? Ist das Auto umweltfreundlich (*environmentally friendly*)? Wie ist der Wiederverkaufswert (*resale value*) des Autos?

Lektion 4A

Auto fahren

die Autobahn, -en *highway*
der Fahrer, - / die Fahrerin, -nen *driver*
der Polizist, -en / die Polizistin, -nen *police officer*
die Straße, -n *street*
die Tankstelle, -n *gas station*
der Verkehr *traffic*
geradeaus fahren *to go straight ahead*
einen Platten haben *to have a flat tire*
einen Unfall haben *to have an accident*
parken *to park*
rechts/links abbiegen (biegt... ab) *to turn right/left*

Auto

das Benzin *gas*
die Bremse, -n *brakes*
der Kofferraum, ¨-e *trunk*
das Lenkrad, ¨-er *steering wheel*
der Mechaniker, - / die Mechanikerin, -nen *mechanic*
der Motor, -en *engine*
die Motorhaube, -n *hood*
das Nummernschild, -er *license plate*
das Öl, -e *oil*
der Scheibenwischer, - *windshield wiper*
der Scheinwerfer, - *headlight*
der Sicherheitsgurt, -e *seatbelt*
die Windschutzscheibe, -n *windshield*
reparieren *to repair*
tanken *to fill up*

die öffentlichen Verkehrsmittel

der Bahnsteig, -e *track; platform*
die Bushaltestelle, -n *bus stop*
der Fahrkartenschalter, - *ticket office*
der Fahrplan, ¨-e *schedule*
das Bußgeld, -er *fine*
die erste/zweite Klasse, -n *first/second class*
der Schaffner, - *ticket collector*
(die Fahrkarte) entwerten *to validate (a ticket)*

das Verkehrsmittel

das Auto, -s *car*
das Boot, -e *boat*
der Bus, -se *bus*
das Fahrrad, ¨-er *bicycle*
der LKW, -s *truck*
das Schiff, -e *ship*
das Taxi, -s *taxi*
die U-Bahn, -en *subway*
der Zug, ¨-e *train*

Das Plusquamperfekt *See pp. 164–165.*
Comparatives and superlatives *See pp. 168–169.*

Lektion 4B

die Technik

der Benutzername, -n *screen name*
der Bildschirm, -e *screen*
die CD, -s *compact disc, CD*
die Datei, -en *file*
die Digitalkamera, -s *digital camera*
das Dokument, -e *document*
der Drucker, - *printer*
die DVD, -s *DVD*
der DVD-Player, - *DVD-player*
die E-Mail, -s *e-mail*
die Fernbedienung, -en *remote control*
der Fernseher, - *television*
die Festplatte, -n *hard drive*
das Handy, -s *cell phone*
der Kopfhörer, - *headphones*
das Ladegerät, -e *battery charger*
der Laptop, -s *laptop (computer)*
die Maus, ¨-e *mouse*
das Mikrofon, -e *microphone*
der MP3-Player, - *mp3 player*
das Passwort, ¨-er *password*
das Programm, -e *program*
der Sender, - *channel*
das Smartphone, -s *smartphone*
die SMS, - *text message*
die Spielkonsole, -n *game console*
die Stereoanlage, -n *stereo system*
das Tablet, -s *tablet*
die Tastatur, -en *keyboard*
das Telefon, -e *telephone*
die Website, -s *Web site*

Technik bedienen

anmachen (macht... an) *to turn on*
aufnehmen (nimmt... auf) *to record*
ausmachen (macht... aus) *to turn off*
drucken *to print*
fernsehen (sieht... fern) *to watch television*
funktionieren *to work, to function*
herunterladen (lädt... herunter) *to download*
klingeln *to ring*
laden (lädt) *to charge; to load*
löschen *to delete*
online sein *to be online*
schicken *to send*
speichern *to save*
starten *to start*
im Internet surfen *to surf the Web*

The genitive case *See pp. 182–183.*
Demonstratives *See pp. 186–187.*

Ressourcen

Appendix A

Appendix B

Appendix C

die Welt

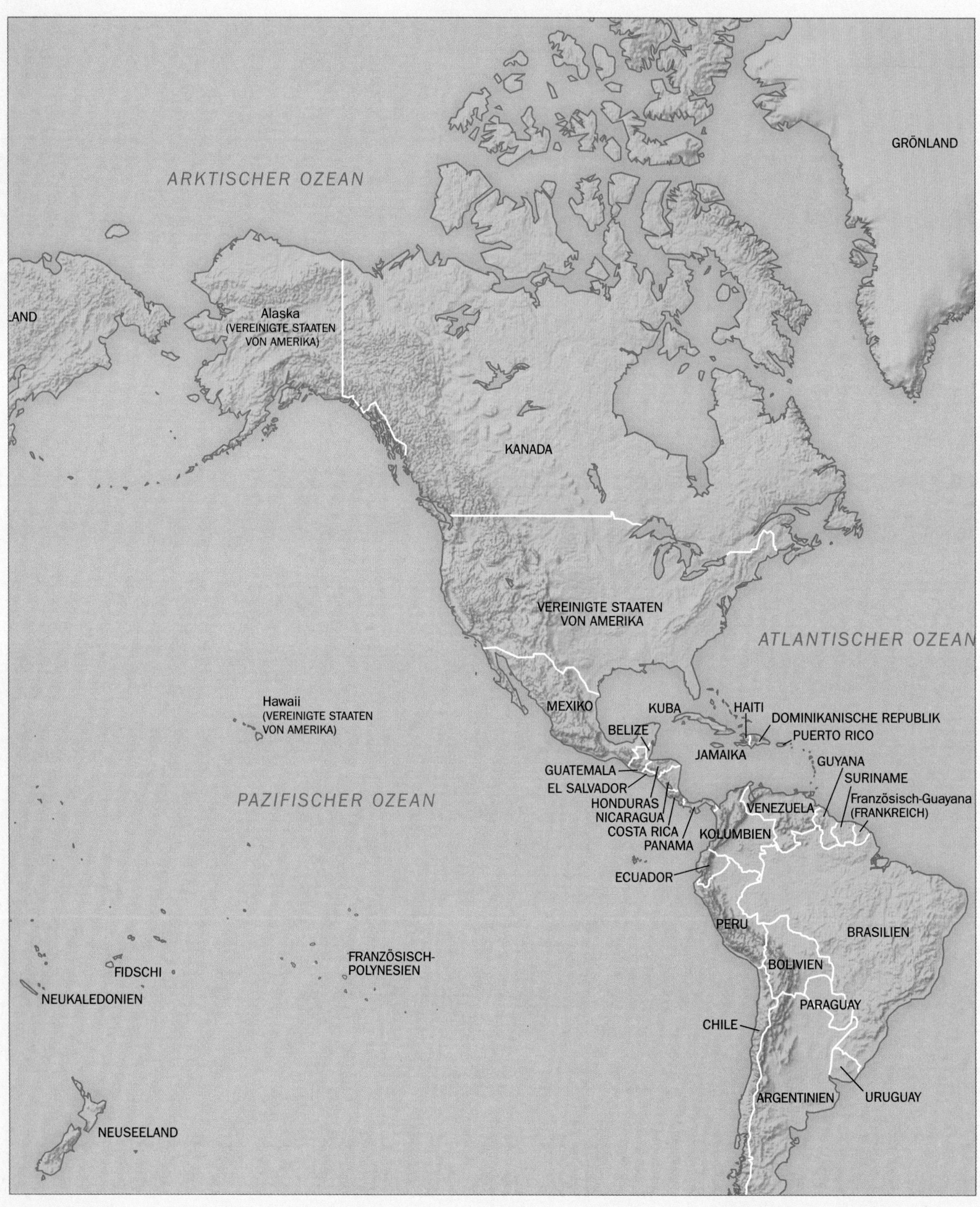

GRÖNLAND
ARKTISCHER OZEAN
LAND
Alaska
(VEREINIGTE STAATEN
VON AMERIKA)
KANADA
VEREINIGTE STAATEN
VON AMERIKA
ATLANTISCHER OZEAN
Hawaii
(VEREINIGTE STAATEN
VON AMERIKA)
MEXIKO
KUBA
HAITI
DOMINIKANISCHE REPUBLIK
PUERTO RICO
BELIZE
JAMAIKA
GUATEMALA
EL SALVADOR
HONDURAS
NICARAGUA
COSTA RICA
PANAMA
GUYANA
SURINAME
Französisch-Guayana
(FRANKREICH)
VENEZUELA
KOLUMBIEN
PAZIFISCHER OZEAN
ECUADOR
PERU
BRASILIEN
BOLIVIEN
PARAGUAY
CHILE
ARGENTINIEN
URUGUAY
FIDSCHI
FRANZÖSISCH-
POLYNESIEN
NEUKALEDONIEN
NEUSEELAND

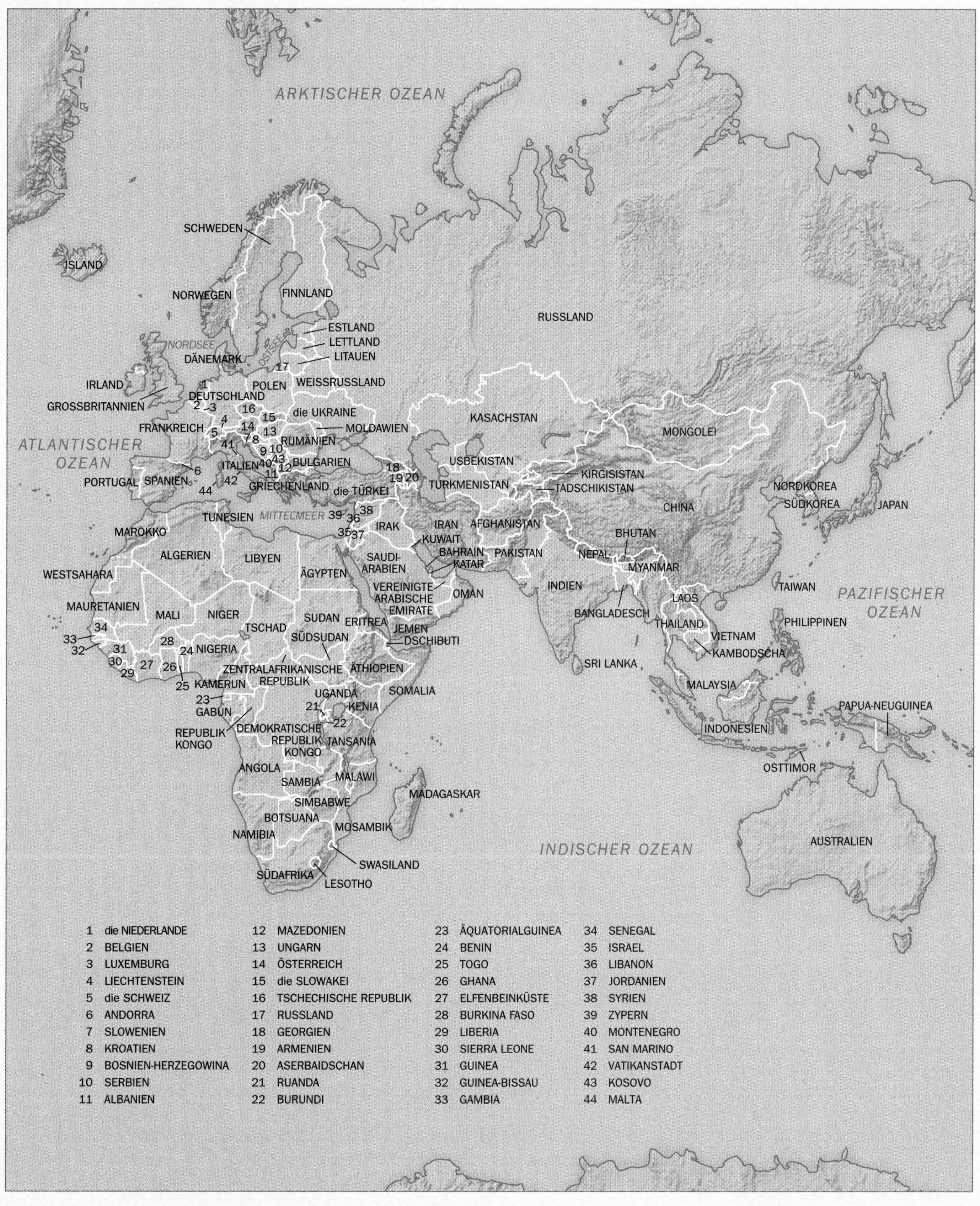

ARKTISCHER OZEAN
ATLANTISCHER OZEAN
PAZIFISCHER OZEAN
INDISCHER OZEAN
NORDSEE
OSTSEE
MITTELMEER
ISLAND
SCHWEDEN
NORWEGEN
FINNLAND
ESTLAND
LETTLAND
LITAUEN
DÄNEMARK
IRLAND
GROSSBRITANNIEN
POLEN
WEISSRUSSLAND
DEUTSCHLAND
die UKRAINE
FRANKREICH
MOLDAWIEN
RUMÄNIEN
BULGARIEN
ITALIEN
PORTUGAL
SPANIEN
GRIECHENLAND
die TÜRKEI
RUSSLAND
KASACHSTAN
MONGOLEI
USBEKISTAN
KIRGISISTAN
TURKMENISTAN
TADSCHIKISTAN
NORDKOREA
SÜDKOREA
JAPAN
CHINA
TUNESIEN
MAROKKO
IRAN
IRAK
AFGHANISTAN
KUWAIT
BAHRAIN
KATAR
PAKISTAN
NEPAL
BHUTAN
ALGERIEN
LIBYEN
SAUDI-ARABIEN
ÄGYPTEN
MYANMAR
WESTSAHARA
VEREINIGTE ARABISCHE EMIRATE
OMAN
INDIEN
TAIWAN
MAURETANIEN
MALI
NIGER
LAOS
BANGLADESCH
SUDAN
ERITREA
JEMEN
TSCHAD
THAILAND
PHILIPPINEN
SÜDSUDAN
DSCHIBUTI
VIETNAM
NIGERIA
KAMBODSCHA
ZENTRALAFRIKANISCHE REPUBLIK
ÄTHIOPIEN
SRI LANKA
KAMERUN
MALAYSIA
UGANDA
SOMALIA
KENIA
GABUN
PAPUA-NEUGUINEA
REPUBLIK KONGO
DEMOKRATISCHE REPUBLIK KONGO
TANSANIA
INDONESIEN
ANGOLA
OSTTIMOR
SAMBIA
MALAWI
MADAGASKAR
SIMBABWE
BOTSUANA
NAMIBIA
MOSAMBIK
AUSTRALIEN
SWASILAND
SÜDAFRIKA
LESOTHO
1 die NIEDERLANDE
2 BELGIEN
3 LUXEMBURG
4 LIECHTENSTEIN
5 die SCHWEIZ
6 ANDORRA
7 SLOWENIEN
8 KROATIEN
9 BOSNIEN-HERZEGOWINA
10 SERBIEN
11 ALBANIEN
12 MAZEDONIEN
13 UNGARN
14 ÖSTERREICH
15 die SLOWAKEI
16 TSCHECHISCHE REPUBLIK
17 RUSSLAND
18 GEORGIEN
19 ARMENIEN
20 ASERBAIDSCHAN
21 RUANDA
22 BURUNDI
23 ÄQUATORIALGUINEA
24 BENIN
25 TOGO
26 GHANA
27 ELFENBEINKÜSTE
28 BURKINA FASO
29 LIBERIA
30 SIERRA LEONE
31 GUINEA
32 GUINEA-BISSAU
33 GAMBIA
34 SENEGAL
35 ISRAEL
36 LIBANON
37 JORDANIEN
38 SYRIEN
39 ZYPERN
40 MONTENEGRO
41 SAN MARINO
42 VATIKANSTADT
43 KOSOVO
44 MALTA

Europa

0 500 Meilen
0 500 Kilometer
Länder, in denen Deutsch eine Amtssprache ist
BARENTSSEE
ISLAND
Reykjavik
EUROPÄISCHES NORDMEER
SCHWEDEN
FINNLAND
NORWEGEN
Helsinki
RUSSLAND
Stockholm
Oslo
Tallinn
ESTLAND
OSTSEE
LETTLAND
Riga
Moskau
NORDSEE
DÄNEMARK
LITAUEN
Vilnius
Kopenhagen
RUSSLAND
Minsk
ÖSTERREICH
LIECHTENSTEIN
Vaduz
die SCHWEIZ
Dublin
IRLAND
die NIEDERLANDE
WEISSRUSSLAND
GROSS-BRITANNIEN
Berlin
Warschau
London
Amsterdam
POLEN
Kiew
Brüssel
DEUTSCHLAND
die UKRAINE
LUXEMBURG
BELGIEN
die SLOWAKEI
Prag
Luxemburg
TSCHECHISCHE REPUBLIK
Paris
MOLDAWIEN
ATLANTISCHER OZEAN
Bratislava
Kischinau
LIECHTENSTEIN
Wien
FRANKREICH
ÖSTERREICH
Budapest
Bern
Vaduz
SLOWENIEN
UNGARN
die SCHWEIZ
Zagreb
RUMÄNIEN
SCHWARZES MEER
Ljubljana
KROATIEN
Bukarest
BOSNIEN-HERZEGOWINA
Belgrad
ITALIEN
SERBIEN
KOSOVO
Monaco
SAN MARINO
Sarajevo
Pristina
BULGARIEN
Andorra la Vella
MONTENEGRO
Sofia
PORTUGAL
MONACO
Podgorica
Skopje
Ankara
ANDORRA
Rom
Tirana
MAZEDONIEN
Madrid
Korsika
ALBANIEN
die TÜRKEI
Lissabon
VATIKANSTADT
SPANIEN
GRIECHENLAND
Sardinien
Balearische Inseln
Athen
Sizilien
Nicosia
Algier
ZYPERN
Tunis
Kreta
Rabat
Valletta
MALTA
MITTELMEER
MAROKKO
TUNESIEN
ALGERIEN
Tripolis
Kairo
LIBYIEN
ÄGYPTEN

Deutschland

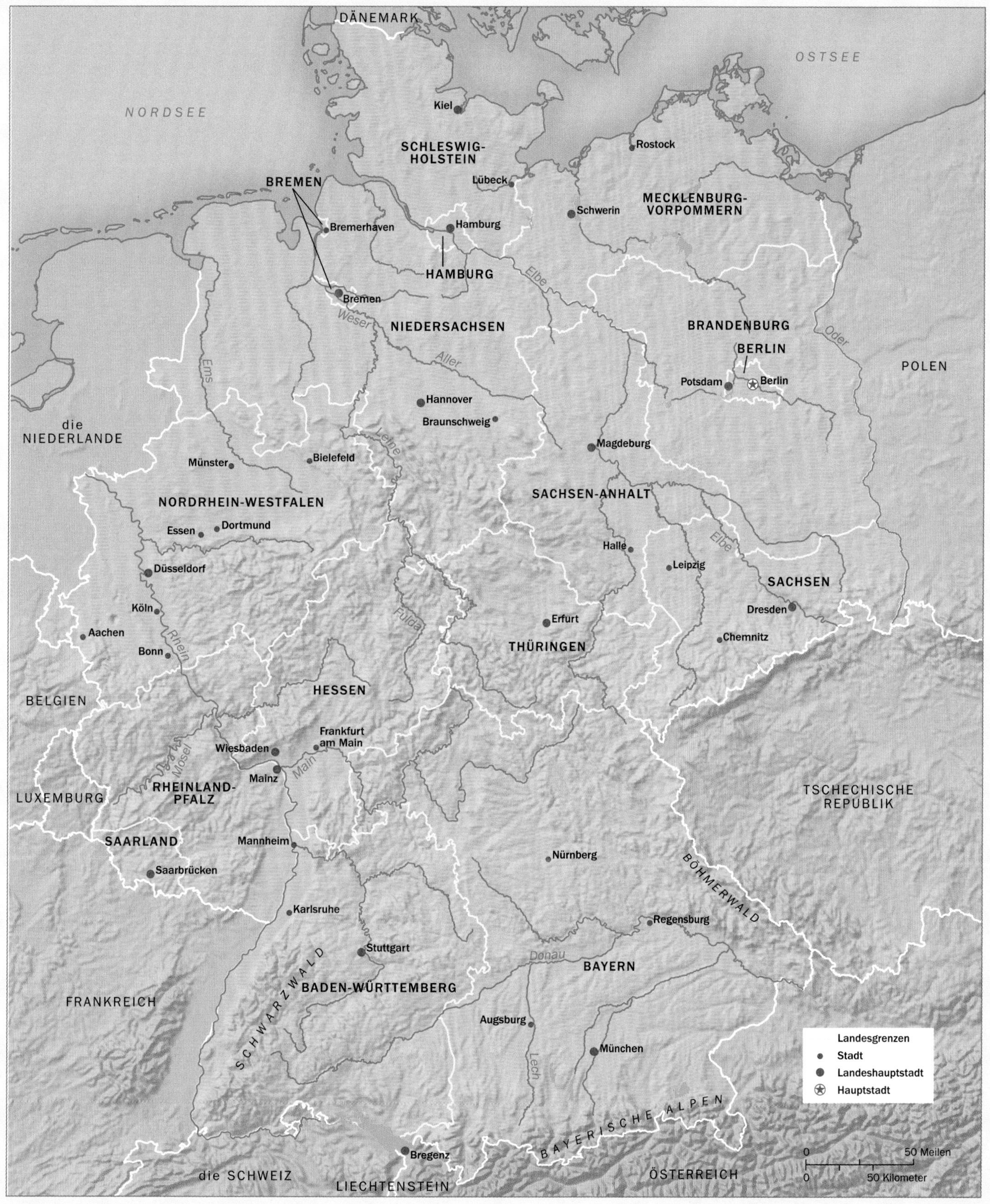

Österreich

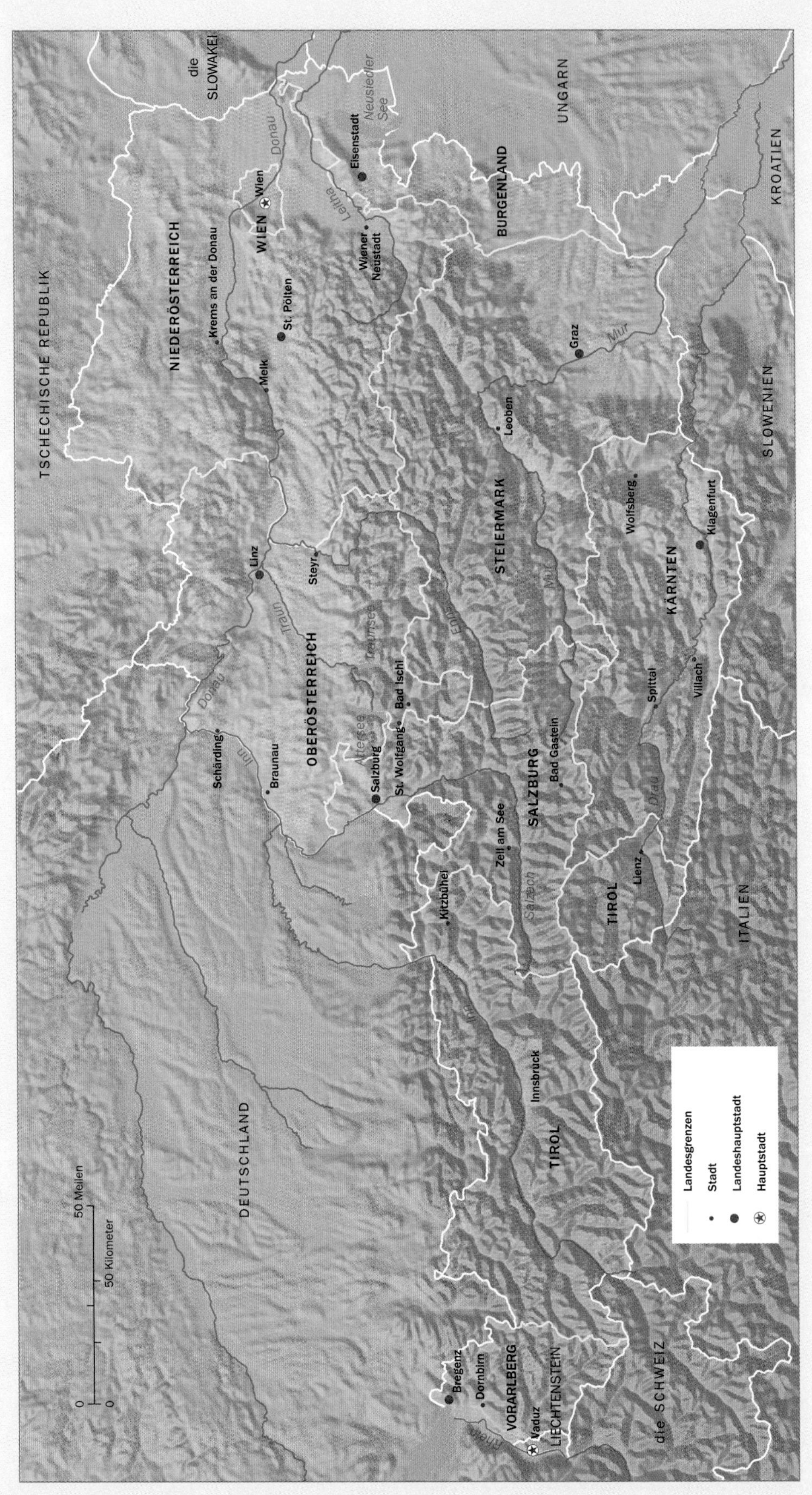
TSCHECHISCHE REPUBLIK
die SLOWAKEI
UNGARN
KROATIEN
SLOWENIEN
ITALIEN
die SCHWEIZ
LIECHTENSTEIN
DEUTSCHLAND
NIEDERÖSTERREICH
WIEN
BURGENLAND
OBERÖSTERREICH
STEIERMARK
SALZBURG
KÄRNTEN
TIROL
TIROL
VORARLBERG
Krems an der Donau
Wien
St. Pölten
Melk
Wiener Neustadt
Eisenstadt
Neusiedler See
Donau
Leitha
Graz
Mur
Leoben
Linz
Steyr
Traun
Traunsee
Enns
Mur
Wolfsberg
Klagenfurt
Villach
Spittal
Drau
Schärding
Braunau
Inn
Salzburg
St. Wolfgang
Bad Ischl
Attersee
Bad Gastein
Zell am See
Salzach
Lienz
Kitzbühel
Innsbruck
Inn
Bregenz
Dornbirn
Vaduz
Rhein
0 50 Meilen
0 50 Kilometer
Landesgrenzen
Stadt
Landeshauptstadt
Hauptstadt

die Schweiz

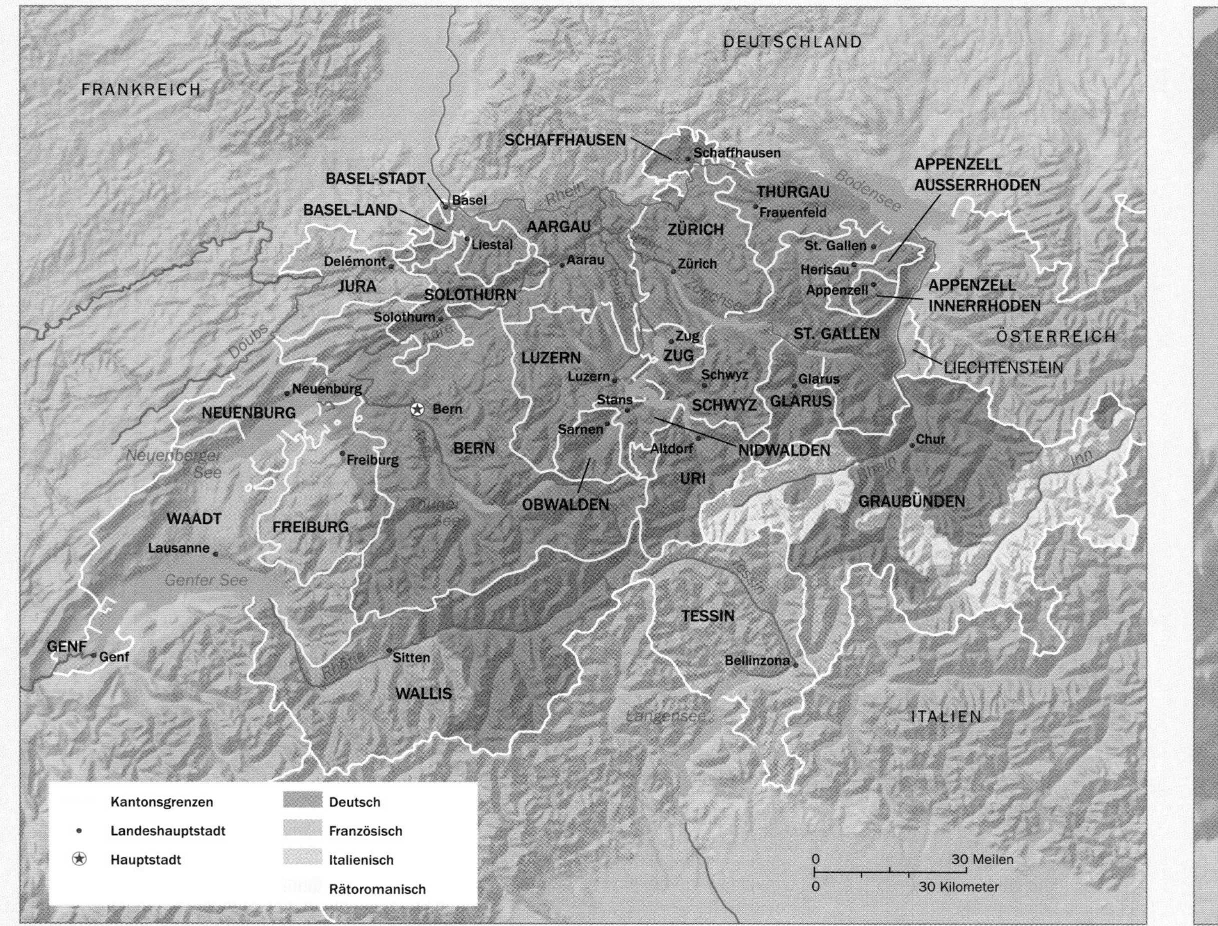

Liechtenstein

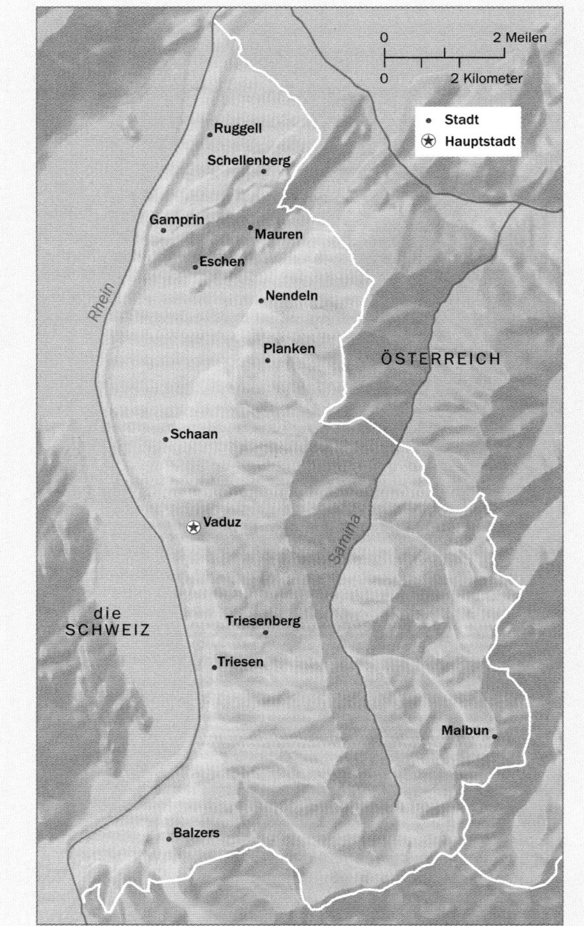

Declension of articles

definite articles				
	masculine	**feminine**	**neuter**	**plural**
nominative	der	die	das	die
accusative	den	die	das	die
dative	dem	der	dem	den
genitive	des	der	des	der

der-words				
	masculine	**feminine**	**neuter**	**plural**
nominative	dieser	diese	dieses	diese
accusative	diesen	diese	dieses	diese
dative	diesem	dieser	diesem	diesen
genitive	dieses	dieser	dieses	dieser

indefinite articles				
	masculine	**feminine**	**neuter**	**plural**
nominative	ein	eine	ein	-
accusative	einen	eine	ein	-
dative	einem	einer	einem	-
genitive	eines	einer	eines	-

ein-words				
	masculine	**feminine**	**neuter**	**plural**
nominative	mein	meine	mein	meine
accusative	meinen	meine	mein	meine
dative	meinem	meiner	meinem	meinen
genitive	meines	meiner	meines	meiner

Declension of nouns and adjectives

nouns and adjectives with *der*-words				
	masculine	**feminine**	**neuter**	**plural**
nominative	der gute Rat	die gute Landschaft	das gute Brot	die guten Freunde
accusative	den guten Rat	die gute Landschaft	das gute Brot	die guten Freunde
dative	dem guten Rat	der guten Landschaft	dem guten Brot	den guten Freunden
genitive	des guten Rates	der guten Landschaft	des guten Brotes	der guten Freunde

nouns and adjectives with *ein*-words				
	masculine	**feminine**	**neuter**	**plural**
nominative	ein guter Rat	eine gute Landschaft	ein gutes Brot	meine guten Freunde
accusative	einen guten Rat	eine gute Landschaft	ein gutes Brot	meine guten Freunde
dative	einem guten Rat	einer guten Landschaft	einem guten Brot	meinen guten Freunden
genitive	eines guten Rates	einer guten Landschaft	eines guten Brotes	meiner guten Freunde

unpreceded adjectives				
	masculine	**feminine**	**neuter**	**plural**
nominative	guter Rat	gute Landschaft	gutes Brot	gute Freunde
accusative	guten Rat	gute Landschaft	gutes Brot	gute Freunde
dative	gutem Rat	guter Landschaft	gutem Brot	guten Freunden
genitive	guten Rates	guter Landschaft	guten Brotes	guter Freunde

Declension of pronouns

personal pronouns										
nominative	ich	du	Sie	er	sie	es	wir	ihr	Sie	sie
accusative	mich	dich	Sie	ihn	sie	es	uns	euch	Sie	sie
accusative reflexive	mich	dich	sich	sich	sich	sich	uns	euch	sich	sich
dative	mir	dir	Ihnen	ihm	ihr	ihm	uns	euch	Ihnen	ihnen
dative reflexive	mir	dir	sich	sich	sich	sich	uns	euch	sich	sich

Glossary of Grammatical Terms

ADJECTIVE Words that describe people, places, or things. An attributive adjective comes before the noun it modifies and takes an ending that matches the gender and case of the noun. A predicate adjective comes after the verb **sein**, **werden**, or **bleiben** and describes the noun that is the subject of the sentence. Predicate adjectives take no additional endings.

Thomas hat eine sehr **gute** Stelle gefunden.
*Thomas found a really **good** job.*

Hast du mein **kleines** Adressbuch gesehen?
*Have you seen my **little** address book?*

Mein Bruder ist **klein**.
*My brother is **short**.*

Deine Schwester wird **groß**.
*Your sister is getting **tall**.*

Possessive adjectives Words that are placed before a noun to indicate ownership or belonging. Each personal pronoun has a corresponding possessive adjective. Possessive adjectives take the same endings as the indefinite article **ein**.

Meine Schwester ist hier.
***My** sister is here.*

Wo ist **dein** Vater?
*Where is **your** father?*

ADVERB Words or phrases that modify a verb, an adjective, or another adverb. Adverbs and adverbial phrases describe *when*, *how*, or *where* an action takes place.

Der Kuchen ist **fast** fertig.
*The cake is **almost** ready.*

Du isst **viel zu** schnell.
*You eat **much too** quickly.*

ARTICLE A word that precedes a noun and indicates its gender, number, and case.

Definite article Equivalent to *the* in English. Its form indicates the gender and case of the noun, and whether it is singular or plural.

der Tisch (*m. s.*)
the table
die Tische (*m. pl.*)
the tables
die Tür (*f. s.*)
the door

die Türen (*f. pl.*)
the doors
das Fenster (*n. s.*)
the window
die Fenster (*n. pl.*)
the windows

Indefinite article Corresponds to *a* or *an* in English. It precedes the noun and matches its gender and case. There is no plural indefinite article in German.

ein Tisch (*m.*)
a table
eine Tür (*f.*)
a door

ein Fenster (*n.*)
a window

CASE There are four cases in German. The case indicates the function of each noun in a sentence. The case of a noun determines the form of the definite or indefinite article that precedes the noun, the form of any adjectives that modify the noun, and the form of the pronoun that can replace the noun.

Nominativ (*nominative*)**: Der Professor** ist alt.
***The professor** is old.*

Akkusativ (*accusative*)**:** Ich verstehe **den Professor**.
*I understand **the professor**.*

Dativ (*dative*)**:** Der Assistent zeigt **dem Professor** den neuen Computer.
*The assistant is showing **the professor** the new computer.*

Genitiv (*genitive*)**:** Das ist der Assistent **des Professors**.
*This is **the professor's** assistant.*

The nominative case The grammatical subject of a sentence is always in the nominative case. The nominative case is also used for nouns that follow a form of **sein**, **werden**, or **bleiben**. In German dictionaries, nouns, pronouns, and numbers are always listed in their nominative form.

Das ist **eine gute Idee.**
*That's **a good idea.***

Die Kinder schlafen.
***The kids** are sleeping.*

The accusative case A noun that functions as a direct object is in the accusative case.

Der Lehrer hat **den Stift**.
*The teacher has **the pen**.*

Ich kaufe **einen Tisch**.
*I'm going to buy **a table**.*

Sie öffnet **die Tür**.
*She's opening **the door**.*

Ich habe **ein Problem**.
*I have **a problem**.*

The dative case An object in the dative case indicates to whom or for whom an action is performed.

Ich bringe **dem Lehrer** einen Apfel.
*I'm bringing **the teacher** an apple.*

Zeig **der Professorin** deine Arbeit.
*Show your work **to the professor**.*

The genitive case A noun in the genitive case modifies another noun. The genitive case indicates ownership or a close relationship between the genitive noun and the noun it modifies, which may be a subject or an object.

Thorsten hat die Rede **des Bundespräsidenten** heruntergeladen.
*Thorsten downloaded **the president's** speech.*

Das Mikrofon **der Professorin** funktioniert nicht.
***The professor's** microphone doesn't work.*

CLAUSE A group of words that contains both a conjugated verb and a subject, either expressed or implied.

Main (or independent) clause A clause that can stand alone as a complete sentence.

Ich bezahle immer bar, weil ich keine Kreditkarte habe.
I always pay cash, *because I don't have a credit card.*

Subordinate clause A subordinate clause explains how, when, why, or under what circumstances the action in the main clause occurs. The conjugated verb of a subordinate clause is placed at the end of that clause.

Ich lese die Zeitung, **wenn** ich Zeit **habe**.
*I read the newspaper **when** I **have** the time.*

COMPARATIVE The form of an adjective or adverb that compares two or more people or things.

Meine Geschwister sind alle **älter** als ich.
*My siblings are all **older** than I am.*

Die Fahrt dauert mit dem Auto **länger** als mit dem Zug.
*The trip takes **longer** by car than by train.*

CONJUNCTION A word used to connect words, clauses, or phrases.

Coordinating conjunctions Words that combine two related sentences, words, or phrases into a single sentence. There are five coordinating conjunctions in German: **aber** (*but*), **denn** (*because; since*), **oder** (*or*), **sondern** (*but, rather*), **und** (*and*). All other conjunctions are subordinating.

Ich möchte eine große Küche, **denn** ich koche gern.
*I want a big kitchen, **because** I like to cook.*

Lola braucht einen Schrank **oder** eine Kommode.
*Lola needs a closet **or** a dresser.*

Subordinating conjunctions Words used to combine a subordinate clause with a main clause.

Ich lese die Zeitung, **wenn** ich Zeit **habe**.
*I read the newspaper **when** I **have** the time.*

DEMONSTRATIVE Pronouns or adjectives that refer to something or someone that has already been mentioned, or that point out a specific person or thing.

Ist Greta online? –Ja, **die** schreibt eine E-Mail.
*Is Greta online? –Yes, **she's** writing an e-mail.*

Gefällt dir dieser Sessel? –Ja, **der** ist sehr bequem!
*Do you like that chair? –Yes, **it's** very comfortable!*

DER-WORDS Words that take the same endings as the forms of the definite article **der**. These include the demonstrative pronouns **dieser** (*this; that*), **jeder** (*each, every*), **jener** (*that*), **mancher** (*some*), and **solcher** (*such*), and the question word **welcher** (*which*).

Welcher Laptop gefällt dir am besten?
***Which** laptop do you like best?*

Ich finde **diesen** Laptop am schönsten.
*I think **this** laptop is the nicest.*

DIRECT OBJECT A noun or pronoun that directly receives the action of the verb. Direct objects are in the accusative.

Kennst du **diesen Mann**?
*Do you know **that man**?*

Ich mache **eine Torte**.
*I'm making **a cake**.*

EIN-WORDS Words that take the same endings as the forms of the indefinite article **ein**. These include the negation **kein** and all of the possessive adjectives.

Hast du **einen** Hund?
*Do you have **a** dog?*

Ich habe **keinen** Fußball.
*I **don't** have **a** soccer ball.*

GENDER The grammatical categorization of nouns, pronouns, and adjectives as masculine, feminine, or neuter.

Masculine
articles: **der**, **ein**
pronouns: **er**, **der**
adjectives: **guter**, **schöner**

Feminine
articles: **die**, **eine**
pronouns: **sie**, **die**
adjectives: **gute**, **schöne**

Neuter
articles: **das**, **ein**
pronouns: **es**, **das**
adjectives: **gutes**, **schönes**

HELPING VERB *See VERB, Auxiliary verb.*

IMPERATIVE Imperatives are verb forms used to express commands, requests, suggestions, directions, or instructions.

Mach deine Hausaufgaben!
***Do** your homework!*

Backen wir einen Kuchen!
***Let's bake** a cake!*

INDIRECT OBJECT A noun or pronoun that receives the action of the verb indirectly. The indirect object is often a person to whom or for whom the action of the sentence is performed. Indirect objects are in the dative case.

Manfred hat **seinem Bruder** ein Buch geschenkt.
*Manfred gave **his brother** a book.*

INFINITIVE The basic, unconjugated form of a verb. Most German infinitives end in **-en**. A few end in **-ern** or **-eln**.

sehen, **essen**, **lesen**, **wandern**, **sammeln**
to see, to eat, to read, to hike, to collect

NOUN A word that refers to one or more people, animals, places, things, or ideas. Nouns in German may be masculine, feminine, or neuter, and are either singular or plural.

der **Junge**, die **Katze**, das **Café**
*the **boy**, the **cat**, the **café***

Compound noun Two or more simple nouns can be combined to form a compound noun. The gender of a compound noun matches the gender of the last noun in the compound.

die Nacht + das Hemd = **das Nachthemd**
*night + shirt = **nightshirt***

NUMBER A grammatical term that refers to the quantity of a noun. Nouns in German are either singular or plural. The plural form of a noun may have an added umlaut and/or an added ending. Adjectives, articles, and verbs also have different endings, depending on whether they are singular or plural.

Singular:
der **Mann**, die **Frau**, das **Kind**
*the **man**, the **woman**, the **child***

Plural:
die **Männer**, die **Frauen**, die **Kinder**
*the **men**, the **women**, the **children***

NUMBERS Words that represent quantities.

Cardinal numbers Numbers that indicate specific quantities. Cardinal numbers typically modify nouns, but do not add gender or case endings.

zwei Männer, **fünfzehn** Frauen, **sechzig** Kinder
***two** men, **fifteen** women, **sixty** children*

Ordinal numbers Words that indicate the order of a noun in a series. Ordinal numbers add the same gender and case endings as adjectives.

der **erste** Mann, die **zweite** Frau, das **dritte** Kind
*the **first** man, the **second** woman, the **third** child*

PARTICIPLE A participle is formed from a verb but may be used as an adjective or adverb. Present participles are used primarily in written German. Past participles are used in compound tenses, including the **Perfekt** and the **Plusquamperfekt**.

Der **aufgehende** Mond war sehr schön.
*The **rising** moon was beautiful.*

Habt ihr schon **gegessen**?
*Have you already **eaten**?*

PREPOSITION A preposition links a noun or pronoun to other words in a sentence. Combined with a noun or pronoun, it forms a prepositional phrase, which can be used like an adverb to answer the question *when*, *how*, or *where*. In German, certain prepositions are always followed by a noun in the accusative case, while others are always followed by a noun in the dative case. A small number of prepositions are used with the genitive case.

ohne das Buch
***without** the book*

mit dem Auto
***by** car*

trotz des Regens
***in spite of** the rain*

Two-way prepositions can be followed by either the dative or the accusative, depending on the situation. They are followed by the accusative when used with a verb that indicates movement toward a destination. With all other verbs, they are followed by the dative.

Stell deine Schuhe nicht **auf den Tisch**!
*Don't put your shoes **on the table**!*

Dein Schal liegt **auf dem Tisch**.
*Your scarf is lying **on the table**.*

PRONOUN A word that takes the place of a noun.

Subject pronouns Words used to replace a noun in the nominative case.

Maria ist nett.
***Maria** is nice.*

Der Junge ist groß.
***The boy** is tall.*

Sie ist nett.
***She** is nice.*

Er ist groß.
***He** is tall.*

Accusative pronouns Words used to replace a noun that functions as the direct object.

Wer hat **die Torte** gebacken?
*Who baked **the cake**?*

Ich habe **sie** gebacken.
*I baked **it**.*

Dative pronouns Words used to replace a noun that functions as the indirect object.

Musst du **deiner Oma** eine E-Mail schicken?
*Do you need to send an e-mail **to your grandma**?*

Nein, ich habe **ihr** schon geschrieben.
*No, I already wrote **to her**.*

Indefinite pronouns Words that refer to an unknown or nonspecific person or thing.

Jemand hat seinen Personalausweis vergessen.
***Someone** forgot his I.D. card.*

Herr Klein will mit **niemandem** sprechen.
*Mr. Klein **doesn't** want to speak with **anyone**.*

Reflexive pronouns The pronouns used with reflexive verbs. When the subject of a reflexive verb is also its direct object, it takes an accusative reflexive pronoun. When the subject of a reflexive verb is not its direct object, it takes a dative reflexive pronoun.

Ich wasche **mich**.
I'm washing (myself).

Ich wasche **mir** das Gesicht.
I'm washing my face.

SUBJUNCTIVE A verb form (**der Konjunktiv II**) used to talk about hypothetical, unlikely or impossible conditions, to express wishes, and to make polite requests. German also has an additional subjunctive tense, der **Konjunktiv I**, used to report what someone else has said without indicating whether the information is true or false.

Ich **hätte** gern viel Geld.
*I'd **like to have** a lot of money.*

Wenn er sportlicher **wäre**, **würde** er häufiger trainieren.
*If he **were** more athletic, he **would exercise** more.*

SUPERLATIVE The form of an adjective or adverb used to indicate that a person or thing has more of a particular quality than anyone or anything else.

Welches ist **das größte** Tier der Welt?
*What's **the biggest** animal in the world?*

Wie komme ich **am besten** zur Tankstelle?
*What's **the best** way to get to the gas station?*

TENSE A set of verb forms that indicates if an action or state occurs in the past, present, or future.

Compound tense A tense made up of an auxiliary verb and a participle or infinitive.

Wir **haben** ihren Geburtstag **gefeiert**.
*We **celebrated** her birthday.*

VERB A word that expresses actions or states of being. German verbs are classified as *weak, mixed*, or *strong*, based on the way their past participles are formed.

weak: Ich **habe** eine Torte **gemacht**.
*I **made** a cake.*

strong: Wir **haben** Kekse **gegessen**.
*We **ate** cookies.*

mixed: Er **hat** eine CD **gebrannt**.
*He **burned** a CD.*

Auxiliary verb A conjugated verb used with the participle or infinitive of another verb. The auxiliary verbs **haben** and **sein** are used with past participles to form compound tenses including the **Perfekt** and **Plusquamperfekt**. **Werden** is used with an infinitive to form the future tense, and with a past participle to form a passive construction. Modals are also frequently used as auxiliary verbs.

Habt ihr den Tisch **gedeckt**?
*Did you **set** the table?*

Jasmin **war** noch nie nach Zürich **gefahren**.
*Jasmin **had** never **been** to Zurich.*

Wir **werden** uns in einer Woche wieder **treffen**.
*We'**ll** meet again in one week.*

Es **wird** hier nur Deutsch **gesprochen**.
*Only German **is spoken** here.*

Modal verbs Verbs that modify the meaning of another verb. Modals express an attitude toward an action, such as permission, obligation, ability, desire, or necessity.

Ich **muss** Französisch **lernen**.
*I **have to study** French.*

Ich **will** Französisch **lernen**.
*I **want to learn** French.*

Principal parts German verbs are usually listed in dictionaries by their *principal parts* (**Stammformen**): the infinitive, the third-person singular present tense form (if the verb is irregular in the present), the third-person singular **Präteritum** form, and the past participle. Knowing the principal parts of a verb allows you to produce all of its conjugations in any tense.

geben (gibt)	**gab**	**gegeben**
to give (gives)	*gave*	*given*

Reflexive verbs Verbs that indicate an action you do to yourself or for yourself. The subject of a reflexive verb is also its object.

Ich **fühle mich** nicht **wohl**.
*I **don't feel well**.*

Wir **haben uns entspannt**.
*We**'ve been relaxing**.*

Reciprocal reflexive verbs Verbs that express an action done by two or more people or things to or for one another.

Wir rufen **uns** jeden Tag an.
***We** call **each other** every day.*

Meine Großeltern lieben **sich** sehr.
***My grandparents** love **each other** very much.*

Verb conjugation tables

Here are the infinitives of all verbs introduced as active vocabulary in **Mosaik**. Each verb is followed by a model verb that follows the same conjugation pattern. The number in parentheses indicates where in the verb tables, pages **A16–A25**, you can find the conjugated forms of the model verb. The word (***sein***) after a verb means that it is conjugated with **sein** in the **Perfekt** and **Plusquamperfekt**. For irregular reflexive verbs, the list may point to a non-reflexive model verb. A full conjugation of the simple forms of a reflexive verb is presented in Verb table 6 on page **A17**. Verbs followed by an asterisk (*) have a separable prefix.

abbiegen* (*sein*) like schieben (42)
abbrechen* like sprechen (47)
abfahren* (*sein*) like tragen (51)
abfliegen* (*sein*) like schieben (42)
abheben* like heben (29)
abschicken* like machen (3)
abstauben* like machen (3)
(sich) abtrocknen* like arbeiten (1)
adoptieren like probieren (4)
anbieten* like schieben (42)
anfangen* like fangen (23)
angeln like sammeln (5)
ankommen* (*sein*) like kommen (32)
anmachen* like machen (3)
anrufen* like rufen (40)
anschauen* like machen (3)
anstoßen* like stoßen (50)
antworten like arbeiten (1)
(sich) anziehen* like schieben (42)
arbeiten (1)
(sich) ärgern like fordern (26)
aufgehen* (*sein*) like gehen (28)
auflegen* like machen (3)
aufmachen* like machen (3)
aufnehmen* like nehmen (38)
aufräumen* like machen (3)
aufstehen* (*sein*) like stehen (48)
aufwachen* (*sein*) like machen (3)
ausfüllen like machen (3)
ausgehen like gehen (28)
ausmachen like machen (3)
(sich) ausruhen like sich freuen (6)
ausschalten* like arbeiten (1)
(sich) ausziehen* like schieben (42)
backen like mahlen (37)
(sich) baden like arbeiten (1)
bauen like machen (3)
beantworten like arbeiten (1)
bedeuten like arbeiten (1)
bedienen like machen (3)
(sich) beeilen like sich freuen (6)
beginnen like schwimmen (44)
behaupten like arbeiten (1)
bekommen like kommen (32)
belegen like machen (3)
benutzen like machen (3)
berichten like arbeiten (1)
beschreiben like bleiben (20)
besprechen like sprechen (47)
bestehen like stehen (48)
bestellen like machen (3)
besuchen like machen (3)
(sich) bewegen like heben (29)
(sich) bewerben like helfen (31)
bezahlen like machen (3)
bieten like schieben (42)
bleiben (*sein*) (20)
braten like schlafen (43)
brauchen like machen (3)
brechen like sprechen (47)
brennen like rennen (17)
bringen like denken (16)
buchen like machen (3)
büffeln like sammeln (5)
bügeln like sammeln (5)
bürsten like arbeiten (1)
danken like machen (3)
decken like machen (3)
denken like denken (16)
drücken like machen (3)
drucken like machen (3)
durchfallen* (*sein*) like fallen (22)
durchmachen* like machen (3)
dürfen (10)
(sich) duschen like sich freuen (6)
einkaufen* like machen (3)
einladen* like tragen (51)
einschlafen* (*sein*) like schlafen (43)
einzahlen* like machen (3)
empfehlen like stehlen (49)
entdecken like machen (3)
entfernen like machen (3)
entgegennehmen* like nehmen (38)
entlassen like fallen (22)
(sich) entschließen like fließen (25)
(sich) entschuldigen like machen (3)
(sich) entspannen like sich freuen (6)
entwerten like arbeiten (1)
entwickeln like sammeln (5)
erfinden like trinken (52)
erforschen like machen (3)
ergänzen like machen (3)
erhalten like fallen (22)
(sich) erinnern like fordern (26)
(sich) erkälten like arbeiten (1)
erkennen like rennen (17)
erklären like machen (3)
erzählen like machen (3)
essen (21)
fahren (*sein*) like tragen (51)
fallen (*sein*) (22)
fangen (23)
(sich) färben like machen (3)
faulenzen like machen (3)
fegen like machen (3)
feiern (2)
fernsehen* like geben (27)
finden like trinken (52)
fliegen (*sein*) like schieben (42)
folgen (*sein*) like machen (3)
(sich) fragen like machen (3)
(sich) freuen (6)
(sich) fühlen like sich freuen (6)
füllen like machen (3)
funktionieren like probieren (4)
geben (27)
gefallen like fallen (22)
gehen (*sein*) (28)
gehören like machen (3)
genießen like fließen (25)
gewinnen like schwimmen (44)
(sich) gewöhnen like sich freuen (6)
glauben like machen (3)
gratulieren like probieren (4)
grüßen like machen (3)
haben like haben (7)
handeln like sammeln (5)
hängen like machen (3)
heiraten like arbeiten (1)
heißen (30)
helfen (31)
heruntergehen* (*sein*) like gehen (28)
herunterladen* like tragen (51)
(sich) hinlegen* like machen (3)
(sich) hinsetzen* like machen (3)
hinterlassen like fallen (22)
hochgehen* (*sein*) like gehen (28)
hören like machen (3)
husten like arbeiten (1)
(sich) informieren like probieren (4)
(sich) interessieren like probieren (4)
joggen (*sein*) like machen (3)
(sich) kämmen like machen (3)
kaufen like machen (3)
kennen like rennen (17)
klettern (*sein*) like fordern (26)
klingeln like sammeln (5)
kochen like machen (3)
kommen (*sein*) (32)
können (11)
korrigieren like probieren (4)
kosten like arbeiten (1)
küssen like machen (3)
lächeln like sammeln (5)
lachen like machen (3)
laden like tragen (51)
landen (*sein*) like arbeiten (1)
lassen like fallen (22)
laufen (*sein*) (33)
leben like machen (3)
legen like machen (3)
leiten like arbeiten (1)
lernen like machen (3)
lesen (34)
lieben like machen (3)
liegen (35)
löschen like tragen (51)
lügen (36)
machen (3)
meinen like machen (3)
mieten like arbeiten (1)
mitbringen* like denken (16)
mitkommen* (*sein*) like kommen (32)
mitmachen* like machen (3)
mitnehmen* like nehmen (38)
mögen (12)
müssen (13)
nachmachen* like machen (3)
nehmen (38)
(sich) nennen like rennen (17)
niesen like machen (3)
öffnen like arbeiten (1)
packen like machen (3)
parken like machen (3)
passen like machen (3)
passieren (*sein*) like probieren (4)
probieren (4)
putzen like machen (3)

(sich) rasieren like probieren (4)
rauchen like machen (3)
recyceln like sammeln (5)
reden like arbeiten (1)
regnen like arbeiten (1)
reisen (*sein*) like machen (3)
reiten (*sein*) like pfeifen (39)
rennen (*sein*) (17)
reparieren like probieren (4)
retten like arbeiten (1)
sagen like machen (3)
schauen like machen (3)
scheitern (*sein*) like fordern (26)
schenken like machen (3)
schicken like machen (3)
schlafen (43)
schmecken like machen (3)
(sich) schminken like machen (3)
schneien like machen (3)
schreiben like bleiben (20)
schützen like machen (3)
schwänzen like machen (3)
schwimmen (*sein*) (44)
sehen like lesen (34)
sein (*sein*) (8)
(sich) setzen like machen (3)
singen like trinken (52)
sitzen (46)
sollen (14)
sortieren like probieren (4)
spazieren (*sein*) like probieren (4)
speichern like fordern (26)
spielen like machen (3)
sprechen (47)
springen (*sein*) like trinken (52)
spülen like machen (3)
starten (*sein*) like arbeiten (1)
staubsaugen like saugen (41)
stehen (48)
stehlen (49)
steigen (*sein*) like bleiben (20)
stellen like machen (3)
sterben (*sein*) like helfen (31)
(sich) streiten like pfeifen (39)
studieren like probieren (4)
suchen like machen (3)
surfen (*sein*) like machen (3)
tanken like machen (3)
tanzen like machen (3)
tragen (51)
träumen like machen (3)
(sich) treffen (*sein*) like sprechen (47)
treiben (*sein*) like bleiben (20)
(sich) trennen like sich freuen (6)
trinken (52)
tun (53)
üben like machen (3)
(sich) überlegen like machen (3)
übernachten like arbeiten (1)
überqueren like machen (3)
überraschen like machen (3)
umtauschen* like machen (3)
(sich) umziehen* (*sein*) like schieben (42)
untergehen* (*sein*) like gehen (28)
(sich) unterhalten* like fallen (22)
unterschreiben like bleiben (20)
(sich) verbessern like fordern (26)
verbringen like denken (16)
verdienen like machen (3)
vereinbaren like machen (3)
vergessen like essen (21)
verkaufen like machen (3)
verkünden like arbeiten (1)
(sich) verlaufen like laufen (33)
(sich) verletzen like machen (3)
(sich) verlieben like machen (3)
verlieren like schieben (42)
verschmutzen (*sein*) like machen (3)
(sich) verspäten like sich freuen (6)
(sich) verstauchen like machen (3)
verstehen like stehen (48)
versuchen like machen (3)
(sich) vorbereiten* like arbeiten (1)
vormachen* like machen (3)
vorschlagen* like tragen (51)
(sich) vorstellen* like machen (3)
wachsen (*sein*) like waschen (54)
wandern (*sein*) like fordern (26)
warten like arbeiten (1)
(sich) waschen (54)
wegräumen* like machen (3)
wegwerfen* like helfen (31)
weinen like machen (3)
werden (*sein*) (9)
wettmachen* like machen (3)
wiederholen like machen (3)
wiegen like schieben (42)
wischen like machen (3)
wissen (55)
wohnen like machen (3)
wollen (15)
(sich) wünschen like machen (3)
zeigen like machen (3)
ziehen (*sein*) like schieben (42)
zubereiten* like arbeiten (1)
zumachen* like machen (3)
(sich) zurechtfinden* like trinken (52)
zurückkommen* (*sein*) like kommen (32)
zuschauen* like machen (3)

Regular verbs: simple tenses

	Infinitiv Partizip I Partizip II Perfekt	INDIKATIV Präsens	INDIKATIV Präteritum	INDIKATIV Plusquamperfekt	KONJUNKTIV I Präsens	KONJUNKTIV II Präsens	KONJUNKTIV II Perfekt	IMPERATIV
1	**arbeiten**	arbeite	arbeitete	hatte gearbeitet	arbeite	arbeitete	hätte gearbeitet	
	(to work)	arbeitest	arbeitetest	hattest gearbeitet	arbeitest	arbeitetest	hättest gearbeitet	arbeite
		arbeitet	arbeitete	hatte gearbeitet	arbeite	arbeitete	hätte gearbeitet	
	arbeitend	arbeiten	arbeiteten	hatten gearbeitet	arbeiten	arbeiteten	hätten gearbeitet	arbeiten wir
	gearbeitet	arbeitet	arbeitetet	hattet gearbeitet	arbeitet	arbeitetet	hättet gearbeitet	arbeitet
	gearbeitet haben	arbeiten	arbeiteten	hatten gearbeitet	arbeiten	arbeiteten	hätten gearbeitet	arbeiten Sie
2	**feiern**	feiere	feierte	hatte gefeiert	feiere	feierte	hätte gefeiert	
	(to celebrate)	feierst	feiertest	hattest gefeiert	feierest	feiertest	hättest gefeiert	feiere
		feiert	feierte	hatte gefeiert	feiere	feierte	hätte gefeiert	
	feiernd	feiern	feierten	hatten gefeiert	feiern	feierten	hätten gefeiert	feiern wir
	gefeiert	feiert	feiertet	hattet gefeiert	feiert	feiertet	hättet gefeiert	feiert
	gefeiert haben	feiern	feierten	hatten gefeiert	feiern	feierten	hätten gefeiert	feiern Sie
3	**machen**	mache	machte	hatte gemacht	mache	machte	hätte gemacht	
	(to make; to do)	machst	machtest	hattest gemacht	machest	machtest	hättest gemacht	mache/mach
		macht	machte	hatte gemacht	mache	machte	hätte gemacht	
	machend	machen	machten	hatten gemacht	machen	machten	hätten gemacht	machen wir
	gemacht	macht	machtet	hattet gemacht	machet	machtet	hättet gemacht	macht
	gemacht haben	machen	machten	hatten gemacht	machen	machten	hätten gemacht	machen Sie
4	**probieren**	probiere	probierte	hatte probiert	probiere	probierte	hätte probiert	
	(to try)	probierst	probiertest	hattest probiert	probierest	probiertest	hättest probiert	probiere/probier
		probiert	probierte	hatte probiert	probiere	probierte	hätte probiert	
	probierend	probieren	probierten	hatten probiert	probieren	probierten	hätten probiert	probieren wir
	probiert	probiert	probiertet	hattet probiert	probieret	probiertet	hättet probiert	probiert
	probiert haben	probieren	probierten	hatten probiert	probieren	probierten	hätten probiert	probieren Sie
5	**sammeln**	sammle	sammelte	hatte gesammelt	sammle	sammelte	hätte gesammelt	
	(to collect)	sammelst	sammeltest	hattest gesammelt	sammlest	sammeltest	hättest gesammelt	sammle
		sammelt	sammelte	hatte gesammelt	sammle	sammelte	hätte gesammelt	
	sammelnd	sammeln	sammelten	hatten gesammelt	sammlen	sammelten	hätten gesammelt	sammeln wir
	gesammelt	sammelt	sammeltet	hattet gesammelt	sammlet	sammeltet	hättet gesammelt	sammelt
	gesammelt haben	sammeln	sammelten	hatten gesammelt	sammlen	sammelten	hätten gesammelt	sammeln Sie

Reflexive verbs

Infinitiv Partizip I Partizip II Perfekt	INDIKATIV Präsens	Präteritum	Plusquamperfekt	KONJUNKTIV I Präsens	KONJUNKTIV II Präsens	Perfekt	IMPERATIV
6 **sich freuen**	freue mich	freute mich	hatte mich gefreut	freue mich	freute mich	hätte mich gefreut	
(to be happy)	freust dich	freutest dich	hattest dich gefreut	freuest dich	freutest dich	hättest dich gefreut	freue/freu dich
	freut sich	freute sich	hatte sich gefreut	freue sich	freute sich	hätte sich gefreut	
sich freuend	freuen uns	freuten uns	hatten uns gefreut	freuen uns	freuten uns	hätten uns gefreut	freuen wir uns
sich gefreut	freut euch	freutet euch	hattet euch gefreut	freuet euch	freutet euch	hättet euch gefreut	freut euch
sich gefreut haben	freuen sich	freuten sich	hatten sich gefreut	freuen sich	freuten sich	hätten sich gefreut	freuen Sie sich

Auxiliary verbs

Infinitiv Partizip I Partizip II Perfekt	INDIKATIV Präsens	Präteritum	Plusquamperfekt	KONJUNKTIV I Präsens	KONJUNKTIV II Präsens	Perfekt	IMPERATIV
7 **haben**	habe	hatte	hatte gehabt	habe	hätte	hätte gehabt	
(to have)	hast	hattest	hattest gehabt	habest	hättest	hättest gehabt	habe/hab
	hat	hatte	hatte gehabt	habe	hätte	hätte gehabt	
habend	haben	hatten	hatten gehabt	haben	hätten	hätten gehabt	haben wir
gehabt	habt	hattet	hattet gehabt	habet	hättet	hättet gehabt	habt
gehabt haben	haben	hatten	hatten gehabt	haben	hätten	hätten gehabt	haben Sie
8 **sein**	bin	war	war gewesen	sei	wäre	wäre gewesen	
(to be)	bist	warst	warst gewesen	seiest/seist	wärst/wärest	wärst/wärest gewesen	sei
	ist	war	war gewesen	sei	wäre	wäre gewesen	
seiend	sind	waren	waren gewesen	seien	wären	wären gewesen	seien wir
gewesen	seid	wart	wart gewesen	seiet	wärt/wäret	wärt/wäret gewesen	seid
gewesen sein	sind	waren	waren gewesen	seien	wären	wären gewesen	seien Sie
9 **werden**	werde	wurde	war geworden	werde	würde	wäre geworden	
(to become)	wirst	wurdest	warst geworden	werdest	würdest	wärst geworden	werde
	wird	wurde	war geworden	werde	würde	wäre geworden	
werdend	werden	wurden	waren geworden	werden	würden	wären geworden	werden wir
geworden	werdet	wurdet	wart geworden	werdet	würdet	wärt geworden	werdet
geworden sein	werden	wurden	waren geworden	werden	würden	wären geworden	werden Sie

Compound tenses

Hilfsverb	INDIKATIV				KONJUNKTIV I		KONJUNKTIV II	
	Perfekt		**Plusquamperfekt**		**Präsens**	**Perfekt**	**Präsens**	**Perfekt**
haben	habe		hatte		habe		hätte	
	hast	gemacht	hattest	gemacht	habest	gemach	hättest	gemach
	hat	gearbeitet	hatte	gearbeitet	habe	gearbeitet	hätte	gearbeitet
	haben	studiert	hatten	studiert	haben	studiert	hätten	studiert
	habt	gefeiert	hattet	gefeiert	habet	gefeiert	hättet	gefeiert
	haben	gesammelt	hatten	gesammelt	haben	gesammelt	hätten	gesammelt
sein	bin gegangen		war gegangen		sei gegangen		wäre gegangen	
	bist gegangen		warst gegangen		seiest/seist gegangen		wärst/wärest gegangen	
	ist gegangen		war gegangen		sei gegangen		wäre gegangen	
	sind gegangen		waren gegangen		seien gegangen		wären gegangen	
	seid gegangen		wart gegangen		seiet gegangen		wärt/wäret gegangen	
	sind gegangen		waren gegangen		seien gegangen		wären gegangen	

	Futur I/II	**Futur I/II**	**Futur I/II**
werden	werde machen / gemacht haben	werde machen / gemacht haben	würde machen / gemacht haben
	wirst machen / gemacht haben	werdest machen / gemacht haben	würdest machen / gemacht haben
	wird machen / gemacht haben	werde machen / gemacht haben	würde machen / gemacht haben
	werden machen / gemacht haben	werden machen / gemacht haben	würden machen / gemacht haben
	werdet machen / gemacht haben	werdet machen / gemacht haben	würdet machen / gemacht haben
	werden machen / gemacht haben	werden machen / gemacht haben	würden machen / gemacht haben

Modal verbs

	Infinitiv Partizip I Partizip II Perfekt	INDIKATIV			KONJUNKTIV I	KONJUNKTIV II		IMPERATIV
		Präsens	**Präteritum**	**Plusquamperfekt**	**Präsens**	**Präsens**	**Perfekt**	
10	**dürfen**	darf	durfte	hatte gedurft	dürfe	dürfte	hätte gedurft	*Modal verbs are not used in the imperative.*
	(to be permitted to)	darfst	durftest	hattest gedurft	dürfest	dürftest	hättest gedurft	
		darf	durfte	hatte gedurft	dürfe	dürfte	hätte gedurft	
	dürfend	dürfen	durften	hatten gedurft	dürfen	dürften	hätten gedurft	
	gedurft/dürfen	dürft	durftet	hattet gedurft	dürfet	dürftet	hättet gedurft	
	gedurft haben	dürfen	durften	hatten gedurft	dürfen	dürften	hätten gedurft	
11	**können**	kann	konnte	hatte gekonnt	könne	könnte	hätte gekonnt	*Modal verbs are not used in the imperative.*
	(to be able to)	kannst	konntest	hattest gekonnt	könnest	könntest	hättest gekonnt	
		kann	konnte	hatte gekonnt	könne	könnte	hätte gekonnt	
	könnend	können	konnten	hatten gekonnt	können	könnten	hätten gekonnt	
	gekonnt /können	könnt	konntet	hattet gekonnt	könnet	könntet	hättet gekonnt	
	gekonnt haben	können	konnten	hatten gekonnt	können	könnten	hätten gekonnt	
12	**mögen**	mag	mochte	hatte gemocht	möge	möchte	hätte gemocht	*Modal verbs are not used in the imperative.*
	(to like)	magst	mochtest	hattest gemocht	mögest	möchtest	hättest gemocht	
		mag	mochte	hatte gemocht	möge	möchte	hätte gemocht	
	mögend	mögen	mochten	hatten gemocht	mögen	möchten	hätten gemocht	
	gemocht /mögen	mögt	mochtet	hattet gemocht	möget	möchtet	hättet gemocht	
	gemocht haben	mögen	mochten	hatten gemocht	mögen	möchten	hätten gemocht	
13	**müssen**	muss	musste	hatte gemusst	müsse	müsste	hätte gemusst	*Modal verbs are not used in the imperative.*
	(to have to)	musst	musstest	hattest gemusst	müssest	müsstest	hättest gemusst	
		muss	musste	hatte gemusst	müsse	müsste	hätte gemusst	
	müssend	müssen	mussten	hatten gemusst	müssen	müssten	hätten gemusst	
	gemusst /müssen	müsst	musstet	hattet gemusst	müsset	müsstet	hättet gemusst	
	gemusst haben	müssen	mussten	hatten gemusst	müssen	müssten	hätten gemusst	
14	**sollen**	soll	sollte	hatte gesollt	solle	sollte	hätte gesollt	*Modal verbs are not used in the imperative.*
	(to be supposed to)	sollst	solltest	hattest gesollt	sollest	solltest	hättest gesollt	
		soll	sollte	hatte gesollt	solle	sollte	hätte gesollt	
	sollend	sollen	sollten	hatten gesollt	sollen	sollten	hätten gesollt	
	gesollt /sollen	sollt	solltet	hattet gesollt	sollet	solltet	hättet gesollt	
	gesollt haben	sollen	sollten	hatten gesollt	sollen	sollten	hätten gesollt	
15	**wollen**	will	wollte	hatte gewollt	wolle	wollte	hätte gewollt	*Modal verbs are not used in the imperative.*
	(to want to)	willst	wolltest	hattest gewollt	wollest	wolltest	hättest gewollt	
		will	wollte	hatte gewollt	wollev	wollte	hätte gewollt	
	wollend	wollen	wollten	hatten gewollt	wollen	wollten	hätten gewollt	
	gewollt/wollen	wollt	wolltet	hattet gewollt	wollet	wolltet	hättet gewollt	
	gewollt haben	wollen	wollten	hatten gewollt	wollen	wollten	hätten gewollt	

Mixed verbs

	Infinitiv	INDIKATIV			KONJUNKTIV I	KONJUNKTIV II		IMPERATIV
	Partizip I Partizip II Perfekt	Präsens	Präteritum	Plusquamperfekt	Präsens	Präsens	Perfekt	
16	**denken**	denke	dachte	hatte gedacht	denke	dächte	hätte gedacht	
	(to think)	denkst	dachtest	hattest gedacht	denkest	dächtest	hättest gedacht	denke/denk
		denkt	dachte	hatte gedacht	denke	dächte	hätte gedacht	
	denkend	denken	dachten	hatten gedacht	denken	dächten	hätten gedacht	denken wir
	gedacht	denkt	dachtet	hattet gedacht	denket	dächtet	hättet gedacht	denkt
	gedacht haben	denken	dachten	hatten gedacht	denken	dächten	hätten gedacht	denken Sie
17	**rennen**	renne	rannte	war gerannt	renne	rennte	wäre gerannt	
	(to run)	rennst	ranntest	warst gerannt	rennest	renntest	wärest gerannt	renne/renn
		rennt	rannte	war gerannt	renne	rennte	wäre gerannt	
	denkend	rennen	rannten	waren gerannt	rennen	rennten	wären gerannt	rennen wir
	gerannt	rennt	ranntet	wart gerannt	rennet	renntet	wärt gerannt	rennt
	gerannt sein	rennen	rannten	waren gerannt	rennen	rennten	wären gerannt	rennen Sie
18	**senden**	sende	sandte	hatte gesandt	sende	sendete	hätte gesandt	
	(to send)	sendest	sandtest	hattest gesandt	sendest	sendetest	hättest gesandt	sende
		sendet	sandte	hatte gesandt	sende	sendete	hätte gesandt	
	sendend	senden	sandten	hatten gesandt	senden	sendeten	hätten gesandt	senden wir
	gesendet	sendet	sandtet	hattet gesandt	sendet	sendetet	hättet gesandt	sendet
	gesendet haben	senden	sandten		senden	sendeten	hätten gesandt	senden Sie

Irregular verbs

	Infinitiv	INDIKATIV			KONJUNKTIV I	KONJUNKTIV II		IMPERATIV
	Partizip I Partizip II Perfekt	Präsens	Präteritum	Plusquamperfekt	Präsens	Präsens	Perfekt	
19	**bitten**	bitte	bat	hatte gebeten	bitte	bäte	hätte gebeten	
	(to ask)	bittest	batest	hattest gebeten	bittest	bätest	hättest gebeten	bitte
		bittet	bat	hatte gebeten	bitte	bäte	hätte gebeten	
	bittend	bitten	baten	hatten gebeten	bitten	bäten	hätten gebeten	bitten wir
	gebeten	bittet	batet	hattet gebeten	bittet	bätet	hättet gebeten	bittet
	gebeten haben	bitten	baten	hatten gebeten	bitten	bäten	hätten gebeten	bitten Sie
20	**bleiben**	bleibe	bliebe	war geblieben	bleibe	bliebe	wäre geblieben	
	(to stay)	bleibst	bliebst	warst geblieben	bleibest	bliebest	wärest geblieben	bleibe/bleib
		bleibt	blieb	war geblieben	bleibe	bliebe	wäre geblieben	
	bleibend	bleiben	blieben	waren geblieben	bleiben	blieben	wären geblieben	bleiben wir
	geblieben	bleibt	bliebt	wart geblieben	bleibet	bliebet	wärt geblieben	bleibt
	geblieben sein	bleiben	blieben	waren geblieben	bleiben	blieben	wären geblieben	bleiben Sie

	Infinitiv	**INDIKATIV**			**KONJUNKTIV I**	**KONJUNKTIV II**		**IMPERATIV**
	Partizip I **Partizip II** **Perfekt**	**Präsens**	**Präteritum**	**Plusquamperfekt**	**Präsens**	**Präsens**	**Perfekt**	
21	**essen**	esse	aß	hatte gegessen	esse	äße	hätte gegessen	
	(to eat)	isst	aßest	hattest gegessen	essest	äßest	hättest gegessen	iss
		isst	aß	hatte gegessen	esse	äße	hätte gegessen	
	essend	essen	aßen	hatten gegessen	essen	äßen	hätten gegessen	essen wir
	gegessen	esst	aß	hattet gegessen	esset	äßet	hättet gegessen	esst
	gegessen haben	essen	aßen	hatten gegessen	essen	äßen	hätten gegessen	essen Sie
22	**fallen**	falle	fiel	war gefallen	falle	fiele	wäre gefallen	
	(to fall)	fällst	fielst	warst gefallen	fallest	fielest	wärest gefallen	falle/fall
		fällt	fiel	war gefallen	falle	fiele	wäre gefallen	
	fallend	fallen	fielen	waren gefallen	fallen	fielen	wären gefallen	fallen wir
	gefallen	fallt	fielt	wart gefallen	fallet	fielet	wäret gefallen	fallt
	gefallen sein	fallen	fielen	waren gefallen	fallen	fielen	wären gefallen	fallen Sie
23	**fangen**	fange	fing	hatte gemacht	fange	finge	hätte gefangen	
	(to catch)	fängst	fingst	hattest gemacht	fangest	fingest	hättest gefangen	fange/fang
		fängt	fing	hatte gemacht	fange	finge	hätte gefangen	
	fangend	fangen	fingen	hatten gemacht	fangen	fingen	hätten gefangen	fangen wir
	gefangen	fangt	fingt	hattet gemacht	fanget	finget	hättet gefangen	fangt
	gefangen haben	fangen	fingen	hatten gemacht	fangen	fingen	hätten gefangen	fangen Sie
24	**flechten**	flechte	flocht	hatte geflochten	flechte	flöchte	hätte geflochten	
	(to braid)	flichtst	flochtest	hattest geflochten	flechtest	flöchtest	hättest geflochten	flicht
		flicht	flocht	hatte geflochten	flechte	flöchte	hätte geflochten	
	flechtend	flechten	flochten	hatten geflochten	flechten	flöchten	hätten geflochten	flechten wir
	geflochten	flechtet	flochtet	hattet geflochten	flechtet	flöchtet	hättet geflochten	flechtet
	geflochten haben	flechten	flochten	hatten geflochten	flechten	flöchten	hätten geflochten	flechten Sie
25	**fließen**	fließe	floss	war geflossen	fließe	flösse	wäre geflossen	
	(to flow)	fließt	flossest/flosst	warst geflossen	fließest	flössest	wärest geflossen	fließe/fließ
		fließt	floss	war geflossen	fließe	flösse	wäre geflossen	
	fließend	fließen	flossen	waren geflossen	fließen	flössen	wären geflossen	fließen wir
	geflossen	fließt	flosst	wart geflossen	fließet	flösset	wärt geflossen	fließt
	geflossen sein	fließen	flossen	waren geflossen	fließen	flössen	wären geflossen	fließen Sie
26	**fordern**	ford(e)re	forderte	hatte gefordert	fordere	forderte	hätte gefordert	
	(to demand)	forderst	fordertest	hattest gefordert	forderest	fordertest	hättest gefordert	fordere/fordre
		fordert	forderte	hatte gefordert	fordere	forderte	hätte gefordert	
	fordernd	fordern	forderten	hatten gefordert	forderen	forderten	hätten gefordert	fordern wir
	gefordert	fordert	fordertet	hattet gefordert	forderet	fordertet	hättet gefordert	fordert
	gefordert haben	fordern	forderten	hatten gefordert	forderen	forderten	hätten gefordert	fordern Sie
27	**geben**	gebe	gab	hatte gegeben	gebe	gäbe	hätte gegeben	
	(to give)	gibst	gabst	hattest gegeben	gebest	gäbest	hättest gegeben	gib
		gibt	gab	hatte gegeben	gebe	gäbe	hätte gegeben	
	gebend	geben	gaben	hatten gegeben	geben	gäben	hätten gegeben	geben wir
	gegeben	gebt	gabt	hattet gegeben	gebet	gäbet	hättet gegeben	gebt
	gegeben haben	geben	gaben	hatten gegeben	geben	gäben	hätten gegeben	geben Sie

	Infinitiv Partizip I Partizip II Perfekt	INDIKATIV Präsens	 Präteritum	 Plusquamperfekt	KONJUNKTIV I Präsens	KONJUNKTIV II Präsens	 Perfekt	IMPERATIV
28	**gehen**	gehe	ging	war gegangen	gehe	ginge	wäre gegangen	
	(to go)	gehst	gingst	warst gegangen	gehest	gingest	wärest gegangen	gehe/geh
		geht	ging	war gegangen	gehe	ginge	wäre gegangen	
	gehend	gehen	gingen	waren gegangen	gehen	gingen	wären gegangen	gehen wir
	gegangen	geht	gingt	wart gegangen	gehet	ginget	wäret gegangen	geht
	gegangen sein	gehen	gingen	waren gegangen	gehen	gingen	wären gegangen	gehen Sie
29	**heben**	hebe	hob	hatte gehoben	hebe	höbe	hätte gehoben	
	(to lift)	hebst	hobst	hattest gehoben	hebest	höbest/höbst	hättest gehoben	hebe/heb
		hebt	hob	hatte gehoben	hebe	höbe	hätte gehoben	
	hebend	heben	hoben	hatten gehoben	heben	höben	hätten gehoben	heben wir
	gehoben	hebt	hobt	hattet gehoben	hebet	höbet/höbt	hättet gehoben	hebt
	gehoben haben	heben	hoben	hatten gehoben	heben	höben	hätten gehoben	heben Sie
30	**heißen**	heiße	hieß	hatte geheißen	heiße	hieße	hätte geheißen	
	(to be called)	heißt	hießest	hattest geheißen	heißest	hießest	hättest geheißen	heiß/heiße
		heißt	hieß	hatte geheißen	heiße	hieße	hätte geheißen	
	heißend	heißen	hießen	hatten geheißen	heißen	hießen	hätten geheißen	heißen wir
	geheißen	heißt	hießt	hattet geheißen	heißet	hießet	hättet geheißen	heißt
	geheißen haben	heißen	hießen	hatten geheißen	heißen	hießen	hätten geheißen	heißen Sie
31	**helfen**	helfe	half	hatte geholfen	helfe	hälfe	hätte geholfen	
	(to help)	hilfst	halfst	hattest geholfen	helfest	hälfest/hälfst	hättest geholfen	hilf
		hilft	half	hatte geholfen	helfe	hälfe	hätte geholfen	
	helfend	helfen	halfen	hatten geholfen	helfen	hälfen	hätten geholfen	helfen wir
	geholfen	helft	halft	hattet geholfen	helfet	hälfet/hälft	hättet geholfen	helft
	geholfen haben	helfen	halfen	hatten geholfen	helfen	hälfen	hätten geholfen	helfen Sie
32	**kommen**	komme	kam	war gekommen	komme	käme	wäre gekommen	
	(to come)	kommst	kamst	warst gekommen	kommest	kämest	wärest gekommen	komme/komm
		kommt	kam	war gekommen	komme	käme	wäre gekommen	
	kommend	kommen	kamen	waren gekommen	kommen	kämen	wären gekommen	kommen wir
	gekommen	kommt	kamt	wart gekommen	kommet	kämet	wäret gekommen	kommt
	gekommen sein	kommen	kamen	waren gekommen	kommen	kämen	wären gekommen	kommen Sie
33	**laufen**	laufe	lief	war gelaufen	laufe	liefe	wäre gelaufen	
	(to run)	läufst	liefst	warst gelaufen	laufest	liefest	wärest gelaufen	laufe/lauf
		läuft	lief	war gelaufen	laufe	liefe	wäre gelaufen	
	laufend	laufen	liefen	waren gelaufen	laufen	liefen	wären gelaufen	laufen wir
	gelaufen	lauft	lieft	wart gelaufen	laufet	liefet	wäret gelaufen	lauft
	gelaufen sein	laufen	liefen	waren gelaufen	laufen	liefen	wären gelaufen	laufen Sie
34	**lesen**	lese	las	hatte gelesen	lese	läse	hätte gelesen	
	(to read)	liest	la(se)st	hattest gelesen	lesest	läsest	hättest gelesen	lies
		liest	las	hatte gelesen	lese	läse	hätte gelesen	
	lesend	lesen	lasen	hatten gelesen	lesen	läsen	hätten gelesen	les en wir
	gelesen	lest	last	hattet gelesen	leset	läset	hättet gelesen	lest
	gelesen haben	lesen	lasen	hatten gelesen	lesen	läsen	hätten gelesen	lesen Sie

	Infinitiv Partizip I Partizip II Perfekt	INDIKATIV Präsens	 Präteritum	 Plusquamperfekt	KONJUNKTIV I Präsens	KONJUNKTIV II Präsens	 Perfekt	IMPERATIV
35	**liegen**	liege	lag	hatte gelegen	liege	läge	hätte gelegen	
	(to lie; to be lying)	liegst	lagst	hattest gelegen	liegest	lägest	hättest gelegen	liege/lieg
		liegt	lag	hatte gelegen	liege	läge	hätte gelegen	
	liegend	liegen	lagen	hatten gelegen	liegen	lägen	hätten gelegen	liegen wir
	gelegen	liegt	lagt	hattet gelegen	lieget	läget	hättet gelegen	liegt
	gelegen haben	liegen	lagen	hatten gelegen	liegen	lägen	hätten gelegen	liegen Sie
36	**lügen**	lüge	log	hatte gelogen	lüge	löge	hätte gelogen	
	(to lie)	lügst	logst	hattest gelogen	lügest	lögest	hättest gelogen	lüge/lüg
		lügt	log	hatte gelogen	lüge	löge	hätte gelogen	
	lügend	lügen	logen	hatten gelogen	lügen	lögen	hätten gelogen	lügen wir
	gelogen	lügt	logt	hattet gelogen	lüget	löget	hättet gelogen	lügt
	gelogen haben	lügen	logen	hatten gelogen	lügen	lögen	hätten gelogen	lügen Sie
37	**mahlen**	mahle	mahlte	hatte gemahlt/gemahlen	mahle	mahlte	hätte gemahlt/gemahlen	
	(to grind)	mahlst	mahltest	hattest gemahlt/gemahlen	mahlest	mahltest	hättest gemahlt/gemahlen	mahle/mahl
	mahlend	mahlt	mahlte	hatte gemahlt/gemahlen	mahle	mahlte	hätte gemahlt/gemahlen	
	gemahlt/gemahlen	mahlen	mahlten	hatten gemahlt/gemahlen	mahlen	mahlten	hätten gemahlt/gemahlen	mahlen wir
	gemahlt/gemahlen	mahlt	mahltet	hattet gemahlt/gemahlen	mahlet	mahltet	hättet gemahlt/gemahlen	mahlt
	haben	mahlen	mahlten	hatten gemahlt/gemahlen	mahlen	mahlten	hätten gemahlt/gemahlen	mahlen Sie
38	**nehmen**	nehme	nahm	hatte genommen	nehme	nähme	hätte genommen	
	(to take)	nimmst	nahmst	hattest genommen	nehmest	nähmest	hättest genommen	nimm
		nimmt	nahm	hatte genommen	nehme	nähme	hätte genommen	
	nehmend	nehmen	nahmen	hatten genommen	nehmen	nähmen	hätten genommen	nehmen wir
	genommen	nehmt	nahmt	hattet genommen	nehmet	nähmet	hättet genommen	nehmt
	genommen haben	nehmen	nahmen	hatten genommen	nehmen	nähmen	hätten genommen	nehmen Sie
39	**pfeifen**	pfeife	pfiff	hatte gepfiffen	pfeife	pfiffe	hätte gepfiffen	
	(to whistle)	pfeifst	pfiffst	hattest gepfiffen	pfeifest	pfiffest	hättest gepfiffen	pfeife/pfeif
		pfeift	pfiff	hatte gepfiffen	pfeife	pfiffe	hätte gepfiffen	
	pfeifend	pfeifen	pfiffen	hatten gepfiffen	pfeifen	pfiffen	hätten gepfiffen	pfeifen wir
	gepfiffen	pfeift	pfifft	hattet gepfiffen	pfeifet	pfiffet	hättet gepfiffen	pfeift
	gepfiffen haben	pfeifen	pfiffen	hatten gepfiffen	pfeifen	pfiffen	hätten gepfiffen	pfeifen Sie
40	**rufen**	rufe	rief	hatte gerufen	rufe	riefe	hätte gerufen	
	(to call)	rufst	riefst	hattest gerufen	rufest	riefest	hättest gerufen	rufe/ruf
		ruft	rief	hatte gerufen	rufe	riefe	hätte gerufen	
	rufend	rufen	riefen	hatten gerufen	rufen	riefen	hätten gerufen	rufen wir
	gerufen	ruft	rieft	hattet gerufen	rufet	riefet	hättet gerufen	ruft
	gerufen haben	rufen	riefen	hatten gerufen	rufen	riefen	hätten gerufen	rufen Sie
41	**saugen**	sauge	saugte/sog	hatte gesaugt/gesogen	sauge	saugte/söge	hätte gesaugt/gesogen	
	(to suck)	saugst	saugtest/sogst	hattest gesaugt/gesogen	saugest	saugtest/sögest	hättest gesaugt/gesogen	sauge/saug
	saugend	saugt	saugte/sog	hatte gesaugt/gesogen	sauge	saugte/söge	hätte gesaugt/gesogen	
	gesaugt/gesogen	saugen	saugten/sogen	hatten gesaugt/gesogen	saugen	saugten/sögen	hätten gesaugt/gesogen	saugen wir
	gesaugt/gesogen	saugt	saugtet/sogt	hattet gesaugt/gesogen	sauget	saugtet/söget	hättet gesaugt/gesogen	saugt
	haben	saugen	saugten/sogen	hatten gesaugt/gesogen	saugen	saugten/sögen	hätten gesaugt/gesogen	saugen Sie

	Infinitiv Partizip I Partizip II Perfekt	INDIKATIV			KONJUNKTIV I	KONJUNKTIV II		IMPERATIV
		Präsens	Präteritum	Plusquamperfekt	Präsens	Präsens	Perfekt	
42	**schieben**	schiebe	schob	hatte geschoben	schiebe	schöbe	hätte geschoben	
	(to push)	schiebst	schobst	hattest geschoben	schiebest	schöbest	hättest geschoben	schiebe/schieb
		schiebt	schob	hatte geschoben	schiebe	schöbe	hätte geschoben	
	schiebend	schieben	schoben	hatten geschoben	schieben	schöben	hätten geschoben	schieben wir
	geschoben	schiebt	schobt	hattet geschoben	schiebet	schöbet	hättet geschoben	schiebt
	geschoben haben	schieben	schoben	hatten geschoben	schieben	schöben	hätten geschoben	schieben Sie
43	**schlafen**	schlafe	schlief	hatte geschlafen	schlafe	schliefe	hätte geschlafen	
	(to sleep)	schläfst	schliefst	hattest geschlafen	schlafest	schliefest	hättest geschlafen	schlafe/schlaf
		schläft	schlief	hatte geschlafen	schlafe	schliefe	hätte geschlafen	
	schlafend	schlafen	schliefen	hatten geschlafen	schlafen	schliefen	hätten geschlafen	schlafen wir
	geschlafen	schlaft	schlieft	hattet geschlafen	schlafet	schliefet	hättet geschlafen	schlaft
	geschlafen haben	schlafen	schliefen	hatten geschlafen	schlafen	schliefen	hätten geschlafen	schlafen Sie
44	**schwimmen**	schwimme	schwamm	war geschwommen	schwimme	schwömme	wäre geschwommen	
	(to swim)	schwimmst	schwammst	warst geschwommen	schwimmest	schwömmest	wärest geschwommen	schwimme/schwimm
		schwimmt	schwamm	war geschwommen	schwimme	schwömme	wäre geschwommen	
	schwimmend	schwimmen	schwammen	waren geschwommen	schwimmen	schwömmen	wären geschwommen	schwimmen wir
	geschwommen	schwimmt	schwammt	wart geschwommen	schwimmet	schwömmet	wäret geschwommen	schwimmt
	geschwommen sein	schwimmen	schwammen	waren geschwommen	schwimmen	schwömmen	wären geschwommen	schwimmen Sie
45	**schwören**	schwöre	schwor	hatte geschworen	schwöre	schwüre	hätte geschworen	
	(to swear)	schwörst	schworst	hattest geschworen	schwörest	schwürest/schwürst	hättest geschworen	schwöre/schwör
		schwört	schwor	hatte geschworen	schwöre	schwüre	hätte geschworen	
	schwörend	schwören	schworen	hatten geschworen	schwören	schwüren	hätten geschworen	schwören wir
	geschworen	schwört	schwort	hattet geschworen	schwöret	schwüret	hättet geschworen	schwört
	geschworen haben	schwören	schworen	hatten geschworen	schwören	schwüren	hätten geschworen	schwören Sie
46	**sitzen**	sitze	saß	hatte gesessen	sitze	säße	hätte gesessen	
	(to sit)	sitzt	saßest	hattest gesessen	sitzest	säßest	hättest gesessen	sitze/sitz
		sitzt	saß	hatte gesessen	sitze	säße	hätte gesessen	
	sitzend	sitzen	saßen	hatten gesessen	sitzen	säßen	hätten gesessen	sitzen wir
	gesessen	sitzt	saßet	hattet gesessen	sitzet	säßet	hättet gesessen	sitzt
	gesessen haben	sitzen	saßen	hatten gesessen	sitzen	säßen	hätten gesessen	sitzen Sie
47	**sprechen**	spreche	sprach	hatte gesprochen	spreche	spräche	hätte gesprochen	
	(to speak)	sprichst	sprachst	hattest gesprochen	sprechest	sprächest	hättest gesprochen	sprich
		spricht	sprach	hatte gesprochen	spreche	spräche	hätte gesprochen	
	sprechend	sprechen	sprachen	hatten gesprochen	sprechen	sprächen	hätten gesprochen	sprechen wir
	gesprochen	sprecht	spracht	hattet gesprochen	sprechet	sprächet	hättet gesprochen	sprecht
	gesprochen haben	sprechen	sprachen	hatten gesprochen	sprechen	sprächen	hätten gesprochen	sprechen Sie
48	**stehen**	stehe	stand	hatte gestanden	stehe	stünde/stände	hätte gestanden	
	(to stand)	stehst	standest/standst	hattest gestanden	stehest	stündest/ständest	hättest gestanden	stehe/steh
		steht	stand	hatte gestanden	stehe	stünde/stände	hätte gestanden	
	stehend	stehen	standen	hatten gestanden	stehen	stünden/ständen	hätten gestanden	stehen wir
	gestanden	steht	standet	hattet gestanden	stehet	stündet/ständet	hättet gestanden	steht
	gestanden haben	stehen	standen	hatten gestanden	stehen	stünden/ständen	hätten gestanden	stehen Sie

	Infinitiv Partizip I Partizip II Perfekt	INDIKATIV Präsens	Präteritum	Plusquamperfekt	KONJUNKTIV I Präsens	KONJUNKTIV II Präsens	Perfekt	IMPERATIV
49	**stehlen**	stehle	stahl	hatte gestohlen	stehle	stähle/stöhle	hätte gestohlen	
	(to steal)	stiehlst	stahlst	hattest gestohlen	stehlest	stählest/stöhlest	hättest gestohlen	stiehl
		stiehlt	stahl	hatte gestohlen	stehle	stähle/stöhle	hätte gestohlen	
	stehlend	stehlen	stahlen	hatten gestohlen	stehlen	stählen/stöhlen	hätten gestohlen	stehlen wir
	gestohlen	stehlt	stahlt	hattet gestohlen	stehlet	stählet/stöhlet	hättet gestohlen	stehlt
	gestohlen haben	stehlen	stahlen	hatten gestohlen	stehlen	stählen/stöhlen	hätten gestohlen	stehlen Sie
50	**stoßen**	stoße	stieß	hatte gestoßen	stoße	stieße	hätte gestoßen	
	(to bump)	stößt	stießest/stießt	hattest gestoßen	stoßest	stießest	hättest gestoßen	stoße/stoß
		stößt	stieß	hatte gestoßen	stoße	stieße	hätte gestoßen	
	stoßend	stoßen	stießen	hatten gestoßen	stoßen	stießen	hätten gestoßen	stoßen wir
	gestoßen	stoßt	stießt	hattet gestoßen	stoßet	stießet	hättet gestoßen	stoßt
	gestoßen haben	stoßen	stießen	hatten gestoßen	stoßen	stießen	hätten gestoßen	stoßen Sie
51	**tragen**	trage	trug	hatte getragen	trage	trüge	hätte getragen	
	(to carry)	trägst	trugst	hattest getragen	tragest	trügest	hättest getragen	trage/trag
		trägt	trug	hatte getragen	trage	trüge	hätte getragen	
	tragend	tragen	trugen	hatten getragen	tragen	trügen	hätten getragen	tragen wir
	getragen	tragt	trugt	hattet getragen	traget	trüget	hättet getragen	tragt
	getragen haben	tragen	trugen	hatten getragen	tragen	trügen	hätten getragen	tragen Sie
52	**trinken**	trinke	trank	hatte getrunken	trinke	tränke	hätte getrunken	
	(to drink)	trinkst	trankst	hattest getrunken	trinkest	tränkest	hättest getrunken	trinke/trink
		trinkt	trank	hatte getrunken	trinke	tränke	hätte getrunken	
	trinkend	trinken	tranken	hatten getrunken	trinken	tränken	hätten getrunken	trinken wir
	getrunken	trinkt	trankt	hattet getrunken	trinket	tränket	hättet getrunken	trinkt
	getrunken haben	trinken	tranken	hatten getrunken	trinken	tränken	hätten getrunken	trinken Sie
53	**tun**	tue	tat	hatte getan	tue	täte	hätte getan	
	(to do)	tust	tatest	hattest getan	tuest	tätest	hättest getan	tue/tu
		tut	tat	hatte getan	tue	täte	hätte getan	
	tuend	tun	taten	hatten getan	tuen	täten	hätten getan	tun wir
	getan	tut	tatet	hattet getan	tuet	tätet	hättet getan	tut
	getan haben	tun	taten	hatten getan	tuen	täten	hätten getan	tun Sie
54	**waschen**	wasche	wusch	hatte gewaschen	wasche	wüsche	hätte gewaschen	
	(to wash)	wäschst	wuschest/wuschst	hattest gewaschen	waschest	wüschest/wüschst	hättest gewaschen	wasche/wasch
		wäscht	wusch	hatte gewaschen	wasche	wüsche	hätte gewaschen	
	waschend	waschen	wuschen	hatten gewaschen	waschen	wüschen	hätten gewaschen	waschen wir
	gewaschen	wascht	wuscht	hattet gewaschen	waschet	wüschet/wüscht	hättet gewaschen	wascht
	gewaschen haben	waschen	wuschen	hatten gewaschen	waschen	wüschen	hätten gewaschen	waschen Sie
55	**wissen**	weiß	wusste	hatte gewusst	wisse	wüsste	hätte gewusst	
	(to know)	weißt	wusstest	hattest gewusst	wissest	wüsstest	hättest gewusst	wisse
		weiß	wusste	hatte gewusst	wisse	wüsste	hätte gewusst	
	wissend	wissen	wussten	hatten gewusst	wissen	wüssten	hätten gewusst	wissen wir
	gewusst	wisst	wusstet	hattet gewusst	wisset	wüsstet	hättet gewusst	wisst
	gewusst haben	wissen	wussten	hatten gewusst	wissen	wüssten	hätten gewusst	wissen Sie

Irregular verbs

The following is a list of the principal parts of all strong and mixed verbs that are introduced as active vocabulary in **Mosaik**, as well as other sample verbs. For the complete conjugations of these verbs, consult the verb list on pages **A14–A15** and the verb charts on pages **A16–A25**. The verbs listed here are base forms. See **Strukturen Volume 2, 2B.2** and **3A.1** to review **Perfekt** and **Präteritum** forms of separable and inseparable prefix verbs.

Infinitiv		Präteritum	Partizip II
backen	*to bake*	backte	gebacken
beginnen	*to begin*	begann	begonnen
bieten	*to bid, to offer*	bot	geboten
binden	*to tie, to bind*	band	gebunden
bitten	*to request*	bat	gebeten
bleiben	*to stay*	blieb	(ist) geblieben
braten (brät)	*to fry, to roast*	briet	gebraten
brechen (bricht)	*to break*	brach	gebrochen
brennen	*to burn*	brannte	gebrannt
bringen	*to bring*	brachte	gebracht
denken	*to think*	dachte	gedacht
dürfen (darf)	*to be allowed to*	durfte	gedurft
empfehlen (empfiehlt)	*to recommend*	empfahl	empfohlen
essen (isst)	*to eat*	aß	gegessen
fahren (fährt)	*to go, to drive*	fuhr	(ist) gefahren
fallen (fällt)	*to fall*	fiel	(ist) gefallen
fangen (fängt)	*to catch*	fing	gefangen
finden	*to find*	fand	gefunden
fliegen	*to fly*	flog	(ist) geflogen
fließen	*to flow, to pour*	floss	(ist) geflossen
frieren	*to freeze*	fror	(hat/ist) gefroren
geben (gibt)	*to give*	gab	gegeben
gehen	*to go, to walk*	ging	(ist) gegangen
gelten (gilt)	*to be valid*	galt	gegolten
genießen	*to enjoy*	genoss	genossen
geschehen (geschieht)	*to happen*	geschah	(ist) geschehen
gewinnen	*to win*	gewann	gewonnen
gleichen	*to resemble*	glich	geglichen
graben (gräbt)	*to dig*	grub	gegraben
haben (hat)	*to have*	hatte	gehabt
halten (hält)	*to hold, to keep*	hielt	gehalten
hängen	*to hang*	hing	gehangen
heben	*to raise, to lift*	hob	gehoben
heißen	*to be called, to mean*	hieß	geheißen
helfen (hilft)	*to help*	half	geholfen
kennen	*to know*	kannte	gekannt
klingen	*to sound, to ring*	klang	geklungen
kommen	*to come*	kam	(ist) gekommen
können (kann)	*to be able to, can*	konnte	gekonnt
laden (lädt)	*to load, to charge*	lud	geladen
lassen (lässt)	*to let, to allow*	ließ	gelassen
laufen (läuft)	*to run, to walk*	lief	(ist) gelaufen

Infinitiv		Präteritum	Partizip II
leiden	*to suffer*	litt	gelitten
leihen	*to lend*	lieh	geliehen
lesen (liest)	*to read*	las	gelesen
liegen	*to lie, to rest*	lag	gelegen
lügen	*to lie, to tell lies*	log	gelogen
meiden	*to avoid*	mied	gemieden
messen (misst)	*to measure*	maß	gemessen
mögen (mag)	*to like*	mochte	gemocht
müssen (muss)	*to have, to must*	musste	gemusst
nehmen (nimmt)	*to take*	nahm	genommen
nennen	*to name, to call*	nannte	genannt
preisen	*to praise*	pries	gepriesen
raten (rät)	*to guess*	riet	geraten
reiben	*to rub, to grate*	rieb	gerieben
riechen	*to smell*	roch	gerochen
rufen	*to call, to shout*	rief	gerufen
schaffen	*to create*	schuf	geschaffen
scheiden	*to divorce*	schied	geschieden
scheinen	*to shine, to appear*	schien	geschienen
schieben	*to push, to shove*	schob	geschoben
schießen	*to shoot*	schoss	geschossen
schlafen (schläft)	*to sleep*	schlief	geschlafen
schlagen (schlägt)	*to beat, to hit*	schlug	geschlagen
schließen	*to close*	schloss	geschlossen
schlingen	*to loop, to gulp*	schlang	geschlungen
schneiden	*to cut*	schnitt	geschnitten
schreiben	*to write*	schrieb	geschrieben
schwimmen	*to swim*	schwamm	(ist) geschwommen
sehen (sieht)	*to see*	sah	gesehen
sein (ist)	*to be*	war	(ist) gewesen
senden	*to send*	sandte/sendete	gesandt/gesendet
singen	*to sing*	sang	gesungen
sinken	*to sink*	sank	(ist) gesunken
sitzen	*to sit*	saß	gesessen
sollen (soll)	*to be supposed to*	sollte	gesollt
sprechen (spricht)	*to speak*	sprach	gesprochen
stehen	*to stand*	stand	gestanden
stehlen (stiehlt)	*to steal*	stahl	gestohlen
steigen	*to climb, to rise*	stieg	(ist) gestiegen
sterben (stirbt)	*to die*	starb	(ist) gestorben
stoßen	*to push, to thrust*	stieß	(hat/ist) gestoßen
streichen	*to paint, to cancel*	strich	gestrichen
streiten	*to argue*	stritt	gestritten
tragen (trägt)	*to carry*	trug	getragen
treffen (trifft)	*to hit, to meet*	traf	getroffen
treten (tritt)	*to kick, to step*	trat	(hat/ist) getreten
trinken	*to drink*	trank	getrunken
tun	*to do*	tat	getan
vergessen (vergisst)	*to forget*	vergaß	vergessen

Infinitiv		Präteritum	Partizip II
verlieren	*to lose*	verlor	verloren
wachsen (wächst)	*to grow*	wuchs	(ist) gewachsen
waschen (wäscht)	*to wash*	wusch	gewaschen
weisen	*to indicate, to show*	wies	gewiesen
wenden	*to turn, to flip*	wandte/wendete	gewandt/gewendet
werben (wirbt)	*to advertise*	warb	geworben
werden (wird)	*to become*	wurde	(ist) geworden
werfen (wirft)	*to throw*	warf	geworfen
winden	*to wind*	wand	gewunden
wissen (weiß)	*to know*	wusste	gewusst
wollen (will)	*to want*	wollte	gewollt
ziehen	*to pull, to draw, to move*	zog	(hat/ist) gezogen

Glossary

This glossary includes all active vocabulary introduced in **Mosaik**, as well as some additional words and expressions. The singular and plural endings listed for adjectival nouns are those that occur after a definite article. The numbers following each entry are as follows:
(2) **1A** = (**Mosaik** Volume) **Chapter, Lesson**
The entry would be in **Mosaik 2**, Chapter 1, Lesson A.

Abbreviations used in this glossary

acc. accusative
adj. adjective
adv. adverb
conj. conjunction
dat. dative
f. feminine noun
form. formal
gen. genitive
inf. informal
interr. interrogative
m. masculine noun
n. neuter noun
nom. nominative
pl. plural
poss. possessive
prep. preposition
pron. pronoun
sing. singular
v. verb

Deutsch-Englisch

A

abbiegen *v.* to turn (2) **4A**
rechts/links abbiegen *v.* to turn right/left (2) **4A**
abbrechen *v.* to cancel (2) **3B**
Abend, -e *m.* evening (1) **2B**
abends *adv.* in the evening (1) **2A**
Abendessen, - *n.* dinner (1) **4B**
aber *conj.* but (1) **1B**
abfahren *v.* to leave (2) **4A**
Abfall, ¨e *m.* waste (3) **4B**
abfliegen *v.* to take off (2) **3B**
Abflug, ¨e *m.* departure (2) **3B**
abheben *v.* to withdraw (money) (3) **3A**
Absatz, ¨e *m.* paragraph (2) **1B**
abschicken *v.* to send (3) **3B**
Abschied, -e *m.* leave-taking; farewell (1) **1A**
Abschluss, ¨e *m.* degree (1) **2A**
einen Abschluss machen *v.* to graduate (2) **1A**
Abschlusszeugnis, -se *n.* diploma (transcript) (1) **2A**
abstauben *v.* to dust (2) **2B**
sich abtrocknen *v.* to dry oneself off (3) **1A**
acht eight (1) **2A**
Achtung! Attention!
adoptieren *v.* to adopt (1) **3A**
Adresse, -n *f.* address (3) **2A**
Allee, -n *f.* avenue (3) **2B**
allein *adv.* alone; by oneself (1) **4A**
Allergie, -n *f.* allergy (3) **1B**
allergisch (gegen) *adj.* allergic (to) (3) **1B**
alles *pron.* everything (2) **3B**
Alles klar? Everything OK? (1) **1A**
alles Gute all the best (3) **2A**
Alles Gute zum Geburtstag! Happy birthday! (2) **1A**
Alltagsroutine, -n *f.* daily routine (3) **1A**
im Alltag in everyday life
als *conj.* as; when (2) **4A**
als ob as if (3) **2A**
also *conj.* therefore; so (3) **1B**
alt *adj.* old (1) **3A**
Altkleider *pl.* second-hand clothing (3) **4B**
Altpapier *n.* used paper (3) **4B**
Amerika *n.* America (3) **2B**
amerikanisch *adj.* American (3) **2B**
Amerikaner, - / Amerikanerin, -nen *m./f.* American (3) **2B**
Ampel, -n *f.* traffic light (3) **2B**
an *prep.* at; on; by; in; to (2) **1B**, (3) **2B**
Ananas, - *f.* pineapple (1) **4A**
anbieten *v.* to offer (3) **4B**
anfangen *v.* to begin (1) **4A**
Angebot, -e *n.* offer
im Angebot on sale (2) **1B**
angeln gehen *v.* to go fishing (1) **2B**
angenehm *adj.* pleasant (1) **3B**
Angenehm. Nice to meet you. (1) **1A**
angesagt *adj.* trendy (2) **1B**
Angestellte, -n *m./f.* employee (3) **3A**
Angst, ¨e *f.* fear (2) **3A**
Angst haben (vor) *v.* to be afraid (of) (2) **3A**
ankommen *v.* to arrive (1) **4A**
Ankunft, ¨e *f.* arrival (2) **3B**
Anlass, ¨e *m.* occasion (2) **1A**
besondere Anlässe *m. pl.* special occasions (2) **1A**
anmachen *v.* to turn on (2) **4B**
Anruf, -e *m.* phone call (3) **3A**
einen Anruf entgegennehmen *v.* to answer the phone (3) **3A**
anrufen *v.* to call (1) **4A**
sich anrufen *v.* to call each other (3) **1A**
anschauen *v.* to watch, look at (2) **3A**
anspruchsvoll *adj.* demanding (3) **3B**
anstatt *prep.* instead of (2) **4B**
anstoßen *v.* to toast (2) **1A**
Antwort, -en *f.* answer
antworten (auf) *v.* to answer (1) **2A**
Anwendung *f.* application; usage
anziehen *v.* to put on (2) **1B**
sich anziehen *v.* to get dressed (3) **1A**
Anzug, ¨e *m.* suit (2) **1B**
Apfel, ¨ *m.* apple (1) **1A**
Apotheke, -n *f.* pharmacy (3) **1B**
April *m.* April (1) **2A**, (2) **3A**
Arbeit, -en *f.* work (3) **3B**
Arbeit finden *v.* to find a job (3) **3A**
arbeiten (an) *v.* to work (on) (1) **2A**, (2) **3A**
arbeitslos *adj.* unemployed (3) **2A**
Arbeitszimmer, - *n.* home office (2) **2A**
Architekt, -en / Architektin, -nen *m./f.* architect (1) **3B**
Architektur, -en *f.* architecture (1) **2A**
sich ärgern (über) *v.* to get angry (about) (3) **1A**
arm *adj.* poor; unfortunate (1) **3B**
Arm, -e *m.* arm (3) **1A**
Art, -en *f.* species; type (3) **4B**
Artischocke, -n *f.* artichoke (1) **4A**
Arzt, ¨e / Ärztin, -nen *m./f.* doctor (3) **1B**
zum Arzt gehen *v.* to go to the doctor (3) **1B**
Assistent, -en / Assistentin, -nen *m./f.* assistant (3) **3A**
Aubergine, -n *f.* eggplant (1) **4A**
auch *adv.* also (1) **1A**
auf *prep.* on, onto, to (2) **1B**
Auf Wiedersehen. Good-bye. (1) **1A**
aufgehen *v.* to rise (sun) (3) **4A**
auflegen *v.* to hang up (3) **3A**
aufmachen *v.* to open (2) **4B**
aufnehmen *v.* to record (2) **4B**
aufräumen *v.* to clean up (2) **2B**
aufregend *adj.* exciting (3) **4A**
aufrichtig *adj.* sincere (1) **3B**
aufstehen *v.* to get up (1) **4A**
aufwachen *v.* to wake up (3) **1A**
Auge, -n *n.* eye (1) **3A**; (3) **1A**
Augenbraue, -n *f.* eyebrow (3) **1A**
August *m.* August (1) **2A**, (2) **3A**
aus *prep.* from (1) **4A**
Ausbildung, -en *f.* education (3) **3A**
Ausdruck, ¨e *m.* expression
Ausfahrt, -en *f.* exit (2) **4A**
ausfüllen *v.* to fill out (3) **2A**
ein Formular ausfüllen *v.* to fill out a form (3) **2A**
Ausgang ¨e *m.* exit (2) **3B**
ausgefallen *adj.* offbeat (2) **1B**
ausgehen *v.* to go out (1) **4A**
Ausland *n.* abroad (2) **3B**
ausmachen *v.* to turn off (2) **4B**
sich ausruhen *v.* to rest (3) **1A**
ausschalten *v.* turn out, to turn off (3) **4B**
Aussehen *n.* look (style) (2) **1B**
außer *prep.* except (for) (1) **4B**
außerhalb *prep.* outside of (2) **4B**
Aussprache *f.* pronunciation
Aussterben *n.* extinction (3) **4B**
sich ausziehen *v.* to get undressed (3) **1A**
Auto, -s *n.* car (1) **1A**, (2) **4A**
Autobahn, -en *f.* highway (2) **4A**

B

Baby, -s *n.* baby (1) **3A**
Bäckerei, -en *f.* bakery (1) **4A**
Badeanzug, ¨e *m.* bathing suit (2) **1B**
Bademantel, ¨ *m.* bathrobe (3) **1A**
sich baden *v.* to bathe, take a bath (3) **1A**
Badewanne, -n *f.* bathtub (2) **2A**
Badezimmer, - *n.* bathroom (2) **2A**, (3) **1A**
Bahnsteig, -e *m.* track; platform (2) **4A**
bald *adv.* soon
Bis bald. See you soon. (1) **1A**
Balkon, -e/-s *m.* balcony (2) **2A**
Ball, ¨e *m.* ball (1) **2B**
Ballon, -e/-s *m.* balloon (2) **1A**
Banane, -n *f.* banana (1) **4A**

Bank, ¨e *f.* bench (3) **2B**
Bank, -en *f.* bank (3) **2A**
auf der Bank *f.* at the bank (3) **2B**
Bankangestellte, -n *m./f.* bank employee (3) **3B**
bar *adj.* cash (3) **2A**
bar bezahlen *v.* to pay in cash (3) **2A**
Bargeld *n.* cash (3) **2A**
Bart, ¨e *m.* beard (3) **1A**
Baseball *m.* baseball (1) **2B**
Basketball *m.* basketball (1) **2B**
Bauch, ¨e *m.* belly (3) **1A**
Bauchschmerzen *m. pl.* stomachache (3) **1B**
bauen *v.* to build (1) **2A**
Bauer, -n / Bäuerin, -nen *m./f.* farmer (3) **3B**
Bauernhof, ¨e *m.* farm (3) **4A**
Baum, ¨e *m.* tree (3) **4A**
Baumwolle *f.* cotton (2) **1B**
Baustelle, -n *f.* construction zone (2) **4A**
beantworten *v.* to answer (1) **4B**
bedeuten *v.* to mean (1) **2A**
bedeutend *adj.* important (3) **4A**
bedienen *v.* to operate, use (2) **4B**
sich beeilen *v.* to hurry (3) **1A**
Beförderung, -en *f.* promotion (3) **3B**
beginnen *v.* to begin (2) **2A**
Begrüßung, -en *f.* greeting (1) **1A**
behaupten *v.* to claim (3) **4B**
bei *prep.* at; near; with (1) **4A**
Beilage, -n *f.* side dish (1) **4B**
Bein, -e *n.* leg (3) **1A**
Beitrag ¨e *m.* contribution (3) **4B**
bekannt *adj.* well-known (3) **2A**
bekommen *v.* to get, to receive (2) **1A**
belegen *v.* to take (a class) (1) **2A**
benutzen *v.* to use (2) **4A**
Benutzername, -n *m.* screen name (2) **4B**
Benzin, -e *n.* gasoline (2) **4A**
Berg -e *m.* mountain (1) **2B**, (3) **4A**
berichten *v.* to report (3) **4B**
Beruf, -e *m.* profession; job (1) **3B**, (3) **3A**
Berufsausbildung, -en *f.* professional training (3) **3A**
bescheiden *adj.* modest (1) **3B**
beschreiben *v.* to describe (1) **2A**
Beschreibung, -en *f.* description (1) **3B**
Besen, - *m.* broom (2) **2B**
Besitzer, - / Besitzerin, -nen *m./f.* owner (1) **3B**
besonderes *adj.* special (3) **2A**
nichts Besonderes *adj.* nothing special (3) **2A**
besorgt *adj.* worried (1) **3B**
Besorgung, -en *f.* errand (3) **2A**
Besorgungen machen *v.* to run errands (3) **2A**
besprechen *v.* to discuss (2) **3A**
Besprechung, -en *f.* meeting (3) **3A**
besser *adj.* better (2) **4A**
Besserwisser, - / Besserwisserin, -nen *m./f.* know-it-all (1) **2A**
beste *adj.* best (2) **4A**
Besteck *n.* silverware (1) **4B**
bestehen *v.* to pass (a test) (1) **1B**
bestellen *v.* to order (1) **4A**
bestimmt *adv.* definitely (1) **4A**
besuchen *v.* to visit (1) **4A**
Bett, -en *n.* bed (2) **2A**
das Bett machen *v.* to make the bed (2) **2B**
ins Bett gehen *v.* to go bed (3) **1A**
Bettdecke, - n *f.* duvet (2) **2B**
bevor *conj.* before (2) **4A**
sich bewegen *v.* to move (around)
sich bewerben *v.* to apply (3) **3A**
Bewerber, - / die Bewerberin, -nen *m./f.* applicant (3) **3A**
Bewertung, -en *f.* rating (2) **3B**
bezahlen *v.* to pay (for) (1) **4A**
Bibliothek, -en *f.* library (1) **1B**
Bier, -e *n.* beer (1) **4B**
bieten *v.* to offer (3) **1B**
Bild, -er *n.* picture (2) **2A**
Bildschirm, -e *m.* screen (2) **4B**
Bioladen, ¨ *m.* health-food store (3) **1B**
Biologie *f.* biology (1) **2A**
biologisch *adj.* organic (3) **4B**
Birne, -n *f.* pear (1) **4A**
bis *prep.* until (1) **3B**
Bis bald. See you soon. (1) **1A**
Bis dann. See you later. (1) **1A**
Bis gleich. See you soon. (1) **1A**
Bis morgen. See you tomorrow. (1) **1A**
Bis später. See you later. (1) **1A**
bis zu *prep.* up to; until (3) **2B**
Bitte. Please.; You're welcome. (1) **1A**
Blatt, ¨er *n.* leaf (3) **4A**
blau *adj.* blue (1) **3A**
blaue Fleck, -e *m.* bruise (3) **B1**
bleiben *v.* to stay (2) **1B**
Bleiben Sie bitte am Apparat. *v.* Please hold. (3) **3A**
Bleistift, -e *m.* pencil (1) **1B**
Blitz, -e *m.* lightning (2) **3A**
blond *adj.* blond (1) **3A**
blonde Haare *n. pl.* blond hair (1) **3A**
Blume, -n *f.* flower (1) **1A**
Blumengeschäft, -e *n.* flower shop (3) **2A**
Bluse, -n *f.* blouse (2) **1B**
Blutdruck *m.* blood pressure (3) **1B**
Boden, ¨ *m.* floor; ground (2) **2A**
Bohne, -n *f.* bean (1) **4A**
grüne Bohne *f.* green bean (1) **4A**
Boot, -e *n.* boat (2) **4A**
Bordkarte, -n *f.* boarding pass (2) **3B**
braten *v.* to fry (1) **2B**
brauchen *v.* to need (1) **2A**
braun *adj.* brown (2) **1B**
braunhaarig *adj.* brown-haired, brunette (1) **3A**
brechen *v.* to break (1) **2B**
sich (den Arm / das Bein) brechen *v.* to break (an arm / a leg) (3) **1B**
Bremse, -n *f.* brake (2) **4A**
brennen *v.* to burn (2) **1A**
Brief, -e *m.* letter (3) **2A**
einen Brief abschicken *v.* to mail a letter (3) **2A**
Briefkasten, ¨ *m.* mailbox (3) **2A**
Briefmarke, -n *f.* stamp (3) **2A**
Briefträger, - / Briefträgerin, -nen *m./f.* mail carrier (3) **2A**
Briefumschlag, ¨e *m.* envelope (3) **2A**
Brille, -n *f.* glasses (2) **1B**
bringen *v.* to bring (1) **2A**
Brot, -e *n.* bread (1) **4A**
Brötchen, - *n.* roll (1) **4A**
Brücke, -n *f.* bridge (3) **2B**
Bruder, ¨ *m.* brother (1) **1A**
Brunnen, - *m.* fountain (3) **2B**
Buch, ¨er *n.* book (1) **1A**
buchen *v.* to make a (hotel) reservation (2) **3B**
Bücherregal, -e *n.* bookshelf (2) **2A**
Buchhalter, - / Buchhalterin, -nen *m./f.* accountant (3) **3B**
büffeln *v.* to cram (for a test) (1) **2A**
Bügelbrett, -er *n.* ironing board (2) **2B**
Bügeleisen, - *n.* iron (2) **2B**
bügeln *v.* to iron (2) **2B**
Bundespräsident, -en / Bundespräsidentin, -nen *m./f.* (federal) president (2) **4B**
bunt *adj.* colorful (3) **2A**
Bürgermeister, - / Bürgermeisterin, -nen *m./f.* mayor (3) **2B**
Bürgersteig, -e *m.* sidewalk (3) **2B**
Büro, -s *n.* office (3) **3B**
Büroklammer, -n *f.* paperclip (3) **3A**
Büromaterial *n.* office supplies (3) **3A**
Bürste, -n *f.* brush (3) **1A**
bürsten *v.* to brush
sich die Haare bürsten *v.* to brush one's hair (3) **1A**
Bus, -se *m.* bus (2) **4A**
Busch, ¨e *m.* bush (3) **4A**
Bushaltestelle, -n *f.* bus stop (2) **4A**
Businessklasse *f.* business class (2) **3B**
Bußgeld, -er *n.* fine (monetary) (2) **4A**
Butter *f.* butter (1) **4A**

C

Café, -s *n.* café (1) **2A**
Camping *n.* camping (1) **2B**
CD, -s *f.* compact disc, CD (2) **4B**
Chef, -s / Chefin, -nen *m./f.* boss (3) **3B**
Chemie *f.* chemistry (1) **2A**
China *n.* China (3) **2B**
Chinese, -n / Chinesin, -nen *m./f.* Chinese (person) (3) **2B**
Chinesisch *n.* Chinese (language) (3) **2B**
Computer, - *m.* computer (1) **1B**
Cousin, -s / Cousine, -n *m./f.* cousin (1) **3A**

D

da there (1) **1A**
Da ist/sind... There is/are... (1) **1A**
Dachboden, ¨ *m.* attic (2) **2A**
dafür *adv.* for it (2) **2A**
daher *adv.* from there (2) **2A**
dahin *adv.* there (2) **2A**
damit *conj.* so that (3) **2A**
danach *conj.* then, after that (3) **1B**
danken *v.* to thank (1) **2A**
Danke. Thank you. (1) **1A**
dann *adv.* then (2) **3B**
daran *adv.* on it (2) **2A**

darauf *adv.* on it (2) **2A**
darin *adv.* in it (2) **2A**
das *n.* the; this/that (1) **1A**
dass *conj.* that (3) **2A**
Datei, - en *f.* file (2) **4B**
Datum (*pl.* Daten) *n.* date (2) **3A**
davon *adv.* of it (2) **2A**
davor *adv.* before it (2) **2A**
Decke, -n *f.* blanket (2) **2B**
decken *v.* to cover (2) **2B**
den Tisch decken *v.* to set the table (2) **2B**
denken *v.* to think (2) **1A**
denken an *v.* to think about (2) **3A**
denn *conj.* for; because (2) **2A**
der *m.* the (1) **1A**
deshalb *conj.* therefore; so (3) **1B**
deswegen *conj.* that's why; therefore (3) **1B**
deutsch *adj.* German (3) **2B**
Deutsch *n.* German (language) (3) **2B**
Deutsche *m./f.* German (man/woman) (3) **2B**
Deutschland *n.* Germany (1) **4A**
deutschsprachig *adj.* German-speaking
Dezember *m.* December (1) **2A**, (2) **3A**
Diät, -en *f.* diet (1) **4B**
auf Diät sein *v.* to be on a diet (1) **4B**
dick *adj.* fat (1) **3A**
die *f./pl.* the (1) **1A**
Dienstag, -e *m.* Tuesday (1) **2A**
dienstags *adv.* on Tuesdays (1) **2A**
dieser/diese/dieses *m./f./n.* this; these (2) **4B**
diesmal *adv.* this time (2) **3B**
Digitalkamera, -s *f.* digital camera (2) **4B**
Ding, -e *n.* thing
Diplom, -e *n.* diploma (degree) (1) **2A**
diskret *adj.* discreet (1) **3B**
doch *adv.* yes (contradicting a negative statement or question) (1) **2B**
Dokument, -e *n.* document (2) **4B**
Donner, - *m.* thunder (2) **3A**
Donnerstag, -e *n.* Thursday (1) **2A**
donnerstags *adv.* on Thursdays (1) **2A**
dort *adv.* there (1) **1A**
Dozent, -en / Dozentin, -nen *m./f.* college instructor (1) **2A**
draußen *prep.* outside; *adv.* out (2) **3A**
Es ist schön draußen. It's nice out. (2) **3A**
dreckig *adj.* filthy (2) **2B**
drei three (1) **2A**
dritte *adj.* third (1) **2A**
Drogerie, -n *f.* drugstore (3) **2A**
drüben *adv.* over there (1) **4A**
drücken *v.* to push (1) **3B**; to print (2) **4B**
Drucker, - *m.* printer (2) **4B**
du *pron.* (*sing. inf.*) you (1) **1A**
dumm *adj.* dumb (2) **4A**
dunkel *adj.* dark (1) **3A**
dunkelhaarig *adj.* dark-haired (1) **3A**
dünn *adj.* thin (1) **3A**
durch *prep.* through (1) **3B**
durchfallen *v.* to flunk; to fail (1) **1B**
durchmachen *v.* to experience (2) **4B**
dürfen *v.* to be allowed to; may (1) **3B**
(sich) duschen *v.* to take a shower (3) **1A**
Dutzend, -e *n.* dozen (1) **4A**
DVD, -s *f.* DVD (2) **4B**
DVD-Player, - *m.* DVD-player (2) **4B**

E

Ecke, -n *f.* corner (3) **2B**
egoistisch *adj.* selfish (1) **3B**
Ehe, -n *f.* marriage (2) **1A**
Ehefrau, -en *f.* wife (1) **3A**
Ehemann, ¨-er *m.* husband (1) **3A**
Ei, -er *n.* egg (1) **4A**
Eichhörnchen, - *n.* squirrel (3) **4A**
eifersüchtig *adj.* jealous (1) **3B**
ein/eine *m./f./n.* a (1) **1A**
Einbahnstraße, -n *f.* one-way street (2) **4A**
einfach *adj.* easy (1) **2A**
einfarbig *adj.* solid colored (2) **1B**
eingebildet *adj.* arrogant (1) **3B**
einkaufen *v.* to shop (1) **4A**
einkaufen gehen *v.* to go shopping (1) **4A**
Einkaufen *n.* shopping (2) **1B**
Einkaufszentrum, (*pl.* Einkaufszentren) *n.* mall; shopping center (3) **2B**
Einkommensgruppe, -n *f.* income bracket (2) **2B**
einladen *v.* to invite (2) **1A**
einmal *adv.* once (2) **3B**
eins one (1) **2A**
einschlafen *v.* to go to sleep (1) **4A**
einzahlen *v.* to deposit (money) (3) **2A**
Einzelkind, -er *n.* only child (1) **3A**
Eis *n.* ice cream (2) **1A**
Eisdiele, -n *f.* ice cream shop (1) **4A**
Eishockey *n.* ice hockey (1) **2B**
Eiswürfel, - *m.* ice cube (2) **1A**
elegant *adj.* elegant (2) **1B**
Elektriker, - / Elektrikerin, -nen *m./f.* electrician (3) **3B**
elf eleven (1) **2A**
Ell(en)bogen, - *m.* elbow (3) **1A**
Eltern *pl.* parents (1) **3A**
E-Mail, -s *f.* e-mail (2) **4B**
empfehlen *v.* to recommend (1) **2B**
Empfehlungsschreiben, - *n.* letter of recommendation (3) **3A**
endlich *adv.* finally (3) **1B**
Energie, -n *f.* energy (3) **4B**
energiesparend *adj.* energy-efficient (2) **2B**
eng *adj.* tight (2) **1B**
England *n.* England (3) **2B**
Engländer, - / Engländerin, -nen *m./f.* English (person) (3) **2B**
Englisch *n.* English (language) (3) **2B**
Enkelkind, -er *n.* grandchild (1) **3A**
Enkelsohn, ¨-e *m.* grandson (1) **3A**
Enkeltochter, ¨- *f.* granddaughter (1) **3A**
entdecken *v.* to discover (2) **2B**
entfernen *v.* to remove (2) **2B**
entlang *prep.* along, down (1) **3B**
entlassen *v.* to fire; to lay off (3) **3B**
sich entschließen *v.* to decide (1) **4B**
(sich) entschuldigen *v.* to apologize; to excuse
Entschuldigen Sie. Excuse me. (*form.*) (1)**1A**
Entschuldigung. Excuse me. (1) **1A**
sich entspannen *v.* to relax (3) **1A**
entwerten *v.* to validate (2) **4A**
eine Fahrkarte entwerten *v.* to validate a ticket (2) **4A**
entwickeln *v.* to develop (3) **4B**
er *pron.* he (1) **1A**
Erdbeben, - *n.* earthquake (3) **4A**
Erdbeere, -n *f.* strawberry (1) **4A**
Erde, -n *f.* earth (3) **4B**
Erderwärmung *f.* global warming (3) **4B**
Erdgeschoss, -e *n.* ground floor (2) **2A**
Erfahrung, -en *f.* experience (3) **3A**
erfinden *v.* to invent (2) **3A**
Erfolg, -e *m.* success (3) **3B**
erforschen *v.* to explore (3) **4A**
ergänzen *v.* complete
Ergebnis, -se *n.* result; score (1) **1B**
erhalten *v.* to preserve (3) **4B**
sich erinnern (an) *v.* to remember (3) **1A**
sich erkälten *v.* to catch a cold (3) **1A**
Erkältung, -en *f.* cold (3) **1B**
erkennen *v.* to recognize (2) **3A**
erklären *v.* to explain (1) **4A**
erneuerbare Energie, -n *f.* renewable energy (3) **4B**
ernst *adj.* serious (1) **3B**
erster/erste/erstes *adj.* first (1) **2A**
erwachsen *adj.* grown-up (3) **2A**
erzählen *v.* to tell (2) **3A**
erzählen von *v.* to talk about (2) **3A**
es *pron.* it (1) **1A**
Es geht. (I'm) so-so. (1) **1A**
Es gibt... There is/are... (1) **2B**
Essen, - *n.* food (1) **4A**
essen *v.* to eat (1) **2B**
essen gehen *v.* to eat out (1) **2B**
Esslöffel, - *m.* soup spoon (1) **4B**
Esszimmer, - *n.* dining room (2) **2A**
etwas *pron.* something (2) **3B**
etwas anderes something else (3) **2A**
euer (*pl. inf.*) *poss. adj.* your (1) **3A**

F

Fabrik, -en *f.* factory (3) **4B**
Fabrikarbeiter, - / Fabrikarbeiterin, -nen *m./f.* factory worker (3) **3B**
Fach, ¨-er *n.* subject (1) **2A**
fade *adj.* bland (1) **4B**
fahren *v.* to drive; to go (1) **2B**
Auto fahren *v.* to drive a car (2) **4A**
Fahrrad fahren *v.* to ride a bicycle (1) **2B**
geradeaus fahren *v.* to go straight ahead (2) **4A**
Fahrer, - / Fahrerin, -nen *m./f.* driver (2) **4A**
Fahrgemeinschaft, -en *f.* carpool (3) **4B**
Fahrkarte, -n *f.* ticket (2) **4A**
eine Fahrkarte entwerten *v.* to validate a ticket (2) **4A**
Fahrkartenschalter, - *m.* ticket office (2) **4A**
Fahrplan, ¨-e *m.* schedule (2) **4A**
Fahrrad, ¨-er *n.* bicycle (1) **2B**, (2) **4A**
Fahrstuhl, ¨-e *m.* elevator (2) **3B**
fallen *v.* to fall (1)**2B**

Familie, -n *f.* family (1) **3A**
Familienstand, ¨-e *m.* marital status (1) **3A**
Fan, -s *m.* fan (1) **2B**
fangen *v.* to catch (1) **2B**
fantastisch *adj.* fantastic (3) **2A**
Farbe, -n *f.* color (2) **1B**
färben *v.* to dye
sich die Haare färben *v.* to dye one's hair (3) **1A**
fast *adv.* almost (1) **4A**
faul *adj.* lazy (1) **3B**
Februar *m.* February (1) **2A**, (2) **3A**
fegen *v.* to sweep (2) **2B**
feiern *v.* to celebrate (2) **1A**
Feiertag, -e *m.* holiday (2) **1A**
Feinkostgeschäft, -e *n.* delicatessen (1) **4A**
Feld, -er *n.* field (3) **4A**
Fenster, - *n.* window (1) **1A**
Ferien *pl.* vacation (2) **3A**
Fernbedienung, -en *f.* remote control (2) **4B**
fernsehen *v.* to watch television (2) **4B**
Fernsehen *n.* television (programming)
Fernseher, - *m.* television set (2) **4B**
fertig *adj.* ready; finished (3) **3B**
Fest, -e *n.* festival; celebration (2) **1A**
Festplatte, -n *f.* hard drive (2) **4B**
Feuerwehrmann, ¨-er / Feuerwehrfrau, -en (*pl.* Feuerwehrleute) *m./f.* firefighter (3) **3B**
Fieber, - *n.* fever (3) **1B**
Fieber haben *v.* to have a fever (3) **1B**
finden *v.* to find (1) **2A**
Finger, - *m.* finger (3) **1A**
Firma (*pl.* die Firmen) *f.* firm; company (3) **3A**
Fisch, -e *m.* fish (1) **4A**, (3) **4A**
Fischgeschäft, -e *n.* fish store (1) **4A**
fit *adj.* in good shape (1) **2B**
Flasche, -n *f.* bottle (1) **4B**
Fleisch *n.* meat (1) **4A**
fleißig *adj.* hard-working (1) **3B**
fliegen *v.* to fly (2) **3B**
Flug, ¨-e *m.* flight (2) **3B**
Flughafen, ¨- *m.* airport (2) **3B**
Flugticket, -s *n.* (plane) ticket (2) **3B**
Flugzeug, -e *n.* airplane (2) **3B**
Flur, -e *m.* hall (2) (1) **2A**
Fluss, ¨-e *m.* river (1) **3B**, (3) **4A**
folgen *v.* to follow (2) **1A**, (3) **2B**
Form, -en *f.* shape, form
in guter/schlechter Form sein *v.* to be in/out of shape (3) **1B**
Formular, -e *n.* form (3) **2A**
ein Formular ausfüllen *v.* to fill out a form (3) **2A**
Foto, -s *n.* photo, picture (1) **1B**
Frage, -n *f.* question (1) **1B**
fragen *v.* to ask (1) **2A**
fragen nach *v.* to ask about (2) **3A**
sich fragen *v.* to wonder, ask oneself (3) **1A**
Frankreich *n.* France (3) **2B**
Franzose, -n / Französin, -nen *m./f.* French (person) (3) **2B**
Französisch *n.* French (language) (3) **2B**
Frau, -en *f.* woman (1) **1A**; wife (1) **3A**
Frau... Mrs./Ms.... (1) **1A**
Freitag, -e *m.* Friday (1) **2A**
freitags *adv.* on Fridays (1) **2A**
Freizeit, -en *f.* free time, leisure (1) **2B**
Freizeitaktivität, - en *f.* leisure activity (1) **2B**
Fremdsprache, -n *f.* foreign language (1) **2A**
sich freuen (über) *v.* to be happy (about) (3) **1A**
Freut mich. Pleased to meet you. (1) **1A**
sich freuen auf *v.* to look forward to (3) **1A**
Freund, -e / Freundin, -nen *m./f.* friend (1) **1A**
freundlich *adj.* friendly (1) **3B**
Mit freundlichen Grüßen Yours sincerely (1) **3B**
Freundschaft, -en *f.* friendship (2) **1A**
Frischvermählte, -n *m./f.* newlywed (2) **1A**
Friseur, -e / Friseurin, -nen *m./f.* hairdresser (1) **3B**
froh *adj.* happy (1) **3B**
Frohe Ostern! Happy Easter! (2) **1A**
Frohe Weihnachten! Merry Christmas! (2) **1A**
früh *adj.* early; in the morning (1) **2B**
morgen früh tomorrow morning (1) **2B**
Frühling, -e *m.* spring (1) **2B**, (2) **3A**
Frühstück, -e *n.* breakfast (1) **4B**
fühlen *v.* to feel (1) **2A**
sich (wohl) fühlen *v.* to feel (well) (3) **1A**
füllen *v.* to fill
fünf five (1) **2A**
funktionieren *v.* to work, function (2) **4B**
für *prep.* for (1) **3B**
furchtbar *adj.* awful (2) **3A**
Fuß, ¨-e *m.* foot (3) **1A**
Fußball *m.* soccer (1) **2B**
Fußgänger, - / Fußgängerin, -nen *m./f.* pedestrian (3) **2B**

G

Gabel, -n *f.* fork (1) **4B**
Gang, ¨-e *m.* course (1) **4B**
erster/zweiter Gang *m.* first/second course (1) **4B**
ganz *adj.* all, total (2) **3B**
ganztags *adj.* full-time (3) **3B**
Garage, -n *f.* garage (2) **1B**
Garnele, -n *f.* shrimp (1) **4A**
Gartenabfall, ¨-e *m.* yard waste (3) **4B**
Gärtner, - /Gärtnerin, -nen *m./f.* gardener (3) **3B**
Gast, ¨-e *m.* guest (2) **1A**
Gastfamilie, -n *f.* host family (1) **4B**
Gastgeber, - / Gastgeberin, -nen *m./f.* host/hostess (2) **1A**
Gebäck, -e *n.* pastries; baked goods (2) **1A**
Gebäude, - *n.* building (3) **2A**
geben *v.* to give (1) **2B**
Es gibt... There is/are... (1) **2B**
Geburt, -en *f.* birth (2) **1A**
Geburtstag, -e *m.* birthday (2) **1A**
Wann hast du Geburtstag? When is your birthday? (2) **3A**
geduldig *adj.* patient (1) **3B**
Gefahr, -en *f.* danger (3) **4B**
gefährdet *adj.* endangered; threatened (3) **4B**
gefallen *v.* to please (2) **1A**
Gefrierschrank, ¨-e *m.* freezer (2) **2B**
gegen *prep.* against (1) **3B**
gegenüber (von) *prep.* across (from) (3) **2B**
Gehalt, ¨-er *n.* salary (3) **3A**
hohes/niedriges Gehalt, ¨-er *n.* high/low salary (3) **3A**
Gehaltserhöhung, -en *f.* raise (3) **3B**
gehen *v.* to go (1) **2A**
Es geht. (I'm) so-so. (1) **1A**
Geht es dir/Ihnen gut? *v.* Are you all right? (*inf./form.*) (1) **1A**
Wie geht es Ihnen? (*form.*) How are you? (1) **1A**
Wie geht's (dir)? (*inf.*) How are you? (1) **1A**
gehören *v.* to belong to (1) **4B**
Geländewagen, - *m.* SUV (2) **4B**
gelb *adj.* yellow (2) **1B**
Geld, -er *n.* money (3) **2A**
Geld abheben/einzahlen *v.* to withdraw/deposit money (3) **2A**
Geldautomat, -en *m.* ATM (3) **2A**
Geldschein, -e *m.* bill (money) (3) **2A**
gemein *adj.* mean (1) **3B**
Gemüse, - *n.* vegetables (1) **4A**
genau *adv.* exactly
genauso wie just as (2) **4A**
genießen *v.* to enjoy
geöffnet *adj.* open (3) **2A**
Gepäck *n.* luggage (2) **3B**
geradeaus *adv.* straight ahead (2) **4A**
gern *adv.* with pleasure (1) **2B**
gern (*+verb*) to like to (*+verb*) (1) **2B**
ich hätte gern... I would like... (1) **4A**
Gern geschehen. My pleasure.; You're welcome. (1) **1A**
Geschäft, -e *n.* business (3) **3A**; store (1) **4A**
Geschäftsführer, - / Geschäftsführerin, -nen *m./f.* manager (3) **3A**
Geschäftsmann, ¨-er / Geschäftsfrau, -en (*pl.* Geschäftsleute) *m./f.* businessman/businesswoman (1) **3B**
Geschenk, -e *n.* gift (2) **1A**
Geschichte, -n *f.* history (1) **2A**; story
geschieden *adj.* divorced (1) **3A**
Geschirr *n.* dishes (2) **2B**
Geschirr spülen *v.* to do the dishes (2) **2B**
geschlossen *adj.* closed (3) **2A**
Geschmack, ¨-e *m.* flavor; taste (1) **4B**
Geschwister, - *n.* sibling (1) **3A**
Gesetz, -e *n.* law (3) **4B**
Gesicht, -er *n.* face (3) **1A**
gestern *adv.* yesterday (2) **1B**
gestreift *adj.* striped (2) **1B**
gesund *adj.* healthy (2) **4A**; (3) **1B**
gesund werden *v.* to get better (3) **1B**
Gesundheit *f.* health (3) **1B**
geteilt durch divided by (1) **1B**
Getränk, -e *n.* beverage (1) **4B**
getrennt *adj.* separated (1) **3A**
gewaltfrei *adj.* nonviolent (3) **4B**
Gewerkschaft, -en *f.* labor union (3) **3B**
gewinnen *v.* to win (1) **2B**
Gewitter, - *n.* thunderstorm (2) **3A**
sich gewöhnen an *v.* to get used to (3) **1A**
gierig *adj.* greedy (1) **3B**
Giftmüll *m.* toxic waste (3) **4B**
Glas, ¨-er *n.* glass (1) **4B**
glatt *adj.* straight (1) **3A**
glatte Haare *n. pl.* straight hair (1) **3A**

glauben *v.* to believe (2) **1A**
gleich *adj.* same
ist gleich *v.* equals, is (1) **1B**
Glück *n.* happiness (2) **1A**
glücklich *adj.* happy (1) **3B**
Golf *n.* golf (1) **2B**
Grad *n.* degree (2) **3A**
Es sind 18 Grad draußen. It's 18 degrees out. (2) **3A**
Gramm, -e *n.* gram (1) **4A**
Granit, -e *m.* granite (2) **2B**
Gras, ¨-er *n.* grass (3) **4A**
gratulieren *v.* to congratulate (2) **1A**
grau *adj.* grey (2) **1B**
grausam *adj.* cruel
Grippe, -n *f.* flu (3) **1B**
groß *adj.* big; tall (1) **3A**
großartig *adj.* terrific (1) **3A**
Großeltern *pl.* grandparents (1) **1A**
Großmutter, ¨ *f.* grandmother (1) **3A**
Großvater, ¨ *m.* grandfather (1) **3A**
großzügig *adj.* generous (1) **3B**
grün *adj.* green (2) **1B**
grüne Bohne (*pl.* die grünen Bohnen) *f.* green bean (1) **4A**
Gruß, ¨-e *m.* greeting
Mit freundlichen Grüßen Yours sincerely (1) **3B**
grüßen *v.* to greet (1) **2A**
günstig *adj.* cheap (2) **1B**
Gürtel, - *m.* belt (2) **1B**
gut *adj.* good; *adv.* well (1) **1A**
gut aussehend *adj.* handsome (1) **3A**
gut gekleidet *adj.* well-dressed (2) **1B**
Gute Besserung! Get well! (2) **1A**
Guten Appetit! Enjoy your meal! (1) **4B**
Guten Abend! Good evening. (1) **1A**
Guten Morgen! Good morning. (1) **1A**
Gute Nacht! Good night. (1) **1A**
Guten Tag! Hello. (1) **1A**

H

Haar, -e *n.* hair (1) **3A**, (3) **1A**
Haartrockner, - *m.* hair dryer (3) **1A**
haben *v.* to have (1) **1B**
Hagel *m.* hail (2) **3A**
Hähnchen, - *n.* chicken (1) **4A**
halb half; half an hour before (1) **2A**
Halbbruder, ¨ *m.* half brother (1) **3A**
Halbschwester, -n *f.* half sister (1) **3A**
halbtags *adj.* part-time (3) **3B**
Hallo! Hello. (1) **1A**
Hals, ¨-e *m.* neck (3) **1A**
Hals- und Beinbruch! Break a leg! (2) **1A**
Halskette, -n *f.* necklace (2) **1B**
Hand, ¨-e *f.* hand (3) **1A**
handeln *v.* to act
handeln von *v.* to be about; have to do with (2) **3A**
Handgelenk, -e *n.* wrist (3) **1B**
Handgepäck *n.* carry-on luggage (2) **3B**
Handschuh, -e *m.* glove (2) **1B**
Handtasche, -n *f.* purse (2) **1B**
Handtuch, ¨-er *n.* towel (3) **1A**
Handy, -s *n.* cell phone (2) **4B**
hängen *v.* to hang (2) **1B**
Hase, -n *m.* hare (3) **4A**
hässlich *adj.* ugly (1) **3A**
Hauptspeise, -n *f.* main course (1) **4B**
Hauptstraße, -n *f.* main road (3) **2B**
Haus, ¨-er *n.* house (2) **2A**
nach Hause *adv.* home (2) **1B**
zu Hause *adv.* at home (1) **4A**
Hausarbeit *f.* housework (2) **2B**
Hausarbeit machen *v.* to do housework (2) **2B**
Hausaufgabe, -n *f.* homework (1) **1B**
Hausfrau, -en / Hausmann, ¨-er *f./m.* homemaker (3) **3B**
hausgemacht *adj.* homemade (1) **4B**
Hausmeister, - / Hausmeisterin, -nen *m./f.* caretaker; custodian (3) **3B**
Hausschuh, -e *m.* slipper (3) **1A**
Haustier, -e *n.* pet (1) **3A**
Heft, -e *n.* notebook (1) **1B**
Hefter, - *m.* stapler (3) **3A**
heiraten *v.* to marry (1) **3A**
heiß *adj.* hot (2) **3A**
heißen *v.* to be named (1) **2A**
Ich heiße... My name is… (1) **1A**
helfen *v.* to help (1) **2B**
helfen bei *v.* to help with (2) **3A**
hell *adj.* light (1) **3A**; bright (2) **1B**
Hemd, -en *n.* shirt (2) **1B**
herauf *adv.* up; upwards (2) **2A**
heraus *adv.* out (2) **2A**
Herbst, -e *m.* fall, autumn (1) **2B**, (2) **3A**
Herd, -e *m.* stove (2) **2B**
Herr Mr. (1) **1A**
herunter *adv.* down; downwards (2) **2A**
heruntergehen *v.* to go down (3) **2B**
die Treppe heruntergehen *v.* to go downstairs (3) **2B**
herunterladen *v.* to download (2) **4B**
Herz, -en *n.* heart
Herzlichen Glückwunsch! Congratulations! (2) **1A**
heute *adv.* today (1) **2B**
Heute ist der... Today is the… (1) **2A**
Welcher Tag ist heute? What day is it today? (2) **3A**
Der Wievielte ist heute? What is the date today? (1) **2A**
hier *adv.* here (1) **1A**
Hier ist/sind... Here is/are… (1) **1B**
Himmel *m.* sky (3) **4A**
hin und zurück there and back (2) **3B**
sich hinlegen *v.* to lie down (3) **1A**
sich hinsetzen *v.* to sit down (3) **1A**
hinter *prep.* behind (2) **1B**
hinterlassen *v.* to leave (behind)
eine Nachricht hinterlassen *v.* to leave a message (3) **3A**
Hobby, -s *n.* hobby (1) **2B**
hoch *adj.* high (2) **4A**
hochgehen *v.* to go up, climb up (3) **2B**
die Treppe hochgehen *v.* to go upstairs (3) **2B**
Hochwasser, - *n.* flood (3) **4B**
Hochzeit, -en *f.* wedding (2) **1A**
Hockey *n.* hockey (1) **2B**
Höflichkeit, -en *f.* courtesy; polite expression (1) **1A**
Holz, ¨-er *n.* wood (2) **2B**
hören *v.* to hear; listen to (1) **2A**
Hörer, - *m.* receiver (3) **3A**
Hörsaal (*pl.* Hörsäle) *m.* lecture hall (1) **2A**
Hose, -n *f.* pants (2) **1B**
kurze Hose *f.* shorts (2) **1B**
Hotel, -s *n.* hotel (2) **3B**
Fünf-Sterne-Hotel *n* five-star hotel. (2) **3B**
Hotelgast, ¨-e *m.* hotel guest (2) **3B**
hübsch *adj.* pretty (1) **3A**
Hund, -e *m.* dog (1) **3A**
Hundewetter *n.* terrible weather (2) **3A**
husten *v.* to cough (3) **1B**
Hut, ¨-e *m.* hat (2) **1B**
Hybridauto, -s *n.* hybrid car (3) **4B**

I

ich *pron.* I (1) **1A**
Idee, -n *f.* idea (1) **1A**
Ihr (*form., sing/pl.*) *poss. adj.* your (1) **3A**
ihr (*inf., pl.*) *pron.* you (1) **1A**; *poss. adj.* her, their (1) **3A**
immer *adv.* always (1) **4A**
Immobilienmakler, - / Immobilienmaklerin, -nen *m./f.* real estate agent (3) **3B**
in *prep.* in (2) **1B**
Inder, - / Inderin, -nen *m./f.* Indian (person) (3) **2B**
Indien *n.* India (3) **2B**
indisch *adj.* Indian (3) **2B**
Informatik *f.* computer science (1) **2A**
sich informieren (über) *v.* to find out (about) (3) **1A**
Ingenieur, -e / Ingenieurin, -nen *m./f.* engineer (1) **3B**
Innenstadt, ¨-e *f.* city center; downtown (3) **2B**
innerhalb *prep.* inside of, within (2) **4B**
Insel, -n *f.* island (3) **4A**
intellektuell *adj.* intellectual (1) **3B**
intelligent *adj.* intelligent (1) **3B**
interessant *adj.* interesting (1) **2A**
sich interessieren (für) *v.* to be interested (in) (3) **1A**
Internet *n.* Web (2) **4B**
im Internet surfen *v.* to surf the Web (2) **4B**
Internetcafé, -s *n.* internet café (3) **2A**
Italien *n.* Italy (3) **2B**
Italiener, - / Italienerin, -nen *m./f.* Italian (person) (3) **2B**
Italienisch *n.* Italian (language) (3) **2B**

J

ja yes (1) **1A**
Jacke, -n *f.* jacket (2) **1B**
Jahr, -e *n.* year (2) **3A**
Ein gutes neues Jahr! Happy New Year! (2) **1A**
Ich bin... Jahre alt. I am… years old (1) **1B**
Jahrestag, -e *m.* anniversary (2) **1A**
Jahreszeit, -en *f.* season (2) **3A**
Januar *m.* January (1) **2A**, (2) **3A**
Japan *n.* Japan (3) **2B**
Japaner, - / Japanerin, -nen *m./f.* Japanese (person) (3) **2B**
Japanisch *n.* Japanese (language) (3) **2B**
Jeans *f.* jeans (2) **1B**
jeder/jede/jedes *adj.* any, every, each (2) **4B**

jemand *pron.* someone (2) **3B**
jetzt *adv.* now (1) **4A**
joggen *v.* to jog (1) **2B**
Joghurt, -s *m.* yogurt (1) **4A**
Journalist, -en / Journalistin, -nen *m./f.* journalist (1) **3B**
Jugendherberge, -n *f.* youth hostel (2) **3B**
jugendlich *adj.* young; youthful (3) **2A**
Juli *m.* July (1) **2A**, (2) **3A**
jung *adj.* young (1) **3A**
Junge, -n *m.* boy (1) **1A**
Juni *m.* June (1) **2A**, (2) **3A**
Juweliergeschäft, -e *n.* jewelry store (3) **2A**

K

Kaffee, -s *m.* coffee (1) **4B**
Kaffeemaschine, -n *f.* coffeemaker (2) **2B**
Kalender, - *m.* calendar (1) **1B**
kalt *adj.* cold (2) **3A**
sich (die Haare) kämmen *v.* to comb (one's hair) (3) **1A**
Kanada *n.* Canada (3) **2B**
Kanadier, - / Kanadierin, -nen *m./f.* Canadian (3) **2B**
Kandidat, -en *m.* candidate (3) **3A**
Kaninchen, - *n.* rabbit (3) **4A**
Karotte, -n *f.* carrot (1) **4A**
Karriere, -n *f.* career (3) **3B**
Karte, -n *f.* map (1) **1B**, *f.* card (1) **2B**; (2) **1A**
eine Karte lesen *v.* to read a map (2) **3B**
mit der Karte bezahlen *v.* to pay by (credit) card (3) **2A**
Kartoffel, -n *f.* potato (1) **4A**
Käse, - *m.* cheese (1) **4A**
Katze, -n *f.* cat (1) **3A**
kaufen *v.* to buy (1) **2A**
Kaufhaus, ¨-er *n.* department store (3) **2B**
Kaution, -en *f.* security deposit (2) **2A**
kein *adj.* no (1) **2B**
Keine Zufahrt. Do not enter. (1) **3B**
Keks, -e *m.* cookie (2) **1A**
Keller, - *m.* cellar (2) **2A**
Kellner, - / Kellnerin, -nen *m./f.* waiter/waitress (1) **3B**, (1) **4B**
kennen *v.* to know, be familiar with (2) **1B**
sich kennen *v.* to know each other (3) **1A**
(sich) kennen lernen *v.* to meet (one another) (1) **1A**
Keramik, -en *f.* ceramic (2) **2B**
Kernenergie *f.* nuclear energy (2) **1B**
Kernkraftwerk, -e *n.* nuclear power plant (3) **4B**
Kind, -er *n.* child (1) **1A**
Kino, -s *n.* movie theater (3) **2A**
Kiosk, -e *m.* newspaper kiosk (3) **2A**
Kirche, -n *f.* church (3) **2B**
Kissen, - *n.* pillow (2) **2B**
Klasse, -n *f.* class (1) **1B**
erste/zweite Klasse, -n first/second class (2) **4A**
Klassenkamerad, -en / Klassenkameradin, -nen *m./f.* (K-12) classmate (1) **1B**
Klassenzimmer, - *n.* classroom (1) **1B**
klassisch *adj.* classical (3) **2A**
Kleid, -er *n.* dress (2) **1B**
Kleidergröße, -n *f.* clothing size (2) **1B**
Kleidung *f. pl.* clothes (2) **1B**
klein *adj.* small; short (stature) (1) **3A**
Kleingeld *n.* change (money) (3) **2A**
Klempner, - / Klempnerin, -nen *m./f.* plumber (3) **3B**
klettern *v.* to climb (mountain) (1) **2B**
klingeln *v.* to ring (2) **4B**
Klippe, -n *f.* cliff (3) **4A**
Knie, - *n.* knee (3) **1A**
Knoblauch, -e *m.* garlic (1) **4A**
Koch, ¨-e / Köchin, -nen *m./f.* cook, chef (1) **4B**
kochen *v.* to cook (1) **2B**
Koffer, - *m.* suitcase (2) **3B**
Kofferraum, ¨-e *m.* trunk (2) **4A**
Kombi, -s *m.* station wagon (2) **4B**
Komma, -s *n.* comma (1) **1B**
kommen *v.* to come (1) **2A**
Kommilitone, -n / Kommilitonin, -nen *m./f.* (university) classmate (1) **1B**
Kommode, -n *f.* dresser (2) **2A**
kompliziert *adj.* complicated (3) **2A**
Konditorei, -en *f.* pastry shop (1) **4A**
können *v.* to be able, can (1) **3B**
Konto (*pl.* Konten) *n.* bank account (3) **2A**
Konzert, -e *n.* concert (2) **1B**
Kopf, ¨-e *m.* head (3) **1A**
Kopfhörer, - *m.* headphones (2) **4B**
Kopfschmerzen *m. pl.* headache (3) **1B**
Korea *n.* Korea (3) **2B**
der Koreaner, - / die Koreanerin, -nen *m./f.* Korean (person) (3) **2B**
Koreanisch *n.* Korean (language) (3) **2B**
Körper, - *m.* body (3) **1A**
korrigieren *v.* to correct (1) **2A**
Kosmetiksalon, -s *m.* beauty salon (3) **2A**
kosten *v.* to cost (1) **2A**
Wie viel kostet das? *v.* How much is that? (1) **4A**
krank *adj.* sick (3) **1B**
krank werden *v.* to get sick (3) **1B**
Krankenhaus, ¨-er *n.* hospital (3) **1B**
Krankenpfleger, - / Krankenschwester, -n *m./f.* nurse (3) **1B**
Krankenwagen, - *m.* ambulance (3) **1B**
Krawatte, -n *f.* tie (2) **1B**
Kreuzfahrt, -en *f.* cruise (2) **3B**
Kreuzung, -en *f.* intersection (3) **2B**
Küche, -n *f.* kitchen (2) **2A**
Kuchen, - *m.* cake; pie (1) **4A**
Kuh, ¨-e *f.* cow (3) **4A**
kühl *adj.* cool (2) **3A**
Kühlschrank, ¨-e *m.* refrigerator (2) **2B**
Kuli, -s *m.* (ball-point) pen (1) **1B**
Kunde, -n / Kundin, -nen *m./f.* customer (2) **1B**
kündigen *v.* to resign (3) **3B**
Kunst, ¨-e *f.* art (1) **2A**
Kunststoff, -e *m.* plastic (2) **2B**
kurz *adj.* short (1) **3A**
kurze Haare *n. pl.* short hair (1) **3A**
kurze Hose *f.* shorts (2) **1B**
kurzärmlig *adj.* short-sleeved (2) **1B**
Kurzfilm, -e *m.* short film
Kuss, ¨-e *m.* kiss (2) **1A**
küssen *v.* to kiss (2) **1A**
sich küssen *v.* to kiss (each other) (3) **1A**
Küste, -n *f.* coast (3) **4A**

L

lächeln *v.* to smile (1) **3B**
lachen *v.* to laugh (1) **3B**
Ladegerät, -e *n.* battery charger (2) **4B**
laden *v.* to charge; load (2) **4B**
Lage, -n *f.* location (2) **3B**
Laken, - *n.* sheet (2) **2B**
Lampe, -n *f.* lamp (2) **2A**
Land, ¨-er *n.* country (2) **3B**
landen *v.* to land (2) **3B**
Landkarte, -n *f.* map (2) **3B**
Landschaft, -en *f.* landscape; countryside (3) **4A**
lang *adj.* long (1) **3A**
lange Haare *n. pl.* long hair (1) **3A**
langärmlig *adj.* long-sleeved (2) **1B**
langsam *adj.* slow (1) **3B**
Langsam fahren. Slow down. (1) **3B**
langweilig *adj.* boring (1) **2A**
Laptop, -s *m./n.* laptop (computer) (2) **4B**
lassen *v.* to let, allow (1) **2B**
laufen *v.* to run (1) **2B**
leben *v.* to live (1) **2A**
Lebenslauf, ¨-e *m.* résumé; CV (3) **3A**
Lebensmittelgeschäft, -e *n.* grocery store (1) **4A**
lecker *adj.* delicious (1) **4B**
Leder, - *n.* leather (2) **1B**
ledig *adj.* single (1) **3A**
legen *v.* to lay (2) **1B**; *v.* to put; lay (3) **1A**
Lehrbuch, ¨-er *n.* textbook (university) (1) **1B**
Lehrer, - / Lehrerin, -nen *m./f.* teacher (1) **1B**
leicht *adj.* light (1) **4B**; mild (3) **1B**
Leichtathletik *f.* track and field (1) **2B**
leider *adv.* unfortunately (1) **4A**
leiten *v.* to manage (3) **3B**
Lenkrad, ¨-er *n.* steering wheel (2) **4A**
lernen *v.* to study; to learn (1) **2A**
lesen *v.* to read (1) **2B**
letzter/letzte/letztes *adj.* last (1) **2B**
Leute *pl.* people (1) **3B**
Licht, -er *n.* light (3) **4B**
Liebe, -n *f.* love (2) **1A**
Lieber/Liebe *m./f.* Dear (1) **3B**
lieben *v.* to love (1) **2A**
sich lieben *v.* to love each other (3) **1A**
lieber *adj.* rather (2) **4A**
liebevoll *adj.* loving (1) **3B**
Liebling, -e *m.* darling
Lieblings- favorite (1) **4B**
liegen *v.* to lie; to be located (2) **1B**
lila *adj.* purple (2) **1B**
Linie, -n *f.* line
Lippe, -n *f.* lip (3) **1A**
Lippenstift, -e *m.* lipstick (3) **1A**
Literatur, -en *f.* literature (1) **2A**
LKW, -s *m.* truck (2) **4A**
LKW-Fahrer, - / LKW-Fahrerin, -nen *m./f.* truck driver (3) **3B**
lockig *adj.* curly (1) **3A**
lockige Haare *n. pl.* curly hair (1) **3A**
Los! Start!; Go! (1) **2B**
löschen *v.* to delete (2) **4B**
Lösung, -en *f.* solution (3) **4B**

eine Lösung vorschlagen *v.* to propose a solution (3) **4B**
Luft, ⁻e *f.* air (3) **4A**
lügen *v.* to lie, tell a lie
Lust, ⁻e *f.* desire
Lust haben *v.* to feel like (2) **3B**
lustig *adj.* funny (1) **3B**

M

machen *v.* to do; make (1) **2A**
Mach's gut! *v.* All the best! (1) **3B**
Mädchen, - *n.* girl (1) **1A**
Mahlzeit, -en *f.* meal (1) **4B**
Mai *m.* May (1) **2A,** (2) **3A**
Mal, -e *n.* time
das erste/letzte Mal the first/last time (2) **3B**
zum ersten/letzten Mal for the first/last time (2) **3B**
mal times (1) **1B**
Mama, -s *f.* mom (1) **3A**
man *pron.* one (2) **3B**
mancher/manche/manches *adj.* some (2) **4B**
manchmal *adv.* sometimes (2) **3B**
Mann, ⁻er *m.* man (1) **1A**; *m.* husband (1) **3A**
Mannschaft, -en *f.* team (1) **2B**
Mantel, ⁻ *m.* coat (2) **1B**
Markt, ⁻e *m.* market (1) **4A**
Marmelade, -n *f.* jam (1) **4A**
Marmor *m.* marble (2) **2B**
März *m.* March (1) **2A,** (3) **3A**
Material, -ien *n.* material (2) **1B**
Mathematik *f.* mathematics (1) **2A**
Maus, ⁻e *f.* mouse (2) **4B**
Mechaniker, - / Mechanikerin, -nen *m./f.* mechanic (2) **4A**
Medikament, -e *n.* medicine (3) **1B**
Medizin *f.* medicine (1) **2A**
Meer, -e *n.* sea; ocean (3) **4A**
Meeresfrüchte *f. pl.* seafood (1) **4A**
mehr *adj.* more (2) **4A**
mein *poss. adj.* my (1) **3A**
meinen *v.* to mean; to believe; to maintain (3) **4B**
Meisterschaft, -en *f.* championship (1) **2B**
Melone, -n *f.* melon (1) **4A**
Mensa (*pl.* Mensen) *f.* cafeteria (college/ university) (1) **1B**
Mensch, -en *m.* person
Messer, - *n.* knife (1) **4B**
Metzgerei, -en *f.* butcher shop (1) **4A**
Mexikaner, - / Mexikanerin, -nen *m./f.* Mexican (person) (3) **2B**
mexikanisch *adj.* Mexican (3) **2B**
Mexiko *n.* Mexico (3) **2B**
Miete, -n *f.* rent (2) **2A**
mieten *v.* to rent (2) **2A**
Mikrofon, -e *n.* microphone (2) **4B**
Mikrowelle, -n *f.* microwave (2) **2B**
Milch *f.* milk (1) **4B**
Minderheit, -en *f.* minority (3) **4B**
Mineralwasser *n.* sparkling water (1) **4B**
minus minus (1) **1B**
mir *pron.* myself, me (2) **3A**
Mir geht's (sehr) gut. *v.* I am (very) well. (1) **1A**
Mir geht's nicht (so) gut. *v.* I am not (so) well. (1) **1A**
mit with (1) **4B**
Mitbewohner, - / Mitbewohnerin, -nen *m./f.* roommate (1) **2A**
mitbringen *v.* to bring along (1) **4A**
mitkommen *v.* to come along (1) **4A**
mitmachen *v.* to participate (2) **4B**
mitnehmen *v.* to bring with (3) **2B**
jemanden mitnehmen *v.* to give someone a ride (3) **2B**
Mittag, -e *m.* noon (1) **2A**
Mittagessen *n.* lunch (1) **4B**
Mitternacht *f.* midnight (1) **2A**
Mittwoch, -e *m.* Wednesday (1) **2A**
mittwochs *adv.* on Wednesdays (1) **2A**
Möbel, - *n.* furniture (2) **2A**
Möbelstück, -e *n.* piece of furniture (2) **2A**
möbliert *adj.* furnished (2) **2A**
modern *adj.* modern (3) **2A**
modisch *adj.* fashionable (2) **1B**
mögen *v.* to like (1) **4B**
Ich möchte... I would like... (1) **4B**
Monat, -e *m.* month (1) **2A,** (2) **3A**
Mond, -e *m.* moon (3) **4A**
Montag, -e *m.* Monday (1) **2A**
montags *adv.* on Mondays (1) **2A**
Morgen, - *m.* morning (1) **2B**
morgens *adv.* in the morning (1) **2A**
morgen *adv.* tomorrow (1) **2B**
morgen früh tomorrow morning (1) **2B**
Motor, -en *m.* engine (2) **4A**
Motorhaube, -n *f.* hood (of car) (2) **4A**
MP3-Player, - *m.* mp3 player (2) **4B**
müde *adj.* tired (1) **3B**
Müll *m.* trash (2) **2B**; *m.* waste (3) **4B**
den Müll rausbringen *v.* to take out the trash (2) **2B**
Müllwagen, - *m.* garbage truck (3) **4B**
Mund, ⁻er *m.* mouth (3) **1A**
Münze, -n *f.* coin (3) **2A**
Musiker, - / Musikerin, -nen *m./f.* musician (1) **3B**
müssen *v.* to have to; must (1) **3B**
mutig *adj.* brave (1) **3B**
Mutter, ⁻ *f.* mother (1) **1A**
Mütze, -n *f.* cap (2) **1B**

N

nach *prep.* after; to; according to (1) **4B**; *prep.* past (time) (1) **2A**
nach rechts/links to the right/left (2) **2A**
nachdem *conj.* after (3) **2A**
nachmachen *v.* to imitate (2) **4B**
Nachmittag, -e *m.* afternoon (1) **2B**
nachmittags *adv.* in the afternoon (1) **2A**
Nachname, -n *m.* last name (1) **3A**
Nachricht, -en *f.* message (3) **3A**
eine Nachricht hinterlassen *v.* to leave a message (3) **3A**
nächster/nächste/nächstes *adj.* next (1) **2B**
Nacht, ⁻e *f.* night (1) **2B**
Nachtisch, -e *m.* dessert (1) **4B**
Nachttisch, -e *m.* night table (2) **2A**
nah(e) *adj.* near; nearby (3) **2B**
Nähe *f.* vicinity (3) **2B**
in der Nähe von *f.* close to (3) **2B**
naiv *adj.* naïve (1) **3B**
Nase, -n *f.* nose (3) **1A**
verstopfte Nase *f.* stuffy nose (3) **1A**
nass *adj.* wet (3) **4A**
Natur, *f.* nature (3) **4A**
Naturkatastrophe, -n *f.* natural disaster (3) **4A**
Naturwissenschaft, -en *f.* science (1) **2A**
Nebel, - *m.* fog; mist (2) **3A**
neben *prep.* next to (2) **1B**
Nebenkosten *pl.* additional charges (2) **2A**
Neffe, -n *m.* nephew (2) **4B**
nehmen *v.* to take (1) **2B**
nein no (1) **1A**
nennen *v.* to call (2) **1A**
nervös *adj.* nervous (1) **3B**
nett *adj.* nice (1) **3B**
neugierig *adj.* curious (1) **3B**
neun nine (1) **2A**
nicht *adv.* not (1) **2B**
nicht schlecht not bad (1) **1A**
nichts *pron.* nothing (2) **3B**
nie *adv.* never (1) **4A**
niedrig *adj.* low (3) **3A**
niemals *adv.* never (2) **3B**
niemand *pron.* no one (2) **3B**
niesen *v.* to sneeze (3) **1B**
noch *adv.* yet; still; in addition (1) **4A**
normalerweise *adv.* usually (3) **1B**
Notaufnahme, -n *f.* emergency room (3) **1B**
Note, -n *f.* grade (on an assignment) (1) **1B**
Notfall, ⁻e *m.* emergency (3) **3B**
Notiz, -en *f.* note (1) **1B**
November *m.* November (1) **2A,** (2) **3A**
Nummernschild, -er *n.* license plate (2) **4A**
nur *adv.* only (1) **4A**
nützlich *adj.* useful (1) **2A**
nutzlos *adj.* useless (1) **2A**

O

ob *conj.* whether; if (3) **2A**
Obst *n.* fruit (1) **4A**
obwohl *conj.* even though (2) **2A**; *conj.* although (3) **2A**
oder *conj.* or (1) **1B**
Ofen, ⁻ *m.* oven (2) **2B**
öffentlich *adj.* public (2) **4A**
öffentliche Verkehrsmittel *n.* public transportation (2) **4A**
öffnen *v.* to open (1) **2A**
oft *adv.* often (1) **4A**
ohne *prep.* without (1) **3B**
Ohr, -en *n.* ear (3) **1A**
Ökologie *f.* ecology (3) **4B**
ökologisch *adj.* ecological (3) **4B**
Oktober *m.* October (1) **2A,** (2) **3A**
Öl, -e *n.* oil (1) **4A**
Olivenöl, -e *n.* olive oil (1) **4A**
Oma, -s *f.* grandma (1) **3A**
online sein *v.* to be online (2) **4B**

Opa, -s *m.* grandpa (1) **3A**
orange *adj.* orange (2) **1B**
Orange, -n *f.* orange (1) **4A**
ordentlich *adj.* neat, tidy (2) **2B**
Ort, -e *m.* place (1) **1B**
Österreich *n.* Austria (3) **2B**
Österreicher, - / Österreicherin, -nen *m./f.* Austrian (person) (3) **2B**

P

Paar, -e *n.* couple (1) **3A**
packen *v.* to pack (2) **3B**
Paket, -e *n.* package (3) **2A**
Papa, -s *m.* dad (1) **3A**
Papier, -e *n.* paper
Blatt Papier (*pl.* Blätter Papier) *n.* sheet of paper (1) **1B**
Papierkorb, ¨-e *m.* wastebasket (1) **1B**
Paprika, - *f.* pepper (1) **4A**
grüne/rote Paprika *f.* green/red pepper (1) **4A**
Park, -s *m.* park (1) **1A**
parken *v.* to park (2) **4A**
Parkverbot. No parking. (1) **3B**
Party, -s *f.* party (2) **1A**
eine Party geben *v.* to throw a party (2) **1A**
Passagier, -e / Passagierin, -nen *m./f.* passenger (2) **3B**
passen *v.* to fit; to match (2) **1A**
passieren *v.* to happen (2) **1B**
Passkontrolle, -n *f.* passport control (2) **3B**
Passwort, ¨-er *n.* password (2) **4B**
Pasta *f.* pasta (1) **4A**
Patient, -en / Patientin, -nen *m./f.* patient (3) **1B**
Pause, -n *f.* break, recess (1) **1B**
Pension, -en *f.* guesthouse (2) **3B**
Person, -en *f.* person (1) **1A**
Personalausweis, -e *m.* ID card (2) **3B**
Personalchef, -s / die Personalchefin, -nen *m./f.* human resources manager (3) **3A**
persönlich *adj.* personal (1) **3B**
Pfanne, -n *f.* pan (2) **2B**
Pfeffer, - *m.* pepper (1) **4B**
Pferd, -e *n.* horse (1) **2B**
Pfirsich, -e *m.* peach (1) **4A**
Pflanze, -n *f.* plant (2) **2A**
Pfund, -e *n.* pound (1) **4A**
Physik *f.* physics (1) **2A**
Picknick, -s, *n.* picnic (3) **4A**
ein Picknick machen *v.* to have a picnic (3) **4A**
Pilz, -e *m.* mushroom (1) **4A**
Pinnwand, ¨-e *f.* bulletin board (3) **3A**
Planet, -en *m.* planet (3) **4B**
den Planeten retten *v.* to save the planet (3) **4B**
Platten, - *m.* flat tire (2) **4A**
einen Platten haben *v.* to have a flat tire (2) **4A**
Platz, ¨-e *m.* court (1) **1A**
plus plus (1) **1B**
Politiker, - / Politikerin, -nen *m./f.* politician (3) **3B**
Polizeiwache, -n *f.* police station (3) **2A**
Polizist, -en / Polizistin, -nen *m./f.* police officer (2) **4A**
Post *f.* post office; mail (3) **2A**
zur Post gehen *v.* to go to the post office (3) **2A**
Poster, - *n.* poster (1) **2A**
Postkarte, -n *f.* postcard (3) **2A**
Praktikum (*pl.* die Praktika) *n.* internship (3) **3A**
prima *adj.* great (1) **1A**
probieren *v.* to try (1) **3B**
Probieren Sie mal! Give it a try!
Problem, -e *n.* problem (1) **1A**
Professor, -en / Professorin, -nen *m./f.* professor (1) **1B**
Programm, -e *n.* program (2) **4B**
Prost! Cheers! (1) **4B**
Prozent, -e *n.* percent (1) **1B**
Prüfung, -en *f.* exam, test (1) **1B**
Psychologe, -n / Psychologin, -nen *m./f.* psychologist (3) **3B**
Psychologie *f.* psychology (1) **2A**
Pullover, - *m.* sweater (2) **1B**
Punkt, -e *m.* period (1) **1B**
pünktlich *adj.* on time (2) **3B**
putzen *v.* to clean (2) **2B**
sich die Zähne putzen *v.* to brush one's teeth (3) **1A**

Q

Querverweis, -e *m.* cross-reference

R

Radiergummi, -s *m.* eraser (1) **1B**
Rasen, - *m.* lawn, grass (1) **3B**
Betreten des Rasens verboten. Keep off the grass. (1) **3B**
sich rasieren *v.* to shave (3) **1A**
Rasierer, - *m.* razor (3) **1A**
Rasierschaum, ¨-e *m.* shaving cream (3) **1A**
Rathaus, ¨-er *n.* town hall (3) **2A**
rauchen *v.* to smoke
Rauchen verboten. No smoking. (1) **3B**
rausbringen *v.* to bring out (2) **2B**
den Müll rausbringen *v.* to take out the trash (2) **2B**
realistisch *adj.* realistic (3) **2A**
Rechnung, -en *f.* check (1) **4B**
Rechtsanwalt, ¨-e / Rechtsanwältin, -nen *m./f.* lawyer (1) **3B**
Rechtschreibung *f.* spelling
recyceln *v.* to recycle (3) **4B**
reden *v.* to talk (2) **1A**
reden über *v.* to talk about (2) **3A**
Referat, -e *n.* presentation (1) **2A**
Referenz, -en *f.* reference (3) **3A**
Regen *m.* rain (2) **3A**
Regenmantel, ¨- *m.* raincoat (2) **3A**
Regenschirm, -e *m.* umbrella (2) **3A**
Regierung, -en *f.* government (3) **4B**
regnen *v.* to rain (1) **2A,** (2) **3A**
reich *adj.* rich (1) **3B**
Reis *m.* rice (1) **4A**
Reise, -n *f.* trip (2) **3B**
Reisebüro, -s *n.* travel agency (2) **3B**
reisen *v.* to travel (1) **2A**
Reisende, -n *m./f.* traveler (2) **3B**
Reiseziel, -e *n.* destination (2) **3B**
reiten *v.* to ride (1) **2B**
rennen *v.* to run (2) **1A**
Rente, -n *f.* pension
in Rente gehen *v.* to retire (2) **1A**
Rentner, - / Rentnerin, -nen *m./f.* retiree (3) **3B**
reparieren *v.* to repair (2) **4A**
Restaurant, -s *n.* restaurant (1) **4B**
retten *v.* to save (3) **4B**
Rezept, -e *n.* recipe (1) **4A**; prescription (3) **1B**
Richter, - / Richterin, -nen *m./f.* judge (3) **3B**
Richtung, -en *f.* direction (3) **2B**
in Richtung *f.* toward (3) **2B**
Rindfleisch *n.* beef (1) **4A**
Rock, ¨-e *m.* skirt (2) **1B**
rosa *adj.* pink (2) **1B**
rot *adj.* red (1) **3A**
rothaarig *adj.* red-haired (1) **3A**
Rücken, - *m.* back (3) **1A**
Rückenschmerzen *m. pl.* backache (3) **1B**
Rucksack, ¨-e *m.* backpack (1) **1B**
ruhig *adj.* calm (1) **3B**
Russe, -n / Russin, -nen *m./f.* Russian (person) (3) **2B**
Russisch *n.* Russian (language) (3) **2B**
Russland *n.* Russia (3) **2B**

S

Sache, -n *f.* thing (1) **1B**
Saft, ¨-e *m.* juice (1) **4B**
sagen *v.* to say (1) **2A**
Salat, -e *m.* lettuce; salad (1) **4A**
Salz, -e *n.* salt (1) **4B**
salzig *adj.* salty (1) **4B**
Samstag, -e *m.* Saturday (1) **2A**
samstags *adv.* on Saturdays (1) **2A**
sauber *adj.* clean (2) **2B**
saurer Regen *m.* acid rain (3) **4B**
Saustall *n.* pigsty (2) **2B**
Es ist ein Saustall! It's a pigsty! (2) **2B**
Schach *n.* chess (1) **2B**
Schaf, -e *n.* sheep (3) **4A**
Schaffner, - / Schaffnerin, -nen *m./f.* ticket collector (2) **4A**
Schal, -s *m.* scarf (2) **1B**
scharf *adj.* spicy (1) **4B**
schauen *v.* to look (2) **3A**
Scheibenwischer, - *m.* windshield wiper (2) **4A**
Scheinwerfer, - *m.* headlight (2) **4A**
scheitern *v.* to fail (3) **3B**
schenken *v.* to give (a gift) (2) **1A**
schicken *v.* to send (2) **4B**
Schiff, -e *n.* ship (2) **4A**
Schinken, - *m.* ham (1) **4A**
Schlafanzug, ¨-e *m.* pajamas (3) **1A**
schlafen *v.* to sleep (1) **2B**
Schlafzimmer, - *n.* bedroom (2) **2A**
Schlange, -n *f.* line (2) **3B**; *f.* snake (3) **4A**
Schlange stehen *v.* to stand in line (2) **3B**
schlank *adj.* slim (1) **3A**
schlecht *adj.* bad (1) **3B**
schlecht gekleidet *adj.* badly dressed (2) **1B**
schließlich *adv.* finally (2) **3B**
Schlüssel, - *m.* key (2) **3B**

schmecken *v.* to taste (1) **4B**
Schmerz, -en *m.* pain (3) **1B**
sich schminken *v.* to put on makeup (3) **1A**
schmutzig *adj.* dirty (2) **2B**
Schnee *m.* snow (2) **3A**
schneien *v.* to snow (2) **3A**
schnell *adj.* fast (1) **3B**
schon *adv.* already, yet (1) **4A**
schön *adj.* pretty; beautiful (1) **3A**
Schön dich/Sie kennen zu lernen. Nice to meet you. (1) **1A**
Schönen Tag noch! Have a nice day! (1) **1A**
Es ist schön draußen. It's nice out. (2) **3A**
Schrank, ¨-e *m.* cabinet; closet (2) **2A**
schreiben *v.* to write (1) **2A**
schreiben an *v.* to write to (2) **3A**
sich schreiben *v.* to write one another (3) **1A**
Schreibtisch, -e *m.* desk (1) **1B**
Schreibwarengeschäft, -e *n.* paper-goods store (3) **2A**
Schublade, -n *f.* drawer (2) **2A**
schüchtern *adj.* shy (1) **3B**
Schuh, -e *m.* shoe (2) **1B**
Schulbuch, ¨-er *n.* textbook (K–12) (1) **1B**
Schule, -n *f.* school (1) **1B**
Schüler, - / Schülerin, -nen (K–12) *m./f.* student (1) **1B**
Schulleiter, - / Schulleiterin, -nen *m./f.* principal (1) **1B**
Schulter, -n *f.* shoulder (3) **1A**
Schüssel, -n *f.* bowl (1) **4B**
schützen *v.* to protect (3) **4B**
schwach *adj.* weak (1) **3B**
Schwager, ¨- *m.* brother-in-law (1) **3A**
Schwägerin, -nen *f.* sister-in-law (1) **3A**
schwanger *adj.* pregnant (3) **1B**
schwänzen *v.* to cut class (1) **1B**
schwarz *adj.* black (2) **1B**
schwarzhaarig *adj.* black-haired (1) **3A**
Schweinefleisch *n.* pork (1) **4A**
Schweiz (die) *f.* Switzerland (2) **3A**
Schweizer, - / Schweizerin, -nen *m./f.* Swiss (person) (3) **2B**
schwer *adj.* rich, heavy (1) **4B**; *adj.* serious, difficult (3) **1B**
Schwester, -n *f.* sister (1) **1A**
Schwiegermutter, ¨- *f.* mother-in-law (1) **3A**
Schwiegervater, ¨- *m.* father-in-law (1) **3A**
schwierig *adj.* difficult (1) **2A**
Schwimmbad, ¨-er *n.* swimming pool (1) **2B**
schwimmen *v.* to swim (1) **2B**
schwindlig *adj.* dizzy (3) **1B**
sechs six (1) **2A**
See, -n *m.* lake (3) **4A**
sehen *v.* to see (1) **2B**
sehr *adv.* very (1) **3A**
Seide, -n *f.* silk (2) **1B**
Seife, -n *f.* soap (3) **1A**
sein *v.* to be (1) **1A**
(gleich) sein *v.* to equal (1) **1B**
sein *poss. adj.* his, its (1) **3A**
seit since; for (1) **4B**
Sekt, -e *m.* champagne (2) **1A**
selten *adv.* rarely (1) **4A**
Seminar, -e *n.* seminar (1) **2A**
Seminarraum, -räume *m.* seminar room (1) **2A**
Sender, - *m.* channel (2) **4B**
September *m.* September (1) **2A**, (2) **3A**
Serviette, -n *f.* napkin (1) **4B**
Sessel, - *m.* armchair (2) **2A**
setzen *v.* to put, place (2) **1B**; *v.* to put, set (3) **1A**
Shampoo, -s *n.* shampoo (3) **1A**
sicher *adv.* probably (3) **2A**
Sicherheitsgurt, -e *m.* seatbelt (2) **4A**
sie *pron.* she/they (1) **1A**
Sie *pron.* (*form., sing./pl.*) you (1) **1A**
sieben seven (1) **2A**
Silvester *n.* New Year's Eve (2) **1A**
singen *v.* to sing (1) **2B**
sitzen *v.* to sit (2) **1B**
Ski fahren *v.* to ski (1) **2B**
Smartphone, -s *n.* smartphone (2) **4B**
SMS, - *f.* text message (2) **4B**
Snack, -s *m.* snack (1) **4B**
so *adv.* so (1) **4A**
Socke, -n *f.* sock (2) **1B**
Sofa, -s *n.* sofa; couch (2) **2A**
Sofa surfen *v.* to couch surf (2) **3B**
Sohn, ¨-e *m.* son (1) **3A**
solcher/solche/solches *pron.* such (2) **4B**
sollen *v.* to be supposed to (1) **3B**
Sommer, - *m.* summer (1) **2B**, (2) **3A**
sondern *conj.* but rather; instead (2) **2A**
Sonne, -n *f.* sun (3) **4A**
Sonnenaufgang, ¨-e *m.* sunrise (3) **4A**
Sonnenbrand, ¨-e *m.* sunburn (3) **1B**
Sonnenbrille, -n *f.* sunglasses (2) **1B**
Sonnenenergie *f.* solar energy (3) **4B**
Sonnenuntergang, ¨-e *m.* sunset (3) **4A**
sonnig *adj.* sunny (2) **3A**
Sonntag, -e *m.* Sunday (1) **2A**
sonntags *adv.* on Sundays (1) **2A**
Spanien *n.* Spain (3) **3B**
Spanier, - / Spanierin, -nen *m./f.* Spanish (person) (3) **2B**
Spanisch *n.* Spanish (language) (3) **2B**
spannend *adj.* exciting (3) **2A**
Spaß *m.* fun (1) **2B**
Spaß haben/machen *v.* to have fun/to be fun (1) **2B**
(keinen) Spaß haben *v.* to (not) have fun (2) **1A**
spät *adj.* late
Wie spät ist es? What time is it? (1) **2A**
spazieren gehen *v.* to go for a walk (1) **2B**
Spaziergang, ¨-e *m.* walk
speichern *v.* to save (2) **4B**
Speisekarte, -n *f.* menu (1) **4B**
Spiegel, - *m.* mirror (2) **2A**
Spiel, -e *n.* match, game (1)c**2B**
spielen *v.* to play (1) **2A**
Spieler, - / Spielerin, -nen *m./f.* player (1) **2B**
Spielfeld, -er *n.* field (1) **2B**
Spielkonsole, -n *f.* game console (2) **4B**
Spitze! *adj.* great! (1) **1A**
Sport *m.* sports (1) **2B**
Sport treiben *v.* to exercise (3) **1B**
Sportart, -en *f.* sport; type of sport (1) **2B**
Sporthalle, - n *f.* gym (1) **2A**
sportlich *adj.* athletic (1) **3A**
sprechen *v.* to speak (1) **2B**
sprechen über *v.* to speak about (2) **3A**
Spritze, -n *f.* shot (3) **1B**
eine Spritze geben *v.* to give a shot (3) **1B**
Spüle, -n *f.* (kitchen) sink (2) **2B**
spülen *v.* to rinse (2) **2B**
Geschirr spülen *v.* to do the dishes (2) **2B**
Spülmaschine, -n *f.* dishwasher (2) **2B**
Stadion (*pl.* Stadien) *n.* stadium (1) **2B**
Stadt, ¨-e *f.* city (2) **1B**; *f.* town (3) **2B**
Stadtplan, ¨-e *m.* city map (2) **3B**
Stahl *m.* steel (2) **2B**
stark *adj.* strong (1) **3B**
starten *v.* to start (2) **4B**
statt *conj.* instead of
Statue, -n *f.* statue (3) **2B**
staubsaugen *v.* to vacuum (2) **2B**
Staubsauger, - *m.* vacuum cleaner (2) **2B**
stehen *v.* to stand (2) **1B**
Schlange stehen *v.* to stand in line (2) **3B**
stehlen *v.* to steal (1) **2B**
steif *adj.* stiff (3) **1B**
steigen *v.* to climb (2) **1B**
Stein, -e *m.* rock (3) **4A**
Stelle, -n *f.* place, position (3) **2A**; job (3) **3A**
an deiner/Ihrer Stelle *f.* if I were you (3) **2A**
eine Stelle suchen *v.* to look for a job (3) **3A**
stellen *v.* to put, place (2) **1B**
Stellenangebot, -e *n.* job opening (3) **3A**
sterben *v.* to die (2) **1B**
Stereoanlage, -n *f.* stereo system (2) **4B**
Stern -e *m.* star (3) **4A**
Stiefel, - *m.* boot (2) **1B**
Stiefmutter, ¨- *f.* stepmother (1) **3A**
Stiefsohn, ¨-e *m.* stepson (1) **3A**
Stieftochter, ¨- *f.* stepdaughter (1) **3A**
Stiefvater, ¨- *m.* stepfather (1) **3A**
Stift, -e *m.* pen (1) **1B**
Stil, -e *m.* style (2) **1B**
still *adj.* still (1) **4B**
stilles Wasser *n.* still water (1) **4B**
Stipendium, (*pl.* Stipendien) *n.* scholarship, grant (1) **2A**
Stock, ¨-e *m.* floor (2) **2A**
erster/zweiter Stock first/second floor (2) **2A**
stolz *adj.* proud (1) **3B**
Stoppschild, -er *n.* stop sign (2) **4A**
Strand, ¨-e *m.* beach (1) **2B**
Straße, -n *f.* street (2) **4A**
sich streiten *v.* to argue (3) **1A**
Strom, ¨-e *m.* stream (3) **4A**
Student, -en / Studentin, -nen *m./f.* (college/university) student (1) **1A**
Studentenwohnheim, -e *n.* dormitory (1) **2A**
studieren *v.* to study; major in (1) **2A**
Studium (*pl.* Studien) *n.* studies (1) **2A**
Stuhl, ¨-e *m.* chair (1) **1A**
Stunde, -n *f.* lesson (1) **1B**; hour (1) **2A**
Stundenplan, ¨-e *m.* schedule (1) **2A**
Sturm, ¨-e *m.* storm (2) **3A**
suchen *v.* to look for (1) **2A**
eine Stelle suchen *v.* to look for a job (3) **3A**

Supermarkt, ¨-e *m.* supermarket (1) **4A**
Suppe, -n *f.* soup (1) **4B**
surfen *v.* to surf (2) **4B**
im Internet surfen *v.* to surf the Web (2) **4B**
süß *adj.* sweet, cute (1) **3B,** (1) **4B**
Süßigkeit, -en *f.* candy (2) **1A**
Sweatshirt, -s *n.* sweatshirt (2) **1B**
Symptom, -e *n.* symptom (3) **1B**

T

Tablet, -s *n.* tablet (2) **4B**
Tablette, -n *f.* pill (3) **1B**
Tafel, -n *f.* board, black board (1) **1B**
Tag, -e *m.* day (1) **1A,** (2) **3A**
Welcher Tag ist heute? What day is it today? (2) **3A**
täglich *adv.* every day; daily (1) **4A**
Tal, ¨-er *n.* valley (3) **4A**
tanken *v.* to fill up (2) **4A**
Tankstelle, -n *f.* gas station (2) **4A**
Tante, -n *f.* aunt (1) **3A**
tanzen *v.* to dance (1) **2B**
Taschenrechner, - *m.* calculator (1) **1B**
Taschentuch, ¨-er *n.* tissue (3) **1B**
Tasse, -n *f.* cup (1) **4B**
Tastatur, -en *f.* keyboard (2) **4B**
Taxi, -s *n.* taxi (2) **4A**
Taxifahrer, - / Taxifahrerin, -nen *m./f.* taxi driver (3) **3B**
Technik *f.* technology (2) **4B**
Technik bedienen *v.* to use technology (2) **4B**
Tee, -s *m.* tea (1) **4B**
Teelöffel, - *m.* teaspoon (1) **4B**
Telefon, -e *n.* telephone (2) **4B**
am Telefon on the telephone (3) **3A**
Telefonnummer, -n *f.* telephone number (3) **3A**
Telefonzelle, -n *f.* phone booth (3) **2B**
Teller, - *m.* plate (1) **4B**
Tennis *n.* tennis (1) **2B**
Teppich, -e *m.* rug (2) **2A**
Termin, -e *m.* appointment (3) **3A**
einen Termin vereinbaren *v.* to make an appointment (3) **3A**
teuer *adj.* expensive (2) **1B**
Thermometer, - *n.* thermometer (1) **1B**
Thunfisch, -e *m.* tuna (1) **4A**
Tier, -e *n.* animal (3) **4A**
Tierarzt, ¨-e / Tierärztin, -nen *m./f.* veterinarian (3) **3B**
Tisch, -e *m.* table, desk (1) **1B**
den Tisch decken *v.* to set the table (2) **2B**
Tischdecke, -n *f.* tablecloth (1) **4B**
Toaster, - *m.* toaster (2) **2B**
Tochter, ¨ *f.* daughter (1) **3A**
Toilette, -n *f.* toilet (2) **2A**
Tomate, -n *f.* tomato (1) **4A**
Topf, ¨-e *m.* pot (2) **2B**
Tor, -e *n.* goal (in soccer, etc.) (1) **2B**
Tornado, -s *m.* tornado (3) **4A**
Torte, -n *f.* cake (2) **1A**
Touristenklasse *f.* economy class (2) **3B**
tragen *v.* to carry; wear (1) **2B**
Trägerhemd, -en *n.* tank top (2) **1B**
trainieren *v.* to practice (sports) (1) **2B**
Traube, -n *f.* grape (1) **4A**
träumen *v.* to dream (2) **3A**
traurig *adj.* sad (1) **3B**
treffen *v.* to meet; to hit (1) **2B**
sich treffen *v.* to meet (each other) (3) **1A**
treiben *v.* to float; to push
Sport treiben *v.* to exercise (3) **1B**
Treibsand *m.* quicksand (3) **4A**
sich trennen *v.* to separate, split up (3) **1A**
Treppe, -n *f.* stairway (2) **2A**
trinken *v.* to drink (1) **3B**
Trinkgeld, -er *n.* tip (1) **4B**
trocken *adj.* dry (3) **4A**
trotz *prep.* despite, in spite of (2) **4B**
Tschüss. Bye. (1) **1A**
T-Shirt, -s *n.* T-shirt (2) **1B**
tun *v.* to do (3) **1B**
Es tut mir leid. I'm sorry. (1) **1A**
weh tun *v.* to hurt (3) **1B**
Tür, -en *f.* door (1) **1B**
Türen schließen. Keep doors closed. (1) **3B**
Türkei (die) *f.* Turkey (3) **2B**
Türke, -n / die Türkin, -nen *m./f.* Turkish (person) (3) **2B**
Türkisch *n.* Turkish (language) (3) **2B**
Turnschuhe *m. pl.* sneakers (2) **1B**

U

U-Bahn, -en *f.* subway (2) **4A**
übel *adj.* nauseous (3) **1B**
über *prep.* over, above (2) **1B**
übernachten *v.* to spend the night (2) **3B**
überall *adv.* everywhere (1) **4A**
Überbevölkerung *f.* overpopulation (3) **4B**
überlegen *v.* to think over (1) **4A**
übermorgen *adv.* the day after tomorrow (1) **2B**
überqueren *v.* to cross (3) **2B**
überraschen *v.* to surprise (2) **1A**
Überraschung, -en *f.* surprise (2) **1A**
überzeugend *adj.* persuasive (3) **1B**
Übung, -en *f.* practice, exercise
Uhr, -en *f.* clock (1) **1B**
um... Uhr at... o'clock (1) **2A**
Wie viel Uhr ist es? *v.* What time is it? (1) **2A**
um *prep.* around; at (time) (1) **3B**
um... zu in order to (2) **3B**
Umleitung, -en *f.* detour (2) **4A**
umtauschen *v.* to exchange (2) **2B**
Umwelt, -en *f.* environment (3) **4B**
umweltfreundlich *adj.* environmentally friendly (3) **4B**
Umweltschutz *m.* environmentalism (3) **4B**
umziehen *v.* to move (2) **2A,** (3) **1A**
sich umziehen *v.* to change clothes (3) **1A**
unangenehm *adj.* unpleasant (1) **3B**
und *conj.* and (1) **1B**
Unfall, ¨-e *m.* accident (2) **4A**
einen Unfall haben *v.* to have an accident (2) **4A**
Universität, -en *f.* university; college (1) **1B**
unmöbliert *adj.* unfurnished (2) **2A**
unser *poss. adj.* our (1) **3A**
unter *prep.* under, below (2) **1B**
untergehen *v.* to set (sun) (3) **4A**
sich unterhalten *v.* to chat, have a conversation (1) **1A**
Unterkunft, ¨-e *f.* accommodations (2) **3B**
Unterricht, -e *m.* class, instruction (1) **1B**
unterschreiben *v.* to sign (3) **2A**
Unterwäsche *f.* underwear (2) **1B**
Urgroßmutter, ¨ *f.* great grandmother (1) **3A**
Urgroßvater, ¨ *m.* great grandfather (1) **3A**
Urlaub, -e *m.* vacation (2) **3B**
Urlaub machen *v.* to go on vacation (2) **3B**
Urlaub nehmen *v.* to take time off (3) **3B**
USA (die) *pl.* USA (3) **2B**

V

Vase, -n *f.* vase (2) **2A**
Vater, ¨ *m.* father (1) **3A**
Veranstaltung, -en *f.* class; course (1) **2A**
Verb, -en *n.* verb (3) **1A**
verbessern *v.* to improve (3) **4B**
verbringen *v.* to spend (1) **4A**
verdienen *v.* to earn (3) **3B**
Vereinigten Staaten (die) *pl.* United States (3) **2B**
Vergangenheit, -en *f.* past (3) **4A**
vergessen *v.* to forget (1) **2B**
verheiratet *adj.* married (1) **3A**
verkaufen *v.* to sell (1) **4A**
Verkäufer, - / Verkäuferin, -nen *m./f.* salesperson (2) **1B**
Verkehr *m.* traffic (2) **4A**
Verkehrsmittel *n.* transportation (2) **4A**
öffentliche Verkehrsmittel *n. pl.* public transportation (2) **4A**
verkünden *v.* to announce (3) **4B**
sich verlaufen *v.* to get lost (3) **2B**
sich verletzen *v.* to hurt oneself (3) **1B**
Verletzung, -en *f.* injury (3) **1B**
sich verlieben (in) *v.* to fall in love (with) (3) **1A**
verlieren *v.* to lose (1) **2B**
verlobt *adj.* engaged (1) **3A**
Verlobte, -n *m./f.* fiancé(e) (1) **3A**
verschmutzen *v.* to pollute (3) **4B**
Verschmutzung *f.* pollution (3) **4B**
sich verspäten *v.* to be late (3) **1A**
Verspätung, -en *f.* delay (2) **3B**
Verständnis, -se *n.* comprehension
sich (das Handgelenk / den Fuß) verstauchen *v.* to sprain (one's wrist/ankle) (3) **1B**
verstehen *v.* to understand (1) **2A**
verstopfte Nase *f.* stuffy nose (3) **1B**
versuchen *v.* to try (2) **3B**
Vertrag, ¨-e *m.* contract (3) **3A**
verwandt *adj.* related (3) **2A**
Verwandte, -n *m.* relative (1) **3A**
viel *adv.* much, a lot (of) (1) **4A**
Viel Glück! Good luck! (2) **1A**
Vielen Dank. Thank you very much. (1) **1A**
vielleicht *adv.* maybe (1) **4A**
vier four (1) **2A**
Viertel, - *n.* quarter (1) **2A;** neighborhood (3) **2B**
Viertel nach/vor quarter past/to (1) **2A**

Visum (*pl.* Visa) *n.* visa (2) **3B**
Vogel, ¨ *m.* bird (1) **3A**
voll *adj.* full (2) **3B**
  voll besetzt *adj.* fully occupied (2) **3B**
Volleyball *m.* volleyball (1) **2B**
von *prep.* from (1) **4B**
vor *prep.* in front of, before (2) **1B;** *prep.* to (1) **2A**
vorbei *adv.* over, past (2) **3A**
vorbereiten *v.* to prepare (1) **4A**
  sich vorbereiten (auf) *v.* to prepare oneself (for) (3) **1A**
  Vorbereitung, -en *f.* preparation
Vorhang, ¨e *m.* curtain (2) **2A**
Vorlesung, -en *f.* lecture (1) **2A**
vormachen *v.* to fool (2) **4B**
Vormittag, -e *m.* midmorning (1) **2B**
vormittags *adv.* before noon (1) **2A**
Vorspeise, -n *f.* appetizer (1) **4B**
vorstellen *v.* to introduce (3) **1A**
  sich vorstellen *v.* to introduce oneself (3) **1A**
  sich (etwas) vorstellen *v.* to imagine (something) (3) **1A**
Vorstellungsgespräch, -e *n.* job interview (3) **3A**
Vortrag, ¨e *m.* lecture (2) **2B**
Vulkan, -e *m.* volcano (3) **4A**

W

wachsen *v.* to grow (2) **1B**
während *prep.* during (2) **4B**
wahrscheinlich *adv.* probably (3) **2A**
Wald, ¨er *m.* forest (1) **2B**, (3) **4A**
Wand, ¨e *f.* wall (2) **1B**
wandern *v.* to hike (1) **2A**
wann *interr.* when (1) **2A**
  Wann hast du Geburtstag? When is your birthday? (1) **2B**
warm *adj.* warm (3) **2A**
warten *v.* to wait (for) (1) **2A**
  warten auf *v.* to wait for (2) **3A**
  in der Warteschleife sein *v.* to be on hold (3) **3B**
warum *interr.* why (1) **2A**
was *interr.* what (1) **2A**
  Was geht ab? What's up? (1) **1A**
  Was ist das? What is that? (1) **1B**
Wäsche *f.* laundry (2) **2B**
waschen *v.* to wash (1) **2B**
  sich waschen *v.* to wash (oneself) (3) **1A**
  Wäsche waschen *v.* to do laundry (2) **2B**
Wäschetrockner, - *m.* dryer (2) **2B**
Waschmaschine, -n *f.* washing machine (2) **2B**
Waschsalon, -s *m.* laundromat (3) **2A**
Wasser *n.* water (1) **4B**
Wasserfall, ¨e *m.* waterfall (3) **4A**
Wasserkrug, ¨e *m.* water pitcher (1) **4B**
Website, -s *f.* web site (2) **4B**
Weg, -e *m.* path (3) **4A**
wegen *prep.* because of (2) **4B**
wegräumen *v.* to put away (2) **2B**
wegwerfen *v.* to throw away (3) **4B**
weh tun *v.* to hurt (3) **1B**
Weihnachten, - *n.* Christmas (2) **1A**
weil *conj.* because (3) **2A**
Wein, -e *m.* wine (1) **4B**
weinen *v.* to cry (1) **3B**
weise *adj.* wise (1) **3B**
weiß *adj.* white (2) **1B**
weit *adj.* loose; big (2) **1B;** *adj.* far (3) **2B**
  weit von *adj.* far from (3) **2B**
  weiter geht's moving forward
welcher/welche/welches *interr.* which (1) **2A**
  Welcher Tag ist heute? What day is it today? (2) **3A**
Welt, -en *f.* world (3) **4B**
wem *interr.* whom (*dat.*) (1) **4B**
wen *interr.* whom (*acc.*) (1) **2A**
Wende, -n *f.* turning point (3) **4B**
wenig *adj.* little; not much (3) **2A**
wenn *conj.* when; whenever; if (3) **2A**
  wenn... dann if... then (3) **2A**
  wenn... nur if... only (3) **2A**
wer *interr.* who (1) **2A**
  Wer ist das? Who is it? (1) **1B**
  Wer spricht? Who's calling? (3) **3A**
werden *v.* to become (1) **2B**
werfen *v.* to throw (1) **2B**
Werkzeug, -e *n.* tool kit
wessen *interr.* whose (2) **4B**
Wetter *n.* weather (2) **3A**
  Wie ist das Wetter? What's the weather like? (2) **3A**
Wetterbericht, -e *m.* weather report (2) **3A**
wichtig *adj.* important (2) **3B**
wie *interr.* how (1) **2A**
  wie viel? *interr.* how much? (1) **1B**
  wie viele? *interr.* how many? (1) **1B**
  Wie alt bist du? How old are you? (1) **1B**
  Wie heißt du? *(inf.)* What's your name? (1) **1A**
wiederholen *v.* to repeat (1) **2A**
Wiederholung, -en *f.* repetition; revision
wiegen *v.* to weigh (2) **4B**
willkommen welcome (1) **1A**
  Herzlich willkommen! Welcome! (1) **1A**
Windenergie *f.* wind energy (3) **4B**
windig *adj.* windy (2) **3A**
Windschutzscheibe, -n *f.* windshield (2) **4A**
Winter, - *m.* winter (1) **2B**, (2) **3A**
wir *pron.* we (1) **1A**
wirklich *adv.* really (1) **4A**
Wirtschaft, -en *f.* business; economy (1) **2A**
wischen *v.* to wipe, mop (2) **2B**
wissen *v.* to know (information) (2) **1B**
Wissenschaftler, - / Wissenschaftlerin, -nen *m./f.* scientist (3) **3B**
Witwe, -n *f.* widow (1) **3A**
Witwer, - *m.* widower (1) **3A**
wo *interr.* where (1) **2A**
woanders *adv.* somewhere else (1) **4A**
Woche, -n *f.* week (1) **2A**
Wochenende, -n *n.* weekend (1) **2A**
woher *interr.* from where (1) **2A**; (2) **2A**
wohin *interr.* where to (1) **2A**
wohl *adv.* probably (3) **2A**
wohnen *v.* to live (somewhere) (1) **2A**
Wohnheim, -e *n.* dorm (2) **2A**
Wohnung, -en *f.* apartment (2) **2A**
Wohnzimmer, - *n.* living room (2) **2A**
Wolke, -n *f.* cloud (2) **3A**
wolkig *adj.* cloudy (2) **3A**
Wolle *f.* wool (2) **1B**
wollen *v.* to want (1) **3B**
Wörterbuch, ¨er *n.* dictionary (1) **1B**
Wortschatz, ¨e *m.* vocabulary
wünschen *v.* to wish (3) **1A**
  sich (etwas) wünschen *v.* to wish (for something) (3) **1A**
Würstchen, - *n.* (small) sausage (1) **4A**

Z

Zahn, ¨e *m.* tooth (3) **1A**
  sich die Zähne putzen *m.* to brush one's teeth (3) **1A**
Zahnarzt, ¨e / Zahnärztin, -nen *m./f.* dentist (3) **1B**
Zahnbürste, -n *f.* toothbrush (3) **1A**
Zahnpasta (*pl.* Zahnpasten) *f.* toothpaste (3) **1A**
Zahnschmerzen *m. pl.* toothache (3) **1B**
Zapping *n.* channel surfing
Zebrastreifen, - *m.* crosswalk (3) **2B**
Zeh, -en *m.* toe (3) **1A**
zehn ten (1) **2A**
zeigen *v.* to show (1) **4B**
Zeit, -en *f.* time (1) **2A**
Zeitschrift, -en *f.* magazine (3) **2A**
Zeitung, -en *f.* newspaper (2) **3B**, (3) **2A**
Zelt, -e *n.* tent (2) **3B**
Zeltplatz, ¨e *m.* camping area (2) **3B**
Zeugnis, -se *n.* report card, grade report (1) **1B**
ziehen *v.* to pull (1) **3B**
ziemlich *adv.* quite (1) **4A**
  ziemlich gut pretty well (1) **1A**
Zimmer, - *n.* room (2) **1A**
  Zimmer frei vacancy (2) **2A**
Zimmerservice *m.* room service (2) **3B**
Zoll, ¨e *m.* customs (2) **3B**
zu *adv.* too (1) **4A**; *prep.* to; for; at (1) **4B**
  bis zu *prep.* until (3) **2B**
  um... zu (in order) to (2) **3B**
  Zum Wohl! Cheers! (1) **4B**
zubereiten *v.* to prepare (2) **3A**
zuerst *adv.* first (2) **3B**
Zug, ¨e *m.* train (2) **4A**
zumachen *v.* to close (2) **4B**
sich zurechtfinden *v.* to find one's way (3) **2B**
zurückkommen *v.* to come back (1) **4A**
zusammen *adv.* together (1) **3A**
zuschauen *v.* to watch (1) **4A**
Zutat, -en *m.* ingredient (1) **4A**
zuverlässig *adj.* reliable (3) **3B**
zwanzig twenty (1) **2A**
zwei two (1) **2A**
zweite *adj.* second (1) **2A**
Zwiebel, -n *f.* onion (1) **4A**
Zwilling, -e *m.* twin (1) **3A**
zwischen *prep.* between (2) **1B**
zwölf twelve (1) **2A**

Englisch-Deutsch

A

a ein/eine (1) **1A**
able: to be able to können *v.* (1) **3B**
about über *prep.* (2) **1B**
to be about handeln von *v.* (2) **3A**
above über *prep.* (2) **1B**
abroad Ausland *n.* (2) **3B**
accident Unfall, ⸚e *m.* (2) **4A**
to have an accident einen Unfall haben *v.* (2) **4A**
accommodation Unterkunft, ⸚e *f.* (2) **3B**
according to nach *prep.* (1) **4B**
accountant Buchhalter, - / Buchhalterin, -nen *m./f.* (3) **3B**
acid rain saurer Regen *m.* (3) **4B**
across (from) gegenüber (von) *prep.* (3) **2B**
address Adresse, -n *f.* (3) **2A**
adopt adoptieren *v.* (1) **3A**
afraid: to be afraid of Angst haben vor *v.* (2) **3A**
after nach *prep.* (1) **4B**; nachdem *conj.* (3) **2A**
afternoon Nachmittag, -e *m.* (1) **2B**
in the afternoon nachmittags *adv.* (1) **2A**
against gegen *prep.* (1) **3B**
air Luft, ⸚e *f.* (3) **4A**
airplane Flugzeug, -e *n.* (2) **3B**
airport Flughafen, ⸚ *m.* (2) **3B**
all ganz *adj.* (2) **3B**; alle *pron.* (2) **3B**
allergic (to) allergisch (gegen) *adj.* (3) **1B**
allergy Allergie, -n *f.* (3) **1B**
allow lassen *v.* (1) **2B**
to be allowed to dürfen *v.* (1) **3B**
almost fast *adv.* (1) **4A**
alone allein *adv.* (1) **4A**
along entlang *prep.* (1) **3B**
already schon (1) **4A**
alright: Are you alright? Alles klar? (1) **1A**
also auch *adv.* (1) **4A**
although obwohl *conj.* (3) **2A**
always immer *adv.* (1) **4A**
ambulance Krankenwagen, - *m.* (3) **1B**
America Amerika *n.* (3) **2B**
American amerikanisch *adj.* (3) **2B**; **(person)** Amerikaner, - / Amerikanerin, -nen *m./f.* (3) **2B**
American football American Football *m.* (1) **2B**
and und *conj.* (1) **1B**
animal Tier, -e *n.* (3) **4A**
angry böse *adj.*
to get angry (about) sich ärgern (über) *v.* (3) **1A**
anniversary Jahrestag, -e *m.* (2) **1A**
announce verkünden *v.* (3) **4B**
answer antworten *v.* (1) **2A**; beantworten *v.* (1) **4A**; Antwort, -en *f.*
to answer the phone einen Anruf entgegennehmen *v.* (3) **3A**
anything: Anything else? Noch einen Wunsch? (1) **4B**; Sonst noch etwas? (1) **4A**
apartment Wohnung, -en *f.* (2) **2A**
appetizer Vorspeise, -n *f.* (1) **4B**
apple Apfel, ⸚ *m.* (1) **1A**
applicant Bewerber, - / Bewerberin, -nen *m./f.* (3) **3A**
apply sich bewerben *v.* (3) *3A*
appointment Termin, -e *m.* (3) **3A**
April April *m.* (1) **2A**
architect Architekt, -en / Architektin, -nen *m./f.* (1) **3B**
architecture Architektur, -en *f.* (1) **2A**
argue sich streiten *v.* (3) **1A**
arm Arm, -e *m.* (3) **1A**
armchair Sessel, - *m.* (2) **2A**
around um *prep.* (1) **3B**
arrival Ankunft, ⸚e *f.* (2) **3B**
arrive ankommen *v.* (1) **4A**
arrogant eingebildet *adj.* (1) **3B**
art Kunst, ⸚e *f.* (1) **2A**
artichoke Artischocke, -n *f.* (1) **4A**
as als *conj.* (2) **4A**
as if als ob (3) **2A**
ask fragen *v.* (1) **2A**
to ask about fragen nach *v.* (2) **3A**
assistant Assistent, -en / Assistentin, -nen *m./f.* (3) **3A**
at um *prep.* (1) **3B**; bei *prep.* (1) **4A**; an *prep.* (2) **1B**
at...o'clock um...Uhr (1) **2A**
athletic sportlich *adj.* (1) **2B**
ATM Geldautomat, -en *m.* (3) **2A**
Attention! Achtung!
attic Dachboden, ⸚ *m.* (2) **2A**
August August *m.* (1) **2A**
aunt Tante, -n *f.* (1) **3A**
Austria Österreich *n.* (3) **2B**
Austrian österreichisch *adj.* (3) **2B**; **(person)** Österreicher, - / Österreicherin, -nen *m./f.* (3) **2B**
autumn Herbst, -e *m.* (1) **2B**
avenue Allee, -n *f.* (3) **2B**
awful furchtbar *adj.* (2) **3A**

B

baby Baby, -s *n.* (1) **3A**
back Rücken, - *m.* (3) **1A**
backache Rückenschmerzen *m. pl.* (3) **1B**
backpack Rucksack, ⸚e *m.* (1) **1B**
bad schlecht *adj.* (1) **3B**
badly dressed schlecht gekleidet *adj.* (2) **1B**
baked goods Gebäck *n.* (2) **1A**
bakery Bäckerei, -en *f.* (1) **4A**
balcony Balkon, - e *m.* (2) **2A**
ball Ball, ⸚e *m.* (1) **2B**
balloon Ballon, -e *m.* (2) **1A**
ball-point pen Kuli, -s *m.* (1) **1B**
banana Banane, -n *f.* (1) **4A**
bank Bank, -en *f.* (3) **2A**
at the bank auf der Bank *f.* (3) **2B**
bank account Konto (*pl.* Konten) *n.* (3) **2A**
bank employee Bankangestellte, -n *m./f.* (3) **3B**
baseball Baseball *m.* (1) **2B**
basketball Basketball *m.* (1) **2B**
bath: to take a bath sich baden *v.* (3) **1A**
bathing suit Badeanzug, ⸚e *m.* (2) **1B**
bathrobe Bademantel, ⸚ *m.* (3) **1A**
bathroom Badezimmer, - *n.* (3) **1A**
bathtub Badewanne, -n *f.* (2) **2A**
battery charger Ladegerät, -e *n.* (2) **4B**
be sein *v.* (1) **1A**
Is/Are there... Ist/Sind hier...? *v.* (1) **1B**; Gibt es...? (1) **2B**
There is/are... Da ist/sind... *v.* (1) **1A**; Es gibt... (1) **2B**
beach Strand, ⸚e *m.* (1) **2B**
bean Bohne, -n *f.* (1) **4A**
beard Bart, ⸚e *m.* (3) **1A**
beautiful schön *adj.* (1) **3A**
beauty salon Kosmetiksalon, -s *m.* (3) **2A**
because denn *conj.* (2) **2A**; weil *conj.* (3) **2A**
because of wegen *prep.* (2) **4B**
become werden *v.* (1) **2B**
bed Bett, -en *n.* (2) **2A**
to go to bed ins Bett gehen *v.* (3) **1A**
to make the bed das Bett machen *v.* (2) **2B**
bedroom Schlafzimmer, - *n.* (2) **2A**
beef Rindfleisch *n.* (1) **4A**
beer Bier, -e *n.* (1) **4B**
before vor *prep.* (2) **1B**; bevor *conj.* (2) **4A**
before noon vormittags *adv.* (1) **2A**
begin anfangen *v.* (1) **4A**; beginnen *v.* (2) **4A**
behind hinter *prep.* (2) **1B**
believe glauben *v.* (2) **1A**; meinen *v.* (3) **4B**
belly Bauch, ⸚e *m.* (3) **1A**
belong gehören *v.* (1) **4B**
below unter *prep.* (2) **1B**
belt Gürtel, - *m.* (2) **1B**
bench Bank, ⸚e *f.* (3) **2B**
best beste/bester/bestes *adj.* (2) **4A**
All the best! Mach's gut! *v.* (1) **3B**; alles Gute (3) **2A**
better besser *adj.* (2) **4A**
to get better gesund werden *v.* (3) **1B**
between zwischen *prep.* (2) **1B**
beverage Getränk, -e *n.* (1) **4B**
bicycle Fahrrad, ⸚er *n.* (1) **2B**
big groß, weit *adj.* (1) **3A**
bill (money) Geldschein, -e *m.* (3) **2A**
biology Biologie *f.* (1) **2A**
bird Vogel, ⸚ *m.* (1) **3A**
birth Geburt, -en *f.* (2) **1A**
birthday Geburtstag, -e *m.* (2) **1A**
When is your birthday? Wann hast du Geburtstag? (1) **2B**
black schwarz *adj.* (2) **1B**
black board Tafel, -n *f.* (1) **1B**
black-haired schwarzhaarig *adj.* (1) **3A**
bland fade *adj.* (1) **4B**
blanket Decke, -n *f.* (2) **2B**
blond blond *adj.* (1) **3A**
blond hair blonde Haare *n. pl.* (1) **3A**
blood pressure Blutdruck *m.* (3) **1B**
blouse Bluse, -n *f.* (2) **1B**
blue blau *adj.* (1) **3A**
board Tafel, -n *f.* (1) **1B**
boarding pass Bordkarte, -n *f.* (2) **3B**
boat Boot, -e *n.* (2) **4A**
body Körper, - *m.* (3) **1A**
book Buch, ⸚er *n.* (1) **1A**
bookshelf Bücherregal, -e *n.* (2) **2A**
boot Stiefel, - *m.* (2) **1B**
boring langweilig *adj.* (1) **2A**
boss Chef, -s / Chefin, -nen *m./f.* (3) **3B**
bottle Flasche, -n *f.* (1) **4B**
bowl Schüssel, -n *f.* (1) **4B**
boy Junge, -n *m.* (1) **1A**

brakes Bremse, -n *f.* (2) **4A**
brave mutig *adj.* (1) **3B**
bread Brot, -e *n.* (1) **4A**
break brechen *v.* (1) **2B**
to break (an arm / a leg) sich (den Arm/Bein) brechen *v.* (3) **1B**
Break a leg! Hals- und Beinbruch! (2) **1A**
breakfast Frühstück, -e *n.* (1) **4B**
bridge Brücke, -n *f.* (3) **2B**
bright hell *adj.* (2) **1B**
bring bringen *v.* (1) **2A**
to bring along mitbringen *v.* (1) **4A**
to bring out rausbringen (2) **2B**
to bring with mitnehmen *v.* (3) **2B**
broom Besen, - *m.* (2) **2B**
brother Bruder, ¨ *m.* (1) **1A**
brother-in-law Schwager, ¨ *m.* (1) **3A**
brown braun *adj.* (2) **1B**
brown-haired braunhaarig *adj.* (1) **3A**
bruise blauer Fleck, -e *m.* (3) **1B**
brush Bürste, -n *f.* (3) **1A**
to brush one's hair sich die Haare bürsten *v.* (3) **1A**
to brush one's teeth sich die Zähne putzen *v.* (3) **1A**
build bauen *v.* (1) **2A**
building Gebäude, - *n.* (3) **2A**
bulletin board Pinnwand, ¨e *f.* (3) **3A**
burn brennen *v.* (2) **1A**
bus Bus, -se *m.* (2) **4A**
bus stop Bushaltestelle, -n *f.* (2) **4A**
bush Busch, ¨e *m.* (3) **4A**
business Wirtschaft, -en *f.* (1) **2A**; Geschäft, -e *n.* (3) **4A**
business class Businessklasse *f.* (2) **3B**
businessman / businesswoman Geschäftsmann, ¨er / Geschäftsfrau, -en *m./f.* (*pl.* Geschäftsleute) (1) **3B**
but aber *conj.* (1) **1B**
but rather sondern *conj.* (2) **2A**
butcher shop Metzgerei, -en *f.* (1) **4A**
butter Butter *f.* (1) **4A**
buy kaufen *v.* (1) **2A**
by an *prep.* (2) **1B**; bei; von (1) **4B**
Bye! Tschüss! (1) **1A**

C

cabinet Schrank, ¨e *m.* (2) **2A**
café Café, -s *n.* (1) **2A**
cafeteria Cafeteria, (*pl.* Cafeterien) *f.*; **(college/university)** Mensa, Mensen *f.* (1) **1B**
cake Kuchen, - *m.* (1) **4A**; Torte, -n *f.* (2) **1A**
calculator Taschenrechner, - *m.* (1) **1B**
calendar Kalender, - *m.* (1) **1B**
call anrufen *v.* (1) **4A**; sich anrufen (3) **1A**; nennen *v.* (2) **1A**
Who's calling? Wer spricht? (3) **3A**
calm ruhig *adj.* (1) **3B**
(to go) camping campen gehen *n.* (1) **2B**
camping area Zeltplatz, ¨e *m.* (2) **3B**
can können *v.* (1) **3B**
Canada Kanada *n.* (3) **2B**
Canadian kanadisch *adj.* (3) **2B**; **(person)** Kanadier, - / Kanadierin, -nen *m./f.* (3) **2B**
cancel abbrechen, streichen *v.* (2) **3B**
candidate Kandidat, -en *m.* (3) **3A**
candy Süßigkeit, -en *f.* (2) **1A**
cap Mütze, -n *f.* (2) **1B**
car Auto, -s *n.* (1) **1A**
to drive a car Auto fahren *v.* (2) **4A**
card Karte, -n *f.* (1) **2B**
career Karriere, -n *f.* (3) **3B**
caretaker Hausmeister, - / Hausmeisterin, -nen *m./f.* (3) **3B**
carpool Fahrgemeinschaft, -en *f.* (3) **4B**
carrot Karotte, -n *f.* (1) **4A**
carry tragen *v.* (1) **2B**
carry-on luggage Handgepäck *n.* (2) **3B**
cash bar *adj.* (3) **2A**; Bargeld *n.* (3) **2A**
to pay in cash bar bezahlen *v.* (3) **2A**
cat Katze, -n *f.* (1) **3A**
catch fangen *v.* (1) **2B**
to catch a cold sich erkälten *v.* (3) **1A**
celebrate feiern *v.* (2) **1A**
celebration Fest, -e *n.* (2) **1A**
cell phone Handy, -s *n.* (2) **4B**
cellar Keller, - *m.* (2) **2A**
ceramic Keramik, -en *f.* (2) **2B**
chair Stuhl, ¨e *m.* (1) **1A**
champagne Sekt, -e *m.* (2) **1A**
championship Meisterschaft, -en *f.* (1) **2B**
change Kleingeld *n.* (3) **2A**
to change clothes sich umziehen *v.* (3) **1A**
channel Sender, - *m.* (3) **4B**
channel surfing Zapping *n.*
charge laden *v.* (2) **4B**
chat sich unterhalten *v.* (3) **1A**
cheap günstig *adj.* (2) **1B**
check Rechnung, -en *f.* (1) **4B**
Cheers! Prost! **4B**; Zum Wohl! (1) **4B**
cheese Käse, - *m.* (1) **4A**
chemistry Chemie *f.* (1) **2A**
chess Schach *n.* (1) **2B**
chicken Huhn, ¨er n. (3) **4A**; **(food)** Hähnchen, - *n.* (1) **4A**
child Kind, -er *n.* (1) **1A**
China China *n.* (3) **2B**
Chinese (person) Chinese, -n / Chinesin, -nen *m./f.* (3) **2B**; **(language)** Chinesisch *n.* (3) **2B**
Christmas Weihnachten, - *n.* (2) **1A**
church Kirche, -n *f.* (3) **2B**
city Stadt, ¨e *f.* (2) **1B**
city center Innenstadt, ¨e *f.* (3) **2B**
claim behaupten *v.* (3) **4B**
class Klasse, -n *f.* (1) **1B**; Unterricht *m.* (1) **1B**; Veranstaltung, -en *f.* (1) **2A**
first/second class erste/zweite Klasse (2) **2A**
classical klassisch *adj.* (3) **2A**
classmate Kommilitone, -n / Kommilitonin, -nen; Klassenkamerad, -en / Klassenkameradin, -nen *m./f.* (1) **1B**
classroom Klassenzimmer, - *n.* (1) **1B**
clean sauber *adj.* (2) **2B**; putzen *v.* (2) **2B**
to clean up aufräumen *v.* (2) **2B**
cliff Klippe, -n *f.* (3) **4A**
climb steigen *v.* (2) **1B**
to climb (mountain) klettern *v.* (1) **2B**
to climb (stairs) (die Treppe) hochgehen *v.* (3) **2B**
clock Uhr, -en *f.* (1) **1B**
at... o'clock um... Uhr (1) **2A**
close zumachen *v.* (2) **2B**; nah *adj.* (3) **2B**
close to in der Nähe von *prep.* (3) **2B**
closed geschlossen *adj.* (3) **2A**
closet Schrank, ¨e *m.* (2) **2A**
clothes Kleidung *f.* (2) **1B**
cloud Wolke, -n *f.* (2) **3A**
cloudy wolkig *adj.* (2) **3A**
coast Küste, -n *f.* (3) **4A**
coat Mantel, ¨ *m.* (2) **1B**
coffee Kaffee, -s *m.* (1) **4B**
coffeemaker Kaffeemaschine, -n *f.* (2) **3B**
coin Münze, -n *f.* (3) **2A**
cold kalt *adj.* (2) **3A**; Erkältung, -en **f.** (3) **1B**
to catch a cold sich erkälten *v.* (3) **1A**
college Universität, -en *f.* (1) **1B**
college instructor Dozent, -en / Dozentin, -nen *m./f.* (1) **2A**
color Farbe, -n *f.* (2) **1B**
solid colored einfarbig *adj.* (2) **1B**
colorful bunt *adj.* (3) **2A**
comb Kamm, ¨e *m.* (3) **1A**
to comb (one's hair) sich (die Haare) kämmen *v.* (3) **1A**
come kommen *v.* (1) **2A**
to come along mitkommen *v.* (1) **4A**
to come back zurückkommen *v.* (1) **4A**
comma Komma, -s *f.* (1) **1B**
compact disc CD, -s *f.* (2) **4B**
company Firma (*pl.* die Firmen) *f.* (3) **3A**
complicated kompliziert *adj.* (3) **2A**
computer Computer, - *m.* (1) **1B**
computer science Informatik *f.* (1) **2A**
concert Konzert, -e *n.* (2) **1B**
congratulate gratulieren *v.* (2) **1A**
Congratulations! Herzlichen Glückwunsch! (2) **1A**
construction zone Baustelle, -n *f.* (2) **4A**
contract Vertrag, ¨e *m.* (3) **3A**
conversation: to have a conversation sich unterhalten *v.* (3) **1A**
cook kochen *v.* (1) **2B**; Koch, ¨e / Köchin, -nen *m./f.* (1) **4B**
cookie Keks, -e *m.* (2) **1A**
cool kühl *adj.* (2) **3A**
corner Ecke, -n *f.* (3) **2B**
correct korrigieren *v.* (1) **2A**
cost kosten *v.* (1) **2A**
cotton Baumwolle *f.* (2) **1B**
couch Sofa, -s *n.* (2) **3B**
to couch surf Sofa surfen *v.* (2) **3B**
cough husten *v.* (3) **1B**
country Land, ¨er *n.* (2) **3B**
countryside Landschaft, -en *f.* (3) **4A**
couple Paar, -e *n.* (1) **3A**
courageous mutig *adj.*
course Veranstaltung, -en *f.* (1) **2B**; Gang, ¨e *m.* (1) **4B**
first/second course erster/zweiter Gang *m.* (1) **4B**
main course Hauptspeise, -en *f.* (1) **4B**
court Platz, ¨e *m.* (1) **1A**
cousin Cousin, -s / Cousine, -n *m./f.* (1) **3A**
cover decken *v.* (2) **2B**
cow Kuh, ¨e *f.* (3) **4A**

cram (for a test) büffeln *v.* (1) **2A**
cross überqueren *v.* (3) **2B**
to cross the street die Straße überqueren *v.* (3) **2B**
cross-reference Querverweis, -e *m.*
crosswalk Zebrastreifen, - *pl.* (3) **2B**
cruel grausam *adj.*; gemein *adj.* (1) **3B**
cruise Kreuzfahrt, -en *f.* (2) **3B**
cry weinen *v.* (1) **3B**
cup Tasse, -n *f.* (1) **4B**
curious neugierig *adj.* (1) **3B**
curly lockig *adj.* (1) **3A**
curtain Vorhang, ¨-e *m.* (2) **2A**
custodian Hausmeister, - / Hausmeisterin, -nen *m./f.* (3) **3B**
customer Kunde, -n /Kundin, -nen *m./f.* (2) **1B**
customs Zoll *m.* (2) **3B**
cut Schnitt, -e *m.* (2) **1B**
to cut class schwänzen *v.* (1) **1B**
cute süß *adj.* (1) **3B**
CV Lebenslauf, ¨-e *m.* (3) **3A**

D

dad Papa, -s *m.* (1) **3A**
daily täglich *adv.* (1) **4A**
daily routine Alltagsroutine *f.* (3) **1A**
dance tanzen *v.* (1) **2B**
danger Gefahr, -en *f.* (3) **4B**
dark dunkel *adj.* (1) **3A**
dark-haired dunkelhaarig *adj.* (1) **3A**
darling Liebling, -e *m.*
date Datum (*pl.* Daten) *n.* (2) **3A**
What is the date today? Der wievielte ist heute? (1) **2A**
daughter Tochter, ¨- *f.* (1) **3A**
day Tag, -e *m.* (1) **1A**
every day täglich *adv.* (1) **4A**
Dear Lieber/Liebe *m./f.* (1) **3B**
December Dezember *m.* (1) **2A**
decide sich entschließen *v.* (1) **4B**
definitely bestimmt *adv.* (1) **4A**
degree Abschluss, ¨-e *m.* (1) **2A**; Grad *n.* (2) **3A**
It's 18 degrees out. Es sind 18 Grad draußen. (2) **3A**
delay Verspätung, -en *f.* (2) **3B**
delete löschen *v.* (2) **4B**
delicatessen Feinkostgeschäft, -e *n.* (1) **4A**
delicious lecker *adj.* (1) **4B**
demanding anspruchsvoll *adj.* (3) **3B**
dentist Zahnarzt, ¨-e / Zahnärztin, -nen *m./f.* (3) **1B**
department store Kaufhaus, ¨-er *n.* (3) **2B**
departure Abflug, ¨-e *m.* (2) **3B**
deposit (money) (Geld) einzahlen *v.* (3) **2A**
describe beschreiben *v.* (1) **2A**
description Beschreibung, -en *f.* (1) **3B**
desk Schreibtisch, -e *m.* (1) **1B**
despite trotz *prep.* (2) **4B**
dessert Nachtisch, -e, *m.* (1) **4B**
destination Reiseziel, -e *n.* (2) **3B**
detour Umleitung, -en *f.* (2) **4A**
develop entwickeln *v.* (3) **4B**
dictionary Wörterbuch, ¨-er *n.* (1) **1B**
die sterben *v.* (2) **1B**
diet Diät, -en *f.* (1) **4B**
to be on a diet auf Diät sein *v.* (1) **4B**
difficult schwierig *adj.* (1) **2A**
digital camera Digitalkamera, -s *f.* (2) **4B**
dining room Esszimmer, - *n.* (2) **2A**
dinner Abendessen, - *n.* (1) **4B**
diploma Abschlusszeugnis, -se *n.* (1) **2A**; Diplom, -e *n.* (1) **2A**
direction Richtung, -en *f.* (3) **2B**
dirty schmutzig *adj.* (2) **2B**
discover entdecken *v.* (2) **2B**
discreet diskret *adj.* (1) **3B**
discuss besprechen *v.* (1) **4A**
dish Gericht, -e *n.* (1) **4B**
dishes Geschirr *n.* (2) **2B**
to do the dishes Geschirr spülen (2) **2B**
dishwasher Spülmaschine, -n *f.* (2) **2B**
dislike nicht gern (+*verb*) (1) **3A**
divided by geteilt durch (1) **1B**
divorced geschieden *adj.* (1) **3A**
dizzy schwindlig *adj.* (3) **1B**
do machen *v.* (1) **2A**; tun *v.* (3) **1B**
to do laundry Wäsche waschen *v.* (2) **2B**
to do the dishes Geschirr spülen *v.* (2) **2B**
to have to do with handeln von (2) **3A**
doctor Arzt, ¨-e / Ärztin, -nen *m./f.* (3) **1B**
to go to the doctor zum Arzt gehen *v.* (3) **1B**
document Dokument, -e *n.* (2) **4B**
dog Hund, -e *m.* (1) **3A**
door Tür, -en *f.* (1) **1B**
dormitory (Studenten)wohnheim, -e *n.* (2) **2A**
down entlang *prep.* (1) **3B**; herunter *adv.* (2) **2A**
to go down heruntergehen *v.* (3) **2B**
download herunterladen *v.* (2) **4B**
downtown Innenstadt, -¨e *f.* (3) **2B**
dozen Dutzend, -e *n.* (1) **4A**
a dozen eggs ein Dutzend Eier (1) **4A**
drawer Schublade, -n *f.* (2) **2A**
dream träumen *v.* (2) **3A**
dress Kleid, -er *n.* (2) **1B**
to get dressed sich anziehen *v.* (3) **1A**
to get undressed sich ausziehen *v.* (3) **1A**
dresser Kommode, -n *f.* (2) **2A**
drink trinken *v.* (1) **3B**
drive fahren *v.* (2) **4A**
to drive a car Auto fahren *v.* (2) **4A**
driver Fahrer, - / Fahrerin, -nen *m./f.* (2) **4A**
drugstore Drogerie, -n *f.* (3) **2A**
dry trocken *adj.* (3) **4A**
to dry oneself off sich abtrocknen *v.* (3) **1A**
dryer Wäschetrockner, - *m.* (2) **2B**
dumb dumm *adj.* (2) **4A**
during während *prep.* (2) **4B**
dust abstauben *v.* (2) **2B**
duvet Bettdecke, - n *f.* (2) **2B**
DVD DVD, -s *f.* (2) **4B**
DVD-player DVD-Player, - *m.* (2) **4B**
dye (one's hair) sich (die Haare) färben *v.* (3) **1A**

E

ear Ohr, -en *n.* (3) **1A**
early früh *adj.* (1) **2B**
earn verdienen *v.* (3) **3B**
earth Erde, -n *f.* (3) **4B**
earthquake Erdbeben, - *n.* (3) **4A**
easy einfach *adj.* (1) **2A**
eat essen *v.* (1) **2B**
to eat out essen gehen *v.* (1) **2B**
ecological ökologisch *adj.* (3) **4B**
ecology Ökologie *f.* (3) **4B**
economy Wirtschaft, -en *f.* (1) **2A**
economy class Touristenklasse *f.* (2) **3B**
education Ausbildung, -en *f.* (3) **3A**
egg Ei, -er *n.* (1) **4A**
eggplant Aubergine, -n *f.* (1) **4A**
eight acht (1) **2A**
elbow Ell(en)bogen, - *m.* (3) **1A**
electrician Elektriker, - / Elektrikerin, -nen *m./f.* (3) **3B**
elegant elegant *adj.* (2) **1B**
elevator Fahrstuhl, ¨-e *m.* (2) **3B**
eleven elf (1) **2A**
e-mail E-Mail, -s *f.* (2) **4B**
emergency Notfall, ¨-e *m.* (3) **3B**
emergency room Notaufnahme, -n *f.* (3) **1B**
employee Angestellte, -n *m./f.* (3) **3A**
endangered gefährdet *adj.* (3) **4B**
energy Energie, -n *f.* (3) **4B**
energy-efficient energiesparend *adj.* (2) **2B**
engaged verlobt *adj.* (1) **3A**
engine Motor, -en *m.* (2) **4A**
engineer Ingenieur, -e / Ingenieurin, -nen *m./f.* (1) **3B**
England England *n.* (3) **2B**
English (person) Engländer, - / Engländerin, -nen *m./f.* (3) **2B**; **(language)** Englisch *n.* (3) **2B**
enjoy genießen *v.*
Enjoy your meal! Guten Appetit! (1) **4B**
envelope Briefumschlag, ¨-e *m.* (3) **2A**
environment Umwelt, -en *f.* (3) **4B**
environmentally friendly umweltfreundlich *adj.* (2) **4B**
environmentalism Umweltschutz *m.* (3) **4B**
equal (gleich) sein *v.* (1) **1B**
eraser Radiergummi, -s *m.* (1) **1B**
errand Besorgung, -en *f.* (3) **2A**
to run errands Besorgungen machen *v.* (3) **2A**
even though obwohl *conj.* (2) **2A**
evening Abend, -e *m.* (1) **2B**
in the evening abends *adv.* (1) **2A**
every jeder/jede/jedes *adv.* (2) **4B**
everything alles *pron.* (2) **3B**
Everything OK? Alles klar? (1) **1A**
everywhere überall *adv.* (1) **4A**
exam Prüfung, -en *f.* (1) **1B**
except (for) außer *prep.* (1) **4B**
exchange umtauschen *v.* (2) **2B**
exciting spannend *adj.* (3) **2A**; aufregend *adj.* (3) **4A**
Excuse me. Entschuldigung. (1) **1A**
exercise Sport treiben *v.* (3) **1B**
exit Ausgang, ¨-e *m.* (2) **1B**; Ausfahrt, -en *f.* (2) **4A**
expensive teuer *adj.* (2) **2B**
experience durchmachen *v.* (2) **4B**; Erfahrung, -en *f.* (3) **3A**
explain erklären *v.* (1) **4A**
explore erforschen *v.* (3) **4A**
expression Ausdruck, ¨-e *m.*

extinction Aussterben *n.* (3) **4B**
eye Auge, -n *n.* (1) **3A**
eyebrow Augenbraue, -n *f.* (3) **1A**

F

face Gesicht, -er *n.* (3) **1A**
factory Fabrik, -en *f.* (3) **4B**
factory worker Fabrikarbeiter, - / Fabrikarbeiterin, -nen *m./f.* (3) **3B**
fail durchfallen *v.* (1) **1B**; scheitern *v.* (3) **3B**
fall fallen *v.* (1) **2B**; **(season)** Herbst, -e *m.* (1) **2B**
  to fall in love (with) sich verlieben (in) *v.* (3) **1A**
familiar bekannt *adj.*
  to be familiar with kennen *v.* (2) **1B**
family Familie, -n *f.* (1) **3A**
fan Fan, -s *m.* (1) **2B**
fantastic fantastisch *adj.* (3) **2A**
far weit *adj.* (3) **2B**
  far from weit von *adj.* (3) **2B**
farm Bauernhof, ¨-e *m.* (3) **4A**
farmer Bauer, -n / Bäuerin, -nen *m./f.* (3) **3B**
fashionable modisch *adj.* (2) **1B**
fast schnell *adj.* (1) **3B**
fat dick *adj.* (1) **3A**
father Vater, ¨ *m.* (1) **3A**
father-in-law Schwiegervater, ¨ *m.* (1) **3A**
favorite Lieblings- (1) **4B**
fear Angst, ¨-e *f.* (2) **3A**
February Februar *m.* (1) **2A**
feel fühlen *v.* (1) **2A**; sich fühlen *v.* (3) **1A**
  to feel like Lust haben *v.* (2) **3B**
  to feel well sich wohl fühlen *v.* (3) **1A**
fever Fieber, - *n.* (3) **1B**
  to have a fever Fieber haben *v.* (3) **1B**
fiancé(e) Verlobte, -n *m./f.* (1) **3A**
field Spielfeld, -er *n.* (1) **2B**; Feld, -er *n.* (3) **4A**
file Datei, -en *f.* (2) **4B**
fill füllen *v.*
  to fill out ausfüllen *v.* (3) **2A**
  to fill up tanken *v.* (2) **4A**
filthy dreckig *adj.* (2) **2B**
finally schließlich *adv.* (2) **3B**
find finden *v.* (1) **2A**
  to find one's way sich zurechtfinden *v.* (3) **2B**
  to find out (about) sich informieren (über) *v.* (3) **1A**
fine (monetary) Bußgeld, -er *n.* (2) **4A**
  I'm fine. Mir geht's gut. (1) **1A**
finger Finger, - *m.* (3) **1A**
fire entlassen *v.* (3) **3B**; Feuer, - *n.*
firefighter Feuerwehrmann, ¨-er / Feuerwehrfrau, -en (*pl.* Feuerwehrleute) *m./f.* (3) **3B**
firm Firma (*pl.* die Firmen) *f.* (3) **3A**
first erster/erste/erstes *adj.* (1) **2A**; zuerst *adv.* (2) **3B**
  first course erster Gang *m.* (1) **4B**
  first class erste Klasse *f.* (2) **4A**
fish Fisch, -e *m.* (1) **4A**
  to go fishing angeln gehen *v.* (1) **2B**
fish store Fischgeschäft, -e *n.* (1) **4A**
fit passen *v.* (2) **1A**; fit *adj.* (1) **2B**
five fünf (1) **2A**
flat tire Platten, - *m.* (2) **4A**
  to have a flat tire einen Platten haben *v.* (2) **4A**
flavor Geschmack, ¨-e *m.* (1) **4B**
flight Flug, ¨-e *m.* (2) **3B**
flood Hochwasser, - *n.* (3) **4B**
floor Stock, ¨-e *m.*; Boden, ¨ *m.* (2) **2A**
  first/second floor erster/zweiter Stock (2) **2A**
flower Blume, -n *f.* (1) **1A**
  flower shop Blumengeschäft, -e *n.* (3) **2A**
flu Grippe, -n *f.* (3) **1B**
flunk durchfallen *v.* (1) **1B**
fly fliegen *v.* (2) **3B**
fog Nebel, - *m.* (2) **3A**
follow folgen *v.* (2) **1A**
food Essen, - *n.* (1) **4A**
foot Fuß, ¨-e *m.* (3) **1A**
football American Football *m.* (1) **2B**
for für *prep.* (1) **3B**; seit; zu *prep.* (1) **4B**
foreign language Fremdsprache, -n *f.* (1) **2A**
forest Wald, ¨-er *m.* (1) **2B**
forget vergessen *v.* (1) **2B**
fork Gabel, -n *f.* (1) **4B**
form Formular, -e *n.* (3) **2A**
  to fill out a form ein Formular ausfüllen *v.* (3) **2A**
fountain Brunnen, - *m.* (3) **2B**
four vier (1) **2A**
France Frankreich *n.* (3) **2B**
French (person) Franzose, -n / Französin, -nen *m./f.* (3) **2B; (language)** Französisch *n.* (3) **2B**
free time Freizeit, -en *f.* (1) **2B**
freezer Gefrierschrank, ¨-e *m.* (2) **2B**
Friday Freitag, -e *m.* (1) **2A**
  on Fridays freitags *adv.* (1) **2A**
friend Freund, -e / Freundin, -nen *m./f.* (1) **1A**
friendly freundlich *adj.* (1) **3B**
friendship Freundschaft, -en *f.* (2) **1A**
from aus *prep.* (1) **4A**; von *prep.* (1) **4B**
  where from woher *interr.* (1) **2A**
front: in front of vor *prep.* (2) **1B**
fruit Obst *n.* (1) **4A**
fry braten *v.* (1) **2B**
full voll *adj.* (2) **3B**
full-time ganztags *adj.* (3) **3B**
fully occupied voll besetzt *adj.* (2) **3B**
fun Spaß *m.* (1) **2B**
  to be fun Spaß machen *v.* (1) **2B**
  to (not) have fun (keinen) Spaß haben *v.* (2) **1A**
function funktionieren *v.* (2) **4B**
funny lustig *adj.* (1) **3B**
furnished möbliert *adj.* (2) **2A**
furniture Möbel, - *n.* (2) **2A**
  piece of furniture Möbelstück, ,-e *n.* (2) **2A**

G

game Spiel, -e *n.* (1) **2B**
game console Spielkonsole, -en *f.* (2) **4B**
garage Garage, -n *f.* (2) **1B**
garbage truck Müllwagen, - *m.* (3) **4B**
gardener Gärtner, - / Gärtnerin, -nen *m./f.* (3) **3B**
garlic Knoblauch *m.* (1) **4A**
gas Benzin, -e *n.* (2) **4A**
gas station Tankstelle, -n *f.* (2) **4A**
generous großzügig *adj.* (1) **3B**
German (person) Deutsche *m./f.* (3) **2B**; **(language)** Deutsch *n.* (3) **2B**
Germany Deutschland *n.* (1) **4A**
get bekommen *v.* (2) **1A**
  to get up aufstehen *v.* (1) **4A**
  to get sick/better krank/gesund werden *v.* (3) **1B**
gift Geschenk, -e *n.* (2) **1A**
girl Mädchen, - *n.* (1) **1A**
give geben *v.* (1) **2B**
  to give (a gift) schenken *v.* (2) **1A**
glass Glas, ¨-er *n.* (1) **4B**
glasses Brille, -n *f.* (2) **1B**
global warming Erderwärmung *f.* (2) **4B**
glove Handschuh, -e *m.* (2) **1B**
go gehen *v.* (1) **2A**; fahren *v.* (1) **2B**
  to go out ausgehen *v.* (1) **4A**
  Go! Los! (1) **2B**
goal (in soccer) Tor, -e *n.* (1) **2B**
golf Golf *n.* (1) **2B**
good gut *adj.*; nett *adj.* (1) **1A**
  Good evening. Guten Abend! (1) **1A**
  Good morning. Guten Morgen! (1) **1A**
  Good night. Gute Nacht! (1) **1A**
  Good-bye. Auf Wiedersehen! (1) **1A**
  Good luck! Viel Glück! (2) **1A**
government Regierung, -en *f.* (3) **4B**
grade Note, -n *f.* (1) **1B**
grade report Zeugnis, -se *n.* (1) **1B**
graduate Abschluss machen, ¨-e *v.* (2) **1A**
graduation Abschluss, ¨-e *m.* (1) **1B**
gram Gramm, -e *n.* (1) **4A**
  100 grams of cheese 100 Gramm Käse (1) **4A**
granddaughter Enkeltochter, ¨ *f.* (1) **3A**
grandson Enkelsohn, ¨-e *m.* (1) **3A**
grandchild Enkel, - *m.* (1) **3A**; Enkelkind, -er *n.* (1) **3A**
grandfather Großvater, ¨ *m.* (1) **3A**
grandma Oma, -s *f.* (1) **3A**
grandmother Großmutter, ¨ *f.* (1) **3A**
grandpa Opa, -s *m.* (1) **3A**
grandparents Großeltern *pl.* (1) **1A**
grape Traube, -n *f.* (1) **4A**
grass Gras, ¨-er *n.* (3) **4A**
gray grau *adj.* (2) **1B**
great toll *adj.* (1) **3B**; prima *adj.*; spitze *adj.* (1) **1A**
great grandfather Urgroßvater, ¨ *m.* (1) **3A**
great grandmother Urgroßmutter, ¨ *f.* (1) **3A**
greedy gierig *adj.* (1) **3B**
green grün *adj.* (2) **1B**
green bean grüne Bohne (*pl.* die grünen Bohnen) *f.* (1) **4A**
greet grüßen *v.* (1) **2A**
greeting Begrüßung, -en *f.* (1) **1A**; Gruß, ¨-e *m.* (1) **1A**
grocery store Lebensmittelgeschäft, -e *n.* (1) **4A**
ground floor Erdgeschoss, -e *n.* (2) **2A**
grow wachsen *v.* (2) **1B**
grown-up erwachsen *adj.* (3) **2A**
guest Gast, ¨-e *m.* (2) **1A**
  hotel guest Hotelgast, ¨-e *m.* (2) **3B**
guesthouse Pension, -en *f.* (2) **3B**
gym Sporthalle, -n *f.* (1) **2A**

H

hail Hagel *m.* (2) **3A**
hair Haar, -e *n.* (1) **3A**
hair dryer Haartrockner, - *m.* (3) **1A**
hairdresser Friseur, -e / Friseurin, -nen *m./f.* (1) **3B**
half halb *adj.* (1) **2A**
half brother Halbbruder, ¨ *m.* (1) **3A**
half sister Halbschwester, -n *f.* (1) **3A**
hall Flur, -e *m.* (2) **2A**
ham Schinken, - *m.* (1) **4A**
hand Hand, ¨e *f.* (3) **1A**
handsome gut aussehend *adj.* (1) **3A**
hang hängen *v.* (2) **1B**
  to hang up auflegen *v.* (3) **3A**
happen passieren *v.* (2) **1B**
happiness Glück *n.* (2) **1A**
happy glücklich *adj.* (1) **3B** froh *adj.* (1) (1) **3B**
  Happy birthday! Alles Gute zum Geburtstag! (2) **1A**
  Happy Easter! Frohe Ostern! (2) **1A**
  Happy New Year! Ein gutes neues Jahr! (2) **1A**
  to be happy (about) sich freuen (über) *v.* (3) **1A**
hard schwer *adj.* (3) **1B**
hard drive Festplatte, -en *f.* (2) **4B**
hard-working fleißig *adj.* (1) **3B**
hare Hase, -n *m.* (3) **4A**
hat Hut, ¨e *m.* (2) **1B**
have haben *v.* (1) **1B**
  Have a nice day! Schönen Tag noch! (1) **1A**
  to have to müssen *v.* (1) **3B**
he er *pron.* (1) **1A**
head Kopf, ¨e *m.* (3) **1A**
headache Kopfschmerzen *m. pl.* (3) **1B**
headlight Scheinwerfer, -e *m.* (2) **4A**
headphones Kopfhörer, - *m.* (2) **4B**
health Gesundheit *f.* (3) **1B**
health-food store Bioladen, ¨ *m.* (3) **1B**
healthy gesund *adj.* (2) **4A**
hear hören *v.* (1) **2A**
heat stroke Hitzschlag, ¨e *m.* (3) **1B**
heavy schwer *adj.* (1) **4B**
hello Guten Tag!; Hallo! (1) **1A**
help helfen *v.* (1) **2B**
  to help with helfen bei *v.* (2) **3A**
her ihr *poss. adj.* (1) **3A**
here hier *adv.* (1) **1A**
  Here is/are... Hier ist/sind... (1) **1B**
high hoch *adj.* (2) **4A**
highway Autobahn, -en *f.* (2) **4A**
hike wandern *v.* (1) **2A**
his sein *poss. adj.* (1) **3A**
history Geschichte, -en *f.* (1) **2A**
hit treffen *v.* (1) **2B**
hobby Hobby, -s *n.* (1) **2B**
hockey Hockey *n.* (1) **2B**
hold: to be on hold in der Warteschleife sein *v.* (3) **3B**
  Please hold. Bleiben Sie bitte am Apparat! (3) **3A**
holiday Feiertag, -e *m.* (2) **1A**
home Haus, ¨er *adv.* (2) **1B**
  at home zu Hause *adv.* (1) **4A**
home office Arbeitszimmer, - *n.* (2) **2A**
homemade hausgemacht *adj.* (1) **4B**
homemaker Hausfrau, -en / Hausmann, ¨er *f./m.* (3) **3B**
homework Hausaufgabe, -n *f.* (1) **1B**
hood Motorhaube, -en *f.* (2) **4A**
horse Pferd, -e *n.* (1) **2B**
hospital Krankenhaus, ¨er *n.* (3) **1B**
host / hostess Gastgeber, - / Gastgeberin, -nen *m./f.* (2) **1A**
host family Gastfamilie, -n *f.* (1) **4B**
hot heiß *adj.* (2) **3A**
hotel Hotel, -s *n.* (2) **3B**
  five-star hotel Fünf-Sterne-Hotel *n.* (2) **3B**
hour Stunde,-n *f.* (1) **2A**
house Haus, ¨er *n.* (2) **2A**
housework Hausarbeit *f.* (2) **2B**
  to do housework Hausarbeit machen *v.* (2) **2B**
how wie *interr.* (1) **2A**
  How are you? (form.) Wie geht es Ihnen? (1) **1A**
  How are you? (inf.) Wie geht's (dir)? (1) **1A**
  how many wie viele *interr.* (1) **1B**
  how much wie viel *interr.* (1) **1B**
human resources manager Personalchef, -s / die Personalchefin, -nen *m./f.* (3) **3A**
humble bescheiden *adj.*
hurry sich beeilen *v.* (3) **1A**
hurt weh tun *v.* (3) **1B**
  to hurt oneself sich verletzen *v.* (3) **1B**
husband Ehemann, ¨er *m.* (1) **3A**
hybrid car Hybridauto, -s *n.* (3) **4B**

I

I ich *pron.* (1) **1A**
ice cream Eis *n.* (2) **1A**
ice cream shop Eisdiele, -n *f.* (1) **4A**
ice cube Eiswürfel, - *m.* (2) **1A**
ice hockey Eishockey *n.* (1) **2B**
ID card Personalausweis, -e *m.* (2) **3B**
idea Idee, -n *f.* (1) **1A**
if wenn *conj.*; ob *conj.* (3) **2A**
  as if als ob (3) **2A**
  if I were you an deiner/Ihrer Stelle *f.* (3) **2A**
  if... only wenn... nur (3) **2A**
  if... then wenn... dann (3) **2A**
imagine sich (etwas) vorstellen *v.* (3) **1A**
imitate nachmachen *v.* (2) **4B**
important wichtig *adj.* (2) **3B**; bedeutend *adj.* (3) **4A**
improve verbessern *v.* (3) **4B**
in in *prep.* (2) **1B**
  in the afternoon nachmittags *adv.* (1) **2A**
  in the evening abends *adv.* (1) **2A**
  in the morning morgens *adv.* (1) **2A**
  in spite of trotz *prep.* (2) **4B**
India Indien *n.* (3) **2B**
Indian indisch *adj.* (3) **2B**; **(person)** Inder, - / Inderin, -nen *m./f.* (3) **2B**
ingredient Zutat, -en *f.* (1) **4A**
injury Verletzung, -en *f.* (3) **1B**
inside (of) innerhalb *prep.* (2) **4B**
instead sondern *conj.* (2) **2A**
  instead of statt *prep.*; anstatt *prep.* (2) **4B**
intellectual intellektuell *adj.* (1) **3B**
intelligent intelligent *adj.* (1) **3B**
interested: to be interested (in) sich interessieren (für) *v.* (3) **1A**
interesting interessant *adj.* (1) **2A**
internet café Internetcafé, -s *n.* (3) **2A**
internship Praktikum (*pl.* die Praktika) *n.* (3) **3A**
intersection Kreuzung, -en *f.* (3) **2B**
introduce: to introduce (oneself) (sich) vorstellen *v.* (3) **1A**
invent erfinden *v.* (2) **3A**
invite einladen *v.* (2) **1A**
iron Bügeleisen, - *n.* (2) **2B**; bügeln *v.* (2) **2B**
ironing board Bügelbrett, -er *n.* (2) **2B**
island Insel, -n *f.* (3) **4A**
it es *pron.* (1) **1A**
Italian (person) Italiener, - / Italienerin, -nen *m./f.* (3) **2B; (language)** Italienisch *n.* (3) **2B**
Italy Italien *n.* (3) **2B**
its sein *poss. adj.* (1) **3A**

J

jacket Jacke, -n *f.* (2) **1B**
jam Marmelade, -n *f.* (1) **4A**
January Januar *m.* (1) **2A**
Japan Japan *n.* (3) **2B**
Japanese (person) Japaner, - / Japanerin, -nen *m./f.* (3) **2B; (language)** Japanisch *n.* (3) **2B**
jealous eifersüchtig *adj.* (1) **3B**
jeans Jeans, - *f.* (2) **1B**
jewelry store Juweliergeschäft, -e *n.* (3) **2A**
job Beruf, -e *m.* (3) **3B**; Stelle, -n *f.* (3) **3A**
  to find a job Arbeit finden *v.* (3) **3A**
job interview Vorstellungsgespräch, -e *n.* (3) **3A**
job opening Stellenangebot, -e *n.* (3) **3A**
jog joggen *v.* (1) **2B**
journalist Journalist, -en / Journalistin, -nen *m./f.* (1) **3B**
judge Richter, - / Richterin, -nen *m./f.* (3) **3B**
juice Saft, ¨e *m.* (1) **4B**
July Juli *m.* (1) **2A**
June Juni *m.* (1) **2A**
just as genauso wie (2) **4A**

K

key Schlüssel, - *m.* (2) **3B**
keyboard Tastatur, -en *f.* (2) **4B**
kind nett *adj.*
kiosk Kiosk, -e *m.* (3) **2A**
kiss Kuss, ¨e *m.* (2) **1A**; küssen *v.* (2) **1A**
  to kiss (each other) sich küssen *v.* (3) **1A**
kitchen Küche, -n *f.* (2) **2A**
knee Knie, - *n.* (3) **1A**
knife Messer, - *n.* (1) **4B**
know kennen *v.* (2) **1B**; wissen *v.* (2) **1B**
  to know each other sich kennen *v.* (3) **1A**
know-it-all Besserwisser, - / Besserwisserin -nen *m./f.* (1) **2A**
Korea Korea *n.* (3) **2B**
Korean (person) Koreaner, - / Koreanerin, -nen *m./f.* (3) **2B; (language)** Koreanisch *n.* (3) **2B**

L

labor union Gewerkschaft, -en *f.* (3) **3B**
lake See, -n *m.* (3) **4A**
lamp Lampe, -n *f.* (2) **2A**

land landen *v.* (2) **3B**; Land, ¨-er *n.* (2) **3B**
landscape Landschaft, -en *f.* (3) **4A**
laptop (computer) Laptop, -s *m./n.* (2) **4B**
last letzter/letzte/letztes *adj.* (1) **2B**
last name Nachname, -n *m.* (1) **3A**
late spät *adj.* (1) **2A**
to be late sich verspäten *v.* (3) **1A**
laugh lachen *v.* (1) **2A**
laundromat Waschsalon, -s *m.* (3) **4A**
laundry Wäsche *f.* (2) **2B**
to do laundry Wäsche waschen *v.* (2) **2B**
law Gesetz, -e *n.* (3) **4B**
lawyer Rechtsanwalt, ¨-e / Rechtsanwältin, -nen *m./f.* (1) **3B**
lay legen *v.* (2) **1B**
lazy faul *adj.* (1) **3B**
leaf Blatt, ¨-er *n.* (3) **4A**
learn lernen *v.* (1) **2A**
leather Leder, - *n.* (2) **1B**
leave abfahren *v.* (2) **4A**
lecture Vorlesung, -en *f.* (1) **2A**; Vortrag, ¨-e *m.* (2) **2B**
lecture hall Hörsaal (*pl.* Hörsäle) *m.* (1) **2A**
leg Bein, -e *n.* (3) **1A**
leisure Freizeit *f.* (1) **2B**
lesson Stunde, -n *f.* (1) **1B**
let lassen *v.* (1) **2B**
letter Brief, -e *m.* (3) **2A**
to mail a letter einen Brief abschicken *v.* (3) **2A**
letter of recommendation Empfehlungsschreiben, - *n.* (3) **3A**
lettuce Salat, -e *m.* (1) **4A**
library Bibliothek, -en *f.* (1) **1B**
license plate Nummernschild, -er *n.* (2) **4A**
lie liegen *v.* (2) **1B**
to lie down sich (hin)legen *v.* (3) **1A**
to tell a lie lügen *v.*
light hell *adj.* (1) **3A**; leicht *adj.* (1) **4B**; Licht, -er *n.* (3) **4B**
lightning Blitz, -e *m.* (2) **3A**
like mögen *v.* **4B**; gern (*+verb*) *v.* (1) **2B**; gefallen *v.* (2) **1A**
I would like... ich hätte gern... (1) **4A**; Ich möchte... (1) **4B**
line Schlange, -n *f.* (2) (1) **3B**; Linie, -n *f.*
to stand in line Schlange stehen *v.* (2) **3B**
lip Lippe, -n *f.* (3) **1A**
lipstick Lippenstift, -e *m.* (3) **1A**
listen (to) hören *v.* (1) **2A**
literature Literatur, -en *f.* (1) **2A**
little klein *adj.* (1) **3A**; wenig *adj.* (3) **2A**
live wohnen *v.* (1) **2A**; leben *v.* (1) **2A**
living room Wohnzimmer, - *n.* (2) **2A**
load laden *v.* (2) **4B**
location Lage, -n *f.* (2) **3B**
long lang *adj.* (1) **3A**
long-sleeved langärmlig *adj.* (2) **1B**
look schauen *v.* (2) **3A**
to look at anschauen *v.* (2) **3A**
to look for suchen *v.* (1) **2A**
to look forward to sich freuen auf *v.* (3) **1A**
loose weit *adj.* (2) **1B**
lose verlieren *v.* (1) **2B**
to get lost sich verlaufen *v.* (3) **2B**
love lieben *v.* (1) **2A**; Liebe *f.* (2) **1A**
to fall in love (with) sich verlieben (in) *v.* (3) **1A**
to love each other sich lieben *v.* (3) **1A**
loving liebevoll *adj.* (1) **3B**
low niedrig *adj.* (3) **3A**
luggage Gepäck *n.* (2) **3B**
lunch Mittagessen, - *n.* (1) **4B**

M

magazine Zeitschrift, -en *f.* (3) **2A**
mail Post *f.* (3) **2A**
to mail a letter einen Brief abschicken *v.* (3) **2A**
mail carrier Briefträger, - / Briefträgerin, -nen *m.* (3) **2A**
mailbox Briefkasten, ¨- *m.* (3) **2A**
main course Hauptspeise, -n *f.* (1) **4B**
main road Hauptstraße, -n *f.* (3) **2B**
major: to major in studieren *v.* (1) **2A**
make machen *v.* (1) **2A**
makeup: to put on makeup sich schminken *v.* (3) **1A**
mall Einkaufszentrum (*pl.* Einkaufszentren) *n.* (3) **2B**
man Mann, ¨-er *m.* (1) **1A**
manage leiten *v.* (3) **4B**
manager Geschäftsführer, - / die Geschäftsführerin, -nen *m./f.* (3) **3A**
map Karte, -n *f.* (1) **1B**; Landkarte, -n *f.* (2) **3B**
city map Stadtplan, ¨-e *m.* (2) **3B**
to read a map eine Karte lesen *v.* (2) **3B**
marble Marmor *m.* (2) **2B**
March März *m.* (1) **2A**
marital status Familienstand, ¨-e *m.* (1) **3A**
market Markt, ¨-e *m.* (1) **4A**
marriage Ehe, -n *f.* (2) **1A**
married verheiratet *adj.* (1) **3A**
marry heiraten *v.* (1) **3A**
match Spiel, -e *n.* (1) **2B**; passen *v.* (2) **1A**
material Material, -ien *n.* **(2) 1B**
mathematics Mathematik *f.* (1) **2A**
May Mai *m.* (1) **2A**
may dürfen *v.* (1) **3B**
maybe vielleicht *adv.* (1) **4A**
mayor Bürgermeister, - / Bürgermeisterin, -nen *m./f.* (3) **2B**
meal Mahlzeit, -en *f.* (1) **4B**
mean bedeuten *v.* (1) **2A**; meinen *v.* (3) **4B**; gemein *adj.* (1) **3B**
meat Fleisch *n.* (1) **4A**
mechanic Mechaniker, - / Mechanikerin, -nen *m./f.* (2) **4A**
medicine Medizin *f.* (1) **2A**; Medikament, -e *n.* (3) **1B**
meet (sich) treffen *v.* (1) **2B**; **(for the first time)** (sich) kennen lernen *v.* (3) **1A**
Pleased to meet you. Schön dich/Sie kennen zu lernen! (1) **1A**
meeting Besprechung, -en *f.* (3) **3A**
melon Melone, -n *f.* (1) **4A**
menu Speisekarte, -n *f.* (1) **4B**
Merry Christmas! Frohe Weihnachten! (2) **1A**
message Nachricht, -en *f.* (3) **3A**
Mexico Mexiko *n.* (3) **2B**
Mexican mexikanisch *adj.* (3) **2B**; **(person)** Mexikaner, - / Mexikanerin, -nen *m./f.* (3) **2B**
microphone Mikrofon, -e *n.* (2) **4B**
microwave Mikrowelle, -n *f.* (2) **2B**
midmorning Vormittag, -e *m.* (1) **2B**
midnight Mitternacht *f.* (1) **2A**
mild leicht *adj.* (3) **1B**
milk Milch *f.* (1) **4B**
minority Minderheit, -en *f.* (3) **4B**
minus minus (1) **1B**
mirror Spiegel, - *m.* (2) **2A**
mist Nebel, - *m.* (2) **3A**
modern modern *adj.* (3) **2A**
modest bescheiden *adj.* (1) **3B**
mom Mama, -s *f.* (1) **3A**
Monday Montag, -e *m.* (1) **2A**
on Mondays montags *adv.* (1) **2A**
money Geld, -er *n.* (3) **2A**
month Monat, -e *m.* (1) **2A**
moon Mond, -e *m.* (3) **4A**
mop wischen *v.* (2) **2B**
more mehr *adj.* (2) **4A**
morning Morgen, - *m.* (1) **2B**
in the morning vormittags (1) **2A**
tomorrow morning morgen früh (1) **2B**
mother Mutter, ¨- *f.* (1) **1A**
mother-in-law Schwiegermutter, ¨- *f.* (1) **3A**
mountain Berg, -e *m.* (1) **2B**; (3) **4A**
mouse Maus, ¨-e *f.* (2) **4B**
mouth Mund, ¨-er *m.* (3) **1A**
move umziehen *v.* (2) **2A**; sich bewegen *v.*
movie Film, -e *m.*
movie theater Kino, -s *n.* (3) **2A**
mp3 player MP3-Player, - *m.* (2) **4B**
Mr. Herr (1) **1A**
Mrs. Frau (1) **1A**
Ms. Frau (1) **1A**
much viel *adv.* (1) **4A**
mushroom Pilz, -e *m.* (1) **4A**
musician Musiker, - / Musikerin, -nen *m./f.* (1) **3B**
must müssen *v.* (1) **3B**
my mein *poss. adj.* (1) **3A**
myself mich *pron.*; mir *pron.* (3) **1A**

N

naïve naiv *adj.* (1) **3B**
name Name, -n *m.* (1) **1A**
to be named heißen *v.* (1) **2A**
What's your name? Wie heißen Sie? (form.) / Wie heißt du? (inf.) *v.* (1) **1A**
napkin Serviette, -n *f.* (1) **4B**
natural disaster Naturkatastrophe, -n *f.* (3) **4A**
nature Natur, -en *f.* (3) **4A**
nauseous übel *adj.* (3) **1B**
near bei *prep.* (1) **4B**; nah *adj.* (3) **2B**
neat ordentlich *adj.* (2) **2B**
neck Hals, ¨-e *m.* (3) **1A**
necklace Halskette, -n *f.* (2) **1B**
need brauchen *v.* (1) **2A**
to need to müssen *v.* (1) **3B**
neighborhood Viertel, - *n.* (3) **2B**
nephew Neffe, -n *m.* (2) **4B**
nervous nervös *adj.* (1) **3B**
never nie *adv.* **4A**; niemals *adv.* (2) **3 B**
New Year's Eve Silvester *n.* (2) **1A**

newlywed Frischvermählte, -n *m./f.* (2) **1A**
newspaper Zeitung, -en *f.* (2) **3B**
next nächster/nächste/nächstes *adj.* (1) **2B**
next to neben *prep.* (2) **1B**
nice nett *adj.* (1) **3B**
It's nice out. Es ist schön draußen. (2) **3A**
Nice to meet you. Schön dich/Sie kennen zu lernen! (1) **1A**
The weather is nice. Das Wetter ist gut. (2) **3A**
night Nacht, ¨-e *f.* (1) **2B**
to spend the night übernachten *f.* (2) **3B**
night table Nachttisch, -e *m.* (2) **2A**
nine neun (1) **2A**
no nein (1) **1A**; kein *adj.* (1) **2B**
no one niemand *pron.* (2) **3B**
nonviolent gewaltfrei *adj.* (3) **4B**
noon Mittag, -e *m.* (1) **2A**
nose Nase, -n *f.* (3) **1A**
not nicht *adv.* (1) **2B**
Do not enter. Keine Zufahrt. (1) **3B**
not bad nicht schlecht (1) **1A**
not much wenig *adj.* (3) **2A**
note Notiz, -en *f.* (1) **1B**
notebook Heft, -e *n.* (1) **1B**
nothing nichts *pron.* (2) **3B**
November November *m.* (1) **2A**
now jetzt *adv.* (1) **4A**
nuclear energy Kernenergie *f.* (3) **4B**
nuclear power plant Kernkraftwerk, -e *n.* (3) **4B**
nurse Krankenpfleger, - / Krankenschwester, -n *m./f.* (3) **1B**

O

ocean Meer, -e *n.* (3) **4A**
occasion Anlass, ¨-e *m.* (2) **1A**
special occasions besondere Anlässe *m. pl.* (2) **1A**
October Oktober *m.* (1) **2A**
offer Angebot, -e *n.* (2) **1B**; bieten *v.* (3) **1B**; anbieten *v.* (3) **4B**
office Büro, -s *n.* (3) **3B**
office supplies Büromaterial, -ien *n.* (3) **3A**
often oft *adv.* (1) **4A**
oil Öl, -e *n.* (1) **4A**
old alt *adj.* (1) **3A**
How old are you? Wie alt bist du? (1) **1B**
I am... years old. Ich bin... Jahre alt. (1) **1B**
olive oil Olivenöl, -e *n.* (1) **4A**
on an *prep.*; auf *prep.* (2) **1B**
once einmal *adv.* (2) **3B**
one eins (1) **2A**; man *pron.* (2) **3B**
by oneself allein *adv.* (1) **4A**
one-way street Einbahnstraβe, -n *f.* (2) **4A**
onion Zwiebel, -n *f.* (1) **4A**
online: to be online online sein *v.* (2) **4B**
only nur *adv.* (1) **4A**
only child Einzelkind, -er *n.* (1) **3A**
on-time pünktlich *adj.* (2) **3B**
onto auf *prep.* (2) **1B**
open öffnen *v.* (1) **2A**; aufmachen *v.* (2) **4B**; geöffnet *adj.* (3) **2A**
or oder *conj.* (1) **1B**
orange Orange, -n *f.* (1) **4A**; orange *adj.* (2) **1B**
order bestellen *v.* (1) **4A**
organic biologisch *adj.* (3) **4B**
our unser *poss. adj.* (1) **3A**
out draußen *adv.* (2) **3A**; heraus *adv.* (2) **2A**
It's nice out. Es ist schön draußen. (2) **3A**
to go out ausgehen *v.* (1) **4A**
to bring out rausbringen (2) **2B**
outside draußen *prep.* (2) **3A**
outside of außerhalb *prep.* (2) **4B**
oven Ofen, ¨ *m.* (2) **2B**
over über *prep.* (2) **1B**; vorbei *adv.* (2) **3A**
over there drüben *adv.* (1) **4A**
overpopulation Überbevölkerung *f.* (3) **4B**
owner Besitzer, - / Besitzerin, -nen *m./f.* (1) **3B**

P

pack packen *v.* (2) **3B**
package Paket, -e *n.* (3) **2A**
pain Schmerz, -en *m.* (3) **1B**
pajamas Schlafanzug, ¨-e *m.* (3) **1A**
pan Pfanne, -n *f.* (2) **2B**
pants Hose, -n *f.* (2) **1B**
paper Papier, -e *n.* (1) **1B**
sheet of paper Blatt Papier (*pl.* Blätter) Papier *n.* (1) **1B**
paperclip Büroklammer, -n *f.* (3) **3A**
paper-goods store Schreibwarengeschäft, -e *n.* (3) **2A**
paragraph Absatz, ¨-e *m.* (2) **1B**
parents Eltern *pl.* (1) **3A**
park Park, -s *m.* (1) **1A**; parken *v.* (2) **4A**
No parking. Parkverbot. (1) **3B**
participate mitmachen *v.* (2) **4B**
part-time halbtags *adj.* (3) **3B**
party Party, -s *f.* (2) **1A**
to go to a party auf eine Party gehen *prep.* (3) **2B**
to throw a party eine Party geben *v.* (2) **1A**
pass (a test) bestehen *v.* (1) **1B**
passenger Passagier, -e *m.* (2) **3B**
passport control Passkontrolle, -n *f.* (2) **3B**
password Passwort, ¨-er *n.* (2) **4B**
past Vergangenheit, -en *f.* (3) **4A**; nach *prep.* (1) **2A**
pasta Pasta *f.* (1) **4A**
pastries Gebäck *n.* (2) **1A**
pastry shop Konditorei, -en *f.* (1) **4A**
path Weg, -e *m.* (3) **4A**
patient geduldig *adj.* (1) **3B**; Patient, -en / Patientin, -nen *m./f.* (3) **1B**
pay (for) bezahlen *v.* (1) **4A**
to pay by (credit) card mit der Karte bezahlen *v.* (3) **2A**
to pay in cash bar bezahlen *v.* (3) **2A**
peach Pfirsich, -e *m.* (1) **4A**
pear Birne, -n *f.* (1) **4A**
pedestrian Fußgänger, - / Fußgängerin, -nen *m./f.* (3) **2B**
pen Kuli, -s *m.* (1) **1B**
pencil Bleistift, -e *m.* (1) **1B**
people Leute *pl.* (1) **3B**; Menschen *pl.*
pepper Paprika, - *f.* (1) **4A**; Pfeffer, - *m.* (1) **4B**
percent Prozent, -e *n.* (1) **1B**
period Punkt, -e *m.* (1) **1B**
person Person, -en *f.* (1) **1A**; Mensch, -en *m.*
personal persönlich *adj.* (1) **3B**
pet Haustier, -e *n.* (1) **3A**
pharmacy Apotheke, -n *f.* (3) **1B**
phone booth Telefonzelle, -n *f.* (3) **2B**
photo Foto, -s *n.* (1) **1B**
physics Physik *f.* (1) **2A**
picnic Picknick, -s *n.* (3) **4A**
to have a picnic ein Picknick machen *v.* (3) **4A**
picture Foto, -s *n.* (1) **1B**; Bild, -er *n.* (2) **2A**
pie Kuchen, - *m.* (1) **4A**
pigsty Saustall, ¨-e *n.* (2) **2B**
It's a pigsty! Es ist ein Saustall! (2) **2B**
pill Tablette, -n *f.* (3) **1B**
pillow Kissen, - *n.* (2) **1B**
pineapple Ananas, - *f.* (1) **4A**
pink rosa *adj.* (2) **1B**
place Ort, -e *m.* (1) **1B**; Lage, -n *f.* (2) **3B**; setzen *v.* (2) **2B**
in your place an deiner/Ihrer Stelle *f.* (3) **2A**
plant Pflanze, -n *f.* (2) **2A**
plastic Kunststoff, -e *m.* (2) **2B**
plate Teller, - *m.* (1) **4B**
platform Bahnsteig, -e (2) **4A**
play spielen *v.* (1) **2A**
player Spieler, - / Spielerin, -nen *m./f.* (1) **2B**
pleasant angenehm *adj.* (1) **3B**
please bitte **1A**; gefallen *v.* (2) **1A**
Pleased to meet you. Freut mich! (1) **1A**
plumber Klempner, - / Klempnerin, -nen *m./f.* (3) **3B**
plus plus (1) **1B**
police officer Polizist, -en / Polizistin, -nen *m./f.* (2) **4A**
police station Polizeiwache, -n *f.* (3) **2A**
politician Politiker, - / Politikerin, -nen *m./f.* (3) **3B**
pollute verschmutzen *v.* (3) **4B**
pollution Verschmutzung *f.* (3) **4B**
poor arm *adj.* (1) **3B**
pork Schweinefleisch *n.* (1) **4A**
position Stelle, -n *f.* (3) **3A**
post office Post, - *f.* (3) **2A**
to go to the post office zur Post gehen *v.* (3) **2A**
postcard Postkarte, -n *f.* (3) **2A**
poster Poster, - *n.* (2) **2A**
pot Topf, ¨-e *m.* (2) **2B**
potato Kartoffel, -n *f.* (1) **4A**
pound Pfund, -e *n.* (1) **4A**
a pound of potatoes ein Pfund Kartoffeln (1) **4A**
practice (sports) trainieren *v.* (1) **2B**; Übung, -en *f.*
pregnant schwanger *adj.* **(3) 1B**
preparation Vorbereitung, -en *f.*
prepare vorbereiten *v.* (1) **4A**; zubereiten *v.* (2) **3A**
to prepare oneself (for) sich vorbereiten (auf) *v.* (3) **1A**
prescription Rezept, -e *n.* (3) **1B**
presentation Referat, -e *n.* (1) **2A**
preserve erhalten *v.* (3) **4B**
president Präsident, - / Präsidentin, -nen *m./f.* (2) **4B**
federal president Bundespräsident, - / Bundespräsidentin, -nen *m./f.* (2) **4B**
pretty hübsch *adj.* (1) **3A**
pretty well ziemlich gut *adv.* (1) **1A**
principal Schulleiter, - *m.* / Schulleiterin, -nen *f.* (1) **1B**

print drucken *v.* (2) **4B**
printer Drucker, - *m.* (2) **4B**
probably wohl ; wahrscheinlich *adv.*(3) **2A**; sicher *adv.* (3) **2A**
problem Problem, -e *n.* (1) **1A**
profession Beruf, -e *m.* (1) **3B**
professional training Berufsausbildung, -en *f.* (3) **3A**
professor Professor, -en / Professorin, -nen *m./f.* (1) **1B**
program Programm, -e *n.* (2) **4B**
promotion Beförderung, -en *f.* (3) **3B**
pronunciation Aussprache *f.*
propose vorschlagen *v.* (3) **4B**
protect schützen *v.* (3) **4B**
proud stolz *adj.* (1) **3B**
psychologist Psychologe, -n / Psychologin, -nen *m./f.* (3) **3B**
psychology Psychologie *f.* (1) **2A**
public öffentlich *adj.* (2) **4A**
public transportation öffentliche Verkehrsmittel *n. pl.* (2) **4A**
pull ziehen *v.* (1) **3B**
purple lila *adj.* (2) **1B**
purse Handtasche, -n *f.* (2) **1B**
push drücken *v.* (1) **3B**
put stellen *v.* (2) **1B**; legen *v.* (3) **1A**; setzen *v.* (3) **1A**
to put away wegräumen *v.* (2) **2B**
to put on anziehen *v.* (2) **1B**

Q

quarter Viertel, - *n.* (1) **2A**
quarter past/to Viertel nach/vor (1) **2A**
question Frage, -n *f.* (1) **1B**
quicksand Treibsand *m.* (3) **4A**
quite ziemlich *adv.* (1) **4A**

R

rabbit Kaninchen, - *n.* (3) **4A**
rain Regen *m.* (2) **3A**; regnen *v.* (1) **2A**
raincoat Regenmantel, ¨ *m.* (2) **3A**
raise Gehaltserhöhung, -en *f.* (3) **3B**
rarely selten *adv.* (1) **4A**
rather lieber *adj.* (2) **4A**
rating Bewertung, -en *f.* (2) **3B**
razor Rasierer, - *m.* (3) **4A**
read lesen *v.* (1) **2B**
ready fertig *adj.* (3) **3B**
real estate agent Immobilienmakler, - / Immobilienmaklerin, -nen *m./f.* (3) **3B**
realistic realistisch *adj.* (3) **2A**
really wirklich *adv.* (1) **4A**
receive bekommen *v.* (2) **1A**
receiver Hörer, - *m.* (3) **3A**
recess Pause, -n *f.* (1) **1B**
recipe Rezept, -e *n.* (1) **4A**
recognize erkennen *v.* (2) **3A**
recommend empfehlen *v.* (1) **2B**
record aufnehmen *v.* (2) **4B**
recycle recyceln *v.* (3) **4B**
red rot *adj.* (1) **3A**
red-haired rothaarig *adj.* (1) **3A**
reference Referenz, -en *f.* (3) **3A**
refrigerator Kühlschrank, ¨e *m.* (2) **2B**
related verwandt *adj.* (3) **2A**
relative Verwandte, -n *m.* (1) **3A**
relax sich entspannen *v.* (3) **1A**
reliable zuverlässig *adj.* (1) **3B**
remember sich erinnern (an) *v.* (3) **1A**
remote control Fernbedienung, -en *f.* (2) **4B**
remove entfernen *v.* (2) **2B**
renewable energy erneuerbare Energie, -en *f.* (3) **4B**
rent Miete, -n *f.* (2) **2A**; mieten *v.* (2) **2A**
repair reparieren *v.* (2) **4A**
repeat wiederholen *v.* (1) **2A**
repetition Wiederholung, -en *f.*
report berichten *v.* (3) **4B**
report card Zeugnis, -se *n.* (1) **1B**
reservation: to make a (hotel) reservation buchen *v.* (2) **3B**
resign kündigen *v.* (3) **3B**
rest sich ausruhen *v.* (3) **1A**
restaurant Restaurant, -s *n.* (1) **4B**
result Ergebnis, -se *n.* (1) **1B**
résumé Lebenslauf, ¨e *m.* (3) **3A**
retire in Rente gehen *v.* (2) **1A**
retiree Rentner, - / Rentnerin, -nen *m./f.* (3) **3B**
review Besprechung, -en *f.* (2) **4B**
rice Reis *m.* (1) **4A**
rich reich *adj.* (1) **3B**
ride fahren *v.* (1) **2B**; reiten *v.* (1) **2B**
to give (someone) a ride (jemanden) mitnehmen *v.* (3) **2B**
to ride a bicycle Fahrrad fahren *v.* (1) **2B**
ring klingeln *v.* (2) **4B**
rinse spülen *v.* (2) **2B**
rise (sun) aufgehen *v.* (3) **4A**
river Fluss, ¨e *m.* (1) **3B**
rock Stein, -e *m.* (3) **4A**
roll Brötchen, - *n.* (1) **4A**
room Zimmer, - *n.* (2) **1A**
room service Zimmerservice *m.* (2) **3B**
roommate Mitbewohner, - / Mitbewohnerin, -nen *m./f.* (1) **2A**
rug Teppich, -e *m.* (2) **2A**
run laufen *v.* (1) **2B**; rennen *v.* (2) **1A**
Russia Russland *n.* (3) **2B**
Russian (person) Russe, -n / Russin, -nen *m./f.* (3) **2B**; **(language)** Russisch *n.* (3) **2B**

S

sad traurig *adj.* (1) **3B**
salad Salat, -e *m.* (1) **4A**
salary Gehalt, ¨er *n.* (3) **3A**
high/low salary hohes/niedriges Gehalt, ¨er *n.* (3) **3A**
sale Verkauf, ¨e *m.*
on sale im Angebot (2) **1B**
salesperson Verkäufer, - / Verkäuferin, -nen *m./f.* (2) **1B**
salt Salz, -e *n.* (1) **4B**
salty salzig *adj.* (1) **4B**
same gleich *adj.*
Saturday Samstag, -e *m.* (1) **2A**
on Saturdays samstags *adv.* (1) **2A**
sausage Würstchen, - *n.* (1) **4A**
save speichern *v.* (2) **4B**; retten *v.* (3) **4B**
to save the planet den Planeten retten *v.* (3) **4B**
say sagen *v.* (1) **2A**
scarf Schal, -s *m.* (2) **1B**
schedule Stundenplan, ¨e *m.* (1) **2A**; Fahrplan, ¨e *m.* (2) **4A**
scholarship Stipendium (*pl.* Stipendien) *n.* (1) **2A**
school Schule, -n *f.* (1) **1B**
science Naturwissenschaft, -en *f.* (1) **2A**
scientist Wissenschaftler, - / Wissenschaftlerin, -nen *m./f.* (3) **3B**
score Ergebnis, -se *n.* (1) **1B**
screen Bildschirm, -e *m.* (2) **4B**
screen name Benutzername, -n *m.* (2) **4B**
sea Meer, -e *n.* (3) **4A**
seafood Meeresfrüchte *f. pl.* (1) **4A**
season Jahreszeit, -en *f.* (2) **3A**
seatbelt Sicherheitsgurt, -e *m.* (2) **4A**
second zweite *adj.* (1) **2A**
second-hand clothing Altkleider *pl.* (3) **4B**
see sehen *v.* (1) **2B**
See you later. Bis später! (1) **1A**
See you soon. Bis gleich! / Bis bald. (1) **1A**
See you tomorrow. Bis morgen! (1) **1A**
selfish egoistisch *adj.* (1) **3B**
sell verkaufen *v.* (1) **4A**
seminar Seminar, -e *n.* (1) **2A**
seminar room Seminarraum (*pl.* Seminarräume) *m.* (1) **2A**
send schicken *v.* (2) **4B**; abschicken *v.* (3) **3B**
separate (sich) trennen *v.* (3) **1A**
separated getrennt *adj.* (1) **3A**
September September *m.* (1) **2A**
serious ernst *adj.* (3) **3B**; schwer *adj.* (3) **1B**
set setzen *v.* (3) **1A**; **(sun)** untergehen v. (3) **4A**
to set the table den Tisch decken *v.* (3) **4B**
seven sieben (1) **2A**
shampoo Shampoo, -s *n.* (3) **1A**
shape Form, -en *f.* (3) **1B**
in good shape fit *adj.* (1) **2B**
to be in/out of shape in guter/schlechter Form sein *v.* (3) **1B**
shave sich rasieren *v.* (3) **1A**
shaving cream Rasierschaum, ¨e *m.* (3) **1A**
she sie *pron.* (1) **1A**
sheep Schaf, -e *n.* (3) **4A**
sheet Laken, - *n.* (2) **2B**
sheet of paper Blatt Papier (*pl.* Blätter) Papier *n.* (1) **1B**
ship Schiff, -e *n.* (2) **4A**
shirt Hemd, -en *n.* (2) **1B**
shoe Schuh, -e *m.* (2) **1B**
shop einkaufen *v.* (1) **4A**; Geschäft, -e *n.* (1) **4A**
to go shopping einkaufen gehen *v.* (1) **4A**
shopping Einkaufen *n.* (2) **1B**
shopping center Einkaufszentrum, -(*pl.* Einkaufszentren) *n.* (3) **2B**
short kurz *adj.* (1) **3A**; **(stature)** klein *adj.* (1) **3A**
short film Kurzfilm, -e *m.* (3) **2A**
short-sleeved kurzärmlig *adj.* (2) **1B**
shorts kurze Hose, -n *f.* (2) **1B**
shot Spritze, -n *f.* (3) **1B**
to give a shot eine Spritze geben *v.* (3) **1B**
shoulder Schulter, -n *f.* (3) **1A**

show zeigen *v.* (1) **4B**
shower: to take a shower (sich) duschen *v.* (3) **1A**
shrimp Garnele, -n *f.* (1) **4A**
shy schüchtern *adj.* (1) **3B**
sibling Geschwister, - *n.* (1) **3A**
sick krank *adj.* (3) **1B**
to get sick krank werden *v.* (3) **1B**
side dish Beilage, -n *f.* (1) **4B**
sidewalk Bürgersteig, -e *m.* (3) **2B**
sign unterschreiben *v.* (3) **2A**; Schild, -er *n.*
silk Seide, -n *f.* (2) **1B**
silverware Besteck *n.* (1) **4B**
since seit (1) **4B**
sincere aufrichtig *adj.* (1) **3B**
Yours sincerely Gruß, ¨-e (1) **3B**
sing singen *v.* (1) **2B**
single ledig *adj.* (1) **3A**
sink Spüle, -n *f.* (2) **2B**
sister Schwester, -n *f.* (1) **1A**
sister-in-law Schwägerin, -nen *f.* (1) **3A**
sit sitzen *v.* (2) **1B**
to sit down sich (hin)setzen *v.* (3) **1A**
six sechs (1) **2A**
size Kleidergröße, -n *f.* (2) **1B**
ski Ski fahren *v.* (1) **2B**
skirt Rock, ¨-e *m.* (2) **1B**
sky Himmel *m.* (3) **4A**
sleep schlafen *v.* (1) **2B**
to go to sleep einschlafen *v.* (1) **4A**
slim schlank *adj.* (1) **3A**
slipper Hausschuh, -e *m.* (3) **1A**
slow langsam *adj.* (1) **3B**
Please speak more slowly. Sprechen Sie bitte langsamer! (1) **3B**
Slow down. Langsam fahren. (1) **3B**
small klein *adj.* (1) **3A**
smartphone Smartphone, -s *n.* (2) **4B**
smile lächeln *v.* (2) **1A**
smoke rauchen *v.*
No smoking. Rauchen verboten. (1) **3B**
snack Snack, -s *m.* (1) **4B**
snake Schlange, -n *f.* (3) **4A**
sneakers Turnschuhe *m. pl.* (2) **1B**
sneeze niesen *v.* (3) **1B**
snow Schnee *m.* (2) **3A**; schneien *v.* (2) **3A**
so so *adv.* (1) **4A**
so far, so good so weit, so gut (1) **1A**
so that damit *conj.* (3) **2A**
soap Seife, -n *f.* (3) **1A**
soccer Fußball *m.* (1) **2B**
sock Socke, -n *f.* (2) **1B**
sofa Sofa, -s *n.* (2) **2A**
soil verschmutzen *v.* (2) **2B**
solar energy Sonnenenergie *f.* (3) **4B**
solid colored einfarbig *adj.* (2) **1B**
solution Lösung, -en *f.* (3) **4B**
some mancher/manche/manches *pron.* (2) **4B**
someone jemand *pron.* (2) **3B**
something etwas *pron.* (2) **3B**
something else etwas anderes *n.* (3) **2A**
sometimes manchmal *adv.* (2) **3B**
somewhere else woanders *adv.* (1) **4A**
son Sohn, ¨-e *m.* (1) **3A**
soon bald (1) **1A**
See you soon. Bis bald.; Bis gleich. (1) **1A**
sorry: I'm sorry. Es tut mir leid. (1) **1A**
so-so (I'm so-so) Es geht. (1) **1A**
soup Suppe, -n *f.* (1) **4B**
soup spoon Esslöffel, - *m.* (1) **4B**
Spain Spanien *n.* (3) **2B**
Spanish (person) Spanier, - / Spanierin, -nen *m./f.* (3) **2B**; **(language)** Spanisch *n.* (3) **2B**
sparkling water Mineralwasser *n.* (1) **4B**
speak sprechen *v.* (1) **2B**
to speak about sprechen über; reden über *v.* (2) **3A**
special besonderes *adj.* (3) **2A**
nothing special nichts Besonderes *adj.* (3) **2A**
species Art, -en *f.* (3) **4B**
spelling Rechtschreibung *f.*
spend verbringen *v.* (1) **4A**
spicy scharf *adj.* (1) **4B**
split up sich trennen *v.* (3) **1A**
spoon Löffel, - *m.* (1) **4B**
sport Sport *m.* (1) **2B**; Sportart, -en *f.* (1) **2B**
sprain (one's wrist/ankle) sich (das Handgelenk / den Fuß) verstauchen *v.* (3) **1B**
spring Frühling, -e *m.* (1) **2B**
squirrel Eichhörnchen, - *n.* (3) **4A**
stadium Stadion (*pl.* Stadien) *n.* (1) **2B**
stairs Treppe, -n *f.* (2) **2A**
to go up/down stairs die Treppe hochgehen/ heruntergehen *v.* (3) **2B**
stamp Briefmarke, -n *f.* (3) **2A**
stand stehen *v.* (2) **1B**
to stand in line Schlange stehen *v.* (2) **3B**
stapler Hefter, - *m.* (3) **3A**
star Stern, -e *m.* (3) **4A**
start starten *v.* (2) **4B**; anfangen *v.* (1) **4A**; beginnen *v.* (2) **2A**
station wagon Kombi, -s *m.* (2) **4B**
statue Statue, -n *f.* (3) **2B**
stay bleiben *v.* (2) **1B**
steal stehlen *v.* (1) **2B**
steering wheel Lenkrad, ¨-er *n.* (2) **4A**
stepbrother Halbbruder, ¨- *m.* (1) **3A**
stepdaughter Stieftochter, ¨- *f.* (1) **3A**
stepfather Stiefvater, -s¨ *m.* (1) **3A**
stepmother Stiefmutter, ¨- *f.* (1) **3A**
stepsister Halbschwester, -n *f.* (1) **3A**
stepson Stiefsohn, ¨- *m.* (1) **3A**
stereo system Stereoanlage, -n *f.* (2) **4B**
still noch *adv.* (1) **4A**; still *adj.* (1) **4B**
still water stilles Wasser *n.* (1) **4B**
stomachache Bauchschmerzen *m. pl.* (3) **1B**
stop sign Stoppschild, -er *n.* (2) **4A**
store Geschäft, -e *n.* (1) **4A**
storm Sturm, ¨-e *m.* (2) **3A**
stove Herd, -e *m.* (2) **2B**
straight glatt *adj.* (1) **3A**
straight hair glatte Haare *n. pl.* (1) **3A**
straight ahead geradeaus *adv.* (2) **4A**
strawberry Erdbeere, -n *f.* (1) **4A**
stream Strom, ¨-e *m.* (3) **4A**
street Straße, -n *f.* (2) **4A**
to cross the street die Straße überqueren *v.* (3) **2B**
striped gestreift *adj.* (2) **1B**
strong stark *adj.* (1) **3B**
student Schüler, - / Schülerin, -nen *m./f.* (1) **1B**; **(college/university)** Student, -en / Studentin, -nen *m./f.* (1) **1A**
studies Studium (*pl.* Studien) *n.* (1) **2A**
study lernen *v.* (1) **2A**
stuffy nose verstopfte Nase *f.* (3) **1B**
style Stil, -e *m.* (2) **1B**
subject Fach, ¨-er *n.* (1) **2A**
subway U-Bahn, -en *f.* (2) **4A**
success Erfolg, -e *m.* (3) **3B**
such solcher/solche/solches *pron.* (2) **4B**
suit Anzug, ¨-e *m.* (2) **1B**
suitcase Koffer, - *m.* (2) **3B**
summer Sommer, - *m.* (1) **2B**
sun Sonne, -n *f.* (3) **4A**
sunburn Sonnenbrand, ¨-e *m.* (3) **1B**
Sunday Sonntag, -e *m.* (1) **2A**
on Sundays sonntags *adv.* (1) **2A**
sunglasses Sonnenbrille, -n *f.* (2) **1B**
sunny sonnig *adj.* (2) **3A**
sunrise Sonnenaufgang, ¨-e *m.* (3) **4A**
sunset Sonnenuntergang, ¨-e *m.* (3) **4A**
supermarket Supermarkt, ¨-e *m.* (1) **4A**
supposed: to be supposed to sollen *v.* (1) **3B**
surf surfen *v.* (2) **4B**
to surf the Web im Internet surfen *v.* (2) **4B**
surprise überraschen *v.* (2) **1A**; Überraschung, -en *f.* (2) **1A**
sweater Pullover, - *m.* (2) **1B**
sweatshirt Sweatshirt, -s *n.* (2) **1B**
sweep fegen *v.* (2) **2B**
sweet süß *adj.* (1) **3B**
swim schwimmen *v.* (1) **2B**
swimming pool Schwimmbad, ¨-er *n.* (1) **2B**
Switzerland die Schweiz *f.* (2) **3A**
Swiss schweizerisch, Schweizer *adj.* (3) **2B**; **(person)** Schweizer, - / Schweizerin, -nen *m./f.* (3) **2B**
symptom Symptom, -e *n.* (3) **1B**

T

table Tisch, -e *m.* (1) **1B**
to set the table den Tisch decken (2) **2B**
tablecloth Tischdecke, -n *f.* (1) **4B**
tablet Tablet, -s *n.* (2) **4B**
take nehmen *v.* (1) **2B**
to take (a class) belegen *v.* (1) **2A**
to take out the trash den Müll rausbringen (2) **2B**
to take a shower (sich) duschen *v.* (3) **1A**
to take off abfliegen *v.* (2) **3B**
talk reden *v.* (2) **1A**
to talk about erzählen von; sprechen/reden über *v.* (2) **3A**
tall groß *adj.* (1) **3A**
tank top Trägerhemd, -en *n.* (2) **1B**
taste schmecken *v.* (1) **4B**; Geschmack, ¨-e *m.* (1) **4B**
taxi Taxi, -s *n.* (2) **4A**
taxi driver Taxifahrer, - / Taxifahrerin, -nen *m./f.* (3) **3B**
tea Tee, -s *m.* (1) **4B**
teacher Lehrer, - / Lehrerin, -nen *m./f.* (1) **1B**
team Mannschaft, -en *f.* (1) **2B**

teaspoon Teelöffel, - *m.* (1) **4B**
technology Technik *f.* (2) **4B**
to use technology Technik bedienen *v.* (2) **4B**
telephone Telefon, -e *n.* (2) **4B**
on the telephone am Telefon (3) **3A**
telephone number Telefonnummer, -n *f.* (3) **3A**
television Fernsehen *n.*
television (set) Fernseher -*m.* (2) **4B**
tell erzählen *v.* (2) **3A**
to tell a story about erzählen von *v.* (2) **3A**
temperature Temperatur, -en *f.*
What's the temperature? Wie warm/kalt ist es? (2) **3A**
tennis Tennis *n.* (1) **2B**
tent Zelt, -e *n.* (2) **3B**
ten zehn (1) **2A**
terrific großartig *adj.* (1) **3A**
test Prüfung, -en *f.* (1) **1B**
text message SMS, - *f.* (2) **4B**
textbook Lehrbuch, ¨-er *n.*; Schulbuch, ¨-er *n.* (1) **1B**
thank danken *v.* (1) **2A**
Thank you. Danke! (1) **1A**
Thank you very much. Vielen Dank! (1) **1A**
that das **1A**; dass *conj.* (3) **2A**
the das/der/die (1) **1A**
their ihr poss. *adj.* (1) **3A**
then dann *adv.* (2) **3B**
there da (1) **1A**
Is/Are there...? Ist/Sind hier...? (1) **1B**; Gibt es...? (1) **2B**
There is/are... Da ist/sind... (1) **1A**; Es gibt... (1) **2B**
there and back hin und zurück (2) **3B**
over there drüben *adv.* (1) **4A**
therefore also; deshalb *conj.* (3) **1B**
thermometer Thermometer, - *n.* (3) **1B**
these diese *pron.* (2) **4B**
These are... Das sind... (1) **1A**
they sie *pron.* (1) **1A**
thick dick *adj.* (1) **3A**
thin dünn *adj.* (1) **3A**
thing Sache, -n *f.* (1) **1B**; Ding, -e *n.*
think denken *v.* (2) **1A**
to think about denken an *v.* (2) **3A**
to think over überlegen *v.* (1) **4A**
third dritter/dritte/drittes *adj.* (1) **2A**
this das **1A**; dieser/diese/dieses *pron.* (2) **4B**
This is... Das ist... (1) **1A**
three drei (1) **2A**
through durch *prep.* (1) **3B**
throw werfen *v.* (1) **2B**
to throw away wegwerfen *v.* (3) **4B**
thunder Donner, - *m.* (2) **3A**
thunderstorm Gewitter, - *n.* (2) **3A**
Thursday Donnerstag, -e *m.* (1) **2A**
on Thursdays donnerstags *adv.* (1) **2A**
ticket Flugticket, -s *n.* (2) **3B**; Fahrkarte, -n *f.* (2) **4A**
ticket collector Schaffner, - / Schaffnerin, -nen *m./f.* (2) **4A**
ticket office Fahrkartenschalter, - *m.* (2) **4A**
tidy ordentlich *adj.* (2) **2B**
tie Krawatte, -n *f.* (2) **1B**
tight eng *adj.* (2) **1B**
time Zeit, -en *f.* (1) **2A**; Mal, -e *n.* (2) **3B**
for the first/last time zum ersten/letzten Mal (2) **3B**
the first/last time das erste/letzte Mal (2) **3B**
this time diesmal *adv.* (2) **3B**
What time is it? Wie spät ist es?; Wie viel Uhr ist es? (1) **2A**
times mal (1) **1B**
tip Trinkgeld, -er *n.* (1) **4B**
tired müde *adj.* (1) **3B**
tissue Taschentuch, ¨-er *n.* (3) **1B**
to vor *prep.* (1) **2A**; nach; zu *prep.* (1) **4B**; auf, an *prep.* (2) **1B**
(in order) to um...zu (2) **3B**
to the right/left nach rechts/links (2) **2A**
toast anstoßen *v.* (2) **1A**
toaster Toaster, - *m.* (2) **2B**
today heute *adv.* (1) **2B**
Today is... Heute ist der... (1) **2A**
What day is it today? Welcher Tag ist heute? (2) **3A**
toe Zeh, -en *m.* (3) **1A**
together zusammen *adv.* (1) **3A**
toilet Toilette, -n *f.* (2) **2A**
tomato Tomate, -n *f.* (1) **4A**
tomorrow morgen *adv.* (1) **2B**
the day after tomorrow übermorgen *adv.* (1) **2B**
tomorrow morning morgen früh (1) **2B**
too zu *adv.* (1) **4A**; auch *adv.* (1) **1A**
tool kit Werkzeug, -e *n.*
tooth Zahn, ¨-e *m.* (3) **1A**
toothache Zahnschmerzen *m. pl.* (3) **1B**
toothbrush Zahnbürste, -n *f.* (3) **1A**
toothpaste Zahnpasta (*pl.* Zahnpasten) *f.* (3) **1A**
tornado Tornado, -s *m.* (3) **4A**
toward in Richtung *f.* (3) **2B**
towel Handtuch, ¨-er *n.* (3) **1A**
town Stadt, ¨-e *f.* (3) **2B**
town hall Rathaus, ¨-er *n.* (3) **2A**
toxic waste Giftmüll *m.* (3) **4B**
track Bahnsteig, -e *m.* (2) **4A**
track and field Leichtathletik *f.* (1) **2B**
traffic Verkehr *m.* (2) **4A**
traffic light Ampel, -n *f.* (3) **2B**
train Zug, ¨-e *m.* (2) **4A**
transportation Verkehrsmittel, - *n.* (2) **4A**
public transportation öffentliche Verkehrsmittel *n. pl.* (2) **4A**
trash Müll *m.* (2) **2B**
to take out the trash den Müll rausbringen (2) **2B**
travel reisen *v.* (1) **2A**
travel agency Reisebüro, -s *n.* (2) **3B**
traveler Reisende, -n *m./f.* (2) **3B**
tree Baum, ¨-e *m.* (3) **4A**
trendy angesagt *adj.* (2) **1B**
trip Reise, -n *f.* (2) **3B**
truck LKW, -s *m.* (2) **4A**
truck driver LKW-Fahrer, - / LKW-Fahrerin, -nen *m./f.* (3) **3B**
trunk Kofferraum, ¨-e *m.* (2) **4A**
try probieren *v.* (1) **3B**; versuchen *v.* (2) **3B**
Give it a try! Probieren Sie mal!
T-shirt T-Shirt, -s *n.* (2) **1B**
Tuesday Dienstag, -e *m.* (1) **2A**
on Tuesdays dienstags *adv.* (1) **2A**
tuition fee Studiengebühr, -en *f.* (1) **2A**
tuna Thunfisch, -e *m.* (1) **4A**
Turkey die Türkei *f.* (3) **2B**
Turkish (person) Türke, -n / Türkin, -nen *m./f.* (3) **2B**; **Turkish (language)** Türkisch *n.* (3) **2B**
turn abbiegen *v.* (3) **2B**
to turn right/left rechts/links abbiegen *v.* (2) **4A**
to turn off ausmachen *v.* (2) **4B**; einschalten *v.* (3) **4B**
to turn on anmachen *v.* (2) **4B**; auschalten *v.* (3) **4B**
turning point Wende, -n *f.* (3) **4B**
twelve zwölf (1) **2A**
twenty zwanzig (1) **2A**
twin Zwilling, -e *m.* (1) **3A**
two zwei (1) **2A**

U

ugly hässlich *adj.* (1) **3A**
umbrella Regenschirm, -e *m.* (2) **3A**
under unter *prep.* (2) **1B**
understand verstehen *v.* (1) **2A**
underwear Unterwäsche *f.* (2) **1B**
undressed: to get undressed sich ausziehen *v.* (3) **1A**
unemployed arbeitslos *adj.* (3) **2A**
unfortunate arm *adj.* (1) **3B**
unfortunately leider *adv.* (1) **4A**
unfurnished unmöbliert *adj.* (2) **2A**
university Universität, -en *f.* (1) **1B**
unpleasant unangenehm *adj.* (1) **3B**
until bis *prep.* (1) **3B**; bis zu *prep.* (3) **2B**
up herauf *adv.* (2) **2A**
to get up aufstehen *v.* (1) **4A**
to go up hochgehen *v.* (3) **2B**
USA die USA *pl.*; die Vereinigten Staaten *pl.* (3) **2B**
use benutzen *v.* (2) **4A**; bedienen *v.* (2) **4B**
to get used to sich gewöhnen an *v.* (3) **1A**
useful nützlich *adj.* (1) **2A**
useless nutzlos *adj.* (1) **2A**

V

vacancy Zimmer frei *f.* (2) **2A**
vacation Ferien *pl.*; Urlaub, -e *m.* (2) **3B**
to go on vacation Urlaub machen *v.* (2) **3B**
vacuum staubsaugen *v.* (2) **2B**
vacuum cleaner Staubsauger, - *m.* (2) **2B**
validate entwerten *v.* (2) **4A**
to validate a ticket eine Fahrkarte entwerten *v.* (2) **4A**
valley Tal, ¨-er *n.* (3) **4A**
vase Vase, -n *f.* (2) **2A**
vegetables Gemüse *n.* (1) **4A**
verb Verb, -en *n.* (3) **1A**
very sehr *adv.* (1) **3A**
very well sehr gut (1) **1A**
veterinarian Tierarzt, ¨-e / Tierärztin, -nen *m./f.* (3) **3B**
visa Visum (*pl.* Visa) *n.* (2) **3B**
visit besuchen *v.* (1) **4A**
vocabulary Wortschatz, ¨-e *m.*
volcano Vulkan, -e *m.* (3) **4A**
volleyball Volleyball *m.* (1) **2B**

W

wait warten *v.* (1) **2A**
to wait for warten auf *v.* (2) **3A**
waiter / waitress Kellner, - / Kellnerin, -nen *m./f.* (1) **3B**
Waiter! Herr Ober! (1) **4B**
wake up aufwachen *v.* (3) **1A**
walk Spaziergang, ¨-e *m.*
to go for a walk spazieren gehen *v.* (1) **2B**
wall Wand, ¨-e *f.* (2) **1B**
want wollen *v.* (1) **3B**
warm warm *adj.* (3) **2A**
wash waschen *v.* (1) **2B**
to wash (oneself) sich waschen *v.* (3) **1A**
washing machine Waschmaschine, -n *f.* (2) **2B**
waste Müll *m.* (3) **4B**; Abfall, ¨-e *m.* (3) **4B**
wastebasket Papierkorb, ¨-e *m.* (1) **1B**
watch zuschauen *v.* (1) **4A**; anschauen *v.* (2) **3A**
to watch television fernsehen *v.* (2) **4B**
water Wasser *n.*
sparkling water Mineralwasser *n.* (1) **4B**
still water stilles Wasser *n.* (1) **4B**
water pitcher Wasserkrug, ¨-e *m.* (1) **4B**
waterfall Wasserfall, ¨-e *m.* (3) **4A**
we wir *pron.* (1) **1A**
weak schwach *adj.* (1) **3B**
wear tragen *v.* (1) **2B**
weather Wetter *n.* (2) **3A**
What's the weather like? Wie ist das Wetter? (2) **3A**
weather report Wetterbericht, -e *m.* (2) **3A**
Web Internet *n.* (2) **4B**
to surf the Web im Internet surfen *v.* (2) **4B**
Web site Website, -s *f.* (2) **4B**
wedding Hochzeit, -en *f.* (2) **1A**
Wednesday Mittwoch, -e *m.* (1) **2A**
on Wednesdays mittwochs *adv.* (1) **2A**
week Woche, -n *f.* (1) **2A**
weekend Wochenende, -n *n.* (1) **2A**
weigh wiegen *v.* (2) **4B**
welcome (herzlich) willkommen (1) **1A**
You're welcome. Gern geschehen! (1) **1A**
well gut *adv.*
I am (very) well. Mir geht's (sehr) gut. (1) **1A**
I am not (so) well. Mir geht's nicht (so) gut. (1) **1A**
Get well! Gute Besserung! (2) **1A**
well-dressed gut gekleidet *adj.* (2) **1B**
well-known bekannt *adj.* (3) **2A**
wet nass *adj.* (3) **4A**
what was *interr.* (1) **2A**
What is that? Was ist das? (1) **1B**
What's up? Was geht ab? (1) **1A**
when wann *interr.* (1) **2A**
whenever wenn *conj.* (3) **2A**
where wo *interr.* (1) **2A**
where from woher *interr.* (1) **2A**
where to wohin *interr.* (1) **2A**
whether ob *conj.* (3) **2A**
which welcher/welche/welches *interr.* (1) **2A**
white weiß *adj.* (2) **1B**
who wer *interr.* (1) **2A**
Who is it? Wer ist das? (1) **1B**
whom wen *acc. interr.* (1) **2A**; wem *dat. interr.* (1) **4B**
whose wessen *interr.* (2) **4B**
why warum *interr.* (1) **2A**
widow Witwe, -n *f.* (1) **3A**
widower Witwer, - *m.* (1) **3A**
wife Ehefrau, -en *f.* (1) **3A**
win gewinnen *v.* (1) **2B**
wind energy Windenergie *f.* (3) **4B**
window Fenster, - *n.* (1) **1A**
windshield Windschutzscheibe, -n *f.* (2) **4A**
windshield wiper Scheibenwischer, - *m.* (2) **4A**
windy windig *adj.* (2) **3A**
wine Wein, -e *m.* (1) **4B**
winter Winter, - *m.* (1) **2B**
wipe wischen *v.* (2) **2B**
wise weise *adj.* (1) **3B**
wish wünschen *v.* (3) **1A**
to wish (for something) sich (etwas) wünschen *v.* (3) **1A**
with mit (1) **4B**
withdraw (money) (Geld) abheben *v.* (3) **2A**
within innerhalb *prep.* (2) **4B**
without ohne *prep.* (1) **3B**
woman Frau, -en *f.* (1) **1A**
wonder sich fragen *v.* (3) **1A**
wood Holz *n.* (2) **2B**
wool Wolle *f.* (2) **1B**
work Arbeit, -en *f.* (3) **4B**; arbeiten *v.* (1) **2A**; funktionieren *v.* (2) **4B**
at work auf der Arbeit (3) **3B**
to work on arbeiten an *v.* (2) **3A**
world Welt, -en *f.* (3) **4B**
worried besorgt *adj.* (1) **3B**
write schreiben *v.* (1) **2A**
to write to schreiben an *v.* (2) **3A**
to write to one another sich schreiben *v.* (3) **1A**

Y

year Jahr, -e *n.* (2) **3A**
yellow gelb *adj.* (2) **1B**
yes ja **1A**; **(contradicting)** doch *adv.* (1) **2B**
yesterday gestern *adv.* (2) **1B**
yet noch *adv.* (1) **4A**
yogurt Joghurt, -s *m.* (1) **4A**
you du/ihr/Sie *pron.* (1) **1A**
young jung *adj.* (1) **3A**; jugendlich *adj.* (3) **2A**
your euer/Ihr *poss. adj.* (1) **3A**
youth hostel Jugendherberge, -n *f.* (2) **3B**

Index

Understanding the Index references

The numbers following each entry can be understood as follows:

(2A) **51** = (Chapter, Lesson) **page**

So, the entry above would be found in Chapter 2, Lesson A, page 51.

About the Authors

Christine Anton, a native of Germany, is Associate Professor of German and Director of the Language Resource Center at Berry College. She received her B.A. in English and German from the Universität Erlangen and her graduate degrees in Germanic Languages and Literatures from the University of North Carolina at Chapel Hill. She has published two books on German realism and German cultural memory of National Socialism, and a number of articles on 19th and 20th century German and Austrian literature, as well as on second language acquisition. Dr. Anton has received several awards for excellence in teaching and was honored by the American Association of Teachers of German with the Duden Award for her "outstanding efforts and achievement in the teaching of German." Dr. Anton previously taught at the State University of New York and the University of North Carolina, Chapel Hill.

Tobias Barske, a native of Bavaria, is an Associate Professor of German and Applied Linguistics at the University of Wisconsin-Stevens Point. He has a Ph.D. in German Applied Linguistics from the University of Illinois at Urbana-Champaign with emphases on language and social interaction as well as language pedagogy. He has also studied at the Universität Regensburg in Germany. Tobias has over 10 years of experience teaching undergraduate and graduate courses at the university level and has earned numerous awards for excellence in teaching.

Megan McKinstry has an M.A. in Germanics from the University of Washington. She is an Assistant Teaching Professor of German Studies and Co-Coordinator for Elementary German at the University of Missouri, where she received the University's "Purple Chalk" teaching award and an award for "Best Online Course." Ms. McKinstry has been teaching for over fifteen years.

Acknowledgments

On behalf of its authors and editors, Vista Higher Learning expresses its sincere appreciation to the teachers nationwide who reviewed materials from **Mosaik**. Their input and suggestions were vitally helpful in forming and shaping the program in its final, published form. Philippe Radelet from Benjamin Franklin High School, Baton Rouge, Louisiana provided a thorough accuracy check.

We also extend a special thank you to the contributing writers of **Mosaik** whose hard work was central to the publication.

Credits

Every effort has been made to trace the copyright holders of the works published herein. If proper copyright acknowledgment has not been made, please contact the publisher and we will correct the information in future printings.

Photography and Art Credits

All images © Vista Higher Learning unless otherwise noted. All Fotoroman photos provided by Xavier Roy.

Cover: SIME/eStockphoto.

Front Matter (SE): xiii: (l) Digital Vision/Getty Images; (r) Andres Rodriguez/Big Stock Photo; **xiv:** Johannes Simon/Getty Images; **xv:** (l) Konstantin Chagin/123RF; (r) Tyler Olson/Shutterstock; **xvi:** PH3/Patrick Hoffmann/WENN/Newscom.

Front Matter (TE): T11: Jean Glueck/Media Bakery; **T29:** Monkey Business Images/Bigstock; **T30:** Simmi Simons/iStockphoto; **T31:** Getty RF.

Überblick: 1: Xavier Roy; **11:** (t) VHL; (mt) VHL; (mb) VHL; (b) Shutterstock.

Chapter 1: 19: Xavier Roy; **22:** Darío Eusse Tobón; **26:** Nagelestock.com/Alamy; **27:** (l) H. Brauer/Shutterstock; (tr) Vario Images GmbH & Co.KG/Alamy; (br) JTB Media Creation, Inc/Alamy; **30:** (tl) Palladium/AGE Fotostock; (tm) Ana Cabezas Martín; (tr) Pascal Pernixl; (bl) Martín Bernetti; (bml) Dmitriy Shironosov/Shutterstock; (bmr) Martín Bernetti; (br) Paula Díez; **33:** (tl) Nicole Winchell; (tr) Andrew Park/ Shutterstock; (bl) Aspen Stock/AGE Fotostock; bml) Moodboard/Fotolia; (bmr) Katie Wade; (br) Martín Bernetti; **39:** (tl) Vanessa Bertozzi; (tm) José Blanco; (tr) Danilo Calilung/Corbis; (bl) Katie Wade; (bm) Katie Wade; (br) Peter Scholz/Scholz Press/Corbis; **40:** (tl) Rolfbodmer/ iStockphoto; (tm) Martín Bernetti; (tr) Martín Bernetti; (bl) Martín Bernetti; (bml) Darío Eusse Tobón; bmr) Martín Bernetti; (br) Martín Bernetti; **44:** A-way!/Splash News/Newscom; **45:** (l) Free Agents Limited/Corbis; (tr) Thomas Rabsch/laif/Redux; (br) Splash News/ Newscom; **46:** (l) Diego Cervo/123RF; (r) Artur Bogacki/123RF; **54:** (tl) Martín Bernetti; (tr) Marc Pinter/Alamy; (bl) Nicole Winchell; (bml) Celso Diniz/Shutterstock; (bmr) Martín Bernetti; (br) Silky/Shutterstock; **56:** (l) Arbit/Shutterstock; (r) Arbit/Shutterstock; **57:** Javier Larrea/ AGE Fotostock; **58:** (tl) Hirotaka Ihara/123RF; (tr) Vaclav Volrab/Shutterstock; (m) Paha_L/Big Stock Photo; (b) Fabián Montoya; **59:** (tl) Enrico Nawrath/DPA/Corbis; (tr) Maugli/Shutterstock; (m) Tibor Bognár/AGE Fotostock; (b) Bloomberg/Getty Images; **60:** Gordon Welters/ Laif/Redux; **60-61:** (tablet) Petr Z/Shutterstock; **61:** (t) Arnold Morascher/Laif/Redux; (b) Georg Knoll/Laif/Redux; **62:** Masterfile; **63:** SE Media/Shutterstock.

Chapter 2: 65: Xavier Roy; **68:** David Hughes/123RF; **72:** F1 Online/SuperStock; **73:** (l) Canebisca/Shutterstock; (tr) Bettmann/Getty Images; (br) Zoonar GmbH/Alamy; **76:** Anopa/Shutterstock; **77:** (t) Mark Bowden/iStockphoto; (b) Zoe Michelle/Big Stock Photo; **79:** Pushkin/Shutterstock; **80:** (tl) Martín Bernetti; (tr) Clayton Hansen/iStockphoto;(bl) José Blanco; (bm) Vanessa Bertozzi; (br) Rolf Fischer/iStockphoto; **88:** Ricardo Miguel/123RF; **92:** Bernina International AG; **93:** (l) Dream Pictures/VStock/Media Bakery; (tr) Interfoto/ Alamy; (br) Martín Bernetti; **96:** (tl) Pixtal/AGE Fotostock; (tr) Martín Bernetti; (bl) Katie Wade; (bm) Radius Images/Corbis; (br) Adam Kazmierski/iStockphoto; **97:** Sean Locke Photography/Shutterstock; **102:** (tablet) Petr Z/Shutterstock; (hotel) Phillip Minnis/123RF; **103:** Anne Loubet; **104:** (t) Sergey Telegin/Shutterstock; (ml) Hongjiong Shi/AGE Fotostock; (mr) Christian Kober/Robert Harding World Imagery/Corbis; (b) Photo courtesy of National Police of the Principality of Liechtenstein; **105:** (tl) Richard Wareham Fotografie/Alamy; (tr) Yvan Reitserof/Fotolia; (m) Robyn Beck/AFP/Getty Images; (b) GAPS/iStockphoto; **106:** Fotosearch; **107:** (t) Ant Clausen/Shutterstock; (b) Elenarts/Fotolia; **108:** Brian McEntire/iStockphoto; **109:** Purestock/Alamy.

Chapter 3: 111: Xavier Roy; **114:** Notkoo/Shutterstock; **118:** Frank Krahmer/Corbis; **119:** (l) David Ball/Alamy; (tr) LOOK Die Bildagentur der Fotografen GmbH/Alamy; (br) Christian Ohde/Chromorange/Picture Alliance/Newscom; **121:** (l) Martín Bernetti; (r) Banana Stock/ JupiterImages; **122:** (tl) Martín Bernetti; (tr) Nicole Winchell; (bl) IT Stock Free/JupiterImages; (bml) Martín Bernetti; (bmr) Oredia/Alamy; (br) Nicole Winchell; **128:** (tl) Nicole Winchell; (tr) Nicole Winchell; (bl) Darío Eusse Tobón; (bml) Georgios Alexandris/Shutterstock; (bmr) MyasNick/Big Stock Photo; (br) Gudrun Hommel; **131:** Ana Cabezas Martin; **136:** Mlenny Photography/iStockphoto; **137:** (l) DeVIce/Fotolia; (tr) Tupungato/Shutterstock; (br) ImageBrokerSuperStock; **141:** (t) Kameraauge/Shutterstock; (m) Elisabeth Holm/ Shutterstock; (b) Karel Gallas/Shutterstock; **145:** (tl) Nicole Winchell; (tr) Raimund Linke/Media Bakery; (bl) Lance Bellers/Fotolia; (bml) Marekuliasz/Shutterstock; (bmr) Nicole Winchell; (br) Nicole Winchell; **147:** Design Pics Inc/Alamy; **148:** (t) ImageBroker/SuperStock; (ml) Tibor Bognár/AGE Fotostock; (mr) Clearlens/Fotolia; (b) Imagebroker/Alamy; **149:** (tl) David Harding/Shutterstock; (tr) Daniel Bockwoldt/DPA/Picture-Alliance/Newscom; (m) Bronswerk/iStockphoto; (b) ImageBroker/SuperStock; **150-151:** (full pg) Manuel Gutjahr/ Getty Images; **151:** (l) Imagebroker/Alamy; (m) Sabine Lubenow/Media Bakery; (r) INSADCO Photography/Alamy; **152:** (left col) Rob Schoenbaum/ZUMA Press; (right col: background) Bloomua/Shutterstock; (right col: t/window) Bronswerk/iStockphoto; (right col: t/chairs)

Kuttig-RF-Travel/Alamy; (right col: m) Captblack76/Fotolia; (right col: b) Artono9/123RF; **153:** Pascal Pernix.

Chapter 4: 155: Xavier Roy; **157:** (tl) Gudrun Hommel; (tm) Sascha Burkard/Shutterstock; (tr) Nicole Winchell; (bl) Martín Bernetti; (bm) Gudrun Hommel; (br) Herb Greene/Big Stock Photo; **158:** Nicole Winchell; **162:** Manfried Steinbach/Shutterstock; **163:** (l) Nicole Winchell; (r) Taglichtmedia/Ullstein Bild/Getty Images; (b) Imaginechina/Corbis; **164:** (l) Emese/Shutterstock; (r) Naphtalina/iStockphoto; **166:** (t) Nicole Winchell; (bl) Ale Ventura/Media Bakery; (bml) Camilo Torres/Shutterstock; (bmr) Gudrun Hommel; (br) Nicole Winchell; **170:** (tl) Gudrun Hommel; (tr) Vanessa Bertozzi; (ml) Gudrun Hommel; (mml) IDP Manchester Airport Collection/Alamy; (mmr) Aspen Stock/AGE Fotostock; (mr) Aspen Photo/Shutterstock; (bl) Gudrun Hommel; (bml) Gudrun Hommel; (bmr) Olgany/Big Stock Photo; (br) Jack Puccio/iStockphoto; **172:** (tl) Nicole Winchell; (tr) Nicole Winchell; (bl) Nicole Winchell; (br) Gudrun Hommel; **175:** (tl) Dmitry Kutlayev/iStockphoto; (tm) Aleksandr Kurganov/Shutterstock; (tr) Ray Levesque; (bl) Greg Nicholas/iStockphoto; (bm) Ray Levesque; (br) LdF/iStockphoto; **180:** Courtesy of the Bain Collection/The Library of Congress; **181:** (l) Nicole Winchell; (tr) Khabar/Big Stock Photo; (br) Nicole Winchell; **185:** (t) Ronen/iStockphoto; (bl) Annie Pickert Fuller; (bml) Kai Chiang/Media Bakery; (bmr) CandyBox Images/Fotolia; (br) Gudrun Hommel; **190:** Aspen Stock/AGE Fotostock; **191:** (tl) Arbit/Shutterstock; (tr) Arbit/Shutterstock; (b) Robert Kneschke/Shutterstock; **192:** (tl) P.lange/Big Stock Photo; (tr) Pecold/Shutterstock; (m) Zsolt Biczo/Shutterstock; (b) Frieder Blickle/laif/Redux; **193:** (t) AKG-Images/Newscom; (ml) Ina Van Hateren/123RF; (mr) Media Bakery; (b) St. Elizabeth (c. 1529/30), Nikolaus Glockendon. AKG-Images; **196:** Wavebreak Media Ltd/Big Stock Photo; **197:** Lexan/123RF.

Television Credits

37: Courtesy of It's Us Media GmbH.

85: Courtesy of Schweizer Radio und Fernsehen/ Telepool (licensing).

129: Grunen Binnenland Tourist Information Office ; http://www.gruenes-binnenland.de/

173: Courtesy of Mercedes-Benz (Daimler AG).